# RUSSIA IN AFRICA

SAMUEL RAMANI

# Russia in Africa

*Resurgent Great Power or Bellicose Pretender?*

# OXFORD
UNIVERSITY PRESS

Oxford University Press is a department of the
University of Oxford. It furthers the University's objective
of excellence in research, scholarship, and education
by publishing worldwide.

Oxford New York

Auckland Cape Town Dar es Salaam Hong Kong Karachi
Kuala Lumpur Madrid Melbourne Mexico City Nairobi
New Delhi Shanghai Taipei Toronto

With offices in

Argentina Austria Brazil Chile Czech Republic France Greece
Guatemala Hungary Italy Japan Poland Portugal Singapore
South Korea Switzerland Thailand Turkey Ukraine Vietnam

Oxford is a registered trade mark of Oxford University Press
in the UK and certain other countries.

Published in the United States of America by
Oxford University Press
198 Madison Avenue, New York, NY 10016

Copyright © Samuel Ramani, 2024

All rights reserved. No part of this publication may be reproduced,
stored in a retrieval system, or transmitted, in any form or by any means,
without the prior permission in writing of Oxford University Press,
or as expressly permitted by law, by license, or under terms agreed with
the appropriate reproduction rights organization. Inquiries concerning
reproduction outside the scope of the above should be sent to the
Rights Department, Oxford University Press, at the address above.

You must not circulate this work in any other form
and you must impose this same condition on any acquirer.
Library of Congress Cataloging-in-Publication Data is available

ISBN: 9780197782538

Printed in the United Kingdom

# CONTENTS

| | |
|---|---|
| Introduction: Setting the Stage | 1 |
| 1. The Tumultuous 1990s: A Lost Decade for Russian Geopolitical Influence in Africa | 25 |
| 2. The Dawn of Russia's Resurgence in Africa: 2000–08 | 53 |
| 3. The Medvedev Interregnum: The Consolidation of Russia's Ambitions in Africa | 77 |
| 4. Russia's Anti-Western Tilt in Africa | 105 |
| 5. Russia Rebuilds Its Influence in North Africa | 135 |
| 6. Russia Becomes a Continent-Wide Great Power | 163 |
| 7. Russia's New Power Projection Tactics in Africa | 199 |
| 8. Russia's Africa Policy in the Age of COVID-19 | 235 |
| 9. New Frontiers of Russian Security Policy in Africa | 255 |
| 10. The Ukraine War and Russia's Africa Strategy | 293 |
| Epilogue to the Paperback Edition: Russia's Africa Policy in 2023—Seismic Shocks, Small Transformations | 321 |
| *Notes* | 347 |
| *Index* | 445 |

# INTRODUCTION
## SETTING THE STAGE

Three decades after the dissolution of the Soviet Union, Russia is resurgent in Africa. From 23 to 24 October 2019, Russian President Vladimir Putin co-chaired the first Russia-Africa Summit in Sochi, which feted heads of state from forty-three African countries and showcased Moscow's great power ambitions. Russia has signed military-technical agreements with over twenty African countries, and has secured lucrative mining and nuclear energy contracts on the continent. Russian private military contractors (PMCs) have influenced the outcomes of civil wars in Libya and the Central African Republic (CAR), and Russia exports more arms to Africa than the US, France and China combined. These indicators of Russia's expanding influence in Africa are compelling, but a closer examination reveals a murkier picture. Despite Putin's lofty trade targets, Russia's trade with Africa stands at just $20 billion, which is lower than India or Turkey. The alleged involvement of Wagner Group PMCs in alleged war crimes in Libya and CAR, Russia's support for authoritarian regimes in Africa and Moscow's failed COVID-19 vaccine distribution campaign have eroded Russia's soft power. Russia's February 2022 invasion of Ukraine risks undermining its standing as an arms supplier to Africa and curtailing the growth of its investments on the continent. Limited cooperation between Russia and China in Africa, combined with growing pressure from the US and Europe, could further expose the shaky foundations of Moscow's influence on the continent.

Given the split-screen nature of Russia's policy towards Africa, the sustainability of Moscow's influence is an open question. This book addresses this puzzle head-on by posing the following question: Is Russia a resurgent great power, which has a long-term strategic vision in Africa, or a bellicose pretender driven by opportunism and a desire to take revenge on Western powers? This book strikes a middle ground on this question throughout. Contrary to popular accounts, which attribute Russia's resurgence in Africa to its post-2014 confrontation with the West, it reveals that Moscow has consistently aspired to be a great power on the continent since the mid-1990s. However, the story of Russia's resurgence in Africa has been characterized by unfulfilled promises, unrealistically optimistic economic and security objectives, and episodes of overextension. This has consigned Russia to the status of a 'virtual great power' in Africa, as it has many of the trappings of great power status but only occupies a second-tier position of influence on the continent's geopolitical hierarchy. Russia's invasion of Ukraine is poised to prolong this dynamic, as the chasm between Moscow's stated ambitions in Africa and its ability to prosecute them grows inexorably wider.

To corroborate this overarching contention, this book will present a chronological perspective of the evolution of Russia's presence in Africa. This analytical narrative rectifies a significant gap in scholarly literature, as no book-length study of Russia's post-Cold War policy towards Africa has been completed. It also ensures that often-neglected periods, such as the 1990s transition era and Vladimir Putin's first two terms (2000–08), receive adequate consideration. This book will pay special attention to the domestic institutions that drive Russia's policy in Africa, as internal forces have both facilitated and restrained Moscow's great power ambitions; the role of non-material factors, such as shared norms and ideas, in facilitating Russia's partnerships in Africa; perceptions of Russia within Africa; and patterns of interaction between Russia and fellow external powers in Africa. These areas of focus are often neglected in analyses of Russia's Africa policy. These omissions produce accounts that are overly Putin-centric, view Russia's actions through an exclusively transactional prism, deprive agency to African states and incorrectly transpose geopolitical trends from other regions to the African

INTRODUCTION

context. To support its findings, this book will extensively cite Russian-language academic and media sources, as well as English, French and Arabic-language perspectives from African countries. It will also reference interviews with experts, journalists and officials from Russia and Africa, which complement and redress gaps in open-source material.

This chapter will provide a summative assessment of extant scholarship on Russia's policy towards Africa and highlight the original contributions of this book. It will then provide a brief historical overview of Russia's shifting interests and policies towards Africa, which orients non-specialists to the subject and contextualizes contemporary developments discussed in the book. The chapter will conclude with a brief chapter-by-chapter layout of the book, which draws attention to critical junctures in Russia's post-Cold War policy towards Africa.

## A Critical Overview of Existing Scholarship on Russia's Policy towards Africa

Despite the media coverage that surrounds Russia's resurgence in Africa, there is a dearth of extant scholarship on this subject. In stark contrast to the vast array of scholarly literature on the Soviet Union's Africa policy, there is no English-language book on Russia's post-1991 policy towards Africa. The foundation of secondary literature on Russia's contemporary policy in Africa rests on think tank reports and policy journal articles by respected scholars and analysts, such as Kimberly Marten, Chris Alden, Elizabeth Sidiropoulos, Paul Stronski, Sergey Sukhankin and J. Peter Pham. Academic and think tank reports have tended to disproportionately focus on the activities of Russian PMCs, Moscow's interventions in Libya and CAR, Russia's oil, mining and nuclear energy projects in Africa, and Russia's relationships with Egypt, Algeria and South Africa. Moreover, these themes are often explored in an isolated fashion, without placing them into the broader context of Russia's policy towards Africa or Russian conduct as a rising power in the Global South. This book addresses these shortcomings by anchoring its analysis of Russia's bilateral relations with African countries to the

3

context of its continent-wide strategy. Its areas of special attention, which were highlighted at the start of this chapter, were specially selected to redress the empirical slants of extant scholarship.

In addition to these empirical shortcomings, four problematic assumptions guide extant scholarship towards Russia's involvement in Africa. The first assumption is that Russia's resurgence in Africa is a relatively recent phenomenon, which took hold at the tail end of Putin's second term and accelerated after Russia–West relations soured over the 2014 Ukraine crisis.

In an October 2019 Carnegie Endowment for International Peace report entitled 'Late to the Party: Russia's Return to Africa', Paul Stronski stated that for two decades after the Soviet Union's collapse, 'Russian activity in Africa was negligible, apart from intermittent appearances by thuggish arms dealers like Viktor Bout and globally minded businessmen like Oleg Deripaska and Viktor Vekselberg.'[1] Kimberly Marten presents a more nuanced account of Russia's resurgence in Africa, which notes Moscow's growing interest during the early 2000s, but concedes that 'Russia has come roaring back on the continent' since Ukraine-related Western sanctions were imposed in 2014.[2] A confluence of factors, such as a protracted economic depression, the breakdown of law and order and Russia's commitment to engaging with Western countries, forced Moscow to cede its Soviet-era superpower status in Africa. However, key institutions within the Russian government, such as the Federation Council and Ministry of the Economy, and statist intellectuals[3] regretted the abandonment of Africa, and urged the Boris Yeltsin administration to change course. These internationalist perspectives gained traction during the last two years of Andrei Kozyrev's tenure as Foreign Minister (1990–96) and inspired Russian policies in Africa, such as debt forgiveness, engagement with African regional institutions and countering Western isolation campaigns against authoritarian regimes. While the scope of Russia's engagement in Africa has expanded greatly in recent years, these core tactics and policies crystallized during Yevgeny Primakov's tenure as foreign minister (1996–99) and Vladimir Putin's first two terms as president (2000–08). This book will emphasize the continuities in Russia's policy towards Africa in the post-Soviet period and present

4

INTRODUCTION

an incremental 'long resurgence' account of Moscow's return as a great power.

The second assumption is that Russia's forays in Africa are transactional and bereft of strategic foresight. Joseph Siegle, the Director of Research at the Africa Center for Strategic Studies, National Defense University (NDU), summarizes the conventional wisdom as follows: 'Coming in the wake of its annexation of Crimea, Russia's interest in Africa is commonly portrayed as opportunistic, aimed at evading international isolation and gaining access to Africa's vast natural resources.'[4] Headlines supporting this narrative, such as 'Gems, Warlords and Mercenaries' in the *New York Times*[5] and 'Guns, Mercenaries and Minerals' in Voice of America,[6] peaked ahead of the Sochi Summit. Russia's post-2014 economic malaise, the interests of state-owned companies, such as Rosatom and Rosoboronexport and the ambitions of Kremlin-aligned businessmen, such as Oleg Deripaska and Yevgeny Prigozhin, have influenced its theatres of power projection in Africa. Focusing exclusively on these factors is reductionist, however, as it ignores the non-material motives that drive Russian policy towards Africa. These non-material factors include rekindling Soviet-era memories of superpower status, or *derzhavnost*; Russia's normative resistance to Western unilateralism; Moscow's desire to highlight itself as a counterterrorism partner and contributor to international governance; and Russian soft power ambitions in Africa. These non-material factors influenced Russia's relationships from countries spanning from Libya to South Africa, and have at times served as Moscow's entry points into African theatres. Russia's enduring appeal as a partner for African countries, even during periods of weakness such as the 1990s and early 2000s, can be attributed to these non-material factors. Therefore, this book will blend transactional and non-material factors guiding Russia's Africa policy and explore the relative balance between these drivers of Moscow's conduct.

The third assumption is that Russia's policy towards Africa is monolithic and revolves around Vladimir Putin's personal vision. While Putin's actions, such as his 2006 African tour and co-chairmanship of the Sochi Summit, have profoundly impacted the course of Russia's policy towards Africa, a Putin-centric account

5

omits critical domestic drivers of Russian decision-making. The Federation Council, Russian Foreign Ministry figures, the Russian State Duma, Former President Dmitry Medvedev and intellectuals at Moscow's Institute for African Studies of the Russian Academy of Sciences (RAS) have all encouraged Russian assertiveness in Africa, even when Putin's inner circle deemed the continent a low priority. Russian regions, such as Nizhny Novgorod, Tatarstan and Chechnya, have both amplified and pushed back against state policy. Bureaucratic rivalries between the Russian Ministry of Defence and Ministry of Foreign Affairs explain vacillations in Russia's policy towards Libya, while state-aligned businessmen and media outlets do not act as passive executors or mouthpieces of Putin's agenda. While empirical evidence on the domestic drivers of Russian decision-making in Africa is incomplete and varies greatly, this book will make regular use of a multiple-actor approach to Russia's conduct and draw hypothetical conclusions about the domestic drivers of Moscow's conduct. This approach distinguishes between agents and surrogates in Russia's policy towards Africa and could have far-reaching benefits for our understanding of the Kremlin's actions on the world stage.

The fourth assumption is that Russia's systemic-level relationships with external powers seamlessly translate to the African context. In each chapter, this book examines how Russia has situated itself vis-à-vis the US, France and China in theatres of power projection and examines the implications of Moscow's actions in Africa on its bilateral relationships with these countries. While the general trend-line of complementary Russian and Chinese interests in Africa, and tensions between Russia, the US and France holds up, these patterns are not universal. Despite escalating Russia–NATO tensions after the 2008 Georgian War, Russia found common ground with Western countries in the struggle against piracy in Somalia. Tensions over Libya did not immediately spill over to France's Operation Serval campaign in Mali. Similarly, frictions between Russia and the US over Libya and Sudan during the 1990s presaged the open disagreements during the 1999 Kosovo War. Russia's autocracy promotion efforts and arms sales to rival factions in African conflicts have undermined the security of China's stability-dependent Belt and Road Initiative (BRI), even as Moscow-Beijing relations have improved. Similar

INTRODUCTION

discrepancies can be observed in Russia's relationships with Middle Eastern regional powers, such as Turkey and the United Arab Emirates (UAE). These anomalies in Russia's relations with external powers in Africa will be unpacked and explained throughout this book.

In addition to broadening the time horizon of analysis and exploring previously overlooked dimensions of Russia's policy towards Africa, this book also recalibrates traditional assessments of Moscow's objectives on the continent. Throughout its duration, this book contends that Russia's quest to construct a multipolar world order[7] is the driving force behind its engagement with African countries. During the early 1990s, this objective was peripheral in importance and harboured by internationalists within the Kremlin. From the late 1990s onwards, Russia viewed multipolarity as a cardinal principle of its foreign policy towards the Global South and pursued this objective with greater confidence as US hegemony waned. Russia's challenge to Western international legal norms and sanctions, efforts to position itself as an alternative trade partner for African countries, counterinsurgency and conflict resolution efforts are all aimed at shifting the centre of global power away from the West. Russia's central role in promoting multipolarity in Africa also boosted domestic perceptions of its great power status[8] and augmented a key component of Vladimir Putin's legacy as president.

## A Historical Overview of Russia's Policy towards Africa

Now that the book's challenges to conventional thinking on Russia's policy in Africa have been articulated, this section will lay out the primary trends in Moscow's approach towards the continent in a periodized fashion. It will also explore how Russia's power projection tactics in Africa changed in response to geopolitical transformations, such as decolonization, the intensification of the Cold War and the Sino-Soviet Split and contextualize this book's examination of continuities between Soviet and Russian conduct. This section will use the following periodization: The Colonial Era (Pre-1960); The Post-Colonial Era (1960–75); The Era of Soviet Adventurism (1975–85); and The Collapse of Soviet Influence in Africa (1985–91). This temporal delineation is effective, as Moscow

7

was a second-tier power in the pre-1960 era, was mostly engaged in ideological proselytization as colonialism unravelled, expanded its military assertiveness during the last years of Leonid Brezhnev's rule, and pivoted sharply towards restraint under Mikhail Gorbachev. The causes and manifestations of these transitions in Russian and Soviet policy will be examined in the remainder of this chapter.

### Russian and Soviet Policy towards Africa during the Colonial Era

Although Russia frames itself as a 'new power' in Africa which lacks pernicious colonial legacies, its engagement with the continent goes back centuries. Russia's relationships with the Maghreb, Horn of Africa and South Africa have especially long antecedents. Due to bonds between Christian communities, Russia's partnership with Egypt is its oldest in Africa. In 1556, Patriarch Joachim of Alexandria sent a letter to Tsar Ivan IV, urging Russia to aid the St Catherine's Monastery in the Sinai Peninsula, which had been ransacked by Ottoman Turkey. Ivan IV dispatched Smolensk merchant Vasily Poznyakov to Egypt in 1558, providing an improbable foundation for centuries of Christian communal bonding. Poznyakov's memoirs of his travels to Cairo, Alexandria and Sinai profoundly shaped Russian popular perceptions of Africa.[9] Tsar Nicholas II played an instrumental role in consolidating Russia's interest in the Maghreb. Nicholas II began his famed 1890–91 'trip to the east' in Egypt, which suggested that Russia, like Britain, viewed Egypt as a gateway to the Indo-Pacific region.[10] Tsar Alexander III's focus on northeastern Africa was linked to Russia's desire to spread Orthodox Christianity, challenge British hegemony over the Suez Canal and Aden, and use Egypt as a Red Sea access point.[11] Russia's efforts to position itself as a secondary partner to Britain in Egypt foreshadowed its conduct after the consolidation of the US-Egypt partnership during the latter stages of the Cold War. In 1897, Russia established a consulate in Tangier, Morocco. As Morocco became a flashpoint in the Franco–German rivalry, Russia's policy entered a state of flux. Historian Paul de Quenoy contends that Russia initially supported Morocco's independence but when this prospect receded, it ultimately backed French colonial rule.[12]

INTRODUCTION

Russia's presence in the Horn of Africa is similarly long-standing. Due to its Orthodox Christian communal bonds, the Russian Empire established close ties with Ethiopia during the nineteenth century. Kharkiv University began teaching the Amharic language in 1829 and prominent Ethiopians, such as League of Nations representative Tekle Hawariat Tekle Mariyam, received military training in Russia and were acquaintances of Tsar Nicholas II.[13] Russia opened Balcha Hospital and trained Ethiopian nurses.[14] Russia's 'medical diplomacy' during the First Italo-Ethiopian War (1895–96) augmented cultural affinities, such as Ethiopia's admiration for native son Alexander Pushkin, and created an enduring reservoir of Russian soft power.[15] During the 1880s, Russia established political and military ties with Ethiopia. Through his 1889 and 1891 meetings with Emperor Menelik I, V.F. Maskhov helped sell Russian mountain guns to Ethiopia ahead of the 1895 Battle of Adwa and facilitated Russia's establishment of a diplomatic presence in Addis Ababa in 1902. In contrast to its success in Ethiopia, Russia's forays into French Somaliland were a spectacular failure. In 1889, Nikolay Achinov dispatched 165 Cossacks to the Gulf of Tadjoura on the coast of present-day Djibouti. As Achinov lost control over his Cossack settlers, he retreated to Sagallo, where he established New Moscow. French cruisers and gunboats recaptured control of Sagallo in an offensive that killed six Cossack settlers. Since Achinov had refused to surrender to France, which became a crucial Russian ally against Germany, he fell out with Tsar Nicholas II and Russia retreated from Djibouti.

Although Russia's adventurism in the Maghreb and Horn of Africa were driven by opportunism and cultural bonds, its initial forays in South Africa had sharp anti-colonial undertones. Lord Carnarvon invoked the Russian threat to justify the creation of the South African Confederation in 1875. During the late 1870s, British officials expressed fears that Russia would arm the Zulus or capitalize on Britain's quagmire in southern Africa by making a blitz from Central Asia to India.[16] While these extreme scenarios did not come to pass, Russia's policy in South Africa was 'preventive imperialism', as it stymied British colonial expansion in Africa.[17] Beyond sympathizing with their anti-British sentiments, Russia formed a values-based partnership with the Boers, as they were

9

Christians, rural, conservatives and patriotically resisting 'foreign capitalists', which was a euphemism for Jews.[18] In 1900, Leo Tolstoy quipped that 'The war in South Africa is a proof of insignificance of the power of money when pitted against moral force.'[19] In 1896, Russia established diplomatic relations with the Transvaal Republic, which exerted control over northeastern South Africa. During the Second Anglo-Boer War from 1899 to 1902, Russian aristocrats and military figures, such as 'the Russian Boer General' Yevgeny Maximov, fought on the Boer side and Russian newspapers, literature and architecture lionized the Boer cause.[20] Britain's triumph in the Boer War in 1902 set the stage for Russia's marginalization in South Africa, which would persist for nearly a century.

While the 1917 Bolshevik Revolution amplified Russia's standing as an anti-imperial power, the Soviet Union was detached from African affairs until the mid-1950s, with two notable exceptions. The first was the 1935–36 Italian invasion of Ethiopia, which saw the Soviet Union join the US in supporting Ethiopian sovereignty and establish diplomatic relations with Ethiopia in 1943. The second was Joseph Stalin's aborted plan to govern Tripolitania for a ten-year period, which sought to promote the 'collective economy' and transplant Soviet policies on Tajik and Uzbek coexistence to Arabs and Berbers in Libya.[21] The Soviet Union's disengagement has often been attributed to Stalin's personal indifference to Africa and Moscow's focus on combatting fascism and exporting revolutionary socialism in Europe. These factors hold considerable sway, but the Union of Soviet Socialist Republics (USSR)'s disinterest was also explained by its dearth of reliable partners in Africa.[22] Under Vladimir Lenin's leadership from 1917 to 1924, the Soviet Union tried to infiltrate Pan-Africanist movements, which were staunchly capitalist, and relied heavily on British and French communist parties in the anti-colonial struggle. During the 1930s, the Soviet Union broke away from bourgeoisie nationalists and tried to create a 'united front from below', which consisted of local parties and trade unions. These outreaches, which relied heavily on European communist support, stalled during World War II and ensured that the Soviet Union remained a marginal force in African affairs.

INTRODUCTION

In the mid-1950s, Soviet influence in Africa rapidly expanded, as the decolonization process began. During Nikita Khrushchev's tenure as General Secretary, the Soviet Union argued that the 'backwardness' of African countries stemmed from colonialism, and that the triumph of anti-imperialist forces would be a prelude to the victory of socialism over capitalism.[23] Khrushchev believed that if the Soviet Union could capture a 40% trade share with a country, it would embrace socialism. The Director of the Africa Institute of the Soviet Union, Ivan Potekhin, believed that a swift 'peaceful transition' to socialism was possible, and began cultivating ties with Mali, Guinea and Ghana in 1957. These lofty expectations were ultimately not met.[24] Due to the Soviet Union's network of satellites in Eastern Europe, some African countries were wary of the sincerity of Moscow's ideological commitment to anti-imperialism. The 1955 Bandung Conference, which condemned all manifestations of colonialism, included Egypt, Libya, Sudan, Ethiopia, Guinea and Liberia. Soviet officials acknowledged that intelligentsia who supported decolonization in Africa were often anti-Marxist. African socialists, such as Tanzania's Julius Nyerere, were unwilling Soviet partners, as they believed that pre-colonial Africa had 'no classes' and that Marxism generates 'class antagonism'.[25]

Due to these constraints, the Soviet Union prioritized material rather than ideological engagement with African countries during the late 1950s. The Soviet Union's backing of Egyptian President Gamal Abdel Nasser, who engaged in anti-imperialist rhetoric after the 1952 Free Officers Coup and nationalized the Suez Canal in 1956, exemplified this strategy. As tensions between Egypt and Britain boiled over, the Soviet Union struck a weapons deal with Cairo in 1955, Czechoslovak technicians trained Egyptian military personnel in the use of Soviet weapons and Moscow backed Nasser during the 1956 Suez Crisis. The Soviet Union's purchase of 40,000 tons of cocoa from Ghana after its independence declaration in 1957 and inauguration of an embassy in Accra after Kwame Nkrumah's takeover, mirrored its conduct in Egypt.[26] These partnerships persisted, even though Nasser's Arab socialist regime repressed communism and Nkrumah believed that reform was a more effective agent of change than Soviet-style revolutions. The Soviet Union's

11

support for national liberation movements was also not universal, as it wished to avoid proxy wars with European powers. This imperative explains Soviet Union's restrained conduct during the Algerian War of Independence, as it only supported Algeria's National Liberation Army when it deemed France's surrender inevitable.[27] The Soviet Union's pragmatic anti-imperialism paved the way for Sino-Soviet contestation in Africa and Moscow's reliance on Warsaw Pact surrogates in the proxy conflicts of the latter Cold War.

## The Soviet Union's Post-Colonial Forays in Africa

In the early 1960s, the Soviet Union designed its strategy towards Africa around the colonial order's gradual decay. Citing US experts, such as Stefan Possony, Soviet academic E.D. Modrzhinskaia opined that European colonial powers would remain in Africa and justify their retention of power by insisting that African countries were not ready for self-government.[28] The rapid pace of decolonization in Africa, which accelerated after British Prime Minister Harold Macmillan's February 1960 Winds of Change speech and France's reverses in Algeria, presented the Soviet Union with a mixture of opportunities and challenges. The Soviet Union viewed post-colonial African states as valuable ideological and commercial partners. Accordingly, Nikita Khrushchev stated in September 1960, 'We have stood, we stand and always will stand for the right of the peoples of Africa' to establish governments of their choice and to 'attain their freedom from colonial oppression'.[29] However, the Soviet Union was unprepared for the intensity of superpower rivalries in Africa and was forced to spontaneously develop a set of tactics that would be conducive to long-term influence.

The 1960 Congo crisis, which saw Soviet-aligned Prime Minister Patrice Lumumba clash with army chief Mobutu Sese Seko, revealed both the opportunities and pitfalls of rapid decolonization. Due to its exceptionally brutal history of Belgian colonial rule, Congo was deemed to be a prime target for Soviet assistance.[30] Although Lumumba was not an avowed Marxist, he had established close ties with Soviet Ambassador to Guinea Pavel Gerasimov in April 1959 and pledged to strengthen relations with Moscow if he took power.[31]

12

## INTRODUCTION

As Lumumba also had close ties with Nkrumah and Guinea's Soviet-aligned President Ahmed Sékou Touré, Moscow viewed Congo as the fulcrum in its axis of newly decolonized partners in Africa. Despite these high geopolitical stakes, the Soviet Union was restrained in its military support for Lumumba after UN peacekeepers refused to support him in August 1960, and Lumumba was toppled on 5 September. The Soviet Union used its UN Security Council seat to unsuccessfully lobby for Lumumba's release in December 1960 and block a UN-mandated intervention by Western powers in Congo. Lumumba's execution in January 1961 paved the way for Congo to be an anti-communist bulwark under Mobutu. Due to this adverse outcome, the Congo crisis is viewed ambiguously in Russia's academic community. Sergei Mazov contends that the Congo Crisis illustrated the uneasy blend of adventurism and caution in Soviet policy towards Africa, as he believes that Moscow 'fought with one hand' in support of revolutionary values and failed to develop the Congolese armed forces into anything more than a 'junk' fighting force.[32]

Despite the Soviet Union's botched Congo Crisis response, Khrushchev was undeterred in his efforts to expand Moscow's influence in Africa. The Soviet Union blended economic development aid and military-technical assistance to expand its array of partners in Africa. In 1964, Nikolay Fedorenko, the head of the USSR's permanent mission to the UN, extolled the Soviet Union's commitment to 'assist the African countries in attacking and ending backwardness'.[33] The Soviet Union's development strategy consisted of nationalizations of foreign assets, supporting local industries, strengthening state-owned sectors of African economies and encouraging radical agricultural reforms. While these ideas hewed closely to Marxist-Leninism, Soviet officials did not make economic development assistance conditional on ideological compliance. Instead, the Soviet Union's focus on being a continent-wide superpower meant that it supported non-aligned countries that possessed varying degrees of commitment to socialism, such as Egypt, Guinea, Ghana, Mali and Somalia.[34] This pragmatism stemmed from the perceived disloyalty of client states, and by the late 1960s, Soviet foreign aid ebbed at the precise moment Western assistance expanded.[35] The Soviet Union's security assistance to African countries mirrored these pragmatic patterns. Despite Nigeria's pro-Western foreign policy orientation and rumours of Soviet support for Biafra, Moscow transferred war materiel to the Nigerian armed forces, such as MiG-15 fighter jets and six L-29 fighter jets, and deployed 200 military technicians to Nigeria.[36] As the US backed decolonization processes to counter Soviet influence, Moscow responded with military support for national liberation movements, such as the People's Movement for the Liberation of Angola (MPLA).

While the Soviet Union pursued opportunities throughout Africa, its influence was concentrated in the Maghreb and West Africa. The Soviet Union aided Egypt against Israeli air attacks during the 1967–70 War of Attrition, and contrary to rumours that Egypt expelled Soviet advisors in July 1972, Moscow supported Egyptian forces during the 1973 Yom Kippur War.[37] The Soviet Union also strengthened its relationship with Libya after the 1969 coup, but Muammar al-Gaddafi's belief that communism was incompatible with his brand of Islamism and socialism stalled the partnership. The Soviet Union also signed an economic development agreement with Algeria in December 1963, which led to projects like the Annaba metallurgical plant, and supplied Algeria with 70–80% of its weaponry. After the 1967 war, Sudan-US relations soured and Gafaar Nimeiry, who took power through the 1969 coup, hired 2,000 Soviet advisors and reoriented the Sudanese economy towards Moscow. In West Africa, the USSR's core partners were Guinea and, more inconsistently, Ghana, Mali and Nigeria. Under Sékou Touré's leadership, Guinea severed all relations with France from 1965 to 1975 and embraced a Soviet-inspired planned economy. Ghana maintained close relations with the Soviet Union until Nkrumah's overthrow in a 1966 coup. Mali's first President Modibo Keita pursued a robust partnership with Moscow and his pro-Western successor Moussa Traore continued to purchase Soviet weaponry. The Soviet Union's even-keeled approach to the Biafra War laid the foundations for cordial Russia-Nigeria relations to this date. Elsewhere in Africa, Soviet influence stagnated. The USSR was largely isolated from Central Africa, aside from its close relationship with the Republic of Congo, withdrew its ambassador from South Africa after the 1960 Sharpeville Massacre and had a frosty relationship with Ethiopia.

14

## INTRODUCTION

Although the Soviet Union was primarily focused on countering the US and France's influence in Africa, the Sino-Soviet Split created new complications for Moscow's power projection ambitions. As Mao Zedong believed that countries in self-described 'intermediate zones' (Africa, Latin America, Asia and Europe) were genuinely resistant to US and Soviet hegemony, China immediately regarded non-aligned post-colonial African countries as prospective partners.[38] From December 1963 to February 1964, Chinese Premier Zhou En-Lai visited Egypt, Algeria, Morocco, Tunisia, Ghana, Mali, Guinea, Sudan, Ethiopia and Somalia. While Zhou publicly refrained from condemning the Soviet Union, competing Soviet and Chinese expeditions in Mali, and the distribution of pro-Soviet leaflets during his trip underscored the extent of the rivalry in Africa.[39] Khrushchev's May 1964 trip to Egypt escalated tensions between China and the Soviet Union. During his visit to Cairo, Khrushchev hailed the Soviet Union's commitment to 'true proletarian internationalism', which was regarded as a jab at China's agrarian model of Marxist-Leninism, and implicitly decried China's exacerbation of racial divisions in the Third World.[40]

China's limited material capabilities meant that it could not convert its warnings about Soviet ideological revisionism into sweeping partnerships. The Soviet Union's loans to Algeria, Somalia, Ghana, Mali and Guinea were $100 million, $44 million, $81 million, $55 million and $80 million, which surpassed China's $50 million, $20 million, $20 million, $19.6 million and $24 million, respectively.[41] China also lagged behind the Soviet Union in the competition for African students. After Nkrumah's overthrow, China's main partners were Algeria's National Liberation Front (FLN) and Tanzania's President Julius Nyerere, and Beijing's clout was more pronounced within pre-independence rather than post-colonial African countries. The growth of US engagement with China during the Nixon administration eventually laid the foundation for tactical Sino-American cooperation against Soviet influence in Africa.

## The Peak of Soviet Influence in Africa under Leonid Brezhnev

In keeping with what academic Seweryn Bialer described as the 'Soviet paradox' of external expansion and internal decline,[42] Soviet influence in Africa peaked during the late 1970s and early 1980s for three reasons. First, the Soviet Union increased its arms exports and development assistance to African countries, reversing the commercial stagnation it experienced in the late 1960s. The Soviet Union's transition from using arms sales as an instrument of geopolitical influence to a means of generating hard currency expanded Moscow's array of partners in Africa.[43] The Soviet Union, which became the world's largest arms vendor by 1980, accrued lucrative contracts with Ethiopia, Algeria and Libya. The Soviet Union developed a four-plank economic assistance policy in Africa, which included loans, trade credits to governments, short-term credits granted by Soviet foreign trade organizations and scholarship programmes.[44] Second, Soviet power projection relied extensively on Marxist-Leninist surrogates, which reduced the cost of intervention in Africa. Cuba's military interventions in Ethiopia and Angola were especially striking, but the Soviet Union also received support from Warsaw Pact countries, such as Czechoslovakia, East Germany and Bulgaria. Third, China transformed from an ideological challenger to a spoiler of Soviet interests in Africa. Although China transferred $142 million in arms to Africa from 1967 to 1976, these weapons transfers tapered off considerably as Deng Xiaoping became increasingly focused on economic reform.

The expansion of Soviet influence was especially pronounced in the Horn of Africa and southern Africa. During the mid-1970s, the Soviet Union's partnership with Somalia undergirded its presence in the Horn of Africa. The Soviet Union had trained the Somali National Army since 1962, provided humanitarian assistance to drought victims in northern Somalia and signed a twenty-year Treaty of Friendship and Cooperation with Somalia in July 1974. Although the Derg regime in Ethiopia, which overthrew Emperor Haile Selassie in September 1974, embraced Marxist-Leninist economic reforms, the Soviet Union viewed Ethiopia's arms purchases from the US and the pro-Western leanings of Derg officials with trepidation. During

INTRODUCTION

the July 1977 to March 1978 Ogaden War, which was triggered by the Somali invasion of eastern Ethiopia's Ogaden region, the Soviet Union reoriented its regional foreign policy towards Ethiopia. Cuba's deployment of 15,000 troops on Ethiopia's behalf helped turn the tide of the Ogaden War, while East Germany established robust economic and security ties with Ethiopia in 1979.[45] The Soviet Union's support for Ethiopia stemmed from its desire to maintain stability in the Horn of Africa, which was jeopardized by Somali revanchism.[46] The reactive nature of Soviet policy in the Horn of Africa was lost on US officials and resulted in intensified geostrategic competition.[47] Building on the deployment of Soviet technical advisors during the Ogaden War, the Soviet Union exported $11 billion in arms to Ethiopia, established a naval base in Nokra Island and air field in Asmara, and shepherded its socialist economic development model.[48]

Although it was sandwiched between anti-communist bulwarks, Mobutu's Zaire and apartheid South Africa, the Soviet Union viewed southern Africa as a fruitful new frontier for power projection. Towards the end of Angola's war of independence from Portuguese colonial rule, the Soviet Union backed the MPLA. The Soviet Union's support for the MPLA was erratic, however, as it supplied war materiel during the late 1960s but suspended these weapons transfers in 1973 before resuming them in March 1975. After Angola obtained its independence in November 1975, the Soviet-aligned MPLA became embroiled in civil war with the National Front for the Liberation of Angola (FNLA) and National Union for the Total Independence of Angola (UNITA), which were backed by the US, Zaire, South Africa and, intermittently, China. Alongside support from the Soviet Union and non-military aid from East Germany and Romania, the MPLA was backed by 36,000 Cuban troops, which resisted South Africa's expansionist designs and bombing raids. The Soviet Union also adopted a prominent position in Mozambique, where it provided large-scale development aid and collaborated with Cuba in giving military-technical assistance to the nascent People's Republic. Soviet forays elsewhere in southern Africa were less successful. After the Rhodesian Bush War, which resulted in the overthrow of white-minority rule in Zimbabwe in December 1979,

17

the Soviet-aligned Zimbabwe African People's Union (ZAPU) led by Joshua Nkomo unsuccessfully vied for power against the Chinese-aligned Zimbabwe African National Union (ZANU) led by Robert Mugabe. Frank Wisner, who served as US Ambassador to Zambia from 1979 to 1982, recalls that a US-China axis formed to pry Zambia away from the Soviet Union after its President Kenneth Kaunda authorized the purchase of sixteen MiG-21 jets from Moscow in 1980.[49]

Outside these two regions, the Soviet Union maintained pockets of influence but struggled to establish durable patron-client relationships. The Soviet Union's inability to convert transactional and situational partnerships into hardened alliances stemmed from the proliferation of non-aligned socialist African countries. From 1976 to 1985, Soviet-Libyan relations reached their Cold War-era apogee, as 11,000 Soviet soldiers transited through Libya and Gaddafi regime officials routinely partook in specialized training courses in Moscow.[50] Gaddafi's diverse array of international partners also benefited Soviet policy, as he backed pro-Moscow factions, such as the Sandinistas in Nicaragua and the Palestinian Liberation Organization. Nevertheless, Gaddafi's staunch defence of non-alignment, which saw him deplore Cuba's President Fidel Castro for being too pro-communist at the 1973 Algiers Summit, placed a natural cap on Moscow-Tripoli cooperation.[51] Burkina Faso, which underwent a sharp ideological pivot towards Marxist-Leninism after Thomas Sankara's 1983 coup, exemplified this trend in an even starker fashion. Under Sankara's leadership, Burkina Faso repressed the pro-Soviet Patriotic League for Development and condemned the Soviet war in Afghanistan but continued to purchase arms from the Eastern Bloc. The Soviet Union also experienced an erosion of traditional partnerships in North and West Africa. Egypt's abrogation of its friendship treaty with the Soviet Union in March 1976 and subsequent support for the mujahideen in Afghanistan was an especially significant blow to Moscow's interests. Robert Grey questions the notion of a 'new Soviet policy' towards Africa in the late 1970s, as he notes that just twenty-three African countries purchased Soviet arms from 1976 to 1980, compared to twenty-one during the previous decade.[52] Therefore, the depth of Moscow's

18

INTRODUCTION

penetration in Africa increased much more significantly than its breadth of partnerships, and the Soviet Union could not claim continent-wide superpower status.

Although the Soviet Union's assertiveness in Africa was superficially at unprecedented heights, there were signs that the long-term direction of Moscow's policy would pivot towards restraint. Neil MacFarlane's analysis of shifts in Soviet policy towards Angola from 1975 to 1990 compellingly illustrates the changes that occurred in the late Brezhnev era.[53] During the mid-1970s, Soviet policy was highly ambitious, as it sought to 'establish new positions of influence, effect socialist-oriented transformation and promote the process of national liberation'. By 1982, the Soviet Union focused on sustaining established positions, de-escalating superpower rivalries, and cutting cost-inefficient relationships in Africa. This dramatic transformation in Soviet policy towards Africa was not only necessitated by economic stagnation but also reflected profound internal changes in Soviet foreign policy decision-making. Chester Crocker, who served as US Assistant Secretary of State for African Affairs from 1981 to 1989, recalls that there were 'three voices in Moscow' on African policy, as it was shaped by the Soviet Foreign Minister, the Communist Party of the Soviet Union's Africa department and state-aligned Soviet intellectuals.[54] Influential members of the Soviet foreign policy community, such as Deputy Head of the International Department of the Central Committee of the Communist Pary of the Soviet Union (CPSU) Karen Brutents and the head of Moscow's Latin American Institute Viktor Volskii, urged Moscow to pivot away from the indiscriminate spread of revolutionary socialism towards newly liberated countries following a capitalist development path.[55] This provides vital context for the strategic transformations in Soviet conduct towards Africa during Mikhail Gorbachev's fateful tenure as General Secretary.

*The Collapse of Soviet Influence in Africa under Mikhail Gorbachev*

During Mikhail Gorbachev's tenure as General Secretary, the Soviet Union's superpower status in Africa unravelled in dramatic fashion. The Soviet Union suspended its financial support for its regional clients, such as Ethiopia, ended its surrogate warfare interventions in southern Africa through a political settlement, and distanced itself from anti-Western partners, such as Muammar al-Gaddafi in Libya. The Soviet Union's pivot towards a cold peace with South Africa in the late 1980s and de-escalation of tensions with Egypt brought some respite, but the Gorbachev era's overarching narrative was one of inexorably declining influence in Africa. This surrender of the Soviet Union's superpower status in Africa can be explained by geopolitical transformations, such as the erosion of the bipolar order and the easing of Cold War tensions, but was even more profoundly shaped by Gorbachev's worldview and leadership qualities. Gorbachev's conditional support for states of socialist orientation was apparent from his actions in the first year of his tenure. The CPSU and FLN in Algeria held central committee-level talks in March 1985, instead of executive-level negotiations, and Gorbachev's perceived unreliability as a partner convinced Algerian President Chadli Bendjedid to request lethal arms from the United States a month later.[56] The April 1985 coup against Gafaar Nimeiry in Sudan, which gave more political rights to the Sudanese Communist Party, was received circumspectly by Soviet officials.[57] Gorbachev stridently condemned the April 1986 US bombing of Libya and advocated Libya's inclusion in an inclusive Mediterranean collective security system, but relations between Moscow and Tripoli cooled considerably in the mid-1980s. The November 1986 Soviet Union-Benin Friendship Accord did not result in Soviet economic assistance for its faltering planned economy.

The dramatic unravelling of the Soviet Union's alliance with Ethiopia laid bare the seismic nature of Gorbachev-era policy changes towards socialist regimes. During the mid-1980s, Soviet media outlets and academic literature abandoned their uncritical support for Derg leader Mengistu Haile Mariam's policies, and highlighted adverse developments, such as the 1983–85 famine and civil war against Tigrayan and Eritrean separatism.[58] Soviet experts began pressuring Ethiopia to engage in economic reforms, such as decollectivization of agriculture and looser restrictions on foreign investment. When Gorbachev reprised these criticisms of Mengistu's policies, the Soviet-Ethiopian relationship soured.

20

## INTRODUCTION

The Soviet Union publicly distanced itself from Ethiopia, which contrasted with Mengistu's seven visits to Moscow from 1977 to 1984, and token gestures, such as Mengistu's adoption of a Soviet-style constitution in September 1987, did not turn the tide of this relationship. Galina Krylova, an influential Soviet Africanist, warned in 1988 that Mengistu's limited popular support would hasten the collapse of his regime and presented Ethiopia's failed 'barracks socialism' and descent into backwardness as a cautionary tale for the Soviet Union.[59] Mengistu's bans on discussions about glasnost and perestroika in Ethiopia was the final straw for his relationship with Gorbachev, and the Soviet Union began scaling back military assistance to Addis Ababa in mid-1989. Mengistu's half-hearted economic liberalization efforts after the 1989 revolutions in Eastern Europe were insufficient, and by early 1990, the Soviet Union welcomed US participation in peace talks on Tigray and Eritrea. In one stroke, Ethiopia and, by extension, the Horn of Africa had transformed from a theatre of superpower contestation to an area of US-Soviet cooperation.

These sweeping changes in Soviet policy also extended to southern Africa. Chester Crocker's linkage policy, which tied Namibia's independence from South Africa to the withdrawal of Cuban forces from Angola, was initially met with deaf ears in Moscow. The Soviet Union's failed export of socialism to Angola meant that its influence in southern Africa depended on a military footprint and its influence would be marginalized in a peacetime scenario. This assumption initially persisted under Gorbachev, as the Soviet Union provided military support for the MPLA's 1985 offensive in Jamba on the Angola-Namibia border, and Soviet Foreign Minister Eduard Shevardnadze reaffirmed Moscow's commitments under the 1976 Friendship Treaty.[60] Ultimately, the stagnant progress of MPLA offensives against UNITA assets, and Gorbachev's belief that de-escalating tensions with the US in Angola would advance 'new thinking', changed Soviet policy.[61] The Soviet Union played a vital role in the four-party negotiations that led to Namibia's independence and pressured Cuba to withdraw its 50,000 troops from Angola in July 1988.[62] The Soviet Union's retrenchment from Angola also extended to Mozambique. Although the Mozambican National

Resistance Movement (RENAMO) emerged as a major political force in 1985–86, the Soviet Union did not provide additional economic assistance to Mozambique's embattled Marxist-Leninist regime.[63] Despite its hostility towards its apartheid system, Mozambique was forced to maintain commercial links with South Africa to forestall an economic collapse. Mozambique also strengthened relations with Western countries and the International Monetary Fund (IMF) during the late 1980s.

Although the Soviet Union's state-building projects and military interventions in Africa came to an abrupt halt, Gorbachev was committed to humanitarian initiatives and resetting Moscow's fraught relations with regional powers in Africa. Building on the Soviet Union's prior contributions to public health in Africa, which included a lead role in the smallpox vaccination campaign, Moscow paid growing attention to food insecurity and humanitarian crises in conflict zones. On 21 January 1985, a *Pravda* commentary praised the Soviet Union's construction of a field hospital to treat drought victims in Ethiopia and declared that 'a new page has been opened in the glorious chronicle of good deeds'.[64] While these propagandistic statements aimed to whitewash Soviet military support for the Derg, Gorbachev immediately reaffirmed his commitment to these facets of humanitarian assistance. At the March 1985 UN Conference on the Emergency Situation in Africa, the Soviet Union reaffirmed its desire to combat drought in Africa and Gorbachev subsequently backed Prime Minister Valery Tikhonov's plans to expand Soviet development assistance to African countries.[65] This suggests that the collapse of Soviet economic assistance in Africa was likely due to unexpected financial constraints rather than Gorbachev's strategic design. The re-establishment of Soviet-Egyptian diplomatic relations in 1984 predated Gorbachev's arrival but Eduard Shevardnadze's February 1989 visit to Cairo helped reset bilateral relations. The Soviet Union's resolute support for the African National Congress (ANC) and scathing criticisms of apartheid prevented a similar re-engagement with South Africa, but the de-escalation in Angola paved the way for Moscow's establishment of diplomatic relations with Pretoria in 1992. By the end of Gorbachev's tenure, Soviet influence in Africa atrophied, and this trajectory of decline would

INTRODUCTION

be increasingly pronounced during Russia's early 1990s transition from communism.

## A Chapter-by-Chapter Layout of this Book

As noted earlier in this introductory chapter, this book will examine Russia's post-1991 foreign policy towards Africa in a chronological fashion. The first three chapters will provide context for contemporary developments in Russia's Africa policy. Chapter One will focus on the post-communist transition during the 1990s. Russian influence in Africa witnessed a dramatic collapse during the first half of the decade before experiencing an incremental resurgence during the mid-1990s, which accelerated after Yevgeny Primakov became foreign minister in 1996. Chapter Two will examine Russia's policy towards Africa during Vladimir Putin's first two terms as president from 2000 to 2008. This period built on Primakov-era foundations, as Russia deepened its engagement with regional institutions, established partnerships with the continent's leading regional powers, strengthened its relationships with anti-Western regimes and experienced a resurgence in North Africa. Chapter Three will explore developments in Russian foreign policy during Dmitry Medvedev's tumultuous tenure as president from 2008 to 2012. Under Medvedev, Russia reasserted itself as a great power in Africa, struck a delicate balance between accommodation and resistance to Western norms, and leveraged its counter-revolutionary positions during the Arab Spring to broaden its array of continental partnerships.

Once this context has been provided, the remainder of the book will examine Russia's resurgence in Africa during Putin's third and fourth terms as president. Chapter Four will examine how the systemic crisis between Russia and the West, which was exacerbated by Moscow's interventions in Ukraine and Syria, shaped Russian policy towards Africa. It will explain why Russia's influence in Africa endured and even expanded during this period, as Moscow deepened its bonds with anti-Western countries, controversially strengthened its relationship with South Africa and gained prestige in the counterterrorism sphere. Chapter Five will explore the resurgence

23

of Russia's influence in North Africa, as Moscow adapted to the post-Arab Spring regional order, and consolidated its relationships with Egypt, Algeria, Libya and Morocco. Chapter Six will examine Russia's emergence as a continent-wide great power at the dawn of Putin's fourth term, which laid the foundations for the 2019 Russia-Africa Summit in Sochi. Chapter Seven will provide a deep dive into Russia's tools of influence projection in target countries, such as private military contractor deployments, election interference campaigns and investments by state-owned companies. It will examine how those tactics were applied successfully in Guinea and the Central African Republic (CAR), with moderate efficacy in Libya and Sudan, and why they failed in Madagascar and Mozambique.

The final two chapters of the book will examine new frontiers in Russia's foreign policy towards Africa during the age of COVID-19. Chapter Eight will examine Russia's coronavirus and vaccine diplomacy campaigns in Africa, and how Moscow has carried forward the Sochi Summit's legacy against countervailing headwinds from the pandemic and external powers. Chapter Nine will examine new developments in Russian security policy, such as the recalibrations of its military interventions in Libya and the Central African Republic, pursuit of a Red Sea naval base in Sudan, and reaction to insecurity in the Sahel. Chapter Ten will examine the responses of African countries to the February 2022 Russian invasion of Ukraine, and Russia's strategy to sustain its influence in Africa in an era of sanctions. The book will culminate with a succinct conclusion that lays out the future direction of Russia's Africa policy.

# 1

# THE TUMULTUOUS 1990s
## A LOST DECADE FOR RUSSIAN GEOPOLITICAL INFLUENCE IN AFRICA

Russia's influence in Africa reached its contemporary nadir during the early 1990s. The trajectory of Soviet decline, which was set into motion by the collapse of Ethiopia's Marxist-Leninist Derg regime in 1991 and Mikhail Gorbachev's economic divestment from Africa, advanced into a full-fledged collapse of Russian influence in the spring of 1992. The remainder of Russia's Lost Decade in Africa was largely characterized by ruptured partnerships, embassy closures and economic marginalization. Within the Russian foreign policy establishment, Africa emerged as a periodic source of internal discord. The 'pragmatist camp', which was led by Andrei Kozyrev, viewed Africa as a region of marginal importance and urged Russia to focus on strengthening relations with the United States, Europe and Japan. The 'internationalist camp', which was led by Yevgeny Primakov, lamented Russia's passive acquiescence to US policies in Africa and urged Moscow to uphold the values that undergirded Soviet policy in the Third World. Contestation between these two factions persisted throughout Boris Yeltsin's tenure as Russian president, but by the end of the decade, the internationalist camp was firmly ascendant.

25

This chapter will begin by exploring how the Soviet Union's dissolution transformed Russia's patterns of engagement with Africa and placing these radical changes in the context of Moscow's broader strategic transformations in the Third World. It will then lay out Andrei Kozyrev's transformation from a measured supporter of Russian engagement with Africa to the architect of Russia's divestment from the continent. This transformation of Kozyrev's worldview partially reversed itself during the mid-1990s, but Russia remained a fringe player in African affairs. The chapter will conclude by examining how Yevgeny Primakov's tenure as Foreign Minister (1996 to 1998) and Prime Minister (1998 to 1999) laid the foundations for a revival of Russian influence in Africa under Vladimir Putin.

## The Collapse of the Soviet Union and Russia's Strategic Reassessment in Africa

During the summer of 1991, the Soviet Union's claims to superpower status atrophied in a dramatic fashion. On 12 July, the *New York Times* reported that the USSR's external debt levels had soared to $70 billion,[1] placing the Soviet Union on the verge of financial ruin. On 19 August, hard-line opponents of perestroika coalesced under the State Committee on the State of Emergency (GKChP) umbrella and staged a coup d'état against Mikhail Gorbachev. The GKChP's seizure of power was nullified on 21 August, as GKChP acting President Gennady Yanayev resigned. The remaining coup plotters were arrested over the next two days, except for acting Minister of the Interior Boris Pugo, who committed suicide on 22 August. Mikhail Gorbachev's standing as leader of the Soviet Union did not recover, as he stepped down as General Secretary of the CPSU on 24 August. In the ten days that followed the GKChP's coup, Ukraine, Moldova, Uzbekistan, Kyrgyzstan and Tajikistan seceded from the Soviet Union. These secessions culminated in the USSR's formal dissolution on 26 December 1991. Under Boris Yeltsin's leadership, Russia inherited the USSR's hyperinflation crisis, spiralling external debt and ethno-nationalist cleavages, but ceased to be a global superpower.

26

## THE TUMULTUOUS 1990s

The severity of Russia's socioeconomic and political crises forced it to scale back its strategic presence in the Third World. In an October 1991 interview with *Izvestia*, Andrei Kozyrev stated that Russia 'would tackle conflict zones' in the Third World, but it would only maintain cultural ties to countries where it had no economic interests.[2] Kozyrev admitted that participation in Third World aid programmes was a desirable long-term objective, but Russia needed to 'first overcome our own underdevelopment'. Kozyrev's materialistic approach to Russian engagement with the Third World repudiated the Soviet Union's emphasis on forging ideological partnerships and extensive reliance on development assistance. Kozyrev's Third World policy aligned with the perspectives of many prominent Russian political commentators, who urged Moscow to divest from Africa. Soviet Ambassador to Israel Aleksandr Bovin argued Russia should abandon Soviet clients in Africa, such as Mozambique and Guinea-Bissau, and focus on courting new partners, such as Israel.[3] Alexander Golts, a leading defence analyst, was even more pessimistic than Kozyrev. He argued that Russia's participation in resolving conflicts in Third World theatres like Africa is 'exclusively of a nominal nature'.[4] Golts predicted that Russia and Ukraine would not emulate the USSR's power projection techniques in Third World conflict zones, such as weapons deliveries or technical advisor deployments.

The emerging consensus in the Kremlin around the need for a partial retrenchment from the Global South overhauled the foundations of long-standing Soviet policy towards Africa. The USSR's cordial relationships with anti-Western regimes in Africa, such as Muammar al-Gaddafi's Libya and Omar al-Bashir's Sudan, abruptly collapsed. Following the August 1991 coup against Gorbachev, Gaddafi praised Gennady Yanayev for carrying out a 'brave historical action' and a 'great deed' that was supported throughout the Third World. Gaddafi accused 'imperialist forces' of pressuring the USSR to abandon its opposition to colonialism. Gaddafi also expressed confidence that the GKChP would prevent the USSR's disintegration and preserve Moscow's standing as the main challenger to the 'monopoly of a single barbaric power in the world', the United States.[5] Libyan state media outlet JANA

27

condemned President George Bush's communications with Boris Yeltsin following the coup as a violation of international law that would 'place the entire world at the threshold of anarchy'.[6] As the Supreme Soviet's Chairman of the Council of Nationalities Rafik Nishanov praised Libya's model of direct democracy during his May 1991 visit to Tripoli,[7] Soviet officials were surprised by Gaddafi's strident support for Yanayev. Consequently, Kozyrev's November 1990 proclamation that Soviet military aid to Libya, Cuba and Syria 'reflects neither their interests nor ours'[8] became a mainstream view in the Kremlin. Russia's partnerships with Libya and Sudan, which also supported the 1991 coup, were accordingly downgraded.

Unlike the USSR's policy of leveraging political instability in Africa to enhance its geopolitical influence and ideological reach, Russia disengaged itself from the frontlines of intra-state conflicts. This retrenchment was especially apparent in Russia's responses to the Ethiopian and Algerian civil wars. Gorbachev embraced a policy of stringent non-alignment during the Ethiopian civil war. This position is striking, as Ethiopian People's Revolutionary Democratic Front (EPRDF)'s overthrow of Mengistu triggered mass anti-American demonstrations throughout Ethiopia in May 1991 and the new Ethiopian President Meles Zenawi had praised Joseph Stalin and Albanian dictator Enver Hoxha. The USSR emphasized dialogue promotion between all conflicting parties in Ethiopia, assisted European efforts to establish positive relations with Zenawi and endorsed Italy's plan to establish a 'broad-based Ethiopian government'.[9] Russia's response to the Algerian civil war's outbreak on 26 December 1991 was similarly cautious. This conflict, which resulted in 150,000 casualties and lasted until February 2002, was triggered by the Algerian military's annulment of the Islamic Salvation Front (FIS)'s election victory. Although Russian experts positively described President Chadli Bendjedid as the 'Algerian Gorbachev' due to his co-option of Islamists into the FLN and resistance to the Algerian military's authoritarian instincts, Russia did not condemn the coup which overthrew him on 11 January 1992.[10] Russia subsequently viewed the participation of the Islamic extremist Armed Islamic Group (GIA) in the Algerian civil war with trepidation, as the GIA was founded by Afghan mujahideen veterans.

Nevertheless, Russia confined its involvement in the Algerian civil war to arms sales, even as France, Saudi Arabia and Iran assisted the Algerian military, FIS and GIA, respectively.

Although these strategic shifts undermined the time-tested foundations of Moscow's influence in the Third World, Russia initially tried to maintain its geopolitical foothold in Africa. Kozyrev's reluctant elevation of Africa's place in Russia's foreign policy agenda was inspired by two main factors. First, Russian officials were alarmed by the rapid progress of diplomatic engagement between Moscow's post-Soviet neighbours and African countries. On 15 February, an editorial in *Pravda* extolled Kazakhstan's expeditious normalization of diplomatic relations with South Africa, as a stark contrast to Moscow's protracted negotiations with Pretoria.[11] As CIS countries also expanded their diplomatic links with the Middle East and Northeast Asia, Russia believed that it needed to match their engagements in the Global South to preserve its long-term hegemony over the post-Soviet space. Second, Russian commentators believed that African countries were nostalgic for Soviet influence in the Third World and disillusioned with Moscow's passive acquiescence to US foreign policy goals. In an article for *Pravda* on 18 January, journalist Igor Tarutin noted that African countries had historically counted on Russia to take their side in disagreements with the United States. Mikhail Gorbachev's alignment with the US during the 1991 Gulf War damaged Moscow's image as a crisis-proof partner in Africa and caused potential anti-imperialist partners, such as Zimbabwe, to delay normalizations with Russia. Tarutin argued that the USSR's collapse contributed to instability in Africa as Western countries no longer saw the need to quell unrest in former Cold War allies, such as Zaire.[12]

As concerns about Russia's disengagement from Africa mounted, Russian officials recognized the imperative of developing a coherent strategy for engagement with the continent. On 2 February 1992, a Russian State Duma report listed Angola, Nigeria and South Africa as Moscow's three most promising partners in Africa. The Duma's advocacy for targeted engagement with Africa resembled its policy recommendations for Russian cooperation with Latin America, which emphasized positive relations with Brazil, Argentina and Mexico. The Duma report also urged Russia to strengthen its relationship with 'moderate regimes in the Middle East',[13] such as Egypt, to expand its influence over the resolution of the Arab-Israeli conflict. Andrei Kozyrev viewed the Duma's recommendations as a reasonable middle ground between the views of the internationalist and pragmatist camps. The sustainability of Kozyrev's compromise was swiftly put to the test when he embarked on his fateful African tour in February 1992.

## Andrei Kozyrev's February 1992 Trip to Africa: A Failed Gambit

From 26 February to 1 March 1992, Andrei Kozyrev visited Angola, South Africa and Egypt. Kozyrev sought to formalize Russia-South Africa relations, illustrate Russia's arbitration role in the Angolan civil war and Arab-Israeli conflict, and strengthen Russian commercial links with all three countries. This ambitious agenda was partially realized, as Russia and South Africa established diplomatic relations on 28 February 1992, but Moscow did not obtain lucrative commercial contracts or achieve transformative results in the diplomatic sphere. The first leg of Kozyrev's African tour, Angola, was arguably his least successful. Prior to Kozyrev's arrival in Angola, Russian officials emphasized how the USSR, along with the United States and Portugal, had spearheaded conflict resolution initiatives in Angola. Despite his dismissal of Russia's 'superpower notions', Kozyrev declared that arbitration in Angola was a continuation of Moscow's global role and part of Russia's 'responsibility to the world'.[14] To exemplify Russia's parity with the United States as a diplomatic stakeholder in Angola, Kozyrev discussed the peace process with US Secretary of State James Baker on 24 February.

During his trip to Angola, Andrei Kozyrev met with President José Eduardo dos Santos, UNITA leader Jonas Savimbi, and an array of other MPLA officials. The lukewarm character of Russia-Angola relations, which was exemplified by uncertainties about Angolan students continuing their education in Moscow and Luanda's reluctance to immediately normalize with Russia, spilt over into Kozyrev's visit.[15] Dialogue on the May 1991 Lisbon Peace Process reached an impasse, but even more concerningly, Russia-Angola

## THE TUMULTUOUS 1990s

bilateral relations did not appreciably advance. As Angola owed $4 billion to Russia, which amounted to approximately 50% of Moscow's outstanding loans to Sub-Saharan Africa, Kozyrev hoped to strike a debt repayment agreement with Dos Santos. Their meeting was inconclusive, as both sides vaguely agreed to find a 'civilized solution' to their debt dispute. Angolan representatives contended that military debt was often not repaid, but Kozyrev insisted that 'Russia and other countries had to pay their debts'.[16] The basis of Russia-Angola security cooperation also unravelled, as Kozyrev announced the closure of the USSR's former military mission in Angola. Despite the Russian Foreign Ministry's assurances that Russia and Angola would continue to engage in peacetime security cooperation, Angola relied increasingly on security assistance from Britain, France and Portugal.[17]

Andrei Kozyrev's 28 February trip to South Africa was much more successful. During his visit to Pretoria, Kozyrev had cordial meetings with State President of South Africa F.W. de Klerk and ANC President Nelson Mandela. Russia and South Africa normalized diplomatic relations and agreed to establish consulates in Cape Town and St Petersburg. This breakthrough was the culmination of one year of shuttle diplomacy between Russia and South Africa. In February 1991, representatives of the International Projects Centre (IPC), a non-governmental organization, met with South African Foreign Minister Pik Botha in Cape Town and discussed potential commercial opportunities with South African elites. The IPC distinguished Boris Yeltsin and Mikhail Gorbachev's positions on South Africa. Its representatives noted that the USSR had imposed sanctions on South Africa, which Russia no longer supported.[18] As the May 1991 Lisbon Agreement on Angola removed a key source of tension between Moscow and Pretoria, Soviet and Russian policies towards South Africa converged. In July 1991, South Africa's Anglo-American Corporation entered the Soviet market, fuelling speculation about the development of a Soviet-South African precious metals cartel.[19] In November 1991, Pik Botha informally met with Eduard Shevardnadze in Moscow. In an interview with *Rabochaya Tribuna*, Botha offered to normalize relations with the USSR, as South Africa was abandoning apartheid and the USSR was turning its back on communism.[20] Botha's offer facilitated the February 1992 normalization of Russia-South Africa relations.

During his stay in Pretoria, Kozyrev and de Klerk praised Russia and South Africa's simultaneous transitions to democracy as a driver of future cooperation. Vitaly Churkin optimistically mused about mining sector deals between Russia and South Africa, but no major contracts were signed. To illustrate his commitment to strengthening Russia-South Africa relations, Kozyrev invited de Klerk for a meeting with Boris Yeltsin in Moscow in July 1992. De Klerk enthusiastically accepted Kozyrev's offer. This pledge created frictions between Russia and the ANC, as de Klerk was assured that Nelson Mandela would be greeted in Moscow as 'an international figure, a fighter for human rights', rather than as ANC president.[21] This controversy tarnished Kozyrev's diplomatic triumph in South Africa and prompted internationalists to warn that Russia would have a tense relationship with a future ANC government.

On 1 March, Andrei Kozyrev concluded his African tour by meeting with Egyptian President Hosni Mubarak in Cairo. Much like his visits to Angola and South Africa, Russian officials had high expectations for Kozyrev's visit to Egypt. Mikhail Bogdanov, who served as Russia's Ambassador to Egypt from 2005 to 2011, argues that Russia's courtship of Mubarak was a reaction to strengthening US-Egypt relations and the European Union's integration of Egypt into its Mediterranean strategy. Bogdanov notes that the US and Europe were filling the vacuum left by the Soviet Union's collapse and this trend caused Russia to extinguish the negative memories of Soviet-Egyptian tensions in the 1970s and 1980s.[22] Egypt's opposition to the August 1991 coup against Gorbachev and praise for Moscow's constructive role in the November 1991 Madrid Conference on the Israel-Palestine process, which was co-sponsored by the Soviet Union, underscored the cordial relationship between Mubarak and Kozyrev. Russian commentators warned that Egyptian intellectuals viewed Russia and the United States as partners and disdained external power interference in the Arab-Israeli conflict.[23] Nevertheless, Kozyrev believed that camaraderie between Russian and Egyptian officials would marginalize these dissenting voices.

32

## THE TUMULTUOUS 1990s

Andrei Kozyrev's visit to Egypt did not result in ground-breaking commercial or diplomatic agreements. However, it reaffirmed the cordiality of Russia-Egypt relations and resulted in Kozyrev inviting Hosni Mubarak to visit Moscow. In a clear appeal to Egypt's international status aspirations, Kozyrev praised Mubarak's insights on developments in the Persian Gulf and CIS regions. As the Russia-South Africa normalization deal rankled the internationalist camp, Kozyrev's rhetoric in Cairo consisted of numerous veiled olive branches to his domestic critics. In particular, Kozyrev emphasized the centrality of Egypt's place in Russian diplomacy towards the Arab world,[24] which invoked memories of Soviet-era superpower status, and highlighted Egypt's status as a 'fortress that confronts all forms of extremism', which appeased domestic concerns about violence in the North Caucasus.

Although dialogue between Russia and Egypt on the Arab-Israeli conflict produced few results, Libya emerged as a surprise agenda item. In a meeting with Egyptian Foreign Minister Amr Moussa, Andrei Kozyrev unveiled Russia's plan to address Libya's state sponsorship of terrorism. Kozyrev urged Libya to hand over the two main suspects in the Pan Am Flight 103 bombing to the United Nations, as the UN Secretary General was the sole legitimate adjudicator of the Lockerbie case. Although Moussa did not publicly endorse Russia's plan, Kozyrev took his proposal a step further by meeting with a senior Libyan official in Cairo. After this meeting, Andrei Kozyrev praised Tripoli's 'civilized position' on the Lockerbie case and vowed to strengthen Russia-Libya bilateral relations.[25] Russia's surprise olive branch to Muammar al-Gaddafi's isolated regime challenged US demands for sweeping multilateral sanctions against Libya. It also temporarily reassured Russian internationalists and African leaders, who feared that Russian and American foreign policy goals were becoming indistinguishable.

### The Collapse of Great Power Ambitions in Africa: Spring 1992 to Summer 1993

Despite Andrei Kozyrev and Vitaly Churkin's triumphalist rhetoric on Russia's ambitions in Africa, Russian officials were privately disappointed by the outcome of Kozyrev's African tour. Robert Donaldson, a Russian foreign policy expert at the University of Tulsa, aptly notes that 'Kozyrev's trip was intended to demonstrate that Russia was not giving up on its global interests, but the facts argued otherwise.'[26] As Africa constituted just 2% of Russia's external trade and Kozyrev's meetings in Angola, South Africa and Egypt produced no commercial breakthroughs, Russia decided to reduce its diplomatic presence in Africa. On 29 April 1992, Russia downgraded its embassies in Burkina Faso, Equatorial Guinea, Lesotho, Liberia, Niger, São Tomé and Príncipe, Somalia, Togo and Sierra Leone into 'honorary consuls'. The Russian Foreign Ministry stated that these embassy closures were motivated purely by 'financial and economic reasons', as Russia inherited the entire USSR's embassy maintenance costs in 1992.[27]

The massive reduction of Russia's diplomatic and military presence in Africa received a poor reception on the continent. During Boris Yeltsin's June 1992 speech to the US Congress, which included the declaration that 'freedom and communism are incompatible', some African ambassadors did not applaud the Russian President.[28] On 13 June 1992, a senior Libyan official decried the illegitimacy of Russia's UN Security Council (UNSC) permanent membership, as Russia was not designated as the Soviet Union's successor through a UNSC resolution or by the approval of other post-Soviet republics.[29] Similar sentiments proliferated in South Africa, in spite of Russia's enthusiastic courtship of Pretoria. Supporters of de Klerk's ruling National Party viewed Russia and the United States as two leaders of the 'ultimate world state', which crowded out dissenting voices within the international system.[30] Despite this backlash, Russia's retrenchment in Africa continued. In November 1992, First Deputy-Head of the Russian Foreign Ministry's Africa Department Alexander Smirnov announced closures of consulates in Niger, Mozambique, Angola, Madagascar and Congo, and hinted at more shutdowns in 1993.[31] The Russian Foreign Ministry's decision to label Africa as a lower strategic priority than Latin America or Australia underscored Russia's growing indifference to African affairs.[32] Margarita Obraztsova, an expert at Moscow's Institute for African Studies, stated that the Ministry of Foreign Affairs

(MFA) of the Russian Federation regarded Africa as a 'black hole of insurmountable backwardness, crises and conflicts', rather than a potential partner for Russia.[33]

Russia compounded these diplomatic withdrawals with a drastic reduction in arms sales to Africa. From 1988 to 1991, the USSR provided Sub-Saharan Africa with 54.4% of its total arms supplies. This figure was more than double the shares of Western Europe (10%), China (5.7%) and the United States (2.7%) combined. Even as the USSR disintegrated in 1991, it was the second largest arms vendor to the Third World, with $5 billion in new contracts.[34] In 1992–93, Russia's arms exports to the developing world declined drastically, as it shipped only $1.3 billion in 1992 (5.76%) and $1.2 billion in 1993 (4.81%). Russia's weapons sales to Africa amounted to only $600 million from 1992 to 1995, compared to $3.5 billion from 1988 to 1991.[35] Boris Yeltsin's appointment of inexperienced civilians to leadership positions in Russian main defence companies, Spetzvneshtechnika and Oboronexport, contributed to this decline in weapons sales.[36] Russia's reduced arms sales to African countries, which possessed Soviet-era military debt, sharpened this ebb. In January 1991, five African countries represented more than $1 billion in military debt in Africa: Ethiopia, Algeria, Angola, Egypt and Libya.[37]

These arms export cuts reduced Russia's presence in conflict zones. On 13 November, Alexander Smirnov stated that 'modern offensive weapons will be crossed out from the list of exported armaments' and that 'weapons will not be supplied to hotbeds of tension'.[38] This policy immediately reduced Russia's arms exports to Algeria. The Algerian military relied heavily on Soviet equipment, such as T-72 tanks, SA-6 missiles and MiG-25 aircraft. Algeria also had 1,065 technical advisors from the USSR and Eastern Bloc on its payroll in 1990. From 1989 to 1992, Algeria purchased $900 million in Russian arms, but these sales declined to $300 million from 1993 to 1996.[39] Due to these abrupt cuts, the Algerian military needed to procure spare parts for Russian equipment from other CIS countries, South Africa and Turkey.[40] Akram Kharief, an Algiers-based political analyst, contends that Russia's policies soured its relationship with Algeria's Department of Intelligence and Security (DRS). Kharief notes that Algeria-Russia intelligence cooperation on Afghanistan persisted during the 1980s, as Algerian operatives worked for the Committee for State Security (KGB). The DRS began to rely on US intelligence cooperation after 1990, and Kharief argues that Russia-Algeria intelligence cooperation did not recover until 2014, when both sides resumed dialogue over Syria.[41]

In addition to overseeing Russia's disengagement from Africa, Andrei Kozyrev aligned with the United States on every UNSC resolution pertaining to Africa during his tenure as Russian Foreign Minister. The consistency of Russia-US coordination in the UN on African affairs is noteworthy, as Russia periodically abstained from UNSC resolutions that imposed sanctions on Yugoslavia and called for the reinstatement of Haiti's deposed President Jean-Bertrand Aristide. Russia's vote for UNSC Resolution 748 on 31 March 1992 underscored Moscow's willingness to align with Western powers in multilateral institutions. This resolution expanded multilateral sanctions on Libya, called on states to withdraw their diplomatic personnel from Tripoli and denied flight permission to Libyan aircraft. As five countries (China, India, Morocco, Zimbabwe and Cape Verde) abstained from UNSC Resolution 748, Russia's vote departed from the non-Western consensus in the United Nations. Russia's condemnations of Libya's refusal to prosecute terrorism suspects notably contradicted Andrei Kozyrev's praise for Muammar al-Gaddafi's cooperative attitude in Cairo on 1 March.[42] The adverse impacts of UNSC Resolution 748 on the Russian economy were immediate. Although Alexei Vasiliev contends that Russian officials 'practically ignored Libya' after Tripoli reneged on military loans to Russia in early 1992,[43] the UN sanctions dealt a crushing blow to Russian economic interests in Libya. The USSR authorized $1.5 billion in arms sales to Libya from 1989 to 1992, but Russia sold Libya $50 million in arms from 1993 to 1996 and completely suspended arms transfers from 1995 to 1998.[44] The collapse of Russian arms sales to Tripoli also halted Moscow's privileged access to Libya's oil industry, as Gaddafi reportedly agreed to provide the USSR with proceeds for 70,000 to 80,000 barrels of oil in exchange for Soviet weaponry.[45]

## THE TUMULTUOUS 1990s

Unlike their public criticisms of Russia's vote for the 1992 arms embargo on Slobodan Milošević's Yugoslavia and support for multilateral sanctions against Iraq, internationalists showcased their opposition to Kozyrev's Libya policy in a variety of ways. Senior diplomats typically made use of behind-the-scenes pressure. Veniamin Popov, Russia's Ambassador to Libya from 1991 to 1992, foresaw adverse potential consequences from the sanctions. Popov noted that Russia viewed Gaddafi's regime as 'friendly', due to its experimentation with socialism and reliability as a purchaser of Russian weaponry. Popov contends that Russia voted for UNSC Resolution 748 to please the United States and exposed itself to backlash from the Libyan people, as a crowd of Gaddafi loyalists tried to storm the Russian embassy after the sanctions were ratified.[46] Alexey Podtserob, who succeeded Popov as Russian Ambassador to Libya from 1992 to 1996, was concerned about Muammar al-Gaddafi's 'moral support for Chechen separatists', but conceded that 'the sanctions imposed by the Security Council hit us harder than any other power'.[47]

Opposition from diplomats to Russia's policy in Libya was compounded by public backlash from Kozyrev's established critics. Vladimir Zhirinovksy was the main public opponent of Kozyrev's pro-American policies in Libya. The Liberal Democratic Party of Russia (LDPR) leader established a robust personal relationship with Muammar al-Gaddafi, which persisted until his overthrow in 2011, and extolled Libya's opposition to Zionism and imperialism during his frequent visits to Tripoli. On 3 November 1993, an article in *Rossiyskaya Gazeta* contended that Russia opposed efforts by the United States, Britain and France to impose an oil embargo on Libya and bar Libyan assets from being deposited in foreign banks.[48] Oleg Davydov, Russia's Minister of Foreign Economic Relations, dispatched a delegation of Russian private entrepreneurs to Tripoli in November 1993, and stated that 'Today, we are betting on Libya as a future economic partner.'[49] The synchronous timing between Davydov's trip to Libya and Andrei Kozyrev's support for UNSC Resolution 883, which reaffirmed Resolution 748, signified a rift between the two ministries. The Russian Ministry of Foreign Economic Relations subsequently criticized the Russian Foreign

Ministry's neglect of Africa's innovation potential. Leonid Safonov, a Ministry of Foreign Economic Relations official, quipped derisively in December 1993 that 'Russian entrepreneurs' ideas about Africa are shaped on the novels of Louis Boussenard.'[50]

Although the debates over sanctioning Libya prompted the deepest rift between Russia's pragmatists and internationalist factions, Moscow's support for UNSC Resolution 794 on the crisis in Somalia augmented these factional divisions. UNSC Resolution 794, which was passed unanimously in December 1992, authorized the deployment of United Task Force (UNITAF) to Mogadishu to provide a 'secure environment' for humanitarian relief operations. Much like on Libya, Russia sided with the US legal arguments for intervention on Somalia and departed from the views of the China-led non-Western bloc. In the UNSC debates, Russia viewed UNITAF's arrival as a positive precedent for peacekeeper deployments in humanitarian crisis areas, but China saw UNITAF's participation as an 'exceptional action', which should cease as soon as the humanitarian crisis abated.[51] The internationalist camp immediately resisted this position. Grigory Karasin, the head of the Russian Foreign Ministry's Africa administration, called the UN deployment an 'extraordinary measure' and was frustrated by the US refusal to inform Russia of the size of its deployment to Somalia.[52]

Russia's marginalization in Somalia caused internationalist intellectuals to criticize Andrei Kozyrev's approach to humanitarian intervention in Africa. These academics did not present a united front against Kozyrev's policies, as they were divided between interventionists and isolationists. However, post-facto assessments of these crises from prominent Kozyrev-era internationalists reveal that they generally opposed Russia's approach to humanitarian intervention. Moscow State Institute of International Relations (MGIMO) Professor Alexei Bogaturov contended that Boris Yeltsin should have encouraged joint Russia-NATO participation in peacekeeping missions in Africa.[53] Moscow's Institute of World Economy and International Relations (IMEMO) security policy expert Dina Malysheva supported non-interference, as she argued that the humanitarian mission was doomed to fail due to widespread anarchy in Somalia.[54] These normative disagreements lingered

# THE TUMULTUOUS 1990s

during the late 1990s, but Russia struck a middle-ground solution by expanding its involvement in conflict resolution processes and championing non-interference throughout Africa.

## A Slight Recovery of Russia's Diplomatic Presence in Africa: 1993–96

During the mid-1990s, Russia's presence in Africa began to recover from the marginalization that it experienced at the start of the decade. To re-establish itself as an influential player, Russia focused its diplomatic efforts on rebuilding ties with regional powers like South Africa, Egypt and Nigeria. As Moscow-Pretoria relations took uneasy steps forward during the early 1990s, Russia viewed improved ties with South Africa as the natural starting point for its resurgence. The Russian Ministry of Foreign Economic Relations intensely lobbied Kozyrev to acknowledge South Africa's value as an economic partner, as it saw Pretoria's resilient reaction to economic sanctions as an exceptional quality. The ministry highlighted innovations that occurred in South Africa, such as Sasol firm's production of liquid fuel from coal to overcome an oil embargo, South Africa's five-kilometre-deep mining operations and the first-ever human heart transplant. The Russian Embassy in South Africa and the Russian Trade and Industry Chamber, which sought to export metallurgical equipment and aviation technology to South Africa, also pressured Kozyrev for stronger Moscow-Pretoria relations.[55]

While these lobbying campaigns could not be ignored by the Russian Foreign Ministry, person-to-person links facilitated a revival of Russia-South Africa relations. Gerrit Olivier, who was appointed as South Africa's first ambassador to Russia in 1992, viewed Kozyrev as 'soft-spoken, colourless, abstract, generally unimpressive and without charisma' but held his eventual successor Yevgeny Primakov in much higher esteem.[56] The South African Bureau of State Security shared Olivier's views and invited Primakov to meet with de Klerk in Pretoria in 1993. Olivier also engaged with Vitaly Churkin and representatives of Anatoly Adamishin, who reassured him that the ANC office in Moscow had no purpose. These informal discussions

39

paved the way for comprehensive official talks between Russia and South Africa, which saw Moscow deftly balance ties with the outgoing de Klerk Cabinet and the ANC. In May 1993, Russian Deputy Foreign Minister Boris Kolokolov held meetings with F.W. de Klerk and Nelson Mandela about South Africa's political reconciliation process over a five-day trip and vowed to reverse the slow pace of Russia-South Africa trade links.[57]

In May 1994, Nelson Mandela was inaugurated as South Africa's president and set out to improve relations with Russia. Mandela's August 1994 speech at the opening of the Centre for Russian Studies in Cape Town was heralded in Moscow as a historic breakthrough. During his speech, Mandela claimed that Russia and South Africa should be 'united by the future' and not separated by 'geographic remoteness, past delusion or political myth'. Mandela's positive descriptions of Russian scientists, praise of the Soviet Union's resistance to racism in southern Africa and recollections of Russian assistance to Transvaal in the Boer War fuelled an upsurge of interest in South African history in Moscow.[58] Despite this fanfare, Russia-South Africa economic cooperation did not immediately increase. Olivier cites periodic declines in trade during the mid-1990s, the absence of a tourism boom and Aeroflot's suspension of its new commercial route to South Africa as proof of this gap in rhetoric and policy.[59] This reflected the ANC's mistrust of Boris Yeltsin, who was regarded unfavourably as the architect of the Soviet Union's demise, but the eventual resurgence of internationalism within the Kremlin played a critical role in alleviating frictions in the Russia-South Africa relationship.

Russia also built on the promising foundations left by Kozyrev's trip to Cairo and deepened its partnership with Egypt. In March 1995, Kozyrev travelled to Egypt as part of a Middle Eastern tour, which also included visits to Israel, Syria, Lebanon and the Palestinian Territories. The main subject was Mubarak's regional effort to create a nuclear-free Middle East. Although Israel resisted pressure to disarm its covert nuclear arsenal, as it was threatened by Iran, Iraq, Syria and Libya, Egypt insisted that it and other Arab League countries would not renew the Nuclear Non-Proliferation Treaty (NPT) unless Israel complied with its terms. While the US aligned with Israel, Russia

# THE TUMULTUOUS 1990s

saw a golden opportunity to back Egypt on a critical foreign policy issue. During his visit to Cairo, Andrei Kozyrev stated, 'There is a feeling here that we will find an appropriate solution, which will be beneficial rather than detrimental to the Nuclear Non-Proliferation Treaty.'[60] Russia engaged in shuttle diplomacy with Israel and its Arab neighbours to demonstrate its standing as a regional power to Egyptian officials. This status-seeking gambit coincided with a major Russian economic project in Egypt. In 1995, Lukoil spearheaded the development of the Meleiha oil fields in Egypt's Western Desert, which led to the construction of a 100 km oil pipeline on the western coast of the Red Sea in 2004.[61]

Russia also tried to reboot its relationship with Nigeria, but these forays proved controversial. As Nigeria was ruled by Sani Abacha, an internationally isolated dictator, from 1993 to 1998, Russian policy reflected a delicate balance between the views of pro-engagement internationalists and sceptical pragmatists. Initially, Russia pressured Nigeria over its detention of regime opponents, such as Olusegun Obasanjo, who was imprisoned in 1995 for allegedly planning a coup against Abacha's regime. Despite these human rights critiques, Russia presented a qualified endorsement of Abacha's three-year plan to transition towards a multi-party system. In October 1995, the Russian Foreign Ministry's Grigory Karasin emphasized 'the transition of such a gigantic country as Nigeria to democracy is a complex process',[62] which was a subtle criticism of US concerns about the longevity of Abacha's proposed transition process. The hanging of environmental activist Ken Saro-Wiwa in November 1995, which resulted in Nigeria's suspension from the Commonwealth of Nations, caused Russia to firmly realign with the international consensus on isolating Abacha's regime. The Russian Foreign Ministry claimed that Abacha's actions had 'sown serious doubts' about Nigeria's democratic transition and Russia recalled its ambassador to Nigeria for consultations.[63] This U-turn ensured that Russia-Nigeria relations would only normalize after Obasanjo's inauguration in 1999.

## The Internationalists Strike Back under Yevgeny Primakov: 1996–1999

During Yevgeny Primakov's tenure as Foreign Minister, the globalists were firmly ascendant. This globalist resurgence caused Russia to abandon Kozyrev's pursuit of transatlantic cooperation at all costs. Instead, Russia wanted to reassert itself as a great power provided it did not lead to a systemic confrontation with the West. This state of 'resistance without confrontation' encouraged Russia to broaden its array of non-Western partners and partially realign its normative agenda in the UN with the non-Western consensus. By early 1998, Primakov became convinced that Russia needed to construct a multipolar world order to recover its international standing. The Russia-China-India strategic triangle was the cornerstone of Primakov's vision for a non-Western counterweight to US hegemony, but Africa had a secondary place in a multipolar world order. After his April 1998 meeting with Angola's Foreign Minister Venâncio de Sylva Moura, Yevgeny Primakov declared that 'the period has passed when Russia paid attention to Africa to a lesser extent than this continent deserves'.[64]

Yevgeny Primakov's belief in Africa's potential to serve as Russia's partner in the construction of a multipolar world order received enthusiastic support from Russian academics. Andranik Migranyan, a MGIMO Professor and member of Boris Yeltsin's presidential council, regarded Russia's departure from Africa as an undesirable trade-off for its decision to enter Western civilization.[65] While an admitted sceptic of Africa's short-term economic potential, Higher School of Economics (HSE) Professor Sergei Karaganov, who was a close associate of Yevgeny Primakov, lamented developments in Africa during the early 1990s. In a 2013 interview with *Vedomosti*, Sergei Karaganov noted that, during the Cold War, Western powers paid attention to humanitarian atrocities out of fear of 'strengthening the enemy'. Without a counterweight to Western dominance, Karaganov opined that 'the former colonial powers decided not to notice the genocide of the Hutu and Tutsi peoples' in Rwanda.[66]

Yevgeny Primakov was uniquely suited to construct an internationalist grand coalition of academics, Russian Foreign

THE TUMULTUOUS 1990s

Ministry personnel and security establishment figures. Primakov was highly regarded by these groups as an internationally respected Arabist at IMEMO, and in his role as Mikhail Gorbachev's Special Envoy to Iraq during the 1991 Gulf War and Director of the Foreign Intelligence Service. The widespread popularity of Primakov's multipolarity vision was striking, as the late 1990s were years of extraordinary economic hardship and political turmoil in Russia. As economic reforms were stymied by left-wing parties in the Russian State Duma and organized labour unrest, an increasingly erratic Boris Yeltsin exerted his presidential authority by decree. In August 1998, the Russian government and Russian Central Bank defaulted on their debt. This crisis resulted in a sustained devaluation of the Russian ruble and marked the low ebb of Russia's transition-era depression. The drastic contrast between Russia's 1992–93 divestment from Africa and 1998–99 re-engagement with the continent underscores the primacy of domestic politics, rather than material capabilities in guiding Moscow's approach to Africa. The dimensions of Russia's Primakov-era policies towards Africa, which are a mirror image of the early-to-mid Kozyrev era, will now be explored.

*The Expansion of Russia's Commercial Relationships in Africa*

Under Yevgeny Primakov's watch, Russia's economic policy in Africa transformed from an emphasis on accruing short-term revenues to capitalizing on Africa's long-term economic potential. Vladimir Lopatov, the head of Moscow's Institute for African Studies, spearheaded this ideational transformation. In his 1996 article for *International Affairs*, Lopatov argued that Russia's commercial links were confined to the Maghreb and a handful of Sub-Saharan African countries, such as Guinea and Nigeria. Russia's slide to near commercial irrelevancy required an immediate strategic overhaul. In a rebuke of Andrei Kozyrev's policies, Lopatov contended that Soviet-era debt presented an opportunity, rather than an impediment for Russian commercial relations in Africa. Lopatov argued that Russia should offer debt relief in exchange for preferential access to African markets and the creation of joint enterprises. Lopatov also called for the expanded role of private companies in Africa's mining sector and for an easing of restrictions on Russian arms sales to African countries.[67] These policy recommendations rapidly became mainstream within Russian foreign policy circles, and have consistently guided Vladimir Putin's approach to commercial relations with Africa.

Although Russia's GDP dropped by 3.8% in 1996, which was the seventh consecutive year of economic decline, the Kremlin swiftly implemented Vladimir Lopatov's debt forgiveness recommendations. In November 1996, Russia signed an agreement with Angola that cut the $5 billion figure in Soviet-era debt by 70% and gave Angola until 2016 to pay its remaining $1.5 billion in debt. This deal was implemented in a highly opaque fashion, which established grey zone financial links between Russia and Angola. Even though there was no apparent need for a financial intermediary, the Kremlin established a shell company to oversee Angola's debt repayment to Russia. The Russian Ministry of Finance received just $161 million in cash transfers in 1997 and 1998, as the shell company and its co-owners allegedly siphoned off $774 million from 1997 to 2000.[68] These revenues were accrued by a series of transactions between the shell company and the Russian state, which saw the Kremlin wilfully pay above market value for Angolan debt holdings. These cash transfers rebooted the Russia-Angola partnership and realigned Russian business leaders, who were disillusioned with Kozyrev's restrictions on commerce in Africa, with the Kremlin.

As Russia's debt forgiveness deal with Angola strengthened their historic partnership, the Kremlin proceeded to renegotiate Soviet-era debts with other African countries. Although Russia faced a sovereign debt crisis of its own from August to November 1998, Moscow cancelled 67% of CAR debts in September 1998[69] and 80% of Zambia's $700 million debt to Russia in April 1999. As Russia's economy recorded 6.4% growth in 1999, which placed it on the road to recovery from its nadir, Moscow sought membership in the Paris Club. This organization facilitates debt repayment from countries facing capital shortages to creditor countries. To secure Paris Club membership, Russia was asked to offer deep reductions in its non-productive military loans to Mozambique.[70] Russia subsequently

## THE TUMULTUOUS 1990s

used its participation in the Paris Club to create a rigid schedule for debt relief. In June 1999, Russia pledged to write off 60–90% of the debts from African countries, such as Benin, Guinea-Bissau, Madagascar, Mali, Mozambique, Tanzania, São Tomé and Príncipe and Equatorial Guinea, from 2000 to 2003. Russia's debt cancellations would occur through inter-governmental agreements that awarded these African countries an instalment plan of up to 30 years.[71] In September 1999, Russia fulfilled its Paris Club commitments by agreeing to forgive 90% of Mozambique's $2.42 billion debt burden to Russia. While the 2000 Paris court arrest warrant against Arcadi Gaydamak revealed the endemic corruption that accompanied Russia's debt forgiveness deal with Angola and raised doubts about its other debt cancellation contracts on the continent, the Kremlin adhered to its Paris Club commitments during Vladimir Putin's first term in office.

In addition to debt forgiveness, Russia pursued closer economic ties with Egypt and Nigeria. In September 1997, Russian Vice-Premier Boris Nemtsov discussed economic relations with Hosni Mubarak and a delegation of Egyptian business leaders and sought to reverse the Kozyrev-era decline in Russia-Egypt trade from $1 billion to $400 million. This trade decline exacerbated the Russia-Egypt trade imbalance, as Egypt imported just $40 million in Russian goods in 1996. To jumpstart Russia-Egypt commercial links, Nemtsov proposed Russian Tu-204 plane shipments and investments in electricity generation projects that would contribute to the development of southern Egypt.[72] Russia's February 1996 endorsement of Sani Abacha's democratic transition plan paved the way for an expansion of its economic ties with Nigeria. Boris Yeltsin saw the revival of the unfinished Ajaokuta Steel Project, which the USSR initiated in 1979, as a potential catalyst for expanded trade links.[73] Russia's outreach defied US calls for an industrialized world boycott on new foreign investments, the freezing of Abacha regime financial assets in Western banks and a cessation of government-sponsored sporting and cultural connections.[74] In December 1998, Russian Fuel and Energy Ministry sources announced plans to construct a 'strategic alliance' between Gazprom, Lukoil and Nigeria's state-owned oil industry. To kickstart this energy alliance,

45

Nigeria planned to invest $2 billion in the project and offer concessions of up to 50% to Russian oil and gas companies.[75]

## The Expansion of Russia's Security Presence in Africa

Although Germany surpassed Russia as the largest arms exporter to Africa from 1998 to 2001, Moscow's transfers of $1.2 billion in weaponry or 12.3% of the continent's total, demonstrated its enduring relevance as a weapons vendor.[76] The numerical statistics belie the transformation of Russia's arms sale patterns from Kozyrev to Primakov. From 1996 to 1999, Russia revived its arms deliveries to core Soviet-era partners in Africa, such as Egypt, Angola and Ethiopia, and resumed the sale of weaponry to fragile states and civil war zones. Even as US-Russia relations deteriorated over the crisis in Yugoslavia, Moscow actively courted US partners for arms contracts. These overtures succeeded in Egypt, as a Russian military delegation had re-established ties with Cairo in July 1995. In 1997, Egypt purchased thirty-four T-80U tanks, twenty Mi-17-1V military transport helicopters and Mi-172s. From 1998 to 2000, Egypt added Volga-3 anti-aircraft missile systems, Kvadrat air defence system missiles, Oborona-14 early warning radars and modernized P-18 radars to its military arsenal.[77]

While Russia had carried out isolated arms transfers to Angola under Kozyrev's watch, such as its March 1995 T-55 tank transfers and M-46 artillery, these transfers soared under Primakov's watch. In 1997–98, Russia supplied Angola with six Mi-17 combat helicopters, eighteen MiG-23 fighter bombers and sixty-five BMPs, and these sales overlapped with a military cooperation agreement between the two countries in January 1998.[78] A follow-up agreement was signed in August 1998, which helped Angola modernize Soviet and Russian-made weapons. These agreements partially reflected Russia's residual alignment with the MPLA government. This partnership was exhibited by visits to Moscow in quick succession by three senior Angolan military officials (December 1997), Angola's Foreign Minister Venâncio de Sylva Moura (April 1998) and President Dos Santos (June 1998).[79] Russian media outlets supported Dos Santos's rationale that he was 'launching a major military operation to

## THE TUMULTUOUS 1990s

protect sovereignty', and argued that UNITA's obstructionism on territorial handovers and militia disarmaments were the principal causes of Angola's security crisis.[80] The absence of Russian military support for the MPLA lends credence to Vice-Minister for Russian Foreign Affairs Boris Kolokolov's January 1996 claims that Moscow's arms transfers were 'purely of a commercial nature'.[81] Russia's 1996–98 arms deals with Angola revealed its ability to leverage historical legacies for material gain, which is now a cornerstone of Putin's policies.

Russia provided military technology to both warring parties during the Eritrean-Ethiopian War of May 1998 to June 2000. From 1998 to 1999, Russia sold Ethiopia $245 million in military equipment, which included eight Su-27 interceptor fighters, four Su-25 attack aircraft, four Mi-24 helicopters and eight Mi-17 helicopters. Promexport, a Russian state-owned company, also struck an agreement to sell Ethiopia $200 million in armoured vehicles. Although Ethiopia paid for an initial tranche of weapons, the 2000 arms embargo froze Russia's transfers. These arms sales ensconced Russia's position as a reliable arms provider to Ethiopia during security crises. Russia also signed a military-technical agreement with Eritrea in 1995 and supplied four Mi-24 and Mi-17 helicopters in 1996. This provided legal grounding for Russia to ship four additional Mi-17 helicopters and 200 Igla MANPADS to Eritrea when Ethiopia launched a counter-offensive to seize control of Badme, a town in Tigray Province that Eritrea annexed at the start of the war.[82] These arms sales crystallized Russia's place as one of Eritrea's few international partners as President Isaias Afwerki battled international isolation during the first two decades of the new millennium.

Russia's restoration of arms deliveries to African conflict zones was accompanied by unofficial economic activities that both reinforced and contradicted state policy. This uneasy balance was observable in the Sierra Leone Civil War, which lasted from 1991 to 2002 and resulted in at least 50,000 fatalities. This war pitted government forces, which included President Joseph Momoh (1991–92), military dictator Valentine Strasser (1992–96) and the Sierra Leone People's Party (1996–2002), against Revolutionary United Front

47

rebels backed by Liberia's President Charles Taylor and Muammar al-Gaddafi. Russia officially supported Sierra Leone's government in this struggle, as it believed that the Revolutionary United Front rebels were waging an illegal war against their own people.[83] Charles Ray, the deputy chief of mission of the US Embassy in Freetown, Sierra Leone from 1993 to 1996, notes that Sierra Leone's military junta hired South African mercenaries to fly Russian aircraft and former Russian air force personnel operated a ferry service from Freetown to Sierra Leone's main airport on Lungi Peninsula.[84] In contrast to these Kremlin-sponsored policies, Russian arms dealer Viktor Bout became a major supplier of small arms to forces aligned with the Revolutionary United Front. Bout's sanctions-busting activities extended beyond Sierra Leone to other African countries, such as Liberia, Angola and the Democratic Republic of the Congo (DRC). Bout's network of small arms transfers operated in concert with Russia's presence in Sierra Leone's conflict diamonds trade. Charles Ray recalls that, from 1993 to 1996, at least two Russian nationals were actively involved in smuggling diamonds out of Sierra Leone.

An elaborate nexus of official and surreptitious Russian arms transfers was visible during the First Congo War, which featured extensive interference from Rwanda and Zimbabwe. In 1997, Russian jets worked in concert with planes from Ukraine, Ghana and Nigeria to transfer illegal arms from Bulgaria and Albania to ex-Rwandan army Hutu militants.[85] A senior US official informed me that ex-KGB personnel of Russian, Ukrainian and Belarusian nationalities and Il-76 aircraft, which transported rifles and ammunition, assisted Rwanda's military interference during the First Congo War that propelled Laurent Kabila to power.[86] These arms transfers occurred in tandem with Russia's export of six to nine Mi-24 jets, which were used during the 1980s Soviet war in Afghanistan, to Zimbabwe, which was a critical supporter of Rwanda's military intervention in the DRC. Russia also hosted training sessions for six Zimbabwean officers in Rostov-on-Don.[87] As Russia's military assistance helped Rwanda, a country of just 6.4 million people, play a critical role in Mobutu's overthrow, the US official concluded that this military assistance occurred with at least the tacit consent of the Kremlin. This ambiguous military assistance foreshadowed Russia's use of

## THE TUMULTUOUS 1990s

deniable interventions in Sub-Saharan Africa during Putin's third and fourth terms.

### Russia's Revival as a Normative Challenger in Africa

During his tenure as Foreign Minister and Prime Minister, Yevgeny Primakov sought to restore Russia's normative autonomy in Africa and realign Moscow's approach to international law with that of its non-Western civilizational partners. Russia's most consistent normative positions were its resolute opposition to unilateral sanctions and US-led military interventions. This normative agenda allowed Russia to strengthen its alignments with authoritarian regimes across Africa and cooperate with African countries on collective security challenges. Although Russia's ability to achieve its preferred outcomes in the UNSC and in crisis zones was limited, Primakov's normative agenda has defined Russian public discourse and partnership-building efforts throughout the Putin era. Policy decisions, which will be described later in the book, such as Russia's veto of UN sanctions against Zimbabwe in 2008 and opposition to Muammar al-Gaddafi's overthrow in 2011, are long-term applications of Primakov-era discourse.

Yevgeny Primakov's commitment to Russia's normative autonomy was on display from the outset of his tenure as Foreign Minister. On 26 April 1996, Russia abstained from UNSC Resolution 1054, which imposed sanctions on Sudan for Bashir's refusal to extradite terrorists that planned an assassination attempt against Hosni Mubarak. Russia's Permanent Representative to the United Nations Sergei Lavrov justified this vote by stating that UNSC Resolution 1054 was 'intended not to locate the suspects, but to isolate Sudan internationally'. Lavrov also stated that Russia opposed the use of sanctions to 'punish certain regimes' and warned that sanctioning Sudan without clear proof of Omar al-Bashir's involvement in Mubarak's attempted assassination 'could do real damage to the authority of the Security Council'.[88] Lavrov's justification for abstaining from UNSC Resolution 1054 mirrored his Chinese counterpart Qin Huasun's statement and ensconced a Sino-Russian normative alignment on African affairs in the UN. To highlight the

49

firmness of its normative convictions, Russia abstained from UNSC Resolution 1070, which imposed aviation sanctions on Sudan.

A similar dispute between Russia and the United States surfaced in a March 1998 UN debate on sanctions against Libya. Despite strenuous US objections, Sergei Lavrov argued that Libya had cooperated sufficiently to warrant 'humanitarian exemptions' from sanctions on pilgrimages, agricultural flights and medical evacuations.[89] Russia viewed its moderate approach to sanctioning Libya as a means of bolstering its soft power in Africa. In 1998, the Organization of African Unity turned against UN sanctions on Libya and Muammar-al Gaddafi underwent an ideological transition from Pan-Arabism to Pan-Africanism.[90] Communist Party of Russia General Secretary Gennady Zyuganov played an instrumental role in communicating Russia's policy shift. In December 1998, Zuganov visited Tunisia to reassure officials of the constructive nature of its pushback against US sanctions on Libya and subsequently met with Gaddafi in Tripoli.[91] Despite its conduct in Sudan and Libya, Russia was not a universal champion of sanctions relief. In the UN, Russia was often a cautious challenger to US sanctions policy in Africa and confined its most vociferous obstructionism to debates on Yugoslavia and Iraq. Russia periodically facilitated the strengthening of sanctions regimes in Africa, such as its engagement with Zambia's Foreign Minister Keli Walubita on punishing Angola's UNITA faction.

Russia's critical response to Operation Infinite Reach, a US cruise missile strike on Al-Shifa pharmaceutical factory in Khartoum on 20 August 1998, broadened its normative autonomy in Africa. The United States justified its attack on Sudan by stating that the Al-Shifa factory was producing chemical weapons for al-Qaeda. The Russian Foreign Ministry responded to the Al-Shifa attack by warning that a US strike on Sudan would not help eradicate terrorism and could trigger a 'chain reaction', which could 'undermine the legal framework of international relations'.[92] This statement reflected Yevgeny Primakov's worldview but also sought to assuage more extreme perspectives from Yeltsin's domestic critics. Gennady Zuganov described the US strike in Khartoum as 'state terrorism' and accused the United States of acting as a 'judge and executioner'.[93] Vladimir Zhirinovsky described the United States as 'worse than

# THE TUMULTUOUS 1990s

Hitler' and urged Boris Yeltsin to cancel President Bill Clinton's state visit to Russia.[94] In a similar vein, the Union of Muslims of Russia chairman Nadirshakh Khachilayev called for the recognition of Bill Clinton as an 'international terrorist'.[95] Chechnya's Foreign Minister Movladi Udugov warned of potential reprisals against the US over its Sudan strikes.[96]

After the Al-Shifa attack, Russia attempted to construct an ideational coalition in Africa, which consisted of countries that opposed US unilateralism. During the December 1998 US Operation Desert Fox airstrikes on Iraq, which were triggered by Saddam Hussein's interference with UN weapons inspections, Russia found ideational common ground with Egypt. On 19 December, Russian Foreign Minister Igor Ivanov and his Egyptian counterpart Amr Moussa stated their 'strong opposition to US and British airstrikes on Iraq' and emphasized the need for UN leadership in disarming Iraq's weapons of mass destruction (WMDs).[97] This alignment on Iraq built on Russian State Duma speaker Gennady Seleznyov's September 1997 endorsement of Mubarak's calls for a UN-led destruction of nuclear weapons in the Middle East.[98] Russia's ideational coalition-building efforts intensified after the start of NATO's military intervention in Kosovo in March 1999. Senior Russian officials, such as Colonel-General Leonid Ivashov from the Ministry of Defence, viewed the Kosovo War as a gateway to expanded US military involvement in Africa.[99] These concerns were communicated to African countries. Due to its recent experience with US coercion, Sudan became an important early member of Russia's normative coalition. During a meeting with a Russian parliamentary delegation in Khartoum on 5 April 1999, Omar al-Bashir condemned NATO airstrikes in Kosovo as a 'gross violation of international law'.[100]

As the Kosovo War continued, the fulcrum of Russia's normative alliance became South Africa. On 30 April 1999, Boris Yeltsin met with Nelson Mandela to upgrade Russia-South Africa bilateral relations. The real agenda item, however, was the Kosovo crisis. During his press conference with Mandela, Boris Yeltsin made a highly publicized gaffe that confused South Africa with Yugoslavia and vowed to cooperate with Pretoria on 'standing up for a multipolar world, against the dictate of force'.[101] South Africa's opposition

51

to NATO's intervention in Kosovo without UN approval aligned closely with Russia's views, even though ANC officials privately conceded airstrikes were the only effective deterrent against Slobodan Milošević.[102] This stance caused Russia to view South Africa as an indispensable partner in both Africa and the world stage. Russian Foreign Minister Igor Ivanov's September 1999 listing of South Africa, alongside China and India, as a leading opponent of the multipolar world order foreshadowed the normative foundations of BRICS (Brazil, Russia, India, China and South Africa).[103] Although other opponents of NATO's military intervention in Kosovo, such as Libya and Zimbabwe, did not engage with Moscow in such a public fashion, Russian officials saw first-hand how shared ideas could create new partnerships for Russia in Africa. This realization would be taken to new heights during Vladimir Putin's first two terms in office.

2

# THE DAWN OF RUSSIA'S RESURGENCE
# IN AFRICA
## 2000–08

During the first decade of the new millennium, Russia overcame its transition-era economic and political turmoil and reasserted itself as a great power on the world stage. Russia's efforts to re-establish its hegemony over the post-Soviet space, accrue status recognition from the United States and Europe, and strengthen its partnership with China were its defining geopolitical ambitions. Initially, Russia's resurgence in Africa was less pronounced than in other former Third World theatres, such as the Middle East and South Asia, as Vladimir Putin continued to build on Yevgeny Primakov's blueprint. However, Russia began paying increased attention to Africa during the mid-2000s, as US-Russia relations deteriorated over the Iraq War and the colour revolutions occurred in Georgia and Ukraine. Through state visits to Algeria in 2006 and Libya in 2008, Vladimir Putin re-established Russia as a great power in North Africa and repaired the soft power damage caused by its heavy-handed response to the Second Chechen War. Russia also established close relationships with anti-Western regimes, such as Sudan and Zimbabwe, with its politics-blind approach to arms sales and commercial engagement on the continent.

The expansion of Russia's array of bilateral partnerships in Africa was complemented by Moscow's growing engagement with the African Union (AU), which ensconced the continent as a pole in Putin's vision of a multipolar world order. These changes suggest that Putin's first two terms should be viewed as a transition period from the 1990s era of Russian marginalization in Africa to the renewed pursuit of continent-wide great power status, which began with Dmitry Medvedev's June 2009 African tour. To illustrate the formative role of the early 2000s in Russia's Africa policy, this chapter will begin by briefly outlining the domestic forces and factors that inspired Putin's pursuit of expanded influence in Africa. It will then examine Russia's efforts to revive its core partnerships in Africa, establish ties with anti-Western regimes and present itself as a potential hedge partner for traditionally pro-Western countries in Africa. The chapter will conclude with an examination of the forces that shaped the recovery of Russia's influence in North Africa, encapsulated in Putin's trips to Morocco, Egypt, Libya and Algeria from 2005 to 2008.

### Vladimir Putin as Yevgeny Primakov 2.0: Russia's Africa Policy, 2000–04

After his inauguration as President of Russia in May 2000, it appeared unlikely that Vladimir Putin would oversee Russia's return to great power status in Africa. The June 2000 Foreign Policy Concept of the Russian Federation highlighted Russia's commitment to stability in North Africa, resolving regional conflicts in Africa and cooperating with the Organization of African Unity (OAU).[1] These plans were ambiguous and contrasted markedly with the targeted outreaches of other great powers to Africa. The April 2000 EU-Africa Summit and October 2000 Forum on China-Africa Cooperation Forum were especially prominent forays by great powers in Africa. These forums predominantly discussed commercial deals, but the EU and China also used these summits to assert themselves as counterweights to US hegemony. Russia viewed these summits positively, as they furthered its vision of a multipolar world order. Outside of the public eye, France's President Jacques Chirac's frustrations with

## THE DAWN OF RUSSIA'S RESURGENCE IN AFRICA

US unilateralism inspired back-channel dialogue between Paris and Moscow. Vladimir Shubin, who was appointed to the Federation Council Foreign Affairs Committee Advisory Council in 2002, recalls French diplomats expressing regret about Russia's 1990s retrenchment from Africa, as it meant that France would have to contain the US alone.[2]

In response to cues from Russia's great power counterparts and prodding from French officials, Vladimir Putin elevated Africa's place in Moscow's foreign policy in 2001. During that year, Putin hosted delegations from major regional powers, such as Algeria, Egypt, Ethiopia and Nigeria; traditional partners, such as Guinea and Libya; and nascent partners, such as Gabon. In April 2001, Putin declared that Russia wanted to establish friendly relations with all regions of the world and insisted that Africa was no less important than other regions.[3] This countered the visible denigration of Africa's importance during the early Yeltsin era. Deputy Foreign Ministers Vasilii Sredin[4] and Alexander Saltanov[5] provided vital support for Putin's re-engagement with Africa. Their perspectives were articulated in *International Affairs* articles, which were published in 2001 and 2004, respectively. Sredin was particularly forceful in his support for Russia's resurgence in Africa, as he argued it was in Moscow's national security interests. Stating that 'Russia's participation in settling conflicts in Africa is not altruism', Sredin urged the Kremlin to thwart the diffusion of terrorism, illegal arms and drugs from Africa to Russia. This national security narrative for expanded engagement in Africa resonated with the Russian foreign policy establishment, as Russia was embroiled in the Second Chechen War and Putin sought to restore law and order by creating a stable authoritarian regime. Sredin and Saltanov were joined by prominent figures in the Federation Council, such as Vladimir Shubin, and influential members of the Russian expert community, such as Alexei Vasiliev, in steering Vladimir Putin towards furthering Primakov's re-engagement with Africa.

Despite Putin's emphasis on a new dawn in Russia-Africa relations, his preferred playbook, which was championed by the Russian MFA, mirrored Primakov-era policies. The resemblance did not just extend to Russia's support for anti-Western regimes and non-normative approach to arms sales, but also extended to Moscow's soft power-building tactics. Sredin argued that Russia's debt forgiveness in Africa during the June 1999 G8 meeting in Cologne and support for debt restructuring in Mozambique in April 2000 had far-reaching positive impacts, such as the dispatch of payment grants to 700 young African scholars. Vladimir Putin continued these policies at the start of his presidency. While details on the timing and scope of its debt forgiveness are unknown, Putin has described Russia's forgiveness of Tanzania's debt in the early 2000s as 'not only an act of generosity, but also a manifestation of pragmatism'.[6] This paved the way for Russian debt renegotiations in Algeria and Libya in 2006 and 2008, respectively. Although Russia's 1996 scholarship programme in Africa struggled for uptake, the Kremlin offered scholarships to African students. The Russian Interior Ministry's education programmes, which trained 78 Africans in peacekeeping and 150 African security experts in Moscow, Volgograd and St Petersburg, were especially noteworthy. This initiative progressed with difficulties, as Russia was only able to expand its array of students to 4,500 by 2007, and modest Russian government scholarships only covered tuition fees.[7]

In addition to educational diplomacy, Russia viewed peacekeeping and humanitarian assistance as fertile areas of cooperation with Africa. Sredin believed that Moscow should expand its peacekeeping role through direct cooperation with the OAU. Saltanov also promoted Russia's expanded role in peacekeeping missions in Africa, as they built on Moscow's standing as a guarantor of peace in Angola. During the late 1990s and early 2000s, Russia participated in UN peacekeeping missions in the Western Sahara, Sierra Leone, Ethiopia, Eritrea, Côte d'Ivoire and Liberia. The scale of Russian participation in peacekeeping missions in Africa reached 230 by 2007. These peacekeeping deployments occurred in tandem with Russia's support for the implementation of truces in the United Nations. Saltanov also steered Russian officials towards backing the expansion of humanitarian aid and contributions to public health in Africa. Aside from Russia's emergency food aid to Sudan, this policy struggled to take root during Putin's first two terms but emerged as a central feature of Moscow's playbook during the subsequent Dmitry Medvedev era.

THE DAWN OF RUSSIA'S RESURGENCE IN AFRICA

Russian officials also emphasized Africa's place as an integral pole in the international system. Although Sredin and Saltanov supported Russia's engagement with the G8 on African affairs, Saltanov was especially forceful in his support for 'African solutions to African problems'. During the mid-2000s, Stronski astutely noted that Russia's outreaches 'focused mainly on South Africa and the African Union—two entities it hoped could serve as partners to support its vision for a multipolar world'.[8] Russia illustrated its commitment to Africa's agency in international affairs in two ways. First, Russia embraced African development agendas, such as the New Partnership for Africa's Development (NEPAD) programme, which was intertwined with its prior support for the African Action Plan (AAP) at the 2002 G8 summit in Kananakis, Canada.[9] Second, Russia strengthened its relationships with regional institutions in Africa, such as the Southern African Development Community (SADC), which was facilitated by its partnerships with South Africa and Angola, and the Economic Community of West African States (ECOWAS), driven by its growing ties with Nigeria. In March 2001, Russia attended an Intergovernmental Development Authority (IGAD) meeting on Somalia and Sudan as an observer, which contributed to the France-led Ethiopia-Eritrea peace initiative.[10] Russia's engagement with IGAD would grow as countries within the bloc faced Western sanctions, which persist to this date.[11] While these outreaches were largely symbolic, they set the tone for Russia's future empowerment of the AU in crises spanning from Libya's 2011 revolution to the Central African Republic civil war.

Despite these ambitious policies, optimism about the scale of Russia-Africa cooperation was initially concentrated in the Russian Foreign Ministry and had little external resonance. In 2001, Sredin was bullish about Russia-Africa relations and boasted that 'relations with very few other world regions have been developing as rapidly over the past four decades'. In 2004, Saltanov stated 'the basic line towards consolidating relations with African countries and their regional and subregional organizations, and mutually expanding beneficial cooperation in various fields remains immutable'. By the mid-2000s, Russia had indisputably turned the corner in its engagement with Africa. Angola's Foreign Minister Téte António

57

argues that 'Since 2005, the friendly ties between the Russian Federation and Africa have been restoring dynamism', as 'countries of strategic importance on the continent were identified'.[12] Vladimir Lopatov's transition from a sceptic to supporter of Putin's Africa policy reflects this growing optimism. In a 2006 article, Lopatov expressed frustration with Africa's stagnant position at 1% of Russia's trade, and explored the intrinsic factors which explain the low appeal of African markets in Russia.[13] One year later, Lopatov argued that Putin had 'returned Africa to its rightful place in Russian foreign policy', as he established diversified cooperation with African partners' and abandoned a 'hypertrophied orientation towards the West'.[14] Lopatov also believed that Putin's personal interest in African affairs, which was illustrated by his visits to Algeria, Egypt, South Africa and Morocco, would lead to major commercial breakthroughs.

After Putin's 2006 trip to Africa, Russia continued to publicly highlight its growing momentum on the continent. In March 2007, Russian Prime Minister Mikhail Fradkov visited Angola, Namibia and South Africa, and the number of intra-parliamentary exchanges between Russia and African countries intensified. These political exchanges were paired with the rapid growth of economic and cultural interactions between Russia and Africa. The Russia-Africa Business Council, which was formed in 2002, and the Russia-South Africa Business Council, which was inaugurated in November 2006, became critical agents of Moscow's commercial ambitions in Africa. Cultural events, such as Mir Afriki (Africa World) and Afrika Sevodnya (Today's Africa) also strengthened Russia-Africa cooperation. A March 2007 Russian Foreign Ministry paper entitled 'A Comprehensive Look at Russian Federation Foreign Policy' codified Sredin and Saltanov's policy prescriptions on debt forgiveness and humanitarian assistance into official policy, and formalized Africa's rising profile as a region of Russia's power projection.[15] This spirit of optimism would reach new heights during Dmitry Medvedev's presidency, as Russia laid the foundation for a return to continent-wide great power status.

## THE DAWN OF RUSSIA'S RESURGENCE IN AFRICA

*Russia Strengthens Its Core Partnerships in Sub-Saharan Africa*

Building on its AU outreaches, Russia established a core network of partnerships with regional powers in Sub-Saharan Africa. The expansion of Russia's relationships with Nigeria, Ethiopia and South Africa was especially pronounced. Although Russia dispatched a representative to Nigerian President Olusegun Obasanjo's 1999 inauguration, Obasanjo's March 2001 visit to Moscow was a seminal moment in Russia-Nigeria relations.[16] Obasanjo expressed frustration with the $50 million trade volume, which was less than one-quarter of Soviet-era levels.[17] Obasanjo targeted an expansion of Russia-Nigeria trade to $500 million by 2006 and signed a military-technical agreement with Russia, which would remain in effect until 2005. Russia also announced plans to construct a metallurgical plant to extract Nigerian oil and agreed to test advanced satellites in Nigeria. Beyond these material targets, Obasanjo sought to establish personal ties with Putin. Obasanjo's decision to visit Russia on his birthday was regarded favourably, as was his praise for Russia's development of democratic institutions and defeat of separatist movements.[18] As Nigeria was experiencing similar political developments, these comments were hailed in Moscow, and *Kommersant* headlined Obasanjo's visit with the sub-caption 'We realize how similar we are.' Putin also acknowledged Nigeria's regional power status in Africa by calling it an 'authoritative state not only in Africa, but also the world'.

Despite these grand gestures, John Campbell, US Ambassador to Nigeria from 2004 to 2007, notes that Russia maintained a 'very low profile', aside from ceremonial events.[19] Obasanjo's October 2004 meeting with Russian Deputy Foreign Minister Yuri Fedorov in Abuja was the most significant Russia-Nigeria foreign policy exchange during his tenure. Campbell notes that Obasanjo's close relationship with President George W. Bush could have impeded cooperation with Russia, as Nigeria vowed to compensate for shortfalls in Middle Eastern oil exports to the US and the US supported Nigeria's democratic transition and peacekeeping role. As President Umaru Yar'Adua lacked Obasanjo's interest in international affairs and Nigerian foreign policy decision-making is concentrated in the president's hands, Nigeria was not expected to overhaul its relationships with great powers.[20] Nevertheless, Putin wrote a letter to Yar'Adua in April 2007 requesting energy sector cooperation with Nigeria. In July 2007, Yar'Adua met with Putin on the sidelines of the G8 summit and agreed to visit Russia. Nigerian officials reportedly hailed Putin's energy offers as 'mind-boggling' and declared that Gazprom was seeking to squeeze Europe out of the picture, while out-competing China, India and the United States.[21] In January 2008, Gazprom unveiled a formal bid to develop Nigeria's energy infrastructure in exchange for access to its vast reserves. This followed Rusal's February 2007 $250 million 77.5% stake in the Aluminium Smelter Company of Nigeria (ALSCON).[22] Putin's outreaches to Yar'Adua, which occurred in tandem with Western discontent about Yar'Adua's fraudulent 2007 election victory, paved the way for Medvedev's historic 2009 visit to Nigeria.

As the 1998–2000 Ethiopia-Eritrea War wound down, Russia's engagement with Ethiopia expanded. Ethiopia's Deputy Foreign Minister, Vice-Premier and Defence Minister held high-level discussions with Russian officials in 2000. In December 2001, Ethiopian Prime Minister Meles Zenawi met with Putin in Moscow to 'restore the pre-existing excellent economic and trade relations with Russia', which had dwindled to just $56.6 million in 2000.[23] Although Derg-era Soviet-Ethiopian relations remained a polarizing issue, Zenawi recalled 'the glorious history of Russian-Ethiopian relations, which began in the late nineteenth century', and claimed that 'a whole generation of Ethiopian people believed that the help and friendship of the Russian people was a matter of course'. The Ethiopian diplomatic delegation that accompanied Zenawi predicted that 'The Horn of Africa will once again be a cornucopia', and declared that Russia and Ethiopia 'intend to contribute to the strengthening of strategic stability in the world'.[24] This ebullient rhetoric was complemented by major breakthroughs in the Russia-Ethiopia relationship. Building on July 1999 negotiations, Russia agreed to cancel Ethiopia's debt via the IMF and Paris Club framework. Ethiopia vowed to expand cooperation with Russia's regions, which built on Tatarstan truck manufacturing company KamAZ's establishment of a workshop in Mekele.[25]

## THE DAWN OF RUSSIA'S RESURGENCE IN AFRICA

Ethiopia also requested a $150 million arms package from Russia consisting of 6 Mi-35 helicopters, 100 anti-aircraft missile systems, 20 BTR-90 armored personnel carriers and ammunition for small arms and artillery. Although Bulgaria had delivered 100 T-55 tanks prior to the 2000 embargo, Russia was once again Ethiopia's overwhelmingly dominant arms supplier.

Mirroring trends in Russia's other African partnerships, these pledges took a long time to come to fruition. Citing prominent Moscow-based defence experts, such as Maxim Pyadushkin, an *Izvestia* article on 4 December predicted that 'the volume of new supplies from Russia will not be too large'.[26] Contrary to the sweeping array of purchases that were anticipated after Zenawi's trip, Pyadushkin predicted that Ethiopia would merely satisfy its urgent need for spare parts and artillery to replace antiquated Soviet-era T-54s, T-55s and T-62s, which built on other deliveries. These predictions appeared to hold until tensions between Ethiopia and Eritrea reheated in 2003–05. In response to this escalation, Ethiopia purchased $407 million in Russian weaponry and Addis Ababa subsequently courted Russian support against Islamic extremism, ethno-confessional conflicts and piracy.[27]

Outside the military-technical sphere, Russia-Ethiopia relations faced major setbacks. While 80% of its debt was cancelled in 2001, Russia's cancellation of $1.1 billion of $1.26 billion Ethiopia's debt and renegotiation of the remaining $160 million to a thirty-year term only occurred in March 2005.[28] As the October 2004 Paris Club meeting caused Ethiopia's main international creditors to cancel their loans, Russia diluted its first-mover debt forgiveness advantage. Prime Minister Mikhail Kasyanov visited Ethiopia in 2002, which resulted in a visa-free travel agreement and Russian pledges to invest in Ethiopia's natural gas deposits, but Putin's much-speculated trip to Ethiopia did not take place. Ethiopia advertised itself as a potentially appealing tourism destination for Russians, as it is Africa's oldest Christian civilization, but the high cost of tours meant that just 100 Russians visited each year in the mid-2000s.[29] These setbacks were compounded by Russia's close ties with Eritrea and ensured that Russia-Ethiopia relations struggled to gain serious traction until Putin's fourth term.

61

Russia greeted Thabo Mbeki's takeover as South Africa's president with apprehension. During the late 1980s and early 1990s, Mbeki converted the ANC from a Soviet-dependent organization that was bent on armed struggle to a non-aligned entity that sought a negotiated end to apartheid.[30] The removal of Soviet fighters from Angola via airlift to Uganda, which signified Gorbachev's desire for deconfliction in southern Africa, crystallized Mbeki's pivot towards non-alignment.[31] Mbeki's actions as president assuaged Russia's concerns, as he elevated pro-Russian figures to senior posts. Ronnie Kasrills, South Africa's Minister of Intelligence from 2004 to 2008, claimed the Soviet Union 'was like a dream' and 'was held with much love and respect'.[32] Pallo Jordan, a cabinet minister from 1994 to 2009, notes that Mbeki's foreign policy towards great powers was pragmatic, and that Mbeki aimed to insert South Africa as an important stakeholder in African affairs, even when the AU was unwilling to follow suit.[33] Russia believed that close ties with South Africa would advance its continental ambitions and welcomed the stability that Mbeki brought to Russia-South Africa relations.

Mbeki's lead role in converting the OAU into the African Union strengthened Russia-South Africa relations, and in July 2002, Putin wrote a letter congratulating Mbeki for his chairmanship of the AU. On 5 September 2006, Vladimir Putin arrived in South Africa for a two-day state visit. During his trip, Putin and Mbeki signed a five-page Treaty of Friendship and Partnership, while Russia agreed to invest $1 billion in the South African economy. These investments gave Russia a foothold in South Africa's energy markets, which presaged its Zuma-era nuclear energy outreaches, and allowed Russia to construct an aluminium plant in South Africa. Due to the initiative of Gijima Technologies chairman Robert Gumede and Russian businessman Vladimir Kremer, a Russia-South Africa Business Council was also established.[34] South Africa's Foreign Minister Nkosazana Dlamini-Zuma claimed that cooperation with Russia will enable Russia to 'have its voice heard' on international issues, and the agenda of Putin's visit fittingly included discussions on Middle East peace and the Iran nuclear programme.[35] Security cooperation between Russia and South Africa also deepened, as both countries pledged to cooperate against terrorism, organized crime

## THE DAWN OF RUSSIA'S RESURGENCE IN AFRICA

and against the weaponization of space.[36] While the Putin-Mbeki relationship spearheaded diplomatic cooperation between Moscow and Pretoria, Fradkov strengthened Russia-South Africa economic cooperation during his March 2007 visit with preliminary discussions about Russian nuclear energy exports and the pursuit of a financial sector agreement between Russia's financial system and Standard Bank.[37] This synthesis of commercial deals, security cooperation and collaboration on international issues set the stage for more expansive Russia-South Africa coordination under Zuma.

### Russia's Embrace of Cautious Anti-Westernism in Sub-Saharan Africa

Despite the cordial state of US-Russia relations during the early 2000s, Russia expanded its network of anti-Western partners. Russian newspaper *Trud* stated that 'in choosing partners, Russia will now be guided exclusively by its own interests'.[38] As a result, Russia engaged with Iraq's Deputy Prime Minister Tariq Aziz and restored highest level 'working contacts' with North Korea. Russia's engagement with Sudan and Zimbabwe extended this policy to Africa. During Putin's tenure, Russia countered US efforts to isolate Sudan. A Stockholm International Peace Research Institute (SIPRI) report from 2003 to 2007 showed that Russia supplied 87% of conventional weapons, which far exceeded China's 8% market share.[39] In March 2005, the UN tightened multilateral sanctions against Sudan over the escalating conflict in Darfur. Russia abstained from UNSC Resolution 1591 alongside China and Algeria but criticized these new sanctions. Andrei Denisov warned that the sanctions could deter the Sudanese authorities from pushing for a speedy resolution to the Darfur war or participating in the Abuja peace talks and noted African Union and Arab League opposition to additional sanctions.[40]

In April 2006, Russia joined China in blocking the imposition of UN sanctions against four Sudanese government officials. In October 2006, Sudan's Defence Minister Abdel Rahim Mohammed Hussein travelled to Moscow, and asked Sergei Lavrov for a $1 billion loan to purchase Russian equipment.[41] Hussein's visit followed a correspondence between Bashir and Putin, which saw the Sudanese leader request a 'large consignment' of Russian aircraft and helicopters.[42] Bashir and Hussein's long-term plan was to oversee a twenty-five-year modernization of Sudan's armed forces, which would be spearheaded by Russian weapons and technical expertise and allow Sudan to be Russia's foothold in Africa. In response to criticisms, Russian experts turned the tables on Western countries by accusing them of turning a blind eye to Ukrainian arms transfers to Sudan via Kenya, which could fan the flames of a 'serious war'.[43] Russian shipments of humanitarian aid to Sudan, which included a July 2006 cargo of 30 tons of rice to Darfur, illustrated its willingness to correct the wrongs imbued by Western sanctions.[44]

During the mid-2000s, Russia's partnership with Zimbabwe strengthened considerably. This improvement in relations appeared to be an unlikely prospect at the dawn of the new millennium, as Robert Mugabe's land seizures from white farmers were fiercely condemned in Russia, especially by liberals. April 2000, a *Kommersant* article accused Mugabe of partnering with 'black fascists' and 'evil and envious loafers', and compared the Zimbabwe African National Union-Patriotic Front (ZANU-PF) revolutionary Chenjerai Hunzvi to Adolf Hitler.[45] March 2002, a *Kommersant* article warned that Zimbabwe was turning into a police state and called Robert Mugabe an 'African Slobodan Milošević'.[46] After Zimbabwe's 2003 withdrawal from the Commonwealth of Nations, Mugabe tried to upgrade Russia-Zimbabwe relations. Mugabe's 2004 *Nezavisimaya Gazeta* article, which highlighted Russia's interests in eastern Zimbabwe's gold reserves as stepping stones for broader cooperation,[47] and post-2005 Look East policy strengthened relations with Russia. In October 2006, Russia and Zimbabwe signed five deals worth $300 million, which gave Moscow a foothold in the electricity, aviation and mining sectors, and military cooperation was upgraded in 2007. Despite Putin's wariness of acting as Zimbabwe's crisis-proof patron, Russia's opposition to UN sanctions against Zimbabwe on non-interference grounds in 2008 was a catalyst for bilateral cooperation.

Russia also capitalized on discontent amongst African countries with US foreign policy and tried to establish itself as a hedge partner for traditional pro-Western African countries. While Conte welcomed the US's imposition of sanctions on Liberia, which

## THE DAWN OF RUSSIA'S RESURGENCE IN AFRICA

trained rebel groups in southern Guinea, he believed that the US's economic assistance was insufficient. Fearing a potential war with Liberia, Lansana Conte visited Moscow in July 2001. During Conte's trip, Guinea struck deals to upgrade its existing stockpile of Russian military technology, such as its eight MiG-17 and MiG-21 fighter jets, and purchased a new fleet of combat helicopters.[48] To accelerate these arms deliveries, Conte gave Russian aluminium giant Rusal development rights to Dian-Dian, which is one of the world's largest bauxite reserves. Dian-Dian has 1 billion tons of high-quality bauxite, and produces 11 million tons of bauxite and 1.2 million tons of alumina each year.[49] As Russia already possessed a 12% stake in the global aluminium market, this deal expanded Moscow's influence over world aluminium prices. Despite close ties with France and the US, which expanded in the early 2000s, Omar Bongo met with Vladimir Putin in Moscow. *Kommersant* noted that the Soviet Union established diplomatic relations with Gabon in 1973, but Gabon's close relationship with France meant that both countries were 'on opposite sides of the barricades'.[50] As Ukraine provided manganese to the Soviet Union, Russia took great interest in Gabon's manganese reserves and the visit of a Russian commercial delegation to Libreville preceded Bongo's visit to Moscow.[51] Bongo also asked Putin to create a repair and maintenance centre for Russian-manufactured aircraft in Africa.[52]

### Russia Repairs Its Historic Partnerships in North Africa

During Putin's first two terms, Russia rebuilt its Soviet-era network of partners in North Africa. The revitalization of Russia's presence in Maghreb appeared unlikely when Putin arrived on the political scene in 1999. The combined effect of lingering debt disputes, the Algerian civil war, UN sanctions against Libya and the US security partnership with Egypt marginalized Russia in the Maghreb during the 1990s. Regional backlash against Putin's heavy-handed response to the Second Chechen War compounded this crisis. Alexander Shumilin, the director of the Center for the Analysis of Middle East Conflicts at the RAS Institute for US and Canadian Studies, pinpoints two key factors that shaped Russia's resurgence in North Africa.[53] The first was the personal influence of Yevgeny Primakov, who valued Russia's historic partnerships with Egypt and Algeria, and continued to strengthen Moscow's presence in North Africa through his travels as a private citizen in the early 2000s. The second was the close relationship between Russia and secular authorities in North Africa, which was ensconced by Moscow's solidarity with the FLN in the Algerian civil war, and parallel strengthening of ties between Russian and North African Sunni Islamic communities.

The incremental growth of person-to-person relations between Russian and North African officials, the Maghreb's support for a multipolar world order and the pursuit of mutually beneficial commercial opportunities helped reverse this tide of Russian marginalization. Russia's support for a 'dialogue of civilizations' approach with North African countries on the issue of terrorism boosted its soft power, as Moscow detached itself from its past reliance on cultural and religious stereotypes.[54] These successes were most apparent in Russia's relationships with Egypt, Algeria and Libya, but Moscow did not completely neglect Morocco and Tunisia. In September 2006, Putin met with King Mohammed VI in Rabat, as he sought to capitalize on the growth of mining and agriculture sector trade between the two countries. Russia's nuclear power monopoly Atomstroyexport announced plans to bid for the construction of Morocco's first nuclear power plant.[55] Sergei Lavrov made a state visit to Tunisia in November 2005, which followed the revival of intra-parliamentary delegation meetings in 2003. As Russia's outreaches to Morocco and Tunisia remained on the fringes of its African strategy, this section will focus on Russia's partnerships with Egypt, Algeria and Libya.

### Russia Deepens Its Partnership with Egypt

Although the War on Terror strengthened Hosni Mubarak's ties with the US, Putin's first two terms witnessed a substantial, if uneven, consolidation of Russia-Egypt relations. HSE academic Leonid Issaev notes that Egypt was committed to positive relations with Russia, as it embraced a position of 'positive neutrality' during the Second Chechen War, courted Russia's support on UNSC reform, and

## THE DAWN OF RUSSIA'S RESURGENCE IN AFRICA

shared Moscow's opposition to US unilateralism. Russia and Egypt also created a bilateral working group on counterterrorism after the 9/11 attacks, and Putin called Mubarak on 20 September 2001 to elevate this collaboration. Despite these successes, Issaev notes that Egypt's dependence on US economic and military aid prevented it from becoming Russia's gateway to the Middle East. While Russia and Egypt devised a long-term framework for commercial relations during Mubarak's 2001 trip, economic links did not reach the expected heights. The Second Chechen War prompted a sharp backlash from Egypt's Islamist movements, which clashed with Mubarak's moderate position. The Muslim Brotherhood described Russia's conduct in Chechnya as 'deviant savagery', while Mufti Sheikh Wassel urged Islamic countries to boycott Russia 'politically and economically'.[56] Russia's designation of the Muslim Brotherhood as a terrorist organization in 2003 was a step too far even for Mubarak, as Muslim Brotherhood members sat in the Egyptian parliament.[57] For these reasons, Alexei Vasiliev describes Russia-Egypt relations as a 'partnership but not an alliance'.[58]

Russia's observer status in the Organisation of Islamic Cooperation (OIC) and revived interest in Middle East affairs strengthened its cooperation with Egypt ahead of Putin's 2005 trip. The Israel-Palestine conflict was a key vector of Russia-Egypt diplomatic cooperation. In November 2000, Igor Ivanov praised Egypt's ceasefire efforts and claimed that Russia could assist the Egypt-Jordan peace initiative, as overreliance on a single peace process might result in diplomatic stagnation.[59] Ivanov's statements caused Russia to convene multilateral negotiations on the Middle East in January 2001, which allowed it to engage with Egypt alongside Western countries. These statements culminated in April 2005 in Putin's visit to Egypt, Israel and Palestine, which aimed to insert Russia as an intermediary in the implementation of the Roadmap for Peace plan.[60] Russia and Egypt's shared opposition to the 2003 Iraq War also created normative bonding. Egypt's engagement with Russia on the Iraq War stemmed from its inflated assessment of Moscow's willingness to resist US policy. At a Civic Debates club meeting in January 2003, an Egyptian journalist stated that 'The entire Arab world is looking at Russia, which can say no to

67

RUSSIA IN AFRICA

America.'[61] As Coptic Church head Pope Shenouda III of Alexandria opposed the Iraq War, Coptic Christians in Egypt viewed Russia's resistance to US unilateralism as a positive gesture.[62] In May 2004, Putin and Mubarak described the Coalition Provisional Authority's rule as incompatible with Iraqi sovereignty and demanded a swift departure of foreign forces from Iraq.[63]

As Russia's diplomatic cooperation with Egypt outstripped its economic partnership, Putin's April 2005 visit to Cairo focused on ensuring the implementation of recently signed commercial deals. These efforts were underwhelming. The Bush administration pressured Egypt to avoid nuclear energy cooperation with Russia. Mubarak acceded to US pressure, as signing non-proliferation agreements would prevent Cairo from ever obtaining a nuclear weapon.[64] Egypt was expected to purchase MANPADs from Rosoboronexport but the Putin-Bush agreement barring MANPAD exports to 'sensitive regions of the world' would preclude sales to Egypt, which had a known al-Qaeda presence.[65] Russia countered by offering Egypt stationary air defence systems, which it already sold to Syria, but Cairo's reticence sparked concerns that Moscow was being outmaneuvered by China in the air defence sphere.[66]

Despite this ambiguous record, Alexei Vasiliev believes that Putin's visit to Cairo strengthened the Russia-Egypt relationship.[67] In the economic arena, Egyptian businessman Ibrahim Kamal invested in Russia's Tu-204 jet and Russian tourism to Egypt expanded. In 2006, Russian students began arriving in Al-Azhar University and a 15,000-strong Russian diaspora in Egypt emerged. These cultural exchanges spilt over to religious diplomacy, as bonds between Coptic Christians and the Russian Orthodox Church, as well as Russian and Egyptian Muslim communities, featured prominently at the Dialogue of Civilizations forum. As trade between Russia and Egypt increased by 52% from 2005 to 2006 to $1.6 billion, Mubarak met with Putin in November 2006 to capitalize on the economic and cultural partnership's momentum.[68] Diplomatic cooperation between Russia and Egypt also continued to expand, albeit at a more incremental pace. Egypt's offer to facilitate the release of Russian citizens captured in Iraq in 2006 further strengthened bonds, even though Cairo's offer had no tangible impact. Russia and Egypt's common

## THE DAWN OF RUSSIA'S RESURGENCE IN AFRICA

views on Syria and Lebanon after the 2005 Cedar Revolution, and the Iran nuclear issue emerged as new areas of common ground.[69] These breakthroughs laid the groundwork for Medvedev's 2009 trip to Cairo and provided a material foundation for Russia's counter-revolutionary response to the Arab Spring.

### The Revitalization of the Russia-Algeria Partnership under Vladimir Putin

Although Vladimir Putin's March 2006 visit to Algiers strengthened the Russia-Algeria partnership, an upward trend in the bilateral relationship was detectable from the inception of his presidency. Abdelaziz Bouteflika's ascension to power as Algeria's president in April 1999 coincided with this improvement. Vasily Kuznetsov, a North Africa expert at the Moscow Institute of Oriental Studies of the Russian Academy of Sciences (RAS), notes that many Russian experts viewed the Algerian civil war as a counterterrorism struggle, and therefore viewed Bouteflika's victory over extremism as a resounding success.[70] E.M. Bogucharskiy claims that Russian officials positively viewed Bouteflika's efforts to 'return Algeria to the international arena'. Algeria's international return was exemplified by its hosting of the 35th OAU Summit and organization of the Western Mediterranean Interior Ministers conference in June 1999. While these efforts bolstered Algeria's prestige in Western capitals, Bogucharskiy noted Bouteflika's aversion to a 'trusteeship' relationship with the West and pragmatic desire to engage with traditional partners like Russia.[71] Despite his commitment to multipolarity, Bouteflika was not immune to criticism. Orientalist Boris Dolgov warned that Bouteflika did not address factors which exacerbated the Algerian civil war, such as youth unemployment and discrimination against Berbers, and this neglect could lead to 'spontaneous unrest, which can take on various, even extremist forms'.[72] Russian media outlets also criticized Bouteflika's participation in NATO's Mediterranean dialogue alongside Egypt, Israel, Jordan, Morocco, Tunisia and Mauritania.[73] These ambiguous assessments of Bouteflika's domestic and foreign policy ensured that the Russia-Algeria rapprochement was gradual and inconsistent during the early 2000s.

Although scepticism abounded about Algeria's long-term prospects for stability and foreign policy orientation, the Russia-Algeria partnership strengthened due to powerful domestic forces. Kuznetsov notes that Russian experts viewed the Algerian civil war as a period akin to the post-Communist transition in Russia, which also witnessed separatist conflicts in Chechnya, and therefore, special attention was paid to Algeria's political future.[74] These parallels resonated at a popular level, as social disorder in Russia and Algeria was triggered in part by the return of soldiers from the Soviet war in Afghanistan.[75] A groundswell of support for Russia-Algeria relations developed, as both countries were believed to possess common destinies. Russian-Algerian business forums, which were held in Algeria in May 1998 and Russia in March 1999; the arrival of a Russian artistic delegation to Algeria in 1999 and Gennady Seleznev-led intra-parliamentary delegation trips strengthened bilateral ties.[76] These gatherings facilitated Igor Ivanov's 2000 visit to Algeria and Bouteflika's reciprocal 2001 visit to Russia. After the Bouteflika-Putin meeting, Russia signed a strategic partnership agreement with Algeria, which was its first in the Arab world, agreed to invest in Algeria's energy sector and sold twenty-two Su-24MKs to Algeria.[77] This strategic partnership agreement was the green light for the entry of Russian energy companies Stroitransgaz and Zarubezhvodstroi into Algeria's market.

Despite these breakthroughs, the Russia-Algeria partnership flatlined after Bouteflika's meeting with Putin. From 2001 to 2004, the Russian ambassador to Algeria bemoaned the partnership's failure to 'bring the expected results'.[78] George Mason University Professor Mark Katz, a leading expert on Russia-Middle East relations, explains the stagnation of Russia-Algeria cooperation by highlighting two limiting factors. First, Bouteflika acknowledged that Algeria needed to pay back Soviet-era loans to Russia but disagreed with Putin on the amount of debt owed. This exacerbated bilateral tensions, which began with Algeria's non-repayment of Russian debt in 1998 and subsequent repayment of loans to other external creditors.[79] During Sergei Lavrov's visit to Algeria in November 2005, the debt issue was finally addressed. Algeria agreed to return $1 billion of the $4.7 billion in debt to Russia and the remaining debt would be

70

## THE DAWN OF RUSSIA'S RESURGENCE IN AFRICA

repaid through purchases of Russian weapons.[80] Second, Russia and Algeria possessed an uneasy relationship in the natural gas sphere, which rendered them as simultaneous partners and rivals. Russia pressured Algeria to form a gas cartel, which would regulate prices in an OPEC-style fashion, but Algeria did not accept this proposal, as it feared offending European countries. Algerian officials opposed Russia's use of 'pipeline diplomacy' against Ukraine in 2006, as it feared that European countries would find alternative suppliers to counter the Russian threat, and cut out established exporters, such as Algeria and Norway.[81] Algeria's preference for lower gas prices, which would facilitate its exports to Eastern Europe via Italy, also clashed with Russia's price inflation tactics.

Vladimir Putin's visit to Algeria in March 2006 sought to rectify these areas of tension. As Algeria had struck a free trade deal with the EU in September 2005 and had received arms sale offers from the US and France, Putin faced an uphill task to reboot Russia-Algeria relations. Federation Council International Affairs committee chair Mikhail Margelov was especially concerned that Putin's visit would have little impact, as he believed that Russia's re-engagement with Algeria was five years too late. While France's debt forgiveness and Russia's Paris Club commitment made Moscow's debt deal with Algeria justifiable, *Nezavisimaya Gazeta* columnist Alexander Babakin expressed frustration with Algeria handing money to defence companies and not to the Russian state budget.[82] Despite these doubts, visits from Sergei Lavrov, Defence Minister Sergei Ivanov, Igor Ivanov and Finance Minister Alexei Kudrin to Algeria in 2005–06 underscored the seriousness of Russia's efforts to compete with Western powers. The participation of Chechnya's President Alu Alkhanov in the Putin-led delegation to Algeria underscored the significance of the trip for Russia's outreaches to the Islamic world. Alkhanov's presence laid the groundwork for his successor Ramzan Kadyrov to engage in surrogate diplomacy on Russia's behalf in the Middle East.

Putin's trip to Algeria was characterized by a mixture of successes and failures. The debt-for-arms deal struck between Russia and Algeria was more lucrative than expected for the Russian defence industry. Prior to Putin's trip, Russia was expected to sell $1.6 billion

71

worth of thirty-six MiG-29SMT fighters and a batch of antiquated MiG-29s, which would complement the thirty-six jets of that class in Algeria's Air Force.[83] Rosoboronexport chief Sergei Chemezov announced that Russia had signed $7.5 billion in preliminary contracts with Algeria, and Putin's trip laid the foundations for $14 billion in arms deals.[84] Contrary to expectations, Algeria agreed to purchase modern Russian equipment, such as twenty-eight Su-30 fighter jets, eight S-300 surface-to-air missile batteries and T-90S battle tanks.[85] These deals were marred by delivery delays, but set the tone for Algeria's emergence as Russia's largest arms purchaser in Africa.

The prospects for Russia-Algeria energy cooperation were dimmer. Although Lavrov had tried to link Russian debt forgiveness to favourable oil exploitation terms, Algerian state-owned energy company Sonatrach did not sign a memorandum of understanding (MOU) with Lukoil, Soyuzneftgaz or Itera,[86] and belatedly struck an agreement with Gazprom. Rosneft's October 2006 proposal to transfer refined Algerian oil to Israel and Gazprom's plans to facilitate gas exports from Libya, an energy rival of Algeria, to Europe exacerbated these frictions.[87] Bouteflika's visit to Moscow in February 2008 did not change the overall tenor of Russia-Algeria relations. Ahead of that trip, Algeria made a request to return fifteen MiG-29 fighter jets due to their low quality, while Bouteflika's pledge to create an Algeria-Qatar-Russia natural gas cartel was not fulfilled.[88] This suggests that Russia-Algeria relations improved significantly under Putin but fell short of the strength of cooperation implied by a strategic partnership.

### Russia Resets Its Relationship with Libya

In line with its broader re-engagement with anti-Western governments in Africa, Russia revitalized its near-moribund economic partnership with Libya. In July 2000, Vladimir Putin met with Libyan Foreign Minister Abdel Shalkam in Moscow, and accepted an invitation from Muammar al-Gaddafi to visit Tripoli.[89] Putin expressed support for an immediate removal of Western sanctions against Libya and scheduled a Russian-Libyan Intergovernmental

## THE DAWN OF RUSSIA'S RESURGENCE IN AFRICA

Commission on Trade and Economic Cooperation meeting for October 2000. This economic forum gave Russia an opportunity to build a thermal power plant in Tripoli.[90] Putin and Shalkam notably did not discuss the revival of military-technical cooperation between Russia and Libya,[91] and Russia's re-engagement with Libya had shallow foundations. Vladimir Putin did not make plans to visit Tripoli, which reneged on his promise to Shalkam. Russia's 2007 arrest of Deputy Finance Minister Sergei Storchak, who spearheaded Libya's debt renegotiations, underscored the Kremlin's apathetic attitude towards the Moscow-Tripoli relationship.

Trade between Russia and Libya remained modest, as it rose from $1.7 million in 1997 to $155 million in 2001, receded to $130 million in 2006 and surged to $232 million in 2007. As Libya's total external trade was $41.6 billion in 2005, Russia's share was extremely small. More American and British workers resided in Libya than Russians, even though the US and Britain retained sanctions against Tripoli, and Russia's contracts with Libya were small-scale.[92] In April 2004, an *Izvestia* article warned that Russian oil and gas companies 'were already late for the division of the Libyan pie', as the West was prepared for a 'massive invasion' of Libya's oil technology.[93] The most commercially lucrative components of the Russia-Libya relationship were its 117 km pipeline construction deal and Promeksport's contracts in 1999–2000 to repair Soviet-supplied armoured vehicles and air defence systems. Russia also supplied Libya with $100 million worth of weapons in 2001. Despite these marginal successes, Libya's uncertainties about 'priority areas' of military modernization restricted its defence cooperation with Russia.[94]

To reverse this stagnation, Russia's regions initiated economic cooperation with Libya. In November 2002, Nizhny Novgorod Governorate organized an industrial products exhibition in Tripoli and used its Sokol Aircraft Plant enterprise to modernize eighty MiG-25 jets in the Libyan Air Force and secure purchases of MiG-31 jets.[95] Tatarstan's President Mintimer Shaimiev invited Libyan Air Force and Defence commanders to Kazan in November 2002, and encouraged companies, such as Tatneft in the oil sector and Kamaz in the automobile sector, to invest in Libya.[96] Although Tatarstan aided Russian commercial breakthroughs in other Middle Eastern

73

countries, such as the UAE and Turkey, it was less successful in Libya. Aside from Libya's $4.6 billion debt burden, *Russkiy Mir* Editor-in-Chief Georgy Bovt linked Russia's disengagement from Libya to its focus on securing contracts in post-war Iraq and inadequate coordination between big business and diplomats.[97] MGIMO academic Eldar Kasaev expressed scepticism about Libya's synthesis of personalistic authoritarian rule and compliance with international norms and revealed Moscow's concerns about Gaddafi's potential to revive his destabilizing policies.[98] Due to these sentiments, energy sector breakthroughs, like Tatneft and Gazprom's joint purchase of four blocks of natural gas in December 2006 and Gazprom's production-sharing agreement with Libya in February 2008, were exceptions and did not indicate a trend of closer relations.[99]

Vladimir Putin's historic visit to Tripoli in April 2008 added new life to the Russia-Libya partnership. This trip, which was the first by a Russian leader since 1985, was accompanied by effusive words of praise from Muammar al-Gaddafi. After calling Putin 'our great guest', Gaddafi indirectly criticized Western powers for perpetuating a Cold War-style arms race and expressed hope that a 'Russian superpower' would counter US hegemony.[100] Gaddafi's highlighting of Western double standards towards the Islamic world, which cause the US and Europe to 'support' Muslims in Bosnia and Chechnya, while launching wars in Iraq and Afghanistan, resonated with Putin's worldview.[101] Gaddafi also invited Putin for breakfast next to television stations airing RT Arabic, which underscored his desire to build a personal relationship with the Russian president. Putin pandered to Gaddafi's desire for greater international influence by pledging to cooperate with Libya as a non-permanent UNSC member from 2008 to 2009 and visited the 'Barbarian Imperialist Aggression', which commemorated the 1986 US bombing in Libya.[102] This cordial relationship between Putin and Gaddafi would persist until the Libyan dictator's assassination in October 2011.

After the Putin-Gaddafi meeting, Russia cancelled Libya's Soviet-era debt. This debt cancellation was accompanied Libya's signing of ten contracts with Russia, which mirrored Moscow's approach to debt forgiveness in Algeria. The most significant contract was a €2.2 billion agreement to construct a 550 km section of the

## THE DAWN OF RUSSIA'S RESURGENCE IN AFRICA

Benghazi-to-Sirte railway, which also required Libya to purchase 70% of the equipment, machinery and metals for the rail-line from Russia. Gazprom also signed a memorandum of cooperation with Libya's National Oil Company (NOC). This MOU handed Gazprom some assets that were held by Italy's Eni and, in July 2008, Gazprom proposed buying all Libyan petroleum intended for export.[103] As Lukoil's representative in Tripoli was detained without charge by the Libyan authorities in November 2007, Gazprom was the unquestioned engine of Russia-Libya energy sector cooperation.[104] Russia also eyed sales of €2.5 billion worth of anti-aircraft systems, jet fighters, helicopters and warships. Although Russia trailed the US and China in its Libyan investments, Alexei Kudrin hailed these contracts as a major success and boasted that 'No country in the world can compare with the contracts that Russia has received today.'[105] While Kudrin's comments were undeniably hyperbolic, Putin's trip resulted in a durable reset in Russia-Libya relations, which was only derailed by the 2011 Arab Spring protests.

During the early 2000s, Putin deftly balanced domestic forces and spearheaded the transition from a marginalized Russian presence in Africa following the collapse of the Soviet Union and the Kozyrev-era disengagement. Russia began its re-emergence as a great power in the continent and successfully built a more durable set of relationships and presence in Africa during Putin's first and second term. The next decade would showcase Russia's power projection capabilities, normative challenges to Western liberalism and resistance to popular uprisings that also allowed for stronger relationships with authoritarian countries in Africa. These policies underpinned the successes of Russia's African policy during the Medvedev interregnum, which will be explored in the next chapter.

3

# THE MEDVEDEV INTERREGNUM
## THE CONSOLIDATION OF RUSSIA'S AMBITIONS IN AFRICA

On 7 May 2008, Dmitry Medvedev replaced Vladimir Putin as President of Russia. Medvedev's triumph during the March 2008 presidential elections attracted international controversy, as media suppression of opposition candidates, voting irregularities and the obstruction of Organization for Security and Cooperation in Europe (OSCE) observers undermined the fairness of the results. Nevertheless, Medvedev smoothly transitioned to the presidency and Russia did not succumb to mass demonstrations. As Vladimir Putin was Prime Minister, Medvedev struggled to assert his independent mark on the trajectory of Russian domestic and foreign policy. The 2008 Georgian War escalated tensions between Russia and the West, but the election of a new US President, Barack Obama, resulted in a swift reset of US-Russia relations. Despite the newfound optimism surrounding US-Russia relations and the deleterious economic impact of declining oil prices, Medvedev capitalized on doubts about US global leadership that emerged from the 2008 financial crisis and devoted more attention to African affairs than either of his predecessors. Medvedev's African tour of June 2009, which included visits to Egypt, Nigeria, Angola and Namibia, underscored Russia's aspirations for lasting influence in Africa. The 2011 Arab

77

Spring uprisings in Tunisia, Egypt and Libya caused Russia to sharpen its focus on protecting its vital interests in North Africa. The collapse of the US-Russia reset, which was expedited by the death of Muammar al-Gaddafi in October 2011, caused Russia to sharpen its opposition to US norms and its anti-Westernism as a selling point for African countries.

*Dmitry Medvedev Arrives: Russia and the West Clash and Cooperate in Africa*

The initial months of Medvedev's presidency were defined by a spirit of economic optimism in Russia. Record-high oil prices, which peaked at $147 a barrel in July 2008, and a year of 8.5% GDP growth in 2007 encouraged greater Russian assertiveness on the world stage. The 2008 Bucharest Summit, which created a path for Ukraine and Georgia to join NATO, caused Russia's assertiveness to be channeled in an increasingly anti-Western direction. These anti-Western sentiments reached a crescendo during the August 2008 Georgian War, which saw the US and many European countries condemn Russia, while the developing world refrained from criticizing Moscow's actions in South Ossetia. This stark divide encouraged Russia to step up its diplomatic overtures towards non-Western countries and benefited Moscow's policy towards Africa. In a throwback to the Primakov era, Russia's anti-Western sentiments were revealed in normative resistance in Africa and alignment with US-designated rogue states, such as Zimbabwe and Sudan. The Somalia piracy crisis illustrated Russia's capacity to pragmatically compartmentalize its disagreements with Western countries and reinforced the spirit of cooperation that surrounded the Obama-era reset of US-Russia relations.

The 2008 Zimbabwe elections provided an ideal testing ground for Russia's normative resistance. After defeating the ZANU-PF in the first run-off, which was followed by political violence that resulted in at least 100 casualties, Movement for Democratic Change (MDC) leader Morgan Tsvangirai boycotted the second run-off. This paved the way for Robert Mugabe to triumph with 85.5% of the vote. The United States and numerous European countries accused the ZANU-

## THE MEDVEDEV INTERREGNUM

PF of instigating post-election violence to guarantee Mugabe's victory. Although the ZANU-PF hired Russian election observers to serve alongside counterparts from China, Iran, Venezuela and a select group of African countries,[1] Russia acknowledged the sharp polarizations over Zimbabwe in the African Union. Therefore, it did not enthusiastically support the fairness of Mugabe's triumph. In July 2008, the debate over UN sanctions against Zimbabwe would have resulted in an arms embargo and asset freezes on thirteen senior ZANU-PF officials involved in orchestrating the post-election violence. Along with China, Libya, South Africa and Vietnam, Russia blocked the imposition of sanctions against Zimbabwe. Vitaly Churkin justified this decision by stating that the crisis in Zimbabwe did not threaten international instability, which was the main criterion for the use of UN sanctions and arguing that sanctions would violate Zimbabwe's sovereignty.

Russian media reports supported Churkin's legal arguments on Zimbabwe, as they emphasized that no country had ever faced UN sanctions for holding a controversial election.[2] While Churkin's position strengthened the Sino-Russian normative axis, Western officials strongly condemned Russia's veto of UN sanctions against Zimbabwe. US Permanent Representative to the UN, Zalmay Khalilzad, argued that Russia's shielding of Mugabe's regime was at odds with its G8 partnership commitments. British Foreign Minister David Miliband accused Russia of reneging on its pledge at the 7–9 July 2008 G8 summit in Hokkaido to sanction Zimbabwe.[3] As Britain was the most outspoken supporter of isolating Mugabe, acute strains in UK-relations, which developed following Alexander Litvinenko's poisoning in 2006, contributed to Russia's UN vote. The chasm between Russian and Western policies towards Zimbabwe grew further, as Moscow compounded its resistance to multilateral sanctions with provisions of humanitarian assistance to Harare.

Russia also deviated from the Western normative consensus by stridently opposing the extradition of Omar al-Bashir to the International Criminal Court (ICC). In spite of mounting evidence of Bashir's involvement in the deaths of between 35,000 to 100,000 Darfurians and the displacement of 2.5 million people from Darfur, Russia supported the African Union and Arab League's calls to suspend the indictment of Bashir for war crimes. Churkin proposed implementing an Article 16 suspension of the ICC indictment, which would delay legal proceedings by one year, and argued that prosecuting Bashir would foment instability in eastern Africa.[4] This stance revealed Russia's scepticism of the ICC, which was evidenced by its refusal to ratify the Treaty of Rome after signing it in 2000, but also underscored Moscow's willingness to upgrade its normative partnership with Sudan that originated with the UN sanctions debates of 1996. Sudan returned this favour by defending Russia during its August 2008 military intervention in Georgia's autonomous region of South Ossetia. The Sudanese National Assembly accused Georgia of carrying out 'genocide' against elders, children, women and the sick, and emphasized the double standards between the Bush administration's invasions of Iraq and Afghanistan, and condemnations of Russian conduct in Georgia.[5]

As Sudan bucked the trend of African silence on Russia's actions in Georgia, which mirrored China's ambiguous calls for de-escalation and India's strict neutrality, optimism abounded about a Russia-Sudan partnership. Mikhail Margelov, Russia's special representative to Sudan, described Sudan as the 'gateway to Africa'. The historic bonds between Russia and Sudan, which included the sojourns of researchers like A.S. Norov and O.I. Senkovsky, who visited Sudan after its conquest by the Turkish-Egyptian army in 1821, were more rigorously explored in Russian academic discourse.[6] In early 2009, Margelov embarked on a tour to Khartoum, Al-Fashir and Juba to meet with leading Sudanese political figures.[7] Margelov's trip fell short of expectations, as no major commercial deals were signed with Sudan, and journalists, rather than business leaders, accompanied him during his trip. Despite this disappointment, Russia sharpened its solidarity with Bashir's regime in March 2009 when the ICC arrest warrant against the Sudanese dictator was finalized. Margelov accused the ICC of systematic bias by exempting Sudanese rebel groups from prosecution for war crimes and claimed that Bashir was trying to ameliorate the security crises in Darfur and South Sudan. Margelov also warned that the African Union-UN mixed operation's activities in Sudan would be blocked by the ICC warrant, and the ICC decision 'could put Sudan on the

THE MEDVEDEV INTERREGNUM

brink of humanitarian catastrophe' by thwarting food and medical aid shipments.[8]

The intensification of Russia-West tensions in Africa during the summer of 2008 also spilt over to the energy markets. In January 2008, Gazprom offered to invest $1.5–2 billion in the Nigerian economy in exchange for access to Nigeria's natural gas reserves. Gazprom executives noted that Nigeria's poor infrastructure caused its production to lag behind that of Egypt and Algeria and saw investments as a means of rectifying this problem.[9] The EU Energy Commissioner Andris Piebalgs travelled to Nigeria after Gazprom's deal. On 17 September, the EU claimed that Nigeria 'could be an important partner in the EU's diversification efforts' and offered financial support for the Sahara gas pipeline, which would cost €15 billion.[10] The EU Energy Commission insisted that Gazprom's overtures towards Nigeria did not factor into Piebalgs's trip and stated that the EU viewed Gazprom as no different from ExxonMobil. Nevertheless, concerns about an EU-Russia competition for gas in Nigeria lingered and resurfaced during Medvedev's trip to Abuja in June 2009.

Although Africa emerged as a front-line theatre in the Russia-West systemic confrontation, Medvedev saw the common threat of piracy in Somalia as a rare opportunity for Russian cooperation with the EU and NATO. The Gulf of Aden and Somalia's eastern coast became the world's largest piracy hot-spot in 2008, as one-third of all global attacks on ships occurred in this region.[11] In February 2008, senior Russian Navy official Igor Dygalo stated that Russian warships needed to be present at all major maritime transit zones. This statement was greeted with trepidation in the West. Danish company Svitzer, which saw its ships captured by Somali pirates, urged Russia not to interfere in their negotiations.[12] In the spring of 2008, Somali pirates captured the Dutch Amiya Scan dry cargo ship, which included five Russian nationals, and captured the German MV Lehmann Timber dry cargo ship, which was manned by a Russian captain.[13] These events caused Russia to view the Somali piracy crisis as a threat to its national security and economic interests, and prodded Moscow to action. On 3 June 2008, Russia aligned with France and the United States in the UN Security Council, and against

81

its non-Western partners, China, Vietnam and Libya, in support of external power interventions in the Somali piracy crisis.[14]

This UNSC vote, which strikingly contrasted with its deviance on Zimbabwe and Sudan, caused Russia to gradually abandon its military restraint in the Somali piracy crisis. To counter the threat to maritime shipping in the Gulf of Aden, Russia expanded its security cooperation with Western countries and respected Somalia's sovereignty by working closely with local authorities. The capture of Ukraine's MV Faina ship, which included three Russian nationals, caused the Russian Navy to deploy its Neutrashimy frigate to the Gulf of Aden in September 2008.[15] In a show of Russia's intention to combat piracy, Sergei Lavrov stated on 3 October that 'Russia aims to stop the outrageous actions of Somali pirates', and called for a more expansive UNSC resolution to address the piracy crisis.[16] Russia believed that NATO efforts to protect ships bearing humanitarian aid and soon-to-be-unveiled EU Atalanta patrol mission would only be able to temporarily alleviate, rather than eviscerate, the threat of Somali piracy. Due to these limitations, the commander-in-chief of the Russian Navy, Vladimir Vystovsky, suggested that the Russian military could escort ships in the Gulf of Aden.[17] While this escorting role did not immediately take hold, Russia's Neustrashimy warship began patrols on the Gulf of Aden on 6 November. These patrols swiftly escalated into full-blown combat missions. In February 2009, Russia's Peter the Great warship captured ten pirates in three ships off the coast of Somalia and prevented pirates from attacking an Iranian fishing trawler.[18] This military operation, which followed a smaller success against pirates in the Gulf of Aden in January 2009, illustrated the strength of the Russian Navy to a domestic and international audience. The ability of the Russian Navy and helicopters to cooperate effectively in a hostile foreign setting also appeased concerns about the interoperability of the Russian Armed Forces, which surfaced after the Georgian War.

In tandem with these military campaigns, Russia saw the anti-piracy struggle as a unique opportunity to engage with NATO and the EU as a peer military power. In his capacity as Russia's Permanent Representative to NATO, Dmitry Rogozin was an especially outspoken supporter of Russia-West cooperation against the piracy

THE MEDVEDEV INTERREGNUM

threat, as he urged the EU and NATO to coordinate with Russia on joint attacks against terrestrial pirate bases. Rogozin's calls for Russia-West cooperation translated into a coordinated anti-piracy policy, as Britain's HMS Cumberland and Russia's Neustrashimy warships jointly blocked pirates from seizing a Danish vessel on 12 November.[19] This experience created a framework for Russia-West cooperation against piracy in Somalia, which culminated in Australia-Russia military cooperation to liberate the MV Moscow University tanker in May 2010. The synthesis of Russia's augmentation of EU and NATO anti-piracy efforts and direct Anglo-Russian cooperation in Somalia helped alleviate tensions with Western countries that grew in the summer of 2008. It also acted as a harbinger for greater Russia-West cooperation that was inspired by the Obama-era reset.

Russia was also more willing than the United States and most European countries to directly cooperate with the Somali government in the struggle against piracy. The escalation of the piracy crisis occurred in tandem with instability in Somalia, as President Abdullahi Yusuf Ahmed and Prime Minister Nur Hassan Hussein openly clashed over the appointment of a new cabinet. Despite this dissent, Russia respected Somalia's sovereignty by urging President Ahmed to grant it 'cooperating state' status in the anti-piracy struggle and championed a whole-of-government, rather than a purely military, solution to the crisis. In a UNSC debate in December 2008, Sergei Lavrov admitted that piracy was the 'tip of the iceberg' of Somalia's challenges and claimed that the 'economic, social and political stabilization' of Somalia needed to occur with international support.[20] This rhetoric was enthusiastically received in Mogadishu. Somali Ambassador to Russia Mohammed Handule stated that Somalia would give Russia free reign to attack pirates on land and at sea and claimed that he was negotiating with Moscow on allowing Russian ships to adopt a Coast Guard function off Somalia's waters.[21]

Russia's cooperation with Somalia against piracy did not immediately eviscerate the legacy of Soviet-era frictions between the two countries. Abukar Arman, who was appointed as Somali Special Envoy to the United States in February 2010, stated that 'a dark cloud of suspicion still hangs over Russia' and the 'majority of

83

the Somali people considered Russia the grandmaster of deception that could not be trusted as a strategic partner'.[22] Russia's capture of Somali pirates in May 2010 off Yemen's coast and denial of these pirates the right to a fair trial in Somalia underscored these hostilities. Abdirisak Aden, Somalia's Information Ministry spokesman, claimed that Russia violated international human rights law and warned of a potential downgrade in Somalia-Russia relations.[23] This setback notwithstanding, Rashid Abdi, a former Horn of Africa project director at the International Crisis Group, noted a generational divide on Somalia's perceptions of Russia. The older generation of Somalis vividly recalled the Soviet Union's refusal to supply necessary equipment to Somalia during the Ogaden War as an act of betrayal, but younger Somalis did not see this historical baggage as an impediment to cooperation with Moscow.[24] The pragmatic views of the post-Ogaden generation of Somalis prevailed during the 2008–09 piracy crisis and continue to fuel closer Somalia-Russia relations to this date. Beyond its lasting impact on Russia-Somalia relations, Moscow's approach to the piracy crisis set a precedent for state-to-state consultations between Russia and African countries on non-traditional security threats, which contrasted with the more brazen unilateralism of the United States.

## Dmitry Medvedev's June 2009 Tour of Africa

As Russia's normative resistance and expanded security involvement in Africa became increasingly visible, Medvedev also sought to shore up Moscow's bilateral relationships on the continent. Russia's desire to be a continent-wide great power was evidenced by Sergei Lavrov's shuttle diplomacy in Africa during the first half of 2009 and Medvedev's historic June 2009 African tour. On 17 February, Sergei Lavrov travelled to Egypt to discuss the Israel-Palestine peace negotiations with Hosni Mubarak. After the 2008–09 Israel-Gaza war, which was dubbed Operation Cast Lead, Egypt tried to broker a lasting Israel-Hamas ceasefire and facilitate intra-Palestinian unity. Russia also saw an opportunity to expand its diplomatic influence in the Israel-Hamas conflict and Deputy Foreign Minister Alexander Saltanov embarked on a shuttle diplomacy campaign in the Middle

## THE MEDVEDEV INTERREGNUM

East. Lavrov's Cairo trip aimed to bridge the Russian and Egyptian diplomatic objectives together. This gambit succeeded, as Egyptian Foreign Minister Ahmed Aboul-Gheit endorsed a Moscow-hosted Israel-Palestine peace process and chastised France for trying to compete with Russia's diplomatic role in the conflict.[25] Lavrov's other diplomatic forays in Africa were less impactful but nonetheless revealed Russia's growing commitment to African affairs. On 17 March, Lavrov welcomed Nigerian Foreign Minister Ojo Maduekwe to Moscow to discuss trade and investment prospects. Lavrov's emphasis on an AU-brokered solution to the political crisis in Madagascar, which saw Antananarivo mayor Andry Rajoelina extra-legally seize power, underscored Russia's commitment to supporting 'African solutions for African problems'. During DRC Foreign Minister Alexis Thambwe Mwamba's visit to Moscow on 7 April, Lavrov emphasized Russia's desire to expand mining sector cooperation with Kinshasa. This underscored Russia's desire to re-enter Central Africa where it had been a fringe player in the post-Cold War era.

In June 2009, Medvedev embarked on a four-country tour of Egypt, Nigeria, Namibia and Angola. This tour primarily aimed to expand Russia's commercial interests in Africa, which were especially pronounced in the mining and energy sectors. It also aimed to highlight Russia's dedication to becoming a great power in Africa, as Barack Obama had just spoken at the American University in Cairo and China and announced a slew of new investments across the continent. Russian state media coverage of Medvedev's trip emphasized Moscow's desire to conclusively turn the page on its 1990s disengagement from Africa. A *Channel One* report argued that 'Russia unjustly abandoned all of the Soviet Union's African projects' and claimed that the only Russians most young Africans knew were wealthy tourists and game hunters.[26] In line with Primakov's thinking, Medvedev recognized that the expansion of Russia's economic interests in Africa hinged on the simultaneous expansion of Russian soft power. On 26 June, a *Rossiyskaya Gazeta* article reflecting on Medvedev's trip emphasized Russia's lack of a 'dark colonial history' in Africa and saw Medvedev's determination to redress Moscow's past neglect of African affairs as constructive.[27] Medvedev also tried

85

to frame himself as a new kind of Russian president who was more approachable than his predecessors through a visit to the Pyramids of Giza and undertaking a safari in Namibia.

Dmitry Medvedev's synthesis of economic ambition, great power status projection and soft power promotion was apparent in each stop on his African tour. As Egypt was Russia's largest trade partner in Africa with $4.5 billion in total trade in 2008, Medvedev's arrival in Egypt was greeted with high expectations. On 23 June, Medvedev announced that the Russia-Egypt relationship would be upgraded into a strategic partnership which would lead to the construction of a free trade zone between the two countries and an expansion of bilateral military-technical cooperation.[28] Rosatom chief Sergei Kiriyenko accompanied Medvedev to Cairo. Kiriyenko announced that Egypt would construct two to four nuclear power reactors with Russian assistance and that Russia would prepare a 'tender proposal' by late 2010.[29] This deal was expected to net Russia $3.5 billion in profits and expanded Russia's stake in Egypt's uranium reserves, as Rosatom outbid competition from China, France and Kazakhstan. Medvedev also used his trip to Cairo to strengthen Russia's sub-state relationships in Egypt. The Russian president's speech at the headquarters of the Arab League, meeting with Patriarch Theodore II of Alexandria and discussion with Fathi Surur, the head of the Egyptian parliament and Russia-Egypt Friendship Society, underscored Russia's ability to leverage diplomatic and religious soft power in Egypt.[30] Medvedev appealed to historical memory during these meetings, as he reminded Egyptians of Soviet support for decolonization and Egypt's support for Russian territorial integrity during the 1990s.[31] Russian commentator Jana Borisova noted that Egyptian officials received Medvedev as an 'old friend' and this illustrated that Mubarak had turned the page on Chechnya.[32]

Medvedev's meeting with Nigerian President Umaru Yar'Adua on 25 June was initially overshadowed by a devastating act of terrorism. The Movement for the Emancipation of the Niger Delta (MEND) attacked Shell Oil infrastructure in Nigeria and claimed that Russia was contributing to Nigeria's structural inequality, as foreign investors favor Abuja and ignored the Niger Delta.[33] In spite of this attack, Medvedev and Yar'Adua achieved noteworthy

THE MEDVEDEV INTERREGNUM

diplomatic breakthroughs. The memorandum between the Nigerian National Petroleum Corporation (NNPC) and Gazprom was the flagship success of Medvedev's trip to Abuja. A RT article on 24 June claimed that Nigerian officials viewed the deal as the 'largest that the country has ever signed with a foreign partner'.[34] Yar'Adua hailed the agreement, as he said that Nigeria was 'more a gas nation than an oil nation', and argued that it would help the West African gas pipeline project that started in Ghana and the Sahara gas pipeline, which pumped Nigerian gas to Spain and Italy.[35] Nigaz, the NNPC-Gazprom joint venture, was worth $2.5 billion and paved the way for Russia to build pipelines, refineries and gas power stations in Nigeria.[36] The name Nigaz sparked controversy due to its racist undertones. However, the substance of the agreement was positively received by the Lagos business establishment.[37] Nigeria also expressed interest in Russian civilian nuclear energy reactors but the progress of negotiations between Moscow and Abuja paled in comparison with the breakthroughs achieved in Egypt. Dmitry Medvedev also pledged Russia's support for African representation in the UN Security Council. This was popular in Nigeria, as it reinforced Yar'Adua's September 2007 claims that Africa's exclusion from the UNSC was 'unfair and untenable'.[38]

Dmitry Medvedev's choice of Namibia as the third destination of his African tour appeared counterintuitive. As Namibia had just 2 million people and $6.4 million in bilateral trade with Russia, Yeltsin and Putin had both treated it as a peripheral partner in Africa. To facilitate an upgrade of Russia's partnership with Namibia, Medvedev appealed to the Soviet Union's vital backing of Namibia's national liberation struggle.[39] The USSR's support for Namibia's independence had exceptional resonance for Namibian President Hifikepunye Pohamba, who was a founding member of South West Africa People's Organization (SWAPO) in 1960, studied politics in the Soviet Union in the early 1980s and acted as SWAPO's de facto envoy in Africa later in that decade. Accusations in Kremlin-backed media of US hypocrisy, which were exemplified by US-Iran commercial collaboration in Namibia's uranium sector, reinforced Medvedev's focus on the exceptional Russia-Namibia partnership.[40] Medvedev, however, saw Namibia's status as the world's fourth largest

87

uranium producer as a major strategic asset. The value of Namibia's uranium reserves dominated Russia's commercial overtures even though Moscow also had one eye on Namibia's vast mineral reserves, such as diamonds, gold, copper and zinc.

Russia's approach to expanding its access to Namibia's uranium reserves differed in two ways from Medvedev's bargaining tactics in Egypt and Nigeria. First, in contrast to his efforts to downplay competition with the US in Egypt or with Europe in Nigeria, Medvedev was much more up-front about Russia's entry into the great power scrum for uranium reserves. Medvedev's admission that Russia had 'nearly missed' entering Namibia, which had signed deals with China and Western countries, underscored this messaging shift.[41] Second, Russian officials focused on win-win cooperation with Namibia in the nuclear energy sphere rather than grandiose investment projects. To reassure Namibia that its intentions were not extractive, Assistant to the President of the Russian Federation Sergei Prikhodko emphasized Russia's commitment to alleviating Namibia's over-dependence on South African electricity, which stemmed from a paralyzing internal debate on the efficacy of hydropower or nuclear energy.[42] Gazprom reinforced Prikhodko's message by agreeing to invest $1–1.2 billion in Namibia's Kudu gas field, which would allow Namibian energy company Namcor to construct a power plant and help Namibia export large quantities of electricity to South Africa for the first time.[43] In order to illustrate their strategic commitment to Namibia, Russian officials linked their uranium investments to Medvedev's vision for the construction of nuclear power plants in Russia. Medvedev's synthesis of soft power, showcasing Russia's great power ambitions and emphasis on win-win cooperation in Namibia have been repeatedly replicated since Putin's return to power.

The last destination of Dmitry Medvedev's African tour was Angola. Although Russian companies had steadily expanded their presence in Angola since the late 1990s, trade between Russia and Angola was mired at just $76 million in 2008. Medvedev's trip was replete with historical references, as Angola saw Russia's support during the global financial crisis as a continuation of loyalty that dated back to the independence struggle against Portugal. In keeping with their Namibian model, Russia saw win-win investment

THE MEDVEDEV INTERREGNUM

projects as the gateway to expanded trade. Beyond expanding the Zarubezhneft-Sonangol partnership on oil exploration, Russia targeted the construction of two major dams on Angola's Kwanza River and proposed lending Luanda $300 million to build the Angosat satellite. Alrosa head Sergei Vybornov accompanied Medvedev to Angola as he sought to secure new diamond sector investments. From a hard currency standpoint, Medvedev's trip to Angola was the least productive but it nonetheless contributed to tighter bilateral relations.

## The Enduring Impact of Dmitry Medvedev's African Tour

Dmitry Medvedev's African tour received little attention in the United States. In Europe, Russia's assistance to Nigeria's Sahara pipeline plan attracted attention, as it would make European countries even more dependent on Russian gas, but other aspects of Medvedev's African tour were largely ignored. China ascribed greater significance to Russia's African forays than the US or Europe. The coincidence in timing between the Nigaz deal and Sinopec's $7.2 billion bid for oil exploration firm Addax, which operates in the Middle East and Africa, underscored the potential for Sino-Russian energy sector competition in Africa.[44] Nevertheless, the prevailing view in Beijing was that Russia was a complementary junior partner to China in Africa. Chinese experts saw Russia's 2008 foreign policy concept's emphasis on entering new markets as a sign of Moscow's pivot to Africa and argued that Medvedev was inheriting the USSR's political capital to expedite Russia's resurgence. Reflecting on the underwhelming long-term impact of Medvedev's trip, Xu Guoqing, an academic at the Institute of West Asian and African studies at the Beijing Chinese Academy of Social Sciences, argued that the Kremlin's understanding of Africa was trapped in the past and that 'prejudice and racist arrogance' diluted Russia's image-building efforts in Africa.[45] These perceptions partially explain why Sino-Russian cooperation in Africa has significantly trailed the bilateral expansion of the Russia-China strategic partnership.

Despite numerous commercial breakthroughs that were announced during Medvedev's African tour, his trip produced mixed

89

long-term results. The much-discussed Russia-Egypt strategic partnership agreement was never ratified due to bureaucratic dissension in both countries and the expansion of Russian trade and investment in Egypt lagged behind Cairo's outreaches with other G8 countries.[46] Russian tourism to Egypt also trailed expectations and in November 2010 an article in state-backed business news agency Prime called Egypt the most dangerous country for Russian tourists.[47] Russia's relationship with Nigeria achieved greater momentum, especially in the energy and technology sectors. In August 2011, Nigeria launched two satellites aboard a Russian Dnepr rocket from a launchpad in southern Russia's city of Yasny, which helped it manage the climactic crises that disrupted Nigerian agriculture.[48] However, the perception that Russia was staging a comeback in Africa helped strengthen bilateral partnerships elsewhere on the continent. The expansion of commercial meetings between Russian and Congolese officials in 2010, which gave Moscow a foothold in Central Africa, was one secondary impact of Medvedev's African tour.

The growth of Russian soft power in Africa after Dmitry Medvedev's June 2009 tour had a greater long-term impact on its power projection than any commercial deal that Russia struck on the continent. The turnaround in Russia's image amongst South African officials from 2008 to 2010 was Medvedev's crowning soft power achievement. Dmitry Medvedev presided over some early economic achievements in the Russia-South Africa relationship, such as the earth-remote sensing project in late 2008 and Moscow's agreement to supply uranium to South African nuclear power plants.[49] However, Russia had a striking soft power deficit in South Africa. Vladimir Shubin contends that the 'distorted picture of Russia' presented by South African media outlets and academics undermined trade and cultural ties between the two countries. Shubin cites former South African ambassador to Russia Gerritt Olivier's description of Russia as an 'undemocratic authoritarian regime' as an example of the anti-Russian rhetoric that was mainstream in South African academic discourse.[50]

South Africa's exclusion from the Yekaterinburg BRICS summit in 2009 was viewed within the ANC leadership as a sign that Russia was snubbing Africa's important role in world affairs. Anti-Russian

THE MEDVEDEV INTERREGNUM

voices in Pretoria's expert community, such as Francis Cornegay, who saw Russia as the 'main culprit' in a conspiracy to exclude South Africa from BRICS and undermine cohesion within the Global South.[51] During Jacob Zuma's visit to Russia in August 2010, Dmitry Medvedev became the first BRICS head of state to unequivocally endorse South Africa's inclusion in the organization. Russia's endorsement of South African BRICS membership paved the way for China, Brazil and India to follow suit. South African officials hailed Russia's support for its accession to BRICS, as they viewed Russia as a bridge between the developed world and the Global South.[52] South African Ambassador to Russia Mandisi Mpahlwa saw South Africa's participation in BRICS as a means of establishing links between Russia and the India-Brazil-South Africa (IBSA) dialogue forum.

Dmitry Medvedev's focus on reviving Russian development assistance in Africa had even more far-reaching impacts. The Russian president's June 2009 pronouncement that 'Africa is waiting for our support' heralded a shift in Russian foreign assistance policy, which was previously centred almost entirely around the post-Soviet space. As Russia did not regard itself as a member of the Global South and Russian overseas development assistance fell sharply from $785 million in 2009 to $472.32 million in 2010, there was a great deal of scepticism surrounding Medvedev's plans to entrench Russia as an aid donor in Africa.[53] However, Russia developed a customized foreign aid strategy that eschewed multilateral institutions, such as the World Bank, and replicated China's leveraging of bilateral development assistance deals in Africa.[54] The establishment of the Russian International Aid Agency in January 2012 allowed Russia to provide strategic development assistance to Africa for the first time since the Soviet Union's collapse.

While Medvedev's contribution to development assistance programmes in Africa was largely confined to his bureaucratic reorganization, Russia established itself as a reliable supplier of humanitarian aid during his presidency. Russian foreign aid was particularly impactful in Zimbabwe and Ethiopia. After Mugabe's re-election, Zimbabwe's hyperinflation crisis worsened, unemployment rates skyrocketed to between 80 to 94%, and a nascent cholera epidemic compounded long-standing food insecurity. In February

2009, Russia supplied urgent humanitarian aid and food shipments to the UN World Food Programme (WFP) in Harare.[55] These aid deliveries gained widespread coverage in the Russian media, which enthusiastically hailed Medvedev's commitment to humanitarian assistance in Africa. A Gazeta.ru headline on 27 February boasted that 'Russia will save Zimbabwe', even though Moscow had ruled out the provisions of financial assistance to Zimbabwe.[56]

Russia subsequently pivoted its attention towards Ethiopia, which was the primary locus of Soviet development assistance in Africa. In 2008, Russia had donated $4 million to land rehabilitation programmes in Ethiopia and, in July 2010, Russia worked with the WFP to supply $2 million in humanitarian assistance to Ethiopians facing drought.[57] These aid provisions resulted in a spike in pro-Russian sentiments in Ethiopia. The Soviet-funded Dejazmach Balcha hospital in Addis Ababa, which treated 20,000 Ethiopian patients a year, erected a portrait of Dmitry Medvedev on its walls.[58] Ethiopian President Meles Zenawi told the Russia-Africa Business Forum in December 2011 that 'Africa welcomes back Russian economic engagement with an open heart'.[59] Medvedev's use of foreign aid as an instrument of soft power in Africa was swiftly paired with ideational synergies during the Arab Spring, which will be discussed in the remainder of this chapter.

*Russia's Responses to the 2011 Arab Spring Revolutions in North Africa*

The 2011 Arab Spring protests in North Africa, which resulted in the overthrow of Zine Abedine Ben Ali in Tunisia, Hosni Mubarak in Egypt and Muammar al-Gaddafi in Libya, further enhanced Russia's resistance to Western norms in Africa. Much like their Western counterparts, Russian officials were surprised by the scope of unrest that swept across North Africa. Alexey Podtserob, who served as Russian Ambassador to Tunisia from 2000 to 2006, stated that Russia's relations with Tunisia 'were not very advanced' and Moscow did not expect Tunisia to become the first Arab country to 'experience the charm of the Islamic winter'.[60] Mikhail Bogdanov similarly notes that, in the fall of 2010, Egyptians were alarmed by rising instability in Palestine, Sudan, Iraq, Lebanon, Yemen and Somalia,[61] and were not inclined to follow that path. The developments in the Maghreb were less surprising to members of Russia's expert community. Vasily Kuznetsov stated that Russian experts thought an Arab Spring scenario was possible in the mid-2000s, but its success depended on the strength of Islamist movements and backlash against the succession strategies of incumbent presidents.[62] Vladimir Sotnikov, director of the Russia-East-West Center for Strategic Studies and Analysis, contends that prominent Russian analysts, such as Alexei Malashenko from the Carnegie Moscow Center and Vitaly Naumkin, who served as academic director of the Institute of Oriental Studies, were especially attuned to the prospect of regime changes through popular unrest in North Africa.[63]

Russia responded ambiguously to the outbreak of mass protests in Tunisia, which were catalyzed by street vendor Mohamed Bouazizi's self-immolation in December 2010. Without praising or condemning the Tunisian revolution, Dmitry Medvedev described Ben Ali's demise on 14 January as a 'big lesson for governments around the world', and urged African governments to pay attention to public opinion.[64] Russian media outlets also presented contradictory messages after Ben Ali's overthrow and flight to Saudi Arabia. An RT article of 18 January argued that socioeconomic deprivation and youth unemployment triggered 'riots' in Tunisia.[65] This perspective aligned broadly with the contentions of international media outlets. Interfax article of 19 January claimed that the Tunisian revolution was a succession from unrest in the post-Soviet space, called the demonstrations violent 'clashes and riots' and described Ben Ali's overthrow as a 'coup d'état'.[66] This rhetoric, with Ben Ali's claims that the Tunisian unrest was triggered by foreign-backed saboteurs, reinforced the Kremlin's narratives to delegitimize the colour revolutions.

Russia's official reaction to Mubarak's overthrow in Egypt was similarly ambiguous as its handling of the events in Tunisia. Although Russia rejected the possibility of a large-scale evacuation of its nationals from Egypt, 132 Russian Al-Ahram University students fled as protests intensified. The wife of a Russian diplomat in Cairo told *The Moscow Times* that 'Everyone is fleeing. It looks like a civil war has begun.'[67] As concerns grew about instability in Egypt, Medvedev became one of the few world leaders to call Mubarak on 3 February. This call reiterated Sergei Lavrov's public support for Egypt's stability and Russia's belief that the Egyptian people, rather than external actors, should decide their country's future.[68] This sharply contrasted with Barack Obama's calls for Mubarak's resignation. On 12 February, Dmitry Medvedev stated that a 'strong democratic Egypt' was essential for the continuation of the Middle East peace process and emphasized the need for 'interfaith concord and harmony to prevail' in Egypt.[69] The subsequent outbreak of popular unrest in Libya caused Medvedev to sharpen his counter-revolutionary rhetoric about the Egyptian revolution. In a February speech in Vladikavkaz in the North Caucasus, Medvedev warned that the Arab uprisings could lead to the 'disintegration of large, densely-populated states' and lead to 'fires for years and the spread of extremism in the future'.[70]

Dmitry Medvedev's volte-face on the consequences of the Arab Spring in Egypt reflected the Kremlin's alignment with the consensus within the expert community. Although Mubarak was a staunch US ally, Russian media outlets praised his legacy, which included a peace treaty with Israel, the suppression of Islamic extremism in Egypt and consistent economic growth.[71] Alexander Ignatenko, a member of the Council for Interaction with Religious Associations, claimed that the 'explosion of popular outrage in Egypt was exploited by the designers and promoters of colour revolutions' and that Mubarak's fall followed unsuccessful 'colour revolutions' in 2005 and 2008.[72] While Ignatenko argued that the Egyptian revolution illustrated the declining influence of political Islam in the Arab world, the consensus within the Russian expert community was that Mubarak's fall would unleash Islamic extremist forces in Egypt. Sergei Markov, a United Russia State Duma deputy, accused the Obama administration of 'stupidity and suicide' for encouraging Mubarak's fall and warned that it would cause radical Islamists to seize power throughout the Middle East.[73] Yevgeny Satanovsky stated that the Muslim Brotherhood's power and Al-Azhar University in Cairo's links with al-Qaeda would result in the 'Islamization of Egypt' and restrict the ability of moderate political figures, such as former International

THE MEDVEDEV INTERREGNUM

Atomic Energy Agency (IAEA) Director General Mohammed el-Baradei to seize power.[74] These narratives were reinforced by alarmist comparisons between the 2011 Egyptian Revolution and the 1979 Iranian Revolution, which was followed by the Iran-Iraq War.

Russia's counter-revolutionary narratives about the revolutions in Egypt and Tunisia, which intensified further with the uprisings in Libya, Bahrain and Syria, eroded its soft power in the MENA region. Alexei Malashenko notes the collapse of favorable perceptions of Russia in MENA countries, such as Turkey (16%), Jordan (25%) and Egypt (30%), after Moscow's counter-revolutionary positions became apparent.[75] While Russia found common cause with Gulf monarchies, such as Kuwait, the UAE and Saudi Arabia, in opposing the Tunisian and Egyptian revolutions, disagreements over Syria prevented a normative alignment from developing. In Sub-Saharan Africa, Russia's counter-revolutionary perspectives aligned with the views of many governments and clashed with the perspectives of civil society movements. Although South Africa cautiously supported Mubarak's resignation, other African countries, such as Nigeria, stayed silent, and authoritarian regimes on the continent, such as Zimbabwe, Gabon and Eritrea, intensified their repression or delegitimized the popular unrest in North Africa. Insecurities about the Arab Spring, which were amplified by backlash in Africa against the NATO military intervention in Libya and the regime change in Côte d'Ivoire in April 2011, helped Russia rebuild its soft power in Africa during Medvedev's final year in power.

## Russia's Response to the Arab Spring in Libya

The 2011 Libyan revolution had a transformative impact on Russian foreign policy and internal politics. Russia's strident opposition to Muammar al-Gaddafi's overthrow hardened its position as a counter-revolutionary actor on the world stage, resulted in the collapse of the Obama-era reset in US-Russia relations and placed Dmitry Medvedev on a long road towards political marginalization. The Medvedev-Putin rift on Libya, which was exposed in the spring of 2011, broke with prior trends, as both men played a key role in strengthening Moscow-Tripoli relations from 2008 to 2011. As oil

95

prices soared in the summer of 2008, Russian officials mused about constructing a gas OPEC, which would consist of Russia, Libya and Qatar.[76] Libya rejected this proposal, which resulted in greater Russia-Iran cooperation in the natural gas sphere, and Moscow rejected Gaddafi's alternative offer to produce Russian gas in Libyan companies. Nevertheless, Russia-Libya relations continued to thrive. In November 2008, Gaddafi met with Putin in Moscow to discuss 'joint activities on the African continent'.[77] This trip presaged Gaddafi's triumph in the African Union chairmanship elections of February 2009, and underscored Libya's desire to frame itself as Russia's gateway to Africa. Gaddafi offered Medvedev a potential Russian base in Benghazi. This base would give Russia's Peter the Great and Admiral Chabanenko ships reliable access to Libya's coast, and rekindle Moscow's superpower status in the Mediterranean, In January 2010, the Libyan Investment Authority purchased a stake in the Hong Kong IPO of Rusal. Days later, Libyan Defence Minister Major General Abu-Bakr Yunis Jabr travelled to Moscow to finalize $1.8 billion in arms purchases from Russia, which included twenty fighter jets, S-300PMU2 air defence systems and prospective purchases of Russian T-90 tanks.[78]

Despite these commercial and strategic interests, Russia did not initially stake out a hardline counter-revolutionary position in Libya. In keeping with its reactions to unrest in Egypt and Tunisia, Russia responded cautiously to the outbreak of mass protests in Benghazi on 15 February and aligned its handling of these demonstrations with the policies of Western countries. Russia voted for UNSC Resolution 1970 on 26 February, which condemned Gaddafi's use of lethal force against Libyan protesters and announced its compliance with the UN arms embargo against Libya on 10 March. Although Russia's refusal to support Gaddafi came at a large financial cost, as Moscow had $4 billion in extant arms contracts with Libya, Medvedev's refusal to side with the Libyan dictator was praised in Kremlin-aligned media outlets. An article in Lenta.ru on 21 February claimed that Gaddafi was 'behaving strangely to say the least, but actually as if he was out of his mind'.[79] To justify Medvedev's non-intervention in Libya, Alexander Ignatenko argued that Gaddafi had financed Chechen separatism and Ukraine's Orange Revolution, while the

## THE MEDVEDEV INTERREGNUM

Libyan opposition sought to create an 'Arabian exclave on Libyan territory'.[80] Vladimir Zhirinovsky, Gaddafi's closest political ally in Russia, claimed on 21 February that 'changes are inevitable in Libya' and urged the Libyan dictator to stop repressing dissent and to seek asylum in Moscow.[81]

Although Medvedev's moderate approach to the Libyan conflict attracted near-unanimous support within Russia's political and media spheres, the memory of internationalist backlash against Andrei Kozyrev's vote for UN sanctions on Libya was all-too vivid. To pre-empt dissent from anti-Western elements within the *siloviki* and Russia's diplomatic corps, Medvedev positioned Russia as a supporter of a political settlement and an opponent of a Western-led military intervention in Libya. In a November 2018 interview with RIA Novosti, Dmitry Medvedev recalled his belief that the 'existing ruling regime stained itself with criminal actions against its citizens' and claimed that his preferred solution to the Libyan conflict was UN-backed intra-Libyan dialogue.[82] In line with this preferred policy, Vitaly Churkin secured a provision in UNSC Resolution 1970 that prevented the US and Europe from using it as a pretext for a military intervention in Libya.[83] To achieve this concession, Russia reluctantly acceded to Gaddafi's potential prosecution by the ICC. Russia also dialed down international pressure for a no-fly zone in Libya by denying that Gaddafi had used helicopters to launch airstrikes on Libyan protesters.[84]

Despite Medvedev's resistance to an external-backed regime change in Libya, Russia surprisingly abstained from UNSC Resolution 1973 on 17 March. UNSC Resolution 1973's pledge to use 'all necessary measures' to protect Libyan civilians opened the door for arms transfers to Libyan rebels and enforced a no-fly zone in Libya. Russia's abstention from UNSC Resolution 1973, which was echoed by China, Brazil, India and Germany, created even sharper polarizations within the Russian foreign policy establishment than Kozyrev's actions in the early 1990s. Dmitry Medvedev insisted that he 'did not consider this resolution to be wrong' and argued that the UNSC resolution was a necessary consequence of Gaddafi's massacres of Libyan civilians.[85] Vitaly Churkin viewed the resolution's calls for an 'immediate ceasefire' in Libya to be constructive, and argued that the

UN could have saved Libyan lives if it had heeded Russia's prior calls for a ceasefire. Churkin was somewhat more critical of the resolution than Medvedev, as he noted that it was 'not in keeping with Security Council practice' and 'many questions remained unanswered'.[86] Unlike Medvedev and Churkin's qualified endorsements of UNSC Resolution 1973, Vladimir Putin called the resolution 'defective and flawed' and claimed that 'it resembles medieval calls for crusades'. Putin's comments mirrored Gaddafi's labelling of the United States, Britain and France as crusader countries. Dmitry Medvedev called Putin's rhetoric 'unacceptable' and warned that it could lead to a 'clash of civilizations'.[87] While Putin had reportedly disagreed with Medvedev's handling of the Georgian War and vote for multilateral sanctions against Iran in 2010, the rift between Putin and Medvedev over Libya exposed unprecedented levels of dissension between the two leaders.

The inception of NATO airstrikes in Libya less than forty-eight hours after UNSC Resolution 1973's passage caused elite and public opinion to swing decidedly in Putin's favour. While the Russian Ministry of Foreign Affairs released a measured call to end NATO's 'indiscriminate use of force', other Russian politicians were more caustic in their criticisms. Vladimir Zhirinovsky called NATO 'murderers and barbarians' and warned that the perpetrators of war against Libya would face a 'new Nuremburg trial'.[88] Russian Deputy Prime Minister Sergei Ivanov subsequently warned that NATO's reliance on a military solution in Libya was 'borrowed from the arsenals of the Cold War' and would sharpen international polarizations.[89] While opposing Medvedev's Libya policy empowered Putin and his allies in the United Russia Party ahead of the 2012 presidential elections, Russian ambassador to Libya Vladimir Chamov's opposition to Medvedev led to his marginalization. Chamov told Medvedev that supporting Western policies towards Libya would lead to the betrayal of Russian interests, and in an interview with *The Moscow Times*, Chamov defended Putin's crusade comment and praised Gaddafi as a 'very adequate person'.[90] Following his dismissal, Chamov's position was widely supported by former Russian diplomats, such as Veniamin Popov, who claimed that Chamov was merely fulfilling his duty as ambassador to advance

## THE MEDVEDEV INTERREGNUM

positive Russia-Libya relations.[91] However, Vladimir Putin did not publicly side with Chamov, as he reaffirmed Medvedev's standing as the leading decision-maker on Russian foreign policy matters[92] and sought to temporarily de-escalate intra-elite rifts ahead of the 2011 legislative elections.

Vladimir Putin's muzzling of intra-elite discord over Libya did not eliminate factional differences within the Kremlin. Dmitry Medvedev's statement on 27 May at the G8 summit in France that 'Gaddafi's regime has lost its legitimacy. He must go' underscored his implicit support for NATO's military intervention in Libya.[93] The June 2011 ICC warrant against Muammar al-Gaddafi, Saif al-Islam Gaddafi and Libyan intelligence chief Abdullah al-Senussi revealed latent polarizations within the Russian foreign policy establishment. State Duma Foreign Affairs Committee chairman Konstantin Kosachev and Dmitry Rogozin's alarmist warnings that the ICC warrant against Gaddafi would derail a peaceful solution in Libya were rebutted by Mikhail Margelov, Medvedev's special envoy to Africa.[94] Moreover, it became clear that Russia's opposition to UNSC Resolution 1973 was driven by political theatre rather than substantive critiques. University of Oxford Professor Roy Allison notes that 'the Russian leadership appears to be fully conscious of the escalatory potential of the resolution that it chose not to veto'.[95] Despite these cleavages, the Russian foreign policy establishment was able to unite around a political resolution to the Libyan crisis, but this proved impossible due to Gaddafi's desire to hold on to power and the escalating NATO intervention.

After political dialogue in Libya failed to take root, the Kremlin's official and unofficial policies bifurcated. Officially, Russia divested from Gaddafi's regime and recognized the National Transitional Council (NTC) as Libya's legitimate authority. Unofficially, it stridently condemned the NATO-led military intervention. While the NTC recognition aligned with the international recognition, the severity of Russia's anti-NATO rhetoric can be explained by two factors that are worthy of deeper analysis. First, Russian elite and public opinion pivoted sharply in a counter-revolutionary direction. After the Tunisian and Egyptian revolutions, Russian media outlets dismissed the potential for unrest on the Arab streets to diffuse to

99

Moscow. A *Vzglyad* commentary of 1 February stated that the 'eternal weakness of the domestic opposition saves us from both the Tunisian and Egyptian versions' of regime change.[96] The Libyan revolution overhauled this climate of indifference, as it coincided with polls which showed that 74% of Russians would participate in a rally or protest.[97] University of Westminster Professor Roland Dannreuther notes that the Kremlin saw both a threat and an opportunity emanating from the events in Libya. On the one hand, Russian officials were alarmed by the prospect of a 'Libyan scenario' being reproduced in Russia or Ukraine. On the other hand, Russia saw Libya's post-Arab Spring instability as an opportunity to highlight the 'virtues of Russia's own model of state-managed political order' and the 'flaws of the imposition of liberal democracy'.[98] The outbreak of mass protests in Moscow's Bolotnaya Square after the Duma elections in December 2011 sharpened these counter-revolutionary narratives.

Second, Russia also viewed its strident defence of Gaddafi as a means of strengthening its relationships with China. The convergence of Russia and China's positions on Libya was initially framed in the context of their shared support for restrained internationalism. Chairman of the Council on Foreign and Defence Policy Fyodor Lukyanov opined that Russia's abstention from UNSC Resolution 1973 revealed that its foreign policy was becoming 'less global, reminiscent of the Chinese approach'.[99] The meeting between Dmitry Medvedev and Chinese President Hu Jintao in June 2011 converted their solidarity into normative resistance, as both leaders warned against the 'willful interpretation and expanded application' of UNSC resolutions.[100] The convergence of Russian and Chinese unofficial narratives on the Libyan crisis was equally pronounced. Zhong Shi, a researcher at the Center for World Socialism Studies at the Chinese Academy of Sciences, claimed that Western countries exported the 'Jasmine Revolution virus' to Libya in order to 'destroy and dismember Libya' and block Asian countries from securing access to its hydrocarbons.[101] This accorded with Kremlin-backed narratives on the NATO intervention in Libya. MGIMO professor Alexey Pushkov was more sceptical of the Sino-Russian alignment in Libya, as he stated that it was 'advantageous for China that the United States invades the Muslim world', as it would strengthen China's

## THE MEDVEDEV INTERREGNUM

power in the Middle East.[102] This scepticism was substantiated by the Chinese Foreign Ministry of Foreign Affairs' more optimistic reaction to Gaddafi's death than the Kremlin. Although Russia and China view the 2011 Libyan war as the main trigger of lasting instability in North Africa and the Sahel, Moscow has more vociferously promoted this theory in its engagement with African countries and used it to ensconce itself as a hedge partner against Chinese hegemony in Africa.

The Kremlin's counter-revolutionary convictions were amplified considerably by Russian official rhetoric after Gaddafi's death on 20 October. Sergei Lavrov focused on the nature of Gaddafi's death, stating 'We have to lean on facts and international laws. They say that a captured participant of an armed conflict should be treated in a certain way. And in any case, a prisoner of war should not be killed.'[103] Lavrov also alluded to NATO's potential violations of the Geneva Convention, which surfaced repeatedly in Russian official statements following the events of 2011. Vladimir Putin initially did not make any political statements on Gaddafi's death but expressed 'disgust' with media coverage of his assassination.[104] Other Russian officials were more dramatic in their condemnations of NATO's reactions to Gaddafi's death. In a fiery tweet, Dmitry Rogozin stated 'The faces of world democracies are so happy, as if they remembered how they hanged stray cats in basements in their childhoods.'[105] These sentiments would profoundly strengthen Russia's solidarity with Syrian President Bashar al-Assad and became a mainstream feature of Russian official foreign policy discourse, which complemented its prior condemnations of NATO conduct in Yugoslavia.

### Russia Leverages Its Opposition to Gaddafi's Overthrow in Africa

The overthrow of Muammar al-Gaddafi split opinion in Africa. Some countries on the democracy-to-hybrid-regime spectrum, such as Botswana and Nigeria, strongly supported Gaddafi's overthrow. They were joined by autocrats, such as Guinea's Alpha Condé, the Gambia's Yahya Jammeh, Rwanda's Paul Kagame and Cameroon's Paul Biya, who urged Gaddafi to resign and banned participation in pro-Gaddafi demonstrations on their soil. South Africa and

101

Nigeria staked out a middle ground, which supported the no-fly zone but deplored NATO's expansion of its mandate to a regime change. Other African leaders, such as Namibia's Hifkepunye Pohamba and Algeria's Abdelaziz Bouteflika, accompanied anti-Western autocrats like Zimbabwe's Robert Mugabe and Uganda's Yoweri Museveni in condemning all aspects of NATO's military intervention in Libya. Russia's opposition to NATO's overreach from the UNSC Resolution 1973 mandate and reaction to Gaddafi's death resonated with a broad coalition of African states. Contrary to popular assumptions, Russia did not build a counter-revolutionary or anti-Western bloc in Africa, but instead engaged in shuttle diplomacy with a diverse group of African countries that supported non-interference.

Russia's shuttle diplomacy in Africa on the Libyan crisis began shortly after the country's devolution into civil war. On 10 March 2011, the Russian Foreign Ministry praised the African Union's peacekeeping plans in Libya. The ratification of UNSC Resolution 1973 and the swift inception of the NATO military intervention in Libya provided Russia with a golden opportunity to strengthen its diplomatic cooperation with African countries. On 20 March, Sergei Lavrov travelled to Egypt and Algeria to discuss NATO's first airstrikes in Libya. During his visit to Egypt, Lavrov engaged with Secretary General of the Arab League Amr Moussa, who insisted that UNSC Resolution 1973 did not mandate an 'invasion' of Libya.[106] Lavrov's description of Egypt as Russia's 'strategic partner' and engagement with its post-Arab Spring head of state Hussein Tantawi eased Moscow-Cairo tensions. Algerian Foreign Minister Murad Medelei supported Russia's view that NATO's actions in Libya were 'disproportionate' and Lavrov warned that the Libyan crisis could create 'new manifestations of international terrorism'.[107] Russia subsequently stepped up its outreaches to the African Union on Libya, as it believed that Western countries, with the exception of Germany, were 'thwarting its plans to carry out a mediation mission'.[108] Andrey Urnov, who served as Russian Ambassador to Namibia from 1990 to 1993, claimed that the UNSC Resolution 1973 was fast-tracked to derail AU diplomacy.[109] Sergei Lavrov also emphasized the AU's ability to work alongside the UN as a peer

## THE MEDVEDEV INTERREGNUM

institution in resolving the Libyan conflict during his meetings with Tripoli and Benghazi delegations in May 2011.[110]

Russia's engagement with South Africa during the Libyan crisis strengthened the Moscow-Pretoria normative axis, which first surfaced during the Yeltsin-Mandela consultations on Kosovo. This outcome appeared unlikely in March 2011, as Russian experts condemned South Africa's vote for UNSC Resolution 1973. Vladimir Shubin described South Africa's vote for a no-fly zone in Libya 'especially deplorable', as it violated the BRICS consensus.[111] Jacob Zuma's condemnation of NATO airstrikes in April 2011 during his first BRICS summit participation facilitated Russia-South Africa cooperation on Libya. On 4 July, Medvedev invited Zuma to Sochi and brokered three-way negotiations between Russia, NATO and South Africa on the crisis in Libya. Even though Lavrov claimed that Zuma's AU-backed plan created a pathway towards political dialogue and NATO vowed to 'study the AU proposals', South Africa's influence on NATO's thinking was negligible.[112] NATO's perceived dismissal of Zuma's ideas on Libya contributed to Pretoria's vocal support for Syrian sovereignty in early 2012, which created a Russia-South Africa alignment on Syria that persists to this day.

Russia's normative resistance in Libya also extended to its handling of the spring 2011 Côte d'Ivoire political crisis. In October 2010, Alassane Ouattara triumphed in Côte d'Ivoire's first presidential elections in a decade, but Laurent Gbagbo, who had held power since 2000, refused to concede. This sparked an intense conflict, which killed 3,000 Ivorians. Aside from their covert Moscow-Abidjan cooperation in the conflict diamond trade, Russia had few material interests in Côte d'Ivoire. Russia aligned with the international consensus by voting for UNSC Resolution 1957 on 29 March, which imposed sanctions on Laurent Gbagbo and his immediate family. Nevertheless, Russia emerged as the international community's main opponent of an external military solution to the crisis in Côte d'Ivoire. In January 2011, Russia blocked a France-sponsored UNSC resolution to increase the United Nations Operation in Côte d'Ivoire (UNOCI) force from 10,000 to 12,000 and demanded the deletion of Ouattara's name from the UN statement.[113] Russia also rejected a proposal from ECOWAS to militarily intervene on Ouattara's behalf.

103

On 31 March, violence intensified after Ouattara attempted to seize control of Abidjan and secure control over Côte d'Ivoire's coffee and cocoa industries, and France intervened on Ouattara's behalf. In response to France's military intervention, Russia emphasized the need for African countries, such as Libya and Côte d'Ivoire, to resolve their security crises through internal mechanisms. During a meeting on 5 April with Gabon's Foreign Minister Paul Toungui, Sergei Lavrov contended that UN peacekeepers might have violated their obligation of neutrality and called for an emergency UNSC meeting on France's military activities in Côte d'Ivoire.[114] RT's coverage of the crisis accused France of putting political interests over humanitarian ones and claimed that the UN aligned with 'western global managers' in Côte d'Ivoire.[115] Laurent Gbagbo's capture on 11 April elicited further rebuke in Russia, as it would lead to his extradition to the ICC. Fyodor Lukyanov argued that the UN violated precedents by implicitly supporting Gbagbo's capture by French and Ivorian forces.[116] Russia's anti-French posturing in Côte d'Ivoire appeased domestic critics of Dmitry Medvedev's abstention from UNSC Resolution 1973 and contextualises Moscow's more assertive campaign against the NATO military intervention in Libya.

During Medvedev's presidency, Russia took major strides towards great power status in Africa and invested considerably in the long-standing expansion of its soft power. Through targeted diplomatic visits, symbolic displays of support for an expanded African role in world affairs and anti-Western normative defiance, the Medvedev era set a tone for the policies that Putin embraced during his third term. The Arab Spring and 2011 NATO military intervention in Libya saw Russia double down on its anti-Western policies and build on its resistance to Western efforts to isolate Zimbabwe and Sudan. Despite these resounding successes, Medvedev's willingness to accommodate rather than emphatically resist Western policy in Libya paved the way for his political marginalization. This ensured that Putin, Russian state-owned companies and anti-Western voices in the foreign and security policy establishments guided Moscow's conduct in the post-2012 period.

# 4

# RUSSIA'S ANTI-WESTERN TILT IN AFRICA

During Vladimir Putin's third term in office from 2012 to 2018, tensions between Russia and the West escalated into a full-blown systemic confrontation. In February 2014, Russia annexed the Crimean Peninsula, which was the first extra-legal seizure of territory in Europe since World War II. The US and EU responded by imposing economic sanctions against Russia, and Russian foreign policy reoriented itself towards the collective non-West. Frictions between Russia and the West intensified further after Moscow's September 2015 military intervention in Syria, which aimed to preserve Bashar al-Assad's hold on power. The persistence of these tensions ensured that Africa became a geopolitical battleground between Russia and the West. It also inspired Russia to deepen its involvement in African affairs, as Moscow positioned itself as a crisis-proof partner for anti-Western authoritarian regimes, a champion of expanded African influence in a multipolar world order and an alternative counterinsurgency partner. This chapter will examine the impact of the Russia-West systemic confrontation on Moscow's ambitions and policies towards Africa. It will begin by exploring how Russia's tensions with the US and EU spilt over to Africa. It will then examine Russia's expanded cooperation with anti-Western countries in Africa and outreaches to South Africa, which became an

105

increasingly important fulcrum of Moscow's strategy towards the continent. The chapter will conclude by examining Russia's efforts to frame itself as an alternative counterinsurgency partner in Africa, efforts to export its 'Syrian model' of counterterrorism on the continent and intervention in the Central African Republic.

## The Russia-West Systemic Confrontation Spills Over to Africa

The Russia-West confrontation over Ukraine created sharp polarizations in Africa but it did not result in drastic shifts in perceptions of Moscow on the continent. Only two African countries, Sudan and Zimbabwe, endorsed the Crimean referendum in a United Nations General Assembly (UNGA) vote 27 March 2014. A bloc of seventeen countries in North Africa (Tunisia and Libya), West Africa (Benin, Chad, Guinea, Guinea-Bissau, Liberia, Niger, Nigeria, Sierra Leone and Togo), Central Africa (Cameroon, CAR and the DRC), as well as Somalia, Malawi and Madagascar, recognized the referendum as illegitimate. Most African countries, including major regional powers like Egypt, Algeria, South Africa and Ethiopia, abstained from the UNGA resolution on Crimea. This favourable breakdown of voting patterns by African countries on Crimea elevated the continent's importance for Russian diplomacy. Brittany Brown, who served as Director for African Affairs at the White House National Security Council from 2016 to 2017, notes that Russia devoted more attention to smaller African countries after this UNGA referendum, as it could yield higher returns than expanding its investments in larger countries, such as Kenya.[1] To rally UNGA votes around anti-Westernism, Russia became the chief obstructionist of US policy towards Africa in the United Nations. Michelle Gavin, who served as US ambassador to Botswana from 2011 to 2014, recalled that Russia 'reflexively opposed' US initiatives on Africa in the UN, even when it did not have major interests at stake or a coherent alternative policy to advance.[2] Russia was especially focused on undermining US sanctions policy in African countries, such as the CAR (Central African Republic) and South Sudan, as the US and EU imposed sweeping economic sanctions against Russia in response to its conduct in Ukraine.

## RUSSIA'S ANTI-WESTERN TILT IN AFRICA

As tensions over African issues mounted between the US and Russia in the UNGA, new Cold War fears reached unprecedented heights. A 2016 Institute for African Studies report declared that 'today we are witnessing an acute geo-economic and geostrategic battle for Africa', which has produced a constantly fluctuating balance of power.[3] The US's successful efforts to thwart Russia from securing a base in Djibouti provided empirical evidence for these contentions. From 2012 to 2013, Russia engaged in intensive negotiations with the Djiboutian authorities on establishing a naval base near Djibouti's international airport, where the US, France, Japan and Italy possessed facilities. A Russian military delegation reportedly visited the Kempinski hotel to finalize the terms of this agreement. Negotiations stalled, as Djibouti offered Russia an insufficiently small land plot of five hectares, and intra-Kremlin divisions surfaced about the merits of the base. The Federal Agency of Special Construction enthusiastically supported the base agreement, while Russian defence officials viewed the regulation of takeoffs and landings by US and French air traffic controllers as problematic. The financial costs of Russia's base gambit in Djibouti also reduced its popularity, as oil prices plunged in 2014. The US capitalized on Russia-Djibouti disagreements and intra-Kremlin divisions by pressuring Djibouti to make an offer to Russia, which would have unacceptable terms. Djibouti offered Russia access to Tajura Bay near Obok, which was a less strategically valuable location than the capital and proposed a plan that would require an initial investment of $1 billion plus base rental fees of between $30 and 70 million per year. Due to the exceptionally high costs and undesirability of this location, Russia rejected Djibouti's US-backed proposal and redirected its attention towards protecting its bases in Syria.[4]

Despite their intense rivalry over Djibouti, the US-Russia relationship in Africa ultimately settled into an unexpected equilibrium of 'hostility without contestation'. While the Obama administration acknowledged Russia's potential to act as a spoiler in Africa, Moscow's presence was viewed as a secondary challenge, as Russian investments lagged Britain, France, China and the United States, and it was unclear whether Russia's arms sales had necessarily destabilizing consequences.[5] Russia capitalized on US neglect of its interests in Africa by stealthily expanding its security presence, ramping up its information war against the United States and capitalizing on US disengagement. Russia signed military-technical agreements with Zimbabwe (October 2015), Ghana (June 2016), Rwanda (October 2016), the Gambia (September 2016), Mozambique (January 2017), Chad (August 2017), Niger (August 2017) and Nigeria (August 2017). These agreements were primarily military training and counterterrorism assistance pacts. Nevertheless, Mozambique security agreement included in-built arms transfers,[6] and Russia's breakthroughs with US partners, such as Nigeria, and France's Operation Barkhane coalition were especially striking. Russian media outlets regularly railed against Western neocolonialism in Africa and claimed that the overthrow of Muammar al-Gaddafi ushered in a new era of neo-imperialism.[7] To amplify these messages, Russian media outlets highlighted commentaries from sympathetic regional voices, such as Tunisian commentator Faouzi Mahbuli, who opposed Ben Ali's overthrow in 2011. Mahbuli claimed that United States Africa Command (AFRICOM) and NATO wanted to entrench US hegemony and expel China from Africa, and this narrative rapidly spread throughout Russian media and academic discourse.[8]

The US's inchoate response to Russia's security agreements and disinformation encouraged Russia to further escalate its tactics in Africa. Jonathan Winer, who served as US Special Envoy to Libya under Barack Obama, argued that Russia's expanded support for Khalifa Haftar was aimed at preventing Hillary Clinton from re-establishing a US foothold in Libya. Winer noted that Donald Trump's unexpected triumph in November 2016 encouraged Russia to expand its support for Haftar, as UAE policy objectives that dovetailed with Moscow's dictated US Libya policy.[9] Outgoing US Ambassador to the EU Anthony Gardner stated that 'To think that Russia is somehow seeking to promote our shared agenda is folly',[10] and this opinion extended to counterterrorism in Libya, which Moscow viewed as a potential area of cooperation as recently as 2015. The US's retention of anachronistic state sponsorship of terrorism sanctions against Sudan and France's suspension of Operation Sangaris in CAR in October 2016 created new opportunities for Russia. Ignoring the consequences of US disengagement from great power competition in Africa, the Trump administration amplified Obama's near-exclusive focus on China and paid little attention to the Russian challenge. Tibor Nagy, who served as Assistant Secretary of State for African Affairs from 2018 to 2021, claimed that the Trump administration 'viewed China as the Great Dane and Russia as the little chihuahua' and saw Russia as an opportunistic power that aimed to poke the US and France wherever possible.[11] This outlook caused the US to design its strategies towards Africa around the Chinese threat and deal with Russia in an ad hoc fashion, thereby underestimating Moscow's sustainability as a great power.

Other major geopolitical trends, such as the escalation of EU-Russia tensions and the strengthening of Russia-China cooperation did not readily transfer to Africa. The EU did not present a unified front against Russia's rising influence, even as a Franco-Russian rivalry intensified in the counterterrorism and nuclear energy spheres. The main flashpoint for Franco-Russian tensions was CAR, and this competition will be explored at the end of this chapter. Mirroring trends in other extra-regional theatres, such as Latin America and Middle East, bilateral policy coordination between Russia and China did not extend to the African context. Russian academics emphasized China's commitment to South-South cooperation in Africa, which would bolster Africa's standing in multilateral institutions, challenge Western neocolonialism and help solve Africa's humanitarian and economic problems.[12] Despite this solidarity, Russia also believed that the legacy of Soviet involvement in Africa would allow it to project influence independently from China,[13] and the Kremlin had few illusions about cooperation with China. Institute for African Studies report of November 2017 noted that 'as the Russian presence in Africa expands, the risks of a clash and rivalry of interests between Russia and China will increase'. China's cooperation with France on thwarting Rosatom's nuclear deal with South Africa underscored the prospects for Sino-Russian contestation.[14]

As Russia tried to distinguish itself from neocolonial Western powers and was unable to free-ride off the BRI, soft power became an increasingly important dimension of its Africa policy. Russia burnished its image in Africa through humanitarian aid and development assistance. In 2015, Russia donated 218 Kamaz trucks to the WFP, which provided vital assistance to CAR, South Sudan and the DRC, and strengthened the WFP's regional truck fleets in Ghana and Uganda.[15] Russia also donated $5 million to the World Health Organization (WHO)'s African aid programme and revived its development assistance provisions to Africa, which were slashed following its steep post-sanctions economic recession. During his September 2017 meeting with Guinea's President Alpha Condé, Vladimir Putin hailed Moscow's $20 billion in debt forgiveness to Africa.[16] Due to its formative role in shaping Russian development assistance measures in Africa, Dmitry Medvedev as prime minister remained the public face of its initiatives on the continent. In October 2017, Medvedev authorized $2 billion in additional development assistance for African countries. Medvedev also tasked Afreximbank—a financial institution registered in Nigeria, based in Egypt, with regional offices in Côte d'Ivoire, Kenya and Zimbabwe—with distributing aid throughout Africa.[17] These ventures strengthened Russia's elite-level relationships in Africa but did not improve its tarnished image at the popular or civil society levels. In August 2017, a Pew Research survey showed Putin's favourability ratings at 32% in Tunisia, 33% in Kenya and South Africa, 34% in Senegal, 36% in Ghana, 39% in Nigeria and 51% in Uganda.[18] The Wagner Group's misconduct and Russia's autocracy promotion efforts would sharpen this soft power deficit in the following years.

### Russia Shores Up Its Anti-Western Partnerships in Africa

Throughout Putin's third term, Russia doubled down on its image as a crisis-proof partner for authoritarian regimes facing international isolation and established diversified strategic partnerships with African countries that had strained relations with Europe and the United States. Russia's support for Burundi's President Pierre Nkurunziza, South Sudan's Salva Kiir and the Gambia's President Yahya Jammeh illustrated Moscow's normative commitment to non-interference and willingness to build bridges with authoritarian regimes that lay outside of its traditional coterie of partners. Russia's solidarity with Uganda's President Yoweri Museveni echoed these

## RUSSIA'S ANTI-WESTERN TILT IN AFRICA

outreaches but had greater strategic intent, as Uganda was a plausible gateway for Russian influence in eastern Africa. As Zimbabwe and Sudan supported Russia's conduct in Ukraine, Moscow also paid particular attention to strengthening its partnerships with both countries. Since Russia had previously backed multilateral sanctions against North Korea and Iran in the Medvedev-era, the scale of Moscow's obstructionism of Western punitive measures in Africa reflected a drastic post-Crimea shift in policy.

### Russia Crystallizes Its Role as a Crisis-Proof Partner for Authoritarian Regimes

Russia's display of loyalty to Burundi's President Pierre Nkurunziza after the outbreak of political violence in 2015, defence of South Sudan's President Salva Kiir against international isolation and the Gambia's PresidentYahya Jammeh cemented its autocracy promotion role in Sub-Saharan Africa. In October 2015, Russia aligned with China in blocking a French-drafted UN Security Council statement on Burundi, and Vitaly Churkin declared that 'it's not the business of the Security Council and the UN Charter to get involved in constitutional matters of sovereign states'.[19] Burundian state-aligned media outlets praised Russia for standing up to the aggression of the US, France and Belgium, pledged to expand cooperation with Russia in the African Great Lakes region and called the protests a 'Burkina Faso-style color revolution'.[20] In the months leading up to Jammeh's departure, Russia-Gambia relations strengthened. Due to the Gambia's strategic location near the Gambia River and the Atlantic Ocean, and the absence of Western competition, Russia viewed the Gambia as a potential foothold in West Africa.[21] In September 2016, Russia and the Gambia signed a military cooperation agreement, which would lead to training and technical assistance. Gambian civil society figures condemned this military cooperation agreement, and one activist, Awa Sey, warned that it would lead to 'more silent deaths'.[22] Russia's desire to strengthen its relations with ECOWAS ultimately trumped its loyalty to Jammeh, as Moscow did not object to the ECOWAS military intervention in January 2017 that installed Adam Barrow as president.

111

Russia's defence of South Sudan from international opprobrium was especially intriguing, as it viewed South Sudan's quest for independence negatively. A 2014 MGIMO report noted that Russia had reluctantly acquiesced to South Sudan's secession, as it had condemned armed separatism for decades, and claimed that South Sudan's constitution reflected the influence of Western governance models.[23] By April 2012, Russia had pivoted towards an official policy of 'positive neutrality' between Sudan and South Sudan. In May 2014, Russia vetoed US-backed sanctions against South Sudan. This vote bolstered Russian soft power in South Sudan, as Foreign Ministry Spokesman Mawien Arik claimed that Russia has been 'helping us, even praying for us' and invited Vladimir Putin to visit South Sudan.[24] Despite its normative case for opposing sanctions, illicit arms sales likely influenced Russia's position. A UN Panel of Experts report of August 2015 revealed that South Sudan's forces used Russian amphibious armoured vehicles, which were capable of moving soldiers through flooded terrain in the rainy season, and Mi-24 attack helicopters.[25] Russia subsequently opposed an arms embargo against South Sudan in January and December 2016, and thwarted Trump administration efforts to sanction South Sudan in November 2017. Russia's Deputy UN Ambassador Petr Ilichev defended its stance by arguing that there was no evidence that Kiir's regime was blocking the entry of regional peacekeepers to South Sudan and noting the ineffectiveness of arms embargoes in CAR.[26]

## The Consolidation of Russia-Uganda Relations

The marked improvement of Russia-Uganda relations was driven by a similar strategic calculus for Burundi, South Sudan and the Gambia, but its durability reflected Uganda's greater strategic significance. During the Cold War, the Soviet Union maintained a close but inconsistent relationship with Uganda. The Soviet Union supplied a $14 million loan to Uganda in 1962 and courted Idi Amin as a counterweight to US-aligned Kenya and Chinese-aligned Tanzania. Under Yoweri Museveni's leadership, Uganda became a US partner in the War on Terror but maintained an independent streak, which was exhibited by its long-standing security

## RUSSIA'S ANTI-WESTERN TILT IN AFRICA

partnership with North Korea. Museveni's private working visit to Moscow in August 2009 boosted Uganda-Russia relations. US President Barack Obama's condemnation of Museveni's anti-LGBT legislation in February 2014 soured US-Uganda relations and caused Kampala to strengthen its partnership with Russia. In February 2015, Uganda asked an RT Global-led consortium, which also included the oil company Tatneft and the investment banking unit of VTB Capital, to construct a 60,000 barrel/day $2.5 billion crude oil refinery.[27]

This deal placed Russia's RT Global in direct competition with Britain's Tullow Oil, France's Total and China's National Offshore Oil Corporation (CNOOC) for access to Uganda's reserves. US Ambassador to Uganda Scott DeLisi called Museveni's acceptance of RT Global's offer 'not a wise decision', and warned that it was placing Uganda's diplomatic and trade relations with the US at stake.[28] However, Museveni called the Obama administration's bluff and proceeded with the contract, which was ultimately met with negligible US pushback. The Russia-Uganda relationship strengthened further, as Western countries sharply criticized Museveni's authoritarian policies. In February 2016, Yoweri Museveni obtained a landslide victory in Uganda's general elections with 60.62% of the vote, but the US and EU challenged the legitimacy of Uganda's elections by criticizing their opacity and the detention of opposition candidates. Russia emphatically rejected Western criticisms and extolled the integrity of Uganda's election process. The Russian Foreign Ministry praised the 'generally open, calm nature of the election campaign and the voting process itself', and noted the 'absence of serious violations' that would compromise the election results.[29] This statement coincided with a commercial dispute between RT Global and Uganda's Ministry of Energy over their $4 billion refinery contract. RT Global accused Uganda of violating the terms of this contract by refusing to give licenses to Total, Tullow and China National Offshore Oil Corporation, or agree to a suitable taxation rate. These disagreements were irreconcilable, as Rostec refused to extend its negotiations beyond 30 June and South Korea's SK Engineering and Construction replaced RT Global on 1 July.[30]

113

Russia's normative bonding with Uganda over Museveni's re-election helped prevent a collapse of Moscow-Kampala relations after this contractual disagreement. In November 2016, Vladimir Putin invited Museveni to visit Moscow, and Museveni spoke with Russian Ambassador to Uganda Alexander Polyakov about the construction of a shipping line from East Africa to Russia.[31] Russian and Ugandan officials also viewed nuclear energy as a sphere of cooperation, which could compensate for the collapse of their oil refinery negotiations. In June 2017, Russia and Uganda signed a framework agreement on developing a nuclear power infrastructure, which included education and training.[32] This agreement created a foundation for long-term Russia-Uganda cooperation, as Museveni approved the peaceful use of nuclear energy in 2002 and established a Nuclear Energy Unit at the Ministry of Energy in 2008 to help Uganda construct a nuclear reactor by 2034.[33] Museveni also called for a Russia-Africa Summit in October 2017, which would discuss 'strategic development issues', and relayed this opinion to a thirty-member Russian delegation.[34] Uganda also courted Russia's assistance in developing a knowledge economy, as Museveni discussed smart cities, information technology and cybersecurity with Vice Minister for Telecommunications and Mass Communications Alexey Volin. The Russia-Uganda relationship's endurance, despite commercial setbacks, underscored the efficacy of Moscow's sovereignty-based outreaches to authoritarian states.

## The Marked Expansion of Russia-Zimbabwe Cooperation

During Putin's third term as president, Russia expanded its strategic footprint in southern Africa. Aside from deepening its relationship with South Africa, Russia was initially focused on adding fresh momentum to its partnership with Angola. In February 2012, the second meeting of the Angola-Russia Bilateral Commission for Economic, Trade, Scientific and Technological Cooperation congregated after a seven-year hiatus.[35] In October 2013, Dmitry Rogozin visited Angola to sign a $1 billion arms deal, which would lead to the export of eighteen Su-30K fighter jets. This arms deal coincided with EU revelations of the extent of corruption in Angola's

## RUSSIA'S ANTI-WESTERN TILT IN AFRICA

debt repayment to Russia but did not dampen Moscow-Luanda cooperation. Russia's relationship with Zimbabwe developed in a similar fashion. In June 2012, Russia and Zimbabwe signed a five-year deal worth $2.8 billion, which gave Moscow access to its platinum mines in exchange for fighter jet sales.[36] The enforcement of Russia's deals with Zimbabwe were often undermined by the ZANU-PF's reckless policies. For example, the ZANU-PF's indigenization policies often disregarded the interests of non-Western investors. This challenge peaked in 2016, as Mugabe authorized a diamond mining nationalization that cost Russia's Zarubezhgeologia valuable assets but was an established issue earlier in the Mugabe era.[37]

Zimbabwe's endorsement of Russia's conduct in Ukraine strengthened their relationship and encouraged Moscow to overcome its frustrations with Mugabe. Zimbabwean Trade and Industry Minister Simbarashe Mumbengegwi praised Russia's 2008 veto of UN sanctions for saving Zimbabwe from potential destruction.[38] ZANU-PF officials saw the Ukraine crisis as an opportunity for Zimbabwe to repay Russia for its loyalty and showcase the success of Mugabe's Look East strategy. In December 2014, Zimbabwean Environment, Water and Climate minister Savior Kasukuwere visited Crimea, which received fierce backlash from Ukrainian officials.[39] Russia repaid Zimbabwe's support with rhetorical solidarity and new commercial deals. During his visit to Harare in September 2014, Sergei Lavrov described Robert Mugabe as a 'legend', and stated that economic sanctions against Zimbabwe 'have no future'.[40] Mugabe's reply that Russia and China had been 'the two main pillars of support' for Zimbabwe's liberation struggle was intriguing.[41] The Soviet Union's alignment with ZAPU against the ZANU-PF in the Rhodesian Bush War caused Mugabe to view Russia with suspicion even after the 2008 veto. In the post-2008 period, Russia attempted to revive the early 1980s spirit of USSR-Zimbabwe cooperation through concerted outreaches to Zimbabwe's students and the Kremlin credited these soft power outreaches with softening Mugabe's anti-Russian sentiments.[42]

To coincide with Sergei Lavrov's visit to Harare, Russian Industry and Trade Minister Denis Manturov announced a joint Russia-Zimbabwe mining operation in Zimbabwe's Darwendale platinum

115

# RUSSIA IN AFRICA

mine. This deal, which originated through exchanges between Zimbabwean and Russian businesspeople in April 2014, would yield $3 billion in profits for both countries. Russia and Zimbabwe also held talks about a platinum refinery which would increase the deal's profits to $4 billion and Alrosa began prospecting for diamonds in Zimbabwe. Manturov stated that these mining sales would be paired with deliveries of Russian military hardware, helicopters and trucks to Zimbabwe, which underscored the growing nexus of mining, energy and arms deals between Russia and African countries.[43] Beyond the economic drivers of the meeting, Sergei Lavrov also used his visit to Zimbabwe to strengthen its engagement with Southern African Development Community (SADC), as Mugabe was chair of the supranational organization.[44] Despite this outreach and the SADC's antipathy towards US and EU sanctions against Zimbabwe, the Russia-SADC relationship was largely dormant in Putin's third term as president. During her tenure as US ambassador to the SADC, Michelle Gavin recalled the Russian ambassador to Zimbabwe's detachment from SADC-sponsored discussions on Zimbabwe's 2013 presidential elections and ambiguous attitude towards the SADC.[45] This suggests that Lavrov's SADC outreach could have been merely appealing to Mugabe's outsized aspirations for influence in African affairs and reassuring the ZANU-PF that Russia did not have purely extractive or neocolonial intentions in Zimbabwe.

During Mugabe's final years in power, Russia-Zimbabwe relations continued to strengthen. In May 2015, Mugabe met with Vladimir Putin in Moscow, and praised the Soviet Union's vital role in Zimbabwe's liberation struggle. This revisionist statement, which framed the Soviet Union and China as equal partners of the ZANU-PF, was accompanied by praise for Russia's resurgence as a world power.[46] Mugabe highlighted Russia and Zimbabwe's common struggle against sanctions by claiming that the US topped the 'imperialist pyramid', while Europe occupied second place. This solidarity facilitated greater Russia-Zimbabwe security cooperation, which compensated for stalled mining sector deals. In October 2015, Russia and Zimbabwe signed a military cooperation agreement, which facilitated arms sales, allowed for joint military exercises and resupply cooperation. This paved the way for Zimbabwe's

116

## RUSSIA'S ANTI-WESTERN TILT IN AFRICA

participation in training drills with Russia, China, Kazakhstan and Armenia in Kubinka, Russia, in 2016. These drills had a largely symbolic impact and goodwill between Russia and Zimbabwe was strained due to racist coverage in Rossiya-24 of Zimbabwe's participation in these drills.[47]

The November 2017 coup, which overthrew Mugabe and propelled Emmerson Mnangagwa to power, was an external shock to Russia-Zimbabwe cooperation. The coup caught Russian officials off guard, as Morgan Tsvangirai and two ZANU-PF officials were in Moscow at the time of Mnangagwa's seizure of power. An Institute for African Studies report written shortly after the coup emphasized Russia's 'wait-and-see' approach to developments in Zimbabwe and lamented the departure of Second Vice-President Phelekezela Mphoko, who received military training in the Soviet Union from 1964 to 1965.[48] The report also lent support to theories about Chinese involvement in the coup, which contradicted express denials from Beijing, and predicted that Mnangagawa would prioritize closer ties with China. Russian state media reactions to the coup presented contradictory messages about the coup. Initial reports uncritically highlighted China's potential role in the coup,[49] which reflected the enduring Sino-Russian rivalry in Zimbabwe. On 25 November, Sputnik claimed that Western speculation about China's hand in the Zimbabwe coup sought to dampen the BRI's appeal in Africa and warned that Mugabe's overthrow could inspire Zuma's critics, such as ANC Chief Whip Jackson Mthembu, to orchestrate a similar coup in South Africa.[50] Despite these lukewarm-to-negative commentaries about Mnangagwa's coup, the Russian Foreign Ministry pledged to cooperate with Zimbabwe's new authorities on 23 November.[51]

### Russia Deepens Its Security Cooperation with Sudan

During Bashir's last year in power, Russia-Sudan relations experienced a peak of solidarity over Ukraine and rare frictions over Syria. In 2012–13, Sudan resisted African Union pressure to cede Abyei to South Sudan and claimed that the nomadic Arab Misseriya tribes were being persecuted by the Ngok Dinka, which supported integration with South Sudan. This resembled Russia's narratives about the illegitimacy of Crimea's handover to Ukraine and contentions that a Ukrainian nationalist government was persecuting ethnic Russians in Donbas. A *Sudan Tribune* article of 27 March opined that 'Just as Moscow insists that Crimea has historically been part of Russia, Khartoum has the same conviction on Abyei.'[52] In December 2014, Sudan hosted the Russian-Arab Forum, which saw Sergei Lavrov discuss the expansion of economic cooperation with Khartoum and the potential creation of a joint investment bank.[53] Sudan's oblique criticisms of Russia's actions in Syria were noteworthy, as they constituted a rare breach in Khartoum's normative alignment with Russia. Ibrahim Omer, Sudan's National Assembly speaker, claimed that Russia's actions were aimed at strengthening Assad, despite opposition from the Gulf monarchies, and urged Moscow to coordinate its counterterrorism efforts in Syria with Arab countries.[54] Omer's position arguably contradicted Sudan's deployment of troops in Yemen at the invitation of a UN-recognized government, but reflected Khartoum's desire to strengthen its partnership with Saudi Arabia even at the cost of its partnership with Russia.

Notwithstanding their divergence over Syria, Russia continued to defend the Sudanese authorities against war crimes allegations in Darfur. In April 2016, Russia blocked a confidential UN report, which revealed that Bashir-aligned militias earned $54 million a year in illegal gold mining operations. This position aligned with Moscow's broader pattern of obstructing or discrediting UN Panel of Experts reports, which extended to North Korean chemical weapons supplies to Syria, allegations of Iranian ballistic missile transfers to the Houthis in Yemen and arms embargo violations in Libya. It also underscored Russia's solidarity with the United Arab Emirates (UAE), which was the destination of illicit gold from Darfur, and aided its path to the landmark Russia-UAE strategic partnership agreement in June 2018.

Despite their relatively consistent alignments on normative issues, Russia-Sudan trade relations experienced a steep decline from 2015 to 2016, and only partially recovered with an 87% boost to $290 million in 2017. This setback was especially jarring for Russian officials, as Turkey-Sudan trade volumes consistently expanded from $200 to $500 million from 2014 to 2017.[55] Russia-Sudan diplomatic

## RUSSIA'S ANTI-WESTERN TILT IN AFRICA

relations were also disrupted by the sudden death of Russian ambassador to Sudan Mirgayas Shirinsky in his pool in August 2017. Shirinsky was a forty-year veteran of the Russian diplomatic corps, and Putin waited until March 2018 to appoint his successor, Vladimir Zheltov. Omar al-Bashir's November 2017 meetings with Russian officials in Sochi reinvigorated the Russia-Sudan partnership. Bashir's meeting with Minister of Defence Sergei Shoigu ensured that Russia would spearhead Sudan's military modernization and resulted in the arrival of new Sudanese military attachés in Moscow. The meeting also resulted in discussions about Russia establishing a base on Sudan's Red Sea coast, which were revealed to RIA Novosti by Al-Hadi Hamid, the head of the Sudanese Parliament's Defence and Security Committee. Hamid also expressed optimism that the Russian base would thwart smuggling and the slave trade, as well as preventing illegal fishing on Sudanese waters.

These developments were publicly revealed in the Bashir-Putin press conference, but the enthusiasm gap between the Russian and Sudanese sides was palpable.[56] Putin was measured in his assessment of Russia-Sudan cooperation and focused on promising economic trends, such as Russia's supply of 1 million tons of grain and potential Sudanese cooperation with Moscow in the civilian nuclear energy sphere. Bashir's support for cooperation with Russia was much more emphatic, as he called Sudan 'Russia's key to Africa' and linked his meeting with Putin to Khartoum's strategic pivot towards the BRICS countries. Bashir also lambasted US interference in the Red Sea region and accused the US of orchestrating the Sudan-South Sudan partition. Bashir urged Russia to help defend Sudan against the threat posed by pernicious US conduct and emphasized Moscow's reliability as a partner by praising its military intervention in Syria and resistance to the 2003 Iraq War.

Russian officials largely refrained from embracing Bashir's requests for assistance. Franz Klintsevich, the First Deputy Chairman of the Federation Council Committee on Defence and Security, was the lone proponent of a Russian naval base in Sudan, which he claimed would 'play an exclusively stabilizing role' on the Red Sea.[57] Klintsevich's comments reflected the Federation Council's exceptional commitment to Red Sea security, which dated back to

Sergei Mironov's 2008 visit to Aden, Yemen. Russian media outlets emphasized the visit's significance for Russia's international status but also acknowledged risks associated with deeper security cooperation with Sudan. Sputnik Radio claimed that Bashir's trip underscored Sochi's role as a 'platform where global issues are solved', as his visit was immediately preceded by trilateral talks between Russia, Iran and Turkey on Syria.[58] Sudan's location at the crossroads of the Middle East and Africa was viewed by Russian academics, such as Boris Dolgov, as especially appealing. Notwithstanding Sudan's strategic location near the Red Sea, Gulf of Aden and Indian Ocean, defence expert Viktor Murakhovsky viewed its conflict in South Sudan as a serious liability and believed that Aden was a much higher quality port than any on Sudan's coast. Murakhovsky also noted that Russia would likely have to compensate the Sudanese military for base access, much like China did in Djibouti and the Soviet Union did in Ethiopia and warned of 'monstrous expenses' associated with a Russian naval base.[59] Despite these misgivings, Bashir's visit paved the way for Russia's deployment of Wagner Group PMCs to Sudan and the consolidation of Moscow's partnership with Khartoum.

## From High Hopes to Dashed Dreams: Russia's Engagement with South Africa

During Putin's third term, Russia-South Africa relations built on the momentum generated from Medvedev-era exchanges. Alexei Vasiliev argued that South Africa was growing in importance as a theatre of power projection, despite postponed contracts with Russia and a fractious entrepreneurial climate.[60] As the Russia-South Africa Business Council waned in importance due to personnel changes, Russian state-owned companies and the Vladimir Putin-Jacob Zuma relationship drove bilateral cooperation. Russian mining companies viewed South Africa as a vital destination for metals that could not be produced domestically, such as manganese, chromium, bauxite, zinc and tin.[61] In August 2012, Renova invested $400 million in South Africa's manganese industry, which brought Viktor Vekselberg's March 2011 plan to launch a manganese mine to fruition.[62] Norilsk Nickel, Evraz Group and Basic Element were other key investors in South Africa. In May 2013, Putin and Zuma met in Sochi to strengthen trade and investment links, as well as strengthening Russia-South Africa cultural ties via an institutionalized programme that would last until 2016.[63]

The expansion of Russia-South Africa relations in 2014 was closely linked to Jacob Zuma's solidarity with Moscow during the Ukraine crisis. Although South Africa emphasized its support for the inviolability of state borders and called for a political solution to the Russia-Ukraine conflict, it refused to criticize Russia's military interventions in Crimea and Donbas.[64] South Africa also flouted Western sanctions against Russia, as bilateral trade increased by 10% in the first half of 2014. Elizabeth Sidiropoulos, the chief executive of the South African Institute of International Affairs (SAIIA) in Johannesburg, contends that South African officials tied their endorsement of Putin's conduct in Ukraine to the key principles of South African foreign policy.[65] South Africa's support for non-interference in the internal affairs of states justified its opposition to unilateral sanctions against Russia and attempted expulsion of Russia from the G20 summit in Brisbane, Australia, in November 2014. South Africa's support for mediation in Ukraine reflected its support for the incremental resolution of political crises, which was exemplified by its handling of Zimbabwe under Robert Mugabe, and desire to export its post-apartheid brand of national reconciliation.[66]

While Zuma sympathized with Russia over Ukraine, South Africa's largest media outlets were sharply polarized on engagement with Russia. In a *Sunday Independent* article of March 2014, Garth Abraham, a professor at Wits Law School in Johannesburg, framed the Ukraine crisis as a primarily geopolitical rather than international legal question and compared Crimea's vote to unite with Russia to the US recognition of Kosovo in 2008.[67] A September 2014 *Mail and Guardian* article openly accused NATO of provoking the Ukraine crisis and cast doubt on the presence of Russian troops in Donbas.[68] In contrast to these sympathetic accounts, Simon Allison, a columnist at *The Daily Maverick*, chastised South Africa for siding with Russia on human rights issues, even though it had vowed to be a counterweight to authoritarian regimes in the UN Human Rights Council.[69] Elizabeth Sidiropoulos attacked Zuma's equivocations on

121

the Ukraine crisis, as she warned that South Africa's soft power would be eroded if it broke with values that it had consistently championed in the post-Cold War period.[70]

During the second half of Jacob Zuma's term, Russia-South Africa relations strengthened considerably. Zuma and Putin held private meetings at the 2014 BRICS summit, UNGA and G20 summits, as well as regular telephone conversations. In August 2014, Zuma made a six-day trip to Moscow. This trip strengthened Russia-South Africa economic cooperation, and addressed international crises like Ukraine, Palestine and Syria. Zuma's trip was poorly received at home. Zuma was seen to be distracting from internal pressures, like Public Prosecutor Thuli Madonsela's investigation of Zuma's Nkandla homestead renovations and Economic Freedom Fighters head Julius Malema's disruption of a parliamentary session.[71] South African media outlets noted that Zuma was accompanied by International Relations and Cooperation Deputy Minister Nomaindia Mfeketo and State Security Minister David Mahlobo, instead of trade-focused Cabinet members, and he travelled without his usual media entourage.[72] The trip also fuelled rumours about Zuma's health, as the first three days of his South Africa trip consisted of 'low-key meetings' and periods of rest.[73] In South Africa, it was widely believed that Putin invited Zuma to Moscow to secure South Africa's endorsement of Russian conduct in Ukraine. Mahlobo wanted the ANC to adopt aspects of Russia's governance model, as Zuma and Putin discussed political survival during an economic recession on the sidelines of the 2014 BRICS summit.[74]

After a month of speculation of what unfolded during the Zuma-Putin meeting, Russia and South Africa signed a comprehensive nuclear energy cooperation agreement on 23 September 2014. This nuclear agreement, which was Rosatom's first in Africa, followed three years of low-profile forays in the South African market. In the summer of 2011, Zuma told his Finance Minister Pravin Gordhan that he wanted Russia to lead South Africa's quest for nuclear energy. Despite intense countervailing pressure from Gordhan, who warned of state capture that could result from engagement with Russia, Rosatom established an office in Johannesburg, its third global office after Ukraine and Singapore, and transformed it from

RUSSIA'S ANTI-WESTERN TILT IN AFRICA

a one-person outpost into a well-organized operation.[75] In March 2013, Putin emphasized the potential for cooperation with South Africa in the nuclear energy space.[76] Putin's statement followed Vice President Kgalema Motianthe's speech at the Nuclear Africa 2013 Conference, which framed nuclear energy as a key driver of South Africa's competitiveness in a globalized economy. This transformation of Rosatom's prospects was striking, as it overcame stiff competition from France. Avenda built South Africa's Koeberg nuclear plant. Until Rosatom entered this market, French companies were expected to construct South Africa's next generation of EPR reactors. Rosatom outbid Avenda in part due to savvy PR moves. While Avenda was embroiled in a contentious struggle with South Africa's trade unionists, Rosatom supported cultural and youth empowerment initiatives that bolstered its image.[77]

Despite concerns about its cost, Russian and South African officials framed this agreement in win-win terms. Sergei Kiriyenko insisted that the agreement would create thousands of jobs in South Africa, provide a $10 billion stimulus to local industries, cause Russia to invest in South African infrastructure development and allow South African students to attend Russian academies.[78] Alexandra Arkhangelskaya, an expert at Moscow's Institute for African Studies, notes that 40–60% localized production would result in 30,000 new jobs, $16 billion in Russian investments in the construction phase and $5 billion in revenues for South Africa's state budget.[79] South African Energy Minister Tina Joemat-Pettersson hailed Russia's role in ensuring that South Africa would produce 9.6 GW of modern nuclear energy.[80] Pettersson's support for clean nuclear energy was justifiable, as South Africa was heavily reliant on coal, shale gas and future projects, such as the DRC's Inga III dam, and South Africa had also mused about nuclear energy since the late 1980s. The 'broad localization' of Rosatom's project, which included giving South African technicians a stake in Rosatom projects in third country markets, added to its appeal.[81] The ANC also emphasized the imperative of avoiding strategic dependence on Western countries.[82] While the ANC did not wish to give Rosatom a complete monopoly over South Africa's nuclear energy projects, it implicitly highlighted Russia's potential to act as a hedge partner against Chinese economic

123

dominance in South Africa. As China was the predominant profiteer from shale gas investment, engagement with Russia in the nuclear energy sphere would have a levelling effect.

Discrepancies about the Rosatom project's cost, which were augmented by contradictory communications from Russian sources, caused widespread disquiet in South Africa. Sergei Kiriyenko stated that South Africa's eight nuclear reactors would cost $50 billion by 2023; however, TASS reported that each reactor cost $5 billion. To burnish its image in South Africa, Rosatom appointed the Magna Carta PR company on a three-month contract in October 2014. As Magna Carta's chairman was Zuma's former spokesman Vincent Magwenya, and the contract cost up to $1 trillion rands, these revelations backfired on Zuma.[83] Due to the controversy surrounding the Magna Carta PR company, Russia was forced to use more insidious disinformation techniques. Dzvinka Kachur, a researcher at the Centre for Complex Systems in Transition at Stellenbosch University in Cape Town, notes that Rosatom and the Russian Orthodox Church partnered to reach Afrikaner communities in South Africa.[84] To appeal to ANC voters, Russia's disinformation machinery called nuclear energy a 'black energy solution' and labelled rival forms of renewable energy 'white energy solutions'. This racialized rhetoric sharpened polarizations and was facilitated by Russia's effective use of NGOs, and RT's widespread availability in South Africa. Revelations that the nuclear deal had been agreed to in February 2014 but was only released to the public later that year entrenched Rosatom's reputation for opacity. The public revelation of the terms of Rosatom's South Africa deal in February 2015 added more fuel to the fire, even though there was more transparency surrounding the Zuma-Putin negotiations.

Due to the controversy surrounding the Zuma-Putin relationship and botched PR attempts, South African public opinion largely aligned with the critical narratives about Russia. A Pew Research survey of July 2014 showed that just 25% of South Africans viewed Russia positively and 51% viewed Russia unfavorably.[85] These figures were almost identical to the 26% positive and 53% negative statistics that were recorded in 2013 and favourability ratings towards Russia that were observed in Britain (25%) and France (26%) after the

## RUSSIA'S ANTI-WESTERN TILT IN AFRICA

Crimea annexation. Vladimir Shubin notes that the Afrikaners mobilized against closer South Africa-Russia relations, as Cold War narratives on the 'Red Menace' coloured this community's perceptions of Putin's Russia, and left-wing elements in South Africa viewed Russia's sole export to be Stalinism.[86] While anti-Russian sentiments were especially pronounced amongst members of the Democratic Alliance Party, which appeals to South Africa's Afrikaners, they also had broad-based support within the ANC rank and file.

Russia and South Africa's shared views on international community created new elite-level bonds within the ANC. David Mahlobo, a Zuma loyalist who was appointed head of South Africa's State Security Agency (SSA) in 2014, met with Secretary of the Russian Security Council Nikolay Patrushev at least four times during his first year in office. In November 2015, Patrushev and Mahlobo discussed 'countering color revolutions and preventing interference in the internal affairs of African states'.[87] Mahlobo believed that the National Endowment for Democracy-funded Democracy Works project and Witwatersrand Institute in Johannesburg, which adhered to Gene Sharp's civil resistance techniques, fomented a colour revolution against Jacob Zuma in 2015.[88] As a result, Russia and South Africa both viewed support for Assad in Syria as a front in their broader struggle against Western-backed destabilization. Despite this solidarity, large swathes of the South African public feared that Russian-orchestrated state capture would be accompanied by autocracy promotion. Therefore, security cooperation between Putin and Zuma's inner circles arguably exacerbated Russia's soft power deficit in South Africa.

Due to the intense political backlash, Rosatom's nuclear energy deal in South Africa ultimately unravelled. In September 2016, the CEO of South Africa's nuclear state agency Necsa Phumzile Tshelane stated that 'Russia is not the frontrunner. It never was' in response to the question of who would spearhead its nuclear energy development.[89] In April 2017, a South African court struck down the Rosatom deal as unlawful, as it ceded favourable taxation benefits to Russia and placed heavy financial obligations on South Africa.[90] This decision followed intense lobbying from progressive South African

125

civil society organizations, such as the Southern African Faith Communities Environment Institute (SAFCEI). Despite the abrupt collapse of the deal, it remained a wedge issue, which restricted the scope of Russia-South Africa cooperation. Vladimir Putin's much-publicized efforts to revive the nuclear deal during a June 2018 meeting with new President Cyril Ramaphosa at the BRICS summit fuelled these polarizations.[91] During the second half of 2018, a judicial inquiry brought more details about Zuma's Rosatom deal to light. In October 2018, South Africa's Finance Minister Nhlanhla Nene told a judicial inquiry that Zuma became hostile towards him at the BRICS summit in Ufa when he refused to sign a guarantee letter for the Rosatom reactor, which Zuma wished to present to Putin.[92] In response to damning testimonies from South African Finance Ministry officials, Jacob Zuma defended the Rosatom agreement in March 2019, as he stated that the deal would have averted South Africa's electricity crisis and that trillions of Rands in initial expenditures would be more than recouped. Despite this defensive rhetoric, the initial potential for collaboration between Russia and South Africa, which was apparent during Zuma's first years in power, waned considerably by the end of his term.

## Russia's Evolving Counterinsurgency Policy in Africa

During the first three years of Putin's third term, a wave of insurgencies swept across Africa. Mali, the Central African Republic, Democratic Republic of the Congo, Somalia and Nigeria were especially impacted by this arc of instability. As these insurgencies swept across the continent, Russia saw opportunities to frame itself as a constructive critic of France and the US's counterterrorism policies and elevate its prestige as a security partner for African countries. To illustrate its role as a counterfoil to Western counterterrorism policy, Russia's response to the 2012 Mali coup emphasized the Arab Spring's destabilizing impact on Africa. Mikhail Margelov claimed that the Arab Spring created a 'green arc of instability' that extended from the Sahel to the Horn of Africa, and that Gaddafi's death ensured that no external force could pacify northern Mali.[93] Sergei Lavrov similarly attributed the Malian crisis to NATO's

## RUSSIA'S ANTI-WESTERN TILT IN AFRICA

subversion of international law in Libya and supported the African Union's condemnation of the Tuareg-led coup.[94] These narratives permeated into Russian media and academic discourse. In March 2012, Gazeta.ru published an article entitled 'Libya came to Mali', which challenged France's depiction of the Malian conflict as an Islamist insurgency and emphasized arms proliferation from Libya.[95] Maria Sapronova, an academic at MGIMO, opined in January 2013 that the Arab Spring is 'assuming more and more bizarre forms' and bringing many 'ethno-confessional, tribal and clan conflicts out of their latent state'.[96]

Notwithstanding Kremlin narratives about Western culpability for the Mali crisis and scepticism about the efficacy of an external military intervention, Russia supported UNSC Resolution 2085 in December 2012 that authorized France's Operation Serval campaign. Russia's legal rationale for backing this resolution stemmed from Mali's invitation of French military assistance and its long-standing policy of supporting interventions that supported domestic state order. These factors made France's intervention in Mali comparable to the 1995 UN peacekeeping operation in Macedonia, which Russia enthusiastically supported, and distinct from interventions that challenged state sovereignty, such as in Kosovo or Libya.[97] Russia's frustrations with the UN's role in enabling Gbagbo's fall in Côte d'Ivoire extended to Mali, as Moscow feared that the UN would greenlight a more expansive French military intervention. Vitaly Churkin warned that deploying UN forces to an active civil war zone would have 'unpredictable and nuclear consequences'.[98] Even though UN activities extended beyond their explicit focus on counterterrorism and France's assurances that it would not maintain a long-term presence in Mali were met with scepticism, Russia backed the UN Multidimensional Integrated Stabilization Mission in Mali (MINUSMA) mission as there was no credible alternative.[99]

As 2013 progressed, Russia's reservations about France's conduct in Mali evolved into a full-blown information war. Although Russia's disinformation machinery had intensely criticized Western conduct in Libya and Syria, the Mali crisis triggered Moscow's first information war in Sub-Saharan Africa. A RT article of August 2013

127

challenged France's counter-terrorism rationale for intervention in Mali by accusing Paris of fomenting extremism in Libya and Syria and asserted that France was manipulating Mali's elections to advance its interests.[100] RT's coverage also accused France of using Operation Serval to seize Mali's gold and uranium reserves, which could provide revenues that would alleviate sluggish economic growth at home.[101] The narrative that France was a neocolonial power in Mali and that François Hollande was trying to boost his flailing image at home by appealing to imperial nostalgia also proliferated in RT's coverage of Operation Serval. To distinguish itself from France's use of military force, Russia supplied thirty-six tons of food and household items to Mali in February 2013.[102] Russia's synthesis of soft power and disinformation in Mali further expanded as France's Operation Barkhane campaign began in August 2014 and led to Russian military-technical agreements in the Sahel from 2017 to 2019.

In response to the Boko Haram insurgency, Russia adopted a more hands-on role and provided military assistance to President Goodluck Jonathan at a time of need. Russian officials saw the Boko Haram insurgency as an opportunity to overcome recent tensions in the Russia-Nigeria relationship and bolster Moscow's status as a reliable counterterrorism partner in Africa. In October 2012, the Nigerian navy had implicated fifteen Russian security personnel affiliated with the Moran Security Group in the smuggling of guns and 8,598 rounds of ammunition.[103] In February 2013, the Nigerian High Court imposed charges on these Russian PMCs, even though the Moran Security Group claimed that it had permission to carry arms and that Lagos was a mere stopover point in their voyage from Madagascar to Guinea.[104] This surprised Russian officials, as Moscow had claimed that it had struck a deal with Nigeria to release Moran Security Group personnel in December 2012. The Russian Foreign Ministry ultimately intervened on behalf of these Russian PMCs, as they advanced state-backed oil interests in Nigeria, and the Nigerian High Court absolved them from criminal charges in October 2013.[105]

Russia also wanted to capitalize on the dearth of international assistance to Nigeria, as the United States and Britain remained

## RUSSIA'S ANTI-WESTERN TILT IN AFRICA

detached from the struggle against Boko Haram. Russian media outlets attributed the indifferent US response to Boko Haram to Nigeria's suspension of oil sales to the United States. A RT report of January 2015 bluntly stated that the lack of US aid to Nigeria 'seems to follow a simple geostrategic logic: no oil, no security support'.[106] A February 2015 Sputnik article alleged that the US 'doesn't obstruct Chad from destroying Boko Haram (despite its interests in keeping the group around)' and claimed that the US views some terrorists as beneficial to its goals.[107] To illustrate its greater reliability as a partner to African countries in crisis, Russia offered military assistance to Nigeria. In September 2014, 1,200 Nigerian Armed Forces, Police and Department of State Services personnel travelled to Russia for a four-month counterinsurgency training course.[108] This course gave Nigeria a core group of trained special forces, which could combat Boko Haram in northern Nigeria's Borno and Adamawa regions.[109] This course also allowed the Nigerian army to learn how to use Russian military technology, as it had been previously dependent on Western weapons, and gave Jonathan the option to suspend the US counterinsurgency training programme in Nigeria.[110]

Nigeria's security engagement with Russia did not necessarily signify a drastic tightening in the Moscow-Abuja partnership, as the Nigerian military also turned to the Czech Republic for surveillance aircraft and Belarus for attack helicopters. Nevertheless, US officials were concerned about the implications of Russia's military training for the struggle against Boko Haram. John Campbell noted that Russia likely imparted its military tactics in Chechnya, Georgia and Ukraine to Nigeria, which would encourage the Nigerian military and police forces to continue to disregard human rights. Without sweeping security sector reforms, Campbell feared that Russia's military training 'will likely fuel support or acquiescence to Boko Haram'.[111] Due to its concerns about the human rights record of the Nigerian security forces, the US rejected Abuja's request to purchase Cobra helicopters. This decision polarized the US foreign policy establishment. Matthew Page, a former US Intelligence and State Department official specializing on Nigeria, noted that some US officials were concerned that Nigeria would purchase jets from

Russia and China, while others felt that the Nigerian government's response to the April 2014 kidnapping of the Chibok girls necessitated a re-evaluation of US arms sales to Nigeria.[112]

In Nigeria, however, there was a widespread perception that the Obama administration had suspended the arms sales in reaction to Jonathan's rejection of US values, such as LGBT rights. This caused Nigeria to view a hard currency-based defence partnership with Russia in a more favourable light.[113] The continuation of US security cooperation with Chad, Mali and Cameroon, which were more authoritarian than Nigeria, fostered concerns about US double standards that Russia could exploit.[114] Russia marketed its Mi-17 and Mi-35 jets to Nigeria, reportedly offered Nigeria a $1 billion line of credit to purchase its fighter jets and emphasized its lack of oversight over the use of Russian equipment.[115] Russia's actions clashed with the Obama administration's concerns that Nigeria would sell its jets to a third party and belief that reforming the Nigerian military would be more effective than attack helicopter sales.[116] Nigeria also reportedly asked Russia to send military advisors to help fight Boko Haram,[117] which suggested its willingness to overcome its past resistance to Russian PMCs and stringent ban on armed private guards travelling by ship.

While Russia's speedy delivery of jets to Nigeria was an advantage of the deal, the Nigerian military had to lay out significant costs to modernize Mi-class jets, which were supplied by the Soviet Union during the 1960s and 1970s. The appeal of potential kickbacks to the Nigerian military, which Russia tolerated, ultimately caused Nigerian officials to downplay these cost considerations.[118] Russia's potential exacerbation of corruption in the Nigerian armed forces was controversial, as arms smuggling strengthened the Boko Haram insurgency and the oil thefts that routinely took place in southern Nigeria. Although Russia's jet deliveries to Nigeria were a major coup in the counterinsurgency sphere, frictions persisted between Moscow and Abuja. In December 2014, Nigeria-Russia relations briefly deteriorated, as the Nigerian military detained a Russian plane in Kano, which allegedly possessed weapons caches.[119] After strenuous denials from the Russian embassy in Nigeria and France, which claimed that that the Russian jet was shipping French army helicopters from Chad to CAR, Nigeria defused a crisis in bilateral relations by releasing the crew members.[120]

Russia's military campaign in Syria gave it an opportunity to transform itself from a counterfoil to US and French policies into a full-fledged counterinsurgency partner in Africa. Most Sub-Saharan African countries neither supported nor condemned Russia's military intervention in Syria. Nigeria's reaction was emblematic of Africa's ambivalence about Russian conduct in Syria. In a speech at the Supporting Syria conference in London, which coincided with Russia's airstrikes in Aleppo, President Muhammadu Buhari expressed solidarity with Syria's struggle against extremism and called for a political solution in Syria.[121] Nevertheless, Russia advertised its military intervention in Syria to African countries facing protracted insurgencies or potential 'color revolutions'. The attractiveness of Russia's counterinsurgency model came from its emphasis on working with extant state institutions, which contrasted with the US's use of unilateral military action and forced democratization to curb extremism. Although the appeal of Russia's intervention in Syria would extend to West African countries, such as Nigeria and Mali, during Putin's fourth term, Somalia was an early supporter of Moscow's conduct. In April 2016, Somali Prime Minister Omar Abdirashid Ali Sharmarke asked Lavrov to equip the Somali military with the necessary technology to fight al-Shabaab and support peacekeeping operations that would strengthen Somalia's military capabilities.[122]

## Russia Enters the Central African Republic

The CAR's descent into state failure, which was instigated by the outbreak of a civil war in December 2012, provided Russia with an unexpected test of its credentials as a counterinsurgency partner. During the early years of the CAR conflict, Russia remained a peripheral player. Russia resisted the imposition of UN sanctions on François Bozizé in April 2014 on the grounds that it would derail the prospects of inter-religious reconciliation in CAR. This position aligned with China's perspective, which presented a sharp normative critique of the effectiveness of sanctions in resolving civil wars.[123]

Russia also engaged in a lower-intensity Mali-style information war against external powers in CAR, which downplayed the role of Islamic extremism and accused France and China of using CAR as a theatre to air out their rivalries.[124] Russia's spectator role in CAR reflected its aversion to large-scale engagement in Central Africa, which was also apparent in its policies towards the DRC. Figures in Russia's business community, such as Dmitry Yermolaev from the Africa Investment Agency, highlighted the DRC's possession of $24 trillion in mineral resources, opportunities for Russian infrastructure companies and Joseph Kabila's amenability to engaging with external powers as major advantages.[125] However, Russia did not develop a Congo peace plan and remained a spectator in the North Kivu crisis.

Russia's breakthrough in CAR was facilitated by the end of France's Operation Sangaris campaign on 30 October 2016. France justified the cessation of its military intervention in CAR by claiming that it had helped stabilize CAR and maintained a residual force of 350 soldiers under the UN Multidimensional Integrated Stabilization Mission in the CAR (MINUSCA) umbrella. While Russian media outlets routinely criticized Operation Sangaris and extensively covered the sexual abuse scandal that besmirched the French military's reputation, Moscow's critiques of French conduct did not translate into a broader intervention in CAR. This trend abruptly changed in the second half of 2017 due to two factors. First, Russia viewed a foothold in CAR as a potential gateway to Central Africa, which would complement its nascent outreaches to the DRC and Burundi. Second, although Russia supported a ban on conflict diamonds via the Kimberly Process in May 2013, it wished to secure preferential access to the CAR's vast mineral reserves and leverage its ground presence to dilute the UN sanctions regime. In 2017, Yevgeny Prigozhin established two CAR-based gold and diamond companies, M Finans and Lobaye Invest, which were administered by Dmitry Sytii, Yevgeny Khodotov and Alexander Kuzin.[126]

In October 2017, Touadéra visited Russia in a private capacity and met with Sergei Lavrov. The ostensible focus of Touadéra's trip was conflict resolution, Russia-CAR diplomatic cooperation in the DRC, South Sudan and Syria, and the pursuit of new economic opportunities, especially in the mining and energy spheres.[127]

## RUSSIA'S ANTI-WESTERN TILT IN AFRICA

While the coincidence in timing between this meeting and Lobaye Invest's establishment is noteworthy, Touadéra's informal requests for Russian security assistance against the ex-Seleka rebels were more impactful. As CAR-Soviet relations were generally cordial during the 1960s and 1970s, but had few strategic foundations, CAR's embrace of Russian assistance is intriguing. Jean-Luc Mara, a CAR parliamentarian who was defeated in the December 2020 elections, noted Russia's preservation of an embassy in Bangui during the post-Cold War era as a mitigating factor and good will established by Soviet construction of schools.[128] Kag Senoussi, a communications advisor to Touadéra, noted that the CAR wanted to diversify its array of military partners to defeat the ex-Seleka rebels and overruling France through cooperation with Russia asserted its sovereignty.[129] Senoussi claimed that the CAR was one of the oldest theatres of Russian diplomatic presence in Africa but conceded that the Russia-CAR partnership was Touadéra-driven and opportunistic in character.[130] At the popular level, Russia's appeal stemmed from it being an alternative to France, which was widely mistrusted, especially in Bangui.[131]

To capitalize on CAR's mistrust of France and desire to find security partners that respected its sovereignty, Russia obstructed Macron's efforts to expand France's military presence in CAR and prioritized state-to-state counterterrorism collaboration over engagement with UN peacekeeping agencies. As France's proposal that CAR purchase old weapons systems had unrealistic costs, French officials offered CAR 1,400 AK-47 assault rifles that it seized off Somalia's coast. Russia thwarted these arms transfers as they contravened UN sanctions against Somalia but proceeded to donate AK-47s, sniper rifles, machine guns and grenade launchers in December 2017.[132] Russia's willingness to deal directly with Touadéra also reflected its discontent with MINUSCA. Russia criticized UN peacekeeping missions, as in Liberia, that heavily relied on military and police support, and viewed MINUSCA as a 'solid peacekeeping mission' that followed the Liberian model.[133] Russia's anti-French rhetoric and uneasy relationship with UN forces in CAR would remain enduring features of the Wagner Group-led military intervention that began in 2018. This combination of anti-Westernism, crisis proof loyalty and

133

assertiveness in the counterinsurgency sphere fed into Russia's great power ambitions in Africa and bolstered its standing as a power in an increasingly multipolar continent.

# 5

# RUSSIA REBUILDS ITS INFLUENCE IN NORTH AFRICA

Although Russia's counter-revolutionary reaction to the Arab Spring initially eroded its influence in North Africa, the Kremlin tried to revive its influence in the Maghreb during Putin's third term. Russia wished to establish closer ties with Egypt's post-Mubarak government, secure lucrative economic contracts in Libya and consolidate its partnerships with Algeria and Morocco, whose regimes withstood the Arab Spring. These efforts produced mixed results. Russia's relationship with Egypt strengthened in the post-Arab Spring period, as Moscow pragmatically adjusted to the ascension of the Muslim Brotherhood and the 2013 coup d'état. The Russia-Libya relationship struggled to gain traction, as Moscow's reluctant acquiescence to Gaddafi's fall bred mistrust with the post-revolutionary authorities. Russia struggled to establish lasting cooperation with the NTC and successor Government of National Accord (GNA), and pivoted towards a sharp alignment with Khalifa Haftar's anti-systemic Libya National Army (LNA). Elsewhere in the Maghreb, Russia-Algeria relations progressed due to their commercial interests and synergistic ideational perspectives on the Arab Spring, while Moscow's partnership with Morocco advanced at a slower pace.

## Russia-Egypt Relations under Morsi and Sisi: A Stop-Start Partnership Consolidation

The Egyptian presidential elections in June 2012 provided Russia with an unexpected opportunity to strengthen its relationship with Egypt. The triumph of Muslim Brotherhood-aligned Freedom and Justice Party (FJP) candidate Mohammed Morsi strained US-Egypt relations and ensured that regional powers, such as Qatar and Turkey, gained leverage over Egypt's economy and foreign policy direction. In late 2012, the Obama administration's engagement with Egypt was hamstrung by Republican calls for conditions on US military aid and a $2.5 billion loan from Qatar in January 2013 saved Egypt's economy from the verge of insolvency. These developments encouraged Morsi to court alternative great power partners to the US and highlight Egypt's capacity to be an independent regional power. Closer ties with Russia furthered both objectives, and accordingly, the Russia-Egypt relationship strengthened under Morsi. Although the strategic rationales for Russia and Egypt to pursue closer relations were sound, Morsi's election was met with trepidation and alarm. Due to resistance from military institutions, such as the Supreme Council of the Armed Forces (SCAF), Russian experts were concerned by the prospect of a second Arab Spring or wave of political violence. In response to the skirmishes in Cairo that preceded the 15 December referendum on a new Egyptian constitution, *Kommersant* announced that a civil war was afoot in Egypt.[1] Alarm about the ideological orientation of Morsi's government also abounded. A RBC article of May 2012 called Morsi a 'radical Islamist' and warned that he would impose Sharia law on Egypt.[2] Gevorg Mirzayan, a Russian international affairs expert and Professor at Moscow's Financial University described the FJP as 'bearded men who intend to build an Islamic state' and argued that political Islam in Egypt would be much more extreme than in Turkey.[3]

In an effort to sully Morsi's international reputation, RT delegitimized Egypt's democratic transition and claimed that Morsi's rule in Egypt would emulate Ayatollah Khomeini's pivot towards dictatorship in Iran.[4] A July 2012 RT article compared Egypt's Muslim Brotherhood to al-Qaeda in Syria and Libya, and predicted that the US would accept an Islamist Egypt if it was subordinate to its interests like Qatar or Saudi Arabia.[5] The close association between Morsi and Islamic extremism could be attributed to an upsurge of violence in the North Caucasus, which heightened Russian public suspicions of the Muslim Brotherhood and Islamist movements.[6] The wave of violence against Egypt's Coptic Christian community also resonated strongly in Russia. Patriarch Kirill, the head of the Russian Orthodox Church, urged Vladimir Putin to strengthen Russia's support for Bashar al-Assad, as a Syrian revolutionary government would emulate Morsi's persecutions of Christians.

Despite its severe reservations about the Egyptian Muslim Brotherhood, Russia opted to pragmatically engage with Morsi's government. On 4 November 2012, Sergei Lavrov travelled to Cairo to consult with Morsi on the Syrian civil war and Libya's reconstruction process. This meeting proved fruitful, even though both sides disagreed on Syria. While Morsi supported Bashar al-Assad's overthrow, Egyptian newspaper *Al-Ahram* allowed Sergei Lavrov to present his case that a foreign-backed regime change in Syria violated international law, and that Russia was merely fulfilling Soviet-era defensive weapon contracts to Syria.[7] In keeping with Russia's Mubarak-era outreaches to Egypt, Putin used their common desire to de-escalate the Israel-Palestine conflict as a gateway to closer relations with Morsi. On 15 November, Vladimir Putin spoke with Mohammed Morsi about Israel's Operation Pillar of Defence operations in the Gaza Strip and endorsed Egypt's efforts to end the Israel-Hamas conflict.[8]

These consultations convinced Lavrov and Putin that they could engage with Mohammed Morsi, and the Kremlin tried to strengthen Russia-Egypt economic relations. During their meeting at the March 2013 BRICS summit in Durban, South Africa, Putin hailed the 70% expansion of Russia-Egypt trade relations in the post-Arab Spring period, and Morsi emphasized the potential for Egyptian gas exports to Russia.[9] These discussions were followed by a meeting between Vladimir Putin and Mohammed Morsi in Sochi on 19 April. After their meeting, Morsi praised the influx of Russian tourists to Egyptian resorts, which rose by 35% after the Arab Spring and topped the world rankings at 2 million in 2012.[10] Morsi also expressed gratitude for the Soviet Union's technological assistance to Egypt's Aswan High Dam construction, steel and aluminium sectors, and emphasized Russia's ability to contribute to Egypt's knowledge economy.[11] Russia responded to Morsi's charm offensive by inviting Egypt to the Moscow-hosted Gas Exporting Countries Forum (GECF) on 30 July, supporting Egypt's plans to produce 4 MW of nuclear energy by 2025 and praising Morsi's 'very new, fresh and interesting ideas' on Syria.[12]

Despite this progress, the designation of the Muslim Brotherhood as a terrorist organization remained a roadblock to strengthened Russia-Egypt relations. In interview with Reuters on 18 December 2012, Mahmoud Ghozlan, a spokesman for Egypt's Muslim Brotherhood, confirmed that he had raised the terrorism designation with the Russian ambassador in Cairo and stated that no real improvement in Russia-Egypt ties would occur as long as the designation remained in effect.[13] Due to this pessimistic assessment, Russian commentators, such as the head of the Religion and Society think tank Alexei Grishin and Fyodor Lukyanov, predicted that the Kremlin would exempt Egypt's Muslim Brotherhood from the terrorism designation and confine the terrorism label to Islamists in the North Caucasus. These predictions did not come to fruition. Russia's efforts to establish closer ties with the FJP clashed with its securitization of political Islam in Syria and Russian officials hedged against Morsi when military-backed mass protests erupted in June 2013.

On 3 July, a coalition led by General Abdel Fattah el-Sisi overthrew Mohammed Morsi. Sisi was allegedly backed by 14 million Egyptian protesters[14] and received financial support from regional actors, such as Saudi Arabia, the UAE and Kuwait, who opposed the 2011 Egyptian revolution. The Russian Foreign Ministry's views broadly aligned with that of the United States, as it refrained from calling Sisi's takeover a coup, and called for the resolution of Egypt's socioeconomic problems in a 'democratic framework without violence'.[15] Russian media commentaries and think tank reports initially reacted with optimism to Morsi's demise. In an interview with Regnum, Alexander Ignatenko called Sisi's takeover a 'new kind of revolution' and claimed that the 'Muslim Brotherhood

138

RUSSIA REBUILDS ITS INFLUENCE IN NORTH AFRICA

stole the victory from the people and instead of democratizing the country, began to propagate their views'.[16] A 12 July IMEMO report predicted that Sisi's coup could strengthen Bashar al-Assad's position in Syria. The report argued that growing US attention to Egypt could detract from its support for the Syrian rebels and the US might gradually acquiesce to the status quo in Syria, if volatility in Egypt destabilizes the eastern Mediterranean.[17]

Although Russian experts viewed the July 2013 coup as a positive development that advanced its strategic interests, concerns swiftly surfaced about Sisi's alleged pro-Western orientation. An *Izvestia* article of 7 July included an interview with an Egyptian man who accused Europe of supporting the enemies of Egyptian democracy and called Sisi 'our Yushchenko' in reference to Kremlin-backed conspiracies about US sponsorship of the Orange Revolution in Ukraine.[18] An RT op-ed claimed that Sisi was a permanent liaison of US Secretary of Defence Chuck Hagel and would not have launched a coup without a 'green light from the Pentagon'.[19] RT also spread the conspiracy that the National Endowment for Democracy and Freedom House backed the Sisi-aligned protesters, as the CIA's covert relationship with the Muslim Brotherhood atrophied. Beyond their suspicions about US support for the coup, Sisi's repressive policies caused Russian officials to fear the imminent destabilization of Egypt. After the 14 August Rabaa Massacre, which saw Egyptian security forces under Interim President Adly Mansour kill over 1,000 civilians, Russian experts became increasingly concerned about prolonged instability in Egypt. A Russian International Affairs Council (RIAC) report of 22 August warned that Sisi's secular Egyptian regime could follow the path of Turkey in the 1950s, which experienced repeated military coups; face a destabilizing Muslim Brotherhood-instigated power struggle in the lead-up to the 2014 Egyptian elections or see Salafists impose radical Islam on Egypt.[20] Sisi's leadership qualities were panned on RT, which claimed that he was 'trying to pose as the new Nasser', and that he was 'essentially an Islamist—but most of all he craves power'.[21]

Due to Russia's concerns about instability and backing the wrong horse in Egypt, Moscow refrained from immediate outreaches to Sisi's regime. The Obama administration's 9 October announcement

139

that it would cut a substantial portion of the $1.5 billion in annual US aid to Egypt created an opening for a reset in Moscow-Cairo relations. Russian officials favourably regarded Sisi's efforts to highlight Egypt's foreign policy independence from the United States, which contrasted with Mubarak's prioritization of the US-Egypt partnership, and believed that the Egyptian military would continue to support him in the 2014 elections even if US-Egypt relations soured further.[22] Russia's shift from a critical to a sympathetic view of Sisi was revealed in its media coverage of Egypt-US relations. RT lambasted the United States for abandoning Egypt during its struggle against Islamic extremism in the Sinai Peninsula and favourably contrasted Russia's loyalty to partners in crisis with the unwillingness of the United States to protect its allies.[23]

The transformation of Sisi's image in Moscow resulted in the expansion of Russia-Egypt diplomatic and security cooperation. On 14 November, Sergei Lavrov and Sergei Shoigu travelled to Cairo for meetings with Egyptian Foreign Minister Nabil Fahmy and Sisi, which fuelled speculation of an impending Russian arms deal with Egypt. Both countries predictably downplayed these rumours, as Russia was reportedly concerned about Egypt's track record of re-selling military equipment to other Global South countries. Nevertheless, the first 2+2 meeting between Russia and Egypt in the post-Soviet era resulted in a flurry of optimistic statements. Fahmy claimed that this summit was 'activating' Russia-Egypt ties but distanced himself from the perception that Egypt viewed Russia as a substitute partner for the United States. In a veiled criticism of the Arab Spring, Lavrov praised the return of a 'stable Egypt with a prosperous economy and an efficient political system', and dubiously praised Egypt's 'right democratic path'.[24] Russia and Egypt also declared their opposition to a foreign military intervention in Syria. This declaration was noteworthy, as Egypt refused to re-establish embassy-level diplomatic relations with Syria after the coup.[25]

Speculation about Russia-Egypt negotiations was confirmed in February 2014, as Sisi travelled to Moscow to expand military-technical cooperation and negotiate a $2 billion arms package from Russia. Sisi sought a diverse array of Russian weapons, such as twenty-four MiG-29 fighters, air defence systems, the Kornet anti-

RUSSIA REBUILDS ITS INFLUENCE IN NORTH AFRICA

tank missile system, Ka-52, Mi-28 and Mi-35 combat helicopters.[26] These arms were the Russian equivalents of the weapons systems that the US had declined to sell Egypt, which included Abrams tanks, F-16 fighter jets and Apache helicopters. Rosoboronexport head Sergei Chemezov claimed that Egypt signed a deal to purchase the S-300 air defence system at the end of 2013, which would be funded by a Russian bridge loan.[27] Beyond their transactional and security implications, these arms deals had broader political and geopolitical significance. Husam Suweilam, retired Egyptian army general and political commentator, believes that Sisi was leveraging his position as Egyptian Defence Minister to negotiate arms sales with Russia and bolster his stature ahead of the Egyptian elections.[28] Vladimir Putin subsequently expressed support for Sisi's presidential bid, which made Russia the first great power to acknowledge the 2013 coup architect as Egypt's president-in-waiting. A *Nezavisimaya Gazeta* article of March 2014 contended that Putin's endorsement bolstered Sisi's electoral prospects, as it demonstrated that he was 'not an updated version of Mubarak', but instead, wished to 'restore dignity and respect to Egypt on the international stage'.[29] This aligned Sisi with Nasser's vision, which emphasized Egyptian foreign policy autonomy and rejected US efforts to make Egypt an 'American satellite'.

Russia also leveraged its arms sales with Egypt to de-escalate tensions with Saudi Arabia, which had intensified over their contrasting positions on Syria. Suweilam noted that Sisi had visited Saudi Arabia and the UAE immediately before visiting Moscow and claimed that both Gulf monarchies would cover the costs of Russian arms transfers to Egypt. Due to Saudi Arabia and Russia's shared support for counter-revolutionary forces, aversion to Qatari influence in Egypt and scepticism of the Muslim Brotherhood, Moscow and Riyadh found common cause in strengthening Sisi's position. Saudi Arabia's alleged financing of Russian arms sales to Egypt signified its desire to embrace Moscow as a hedge partner, as it clashed with the US over Obama's engagement with Iran and flip-flop on military intervention in Syria.[30] The *Saudi Gazette* hailed the Fahmy-Lavrov meeting, as Russia was correcting a 'strategic imbalance in the Middle East', and allowing Egypt to emulate India's

141

non-aligned foreign policy.[31] Egyptian media outlets, such as *El-Watan*, presented Egypt as an intermediary between Saudi Arabia and Russia, and Sisi as the leader of a coalition consisting of Egypt, Russia, Saudi Arabia, Kuwait and the UAE against a Western regional alliance headed by the US, Qatar and Turkey.[32] These fanciful notions strengthened Sisi's domestic position, but Russia-Saudi Arabia cooperation on Egypt did not readily extend elsewhere.

Egypt's response to the Crimea annexation underscored the strategic depth of its partnership with Russia. Unlike Saudi Arabia, which supported Ukraine's territorial integrity, Egypt did not condemn Russia's actions and maintained normal economic and security relations with Russia. Two Russian military delegations visited Egypt in February 2014, with the last departing on 24 February,[33] and in April 2014, Russia's Deputy Defence Minister Anatoly Antonov met with his Egyptian counterpart Muhammad Said al-Assar. Russia also agreed to train Egyptian officers in its defence academies, revive a spare parts deal for legacy Soviet-era equipment, and hold joint counterterrorism exercises with Egypt, which would offset the potentially slow integration of Mi-35s into the Egyptian Air Force.[34] Sisi's landslide victory in the 26–28 May elections, which handed him 97% of the vote, was followed by new Egypt-Russia commercial deals. In May 2014, Gazprom struck a deal with the Egyptian Natural Gas Holding Company (EGAS) to transfer seven tranches of Russian gas. EGAS initially planned to purchase gas from Algeria's Sonatrach but was forced to turn to Gazprom, as Sonatrach needed to redirect its supplies to the European market and aid the EU's divestment from Russian gas.[35] The EGAS-Gazprom deal provided Egypt with secure access to natural gas through 2015 and a flexible compensation schedule with 'grace periods to repay the value of the debt'. Gazprom began shipping LNG to Egypt in December 2014, and initiated talks with EGAS on joint Russia-Egypt gas exploration deals.

## The Cautious Expansion of Russia-Egypt Cooperation (2015–17)

Despite the growth of bilateral cooperation during the first years of Sisi's presidency, Egypt defied predictions that it would replace the

US with Russia as its primary partner. Michelle Dunne and Andrew Miller believe that these predictions were based on a false premise and contend that 'Egypt is no longer a strategic prize for the US or Russia to win.' Instead, Dunne and Miller argue that the US was trying to advance its interests, while preventing a potentially fragile Egyptian state from collapsing.[36] Mark Katz broadly accepts the premise of US-Russia competition in Egypt, but highlights two limiting factors on Russia-Egypt cooperation, which prevented Sisi from making a hard pivot to Moscow.[37] First, Egypt successfully used the threat of Russian arms purchases to convince the US to drop human rights restrictions on arms sales. The Obama administration's decision in June 2014 to greenlight the sale of ten Apache helicopters to Egypt, despite strenuous Congressional opposition, was a key success for Cairo. Katz contends that Russia was cognizant of Egypt's bargaining tactics and viewed its relationship with Sisi as a gambit to boost its status in the Arab world. Second, Saudi Arabia wished to constrain the scope of Egypt-Russia cooperation, despite its initial support for Moscow-Cairo rapprochement. Gazprom's investments in Egypt's offshore natural gas reserves could be aimed at giving Cairo the capital it needed to defy Saudi Arabia and purchase Russian weapons. These constraining factors ensure that Egypt views Russia as a critical vector in a multipolar world order rather than a replacement for the United States.

Although the Russia-Egypt partnership had its limits, economic, security and cultural cooperation between the two countries continued to strengthen. In November 2015, Egypt signed an agreement with Russia, which would allow Rosatom to construct the El Dabaa Nuclear Power Plant. This nuclear reactor would be financed by a Russian loan of unspecified terms, and Sisi stated that it would be completely repaid within thirty-five years. In May 2016, Russia announced plans to lend Egypt $25 billion to finance the construction of the El Dabaa nuclear reactor.[38] In September 2017, Russia and Egypt held an intergovernmental commission meeting on trade and economic cooperation, which addressed the construction of an industrial trade zone at East Port Said in the Suez Canal Special Economic Zone and facilitated the start of negotiations on a free trade agreement with the Eurasian Economic Union (EAEU).[39]

The Suez Canal Industrial Zone was hailed in the Russian media as 'the first major industrial cluster in the far abroad since the Soviet Union times' and was viewed as a potential transit location to other African and Middle Eastern markets.[40] As Russia-Egypt relations had traditionally revolved around Middle Eastern issues, such as Israel-Palestine and Syria, or Maghreb issues, such as Libya, these projects cemented Cairo's standing as Russia's power projection entry point in Africa. In tandem with the expansion of Russia-Egypt economic cooperation, the two countries held joint naval drills in June 2015 and joint military exercises in October 2016, which would become routinized in the years that followed.

Russia's military intervention in Syria also created new opportunities for security cooperation with Egypt. In interview on 3 October with *Al-Arabiya*, Egypt's Foreign Minister Sameh Shoukry stated that 'Russia's entrance, given its potential and capabilities, is something that is going to have an effect on limiting terrorism in Syria and eradicating it.'[41] Egyptian officials backed Russia's military intervention in Syria, as they regarded it to be part of Moscow's attempt to rebuild its Soviet-era Damascus-Cairo-Baghdad axis, and believed that their closest regional partner, Saudi Arabia, would exercise restraint in Syria.[42] Ahmed Dahshan, a Cairo-based Russian foreign policy specialist, notes that Egypt believed that Russia was more serious than Western countries about combatting Islamic extremism, as the US had a history of aligning with Islamist movements against adversaries, such as the Soviet Union.[43] Dahshan acknowledged Egypt's concerns that Syria was on the verge of falling under the Turkish-Qatari orbit, which had already ensconced its hegemony over Tunisia, Libya and the Gaza Strip.[44] Egypt's historic preoccupation with securing its eastern frontier, fear of a sectarian civil war that would marginalize Cairo and alarm about Qatari-Turkish encirclement encouraged Sisi to support Russia's 'stabilization efforts' in Syria.[45]

While Egypt viewed Russia's military intervention in Syria as a development that would advance its geopolitical interests, Moscow's partnership with Iran and Cairo's desire to avoid offending its Gulf partners limited its cooperation with Russia. As Egypt's primary supporters of Assad were also opponents of the January 2011 revolution, Sisi decoupled Egypt's support for the Russian military intervention from an endorsement of Assad's future, and was wary of Iran's growing influence in Syria.[46] In December 2016, Lavrov asked Egypt to join a ceasefire agreement in Syria alongside other Arab countries, such as Saudi Arabia, Iraq, Jordan and Qatar.[47] In October 2017, Russian Presidential Envoy for the Syrian Settlement Alexander Lavrentiyev listed Egypt as a potential observer in the Astana Peace Process alongside China, the UAE, Iraq and Lebanon.[48] Egypt's rejection of Lavrov and Lavrentiyev's invitations underscored the limits of its cooperation with Russia on Syria. However, Egyptian officials acknowledged their common strategic goals with Russia in Syria but remained disengaged due to the slim prospects for a political solution, and unwillingness to enter a conflict where Russia, Iran, Turkey and the US had dissonant views.[49] Libya emerged as a more effective theatre for Russia-Egypt cooperation, and the dynamics of their bilateral relationship in this theatre will be explored later in this chapter.

In addition to these improvements in Russia-Egypt economic, diplomatic and security cooperation, cultural bonds between the Islamic communities of both countries strengthened. Chechnya's Ramzan Kadyrov served as a critical interlocutor between the Russian and Egyptian Islamic communities. The August 2016 Grozny Conference on Sunni Islam, which renounced the Muslim Brotherhood and Wahhabism, featured prominent Egyptian clerics, such as Grand Imam of Al-Azhar Mosque Ahmed el-Tayeb, Grand Mufti of Egypt Shawki Allam and President of Al-Azhar University Ibrahim Salah al-Hudhud. Al-Azhar's participation at the Grozny Conference was controversial, as it sparked calls for Saudi Arabia to divest from Egypt. Al-Azhar responded by claiming that its role in the Grozny Conference was confined to el-Tayeb's speech and that it did not contribute to the final communique.[50] Despite this controversy, cultural bonds between Chechnya and Egypt continued to flourish. The Egypt national football team's decision to visit Grozny during the 2018 FIFA World Cup raised the profile of these cultural bonds to a Russian and Egyptian audience.

## Russia Consolidates Its Partnership with Algeria

As Russia struggled to adjust to the changing political winds in Egypt and Libya, Moscow viewed Algeria's relative stability as beneficial for its post-Arab Spring strategy towards North Africa. The strengthening of Russia's partnership with Algeria was facilitated by shared ideas, as both countries embraced non-interference in internal affairs of state and expressed their aversion to Western-backed regime changes. Russia also appreciated Algeria's desire to preserve existing state borders in the Middle East and was confident that this perspective would continue, as regional instability threatened Algeria's security. Arabist Sergei Balmasov praised Algeria as 'Russia's crisis-proof partner in the Arab world', as it was a rare Arab country that could maintain an independent foreign policy despite regional disruptions.[51] Algeria viewed Russia as an increasingly appealing partner, as its condemnation of the NATO military intervention in Libya cooled its relationship with France and led to the reduction of economic cooperation with the European Union.[52] To cement this narrative, Russia blamed external forces rather than Bouteflika for the expansion of terrorism in Algeria. After the bombing of the In Amenas gas plant in January 2013 by a brigade linked to Algerian militant leader Mokhtar Belmokhtar, Vladimir Putin blamed the destabilization of Libya, Syria and Mali for the attack in Algeria.[53]

Russia's military intervention in Syria would take its ideational partnership with Algeria to new heights. Dalia Ghanem, an Algerian political scientist at the Carnegie Endowment for International Peace, noted that, much like Russia, Algeria viewed the Syrian crisis as a 'Syrian-Syrian problem' and condemned the designation of Hezbollah as a terrorist organization.[54] During the summer 2013 standoff between Syria and Western powers over Assad's use of chemical weapons in eastern Ghouta, Algeria opposed an external military intervention that undermined Syrian sovereignty. Bouteflika's support for Russia's military intervention in Syria broke with Algeria's past policies and exacerbated political cleavages at home. Ismail Maaraf, a political scientist at the University of Algiers, contends that the Algerian military encouraged Bouteflika to overlook the backlash associated with backing Russia's actions in Syria, as it wanted to reward Russia for being a more consistent partner than France, Britain or the United States.[55] This reaction was not shared by Algerian civil society or opposition figures. Algerian journalist Tawfiq cast doubt about Russia's ability to combat ISIS in Syria and claimed that ISIS did not have a state aim of overthrowing Assad.[56] Algerian opposition figures, like Rashad founder Mohamed Zitout and security analyst Karim Moulay, claimed that Bouteflika's support for Russia's military intervention in Syria and France's involvement in Mali undermined Algeria's time-tested commitment to non-interference in the internal affairs of state.[57] Concerns also mounted in Algeria about Russia's newfound assertiveness in Middle Eastern security, as Moscow's actions in Syria could pave the way for anti-ISIS operations in Libya that could threaten Algeria's border security.

Chairman of the State Duma Sergei Naryshkin's November 2015 trip to Algeria underscored Russia's desire to engage North African countries on Syria. Naryshkin linked Algeria's support for Russia's military intervention in Syria to the FLN's struggle against colonialism and claimed that rejecting external interference has become an 'ideological foundation' of Russia-Algeria relations.[58] To elevate these anti-colonial parallels, Naryshkin handed over archival documents to President of the People's National Assembly Mohamed Khelifa, which included pictures of Nikita Khrushchev welcoming Ahmed Ben Bella to Yalta in 1964. Naryshkin also recalled the memory of his uncle's training of Algerians in the Soviet university system. Khelifa responded by praising the Soviet Union's removal of 1.5 million landmines from Algeria and emphasized Algeria's efforts to 'export peace and stability' across the Arab world.[59] While Naryshkin's outreach to Khelifa was rife with symbolism, Russia succeeded in enlisting Algeria as a diplomatic partner in Syria. After Turkey's shoot-down of the Russian Su-24 jet November 2015, Algeria emerged as a dialogue facilitator between Russia and Turkey, and Turkey and Syria. Algerian diplomacy reportedly facilitated a reduction of Russian airstrikes on pro-Turkish militants in Syria and encouraged clandestine Turkey-Syria discussions on the creation of an autonomous Kurdish state.[60] As Algeria was trying to de-escalate tensions with Iran and was deepening links with African powers, such as Nigeria, Ethiopia and South Africa, to upstage Morocco, Russia viewed Algeria's dialogue facilitation role in Syria as a precedent for the deepening of its partnership.[61]

Russia swiftly cashed in on this ideational partnership by aggressively marketing its military equipment to Algeria. Due to its trepidations about the Arab Spring, Algeria agreed to $1 billion in ground force modernization deals with Russia, and in February 2012, Russia confirmed that 120 T-90S tanks would arrive in Algeria. Russia hailed Algeria's tank purchases, as arms sales from China were dropping and these deals were part of Moscow's strategy of surpassing Beijing as the world's leading tank exporter.[62] While the T-90 tank deal made headlines, Russia exported a diverse portfolio of military equipment to Algeria from 2010 to 2015, which included helicopters, tanks and submarines.[63] Algeria's purchase of two new Tiger class corvettes from Russia and two Kilo submarines in 2014 were linked to its naval modernization efforts, which were inspired by its desire to combat smuggling, terrorism and illegal migration.[64] In keeping with its policy of synthesizing arms sales and the transfer of technological knowhow, Russia covertly engaged with Algeria on local production of its weaponry. In 2014, Rosoboronexport signed a deal with the Algerian armed forces to produce 200 T-90 tanks in Algeria, which was described by Moscow Defence Brief Magazine editor Mikhail Barabanov as 'the world's largest export contract for main battle tanks'.[65] SIPRI figures show that Russian technology dominated Algeria's arms markets, as it supplied 67% of its arms from 2010 to 2014 compared to 13% for China and 11% for Germany.[66]

Following Russia's military intervention in Syria, Moscow accelerated its marketing of arms to Algeria. Alexander Golts noted that the low price of Russia's jets made them more appealing than their US counterparts, and the success of Moscow's military intervention in Syria sweetened the deal.[67] In January 2016, Algeria agreed to purchase Su-32 bomber jets, which were an export variant of the Su-34 bombers that Russia used effectively in Syria.[68] This deal did not come to fruition, as the late 2016 purchase target date expired and negotiations between Russia and Algeria resumed in July 2017. The unravelling of this Syrian conflict-inspired arms contract

148

## RUSSIA REBUILDS ITS INFLUENCE IN NORTH AFRICA

was an anomalous failure in Russia's weapons exports to Africa. In 2017, 13% of Russia's $15 billion in global arms sales came from Africa, and many of the weapons that African countries purchased were variants of those used in Syria. Egypt's MiG-29 and Algeria's Iskander-E short-range ballistic missile contracts were especially critical deals. Russia also agreed to export Mi-35s to Nigeria and Mali, two Pantsir S-1 defence systems to Equatorial Guinea, Su-30Ks to Angola and two Mi-171Sh armed helicopters to Burkina Faso.[69]

Beyond its ideational and security dimensions, the Russia-Algeria economic partnership strengthened in a wide variety of spheres. Due to energy, agriculture and construction cooperation, Russia-Algeria trade volumes rose 130% from $885.3 million to $2 billion in 2015.[70] In September 2014, Rosatom signed a deal to construct a nuclear reactor in Algeria and Sergei Kiriyenko pitched the success of Iran's Bushehr reactor to convince Algerian officials of the merits of nuclear energy.[71] Rosatom's Algeria deal was also an early example of Russia's linkage of nuclear energy deals with educational diplomacy, as Kiriyenko announced that ten Algerian specialists would begin postgraduate studies at the Russian National Research Nuclear University MEPhI.[72] This deal reflected Algeria's strategy to adapt its economy to the post-oil age by 2020 and followed years of clandestine negotiations, which dated back to Putin's first meeting with Bouteflika in 2001.[73] Due to these protracted negotiations, Rosatom hoped that Algeria would be its breakthrough country in Africa, as Medvedev-era negotiations with Egypt and Nigeria had ground to a halt.

Notwithstanding these breakthroughs, the Russia-Algeria partnership had limited strategic depth and two fault-lines constrained its development during Putin's third term. First, Russia and Algeria possessed a competitive relationship in the energy market. Gazprom's exploration efforts in the El-Assel gas field did not change the fundamental calculus of Russia-Algeria competition for European gas importers and Moscow's failed efforts to establish energy cooperation with countries in the GECF extended to Algeria.[74] Due to the steady decline in Algerian gas production in the post-2006 period, which was exacerbated by political turmoil in 2014, Russia viewed Algeria's efforts to replace it as a gas

149

exporter during the Ukraine crisis as a strategic miscalculation.[75] Second, Russia was frustrated by the unexpected revival of Algeria's partnerships with Western countries as the memory of the Libyan war receded. French President François Hollande's acknowledgement of colonial-era suffering in Algeria in December 2012 and British Prime Minister David Cameron's visit to Algeria reaffirmed this change. As Algeria opted to strengthen its counterterrorism links with the US, Britain and France, Russia used ideational bonds to challenge Western synergies. Third, Russia's support for Egypt's pro-active counterterrorism strategy in Libya contrasted with Algeria's emphasis on political dialogue.[76] This disagreement foreshadowed the trajectory of Russia-Algeria interactions on Libya in the post-2016 period, which has been characterized by regular engagement and opposing strategic approaches.

### Russia's Relations with Post-Arab Spring Tunisia and Morocco

Although Russia did not publicly condemn Tunisia's Arab Spring revolution, bilateral relations built on their Ben Ali-era stagnation. Russia's efforts to engage Tunisia on Syria were less successful than its outreaches to Algeria and Egypt. During his November 2015 visit to Tunis, Sergei Naryshkin noted Tunisia's experience with instability during the Arab Spring and argued that the restoration of stability in Tunisia could be a helpful model for Syria to follow.[77] This outreach failed, as Tunisia continued to support Assad's ouster through a political settlement. The Russia-Morocco relationship showed initial promise but also resulted in unmet expectations. Although Russia unambiguously viewed Morocco as a secondary partner to Algeria, Moroccan officials became increasingly aware of Moscow's rising presence in Africa. During his fifteenth-anniversary throne day speech in July 2014, King Mohammed VI emphasized the importance of Russia and China as partners and pledged to arrange trips to both countries.[78] This speech followed Moroccan Foreign Minister Salaheddine Mezouar's visit to Russia on 3 July and prior engagement with Sergei Lavrov at the Organization of Islamic Cooperation (OIC) summit, which was hosted in Marrakech in January 2014. However, Moroccan media outlets noted that Rabat's extensive ties with the EU and US could restrict cooperation with Moscow while the Russia-West systemic confrontation persisted.[79] The postponement of Mohammed VI's trip to Russia reflected Morocco's caution about close engagement with Moscow.

While Moscow-Rabat economic relations stagnated, Russia surprisingly expanded its role in the Western Sahara dispute. In February 2015, Mohammed Khaddad, the Polisario Front's coordinator with the UN mission on the Western Sahara, met with Mikhail Bogdanov and a delegation from the Institute of Oriental Studies. During his visit to Moscow, Khaddad claimed that Morocco's intransigence on the Western Sahara endangered the security of North Africa and worsened the crisis in Libya and accused France of 'putting spokes in our wheels and hindering our search for a solution'.[80] Khaddad argued that Russia could leverage its great power status to play a more constructive role than France in the Western Sahara. In an interview with Sputnik Arabic, Khaddad noted that Russian companies could invest in the Western Sahara's fishery sector, phosphate reserves and oil and gas reserves via its established partnerships with Algeria.[81] Despite these conciliatory comments, Vitaly Naumkin, a key advisor to Vladimir Putin on Syria, urged Russia to embrace a restrained approach to the Western Sahara conflict. Naumkin noted Russia's historic relationship with Morocco, the risk of the Sahrawis embracing armed struggle to redress their grievances and rising Egypt-Morocco tensions as proof of Russia's need to maintain an even-keeled approach to North African affairs. If Russia embraced a restrained approach, Naumkin noted that the Western Sahara crisis could be an area of cooperation with the West, which mirrored prior collaboration against Syria's chemical weapons and Iran's nuclear ambitions.[82] Russian policy towards the Western Sahara heeded Naumkin's recommendations, as Moscow combined diplomatic assertiveness with a strict balancing strategy in North Africa.

### Russia Enters the Geopolitical Wilderness in Libya

During the first half of Putin's third term as president, Russia played a peripheral role in Libyan affairs. Ekaterina Stepanova, the Head of the Peace and Conflict Studies unit at IMEMO, noted that 'up until 2015, the only identifiable aspect of Russia's policy on the Libya crisis was diplomatic aversion to external military intervention that stretched the limit of the UNSC mandate and a strong emphasis on the grave consequences resulting from state collapse in Libya'.[83] The rise of instability in Libya, which featured an upsurge of militia activity in Tripoli and Misrata in 2013 and frictions between secularists and Islamists, caused the Russian media to immodestly praise the wisdom of opposing Gaddafi's fall. This self-righteous rhetoric peaked following the Benghazi attack in September 2012, which resulted in the death of Ambassador J. Christopher Stevens and three other US diplomatic and military personnel at the hands of the Salafist group Ansar al-Sharia. As Stevens had regularly travelled to Benghazi in support of the Libyan opposition in 2011, *Kommersant* ran a story on 13 September 2012 entitled 'Libyan revolution devours its fathers'.[84] RT attributed the Benghazi attack to US arms transfers to al-Qaeda-aligned militants in Libya.[85]

Despite Russia's ongoing delegitimization of the 2011 revolution, Moscow attempted to re-establish commercial relations with Libya's new authorities. These efforts were greeted with scepticism in the Russian expert community. A RIAC report of February 2012 claimed that 'any contracts that may be offered to Russia by the new Libyan authorities should be regarded as a courtesy', as Russia was unable to financially support Arab countries, Libyans with Soviet technical training wished to cooperate with Western countries and Russian industrial products were uncompetitive in the Libyan market.[86] Nevertheless, Sergei Lavrov met with Libyan Foreign Minister Mohammed Abdelaziz to discuss possible arms deals in September 2013. After their meeting, Lavrov emphasized Russia's commitment to training the Libyan army and police and called the new government 'our Libyan friends'.[87] Despite this cordial rhetoric, Russia failed to achieve any significant commercial breakthroughs with Libya. The October 2013 breach of the Russian Embassy in Libya by sixty armed rioters who opened fire and tore the Russian flag created new challenges for the Moscow-Tripoli partnership.[88] After this incident, the Libyan government allegedly told Russia that it could not guarantee the safety of its diplomats.[89] Mohammed

RUSSIA REBUILDS ITS INFLUENCE IN NORTH AFRICA

Abdelaziz subsequently denied that this discussion occurred, but Russia relocated its personnel from Libya to Tunisia, and Moscow–Tripoli relations ground to a dead-stop.

During the first half of 2014, Russia was forced to contend with a new actor in Libya: General Khalifa Haftar. On 14 February, Haftar announced the suspension of the General National Congress, government and constitutional declaration, and on 18 May, Haftar-aligned forces and the Zintan militia stormed the Libyan parliament. The Libyan government and much of the international community derided both events as coup attempts. Inside the Kremlin, Haftar's US citizenship was viewed with suspicion, as was the belief that he was an incompetent general who was gaining ground by allegedly bribing Libyan tribal militias.[90] An article in RT of May 2014 facetiously asserted that Haftar's coup was 'NATO-exported democracy to Libya', and claimed that Haftar was a US trojan horse, as he could align with death squads that would coercively advance Western interests.[91] On 20 May, an article in *Rossiyskaya Gazeta* concurred with Haftar's warnings about extremist infiltration of the Libyan government. However, the article noted that 'Haftar did not say a word about the main puppeteers of the authorities in Tripoli, the Americans', speculated that Haftar wanted a deal with the US and sarcastically quipped 'That's all democracy.'[92]

Despite its antipathy towards the Tripoli authorities and Haftar, the February 2015 beheading of twenty-one Coptic Christians by ISIS militants in Libya inspired a change in Russian policy. In early 2015, Russian experts feared the consequences of Islamist militia dominance in Tripoli and mass protests against Omar al-Hassi's National Salvation Government. Former Russian Ambassador to Libya Alexey Podsterob mused openly about a 'Somalization' scenario in Libya, which saw Cyrenaica fight Tripolitana and Fezzan, inter-tribal violence, an Arab-Berber conflict, and clashes between Islamic fundamentalists and Gaddafi loyalists, or a potential partition of Libya, which would result in a Korea or Cyprus.[93] Khalifa urged Russia to condemn the activities of Tripoli-based militias in the UN Security Council and support war crimes trials for the leaders of these informal armed units. On 9 February, Major General Abdulrazek al-Nadoori, a close ally of Khalifa Haftar, met with a

153

senior Russian official in Cairo. This meeting, which occurred in tandem with Vladimir Putin's visit to Egypt, resulted in an agreement to ship Russian equipment to Haftar's forces, which were carrying out counterterrorism operations in Benghazi.[94] LNA Spokesperson Colonel Ahmed al-Mismari subsequently confirmed that Sisi and Putin had discussed Russian arms transfers to Haftar's forces via Egypt.[95] These negotiations expressly violated the UN arms embargo on Libya, which was already being eroded by weapons smuggling from Sudan, but helped consolidate the partnership between Russia and the Tobruk-based government.

These clandestine negotiations swiftly translated into Russian official policy. In a statement of 25 February, Vitaly Churkin predictably praised Russia's judgment in warning against Gaddafi's fall but also proposed transferring weapons to the Libyan army and broached Russian participation in a multi-national coalition to remove ISIS from Libya. Churkin emphasized the decisiveness of Russia's policies, which were exemplified by its supply of weapons to Iraq while the US was deliberating, as proof of its ability to contribute meaningfully to an anti-ISIS coalition. On 26 February, Churkin reaffirmed Russia's commitment to joining a multilateral anti-ISIS coalition against Libya by stating that 'If Russia could take part in an operation off Somalia's coast, why can't it take part in an operation in the Mediterranean?'[96] Russia also called for a modification of the arms embargo, which would allow the House of Representatives (HoR) in Tobruk, which served as Libya's internationally recognized government, to secure arms, and would impose an arms blockade on areas of Libya where ISIS and militants were present.[97]

Russia's official rhetoric was crafted to offer an olive branch to the West during a time of crisis, appeal to Russia's partners in the Arab world, and rally domestic support for its Libya policy. Churkin's implicit calls for Russian cooperation with Britain, France and the US against ISIS in Libya was noteworthy, as it was Russia's first proposed act of security cooperation with Western countries since the Ukraine crisis.[98] Russia also viewed the Libya crisis as a potential gateway to renewed intelligence cooperation with the US and Europe, as EU-sanctioned FSB chief Alexander Bortnikov

## RUSSIA REBUILDS ITS INFLUENCE IN NORTH AFRICA

was participating in dialogue with Western countries about ISIS in Libya.[99] Unlike their prior cooperation in Somalia, most Western countries did not embrace Churkin's offer of cooperation, and Spain and the US opposed Russia's arms embargo modification proposal. Italy was a noteworthy exception to this trend. During a 5 March press conference with Vladimir Putin, Italian Prime Minister Matteo Renzi claimed that 'Russia's role could be decisive' against ISIS in Libya, and that 'without Russia it is much more complicated to find a point of equilibrium'.[100] MGIMO academic Elena Maslova argued that Italy viewed the migration crisis in Libya as much more important to its security than Ukraine, and claimed that Renzi believed that Russia was more interested than the US in solving this crisis.[101] Due to these efforts, Russia viewed Italy as the weakest link in the Western sanctions regime, and saw outreaches to Rome, along with France, as critical to its efforts to escape economic isolation from the West.[102]

Beyond strengthening its relationship with Tobruk and providing a rare outlet for cooperation with the West, Russia's intensified opposition to ISIS in Libya had sweeping domestic political and diplomatic impacts. Russia's linkage of its anti-ISIS campaign to support for Coptic Christians helped strengthen the alignment between the Kremlin and the Russian Orthodox Church. Patriarch Kirill, the Primate of the Russian Orthodox Church, wrote a letter to President Sisi condemning the ISIS attacks.[103] On 17 February, Vladimir Legoida, the chairman of the Russian Orthodox Church's Synodal Information Department, called ISIS 'servants of Satan', and warned that ISIS's actions in Libya would disrupt Christian-Muslim relations in the Middle East.[104] As the Kremlin had emphasized its role as a guardian of Christendom in the Middle East during the Arab Spring, Russia reacted assertively to this attack. On 2 March, Russia co-sponsored a session on the protection of Christians with Lebanon and Armenia on the sidelines of the UN Human Rights Council in Geneva, which saw Sergei Lavrov equate the killing of Coptic Christians in Libya with genocide.[105] Russia's linkage of ISIS's rise in Libya also reinforced its image as a resurgent Mediterranean power, which appealed to Tsarist and Soviet-era legacies, and complemented Moscow's assertiveness in Syria.

Russia's response to the growing ISIS threat in Libya also helped consolidate its partnership with Egypt. On 26 February, Egyptian Foreign Minister Sameh Shoukry claimed that 'Russia plays an important role in this issue since it has a naval fleet in the Mediterranean', and added that he would welcome a Russian naval blockade of Libya.[106] Due to its close relations with Washington and Moscow, Egypt aspired for a coordination role between the US and Russia in Libya, which resembled Iraq's role as a conduit between the US and Iran in the anti-ISIS struggle.[107] While these ambitions for large-scale Russia-Egypt security cooperation in Libya did not come to pass, Vitaly Naumkin noted that Russian officials viewed Egypt, along with Algeria, as a potential stabilizing force in Libya.[108] Therefore, consultations between Russia and Egypt on the ISIS threat in Libya laid the foundations for Moscow-Cairo cooperation from 2016 to 2018, which aided Haftar's triumphs in eastern and southern Libya.

By the spring of 2015, Russia had established a robust partnership with the Tobruk-based government. On 15 April, Prime Minister Abdullah al-Thinni emphasized the strength of the Russia-Libya partnership on RT Arabic by highlighting Moscow's friendship with Libya since the era of King Idris, asking Russia to strike down the UN arms embargo against Libya at the UNSC and urging Russia to revive Gaddafi-era contracts, which only expired in 2020.[109] Thinni also embraced Russian narratives on Libya by accusing Western countries of double standards. Thinni railed against the contradiction between official Western support for the Tobruk-based government and the Western-backed arms embargo, which undermined Libya's sovereignty over its counterterrorism policy.[110] The resonance of al-Thinni's rhetoric in Moscow served as a prelude for Russia's subsequent military intervention in Libya.

## Russia's Expands Its Security Involvement in Libya

During the second half of 2016, Russia's partnership with Libya's Tobruk-based government and Khalifa Haftar strengthened considerably. On 31 May, 4 billion Libyan dinars arrived from Moscow to Al Abraq airport near Bayda for distribution in eastern

Libya. The GNA's reaction to this development was ambiguous, as it feared that the dinars would entrench Libya's east-west tensions, but also acknowledged their role in ameliorating Libya's liquidity crisis. The delayed arrival of British-printed banknotes also increased the appeal of Russian-made dinars. However, the United States argued that the Bayda banknotes could undermine confidence in Libya's currency and the Central Bank of Libya's efforts to create a common monetary policy.[111] Siddiq al-Kabir, the Tripoli-based Central Bank governor, proposed an alternative plan to print 8 billion dinars, and warned that the international community could freeze the central bank's assets if it continued accepting dinars from Russia.[112] These pleas were ignored by the Tobruk-based government, which became increasingly reliant on Russian-made banknotes.

While Russia's dinar shipments revealed a pro-LNA stance, Moscow's strategy towards Libya was much more nuanced. As Russia's military intervention in Syria gained traction and the ISIS threat in Libya loomed large, Moscow viewed Libya as an increasingly important regional theatre for its counterinsurgency goals. During a March 2016 press conference with US Secretary of State John Kerry, Sergei Lavrov warned that Libya had become a 'black hole' for arms transfers to Sub-Saharan Africa and illegal immigration to Europe.[113] To ensure that it possessed a reliable security partner in Libya regardless of who gained the political upper hand, Russia balanced favourable relations with the LNA and GNA. On 29 June, Haftar met with Sergei Shoigu and Nikolay Patrushev in Moscow, which fuelled rumours of imminent Russian arms transfers to the LNA. Russia's reluctance to recognize the GNA's legitimacy until the HoR supported it also played into Haftar's hands.[114] However, Russia also regularly contacted GNA officials, such as Prime Minister Fayez al-Sarraj, defence minister-designate Mahdi al-Barghati and Vice Chairman of the Presidential Council of Libya Ahmad Maiteeq.

Towards the end of 2016, Russia's pivot towards Haftar sharpened dramatically, as Moscow viewed aligning with the LNA chieftain as the most expedient path to influence in Libya. This assessment was triggered by the LNA's wave of military successes, which saw it entrench its hegemony over the oil crescent, and capture the ports of Sidra, Brega and Ras Lanuf in September 2016. *Nezavisimaya Gazeta* article of January 2017 extolled Haftar's possession of control over the Libyan military and efforts to push Libya in a secular direction, and praised his purported achievements, which included reviving the national oil company, increasing hydrocarbon revenues and centralizing control over Libyan ports. The article also condemned the GNA as an organization that was overtaken by Islamists, which spanned from 'moderate' Muslim Brotherhood members, Salafists who were willing to embrace pluralism and, at the extreme end of the spectrum, ISIS.[115] Political commentator Ivan Konovalov claimed that Europe was deliberately turning a blind eye to Haftar's counterterrorism goals, with the possible exception of Italian Foreign Minister Angelino Alfano, who supported the constructive security role of the Russia-LNA axis.[116] Russian academic discourse periodically rebutted these narratives, which noted Haftar's role in dampening turnout in the 2014 Libyan elections, the weakness of the Muslim Brotherhood and Madkhali Salafist support for the LNA,[117] but these perspectives were excluded from Kremlin-backed accounts of events in Libya.

In November 2016, Haftar returned to Moscow to hold talks with Sergei Lavrov about the political situation in Libya. As Haftar's prior engagements with Russian officials were confined to defence and intelligence figures, his meeting with Lavrov underscored Moscow's efforts to normalize the LNA chieftain as a political figure. It also complemented indirect negotiations that were held earlier in the fall between Mikhail Bogdanov and Libya's Ambassador to Saudi Arabia Abdelbassat al-Badri. Following his meeting with Lavrov, Haftar expressed interest in purchasing Russian weapons once the arms embargo expired, and invited Russia to invest in Libya's reconstruction process.[118] These talks culminated in Haftar's visit to the Admiral Kuznetsov aircraft carrier in January 2017, which was off the coast of Tobruk. During this visit, Haftar discussed counterterrorism with Shoigu, but the symbolic impact superseded any policy dialogue. Peter Millett, who served as British Ambassador to Libya from 2015 to 2018, recalled that Haftar merely signed a visitor's guide to Benghazi on the Admiral Kuznetsov but crafted the impression of Russian support to bolster his standing.[119] Other news outlets, such as Italy's RAI, reported that Haftar had offered

## RUSSIA REBUILDS ITS INFLUENCE IN NORTH AFRICA

Russia basing rights in Tobruk and Benghazi in exchange for military support. The post-2011 proliferation of small arms in Libya meant that the LNA was well-stocked, but Haftar wished to inherit Gaddafi-era deals for Su-35, Su-30 and Yak-130 jets, as well as securing access to spare parts for out-of-service Russian equipment that was operated by the LNA.[120]

The Russia-LNA partnership's consolidation advanced Moscow's strategic interests in three ways. First, Russia viewed its alignment with Haftar as a gateway to Libya's strategically valuable port infrastructure. Russian officials viewed Tobruk as an especially valuable base location, as Soviet specialists had operated there during the early 1980s and it was conveniently protected by a deep-water bay, while a Benghazi base was viewed as an extravagant short-term goal but potentially valuable long-term objective.[121] Russia also expanded its involvement in securing eastern Libyan ports, as the private military consulting company RSB Group led by Oleg Kritinsyn engaged in mine clearance in Benghazi at Haftar's behest and protected ships from piracy. The RSB Group's personnel possessed an intelligence, rather than a military background, and were recruited from FSB units Vymphel and Alpha.[122] Russia did not publicly reveal its interest in Libyan ports or bases, as its movements in this sphere were widely scrutinized by Western officials. Maltese Foreign Minister George Vella, who chaired the EU in early 2017, linked Haftar's Admiral Kuznetsov trip to Russia's basing aspirations in the Mediterranean, and urged Western officials to hold strategic discussions on Moscow's threat to Libya, much like they did in Syria.[123]

Viktor Ozerov, the head of the Russian Federation Council Committee on Security and Defence tried to silence this speculation by denying negotiations with Haftar to construct a base in Tobruk or Benghazi.[124] Russian media outlets also noted Libya's long-standing disdain for a foreign military presence on its territory, which dated back to the Italian colonial experience, and any attempt to impose a base on Libyan soil could lead to armed resistance against Russia.[125] Anas El-Gomati, the director of the Sadeq Institute in Tripoli, contends that Russia was aware of the residual popularity of Gaddafi's resistance to foreign interference in Libya and public nostalgia for Libya's ability to punch above its weight in international

159

affairs. This contrasted with widespread disdain amongst Libyans for Gaddafi's economic policies and human rights abuses.[126] Despite this pushback, reports surfaced in December 2017 that talks between Russia and Haftar's representatives reached 'advanced stages' on establishing a military base, as Moscow sought to capitalize on Libya's 'lawlessness' and establish an alternative Middle Eastern foothold to its bases in Syria.[127]

Second, Russia's pro-Haftar stance crystallized its security cooperation with Egypt and Algeria, which had stagnated after their initial support for a military intervention in Syria. Egyptian and US security sources informed Reuters in March 2017 that Russia had used eastern Egypt's Marsa Matrouh base in early February and had deployed a twenty-two-person special forces contingent at Sidi Barrani, which is located 100 km from the Egypt-Libya border.[128] Russia's military deployments sought to strengthen Haftar's position, which was weakened by the 3 March attacks by the Benghazi Defence Brigades on LNA-held oil ports. These special forces primarily had defensive responsibilities, as they sought to protect Russian technicians who helped the LNA operate military technology.[129] This report received widespread attention in the Western media but was immediately downplayed by Russian, Egyptian and LNA officials. Viktor Ozerov called reports on Russia's military presence in Libya 'another information duck', and a distraction from US special forces deployments to Raqqa, Syria.[130] Egyptian officials feared the repercussions of violating its long-standing policy of denying foreign countries access to its bases, while the LNA wanted to keep an open door for counter-terrorism cooperation with the US, such as the August 2016 anti-ISIS attack in Sirte.

Mark Katz acknowledged that the expansion of Russia-Egypt security cooperation in Libya had both opportunities and risks.[131] As Russia's alignment with Haftar was also backed by US partners, such as the UAE, Egypt and France, Washington was unlikely to resist Moscow's policies, and Russia hoped that the close Trump-Sisi relationship could even lead to tacit US support for its actions. The main risk stemmed from uncertainties about the long-term Russia-Egypt coordination in Libya. If Russia backed a large-scale LNA offensive or neglected Egypt's primary border security concerns,

Moscow-Cairo relations could deteriorate. Russia and Egypt's frequent consultations about Libya mitigated these disagreements. However, tensions reheated due to Cairo's cautious support for Haftar's April 2019 offensive on Tripoli and Moscow's unease with Sisi's growing assertiveness on the Egypt-Libya border in the summer of 2020.

Although it was much more serendipitous than Russia-Egypt cooperation, Moscow's growing assertiveness in Libya indirectly strengthened its partnership with Algeria. By January 2017, 150 ISIS militants had congregated in southwestern Libya's Fezzan region, which lies at the intersection between Algeria, Niger and Chad. Algerian officials were alarmed by ISIS's rise in Fezzan, and were concerned that the terrorism problem could escalate if ISIS fighters fled from Iraq and Syria to Libya. While FLN officials viewed Haftar with mistrust, the elimination of hawkish voices during Bouteflika's 2015 military restructuring and tightening UAE-Algeria cooperation caused Algiers to soften its anti-LNA stance.[132] Due to these strategic calculations, Algeria viewed Moscow's military support for Haftar as a positive development, provided that the Russia-LNA alliance exclusively targeted ISIS in Fezzan and Haftar did not launch an offensive on Tripoli. During Haftar's visit to Algiers in December 2016, which preceded his trip to the Admiral Kuznetsov, Algeria reportedly acquiesced to the transfer of Russian arms for the LNA's anti-ISIS campaign.[133] As the UAE and Egypt largely relied on US arms, and the Kremlin wanted deniability around its support for Haftar, the Russia-Algeria nexus became a clandestine plank of its involvement in Libya.

Third, Russia viewed its partnership with Haftar as an entry point to expanded diplomatic influence in Libya, as Moscow wished to become the only great power that could liaise with both Tripoli and Tobruk. In 2016, Russia established the inter-ministerial Contact Group for Libyan reconciliation, which consisted of former Russian diplomats in Libya and members of the State Duma. This contact group increased the frequency of Russia's meetings with GNA officials and aligned militia groups, such as the Misrata Brigades.[134] Businessman Lev Dengov spearheaded the Contact Group's activities and its public communications. Dengov's selection can be explained by his close relationship with Chechnya's leader Ramzan Kadyrov, who extended his expanding role in Arab diplomacy to Libya. Kadyrov vigorously embraced Haftar's anti-Islamist discourse and invited Ahmad Maiteeq to Grozny.[135]

As Russia's military alignment with the LNA gained more scrutiny, the Kremlin muddied the waters by emphasizing its role as an honest broker in Libya. This mirrored Russia's efforts to deflect from its support for Assad in Syria through the more inclusive Astana Process and Sochi peace summits. Dengov emphasized Russia's commitment to preserving Libya's sovereignty, downplayed Moscow's extractive ambitions in the conflict and highlighted the purported popularity of Russian diplomacy amongst Libyan tribes as significant advantages.[136] In September 2017, Russia simultaneously invited GNA Deputy Prime Minister Ahmed Maiteeq and LNA spokesperson Ahmed al-Mismari for talks. A Valdai Discussion Club event in December 2017, which had a Russian Ministry of Foreign Affairs presence, claimed that Russia's Libya policy had a 'fundamentally equidistant position, which allows it to act as a neutral intermediary'.[137] This façade of non-alignment would persist, even as Wagner Group PMCs aided Khalifa Haftar's offensives in southern Libya and Tripoli. During Putin's fourth term, Russia paired its intervention in Libya with upgraded relations with Egypt and Algeria. This trend ensconced the Maghreb's prominence as a pole in Russia's policy in Africa, and bridged Moscow's North African strategy with its policies elsewhere on the continent.

6

# RUSSIA BECOMES A CONTINENT-WIDE GREAT POWER

During Vladimir Putin's fourth term as president, Russia's long-standing goal of re-emerging as a continent-wide great power in Africa finally came to fruition. The expansion of Russian influence in Africa occurred against seemingly tall odds. The US and Europe paid greater attention to Russia's rising influence in Africa, even though it remained a secondary factor to China's growing power. Russia was also forced to navigate serious political shocks, such as the 'second Arab Spring' protests in Algeria and Sudan, and the wave of leadership changes in southern Africa. Through targeted diplomatic engagement and symbolically powerful shows of commitment to Africa, such as the 2018 BRICS summit and the Sochi Summit in October 2019, Russia was able to defy these geopolitical headwinds. Russia's relationships with traditional partners, such as Egypt and Algeria, survived, its partnership with South Africa was partially rebuilt, and Moscow was able to project influence with varying degrees of success in new frontiers, such as the Red Sea region, Central Africa and the Sahel. This chapter will examine these sweeping changes in Russian policy towards Africa and assess how the Sochi Summit capitalized on geopolitical trends during Putin's fourth term.

163

## The Sochi Summit and Russia's Pursuit of Continent-Wide Great Power Status

While Russia's great power ambitions in Africa were evidenced through foreign policy concepts and travel itineraries of senior officials, it was still unclear whether Moscow possessed a grand strategy in Africa. The perception that Russia's actions in Africa were opportunistic and its tendency to set over-ambitious targets restricted the growth of its influence. As France, China, the EU and the US hosted major African summits over the past two decades, Russian officials concluded that a continent-wide conference would expedite the expansion of its influence in Africa. Vladimir Putin formalized the concept of an Africa-wide conference July 2018 at the BRICS summit in Johannesburg, and in the months that followed, officials from Russia, Egypt and the African Union prepared for the events in Sochi.[1] These preparations coincided with a series of symbolic and tangible displays of Russia's strategic commitment to Africa. In May 2019, Egypt confirmed that Sochi would host the first Russia-Africa summit.[2] In June 2019, Russia organized two economic forums, which emphasized its commitment to closer economic ties with Africa and laid the groundwork for the Sochi Summit. The St Petersburg Economic Forum encouraged African business leaders to view Russia as a lucrative investment destination.[3] On 22 June, the 26th annual Afreximbank summit convened in Moscow, which was only the second time it had gathered outside of Africa. Dmitry Medvedev emphasized the need for a strategic partnership between Russia and Africa, as they control half of the world's natural resources. The Russia-Africa Shared Vision 2030 plan was also unveiled in conjunction with the Sochi Summit's announcement.

On 23 October 2019, forty-three African heads of state congregated in Sochi for the first Russia-Africa Summit. This conference, which was co-chaired by Vladimir Putin and Abdel Fattah el-Sisi, underscored the progress of Russia's geopolitical forays in Africa and featured grandiose predictions about the future of Russia-Africa cooperation. Putin declared that strengthening ties with Africa was 'one of the priorities' of Russian foreign policy. Deputy Chairperson of the State Duma Olga Timofeeva declared

## RUSSIA BECOMES A CONTINENT-WIDE GREAT POWER

that a 'completely new page is beginning in the history of relations between Russia and Africa. Russia is returning to Africa'.[4] In a similar vein, Sisi declared it was the 'ideal time' for Russia to expand its investments in Africa, and AUC Commissioner for Infrastructure and Energy Amani Abou-Zeid urged Russian investors to enter partnerships with African businesses.[5] At the Sochi Summit, Russia announced that it had signed $12.5 billion in new deals but these contracts were not legally binding, and it was unclear whether they would convert into investments.[6] Deputy Director of the Russian Foreign Ministry's Africa Department Oleg Ozerov's strident criticisms of Western neocolonialism in Africa and full-throated appeals to Cold War legacies earned widespread acclaim. Malawi's President Peter Mutarika claimed that 'we must put an end to the exploitation of Africa' and called upon Russia to 'turn its eyes to Africa as the center of world production'.[7] These sentiments were echoed by Madagascar's President Andry Rajeolina, who claimed that 'Africa was the workforce of the planet, and now African countries need to become masters of their own destiny.'[8]

Russia's show of intent at the Sochi Summit, which featured pageantry, caustic anti-Western rhetoric and genuine commercial breakthroughs, captured the attention of the international community. Due to the influence of Trump's hawkish national security advisor John Bolton, the US became increasingly attuned to Russia's assertiveness in Africa. In December 2018, during a speech at the Heritage Foundation, Bolton decried Russia's predatory behaviour in Africa and urged the US to target more resources to theatres of great power competition rather than dispersing assets throughout Africa.[9] Bolton accused Russia of using arms and energy to procure votes at the UNGA from African countries, and claimed that these policies kept strongmen in power and stunted Africa's economic growth. Concerns about Russia's rising influence in Africa diffused across the foreign policy community. After the Sochi Summit, James Jonah, a former UN Under-Secretary General for Political Affairs, linked Russia's appeal to the Trump administration's disengagement from the continent.[10] Trump's omission of Africa from his September 2019 UNGA speech and John Bolton's departure caused African leaders to view the US's 'Prosper Africa'

165

strategy to be insincere. Jonah also noted that Africa's embrace of Russia stemmed from its desire to avoid over-reliance on a single partner, which suggested that US disengagement was only one factor in play. While Jonah was convinced that Russia had emerged as a power centre in a multipolar African geopolitical landscape, the US Department of Defence was publicly sceptical of Moscow's power projection capacity. US Army Major General William Gayler, the AFRICOM director of operations, stated in January 2020 that he was 'not worried' about Russia's security agreements in Africa, and insisted that the US could deepen its partnerships on the continent to counter Moscow's resurgence. AFRICOM deputy director of intelligence Gregory Hadfield said that 'China and Russia are not doing much to help counter extremist groups that rob Africans of their future', and exclusively linked Russian arms sales to Africa to the pursuit of hard currency.[11]

Although French President Emmanuel Macron attempted to de-escalate tensions with Russia, Africa emerged as a major theatre of contestation between Moscow and Paris. Julien Nocetti, an Associate Professor at the St Cyr Military Academy, notes that the Ministry of Francophone Affairs Policy Planning office and MoD Strategy Office did not have a firmly developed strategy towards Russian involvement in Africa, as Moscow's conduct was driven by a mixture of strategy and opportunism.[12] Under Macron, this trend experienced significant changes. The Franco-Russian rivalry was explicitly related to Russia's actions in Africa, such as disinformation against French counterterrorism missions in the Sahel and military intervention in the Central African Republic, and also linked to systemic-level developments. France's resolute support for Ukraine, which was shared by its European partners, was viewed as a provocation in Russia that would legitimize an asymmetric response. Igor Delanoe, the Deputy Head of Moscow's French-Russian Analytical Center, claimed that Russia's policy in France's sphere of influence in Africa 'plays with the rules of the game that NATO played with in the post-Soviet space during the 1990s and the beginning of the 2000s'.[13] Former Polish Foreign Minister Anna Fotyga notes that the European Parliament began coordinating a multilateral strategy against the Wagner Group's

## RUSSIA BECOMES A CONTINENT-WIDE GREAT POWER

rising influence, which converted a Franco-Russian rivalry into a Europe-Russia systemic confrontation.[14]

Despite this negative momentum, the outlook for Europe-Russia cooperation in Africa after the Sochi Summit appeared more hopeful than US-Russia collaboration. To assuage France's concerns about the strength of Russia-CAR relations and Moscow's strident condemnations of neocolonialism, Vladimir Putin consulted with Emmanuel Macron about the Sochi Summit's outcomes on 26 October.[15] The Putin-Macron phone call built on France's praise of the Russia-Ukraine prisoner swap in September 2019 and Macron's efforts to spearhead a de-escalation of Russia-West relations. Alexandra Arkhangelskaya, an expert at Moscow's Institute of African Studies, challenged the notion that the Sochi Summit would strain EU-Russia relations, and instead highlighted areas of EU-Russia cooperation in Africa.[16] Arkhangelskaya viewed the EU's experience in developing long-term strategies towards Africa as beneficial for Russia, and urged Russian NGOs to develop joint projects with their European counterparts. Product certification and public health were other areas of immediate EU-Russia cooperation in Africa. Andrei Kortunov urged Britain and Russia to 'exempt' Africa from their geopolitical rivalry, stating in a RIAC report of 28 October: 'an exemption would not be a manifestation of weakness or cynicism, but rather a demonstration of political wisdom and strategic foresight'.[17] A Royal United Services Institute (RUSI) report of 21 October similarly noted that Britain and Russia were both 're-engaging' with Africa, and in spite of disagreements on security issues, such as peacekeeper deployments in Sudan, the two countries did not have a zero-sum rivalry.[18]

China viewed the expansion of Russian influence in Africa with cautious optimism, but was wary of where the Sochi Summit might lead in the long-term. Cui Heng, an academic at East China Normal University's Center for Russian Studies, claimed that Putin's strategy to expand Russian influence in Africa could have a superior track record to the Soviet Union's past tactics. Heng claimed that Russia's 'cooperation based on realism' differed markedly from the Soviet Union's 'aid model', and while it has yielded slower results in Africa, it is more conducive to long-term mutually beneficial relationships.[19] Liu Naiya, an Africa expert at the Chinese Academy of Social Sciences, favourably highlighted Putin's criticisms of Western neocolonialism at the Sochi Summit, and stated that China 'was more of a partner than a competitor' in Africa. Naiya was optimistic that Sino-Russian cooperation in other multilateral forums, such as BRICS and the Shanghai Cooperation Organization (SCO) would contribute to collaboration in Africa.[20] Other Chinese academics viewed Russia's pragmatism in Africa as a mixed blessing or potentially problematic development. In a report for the Shanghai Institute of International Studies, Qiang Xiaoyun viewed the Sochi Summit as a key component of Russia's 'hedging' strategy in world affairs. Xiaoyun stated that Russia's hedging policy in Africa was necessitated by Western sanctions, but also reflected Moscow's concerns about the limits of Sino-Russian cooperation and desire to present itself to African countries as an alternative to China and the West.[21] In November 2019, Wang Jiahao and Luo Jinyi, academics at the Education University in Hong Kong, unfavourably contrasted Russia's military-focused approach to China's economic penetration strategy in Africa, and subsequently concluded that 'Russia and China's strategies in Africa are very different, and there has been no concrete coordination between the two countries to this day.'[22] The absence of a centralized Chinese narrative on the Sochi Summit also reflects Moscow and Beijing's limited degree of interaction on African affairs.

## The Sochi Summit Spotlights Russia-Egypt Cooperation

Prior to the Sochi Summit, Russia-Egypt relations strengthened considerably. During Sisi's October 2018 visit to Moscow, Russia and Egypt signed an agreement on 'comprehensive partnership and strategic cooperation'.[23] The visit was timed with the seventy-fifth anniversary of the Russia-Egypt diplomatic relationship, and Putin designated 2020 an Egypt-Russia cultural year. The comprehensive strategic partnership agreement was hailed in Cairo, as Moscow had few such agreements in the Arab world.[24] Ahmed el-Shami, an economics professor at Cairo's Ain Shams University, claimed that this agreement raised Russia-Egypt cooperation to a 'whole

## RUSSIA BECOMES A CONTINENT-WIDE GREAT POWER

new level', and predicted that Russia-Egypt relations would reach the heights witnessed during the 1960s. Farag Abdel Fattah, an economics professor at Cairo University, stated that the agreement would remove trade barriers between Russia and Egypt, which would jumpstart economic cooperation. Notwithstanding this breakthrough, the Russia-Egypt relationship was not trouble-free. Although Sisi raised the issue with Putin, Russia only lifted travel restrictions on Cairo, and not on the more lucrative Red Sea resort. Russia's access to Egyptian bases, which was codified by a November 2017 agreement, did not come to fruition.[25]

Despite these frictions, Russia-Egypt cooperation advanced in three critical spheres. First, Russia and Egypt diversified the scope of their economic partnership. Sisi's close relationship with Dmitry Medvedev, who spoke with Sisi after the strategic partnership agreement was signed in 2018, helped streamline Russia-Egypt economic cooperation. From 2017 to 2018, Russia-Egypt trade volumes expanded by 62%, to $6.7 billion. The main drivers of this trade expansion were agricultural products, as Egypt imported more Russian potatoes and Russia supplied wheat, vegetable oil and agricultural machinery to Africa.[26] As Russia supplies 7.8 million tons of grain to Egypt each year, which is 70% of its imports, Egypt encouraged Russian private companies to enter its market. In October 2018, Egypt and Russia also announced a quality inspection agreement, which would cause all Russian grain to be assessed in Alexandria and Novorossiysk before entering the Egyptian market. Outside the agriculture sector, Russia-Egypt commercial relations also gained momentum. In September 2018, Russian-Hungarian Consortium Transmashholding landed Egypt National Railway's largest contract, which consisted of 1,300 rail cars at a cost of €1 billion.[27] Egypt also offered itself as a transhipment point for Russian automobiles to other African countries, and constructed a car-building plant in the proposed Russian Industrial Zone of the Suez Canal region. These infrastructure projects were encouraging, but Russia also wished to create a high-tech partnership with Egypt. In 2018, a Moscow Institute for African Studies of the Russian Academy of Sciences report urged Russia to explore new frontiers of commercial cooperation with Egypt, such as small-to-medium-sized business partnerships, the local production of Russian technologies and Internet-based education and health exchanges.[28]

Despite these lofty ambitions, the Sochi Summit resulted in more rhetorical pledges than substantive breakthroughs in the economic sphere. Sisi urged Russian Railways to expand its involvement in Egypt and add to the 1,300 train carriages that Moscow had previously delivered.[29] Russia reacted inconclusively to Sisi's requests, and Egyptian security measures, such as double searches of passengers and the creation of a special exit for Russian-bound flights at Cairo Airport, did not restore cancelled Russia-Egypt flight routes.[30] Putin's promise to visit the El Dabaa nuclear reactor site garnered positive attention, but his similar pledge to visit the Russian Industrial Zone in the Suez Canal was especially underwhelming. After Egypt promised Germany a rival industrial zone in the Suez Canal, companies from Moscow, St Petersburg and Tatarstan announced a slate of investment pledges. Building on his 19 October trip to Abu Dhabi, Putin expressed optimism about a potential breakthrough for UAE investments in the Suez Canal Industrial Zone.[31] The UAE did not react to Putin's statement, and this speculation swiftly died down. Russian companies were sceptical of their ability to invest in the Suez Canal, as the Egyptian government held final sway over capital provisions, and privately did not anticipate a breakthrough for at least five to seven years.[32] The COVID-19 pandemic dashed lingering hopes for an expansion of Russia-Egypt commercial cooperation, and Moscow-Cairo relations suffered from periodic turbulence after the Sochi Summit.

Second, Russia ensconced its position as a crisis-proof partner and staunch defender of authoritarian stability in Egypt. In September 2018, Al-Ahram and Sputnik Arabic signed a media cooperation agreement, which allowed Russia and Egypt to coordinate their narratives on domestic and international issues.[33] The Kremlin's loyalty to Sisi extended to the September 2019 mass protests in Cairo, Alexandria and Damietta. Fulfilling the spirit of this agreement, Sputnik amplified Egyptian state media narratives, such as the allegation that the Muslim Brotherhood had staged protests by using old footage.[34] A *Nezavisimaya Gazeta* article of 24 September extolled Sisi's achievements, such as his restoration of stability, establishment

## RUSSIA BECOMES A CONTINENT-WIDE GREAT POWER

of a 'balanced' Egyptian foreign policy, economic growth and Egypt's growing appeal as an investment destination.[35] Due to its support for his regime against political pressure, Sisi emphasized Russia's reliability as a partner for African countries at the Sochi Summit. Putin returned the favour by engaging with Sisi on the prevention of ISIS migration from Syria to Africa, and brainstorming 'African solutions' to the extremism threat with his Egyptian counterpart.[36] These discussions implicitly highlighted Russia's support for Sisi's crackdown on the Islamist movement and belief in Egypt's reliability as a counterterrorism partner.

Third, Egypt consolidated its position as Russia's bridge to Sub-Saharan Africa. Prior to the Sochi Summit, Egyptian Ambassador to Russia Ehab Nasr and Mikhail Bogdanov regularly discussed development initiatives in Africa. Egyptian commentators and business leaders provided enthusiastic backing for Egypt's position as Russia's gateway to Africa. An article in Cairo's *Al-Shorouk* newspaper of 19 October boasted that 'Russia views Egypt as a pivotal country, a partner and fundamental pillar of stability in the Middle East and the African continent.'[37] The head of the Capital Center for Economic Studies and Research Khaled al-Shafei stated that Egypt is a 'strategic axis to reach the continent of Africa', and no major power, including Russia, will be able to invest in Africa without participating in development and economic projects in Egypt. Gamal Bayoumi, the Secretary-General of the Arab Investors Union (AIU), argued that Egypt could provide technical expertise to Russian projects in Africa, much like it assisted China and Japan.[38] These narratives were inextricably linked to Sisi's legacy of returning Egypt to the forefront of African diplomacy. While Egypt's resurgence as a pan-African power was observable as early as 2005, Sisi's trips to twenty-one African countries from 2014 to 2017 and chairmanship of the African Union in 2019 were signature foreign policy accomplishments.[39] Putin's co-hosting of the Sochi Summit with Sisi gave great power recognition to these achievements, which bolstered Russia's standing in Egypt. This positive momentum would persist in spite of Egypt's frustration that Russia was not championing its position on the Grand Ethiopian Renaissance Dam (GERD) dispute.

## Russia's Response to the 2019 Algerian Revolution

During the penultimate year of Bouteflika's presidency, Russia-Algeria relations continued to strengthen. In February 2018, Abdelkader Messahel visited Moscow, and Lavrov travelled to Algeria for the sixth time in January 2019. These meetings shored up the Moscow-Algiers partnership without reversing its stagnant economic trajectory. The Burkan-2019 military exercises and 9 January Mers el-Kebri naval base ceremony underscored Algeria's continued reliance on Russian arms. The Kornet-EM anti-tank system, which was purchased in 2015, was showcased for the first time. Chief of Staff Lieutenant General Ahmed Gaied Salah unveiled two Russian-built Project 636 submarines, which gave the Algerian Navy six submarines capable of firing Kalibr missiles.[40] While Russia-Algeria relations progressed in a business-as-usual fashion, the Russian expert community was increasingly polarized on Bouteflika's viability and Algeria's long-term reliability as a stable partner. North Africa expert V.V. Kudelev stated that Bouteflika would inevitably win a fifth term as president, as he ended the Algerian civil war, promoted national reconciliation and aided Algeria's economic development.[41] N. Zherlistsyna presented an alternative view that Bouteflika's run for a fifth term would be a 'catalyst of much greater instability than that faced by his regime at the present time'.[42]

Given these intense disagreements, the Algerian Hirak Protest Movement did not come as a complete surprise to Russian officials. The consensus within the Russian foreign and security policy establishment was that the FLN's retention of power or a military-brokered transition would protect Russia's interests in Algeria. Support for the status quo was especially pronounced in the Russian defence industry, as Bouteflika had personally overseen the expansion of Russian arms deals to Algeria, but also extended to the foreign policy establishment.[43] Oleg Barabanov warned that Bouteflika's ouster could result in an Egypt or Tunisia-style Arab Spring, which empowered Islamist movements, and warned that 'if Algeria turns 180 degrees, we do not know how Russian-Algerian relations will develop'.[44] Barabanov's warning was reiterated in Russian state-aligned media coverage of the Algerian Hirak. An

## RUSSIA BECOMES A CONTINENT-WIDE GREAT POWER

article in Gazeta.ru on 16 April warned that 'radical Islamists seize protest movement in Algeria', and interviewed Hirak participants who were alarmed by the Islamist Rashad Party's infiltration.[45] Tatiana Shumeleva, a Middle East expert at RIAC, described the Algerian opposition as an 'aggressive, chaotic crowd', and compared their acts of vandalism to the robbery of the Egyptian Museum during the Arab Spring.[46] Lavrov warned against foreign interference in Algeria's internal affairs, which appeared to be a veiled jab at Western powers.[47]

Although Russia was alarmed by the Algerian Hirak's momentum and supported the status quo in Algeria, it refrained from intervention on Bouteflika's behalf. Lavrov met with newly appointed Algerian Foreign Minister Ramtane Lamamra in March 2019 to show that Russia-Algeria relations were progressing in a business-as-usual fashion, and Russian officials repeatedly emphasized that the situation in Algeria was an 'internal affair'. Even hawkish voices, such as Barabanov, only foresaw a Russian intervention if the Hirak resulted in an Algerian civil war. Russia's restraint in Algeria is intriguing, as it contrasts markedly with Moscow's aggressive response to protests in Sudan. Vasily Kuznetsov contends that foreign powers were unlikely to hijack the Algerian Hirak, and cited Russia's cautious reactions to the 2011 uprisings in Tunisia and Egypt and the 2018 Armenian Revolution as precedents.[48] While this explanation is plausible, it is also worth noting that Russian experts viewed the likelihood of a democratic revolution in Algeria to be very slim. Shumeleva noted that the most likely regime change scenario in Algeria was a military coup, and Ahmed Gaied Saleh was regularly compared to Sisi in Russian state-aligned media commentaries.

The departure of Bouteflika on 2 April caused alarm in Russia, as it coincided with the exit of two key Moscow-friendly Algerian officials, Sonatrach president Abdelmoumem Kaddour and Ramtane Lamamra. Expressions of anti-Russian sentiments amongst supporters of the Algerian Hirak compounded these concerns. The slogan 'The fate of Algeria should be decided not in Rome and Moscow, but on the square of the capital' circulated widely on social media,[49] and Hirak demonstrators held banners criticizing Sergei Lavrov and derisively linking Vladimir Putin with Abdelkader

173

Bensalah.[50] These anti-Russian sentiments were not universal, as supporters of Vladimir Putin's leadership could be found in the Hirak, but reflected disdain for Russian interference in Algeria's political crisis.[51] Hirak supporters were concerned by Franco-Russian collusion in support of the FLN. Akram Kharief noted that Russia and France both opposed the Hirak for different reasons, as Moscow wanted to preserve its arms contracts with Algeria and Macron compared the Algerian protests to the Gilet Jaunes unrest at home.[52] Due to Russia's reliance on Algerian military kickbacks and the tolerance for corruption of some French companies, both Russia and France supported General Ahmed Gaid Salah's symbolic anti-corruption crackdowns.[53]

Concerns in Moscow about the Hirak's short-term impact on Russia-Algeria relations were ultimately unfounded. On 16 April, Lavrov held talks with new Algerian Foreign Minister Sabri Boukadoum, which included consultations on Libya and the Western Sahara. The absence of personnel changes in the Algerian military and the FLN's dominance abated Russia's concerns about Hirak influence on Algerian foreign policy decision-making. Russia's soft power in Algeria also proved to be highly resilient. Despite concerns that purchasing Russian weaponry would lead to US sanctions or derail US investments in Algerian shale gas, Algerian politicians of all ideological orientations supported Algeria's multi-vector foreign policy and continued Russian arms deals. Abderrazak Makri, the head of the Islamist Movement for a Peaceful Society Party, supported intensive negotiations with the US to ensure that Algeria would not be sanctioned for buying Russian arms.[54] The growing popularity of the Russian media aided Moscow's cause. Russian media outlets positioned themselves as the antithesis to French outlets and spread criticisms of French neocolonialism in Algeria. As the Algerian media focused on France's counter-revolutionary media coverage, which was broadcast on France-5 and printed in *Le Monde*, but gave little critical coverage to Russian disinformation, Russia was able to win the information war.[55] Russia's influence in Algeria survived the Hirak with surprising ease, and bilateral relations continued to strengthen in the months that followed.

## RUSSIA BECOMES A CONTINENT-WIDE GREAT POWER

### *Russia Reacts to Political Transitions in Southern Africa*

While Russia was firmly ascendant elsewhere on the continent, Moscow adopted a defensive posture in southern Africa. The September 2017 departure of Angola's President José Eduardo dos Santos, the November 2017 coup d'état that overthrew Zimbabwe's President Robert Mugabe, and the February 2018 resignation of South Africa's President Jacob Zuma transformed the region's political landscape. Russia watched these leadership changes with trepidation, as Dos Santos, Mugabe and Zuma were crucial enablers of Moscow's influence in southern Africa. The upswing in US-Angola relations under João Lourenço, the US's conditional offer to lift sanctions on Zimbabwe and negative aftershocks of the Rosatom controversy in South Africa raised doubts about the sustainability of Russia's regional presence. In March 2018, Sergei Lavrov toured Angola, Zimbabwe, Mozambique and Namibia, which resulted in new commercial deals with all four countries, and Vladimir Putin's visit to Johannesburg for the BRICS summit in July 2018 helped assuage Russia-South Africa tensions. These diplomatic outreaches caused Russia's presence in southern Africa to expand against the odds and strengthened Moscow's geo-strategic position ahead of the Sochi Summit.

### *Russia's Response to Angola's Leadership Transition*

Russia's initial reaction to João Lourenço's takeover as Angola's president was circumspect. As Lourenço studied at Moscow's Lenin Political-Military Academy in 1978 and had previously served as Angola's Defence Minister, he was known to Russian officials. Lourenço's initial emphasis on resetting relations with the US and Europe was viewed with concern in the Kremlin. Lourenço's refusal to side with Russia in a December 2017 UN resolution condemning 'gross violations of human rights in Crimea' caused alarm in Moscow, as Dos Santos had voted against a similar resolution during his last year in office.[56] In January 2018, Russia's VTB bank held talks with Angola on renegotiating the terms of its $1.5 billion loan and extended it by ten years.[57] Although VTB insisted that Angola was

175

one of its most lucrative markets in Africa, as its investments in the country had a 62% return on equity, rumours swirled that the bank would ultimately divest from Angola. Due to a prolonged recession; an oil price collapse-induced budget crisis; structural unemployment exceeding 25%; concerns about epidemic disease; and the Angolan central bank's removal of a kwanza / US dollar peg, Russia's trade and private sector investments in Angola stalled.

To overcome these setbacks, Lourenço made Angola the hub of Russia's aerospace ambitions in Sub-Saharan Africa. Russia's State Corporation for Space Activities Roscosmos was under pressure as its reputation was marred by corruption allegations and failed launches in April 2016 and November 2017.[58] Dmitry Rogozin was a key proponent of Roscosmsos's research and would eventually become its Director-General in May 2018. Despite Roscosmos's poor track record, Angola lent its satellite AngoSat1 for a test launch from Baikonur Cosmodrome, a Russian-leased facility in Kazakhstan, on 26 December 2017. Angola had received a €286.2 million loan from Rosoboronexport to design AngoSat1, which fulfilled a 2009 agreement with Russia on space cooperation and constituted Moscow's most significant aerospace investment in Africa. The AngoSat1 test ended in failure. Communication with the satellite was lost on 27 December, and although Roscosmos confirmed the health of AngoSat1 on 29 December, it was lost again by April 2018. Despite these setbacks, Russia reimbursed Angola for the AngoSat1 and agreed to build AngoSat2 in April 2018.[59] Russia and Angola also signed an aerospace cooperation agreement in April 2019. Russian Ambassador to Angola Vladimir Tatarov claimed that AngoSat made Angola a 'regional power', and noted that Angola earned $70 million from leasing satellite frequencies to neighboring countries.[60]

Lourenco's visit to Moscow in April 2019 underscored Angola's cooperation with Russia in the defence and mining sectors, as well as against emerging challenges, such as climate change. Angola's Defence Minister Salviano de Jesus Sequeira stated that military cooperation with Russia 'would last forever', and Russia delivered eight Su-30K fighter jets to Angola during the first half of 2019.[61] Sequeira also engaged in talks on the local production of Russian

176

## RUSSIA BECOMES A CONTINENT-WIDE GREAT POWER

weaponry and expressed interest in the S-400 air defence system, which had never been sold to an African country. This S-400 pledge was effectively symbolic, as Angola's mounting debt levels precluded serious negotiations.[62] Alrosa also signed an MOU with Angola's national diamond mining company Endiama, which reinforced the joint venture signed between the two companies in 2014 and their partnership which created the Catoca conglomerate.[63] Lourenço also sought to add a post-material dimension to Russia-Angola cooperation. During his State Duma speech, Lourenço emphasized his willingness to cooperate with Russian officials against climate change, as recurrent droughts in southern Angola created food security risks for millions of people.[64]

Despite these breakthroughs, Angola's efforts to balance between East and West hit a snag and Lourenço viewed the Sochi Summit as an opportunity to reverse this trend. Angola's multi-vector foreign policy was compromised by frictions between China and Angola over debt repayment, which forced Lourenço to seek credit from the IMF. This dispute increased Russia's importance to Angola's embrace of a multipolar world order. At the Sochi Summit, Lourenço tried to assuage concerns in Moscow about his outreaches to the US, Britain and France, and neutralize Russia's potential attempt to hedge against his leadership through cooperation with the Dos Santos family.[65] Lourenço claimed that 'Africa is free due to a great extent to the efforts of the Russian people, the efforts of the former Soviet Union', which was widely publicized in the Russian press.[66] Despite this conciliatory rhetoric, the Sochi Summit produced ambiguous outcomes for Angola. On 23 October, Dmitry Shugayev announced that all twelve Su-30K jets had arrived in Angola, but hours later, VTB declared that it would sell 10% of its Angolan assets. The sole noteworthy contract was struck between Angolan Grupo Pitabel company and Russian company Leonarda-Service LLC to distribute medical equipment. In a foreshadowing of Russia's medical diplomacy during the COVID-19 pandemic, Andrey Slepnev, the director of Russia's Export Center, claimed that 'high-tech exports of medical supplies to the countries in southwest Africa have not only economic but also important political significance, sending a signal that Russia is returning to the region'.[67]

177

Isabel dos Santos, José dos Santos's eldest daughter, who was worth $2 billion, caused controversy by attending the Sochi Summit. Lourenço's MPLA anti-corruption crusade, which was announced in September 2018, implicitly targeted the Dos Santos family, and in May 2019, Isabel dos Santos lambasted Lourenço's authoritarian policies. Lourenço retaliated by suspending her from the MPLA central committee, as she had been absent for ninety days in parliament.[68] Lourenço redirected his anti-corruption campaign towards 'banking, telephony, media, diamonds, mass distribution and building materials', which were industries that propped up Isabel dos Santos's fortune. One month later, Dos Santos was feted as a guest at the St Petersburg Economic Forum. At this conference, Dos Santos had dinner with Vladimir Putin alongside business leaders from Huawei, Ericsson, Phillips and Siemens, who informed her of the benefits of investing in Russia and she implored the Russian private sector to play a more active role in investing in Angola. Dos Santos's embrace of closer Angola-Russia relations was unsurprising, as she was born in Baku to José dos Santos's Russian-born first wife Tatiana Kukanova and retained her Russian citizenship. Nevertheless, Dos Santos's calls for investment were noteworthy, as she had previously engaged in alarmist rhetoric about the state of Angolan economy under Lourenço. This volte-face potentially reflected her willingness to protect her business interests by becoming an indispensable interlocutor between Russia and Angola.

The mining sector played a key role in strengthening Russia-Angola cooperation after the Sochi Summit. Alrosa was a leading champion of Lourenço's 2019 anti-corruption reforms, which resulted in an end to monopolies for 'privileged companies' in the diamond sector. These reforms resulted in an immediate 30% boost in Catoca's revenues and caused Angola to boost its diamond production target to 14 million carats by 2023. As a result of these successes, Alrosa expanded its commercial presence in Angola. In December 2019, Alrosa Deputy CEO Vladimir Marchenko targeted the production of 1 million diamond carats worth $90 million from the Luaxe deposit by mid-2020.[69] Alrosa also pledged to spend $9 million on diamond exploration in Angola from 2020 to 2022 and claimed that Angola was its number one priority country in Africa. Marchenko's faith in

## RUSSIA BECOMES A CONTINENT-WIDE GREAT POWER

Angola's diamond sector was swiftly vindicated. Angola's production of 3.1 million diamond carats during the first four months of 2021 edged it closer to its production targets and Lourenço's reforms allowed Angola to proceed with a diamond exchange, which will be unveiled at the end of 2021.

### Russia's Post-Coup Relationship with Zimbabwe

As the ZANU-PF maintained its anti-Western posturing and US sanctions remained intact, Russia-Zimbabwe cooperation was not disrupted by Mugabe's overthrow. During Lavrov's visit to Zimbabwe in March 2018, Russia reaffirmed its mining interests and Zimbabwe courted Russian tourists by easing visa restrictions. Russia's pursuit of closer relations with Zimbabwe's post-coup government stemmed from its belief in China and South Africa's potential vulnerability. Academics Andrey Maslov and Vadim Zaytsev warned that China's projects in Zimbabwe could be inflated as Beijing viewed political stability as a precondition for investment and noted that China accounted for just 5–7% of Zimbabwe's export-import market.[70] China's strategic position in Zimbabwe was weakened further by periodic debt disputes, while South Africa's ability to aid Zimbabwe was constrained by its unwillingness to avoid frictions with the US. To capitalize on this perceived opportunity, Russia actively interfered on Mnangagwa's behalf in Zimbabwe's June 2018 elections, which saw the ZANU-PF president narrowly defeat his Movement for Democratic Change (MDC) rival Nelson Chamisa by a 51.44–45.07% margin.

Much like in South Africa, the merits of the Sochi summit divided opinion in Zimbabwe. Callisto Jokonya, the former head of the Zimbabwe National Chamber of Commerce, believed the summit would lead to major new Russia-Zimbabwe mining deals and Mnangagwa's presence in Sochi would prevent Moscow from striking one-sided agreements with Harare. Tendai Biti, the president of the MDC, rejected this notion, as he argued that Russia had repeatedly promised mega-deals since 2017 but never delivered on its promises.[71] Russia sought to assuage these polarizations by emphasizing the synergies between Sochi summit agenda items and

Zimbabwe's interests. In an interview with the *Zimbabwe Herald*, Russian ambassador to Zimbabwe Nikolai Krasilnikov appealed to the ZANU-PF's opposition to neocolonialism by promising a discussion on addressing 'political dictatorship and currency intimidation in international trade and economic cooperation and insisted that the Sochi Summit would rebuke unilateral sanctions.[72] These partisan appeals merely sharpened divisions within Zimbabwe between the pro-Russian ZANU-PF and Russia-sceptic MDC.

The Sochi summit resulted in a significant commercial breakthrough for Russia-Zimbabwe relations, as first Deputy CEO of Vi Holdings, Alexander Ivanov, announced a $500 million investment in Zimbabwe's Darwendale platinum mine in the second quarter of 2020.[73] In the following months, the most significant developments in Russia-Zimbabwe relations occurred in other spheres. In December 2019, Alrosa signed a joint venture agreement with the Zimbabwe Consolidated Diamond Company (ZCDC), which led to $12 million in new investments from 2020 to 2022.[74] These investments would help Zimbabwe triple its diamond production by 2023. These contracts occurred in tandem with speculation about grey zone barter agreements between Russia and Zimbabwe. On 10 January 2020, the *Zimbabwe Independent* revealed that Mnagagwa had plans to fortify Zimbabwe's military through purchases of Russian MiG-29 and MiG-35 jets to replace the Chinese J-7 fighter jets, and his regular visits to Moscow were aimed at creating a minerals-for-arms pact with Russia.[75] These revelations sparked fierce backlash in Zimbabwe, as Mnangagwa was accused of mortgaging its mineral resources to Russia, but the ZANU-PF refused to clarify or dampen the speculation. On 30 January, Tatneft CEO Nail Maganov was reportedly engaging in a fuel-for-mineral exchange with Zimbabwe, which would alleviate the chronic power outages that disrupted Zimbabwe's industrial operations.[76]

*Russia's Inconsistent Partnership with South Africa*

Although Jacob Zuma had strengthened Russia-South Africa relations, his departure was greeted with optimism in Moscow. Vladimir Shubin stated that 'Zuma's departure could create more favourable conditions for the development of ties between South Africa and Russia.' Shubin decried the extremely distorted image of Russia in the South African media, which he believed was exacerbated by the US and Europe's 'malicious and dirty anti-Russian campaign'. Nevertheless, he expressed optimism that Russia-South Africa energy sector cooperation could revive after Zuma's departure.[77] Initial indicators suggested that Shubin's forecast was overly optimistic. Russian media outlets exacerbated tensions between Russia and South Africa with pointed criticisms of the ANC's leadership. During the 2019 South African elections, RT published articles entitled 'South Africa's economic and social decline the worst of nations not at war',[78] and 'As it re-elects hopeless ANC again, do we finally admit that post-apartheid South Africa has failed?'[79] The latter article acknowledged the injustices of the apartheid regime but praised the National Party for leaving 'first-world institutions and systems, from a functional democracy to a competitive industrial base to a free press'.[80] RT also painted the ANC as an extremist organization by showcasing examples of anti-white intolerance in the party, while paying little attention to moderate voices.[81]

Russia's relationship with South Africa was further strained by a spike in pro-Russian sentiments amongst white farmers. These pro-Russian views reflected individual opinions and clashed with the anti-Kremlin sentiments exhibited by the Democratic Alliance Party, which was popular amongst Afrikaners. Rising outbreaks of violence against white farmers, which included 74 murders and 638 attacks from 2016 to 2017, caused some Afrikaners to consider emigration. Cyril Ramaphosa's pledge to reverse apartheid's legacy by redistributing farmland from white to black South Africans accelerated this trend.[82] Some Afrikaner farmers claimed that Ramaphosa's policies would cause inexperienced workers to populate South Africa's agriculture sector and result in production shortages and food price inflation. Russia was initially not the first-choice destination for emigrating Afrikaners, as many wished to migrate to Canada and Australia, but it eventually rose in popularity. In July 2018, a delegation of thirty South African farming families arrived in Stavropol to escape from violence and death threats. These farmers were economically self-sufficient, as they had $500,000 per

RUSSIA IN AFRICA

person to invest, and swiftly grabbed the attention of local officials. Stavropol's Deputy Commissioner of Human Rights Vladimir Poluboyarenko pledged to immediately resettle fifty Boer farming families and claimed that 15,000 Afrikaners wanted to emigrate to Russia.[83] As the Kremlin wished to strengthen its relations with the ANC government, it remained silent on these settlements, and Polyubarenko claimed that he financed trips for South African farmers from his own savings.[84]

Russian state-aligned media outlets extensively covered the emigration of Afrikaner farmers to Russia. This media coverage emphasized Russia's economic opportunity, highlighted Russia as a compassionate conservative society and augmented the Kremlin's ongoing propaganda war over Crimea. RT and Rossiya-1 extolled these developments as a success for Russia's post-2014 policy of handing over 43 million hectares of unused farmland to settlers and hailed the appeal of Stavropol's temperate climate to farmers across the world. *Vzyglad* highlighted Russia's traditional values as a point of attraction for Afrikaner farmers, as Moscow sought to export its brand of conservatism to African countries.[85] Russian media outlets also leveraged testimonies from Afrikaner farmers to challenge the prevailing notion of Russia as an intolerant and xenophobic society. A September 2018 interview with Johannes du Toit, an Afrikaner farmer with a Russian wife who was visiting Kaluga region, exemplified this narrative, as he claimed to feel so at home in Russia that he wished to adopt a Russian name, Ivan Leonovich Varushev.[86] The travels of Afrikaner farmers to Crimea gave the peninsula a rare escape from international isolation. In August 2018, RT reported that Afrikaner farmers wished to emigrate to Crimea and cited Adi Schlebusch, a farmer who called Crimea a 'good option', to justify this story.[87] Omri van Zyl, the CEO of the South African Agricultural Farmers Union AgriSA, pledged to impart his experience with wine making to Crimea and expand the export of tropical fruits, such as mangoes and lychees, to Russia.[88]

Although the vision of some Afrikaners to establish a colony in Russia was unrealistic and the exact number of Afrikaner farmers who emigrated to Russia was never revealed, Moscow struggled to shake off the perception that it was stoking racial tensions in South

## RUSSIA BECOMES A CONTINENT-WIDE GREAT POWER

Africa. As RT's attention to the Afrikaner farmer issue was linked to its empowerment of right-wing populists in the US and had a minimal impact on racial discord within South African society, its long-term impact on Moscow-Pretoria relations was ultimately dissipated. The alleged mistreatment of Afrikaner farmers was largely ignored by Russian state media outlets after the 2019 elections except for its coverage of the 'Boer Lives Matter' movement in October 2020.[89] Even though this information war cooled by mid-2019, it nonetheless constrained the development of Russia-South Africa cooperation. Russia became a domestic political, as well as foreign policy and national security, issue for South African officials, and restricted Ramaphosa's engagement with Moscow. When South Africa supported Venezuela's under-fire President Nicolás Maduro in early 2019, Ramaphosa emphasized that he was supporting state sovereignty rather than aligning with Russia.[90] This underscored that Ramaphosa remained firmly focused on strengthening Pretoria's relationship with China.[91]

To lay the foundations for closer Russia-South Africa relations ahead of the Sochi Summit, Putin met with Ramaphosa on the sidelines of the G20 summit in July 2019. This meeting was seemingly inconsequential, but it fuelled speculation about a new nuclear energy deal with Russia. These rumours reached a fever pitch in August 2019, as South African Mineral Resources and Energy Minister Gwede Mantashe stated that South Africa must plan for a new nuclear energy plant by 2045 to replace its domestically constructed plant in Koeberg near Cape Town.[92] Speculation intensified due to Mantashe's claim that South Africa should purchase a nuclear reactor at the 'pace and scale that it can afford', which mirrored Ramaphosa's spokeswoman's comments on nuclear energy after his meeting with Putin.[93] South Africa's Minister of International Relations and Cooperation Naledi Pandor reassured a domestic audience that he would be negotiating win-win investments ahead of the Sochi Summit, but this did not ease the nuclear deal speculation.[94]

On the first day of the summit, Russia's deployment of two nuclear capable Tupolev Tu-160M2 bombers to Waterkloof Air Force base in Centurion, South Africa dominated the headlines. The Kremlin's justification for this deployment was to strengthen Russia-

183

# RUSSIA IN AFRICA

South Africa air force cooperation and train South African pilots. However, the recent memory of Russia's dispatch of nuclear-capable jets to Venezuela in December 2018 made it a potent political signal.[95] A *Rossiyskaya Gazeta* article entitled 'A Loud Signal' hailed the Tu-160M2 deployment as proof of Russia's ability 'to urgently relocate nuclear assets to theatres of war located far from its own borders'.[96] South African military officials enthusiastically embraced Russia's showmanship, as it cemented South Africa's place as a key nexus for Russian military cooperation with Africa. Deputy Chief of the South African Air Force (SAAF) General Mzayifani Buthelezi claimed that 'Today is a historic day for Africa and for South Africa' and praised Russia's military training programmes for South African cadets, while Spokesperson for the South African Defence Ministry Major Motsamai Mabote called the Tu-160 arrivals a 'premiere for the whole of Africa'.[97] Compared to this historic event, Ramaphosa's participation in the Sochi summit was anti-climactic and widely criticized at home. Ramaphosa was panned in the South African press for apparently sleeping during the conference, which led to criticisms of the extravagant expenditures that accompanied his trip to Russia.[98] Peter Fabricius, a veteran South African foreign affairs journalist who visited Sochi, confirmed that Ramaphosa rejected Putin's offer for a new nuclear energy deal by 'pleading poverty',[99] and no major economic deals were signed between Russia and South Africa.

The Sochi Summit's long-term impacts were also felt most profoundly in the security sphere, as the November 2019 BRICS summit in Brasília was similarly underwhelming for Russia-South Africa economic cooperation. From 24 to 30 November, Russia, China and South Africa participated in their first-ever trilateral naval drills. These drills saw Russia's Marshall Ustinov naval cruiser establish inter-operability with South Africa's SAS Amatola frigate.[100] In contrast to the Tu-160 deployment, both Russia and South Africa skirted this drill's implications for bilateral security cooperation. Ramaphosa denied that the Tu-160 arrival and naval drills with Russia were timed together to highlight a South Africa-Russia military partnership, and Darren Olivier, a director of South Africa's African Defence Review, emphasized the South African

184

## RUSSIA BECOMES A CONTINENT-WIDE GREAT POWER

navy's core alignment with NATO.[101] Russian defence experts, such as Captain Vasily Dandykin, attributed these drills to Putin's calls for greater military integration between BRICS countries, and argued that Russia wanted to show that it could coordinate with China anywhere in the world.[102] South African officials were sceptical of BRICS cooperation arguments for these drills. Peter Fabricius noted that BRICS military cooperation was unrealistic due to China-India tensions, and Brazilian President Jair Bolsonaro's pro-US stance.[103] Steve Gruzd, head of African Governance and Diplomacy Programme at SAIIA, argues that these drills reflected South Africa's 'blue economy' ambitions, which require expanded naval reach, and growing attention to Indian Ocean security, which was illustrated by South Africa's active participation in the Indian Ocean Rim Association.[104]

### Russia Deepens Its Footprint in West Africa

Although Russia had asserted its opinions on insurgencies and extremism in West Africa, Moscow's influence in the region suffered from underdevelopment. Ahead of the Sochi Summit, Russia and Nigeria sought to upgrade their bilateral partnership. Initially, it appeared as if Russia-Nigeria security cooperation would take centre stage in Sochi. On 11 October, Nigeria's Ambassador to Russia, Steve Ugbah, announced plans to sign a military-technical cooperation deal with Moscow, and confidently predicted 'We're sure that with Russian help, we'll manage to crush Boko Haram, given Russia's experience combatting the Islamic State in Syria.'[105] This military cooperation agreement was not ratified until August 2021, but Russia agreed to sell twelve Mi-35 attack helicopters to Nigeria in Sochi. Nigeria also assiduously courted commercial links with Russia. At the St Petersburg Economic Forum, Olusegun Obasanjo made a full-throated pitch for expanded Russia-Nigeria economic cooperation. Obasanjo highlighted the deficit of Russian companies operating in Nigeria, which persisted despite the 78% increase in bilateral trade that was recorded in 2018.[106] Putin presented a higher 93% trade growth figure between Russia and Nigeria at the Sochi Summit, but also stated that it was below-potential. After meeting with Putin,

185

Muhammadu Buhari effusively praised Russia's economic model.[107] Buhari claimed that there were 'many similarities' between Russia's economic trajectory under Putin's leadership and Nigeria's hopes for the future. Buhari argued that Russia had transformed from an 'oil-dependent economy to a modern, diversified and inclusive economy', converted state-owned companies into well-known commercial brands through privatization and made considerable strides in light industry development.

During the two-day conference, Russia signed a total of thirteen economic agreements with Nigeria.[108] Two significant agreements were struck in the energy sector, as Lukoil signed an MOU with NNPC to overhaul Nigeria's non-functioning refineries. After striking this agreement with NNPC, Lukoil described West Africa as a 'priority region' and appointed a Vice President to oversee its projects in Sub-Saharan Africa, which also included investments in Cameroon, Ghana and Congo.[109] Although Russia framed itself as a partner that could facilitate economic diversification in Nigeria, its non-oil investment pledges fell short of the lofty promises at the Sochi Summit. The gap between rhetorical pledges and implemented contracts was especially stark in the infrastructure, steel manufacturing and nuclear energy sectors. The MOU between Russian Railways and Nigeria's Ministry of Transport, which laid the groundwork for Russian investment in the Lagos-Calabar coastal line and Harcourt-Maiduguri railway project, stalled. Olawale Rasheed, CEO of African Railway Consulting LImited, noted that none of the Sochi Summit projects came to fruition, as China took over these rail-lines.[110] Rasheed stated that Russian railway giant Transmashholding is preoccupied with projects in South Africa and Egypt, and often ignores Nigeria. Rasheed states that Russia's reticence about government-to-government contracts, which China uses for infrastructure investments, and reliance on funds from fickle financial institutions, such as Afrexim bank, underscores Moscow's unwillingness to divert large-scale capital into Nigeria's railways. Rasheed contends that Russia-Nigeria relations are undergirded by Western-style collaborative projects, such as military, science and health cooperation, rather than Chinese-style capital-intensive infrastructure projects.

## RUSSIA BECOMES A CONTINENT-WIDE GREAT POWER

Due to its notorious association with Nigerian state corruption, Putin and Buhari's pledge to revitalize the Ajaokuta steel mill attracted widespread attention. Ajaokuta was a Soviet-era project, which was unveiled by Leonid Brezhnev and then-President Shehu Shagari in 1979 but had failed to produce any steel despite $1 billion in investments.[111] The USSR abandoned Ajaokuta in the 1980s, as the Nigerian government did not pay the Tyazhpromexport construction company on schedule. While Russian engineers carried out a 'technical audit' of Ajaokuta in July 2020 and Moscow pledged to revive the steel mill in July 2021, progress flatlined. Rosatom's nuclear energy ambitions in Nigeria experienced similar roadblocks. In November 2019, the Nigerian Senate passed a resolution urging Buhari to consider nuclear energy and asked him to grant the Nigerian Atomic Energy Commission a mandate to engage in talks with nuclear energy providers.[112] As Rosatom had negotiated with Nigeria since 2009 and signed agreements in 2016 and 2017, which created four nuclear power plants, its plan to construct a $20 billion 4,800 MW reactor by 2035 was at the top of the queue. Rosatom viewed this Senate resolution with cautious optimism. Although the Nigerian Atomic Energy Commission was formed in 1976, its claims that nuclear energy would lead to 'industrialization, shared prosperity and poverty eradication' received little executive branch or public support prior to this resolution. Nigeria's intensified pursuit of Rosatom's nuclear reactor project proved to be a mirage, as it failed to gain traction in the succeeding months.

Aside from Guinea, which will be discussed in the next chapter, Russia's partnerships with other West African countries did not gain serious traction either in the lead-up to or during the Sochi Summit. Russia pinned its hopes on an expansion of cooperation with Côte d'Ivoire, which proved elusive. At the 2019 St Petersburg Economic Forum, Côte d'Ivoire's Vice President Daniel Kablan Duncan expressed interest in Russian investment in capital-intensive deep-seat natural gas projects, which were 3,000 metres below sea level.[113] Alassane Ouattara's attendance at the Sochi Summit was the first visit to Russia by an Ivorian president, and optimism grew about a potential Russian military cooperation deal with Côte d'Ivoire. However, Russia and Côte d'Ivoire did not achieve significant breakthroughs in

187

the natural gas or military cooperation spheres. In June 2019, *Vzyglad* reported that Russia was on the cusp of deploying PMCs to Guinea-Bissau, which would be aimed at combatting the country's role as a trans-shipment point for Latin American cocaine.[114] Talks between Sergei Shoigu and Guinea-Bissau's Defence Minister Eduardo Sanya gained little traction, and this plan was shelved. In June 2019, Russia signed a military cooperation agreement with Mali, which was inked by Generals Ibrahim Dahirou Dembele and Sergei Shoigu.[115] This agreement would lead to the renovation of both Mi-35 fighter jets and Mali's aircraft but did not lead to counterterrorism assistance.

## *A Resurgent Russia in the Red Sea Region*

Russia also expanded its influence in the Red Sea region, which was previously confined to arms sales and open-ended discussions about security assistance. On 18 April, *The Sun* published a bombshell story warning that Russia had plans to establish a 1,500-person naval base in Somaliland to 'support its warships and hunter-killer submarines'. Russia's proposed base was planned for Zeila, which is near the Somaliland-Djibouti border. This facility would complement the UAE's base in Berbera and allow Russia to expand its access to the Suez Canal, as this trade route was located near northern Somalia. While this story was greeted with a mixture of alarm and scepticism in the US and Europe, it was covered in some Russian media outlets. Lenta.ru reported that an employee of the Russian embassy in Djibouti visited Somaliland in 2017 and devised a plan for a dual-purpose naval and air base in Zeila.[116] This Zeila base would have the capacity to include two destroyers, four frigates and two submarines, as well as two runways that would include six military transport aircraft and fifteen fighter jets. While Russia's basing negotiations in Somaliland ultimately did not gain traction, the story catapulted Moscow's ambitions in the Red Sea region to the forefront of the minds of Western officials.

In March 2018, Sergei Lavrov met with Ethiopian Prime Minister Hailemariam Desalegn in Addis Ababa. This meeting coincided with Russia's cancellation of $162 million in Soviet-era Ethiopian debt and Lavrov's request for Russian membership in the African Union's

## RUSSIA BECOMES A CONTINENT-WIDE GREAT POWER

Mechanism for Police Cooperation (AFRIPOL), which appealed to Ethiopia's regional power status.[117] These symbolic gestures, while significant, were overshadowed by discussions on Russia-Ethiopia nuclear energy cooperation. Ethiopia wished to expand its electricity capacity generation from 4,200 MW to 37,000 MW by 2037 and explored hydroelectricity, geothermal, nuclear, solar and wind energy projects.[118] The Grand Ethiopian Renaissance Dam (GERD) undergirded Ethiopia's energy plans, as it would produce 6,000 MW over a four-year period, but frequent droughts underscored the perils of overdependence on hydroelectric power.[119] To steer it away from overreliance on the GERD, Russia struck a nuclear energy cooperation agreement with Ethiopia during Lavrov's March 2018 trip. This pact did not immediately expand Russia's presence in Ethiopia's energy sector, but it was a triumph for Russian educational diplomacy in Africa. Ethiopian Ambassador to Russia Grum Teshome enthusiastically championed Rosatom scholarships for aspiring Ethiopian engineers, as he was one of 24,000 Ethiopian students who benefited from Soviet scholarships to study in Chisinau and Leningrad during the 1980s.[120]

Russia's partnerships with the Red Sea region's economically isolated countries, South Sudan and Eritrea, also witnessed significant breakthroughs. Russia viewed the August 2018 reconciliation and division of powers agreement in South Sudan as a greenlight for investment. On November 2018, Zarubezhneft signed an MOU with South Sudan to explore four of the country's largest oil blocks.[121] This contract inserted Russia as a major player in South Sudan's oil market, which was dominated by countries from the Indo-Pacific region like China, India and Malaysia. This agreement would help South Sudan reach its 200,000-bpd oil production target, and defied IMF recommendations urging Juba to avoid replicating its oil-for-loans deals with China to other countries. To express solidarity with South Sudan in this tumultuous period, Russia defended the Khartoum reconciliation agreement against international criticism and made South Sudan a theatre of its traditional values-based outreaches to African countries. In March 2019, Russia abstained from a US-drafted resolution urging the South Sudan authorities to advance the cause of peace. Russia's Deputy UN Ambassador Dmitry

189

RUSSIA IN AFRICA

Polyanskiy justified this position by accusing the US of not upholding the Khartoum reconciliation agreement and prioritizing gender and human rights over the peace deal's implementation.[122] As China voted for the US-backed resolution, Russia was able to highlight itself as an exceptionally loyal partner to South Sudan and concomitantly strengthen its relationship with Uganda, which helped broker the Khartoum Agreement.

Russia also opposed the continued imposition of UN sanctions against Eritrea. These sanctions were renewed due to Eritrea's alleged support for al-Shabaab, border dispute with Djibouti and insufficient cooperation with the UNSC monitoring group. Russia was especially frustrated by the UNSC's removal of the caveat that there was no recent evidence for Eritrea's support for al-Shabaab. In November 2017, Vasily Nebenzia, Permanent Representative of Russia to the UN, insisted that Eritrea should not be penalized for supporting armed groups, as all other countries in the region had links to militant organizations and claimed that there was no evidence of Eritrea's support for al-Shabaab since 2013.[123] Nebenzia also decried the sanctions regime as 'anti-Eritrean' and called for their phased removal. Russia's stance was praised in Egypt, which had tried to insert a clause praising Eritrea's counterterrorism role, and also paved the way for stronger relations between Moscow and Asmara. Eritrean analyst Abdul Qadir Muhammad Ali described the Russia-Eritrea partnership as a 'relationship of mutual need', as Eritrea felt targeted by the West, while Russia needed a friend in the strategic southern Red Sea region, Bab el-Mandeb Strait and Horn of Africa.[124] This alliance of necessity gained immediate momentum after the July 2018 Ethiopia-Eritrea peace agreement, which paved the way for Eritrea's exit from international isolation. In August 2018, Lavrov visited Eritrea to discuss the construction of a planned logistics centre. This logistics centre was framed in strictly economic terms, as Lavrov stated that it would facilitate the development of trade between Russia and Eritrea.[125] Economic relations between Russia and Eritrea were marginal, and the only notable project on the horizon was EuroChem's June 2018 take-or-pay offtake agreement in Eritrea's potash industry. However, Russian Ambassador to Eritrea Azim Yarakhmedov mused about the creation of 'new transport

190

## RUSSIA BECOMES A CONTINENT-WIDE GREAT POWER

corridors' in Eritrea, which would lead to 'economic integration in the Horn of Africa'.[126]

Russia's rapid expansion of trade relations with Eritrea had broader strategic designs. As the UAE's military presence in Assab depended on the continuation of the Yemen war, Russia viewed this logistics facility as a gateway to uncontested long-term access to Massawa and Assab, which were key Red Sea ports. As Ethiopia targeted access to similar ports, Russia's combination of a presence in Eritrea and military cooperation with Ethiopia would have reciprocal benefits for its relationship with Addis Ababa. Due to these possibilities, prominent US diplomats, such as former Assistant Secretary of State for African Affairs (1989–93) Herman Cohen, urged the US and France to sign new commercial deals with Eritrea to counter Russia's moves.[127] Ultimately, Russia's logistics facility negotiations stagnated, and Moscow's first-mover advantage was diluted. After the Ethiopia-Eritrea peace agreement of July 2018, Afewerki held high-level meetings with delegations from Saudi Arabia, the UAE, Somalia, South Sudan, Germany and Japan, and China presided over the removal of UN sanctions in November 2018. Nevertheless, Eritreans hailed Russia for being the first great power to oppose these punitive measures and Moscow leveraged this momentum during the Sochi Summit and COVID-19 pandemic.

The Sochi Summit did not result in major breakthroughs for Russia's geopolitical standing in the Red Sea and Horn of Africa. However, it allowed Russia to position itself as a potential mediator in the GERD dispute between Egypt, Sudan and Ethiopia. Although the GERD dispute had been a point of contention in the Egypt-Ethiopia relationship since 2011, Russia obscured its official position on the Nile dam issue. A RIAC report of October 2017 highlighted the ambiguities in the Russian expert community's views on the GERD dispute.[128] On the one hand, it argued that the GERD threatened Egypt's 'inviolable right to the water resources of the Nile River' and accused Ethiopia of capitalizing on post-Arab Spring turmoil in Egypt and South Sudan's secession. On the other hand, it defended Ethiopia against Egypt's claims that it violated international law, as it argued that the Watercourses Convention was not universally accepted. At the Sochi Summit, Putin capitalized on Russia's

191

ambiguous and even-handed position on the GERD dispute by raising the issue with Sisi and Ahmed and offering 'assistance' to talks between both leaders. Tarek Fahmy, an academic at the American University in Cairo, praised Russia as a 'real mediator' between Egypt and Ethiopia, and expressed optimism that Moscow would be able to facilitate common ground between the two countries on the GERD.[129] Although Sisi and Ahmed met at the sidelines of the Sochi Summit, Russia's diplomatic efforts were overshadowed by a concurrent US offer to facilitate dialogue between Egypt, Ethiopia and Sudan. Russia swiftly returned to the peripheries of the GERD issue and, much to Egypt's chagrin, became a champion of Ethiopia's AU-led approach.

### Russia's Great Power Reassertion in Central and Eastern Africa

Except for Russia's stop-start commercial engagement with Uganda and dramatic entry into CAR, Moscow remained a peripheral player in Central and Eastern Africa. As the Sochi Summit neared, Russia tried to rectify its marginalization from these regions, as part of its broader goal of becoming a continent-wide great power. Russia continued its humanitarian activities in the region, as it deployed fifty-three KAMAZ trucks to Mombasa, Kenya and aided WFP initiatives in Kampala, Uganda.[130] Russia also provided medical assistance during the Ebola epidemic, which foreshadowed its distribution of COVID-19 vaccines. However, Russian officials also strengthened their personal bonds with officials in both regions and leveraged nuclear energy diplomacy and security agreements to expand Moscow's presence. Russia's influence expansion efforts yielded mixed results and, overall, lagged Moscow's breakthroughs in the Horn of Africa and the Sahel. Russia's relationships with Kenya, Tanzania and Cameroon experienced largely symbolic advancements. Russia's partnerships with the DRC, Rwanda, the Republic of Congo, Uganda and Gabon gained notable traction, but the COVID-19 pandemic raised doubts about the durability of these improvements.

Vladimir Putin and Kenya's President Uhuru Kenyatta discussed commercial opportunities and unveiled a Russia-Kenya business

## RUSSIA BECOMES A CONTINENT-WIDE GREAT POWER

council at the Sochi Summit, but Moscow-Nairobi commercial relations did not appreciably strengthen. Russian Minister of Trade and Industry Denis Manturov expressed hope that Tanzania could serve as Russia's springboard into East Africa.[131] Russia's strategic interest in Tanzania was also linked to its standing as a theatre of geopolitical contestation with France. In May 2010, French nuclear energy giant Areva expressed interest in investing in Tanzania's $4 billion uranium oxide reserves, and it became the front-runner to fulfill Tanzania's ambitions of constructing a nuclear reactor by 2025. In November 2016, Rosatom subsidiary Uranium One upended Areva's ambitions, as it was granted a permit to extract uranium in the Mkuju River in Selous Game Reserve and announced plans to produce uranium in 2018.[132] Aside from this project, Russia's investments in Tanzania were peripheral. Although Cameroon was one of the first African countries to engage with Russia on counterterrorism, Moscow did not rush to its defence on the Anglophone crisis. Instead, Russia signalled its willingness to block UN resolutions that criticized Cameroon on the grounds of non-interference,[133] while still expressing discontent with President Paul Biya's handling of the crisis. Although Biya did not attend the Sochi Summit, Russian and Cameroonian officials held discussions about reconstructing national refining company Sonara, which was destroyed in May 2019 in a fire. Russia's willingness to help reconstruct Sonara, which was evidenced by the arrival of a Lukoil delegation in February 2020, was hailed in Cameroon, as the destruction of four of its production units forced Cameroon to purchase almost all of its refined petroleum.[134]

After nearly two decades of detachment from its security crises, Russia's growing assertiveness in CAR spilt over to the DRC. Prominent Russian and Congolese political figures have presented a mixed view of the current state of Russia-DRC relations. At the Sochi Summit, Putin described the DRC as one of 'Russia's most promising partners in Africa'.[135] In February 2020, Russian Ambassador to the DRC, Alexei Sentebov, quipped that on the sixtieth anniversary of our bilateral relationship, 'we still do not know each other' and blamed Mobutu's pro-Western policies for this predicament.[136] China's growing frustrations with Joseph Kabila's idiosyncratic policies and personalist rule prompted Kinshasa to seek out alternative partners, such as Russia. Congolese opposition leader United Congolese Party President Christian Malanga welcomed Russia's resurgence, stating in May 2019 that 'This is Cold War 2.0', and asserting that 'China is money, and Russia is muscle.'[137] Martin Fayulu, an opposition candidate in the December 2018 elections, highlighted the exploitative character of Russian policy in the DRC, stating 'It's not surprising that Russia is moving into Congo, given our vast mineral wealth.'[138] In October 2018, Congolese newspaper *Le Fontenil* accused Russia of moving military equipment to the DRC to violate its sovereignty and influence the election results in favour of Kabila's hand-picked successor.[139]

Despite this ambiguous rhetoric, the Russia-DRC relationship has strengthened due to Moscow's growing interest in the DRC's economic development, tighter Russia-DRC security cooperation and strengthening political ties. Sergey Sukhankin, a senior fellow at the Jamestown Foundation, noted that Russia and the DRC both emphasized win-win economic cooperation at the Sochi Summit. Putin's castigation of the 'unjust redistribution of profits coming from the exploitation of local natural resources' mirrored DRC President Félix Tshisekedi's condemnation of profit-seeking practices by foreign companies.[140] Russia has growing commercial interests in the DRC's mining and energy sectors. In an April 2019 *Izvestia* interview, DRC Foreign Minister Leonard Okitundu extolled the value of Russian technical expertise in allowing the DRC to profit from its uranium, malachite, gold and columbite-tantalite reserves.[141] While Russia has been tight-lipped about prospective contracts in the DRC, the deaths of two Russian pilots in the mineral-rich Maniema province and rumours that Yevgeny Prigozhin was on board this flight have attracted speculation.[142] Russia has also pursued investments outside of the mining sector to live up to Putin and Tshisedeki's pledges. In 2019, the AU also offered Russia a lead role in developing the Grand Inga Dam, which costs $14 billion and will be the largest hydropower project in the world.

While Okitundu categorically ruled out the erection of a Russian military base in the DRC, he nevertheless praised Russia as an ally in the security sphere.[143] As France, Belgium and the US confined their security assistance to the DRC to military training, Russia pursued

## RUSSIA BECOMES A CONTINENT-WIDE GREAT POWER

a more expansive military-technical agreement with Kinshasa in June 2018.[144] Congolese Minister of Defence Crispin Tabe praised Russia's willingness to provide military equipment to the DRC as a sign of Moscow's commitment to Congolese sovereignty. While Russia-DRC arms sales are yet to be confirmed, Kabila's elevation of a trusted retired general as ambassador to Russia fuelled rumours of imminent contracts.[145] Russia also supported the legitimacy of the controversial December 2018 DRC elections, which resulted in Félix Tshisekedi's triumph. Mikhail Bogdanov hailed the elections as a 'milestone in the gradual normalization of the situation in this important African country', which contrasted with the AU's open scepticism about the results and the EU's neutral statement.[146] The DRC returned the favour by holding parades to commemorate the Soviet triumph over Nazism and legitimizing Russia's extra-legal actions in Ukraine. A Luhansk People's Republic cultural representation office surfaced in Kolwezi, which is near the DRC's Musonoi mine, and a DRC delegation attended the 2019 Yalta Economic Forum in annexed Crimea.[147] This broadened the array of local partnerships between Russian and Congolese officials, as Mikhail Bogdanov and the Russia-DRC Friendship Group, which was established in 2017, were the main bridges between Moscow and Kinshasa.[148]

Russia's relationship with Rwanda strengthened after Paul Kagame visited Moscow for the 2018 World Cup opening ceremony and Sergei Lavrov travelled to Kigali in June 2018. Prior to these visits, Russia-Rwanda cooperation was limited. Russia aided Rwanda's discovery of mineral deposits, but their $100 million trade volume was almost exclusively confined to military equipment and Russian Joint Stock Company Goznak's deal to print Rwandan banknotes. Both countries signed a security cooperation agreement in October 2016, but Lavrov's decision to visit Rwanda ahead of the 2018 BRICS summit was intriguing. Dmitry Bondarenko, an Africa specialist at Moscow's HSE, explained Lavrov's visit by noting Rwanda's efforts to present itself as an 'exemplary African country' on the world stage.[149] After visiting the Rwandan Genocide memorial, Lavrov praised Rwanda's leader, stating 'What President Paul Kagame is doing to strengthen interethnic peace and harmony in his country is invaluable.'[150] Russia's desire to promote Rwanda

195

as an effective illiberal governance model in Africa contrasted with US criticisms of Kagame's authoritarian policies. It also paved the way for deeper commercial ties between Russia and Rwanda. At the Sochi Summit, Russia announced that it would sign a deal to produce a nuclear science research centre in Rwanda, which would lead to the production of radioisotopes for agricultural purposes and the construction of a 10 MW reactor.[151]

Russia also revived its historic partnership with the Republic of Congo. Due to the Congo's socialist orientation from 1963 to 1992, the USSR invested considerably in the country, but the ascension of pro-Western Pascal Lissouba in August 1992 strained bilateral relations. President Denis Sassou Nguesso's rise to power in 1997 changed this dynamic, and as AU chairman, he participated in the G8 summit in St Petersburg in 2006. Bilateral dialogue became more frequent, as Vladimir Putin met with Nguesso in November 2012; Congolese Foreign Minister Jean-Claude Gacosso made two visits to Russia in 2017, and Mikhail Bogdanov visited Congo in 2012, 2013 and 2015.[152] Despite a provisional 2012 agreement to construct a 1,334 km Pointe Noire–Ouesso pipeline, bilateral trade was just $38.4 million in 2018. Given these erstwhile stagnant dynamics, 2019 was a break-out year for Russia-Congo relations. In May 2019, Nguesso signed a security agreement with Vladimir Putin, which would allow Russian military specialists to service Congo's military hardware.[153] While Press Secretary Dmitry Peskov did not categorically answer whether these Russian specialists were government-aligned or PMCs, this agreement meant that Congo was the second country after Sudan to have a Kremlin-confirmed military presence in Africa. At the Sochi Summit, Russian state development bank VEB signed a MOU to invest in the Pointe Noire pipeline project, which would allow for three years of construction and at least forty years of operations. This pipeline would alleviate Central Africa's affordable energy shortages and make Congo a supply nexus for oil shipments to DR Congo and CAR.[154] In December 2019, Russia's Deputy Energy Minister Pavel Sorokin stated that TMK and Congo's national oil company SNPC would proceed on the pipeline construction, while Almaz Antey would supply arms to Congo and explore nuclear energy opportunities.[155]

## RUSSIA BECOMES A CONTINENT-WIDE GREAT POWER

Russia's relationships with Uganda and Gabon also experienced notable improvements. In September 2019, Russia and Uganda signed a nuclear energy cooperation agreement. This deal was an unexpected coup for Rosatom, as the China National Nuclear Corporation (CNNC) had an extant May 2018 agreement with Uganda, and was primed to spearhead Museveni's quest for nuclear power. Museveni was alarmed by CNNC's hurried approach to nuclear energy development, which included intense lobbying of Ugandan officials, and ultimately viewed Rosatom as a preferrable option.[156] While the scope of Uganda's uranium deposits are unclear and western Uganda's 6 billion barrels of oil will dominate its energy needs from 2022, this agreement had a powerful symbolic impact on Moscow-Kampala relations.[157] At the Sochi Summit, Uganda joined Angola as an African partner in Russia's space science development, and sought to cooperate with Gazprom and Aksioma in this sphere. In November 2019, Russia shipped small arms to Gabon to confront wildlife poaching. These arms transfers, which were the first in the history of Russia-Gabon relations, built on a military-technical agreement in 2002 and underscored Moscow's desire to cooperate with African countries on environmental issues.[158] The emergence of cooperation between Russia and Africa on post-material issues provided context for Moscow's coordination with African countries against COVID-19. The diversification of Russia's collaboration with African countries defied sceptical perspectives in the US, Europe and China, and facilitated the deepening of Moscow's great power status during Putin's fourth term.

# 7

# RUSSIA'S NEW POWER PROJECTION TACTICS IN AFRICA

While the Sochi Summit highlighted Russia's geopolitical ambitions and commercial presence in Africa, it failed to shed light on Moscow's shadowy array of power projection tools. Since 2017, Russia has carried out hybrid interventions in African countries, which are aimed at securing commercial profits, outbidding rival great powers for geostrategic influence, securing the futures of its authoritarian allies, and burnishing its image as a counterinsurgency partner. These interventions have resulted in varying degrees of success. In Guinea and the Central African Republic, Russia successfully secured preferential access to strategically valuable mineral deposits, while propping up friendly authoritarian regimes. In Libya and Sudan, Russia achieved tactical successes, and secured positions of leverage but did not see its preferred political actors emerge triumphant. In Madagascar and Mozambique, Russia's hybrid interventions failed spectacularly, and Moscow's prestige in both countries has been damaged. This chapter will analyze Russia's six major hybrid interventions in Africa from 2018 to 2020. The chapter analyzes the tactics that Russia used and the objectives it pursued and explains the role of domestic actors and systemic constraints in determining these outcomes.

Before examining Russia's hybrid interventions in Africa, its preferred tactics should be briefly articulated. Russia's hybrid interventions are carried out by a diverse array of state and independent state-aligned actors. Russia has deployed private military contractors, which carry out deniable operations at the Kremlin's behest in African theatres. These PMCs are involved in guarding stationary commercial assets but also carry out forward counterterrorism and offensive military operations. The dominant private military company is the Wagner Group, which is overseen by Yevgeny Prigozhin, but other PMC operators, such as Shield, and Patriot continue to ply their trade. Russia has also deployed political technologists to spread disinformation in target countries and influence the results of national elections. Above the radar, Russia has used state-owned companies and surrogate businessmen to advance Moscow's economic interest.

## Russia's Hybrid Intervention in Guinea

While Russia's hybrid intervention in Guinea looks like a textbook case of autocracy promotion, it has three dimensions that should be unpacked. First, Russia has established a foothold in Guinea's vast mineral reserves, which provide it with one-third of its economic revenues. Russia has not secured a hegemonic position in Guinea's economy, as China signed a $20 billion infrastructure-for-minerals deal in 2017 and has three companies with bauxite concessions. However, it has witnessed a dramatic increase in its commercial clout due to its close alignment with President Alpha Condé. Amadou Bah, the executive director of Action Mines, contends that Russia has created an oligarchy that wields 'considerable weight in the political and economic affairs' of Guinea.[1] Russian investors have forced Condé to rescind reforms of the conduct of mining companies, such as tax increases and new environmental protections, and stymied the flow of revenues to communities surrounding aluminium and gold mines.[2] While the Kremlin is more vested in autocracy promotion than Guinean companies, Condé has awarded Rusal opaque contracts that last until 2050.

In June 2018, Rusal began shipping bauxite from Guinea's Dian-Dian mine to aluminium refineries across the globe. As the Dian-

## RUSSIA'S NEW POWER PROJECTION TACTICS IN AFRICA

Dian mine has the world's largest bauxite deposits and Guinea possesses 27% of the world's bauxite, Rusal's entry into the Guinean market was a significant coup for Russian mining companies.[3] This deal also demonstrated Rusal's continued clout in international aluminium markets, as its co-owner Oleg Deripaska was sanctioned by the United States in April 2018. Sanctions against Deripaska complicated Rusal's ability to purchase aluminium at affordable prices in the open markets, but Guinea's long-standing cooperation with Rusal, which dated back to 2001, and closer relations with Russia gave it crucial respite.[4] Speaker of the State Duma Vyacheslav Volodin's June 2018 visit to Guinea underscored the Dian-Dian deal's strategic importance and allowed Russia to showcase its commitment to Guinea's economic development. To express his support for the Russia-Guinea partnership, Claude Kondiano, the president of Guinea's National Assembly, boasted that Rusal was embarking on a 'gigantic project that will make all our new friends envious' and openly courted Russian support for Guinea's education system.[5] Nordgold has also emerged as a valuable surrogate for Russia's commercial interests in Guinea. In 2010, Nordgold acquired Guinea's Lefa gold mine and over the past decade, it has invested $1 billion in these deposits. Nordgold's investments have had constructive economic consequences, as the gold company employs 1,200 Guinean workers, and has spearheaded the creation of forty schools and medical facilities that have aided the struggle against Ebola.[6]

Second, Russia has engaged in autocracy promotion, as it has tied its interests to the survival of the existing regime. Alpha Condé's controversial quest for a third term handed Russia an opportunity to upgrade a key partnership in West Africa. In January 2019, Russian Ambassador to Guinea Alexander Bregadze hailed Condé as 'legendary' and endorsed his proposed term extension by stating that 'Constitutions are no dogma, Bible or Koran. It's constitutions that adapt to reality, not realities that adapt to constitutions.'[7] Bregadze also supported Condé's economic rationale for staying in power by presenting exaggerated economic growth statistics and dubiously claiming that Guinea was on course to become 'the most electrified country in Africa'. These claims were widely panned by

201

Guinean civil society and opposition figures. Cellou Dalein Diallo, a Guinean opposition leader, claimed that Bregadze was being manipulated by Condé and praised Russia's role in decolonization and supporting non-interference in the internal affairs of states. Gabriel Haba, the President of the Civil Action Brigade, was much more stridently critical of Bregadze, and openly accused Russia of interference in Guinea's internal affairs.[8] A coalition of Guinean civil society activists proposed holding a sit-in in front of the Russian embassy in Conakry to protest Bregadze's comments. These anti-Russian sentiments intensified after Bregadze became the head of Rusal's Guinea operations following his departure as ambassador in May 2019.

Third, Russia has deepened its informal security links with Guinea, which includes the deployment of PMCs. In April 2018, Russia-Guinea security ties surged to its highest level since the end of the Cold War with the ratification of an intergovernmental military cooperation agreement. Guinea's switch from supporting to abstaining from UN resolutions criticizing Russian conduct in Ukraine and refusal to endorse a UN resolution on refugees in Abkhazia and South Ossetia resulted in the expansion of Russia-Guinea military cooperation.[9] Russia's below-the-radar security cooperation with Guinea was even more consequential. Condé solicited Wagner Group assistance in strengthening his regime's security organs and allowed PMCs to guard Rusal's investments in Guinea. The terms of these PMC deployments are unclear, but they have allowed Moscow to ensconce Guinea as its strongest West African partner.

## Russia's Hybrid Intervention in the Central African Republic

During the first eighteen months of Putin's fourth term, Russia established itself as CAR's primary security partner, and converted its military presence into diplomatic influence and lucrative forays in CAR's vast mineral reserves. In March 2018, Touadéra appointed retired GRU official Valery Zakharov as CAR's national security advisor. Zakharov's arrival resulted in the immediate expansion of Russia's military presence in CAR. In addition to the transfer

# RUSSIA'S NEW POWER PROJECTION TACTICS IN AFRICA

of nine tranches of Russian military equipment, Russia deployed 255 civilian advisors to CAR along with an undisclosed number of military instructors.[10] These Russian PMC deployments were officially tasked with rebuilding the CAR's armed forces, and in October 2018, Vasily Nebenzia praised Russia's role in training 1,000 CAR military personnel.[11] However, the responsibilities of Russian PMCs swiftly extended beyond their military training mandate. At the football stadium ceremony celebrating the second anniversary of Touadéra's ascension to power, Wagner Group PMCs guarded the president and gained complete access to his meeting schedule. Rwandan MINUSCA bodyguards, who had previously protected Touadéra, were subsequently reassigned to parking lots and the Berengo Palace's doors.[12]

This narrative defending Wagner Group PMC deployments became an increasingly hard sell to the international community and Russian liberals. In July 2018, *Novaya Gazeta* war correspondent Orkhan Djemal, opposition film-maker Alexander Rastorguev and photographer Kirill Radchenko were murdered while conducting research on the Wagner Group's activities in CAR. The murders occurred in Sibut, which is 300 km north of Bangui, and followed a protracted ambush of the Russian journalists. Dissident oligarch Mikhail Khodorkovsky dismissed the notion that these journalists were killed in a standard robbery. He stated that Wagner Group-aligned figures tried to block the journalists from visiting the area where they were murdered.[13] Khodorkovsky also accused the CAR authorities of hiding the local driver, whose life was spared during the ambush. The findings of a Dossier Project investigation, which were published by *Novaya Gazeta* in January 2019, revealed damning evidence.[14]

The deaths of the three journalists and these subsequent revelations triggered Western media condemnations of the Wagner Group and caused Russian liberals to raise critical questions about Russia's involvement in CAR. The Kremlin responded to these criticisms by advancing a counter-programming narrative, which whitewashed the Wagner Group's role in CAR. The Russian MFA insisted that the three men were tourists in CAR and placed the burden of culpability on the CAR law enforcement, which they described as 'not

203

functioning'.[15] Russian state-aligned media outlets gagged coverage of their research on the Wagner Group.[16] Russian officials and experts emphasized the constructive role of Russian PMCs in CAR. Nebenzia repeatedly highlighted the humanitarian responsibilities of Russian forces, which included provisions of medical treatment. Sputnik reported that Russia had dispatched a convoy with twenty trucks loaded with medical supplies to local hospitals,[17] while Kirill Romanovsky claimed that his visit to CAR was linked to a ceremony to unveil humanitarian aid deliveries. In October 2018, a Carnegie Moscow Center report contended these responsibilities aligned with Russia's 'African solutions to African problems' mantra, as Moscow was providing security in a transactional fashion that did not compromise the political or economic sovereignty of states.[18] The CAR turned to Russia, as it was disillusioned with France and spent more than its GDP on UN-provided security forces with few results. Russian PMCs cost an estimated seventy to eighty times less than the UN security forces and provided greater security benefits.

To secure new mining concessions in rebel-held areas and ensure that its influence in CAR was not Touadéra-dependent, Russia expanded its diplomatic presence in CAR. In May 2018, anonymous sources within the CAR rebels claimed that they were approached by 'Russian figures', who wished to broker a peace agreement between themselves and the CAR government.[19] The Russian interlocutors also reached out to Touadéra, but the Bangui authorities rejected their overtures. A former CAR parliamentarian stated that Touadéra's rejection of Russian diplomatic assistance in CAR can be explained by two factors.[20] First, some members of Touadéra's inner circle were convinced that the ex-Seleka rebels and their allies could only be defeated through military means. While this contradicted Touadéra's rhetoric that an inter-ethnic settlement was necessary, it influenced his decision-making. Second, the diplomatic efforts of the Russian Embassy in Bangui were viewed as an overstep of its role, as ambassadors should not lecture local officials on how to run their government. Despite Touadéra's objections, Russia convened intra-rebel talks in Khartoum in August 2018. Yevgeny Prigozhin flew to Sudan to participate in these talks, as they impacted his commercial interests. These Russia-hosted negotiations produced

## RUSSIA'S NEW POWER PROJECTION TACTICS IN AFRICA

a diplomatic breakthrough, as a Central African opposition alliance consisting of ex-Seleka and Anti-Balaka rebels was formed.[21] While Prigozhin's mediation efforts were successful, they prompted fierce backlash in France. *Le Monde* accused Russia of 'interfering' with the 'legitimate negotiating process', which is overseen by the African Union.[22] In response to the Khartoum agreement, French Defence Minister Florence Parly stated that 'Africa belongs to Africans and no-one else, applies no more to the Russians than to the French' and warned that the opposition alliance might not help stabilize CAR.[23] These objections did not discourage Russia's diplomatic activities in CAR but instead emboldened them, setting the stage for heightened Franco-Russian competition in Central Africa.

Russia has invested considerably in soft power-building initiatives in the Central African Republic. To supplement its growing diplomatic influence, Russia used cultural diplomacy to burnish its image in CAR. The 2018 Miss Bangui beauty pageant was funded by a Kremlin-aligned entity, and featured Valery Zakharov and First Secretary of the Russian Embassy in Bangui, Viktor Tokmakov, as front-row guests.[24] The Russian-funded Lengo Songo 98.9 FM radio station, which means 'Build Solidarity', was unveiled in 2018, and broadcast music, news and talk shows. The Cup of Hope campaign, a Russian-organized youth football tournament in Bangui, and 'Peace Through Eyes of Children' poetry competition, which was organized by the Russian embassy in Bangui and CAR Ministry of Education, sought to improve Russia's image amongst youths in CAR. The prize for winning these competitions was a beach holiday in Crimea, which complements educational diplomacy initiatives on the continent.

During the Sochi Summit, the strength of Russia-CAR security cooperation was on display. Touadéra urged Russia to support an immediate suspension of the UN arms embargo against CAR, as he claimed that these restrictions allowed rebel groups to receive 'illegal weapons' and prevented the government from gaining control over all of CAR's territory.[25] In a RIA Novosti interview, Touadéra stated that Russia's arms shipments to CAR in 2005 'met all the needs of the republic in the field of small arms', and noted that he had asked the Russian Ministry of Defence to train four helicopter pilots in CAR.[26] Touadéra also sparked controversy by expressing interest in

205

the construction of a Russian base on CAR's territory. This statement was not entirely new. In January 2019, CAR Defence Minister Marie-Noëlle Koyara not only stated that a Russian installation would hypothetically fit within the scope of Moscow's defence treaty with CAR but also insisted that the Berengo training centre fell well short of the definition of a base.[27] Kag Senoussi confirmed that CAR was seriously considering a Russian base proposal and dismissed French objections by stating that 'CAR is sovereign, this is 2021.'[28] Nevertheless, Dmitry Peskov swiftly shot down Touadéra's assertion and stated that the CAR president had not broached this issue with Putin. Nevertheless, some Russian experts saw a base in CAR as strategically valuable. Alexander Perendzhiev, a professor at Plekhanov Russian University of Economics, argued that a CAR base would amplify Moscow's ability to carry out Syria-style diplomatic negotiations and aid its humanitarian operations by protecting field hospitals.[29] The expansion of Russia's military intervention in CAR, which will be discussed in the final chapter of this book, ensures that this base debate could eventually resurface.

*Russia Expands Its Military Intervention in Libya*

Although Russia's economic and diplomatic aspirations in Libya made significant strides in 2017, the Russia-LNA partnership stagnated during the first months of Putin's fourth term. Russia's unwillingness to deploy resources on Haftar's behalf can be explained by two principal factors. First, Russian officials were concerned that the United States was expanding its security presence in Libya and that Trump would find common cause with Haftar. In December 2017, Trump reaffirmed the US's support for the GNA by inviting Serraj to the White House, and in early 2018, the US strengthened its commitment to targeting ISIS in Libya. John Bolton's appointment as US national security advisor in April 2018 also influenced Trump to establish a line of communication with Haftar.[30] Erik Prince, CEO of Blackwater, also urged the US to support Haftar in order to dilute Russian influence over the LNA chieftain. To discredit US involvement in Libya, Russian state media outlets claimed that the US was stoking ISIS's rise in Libya

RUSSIA'S NEW POWER PROJECTION TACTICS IN AFRICA

to seize its oil reserves. This mirrored Russia's narratives on ISIS's rise in Syria and Afghanistan, and was promoted by sympathetic Libyan voices, such as the Tobruk government's ambassador to Saudi Arabia Muhammad Saeed al-Qashat.[31] When it became clear in late 2018 that the Trump administration was disinterested in Libya and had not developed a coherent US strategy, Russia saw a clear opening to fill the vacuum.

Second, the Russian foreign and security policy establishments were sharply polarized on Haftar's reliability as a partner. These disagreements were exposed as Russia mulled deploying Wagner Group PMCs on Haftar's behalf. During her engagements with Russian policymakers, Deputy Head of UN Support Missions in Libya Stephanie Williams noted a distinction between the perspectives of foreign and defence ministry officials. Williams recalls that Lavrov and Bogdanov's policy ideas were informed by Arabic-language-speaking Russian diplomats who served in Libya and were alarmed by the reputational risks associated with Wagner Group PMC deployments on Haftar's behalf. In the Russian MoD, officials believed that Russia's most effective means of advancing its interests in Libya came from 'creating facts on the ground' and viewed Wagner Group PMCs as a deniable source of leverage.[32] Despite his close links with the GRU and MoD, Prigozhin did not share Shoigu's view that Haftar was a reliable Russian surrogate in Libya. In a letter to the MoD, a Prigozhin-aligned strategist stated that 'There are serious reasons to believe that in the event of a military-political victory, Haftar will not be loyal to Russia's interests.'[33] Prigozhin's narrative had supporters within the MoD, who were wary of the LNA chieftain's refusal to renounce his US citizenship and feared that he would become a CIA asset once again.[34] The long-term impact of these inter-agency frictions is unclear. Maxim Suchkov, a MGIMO academic focusing on Russia-Middle East relations, acknowledged the possibility that Russia's Libya policy was shaped by inter-agency rivalries, which saw the MFA back Serraj and MoD back Haftar. However, Suchkov also noted that Russia could be trying to place multiple bets in Libya and, therefore, frame itself as an objective mediator.[35]

Despite these intra-elite disagreements about Haftar's merits, Russian officials eventually concurred that backing the LNA would

207

advance Russia's short-term influence and bargaining position in Libya. The intensification of Russia's support for Haftar became evident in the autumn of 2018, as Moscow backed the LNA with war materiel and PMCs. On 8 October, *The Sun* reported that Russia had established bases in Tobruk and Benghazi, and had deployed sophisticated military equipment, such as Kalibr anti-ship missiles and S-300 air defence missile systems, in Libya. The Whitehall source warned that Russia was securing hegemony over Libya's coast to push an influx of North African migrants across the Mediterranean or exert leverage over Libyan oil exports to southern Europe.[36] These reports were immediately denied by Chairman of the Russian-Libyan Trade House, Lev Dengov, and Chair of the Foreign Affairs Committee of the Russian Federation, Konstantin Kosachev, while the Russian Embassy in Britain sarcastically quipped that Britain was hoping that Russia would clean the mess Western countries created in Libya. As media coverage intensified, Russian experts redirected attention to Italian, French and Sudanese PMCs, and then admitted their PMC deployments were linked to Moscow's guardianship of oil assets.[37]

Notwithstanding these denials, the extent of Russia's alignment with Haftar was revealed by the LNA chieftain's November 2018 trip to Moscow. The timing of Haftar's trip, which occurred less than a week before the Palermo Conference of 12–13 November, illustrated the LNA chieftain's desire to secure Russian diplomatic support.[38] While Russian state media outlets exclusively reported on Shoigu's meeting with Haftar, LNA-aligned social media posts revealed Prigozhin was also in attendance. A Russian military-diplomatic source claimed that Prigozhin 'organized an official lunch' to discuss the Libyan delegation's cultural programme, but rumours swirled that Haftar had requested Wagner Group PMCs. Until late 2018, Haftar had relied on Oleg Krinitsyn, the owner of the RSB Group, to carry out de-mining contracts in Libya. Although the RSB Group denies involvement in armed conflicts, Krinitsyn has boasted that he could mobilize '1,000 fighters ready to take up arms in under a week', and claimed to have access to ex-Russian military personnel with combat experience.[39] The LNA's scepticism of Krinitsyn's claims might have inspired his request for Prigozhin's

RUSSIA'S NEW POWER PROJECTION TACTICS IN AFRICA

support, and the prospect of short-term financial windfalls caused Prigozhin to look past his disdain for Haftar.

During the first few months of 2019, evidence mounted about Russia's clandestine military presence in Libya. In January 2019, a Prigozhin-linked jet entered Libya's airspace.[40] Following this revelation, Yevgeny Shabayev, a Cossack lobbyist for the legalization of Russian PMCs, alleged that Wagner Group PMCs were involved in 'drug and people smuggling'. Although these sensational claims were unproven, *The Telegraph* reported that 300 Wagner Group PMCs were stationed in Cyrenaica by March 2019. The arrival of Russian PMCs aided Haftar's decision to launch a surprise offensive against Tripoli on 4 April 2019. The extent of consultation between the LNA and Russia in the build-up to Haftar's offensive is an open question. Andrey Chuprygin, a professor at the Faculty of World Economy and International Affairs at the Higher School of Economics in Moscow, notes that Haftar's offensive on Tripoli did not surprise Russian officials, as he had been warning of this campaign for years but contended that he acted unilaterally to derail the Ghadames peace conference.[41] Anas el-Gomati, the head of Tripoli's Sadeq Institute, disagrees, and believes that Haftar's offensive required strategic coordination with France, the UAE and Egypt at the outset of the Tripoli attack, and subsequently, Russia.[42]

After the LNA offensive began, Russia defended Haftar from international opprobrium through obstructionism in the UN and the circulation of pro-LNA state media commentaries. In the UN Security Council, Russia blocked a British-backed resolution that urged Haftar to halt his military operations in Tripoli and forged an immediate ceasefire.[43] While France allowed Russia to take the lead in the UNSC, it blocked an EU statement on 10 April calling for a de-escalation in Libya. Behind the scenes, Russia blocked a UN probe into alleged LNA-aligned war crimes in Tarhuna and periodically received the support of China, France and the US.[44] RT Arabic aided the LNA's framing of its Tripoli offensive as a counterterrorism campaign, while ignoring the alleged crimes of Haftar-aligned forces. RT Arabic shared LNA claims that al-Qaeda fighters had migrated from Syria to western Libya to liberate the region.[45] On 4 April, RT Arabic uncritically promoted LNA narratives about Turkish and

209

Qatari terrorism sponsorship and highlighted the concentration of pro-Turkey Muslim Brotherhood affiliates in Misrata.[46] This story was the second most viewed post on Facebook in the early days of the Tripoli offensive. Official support for these narratives from the Kremlin, which included Putin's claim on 4 July that ISIS was migrating from Syria to Libya, created a disinformation nexus between the Russian state and aligned media outlets that aided the LNA's cause.

Notwithstanding this pro-Haftar rhetoric, Russian experts were sceptical of the LNA's ability to seize Tripoli. Due to these concerns, Russia set clear limits on its support for Haftar's offensive. Vitaly Naumkin and Vasily Kuznetsov compellingly highlighted the prevailing wisdom in Moscow about the LNA's vulnerability and the GNA's understated strength.[47] They contended that the LNA's cohesion depended on 'generously paid expeditionary activity' and that when the LNA's expansion stalls, internecine squabbles break out. While the GNA's political power was undermined by its integration of 'criminal militias', these armed groups were nevertheless willing to vigorously defend Tripoli against LNA expansion. The LNA's control over just 25% of the Libyan population and its disparate composition, which consisted of secularists, foreign mercenaries and Madkhali-Salafists, were also cited as critical weaknesses.[48] Even if the LNA could overcome its material limitations, doubts lingered about whether Haftar's triumph would benefit Russia's interests. Orientalists, such as Kirill Semenov and Andrei Ontikov, concluded that Russia's influence over the LNA was maximized in a wartime setting and the establishment of a Haftar-led military dictatorship would place the entirety of Libya under sanctions, which would derail Russia's business interests.[49]

Due to these concomitant risks, Russia's strategy in Libya was to increase Haftar's position at the bargaining table through a short-burst military triumph but not provide the LNA chieftain with adequate support to occupy Tripoli. Russia repeatedly rebuffed Haftar's request for official military support in the form of peacekeepers,[50] and used Wagner Group PMCs to provide additional manpower, sniper support and logistical training for the LNA. Russia also consistently maintained a line of communication with the GNA

## RUSSIA'S NEW POWER PROJECTION TACTICS IN AFRICA

and Bogdanov invited GNA Foreign Minister Mohammed Siyala to the Russian-Arab Cooperation Forum on 16 April. This built on established trends in Russian policy towards Libya. Siyala was feted as a guest at the St Petersburg Economic Forum in May 2018, and after the summit, he stated that Russia was shipping 750,000 tons of wheat to Libya.[51] Russia's balance between the GNA and LNA reflected its desire to frame itself as a mediator in Libya and accrue the status benefits which accompanied that role. A successful diplomatic foray in Libya would compensate for Russian diplomatic failures elsewhere, as talks on a new Syrian constitution had stalled and dialogue facilitation efforts in other theatres, such as Afghanistan and Yemen, had achieved little success.

Russia's restrained support for Haftar was favourably regarded in Egypt and Jordan but created rare frictions with the UAE. Egypt supported Russia's instrumental alignment with Haftar, and questioned France and the UAE's belief in a military solution.[52] Egypt's support for Haftar was predicated on his ability to maintain stability in eastern Libya, and was inspired by the LNA chieftain's expeditious triumph over Islamist movements in Benghazi.[53] Egypt's main objective was to facilitate the creation of a centralized government in Libya, but it viewed Haftar as a 'winning card against Islamists' in the meantime.[54] This shared perception of Haftar as a useful temporary option facilitated Egypt-Russia cooperation on an intra-Libyan political settlement. Andrei Kortunov, the director-general of RIAC, urged Russia and Egypt to work on bringing Haftar into a political settlement, and Lavrov discussed this option with Egyptian Minister of Foreign Affairs Shoukry on 7 April.[55] Lavrov visited Amman on 8 April and Jordan supported Russia's military intervention in Libya by deploying armoured vehicles that were used alongside Wagner Group PMC.[56]

In the UAE, Russia's deployment of Wagner Group PMCs on the LNA's behalf was privately supported. Albadr Alshateri, a retired professor at Abu Dhabi's National Defence College, stated that Russia's intervention in Libya was proof that 'If Vladimir Putin says something, you will have an ironclad commitment that it will be done.'[57] Russia's military response on Haftar's behalf also increased the appeal of its governance model in the UAE, as there

211

was widespread admiration of Putin's ability to make hard decisions without civil society pressure.[58] This ebullient rhetoric belied strategic disagreements between Russia and the UAE. Although both Russia and the UAE wished to roll back the Arab Spring in North Africa, Abu Dhabi's commitment to Haftar was ideological in nature. Haftar was the prototype of a secular authoritarian leader that could quash pluralism and grassroots Islamism and marginalize Turkey and Qatar's ideational visions. Unlike in Syria and Sudan, the ideational dimension of Russia's policy in Libya was a third-order priority behind commercial gains and the pursuit of great power status in the Mediterranean.[59] This meant that Russia viewed the UAE's approach to Libya as undesirably rigid and restricted their partnership to instrumental cooperation.

Beyond these strategic disagreements, Russian officials were also mistrustful of the UAE's growing assertiveness as a regional power. Jalel Harchaoui, Associate Fellow at the Royal United Services Institute (RUSI), contends that Abu Dhabi Crown Prince Mohammed bin Zayed is unable to exert influence over Russia's Libya policy like he does with the US and France.[60] Chuprygin expressed frustration with the UAE's insertion of its rivalry with Qatar into the Libyan theatre, and bluntly claimed that UAE, along with Qatar, Turkey, Italy and France, were pursuing their own interests in Libya at the expense of a broader peace settlement.[61] Russia's concerns about UAE unilateralism in Libya mirrored Russia's frustrations with Emirati conduct in Yemen, which peaked after the May 2018 annexation of Socotra and the August 2019 Aden clashes. Moreover, the fault-lines within the UAE foreign policy establishment on Libya closely mirrored Russia's divisions. Senior diplomats, such as Anwar Gargash and Abdullah bin Zayed, believed in the political process, while Mohammed bin Zayed and Sheikh Tahnoon leaned more firmly towards Haftar.[62] This meant that engagement between Russia and the UAE's foreign and security policy institutions on Libya occurred along parallel tracks. The strategic foundations of Russia-UAE cooperation in Libya further weakened as Haftar's Tripoli offensive unravelled in early 2020.

## RUSSIA'S NEW POWER PROJECTION TACTICS IN AFRICA

### *The Stagnation of Russia's Military Intervention in Libya*

During the second half of 2019, Russia's intervention in Libya suffered from a series of setbacks. The exposure of Russia's political interference soured Moscow-Tripoli relations, latent domestic polarizations about Russia's Libya policy were exacerbated and Moscow faced an increasingly severe challenge from Turkey. In May 2019, Maxim Shugaley and his interpreter Samir Seifan were arrested for attempting to interfere in Libya's elections. The Prigozhin-aligned Foundation for the Protection of National Values lobbied the Libyan authorities for their release and claimed that Shugaley was 'conducting sociological surveys, studying the humanitarian, cultural and political situation in the country'.[63] This façade was swiftly debunked. A search on the Scientific Electronic Database, Russia's largest database of academic research, revealed that Shugaley had no track record of academic publications.[64] Shugaley was also linked to a Prigozhin-led initiative to empower Saif al-Islam Gaddafi. Shugaley relayed polling data back to Russia, which revealed that Gaddafi was Libya's most popular politician, and Haftar was in second place.[65] Shugaley and Seifan's meetings with Gaddafi were the proximate trigger for his arrest. During these meetings, Gaddafi highlighted his father's donations to Western politicians. This narrative resonated with his Russian guests, as France's militant response to the 2011 Arab Spring in Libya was widely attributed in Moscow to Gaddafi's financial links to Nicolas Sarkozy.[66]

While Shugaley insisted that he was working in a private capacity, his pro-Gaddafi efforts had unofficial backing in the Kremlin. In December 2018, Saif al-Islam Gaddafi's representative sent a letter to Mikhail Bogdanov, which revealed that he had been regularly in touch with senior Russian officials. Bogdanov has repeatedly claimed that an inclusive Libyan political process would leave the door open for active participation from Saif al-Islam Gaddafi. As the Kremlin wished to distance itself from Shugaley's interference on Gaddafi's behalf, the Russian Foreign Ministry responded belatedly and cautiously to his detention. The Kremlin's inchoate response to Shugaley's detention caused the GNA to pass the case to the Libyan courts and forced Prigozhin to take matters into his own hands. Alexander Malkevich, the director of the Foundation for the Protection of National Values, wrote a letter to Serraj claiming that the release of Shugaley and Seifan was intertwined with the GNA's Berlin Conference commitments. Libyan Foreign Minister Mohamed Siyala rebutted Malkevich's claims, insisting that Fayez al-Sarraj could not release the two Russian nationals by executive fiat.[67] Serraj's response delayed Shugaley and Seifan's release until December 2020 and underscored Russia's inability to convert dialogue with the GNA into genuine leverage.

During the fall of 2019, revelations about the extent of the Wagner Group's presence in Libya provoked severe backlash from Russian liberals. While Al Jazeera had reported that eight Wagner Group PMCs had been killed in an air raid outside Tripoli in September 2019, a *Meduza* investigation in October 2019 revealed that thirty-five casualties had been inflicted. These casualties were obscured from the families of Wagner Group PMCs and were likely carried out by the GNA's Air Force with Turkish logistical support.[68] The Kremlin's inability to control the narrative around the death of Wagner Group PMCs worsened the impact of these revelations, and *Meduza*'s interviews revealed the disparate accounts circulating within Russia's security establishment. A Russian PMC company manager from Rostov told *Meduza* that twenty casualties 'would be a small price to pay for capturing Tripoli', and another Wagner Group-aligned figure described thirty casualties with complete desecration of the bodies. A Russian Ministry of Defence source insisted that only one casualty had occurred, which happened accidentally as the activities of Russian fighters in Libya were limited to 'training exercises'.[69]

The controversy that surrounded Fayez al-Sarraj's participation in the Sochi Summit further revealed the Kremlin's inability to mollify inter-factional disagreements over Libya. Lev Dengov framed Serraj's visit as a success, as he announced Libya's willingness to purchase 1 million tons of Russian wheat and secure Russian help in constructing a power plant.[70] As Russian officials were wary about inviting unrecognized Libyan officials to Sochi, Khalifa Haftar and Abdullah al-Thani were not invited. These omissions received unprecedented internal pushback. LNA-aligned Russian officials tried to place interviews with eastern Libyan officials on the Sochi Summit's agenda and hold discussions about Turkey's transfer of terrorism from Idlib to Libya.[71] This bloc was aggressively lobbying Russia to follow Egypt and the UAE's non-recognition of the GNA and clashed with Ramzan Kadyrov's pro-GNA tilt.[72] Some Russian defence industry figures also supported Haftar's presence at the Sochi Summit, as Libya was an effective transit base for military equipment to Sub-Saharan Africa and global theatres, such as Venezuela.[73] While these disagreements mostly occurred in private, some displays of discontent were aired in public. Yuri Shvytkin, Deputy Chairman of the State Duma Committee on Defence, lambasted Serraj's invitation to Sochi, as he was linked with terrorist activities and caused civilian deaths, and protests were held in Moscow against his participation in the summit.[74] Prigozhin-aligned media outlets labelled Serraj a 'puppet' leader, while Russia's Investigative Committee head Alexander Bastrykin called for a criminal case against Serraj for abducting Russians.[75]

In December 2019, Russia's ambitions in Libya experienced another setback as Turkey intervened militarily in support of GNA. Turkey's military intervention came after a series of escalatory moves in Libya, such as its controversial energy exploration agreement of November 2019 with the GNA and Erdoğan's pledge to provide military support for the GNA. Nevertheless, the extent of Turkey's military intervention in Libya caught Russian officials off guard. Dmitry Frolovskiy, a Russian political consultant specializing on the Middle East, contends that the Kremlin anticipated Turkey's expanded involvement in Libya, as it wanted 'more cards to influence Russia's positions in Syria and the Caucasus'. Frolovskiy conceded that from his experience engaging with the Russian foreign policy community, 'there was a genuine persuasion that Turkey was not ready to support its proxies to the extent it eventually did or would go so far as deploying troops'.[76]

Russian officials were confident that Turkey's military intervention in Libya would swiftly unravel. They believed that nostalgia for the Gaddafi regime, historical, cultural and ethnic factors would create backlash against Turkish involvement, and argued that Turkey was 'playing geopolitics', which would make its position in Libya

215

more fragile in the medium-term.[77] Russian media commentaries strongly supported this perspective. A RIA Novosti article of 30 December claimed that Erdoğan was trying to emulate Russia's military intervention in Syria, but noted that the GNA's close ties with 'Islamist gangs of the most radical persuasion' had tilted international opinion firmly towards the LNA.[78] Colonel-General Leonid Ivashov, a senior former Russian MoD official, contended that Turkey would not deploy ground troops in Libya, as it would be unable to sustain a two-front war.[79] These assessments explained Russia's slow reciprocal deployment of Wagner Group PMCs, which only gained momentum in the spring of 2020, once the Turkish offensive had gained momentum.

Despite Russia's confidence that Turkey's military intervention would not have a game-changing impact on political developments in Libya, Kremlin-aligned media outlets condemned Erdoğan. On 2 January, a RT article lambasted Turkey's intervention on the GNA's behalf as an 'imperial delusion', and predicted 'Erdoğan may get himself in over his head and find Turkey increasingly isolated.'[80] A RT article on 6 January emphasized Turkey's expansionist ambitions in the eastern Mediterranean energy sector, and claimed that 'Turkey is playing a high-stakes game with very little chance of success.[81] Turkey's *Daily Sabah* responded in kind as it published an article condemning Russian Ambassador to Turkey Alexei Erkhov's false equivalencies between the GNA and LNA, and quipped that 'the just side is never determined by the size of its adherents'.[82] Russia's official statements on Turkey's military campaign were more cautious. In a veiled criticism of Turkey's impending intervention, Dmitry Peskov reiterated Russia's support for non-interference by external powers and a political solution in Libya on 26 December.[83] After talks between Erdoğan and Putin on 8 January, Russia and Turkey announced their joint support for a ceasefire in Libya by 12 January.

To enforce this ceasefire, Russia hosted talks with Libya's warring factions on 12 January. During these negotiations, Fayez al-Sarraj spent over seven hours negotiating with Russian and Turkish officials and signed a draft agreement. Russia was unable to facilitate a meeting between Serraj and Haftar, and the LNA chieftain refused to sign the draft agreement, claiming that he needed more time.

The talks were adjourned until 14 January, but Haftar ultimately left Moscow without signing the agreement.[84] This dramatic unravelling of the Moscow-hosted peace negotiations provoked mixed reactions. Andrey Chuprygin attributed the collapse of the talks to Haftar's refusal to exit Tripoli and Serraj's mistrust of Haftar after the LNA chieftain launched an offensive two months after meeting in Abu Dhabi.[85] Chairman of Libya's High Council of State Khalid al-Mishri accused the UAE charge d'affaires in Moscow, who was present at the peace talks, of orchestrating Haftar's abrupt exit and claimed that the Russian ceasefire proposal aimed to 'satisfy the aggressor'.[86]

Despite this setback, Russia and Turkey expressed interest in long-term cooperation on stabilizing Libya. Ahmet Berat Conkar, an AKP lawmaker and Deputy Head of Turkey's delegation to the NATO Parliamentary Assembly, said Turkey-Russia dialogue on Libya set a 'perfect example' for external powers and stated that their joint efforts to counter the West's 'erroneous attitude' inspires hope.[87] Sergei Lavrov expressed hope that Libya could become a 'second Syria', and indirectly compared Russia-Turkey cooperation in Libya to the Astana Peace Process trilateral meetings between Russia, Iran and Turkey.[88] Turkish foreign policy experts, such as Huriye Yildrim Cinar of the Caucasus Strategic Research Center, urged the US, the UAE, Egypt and the EU to join the Russia-Turkey initiative to stabilize Libya.[89] This cooperation unravelled abruptly as tensions between Russia and Turkey flared over Syria's Idlib Governorate. In an extraordinary rebuke of Moscow's conduct in Libya, Erdoğan accused Russia of 'managing the conflict in Libya at the highest level' on 17 February and implied that Shoigu and Gerasimov were falsely denying their role in directing the Wagner Group's conduct.[90]

From 27 February to 6 March 2020, the Operation Spring Shield Offensive, which placed Turkey in direct conflict with Bashar al-Assad, caused Moscow-Ankara tensions to escalate further. This escalation in Syria further entrenched Russia's belief that Turkey was on the brink of defeat in Libya. Colonel Vladimir Anokhin asserted that Erdoğan would leave Libya if setbacks, such as the defeat in Mitiga airbase mount, and highlighted the unpopularity of Turkey's Neo-Ottomanist 'Adriatic to Tunisia' ideology in the international community.[91] The March 2 Haftar-Assad alliance against Turkey

217

was also expected to strengthen the LNA's position, as Syria had extensive experience countering Turkish UAVs.[92] While tensions between Russia and Turkey simmered down in March 2020, Russian overconfidence in Libya persisted, which ultimately forced the Kremlin to re-evaluate its strategy in the spring of 2020.

*Russia's Response to the Sudanese Revolution and Democratic Transition*

On 19 December 2018, mass protests erupted in Sudan over high inflation and worsening economic conditions. Once support for economic reforms escalated into calls for regime change, Bashir declared a year-long state of emergency, released female opposition activists, and courted financial support from Sudan's international partners. These compromises failed, as Bashir was toppled by a coup d'état on 11 April 2019, and Lieutenant General Abdel Fattah el-Burhan emerged as Sudan's leader. Due to its counter-revolutionary impulses and growing economic ties with Bashir's regime, Russia was alarmed by political turmoil in Sudan. During Bashir's July 2018 visit to Moscow, Putin praised Sudan's purchase of 1.5 million tons of Russian wheat and Bashir announced new discussions about agricultural cooperation with Russia in September 2018. Putin also noted a two-fold increase in Russia-Sudan trade after his meeting with Bashir in Sochi, while Bashir urged Russian companies to enter Sudan's oil industry.[93] The normalization of Sudan-Syria relations, which resulted in Bashir becoming the first Arab leader to visit Damascus since the civil war's outbreak in December 2018, further bolstered Russia's desire to preserve the status quo in Sudan. While Dmitry Peskov responded evasively to reports that Bashir arrived in Syria on a Russian plane, the Russian Foreign Ministry viewed Bashir's visit as a step towards securing Syria's return to the Arab League.[94]

Russia responded to Bashir's growing vulnerability by deploying Wagner Group PMCs to prop up his regime and engaging in shuttle diplomacy with Sudan's main Arab partners, Saudi Arabia and the UAE. Although Wagner Group PMCs were stationed in Sudan for a year prior to the revolution and military delegations shuttled frequently between Moscow and Khartoum, the extent of Russia's

## RUSSIA'S NEW POWER PROJECTION TACTICS IN AFRICA

security footprint was unclear. In July 2018, Bashir acknowledged a 'big number' of Russian military-technical specialists worked in Sudan but did not disclose their duties.[95] On 26 December, Sudanese opposition sources revealed that Russian PMCs were training special operations from Sudan's National Intelligence and Security Services (NISS). However, an NISS source confirmed that the Wagner Group was working with Sudan's mainstream intelligence and security services.[96] The intensification of Sudan's mass protests, which were met with a much-criticized heavy-handed NISS response, resulted in a new influx of Russian PMCs. Vasyl Hrytsak, the head of the Security Service of Ukraine (SSUA), claimed to possess the travel documents and passport information of 149 Wagner Group PMCs.[97] Hrytsak noted that Prigozhin's M-Invest received Tu-154M airliners from the Russian Ministry of Defence to deploy PMCs to Sudan. Russian officials suppressed rumours that Wagner Group PMCs helped the NISS repress demonstrators. Peskov and Bogdanov insisted that Russian PMCs were involved in personnel training, while Maria Zakharova emphasized that Russian security personnel were solely employed in a private capacity.

Documents obtained by the Dossier Center, an organization overseen by dissident oligarch Mikhail Khodorkovsky, discredited these denials and provided a clearer picture of Russian political interference in Sudan.[98] Correspondence between Sudan's Military Industrial Corporation and Valery Gerasimov in June 2018 revealed that M-Invest tried to secure access to Sudanese facilities for the Russian Navy. These outreaches began after Deputy Commander of the Russian Navy Oleg Makarevich visited Sudan in May 2018, and possibly facilitated the Sudanese parliament's January 2019 draft naval facility-sharing agreement.[99] In addition to making outreaches at the Kremlin's behest, M-Invest covertly helped Bashir quash Sudan's burgeoning revolution. M-Invest encouraged Bashir to distribute free bread, flour and grain to bolster his popularity. When Bashir complied with these suggestions, Prigozhin unleashed a wave of pro-Bashir propaganda. The Federal News Agency claimed that Bashir 'is working around the clock to help his fellow citizens',[100] and accused Western countries of doctoring images of 500-person protests into demonstrations with hundreds of thousands of people.[101]

219

When Bashir's popularity-boosting tactics failed to quell the demonstrations, Prigozhin's strategists urged Bashir to aggressively crack down on the opposition. M-Invest urged Bashir to blame Western countries for the protests; extract forced confessions from detainees about Western plots to instigate a civil war in Sudan; and stage the seizure of an opposition-owned car with weapons, foreign currency and propaganda material. M-Invest also asked Bashir to create social media teams of forty to fifty users that would counter the Sudanese opposition's narratives and spread rumours that the Sudanese opposition are 'anti-Islam', 'pro-Israel' and 'pro-LGBT'.[102] The Wagner Group also sought to prepare Bashir for the 2020 Sudanese elections. Prigozhin-aligned strategists planned to create 'For Bashir' and 'Bashir is the Father of the Nation' movements, orchestrate mass arrests of Sudanese officials and assemble one or two pseudo-opposition parties overseen by Bashir allies.[103] These strategists also suggested that Bashir project an image of invulnerability in 2020, while dangling the prospect of political change in 2025.

Russia also strengthened Bashir's political position by coordinating with his leading regional sponsors. The Russia-Saudi Arabia relationship improved after King Salman's October 2017 visit to Moscow, while the June 2018 Russia-UAE strategic partnership agreement augmented the impact of clandestine cooperation in Libya and the normalization of UAE-Syria relations in December 2018. As Russia, Saudi Arabia and the UAE feared the destabilizing consequences of an Arab Spring 2.0 in North Africa, all three countries formed an axis of illiberalism in Sudan. This axis formed ahead of Bashir's visit to Syria, which was covertly facilitated by Russia and Saudi Arabia.[104] Nikolay Patrushev's January 2019 trips to Egypt and the UAE addressed the need to prevent a colour revolution in Sudan and deepened their counter-revolutionary coordination. Kirill Semenov, a Moscow-based defence analyst focusing on the Middle East, opined that Russian PMCs would shore up Bashir's regime, while Saudi Arabia and the UAE provided financial support.[105] Russian media coverage, which emphasized exogenous triggers of Sudan's economic crisis like US sanctions or South Sudan's secession, amplified Saudi Arabia and the UAE's pro-Bashir line. As RT Arabic had larger viewership in Sudan than Al-Arabiya, especially on social media, it could communicate Saudi and Emirati talking points to a local audience, and counter Al-Jazeera's supportive stance towards the Sudanese revolution.[106]

Ultimately, cooperation between these three countries was more oblique, as Russia and the UAE's policies towards Sudan diverged. The UAE gradually distanced itself from Bashir, as he maintained links with Islamist movements, Turkey and Qatar, and aligned with security establishment figures, such as Bashir's national security advisor Salah Gosh and Rapid Support Forces (RSF) head Mohammed Hamdan 'Hemedti' Dagalo.[107] These figures had limited ties with Russia, as the Sudanese military had deeper institutional links with China.[108] Sergei Seregichev, a Sudan expert at the Russian State University of the Humanities, noted that Russia had minimal ties with Hemedti and that delays in the Sudanese base negotiations had tarnished his image.[109] Nevertheless, Russian media outlets framed the Sudan crisis as a triumph for Moscow's engagement with the Gulf monarchies. In May 2019, an article in *Nezavisimaya Gazeta* boasted that the link between Russia, Saudi Arabia and the UAE 'appears to be closer and perhaps stronger than the relationship between the capitals of the region and Western powers', and cited their synergistic support for stability in Sudan as a driver of this partnership.[110]

The April 2019 coup raised doubts about the sustainability of Russia's influence in Sudan and polarized the Russian foreign policy establishment. Key figures in the Federation Council, who had until now spearheaded Russia's ambitions for a Red Sea base, publicly decried Bashir's overthrow. Andrei Klishas, the chairman of the Federation Council Committee on Constitutional Legislation and State Building, decried the 'violent unconstitutional change of power' in Sudan.[111] Konstantin Kosachev did not explicitly condemn the coup but compared it to other insurrections that Russia opposed, such as the 2016 Turkish coup attempt, Euro-Maidan in Ukraine, the Arab Spring in Syria, and January 2019 Venezuela crisis.[112] The Russian State Duma treaded more cautiously about developments in Sudan. Leonid Slutsky, chairman of the State Duma's International Affairs Committee, predicted that Russia-Sudan cooperation would endure, in part due to its geo-strategic location in the Middle East and Africa. Yevgeny Prigozhin likely welcomed the coup, as he had expressed frustration to Bashir in March 2019 over his 'lack of activity' and 'extremely cautious position' towards the Sudanese protests.[113]

The views of Slutsky and Prigozhin ultimately prevailed, as Bogdanov met Burhan in Khartoum and Zakharova declared that Russia-Sudan relations were 'unchanged' on 18 April.[114] Russian media outlets also quelled internal dissent about Moscow's embrace of Burhan by depicting the Sudanese opposition as a greater evil. Except for the liberal newspaper *Novaya Gazeta*, which criticized Russia's counter-revolutionary policy in Sudan, Russian media outlets praised Burhan's technocratic government and denigrated Sudanese demonstrators. While Russian experts, such as Vladimir Fitin from the Russian Institute for Strategic Studies, rebutted comparisons of the Sudan events with Venezuela or the Arab Spring, *Izvestia*'s 11 April headline was 'Maidan in Sudan'.[115] Trade unionists in the Sudanese opposition were described as trojan horses for Western influence, while a Russian diplomat told *Kommersant* that a 'Ukrainian scenario' was unfolding in Sudan, and that a Western-backed campaign to delegitimize the Sudanese military was afoot.[116] Anti-Russian comments from Sudanese opposition figures added fuel to these narratives. The leader of Darfur's Sudan Liberation Movement (SLM-AW) Abdul Wahid al-Nur was an especially strident critic of Russia, as he urged US President Donald Trump to stop decoupling human rights from security policy and acknowledge the threat Moscow posed to AFRICOM in Sudan.[117] RT and Sputnik Arabic promoted counter-revolutionary narratives about Sudanese audience in a milder form, as they emphasized Burhan's willingness to reform and compromise, while depicting the Forces for Freedom and Change (FFC) as single-minded and obstructionist.[118]

After Burhan pledged to maintain military rule for two years and then call elections, Russia resumed its political interference in Sudan. Burhan welcomed Russia's autocracy promotion efforts, as he retained Wagner Group consultants and allowed economists from Moscow State University's Institute of Asian and African Countries to remain in Khartoum.[119] As FFC protests persisted, Prigozhin-aligned strategists urged Burhan to use repression, if it resulted in a 'minimal but acceptable loss of life'. The Khartoum massacre on

# RUSSIA'S NEW POWER PROJECTION TACTICS IN AFRICA

3 June, which saw the RSF kill at least 128 FFC demonstrators, tested Russia's commitment to autocracy promotion in Sudan. While the US and Europe immediately condemned the massacre, Russia defended Burhan. When Britain and Germany circulated a press statement condemning the Burhan-led Transitional Military Council (TMC) in a closed-door press briefing, Dmitry Polyanskiy called it 'unbalanced' and stressed the need to be 'very cautious in this situation'.[120] Polyanskiy also urged the African Union to lead normative deliberations on the Khartoum massacre, which mirrored its empowerment of the AU during the 2011 Libyan civil war. This position was more moderate than China's stronger objections to the draft but mirrored Kuwait's position.

Polyanskiy's words at the UN Security Council aligned with the views of the Russian Foreign Ministry. On 4 June, Mikhail Bogdanov insisted that Sudan needed to repress 'extremists and saboteurs' to facilitate a democratic transition and resisted an 'external intervention' in Sudanese politics.[121] Bogdanov's ambiguous phrases reflected Russia's coded support for the TMC's pursuit of authoritarian stability through repression. Notwithstanding Bogdanov's comments, Russian officials were aware of the reputational damage caused by the Wagner Group's conduct in Sudan and kept a low profile as democratic transition negotiations began. The Russian MFA subsequently praised the August 2019 constitutional declaration between the Sudanese military and opposition as an 'important step to the stability' of Sudan.[122] The Russian expert community was less sanguine about the prospects of a successful democratic transition in Sudan. Igor Gerasimov, a professor at St Petersburg State University, noted that the ambiguous relationships between 'representatives of a certain tribal union and a certain Sufi brotherhood' and the experience of a failed democratic transition from 1985 to 1989 boded poorly for Sudan's future. Gerasimov urged Russia to support the Sudanese military, as it viewed Moscow's support for authoritarian stability in Syria as a model for Sudan.[123] This perspective entered Russian official policy and inspired Moscow's persistently close relationship with Burhan throughout Sudan's at-times turbulent transition process.

223

RUSSIA IN AFRICA

## Russia's Political Interference Campaign in Madagascar

Russia's political interference campaign during Madagascar's 2018 elections was a surprise development. Gaelle Borgia, a Madagascar-based journalist, notes that Russia has deep ties with Madagascar, as Soviet weapons are widely present, Aeroflot flights were very popular and Soviet-era guns are present in rural areas.[124] Russia also viewed Madagascar as a strategically valuable location on the Indian Ocean. Nevertheless, the scale of Russian political interference was striking. On 8 April 2019, a BBC investigation revealed that three Russian political strategists posing as tourists offered money to six candidates in the November 2018 Malagasy presidential elections. The three Russian political strategists were Andrei Kramar, a Kremlin-aligned political technologist; businessman Roman Pozdnyakov; and Vladimir Boyarishchev, who had experience in the diamond trade.[125] Pastor Andre Mailhol signed a contract with these Russian operatives, which bound him to endorse one of the eight to nine pro-Kremlin candidates in Madagascar that reached the second runoff.[126] Maxim Shugaley, a veteran Russian spin doctor and Liberal Democratic Party of Russia candidate in the 2002 St Petersburg elections, aided the campaign of Madagascar's Prime Minister from 2011 to 2014 Omer Beriziky, and offered him 'technical support' to 'get control of the election'.[127] In November 2019, a *New York Times* report confirmed that Vladimir Putin and Yevgeny Prigozhin met with Madagascar's President Hery Rajaonarimampianina in Moscow in 2018, and contended that Prigozhin's stake in Madagascar's chromium reserves motivated Russian election interference.[128]

Russian operatives also manipulated public opinion by supporting protests against Western neocolonialism outside the French embassy in Antananarivo, which featured an orator who declared that 'Africans trust Russia more than America or France.'[129] The slogans 'France must leave Madagascar alone!' and 'France must stop teaching the rest of the world while it engaged in colonialism!' featured prominently in these demonstrations.[130] Niaina, a communications consultant for Pastor Mailhol, noted that Russia also hosted a 'Scattered Islands conference' to reinflame colonial-era grievances against France.[131]

224

## RUSSIA'S NEW POWER PROJECTION TACTICS IN AFRICA

Russia also aimed to distribute a mass-selling newspaper to 2 million people in Madagascar.[132] This project struggled to get off the ground, as the newspaper misspelt Rajaonarimampianina's name and Russian operatives created fake receipts doubling their costs in order to profit from the media outlet.[133] According to leaked documents obtained by the Dossier Center in London, which is backed by Mikhail Khodorkovsky, Russia listed Madagascar as a Level 5 target country, which was on par with Sudan and the Central African Republic and sought to combine political interference with police training and assistance to the Malagasy authorities against opposition protests.

While Russia's interference in Madagascar's elections threatened its democracy, it was a resounding failure. Madagascar's independently wealthy former President Andry Rajoelina, who won the first run-off with 39.23% of the vote and the second run-off with 55.66% of the vote, rebuffed Russian offers of support when the Kremlin realized that its election strategy had backfired.[134] Rajaonarimampianina, Mailhol and Beriziky received 8.82%, 1.27% and 0.31% of the vote respectively in the first runoff. The latter two candidates had unpleasant conclusions to their dealings with Russian political operatives. Mailhol claims that Russian operatives abandoned him after he refused to endorse Rajoelina's re-election and Beriziky claimed that he received only a small fraction of the $2 million that Shugaley promised him.[135] The *New York Times* investigation revealed that Russia's approaches to Mailhol were not triggered by genuine support but rather due to a desire to capitalize on his status as an 'apocalyptic cult leader' and split the opposition vote.[136] Yevgeny Prigozhin's heavy investments in Internet troll farms in Madagascar also sparked accusations of incompetence, as Madagascar's Internet penetration rate is just 9.8% or one-quarter of the average in Africa.[137] Moreover, local backlash against Prigozhin's seizure of chromium, which is viewed in Madagascar as a national asset, and allegations of unpaid wages and cancelled benefits for Malagasy workers in Prigozhin's corporate network undermined Russian soft power in Madagascar.[138]

The response in Moscow to Russian election interference allegations in Madagascar was predictably dismissive. Intriguingly, Russian state-aligned media outlets had pre-empted Western allegations of election interference in Madagascar with their own claims of Western interference. These allegations peaked in late December 2018 and early January 2019, as mass protests by supporters of Marc Ravalomanana, Madagascar's President from 2002 to 2009 and the runner-up in the 2018 elections, erupted in Antananarivo against election fraud. Russia's international media outlets, RT and Sputnik, were largely silent on these allegations. Dmitry Peskov acknowledged them on 11 November 2019, when he stated that it was a 'favoured practice to accuse Russia of interfering everywhere and in everything' and denied that the Putin-Prigozhin-Rajaonarimampianina meeting took place.[139] No Russian official publicly accused the US or France of election interference in Madagascar. Instead, Russian-language outlets for domestic consumption publicized the accusations, as they manipulated the public to mistrust international reports about Russian election interference in the US and Europe, and these accusations were distributed locally through the pro-Kremlin media nexus in Madagascar. On 22 December 2018, Federal News Agency accused Marc Ravalomanana of receiving social media assistance from France and the United States, and Israel of hacking Madagascar's Central Independent Election Commission.[140] The report accused Western media outlets of defaming Rajaonarimapianina and encouraging the Malagasy military to side with Ravalomanana by planting incendiary reports in the *Madagascar Tribune*. It also accused CNN of leading an effort to manufacture Russian interference stories in Madagascar and asserted that 'to find Russians, you have to push your way between the British, French and Jews'.

On 8 January, a Federal News Agency 'investigation' expanded on these conspiracies by claiming that US tourists in Antananarivo were 'employees on a special assignment'. The report listed the names of American paratroopers, cyberwarriors, lawyers and activists who were allegedly present in Madagascar around the time of the elections as proof of a conspiracy.[141] These individuals included the 780th US military intelligence brigade's Matthew Weatherington, who was referred to as the 'mysterious white man' and New York lawyer Betty Lynn-White, who was allegedly tasked with finding loopholes in the election legislation. The report claimed that it had

RUSSIA'S NEW POWER PROJECTION TACTICS IN AFRICA

6,000 text messages in its possession that verified their presence but cited no first-hand interview material from Malagasy sources. This investigation also turned the tables on Western allegations of Russian interference in Madagascar. The Russian state news outlet RIA FAN report accused the US of colluding with Ravalomanana to instigate popular protests in Madagascar. It also claimed that the US co-opted two backup candidates, the Stanford-educated Roseline Rasolovoagy and physicist Stephen Narison, ahead of the elections, and convinced them to accept US military bases in Madagascar. News.ru expounded on the RIA FAN investigation by claiming that Ravalomanana was an after-hours visitor to the US Embassy in Antananarivo, which regularly hosted US and European diplomats in the lead-up to the elections.[142] Notwithstanding these narratives of disinformation, the Madagascar campaign eroded Prigozhin's prestige as an overseer of political technologists and dented Moscow's standing in Africa.

## Russia's Failed Counterterrorism Mission in Northern Mozambique

During the long buildup to its election interference campaign and military intervention in Cabo Delgado, Russia strengthened its economic and security partnership with Mozambique. In 2015, Rosneft and ExxonMobil formed a 20-to-80% share consortium to develop three blocks of offshore natural gas in northern Mozambique. In July 2017, Rosneft's Vice-President Vlada Rusakova announced plans to secure binding gas exploration contracts with Mozambique, but in March 2018, ExxonMobil scaled back its partnership with Rosneft over US sanctions against Russia.[143] This U-turn cost ExxonMobil $200 million and allowed Russian energy companies to expand their presence in Cabo Delgado. After Lavrov's March 2018 meeting with Mozambican counterpart José Pacheco, an intergovernmental commission on trade-economic cooperation was unveiled in Maputo. In October 2018, ExxonMobil and Rosneft revived their consortium partnership in a new arrangement, which saw ExxonMobil secure a 50% stake, Rosneft gain a 20% stake, Mozambique's ENH gain a 20% stake and Qatar Petroleum secure a 10% stake. This paved the way for a more comprehensive

227

Rosneft-ENH MOU during Mozambique President Filipe Nyusi's August 2019 visit to Russia, which was the first trip to Moscow by a Mozambican head of state since 1987.[144] This set the stage for new commercial deals ahead of the Sochi Summit. On 18 October 2019, Russian ambassador to Mozambique Alexander Surikov claimed that Russian companies had the technology to help Mozambique, which had less than 30% of its population with access to electricity, to achieve 'universal electrification' by 2030.[145]

Russia's security partnership with Mozambique progressed in tandem with its commercial relationship. In January 2017, Russia and Mozambique signed a renewable five-year military-technical agreement, which would allow for the transfer of military equipment and spare parts. This agreement did not result in major arms deals between Russia and Mozambique, as SIPRI's records from 1970 to 2019 reveal a $2 million transaction in 1999 and a $7 million transaction in 2019.[146] Nevertheless, it paved the way for the establishment of a working group on military-technical cooperation and the entry of 'several hundred' Mozambican students in educational institutions of Russia's Defence and Interior Ministries.[147] This combination of security and economic cooperation caused Lavrov to support the elevation of the Russia-Mozambique relationship to a strategic partnership during his March 2018 trip. One month later, Sergei Shoigu signed an intergovernmental agreement with his Mozambican counterpart Athanasius Salvador Mtumuke, which would streamline access by Russian warships to Mozambique's ports and strengthen naval cooperation. Mtumuke asked Shoigu to deploy Russian military-technical advisors to Mozambique and noted that Mozambique's national banner depicts a Kalashnikov rifle, which symbolizes its 'eternal' security partnership with Russia.[148] This agreement underscored Russia's intention to gain a foothold in the Mozambique channel, which lies between Madagascar and East Africa. The Northern Fleet's Severomorsk anti-submarine destroyer docked at Maputo in March 2017 and October 2018, which underscored Mozambique's growing importance to Russia's Indian Ocean strategy.

The expansion of Russia-Mozambique cooperation spilt over to the counterterrorism sphere. In October 2017, Islamist militant group Ansar al-Sunna launched an insurgency in northern Mozambique's gas-rich Cabo Delgado region, and allowed ISIS to attack Mozambique's security forces in June 2019. As instability soared in Cabo Delgado, Nyusi considered rival counterterrorism assistance bids from South African private security companies (PSCs) and the Wagner Group. South Africa's Umbria Aviation called for covert airstrikes, helicopters and armoured vehicles, while its competitor OAM focused on providing training and advisory support to Mozambique's armed forces.[149] Anticipating competition from the Wagner Group, South African PSC Black Hawk warned that Russian PMCs lacked knowledge of the local terrain or Mozambican politics. The Wagner Group possessed a significant cost advantage, however, as its employees charged between $1,800 to $4,700/month compared to OAM's $15,000 to $25,000/month rate.[150] Russia's political influence in Mozambique also counted in the Wagner Group's favour, despite concerns about a CAR-style erosion of Mozambique's sovereignty. Russia's pro-active response to terrorism in Mozambique, which was a peripheral issue for other great powers from 2017 to 2018, also aided its cause. During his March 2018 meeting with Pacheco, Lavrov emphasized the need to combat terrorism without double standards,[151] and sold Moscow's 'strong state' model of counterterrorism to Mozambican officials. These factors caused Nyusi to accept Wagner Group assistance in August 2019, and South African PSCs hoped that their knowledge of Mozambique's terrain would allow them to assist their Russian counterpart.

Nyusi's September 2019 visit to Moscow was swiftly followed by the entry of Russian military personnel in northern Mozambique. On 13 September, 160 Russian PMCs arrived in Mozambique on an Antonov An-124 plane, and on 25 September, a second Antonov An-124 carried an Mi-17 helicopter to Nacala Airport. The An-124s belonged to the 224th Flight Unit of the Russian Air Force, and closely resembled 223rd Flight Unit equipment used by Wagner Group forces in Sudan. Russian officials viewed these deployments as a limited-risk mission, as the situation in Cabo Delgado was deemed to be less complicated than other African theatres, but one that could reap extensive economic rewards.[152] Russia's military deployments, which included 200 PMCs and three attack helicopters by 2 October, ended in dismal failure. Prigozhin-aligned spokesman Yevgeny Shabayev confirmed that two PMCs, aged twenty-eight and thirty-one, were killed by Asnar al-Sunna and ISIS insurgents during the first days of their deployment. The killing of five Wagner Group PMCs and twenty Mozambican special forces in an ambush in November 2019 hastened the end of Prigozhin's most ignominious foray into Sub-Saharan Africa.[153] Russia's military intervention in Mozambique likely ended before 25 November.

The Wagner Group's failed counterterrorism mission in Mozambique was attributed to poor relations with the local population, badly organized aerial reconnaissance and insufficient combat experience in Sub-Saharan Africa.[154] The limited training of the Mozambican armed forces in counterinsurgency compounded the Wagner Group's woes.[155] Much like the Soviet technical advisors that preceded them, Wagner Group PMCs were disdained by local armed forces.[156] Despite its brief duration and extenuating circumstances, the Cabo Delgado debacle had costly reverberations. Russia's failure in Mozambique, which coincided with reversals in Libya, undermined its ability to export its 'Syrian model' of counterinsurgency in Africa. The Mozambique misadventure also dented Russia's prestige as a counterterrorism partner in China. A commentary in *Dajunshi*, a Chinese defence website, described Mozambique as 'Wagner's Challenge' in contrast to CAR which was 'Wagner's paradise, and blamed the inability of Russian PMCs to operate in a terrain of 'heavy rains and wild forests' for their failure to combat ISIS.[157] These criticisms frustrated Russian officials, as Moscow hoped that a successful counterterrorism operation in Mozambique might encourage China to entrust the Wagner Group with guarding its natural resource deposits in Africa.[158]

To deflect from the failed mission, Kremlin and Prigozhin-aligned media outlets circulated disinformation about events in Mozambique. Russia's disinformation campaign initially focused on denying the presence of Wagner Group PMCs in Mozambique but has since reframed Moscow's role in Cabo Delgado as a success. On 8 October, Dmitry Peskov stated 'as far as Mozambique is concerned, there are no Russian soldiers there'.[159] RIA FAN alleged that the opposition Mozambican National Resistance Movement (RENAMO) party was spreading false rumours of Russian PMC deployments and casualties from Mozambican forces to discredit Nyusi.[160] RIA FAN's 'evidence' came from tweets by Constantino Cossa and Zimbabwean commentator Liberty Pazvakavambwa, whose accounts were subsequently suspended in Twitter's broader crackdown on Russian disinformation in Africa. Russian revisionism about the counterinsurgency mission in Mozambique persists to this date. In July 2021, Maxim Shugaley said that the sole responsibility of Russian PMCs was to provide security in Mozambique ahead of the 2019 elections and claimed that the Russians 'liberated several cities at once' while suffering only one casualty.[161] This statement echoed unsubstantiated reports from Mozambique's Ministry of Defence, such as its 9 October statement hailing successful operations in 'eliminating criminals' in Mbau region.[162] Shugaley also claimed that the Mozambican military fled from extremist militias, and Russia withdrew from Mozambique as it lacked a suitable partner. These narratives helped silence domestic dissent over Wagner Group activities but were unconvincing on the international stage.

Russia's involvement in Mozambique attracted more negative scrutiny as evidence of Kremlin interference in the October 2019 Mozambican elections mounted. These elections, which handed Nyusi a landslide victory with 73.46% of the vote, were marred by RENAMO's allegations of 'massive electoral fraud' and hundreds of thousands of 'ghost voters'. While Russia was not directly involved in falsifying vote tallies, the Russian International Anticrisis Center (IAC) applied election interference tactics that it used in South Africa to Mozambique. In September 2019, the IAC interviewed 3,124 Mozambicans about their views in Mozambique Liberation Front (FRELIMO) and published polls that gave Nysui unexpectedly high favourability ratings in Nampula.[163] Although pre-election polling is banned in Mozambique, FRELIMO aligned social media accounts amplified these surveys on Facebook ahead of the elections. The Association for Free Research and International Cooperation (AFRIC), a Prigozhin-aligned group, complemented the IAC's efforts to burnish Nyusi's image. Before the elections, AFRIC praised Nyusi's counterterrorism efforts and posted images of vast crowds supporting Nyusi. AFRIC falsely accused RENAMO of allowing China to dispose radioactive waste in Mozambique, which prompted significant backlash within Mozambique. Portuguese-language posts saying 'fake news' or 'I think your tin hat is wound too tightly around your head; this can't be true' pushed back against AFRIC's allegations.[164] AFRIC also dismissed electoral fraud allegations against Nyusi by stating that its representatives at 200 polling stations in Maputo and Mozambique's ten provinces saw no irregularities.[165] The implausible narratives promoted by AFRIC ensured that Russia's election interference efforts in Mozambique were a comparable, if less spectacular, failure to those in Madagascar.

These failures were compounded by a debt dispute between Russia's VTB bank and Mozambique Asset Management, a state-owned company. On 23 December, VTB lodged a lawsuit in Britain's High Court against the Mozambican state, as the latest round of debt restructuring negotiations in October 2019 yielded no breakthroughs.[166] VTB's use of the British court system to recoup $535 million in debt owed by Mozambique was a surprise turn. In March 2020, Mozambique pushed back against VTB's lawsuit by claiming that it did not necessarily need to guarantee or repay debt to Credit Suisse and VTB, as per the loan agreement.[167] VTB countered with a request for a repayment of $817.5 million plus interest on loans, which exacerbated the collapse of Mozambique's credit rating to 'financial default' status over 'hidden debts'.[168] While Russian officials have detached themselves from this legal dispute, this impasse exposed the corruption that undergirded Russia's debt forgiveness schemes and stalled a recovery of Russia-Mozambique relations after the setbacks of late 2019.

Although the Sochi Summit revealed Russia's ascendancy as a great power in Africa, its hybrid military interventions presented a murkier picture. Russia has tried to replicate its successes in Guinea and, to a lesser extent, CAR, while leveraging the flexibility of its policies to maintain influence in Libya and Sudan. Madagascar and Mozambique have emerged as cautionary tales of the limits of Russian influence, especially in the spheres of political interference and counterterrorism. Russia's recalibration of these tactics to new frontiers, such as the Sahel, suggests that these debacles did not steer its policy towards restraint. During the COVID-19 pandemic, Russia tried to reinforce its image as a reliable great power partner, while trying to steer the local situations in fragile African states to its advantage.

8

# RUSSIA'S AFRICA POLICY IN THE
# AGE OF COVID-19

The COVID-19 pandemic presented Russia with a unique opportunity to amplify its great power status in Africa. During the first weeks of the pandemic, Russia avoided its worst effects. A CNN report on 23 March 2020 asked the puzzling question of why Russia, a country of 146 million people, had fewer COVID-19 cases than Luxembourg, a country of 630,000 people.[1] Russia capitalized on this fortuitous position through pledges of personal protective equipment (PPE) assistance to Africa and assertive support for Ethiopian Prime Minister Abiy Ahmed's calls for debt relief to the Global South. By the summer of 2020, Russia's coronavirus diplomacy strategy in Africa was at risk of backfiring. Russia's PPE deliveries lagged other countries, such as China, Turkey and the UAE, and the COVID-19 pandemic swept across the country. Russia's controversial approval of the Sputnik V vaccine on 11 August, which occurred without phase 3 testing, gave Moscow a golden opportunity to arrest the trend of eroding soft power in Africa. While approvals of Russia's Sputnik V vaccine in Africa have been incremental, Moscow began vaccine deliveries to the continent before Western countries, such as Britain, France or the United States, and avoided the inefficacies that undermined China's vaccine rollouts. Delays in vaccine deliveries

235

undermined that initial success and sullied Russian soft power. Russia faced stiffened challenges from external powers, and also found itself mired in an uneasy balancing act between Egypt and Ethiopia on the GERD issue.

### Russia-Africa Relations and the Outbreak of the COVID-19 Pandemic

As COVID-19 swept across the globe, Russian officials swiftly attuned to the pandemic's potential to impact sweeping geopolitical transformations. While the Russian foreign policy community was primarily preoccupied with Moscow's response to a potential US-China Cold War, there were also heated debates about Africa's place in the future international order. A RIAC report of 9 April contended that 'Africa has the potential to be either an essential part of the fundamental problems of this emerging system, or a part of the solutions.'[2] In the 'problem' scenario, the report warned that Africa would be an even greater threat to international stability than the Middle East, but in the 'solution' scenario, Africa could rival East Asia as a key driver of the world economy. Uncertainties about Africa's place within the global order also extended to Russia's ambitions on the continent. Concerns grew that the triple effect of the COVID-19 pandemic, collapsing hydrocarbon prices and an economic crisis would likely force Russia to downsize its plans in Africa.[3] To stem the decline of its influence in Africa, Russia considered leveraging symbolic displays of solidarity, humanitarian assistance through bilateral agreements and multilateral cooperation with Europe and China, and assuming leadership in the resolution of conflicts, such as the Libyan civil war.[4] These actions would capitalize on the EU's decision to relinquish its conflict arbitration roles in Africa during the pandemic and highlight the limitations of the Western development model to an African audience.[5]

Russia's early warnings about the COVID-19 pandemic's spread to Africa clashed with the narratives of African officials. On 11 February, Oleg Ozerov admitted that COVID-19 was present in Africa,[6] which conflicted with the African Union's denials of the virus's spread and Ethiopia's desire to dampen speculation about flight suspensions to China. By early April 2020, Russian and African officials were united

RUSSIA'S AFRICA POLICY IN THE AGE OF COVID-19

on combatting COVID-19, and the Kremlin's policies mirrored the prescriptions that RIAC stipulated. As Russia saw its status elevated by much-publicized medical aid shipments to Italy and the United States in April 2020, it sought to play a decisive role in ameliorating Africa's medical equipment shortage. On 21 April, the Russian Foreign Ministry stated that a number of African states had asked Russia for ventilators, testing kits and PPE, and noted Moscow's track record of assisting African countries during natural disasters and helping Africa contain the Ebola epidemic's spread.[7] On 28 April, Russia stated that it was processing requests for humanitarian assistance from Algeria, Egypt, Libya, Mauritania, Morocco, Sudan and Tunisia.[8] Despite these pledges, Russia's medical aid provisions fell short of expectations, as Russia focused its limited resources on containing cases at home and using medical aid as an instrument of leverage in Europe. Russia's negotiations with Algeria on medical aid abruptly unravelled.[9] South Africa's consultations with Russia on infection control on 4 April, which saw Cyril Ramaphosa praise South Africa's 'long friendship with Russia' and extol Russia's aid deliveries to China, the US and Italy, did not result in medical aid.[10] On 18 June, Ethiopian Ambassador to Russia Alemayehu Aargau admitted that Ethiopia was still waiting for medical aid that Russia pledged to deliver on 16 April.[11]

Russia's efforts to show solidarity with African countries during the pandemic were more effective. On 24 March, Ethiopia's Abiy Ahmed unveiled a three-point proposal for G20 countries to combat COVID-19 in Africa. It consisted of a $150 billion emergency financing package, G20 support for the World Health Organization (WHO) and Africa's Centers for Disease Control (CDC), and a coordinated G20 debt restructuring initiative for African countries.[12] On 7 April, Vladimir Putin spoke with Abiy Ahmed about his proposals and implicitly endorsed the financial planks of Ethiopia's proposals by calling for IMF and World Bank coordination against the COVID-19 pandemic.[13] On this issue, Russia aligned with France, which was the most active supporter of debt restructuring for Africa in the UN Security Council, and conflicted with China's support for limited restructuring rather than blanket debt forgiveness. Russia also championed António Guterres's early calls for a pandemic

237

ceasefire and called for an immediate de-escalation in MENA conflict zones, such as Libya.[14] However, the potential for a UN-mandated pandemic ceasefire resolution to suspend Russia's military interventions in Syria and Libya caused Moscow to abruptly change its position. As the Trump administration also opposed the ceasefire resolution, because it wanted to keep open the option of striking Iran-aligned proxy militias and ISIS in Iraq, Russia sided with the US and against France, which was the main UN Security Council backer of this resolution.[15]

Although Russia's inconsistent policies towards COVID-19 in Africa restricted its soft power gains on the continent, Russian media outlets consistently defended China against racism allegations in Guangzhou. In April 2020, many Africans in Guangzhou were evicted from their apartments and subjected to racial harassment, which was inspired by the popular conspiracy that African migrant workers had spread COVID-19 to China. These racism allegations resulted in an official protest to the Chinese government from the Group of African Ambassadors in Beijing.[16] Mirroring *Xinhua*'s refusal to report on these developments, Sputnik ignored the Guangzhou events, and RT only published the Chinese official response denying structural racism in Guangzhou. RIA Novosti vociferously defended China over the Guangzhou affair, as it claimed that the measures against Africans were solely aimed at preventing a second wave of the pandemic. The outlet accused the US of using 'five Nigerians' to drive a wedge between China and Africa, much like it had used Xinjiang to sully China's partnerships in Asia.[17] Russia's solidarity with China over the Guangzhou racism controversy built on its alignment with Beijing over the origins of COVID-19 and the 30 June Hong Kong national security law, thereby strengthening Sino-Russian relations.

## Russia's Vaccine Diplomacy Efforts in Africa

As the buoyant mood surrounding Russia's influence in Africa, which was so apparent after the Sochi Summit, stalled during the early months of the pandemic, Moscow turned to vaccine diplomacy to revive its fortunes. The Russian Direct Investment Fund (RDIF), which oversees Russia's COVID-19 immunization efforts, aggressively marketed its Sputnik V vaccine throughout Africa in the fall of 2020. These efforts initially struggled to gain traction with the crucial exception of Morocco. After South Africa, Egypt and Tunisia, Morocco suffered the fourth largest number of recorded fatalities from COVID-19, and ranked tenth in Africa for COVID-19 deaths/per capita. The relative severity of Morocco's outbreak caused it to look for a quick-fix solution to its COVID-19 crisis. In September 2020, the RDIF signed a deal with Moroccan pharmaceutical manufacturer Galenica to locally produce the Sputnik V vaccine. On 20 November, Artyom Tsinamdzgvrishvili, the head of Russia's trade mission in Morocco, announced that the RDIF would ship Morocco enough doses to vaccinate 20% of its population, and declared that Morocco's manufacturing plant could act as a hub for vaccine deliveries across the region.[18] Russia viewed Morocco as a viable vaccine hub because of its diverse array of free trade agreements with the US, EU and Turkey, and countries in both Africa and the MENA region. After Morocco, Egypt and Algeria were Sputnik V's next two breakthrough countries in Africa. On 12 November, RDIF had signed a memorandum with Pharco Pharmaceuticals, which would allow Egypt to potentially supersede Morocco as a COVID-19 vaccine hub. While the arrival of Sputnik V was greeted with optimism, Egypt's laboratories lacked the infrastructure to produce the vaccine. Mahmoud Fouad, head of the Egyptian Center of the Right to Medicine, implied that Russia had not passed its technological secrets for vaccine production to Egypt.[19] As Sputnik V's arrival in Morocco and Egypt drew closer, RDIF Director-General Kirill Dmitriev told a UNGA special session on 16 December that Sputnik V was on its way to Algeria, and that Russia was working with Nigeria on the establishment of a local production facility.[20] On 10 January, Algeria authorized Sputnik V and the head of Algeria's Finance Ministry Abdelaziz Fayed announced plans to distribute 500,000 doses of the vaccine free of charge.[21]

Guinea was the first Sub-Saharan African country to authorize Sputnik V, as it had an established track record of cooperating with Russia on matters of public health. Rusal worked with the Russian Ministry of Health on Guinea's Ebola struggle and in December 2018, the aluminium giant tested the GamEvac-Combi Ebola vaccine on 2,000 participants.[22] Due to its twenty years of cooperation with Guinea, Rusal claims that it is the first private company to assist Africa against epidemic disease.[23] Building on this success, Guinean officials began using the Sputnik V vaccine on 31 December, and on 16 January 2021 Alpha Condé became the first African leader to be immunized by Sputnik V.[24] On 29 January, Guinea finalized its authorization of Sputnik V. The rising tide of 'vaccine nationalism' in the US and Europe during the first half of 2021, which saw Western countries refrain from mass donations to the Global South, created more openings for Russia's vaccine distribution to Africa. On 19 February, the African Union announced that the RDIF offered it 300 million Sputnik V doses.[25] By 30 March, Sputnik V was authorized by a total of fifteen African countries (Algeria, Guinea, Tunisia, Gabon, Ghana, Egypt, Angola, Congo, Djibouti, Kenya, Morocco, Cameroon, Seychelles, Mauritius and Mali). By 13 May, Sputnik V had also been authorized by Angola and Namibia. Despite this continent-wide outreach, Russia's Sputnik V deliveries continued to have a two-speed distribution in Africa. The Maghreb continued to lead the way with southern Africa trailing in second place, while the remainder of the continent embraced Sputnik V with greater caution.

As the Maghreb was the secondary epicentre of COVID-19 in Africa, aside from South Africa, Russia's vaccine diplomacy achieved instant success. On 9 March, Tunisian Prime Minister Hichem Mechichi spoke with Lavrov and announced the imminent arrival of 1 million Sputnik V vaccine doses. Tunisia, which had Africa's highest rates of COVID-19 deaths per capita, relied on Sputnik V in part because of its desire to encourage the return of Russian tourists.[26] On 4 April, 100,000 doses of Russia's Sputnik V vaccine arrived in Tripoli's Mitiga airport. Libya's interim Prime Minister Abdul Hamid al-Dbeibah described these vaccine deliveries as a 'first drop of rain', as the war-ravaged Libyan public health system was strained by the burden of an estimated 1,000 daily new COVID-19 infections.[27] Russia also worked around Egypt and Algeria's manufacturing limitations and distinguished itself from China and Western countries, which often supplied vaccines to North Africa without substantive plans to develop local production infrastructure.

240

## RUSSIA'S AFRICA POLICY IN THE AGE OF COVID-19

On 7 April, Algeria confirmed that it had already received 50,000 Sputnik V doses and announced that an Indian laboratory would help state pharmaceuticals company Saidal produce the Russian-made vaccine in the eastern city of Constantine. Lotfi Benhamed, Algeria's pharmaceutical industry minister, stated that three committees facilitated the transfer of Russian vaccine technology to Algeria and would allow Algeria to emerge as a vaccine hub in Africa by the fall 2021.[28] On 22 April, Egypt's pharmaceutical firm Minapharm agreed to produce 40 million doses per year of the Sputnik V vaccine, which would lead to a mass roll-out in the third quarter of 2021.[29]

Alrosa's entrenched presence in Angola and Zimbabwe played a crucial role in facilitating Sputnik V vaccine transfers to southern Africa. In February 2021, Alrosa CEO Sergei Ivanov pledged to buy and donate Sputnik V vaccines to Angola and Zimbabwe, which would be distributed in mid-March.[30] The pausing of AstraZeneca over blood clot concerns caused the Angolan authorities to vaccinate 40,000 people in mid-May with Sputnik V and Angola also was one of the initial countries to test the RDIF's alternative one-shot Sputnik Light vaccine.[31] While Zimbabwe remained heavily reliant on Sinopharm and Sinovac, it also authorized Sputnik V for use on 9 March. Elsewhere in Africa, Russia largely confined its vaccine shipments to smaller and more sporadic doses. Russia's shipment of 12,000 doses to Congo on 23 March typified its vaccine distribution efforts in West, Eastern and Central Africa. One exception to this trend was Ghana, which ordered 1.3 million Sputnik V doses for mid-May 2021 after receiving 600,000 AstraZeneca vaccines from the COVAX initiative for developing countries.[32] Another potential exception is Ethiopia, which announced plans to purchase Sputnik V on 30 April as a part of its broader plans to expand bilateral and multilateral cooperation with Russia against COVID-19.[33]

Although most African countries were reliant on Chinese-made vaccines and India's Novavax scheme for low-income countries, the AU treaded cautiously about accepting mass Sputnik V vaccinations. The comparatively high cost of Sputnik V, which was $9.75/dose or $19.50 for a two-dose vaccination, made it less appealing to African countries than AstraZeneca's $3/dose vaccine, Pfizer's $6.75/dose vaccine and Johnson & Johnson's $10 single-dose vaccine.[34] This

241

contrasted with CEO of RDIF Dmitriev's claims at the UNGA that the RDIF had received requests for 1.2 billion vaccine doses, as it was the world's least expensive vaccine to date. The RDIF regarded local production initiatives in African countries with sufficient infrastructure, such as Morocco and Nigeria, growing availability, and its superior effectiveness to Sinovac, which suffered a high-profile immunization setback in Seychelles, as major selling points. In spite of the RDIF's aggressive sales pitches, authorizations of Sputnik V often did not readily convert into widespread vaccine use and Russia's vaccine distributions often mirrored the slow pace of its allotment of humanitarian aid earlier in the pandemic. The RDIF-AU vaccine distribution deal was postponed to May 2021, Kenya publicly rejected using Sputnik V and Russia had only shipped 100,000 doses to Algeria, Tunisia and Guinea by 12 March.[35] Foreign competition has also diluted Russia's marketing of Sputnik V. In Egypt, Sinopharm and AstraZeneca continued to supersede Sputnik V as the vaccine of choice.[36] Russia's Sputnik V vaccine deliveries to Libya were followed by the arrival of 57,000 AstraZeneca doses from the COVAX initiative and 150,000 Sinovac doses distributed by Turkey.

South Africa's reluctance to authorize Sputnik V was another major blow to Russia's vaccine diplomacy efforts in Sub-Saharan Africa. At the BRICS summit in November 2020, which was hosted by Russia, Vladimir Putin emphasized the importance of collaboration between BRICS countries against COVID-19 and urged all five countries to 'join forces' in the mass production of vaccines.[37] Putin's request for BRICS vaccine cooperation did not gain traction, as Sputnik V was only authorized by India and was publicly rejected by Brazil's regulators. Despite an urgent warning in the April 2021 issue of the *South African Medical Journal*, which implored South Africa to authorize Sputnik V to combat a third wave of infections and boost immunity amongst urban health care workers,[38] South African officials moved slowly on authorizing the Sputnik V vaccine. On 19 February, South Africa's Health Ministry made a request for Sputnik V and Denis Logunov, the deputy head of the Gamaleya National Center for Epidemiology and Microbiology, subsequently emphasized the vaccine's effectiveness against the South

# RUSSIA'S AFRICA POLICY IN THE AGE OF COVID-19

African COVID-19 variant.[39] On 9 April, Alexander Gintsburg, the lead scientist behind Sputnik V, conceded that the vaccine was less effective against the South African variant but admitted that the decline in antibody response was significantly lower than Western-made vaccines.[40] In response to these reports, South African Health Minister Zweli Mkhize announced on 28 April that South Africa would order 10 million doses of Sputnik V and expressed optimism that the regulatory bodies would approve the Russian vaccine.[41]

Despite these pledges, the Sputnik V vaccine did not arrive in South Africa. Vladimir Shubin hoped that South Africa's large immunocompromised population, which included a 19% HIV-AIDS prevalence rate, would lead to a swifter authorization of Sputnik V but decried administrative inefficiencies and a Western smear campaign as a cause for the delay.[42] In South Africa, the prevailing view on Sputnik V follows a different narrative. Gustavo de Carvalho dismisses the notion that South Africa has an aversion to Sputnik V because of its Russian origins, and contends that South Africa's vaccine policy is driven by technical considerations. De Carvalho earmarks two reasons for South Africa's delayed authorization of Sputnik V. First, South Africa's pharmaceutical industry had established links with Johnson & Johnson, which restricted their ability to strike deals with Sputnik V. Second, Sputnik V's potential ineffectiveness against the South African variant of COVID-19 was a serious concern, as South Africa had been forced to send back AstraZeneca vaccines for this reason.[43] South African academic Theodor Neethling contends that South Africa rejected Russia's initial efforts to market Sputnik V because the vaccine was not authorized for use by the WHO.[44] Notwithstanding these rationales, the gap between South Africa's rhetoric and policy towards Sputnik V appears to be creating a new source of friction with Russia.

By the spring of 2021, concerns mounted about Russia's involvement in price-gouging and serious discrepancies between the pledged and delivered supplies of vaccines.

They also coincide with growing disquiet in the continent of Moscow's commercial practices. In November 2020, Rwandan environmental groups and civil society organizations pushed back against Rosatom's nuclear energy forays in Rwanda. Frank

243

Habineza, the leader of Rwanda's opposition Democratic Green Party, spearheaded this charge, warning 'Living near a nuclear energy plant is like living near a nuclear bomb which can explode and cause destruction of life and property for the nation and its neighboring countries.'[45]

These controversies have not prevented African countries from signing new commercial deals with Russia in the public health or nuclear energy spheres. Sputnik V's new one-shot Sputnik Light vaccine is gradually gaining traction in Africa, as it was approved for use in the Republic of Congo in June 2021 and was green-lighted in Egypt in September 2021. Russia and Zimbabwe's MOU on nuclear energy production, which has no binding commitments, suggests that Russian mega-projects still have support from anti-Western or economically isolated African countries.[46] However, they reinforce the image that Russia is opportunistically seeking commercial profit or is actively exporting products that are harmful for their African target markets. As Russia continues to make controversial forays into the telecommunications sector, which included the sale of 'intelligence transport monitoring' surveillance systems to Uganda in July 2021, these doubts will likely continue to grow.[47] Of even greater short-term significance to Russian companies could be Moscow's perceived unreliability as a commercial partner. While Russia's energy, arms and mining projects in Africa have a poor track record of success, as they are often signed from over-ambitious or informal targets, mishaps in the public health sphere are especially deleterious to its image. By early July 2021, Ghana had received just 20,000 out of 3.4 million doses, while Angola had received 40,000 out of 12 million doses.[48] While Russian authorities insist that the doses are arriving 'soon' and there has been no public dispute in Africa, such as the clash between Guatemala and Russia over supply deliveries, these delivery delays undermine a key plank of Moscow's appeal, which is its standing as a crisis-proof partner.

### Russia's Evolving Relationships with External Powers in Africa

Russia's vaccine diplomacy campaigns have largely occurred in a unilateral rather than a coordinated fashion but have nevertheless

## RUSSIA'S AFRICA POLICY IN THE AGE OF COVID-19

profoundly impacted Moscow's standing in Africa. In Western countries, there are sharp divisions of opinion on the viability of Sputnik V transfers. France was the first country to sound the alarm about Russia's vaccine diplomacy in Africa. On 18 February 2021, Emmanuel Macron urged European countries to distribute 5% of their vaccine supplies to Africa to prevent Russia and China from gaining a decisive geopolitical advantage.[49] On 23 March, White House press secretary Jen Psaki claimed that Russia and China were using vaccine deliveries to advance their geopolitical goals. However, US officials presented a more ambiguous picture. Former US Secretary of State for African Affairs Tibor Nagy quipped that when it comes to public opinion, 'health diplomacy is much less effective than building a stadium'. Nagy noted that the US has spent $100 billion on health care in Africa since 2000, which was largely directed to fighting HIV-AIDS, but this has not matched China's conversion of infrastructure spending into soft power. Given this perspective, Nagy predicted that Russia's vaccine diplomacy in Africa would not significantly bolster its long-term influence.[50] Based on her experience aiding the Obama administration's struggle against HIV-AIDS in Africa, Michelle Gavin of the Council of Foreign Relations was more sanguine about the impact of public health investments. Gavin noted that the Chinese state's ability to take credit for privately distributed medical aid was a significant advantage and contended that the US government has often struggled to take credit for transformative public health investments, which have been supported by institutions like the University of Pennsylvania or Harvard University.[51] As Russia has distributed COVID-19 vaccines via state-owned companies but lacks China's investment capabilities, the impact of Russian vaccine diplomacy on its soft power could fall somewhere between the efforts of the US and China.

Although Russia's vaccine diplomacy in Africa has not been an unbridled success, the Kremlin-aligned commentators have highlighted these vaccine deliveries as proof of Russia's rising geopolitical influence. In a November 2020 *International Affairs* article, political scientist Andrey Kadomtsev claimed that an 'officially announced vaccine race is becoming an essential element of interstate rivalry' and 'advanced medical developments embody

245

the most important components of national power and prestige'.[52] In spite of this emphasis on geopolitical contestation, Kadomtsev insisted that Russia did not distribute vaccines to Africa and other regions of the Global South on a quid-pro-quo basis. These comments sparked a fierce backlash from the Kremlin and caused Russia to emphasize win-win cooperation in the vaccine diplomacy sphere instead of Moscow's competitive advantage. In response to Psaki's comments, Lavrov stated on 23 March that allegations of Russian vaccine diplomacy were 'absolutely not true'.[53] On 26 March, Dmitry Peskov condemned Western insinuation that 'Russia and China are engaged in some vaccine war and abuse the coronavirus pandemic and vaccines as a certain leverage.'[54] A RIAC article of 5 April reiterated these criticisms of Macron's comments and claimed that Russia's Sputnik V vaccine deliveries amounted to 'people's diplomacy', which is interstate humanitarian cooperation without political undertones and is akin to US public diplomacy. The report justified this view by stating that Sergei Lavrov's rhetoric at the Russia-Africa Partnership Forum linked Russia's medical aid to Africa to 'principles of humanism and mutual assistance' rather than competition.[55]

Looking ahead to a post-pandemic world order, the outlook for Moscow's relationships with external powers on the continent is bleak. President Joe Biden's inauguration in January 2021 sharpened US-Russia frictions in Africa. The deterioration of Franco-Russian relations in the Central African Republic and the Sahel have sullied prospects for EU-Russia cooperation. Russia's strengthening partnerships with non-Western powers, such as China and Turkey, have not extended to Africa, and Moscow could find itself at loggerheads with Beijing and Ankara in the months ahead. While Russia's diverse array of tactics and strengthening partnerships in Africa are considerable advantages, the absence of Russian cooperation with external powers could place an upper limit on its great power status. As a result, Russia could find itself mired in between second-tier powers in Africa, such as Britain, India, Japan and Turkey, and top-tier powers, the US, China and France, with slim prospects of elevation and a high risk of relegation.

Under Joe Biden's leadership, the United States has countered Russian influence in Africa through targeted sanctions and expanded engagement with African countries. In April 2021, the US Treasury Department imposed sanctions on Petr Byschkov, Yulia Afanasyeva and Taras Pribyshin for spreading disinformation in Africa.[56] These three individuals are the lead figures in AFRIC, which has served as a front for Prigozhin's influence operations in Africa. AFRICOM commander Stephen Townsend, a key supporter of containing Russian influence in Africa, stated that Russia's role is 'self-interested and exploitative' and pointedly targeted the Wagner Group as unhelpful to Africans.[57] The Biden administration has also incorporated the perspectives of House Foreign Affairs Committee chairman Gregory Meeks, who criticized the Trump-era fixation on combatting Russian and Chinese influence in Africa and urged the US to establish a genuinely collaborative relationship with Africa.[58] The expansion of US vaccine deliveries to Africa is a step in this direction, as are growing discussions in Washington about holding a US-Africa Summit, which mirrors continent-wide conferences hosted by Russia, China and France.[59] Jeremy Feltman's appointment as US Special Envoy for the Horn of Africa, which followed Trump's abrupt withdrawal from Somalia, underscores the Biden administration's efforts to fill vacuums that Russia could capitalize on.

Despite these statements of intent, Russian media outlets and experts are not anticipating major changes in US policy. A *Krasnaya Vesna* of 6 April article argued that the tone of US-Africa relations could improve under Biden but noted slim prospects for an expansion of US development assistance or an escalation of US military activities in Africa.[60] On 14 February, an *International Affairs* article noted Biden's expanded attention to human rights in Nigeria, Ethiopia and Uganda, but predicted that Biden would struggle to escape 'Trump's African trap'. The Biden administration's refusal to reverse Trump's recognition of Morocco's sovereignty over the Western Sahara was viewed in Russia as a move that would perpetuate the Trump-era decline in US soft power in Africa.[61] Given these expectations, Russia will likely not adjust its Obama and Trump-era strategies in Africa and will view US passivity in Libya, Sudan, Mali, Chad and the Central African Republic as a green light to continue its policies.

Due to Russia's entrenched military presence in CAR and growing ambitions in Mali and Chad, Franco-Russian relations

247

in Africa are expected to deteriorate further. On 20 November 2020, Emmanuel Macron blamed Russia and Turkey for fomenting anti-French sentiments in Africa and accused both countries of pandering to post-colonial resentment.[62] Russian experts do not view these comments as a sign of Macron's resolve to curb Russia's influence in Africa but instead see them as a sign of French weakness. Vasily Filipov, an expert at the Institute for African Studies, earmarked rising anti-French sentiments amongst African youths, the tendency of Sahelians to sympathize with Islamists over 'French peacekeepers' and France's deteriorating relations with its counterterrorism partners as proof of Paris's weakness.[63] The imminent end of Operation Barkhane will likely further embolden Russia to capitalize on France's detachment from Africa and intensify proxy rivalries between the two countries. While Russia is trying to compartmentalize Europe-Russia relations from Franco-Russian tensions, EU-Russia coordination will likely be confined to dialogue on Libya and multilateral cooperation on maritime security threats in the Indian Ocean.

An examination of the trajectory of Russia-China relations in Africa presents a more ambiguous picture. At first glance, Sino-Russian relations in Africa appear to be thriving. In December 2020, Wu Peng and Vsevolod Tkachenko, the heads of the Chinese and Russian Foreign Ministry's African departments, emphasized cooperation on public health, peacekeeping and economic development, and praised each other's diplomatic achievements in Africa.[64] A March 2021 RIAC-PKU policy report, which was jointly produced by the RIAC and the Peking University (PKU) Institute for International and Strategic Studies (IISS), opined that Russia and China have 'no irreconcilable differences' and 'are not competing for influence in Africa, but on the contrary, can complement each other's positions and approaches'.[65] The report illustrated robust Sino-Russian security and normative cooperation that was diluted by targeted economic cooperation. It listed the strength of Russia-China bilateral relations, the commitment of both countries to stabilizing Africa and the shared threat of terrorism as key sources of cooperation, and itemized bilateral trade, energy exports and military-technical cooperation as major areas of contestation.[66]

## RUSSIA'S AFRICA POLICY IN THE AGE OF COVID-19

Beneath this optimistic rhetoric, the limitations of Russia-China cooperation in Africa are clear. Consultations between Russia and China on African security crises, such as Libya, CAR and Sudan, are limited, especially outside the UN Security Council. China's condemnation of 'the attempt to seek change in power through force and other unusual means'[67] after Mali's August 2020 coup contrasted with Russia's immediate engagement with Assimi Goïta. The tactical divergence between Russia and China, which was noted in the RIAC-PKU report, could also sow the seeds of discord. Paul Goble, an advisor to former US Secretary of State James Baker on Soviet foreign policy, predicted in June 2021 that Russia and China 'are virtually certain to find themselves at odds in the future', as Moscow's strategy of filling vacuums is constricted by the consolidation of Chinese hegemony in Africa.[68] In May 2020, David Shinn opined in a testimony to Congress that Russia's reliance on Wagner Group PMCs in Libya, Sudan and CAR could pose a long-term threat to Chinese interests in Africa.[69] As Russia views instability in Africa as a geopolitical opportunity and China sees security crises as an existential threat to its BRI investments, disagreements between both countries are likely to sharpen.

Turkey's rising influence in Africa, which is exemplified by the increase in its embassy presence from twelve to forty-four under Erdoğan, poses both opportunities and challenges for Russia. Turkey's opposition to French military interventions in Africa, which date back to Operation Serval in Mali, and synergistic anti-colonial narratives from Turkey and Russia are key points of synergy. While Turkey's use of infrastructure, humanitarian aid and targeted military training to expand its influence diverges from Russia's reliance on arms sales and PMCs, both countries could emerge as strategic competitors in Africa. Elem Eyrice, an expert on Turkey-Africa relations at Yasar University in Izmir, contends that relations between Turkey and Russia in Africa are characterized by 'suspicion and crisis' and highlighted rivalries in Libya and Sudan as precedents for their future interactions in Africa.[70] Erkan Sahin, a researcher at Selcuk University in Konya, notes that Turkey-Russia relations in Africa are 'both dependent and competing', and contends that Syria-style disagreements could emerge even in areas of common interest,

249

such as counterterrorism.[71] Regular denunciations of Wagner Group activities in Africa in Turkish media outlets, which extend to areas of peripheral interest to Turkey like the CAR and Mozambique, and Russian media alarmism about Turkish expansionism in Africa suggest that a narrative war is afoot between the two countries that will be difficult to squelch.

## Russia's Balancing Strategy between Egypt and Ethiopia

Despite the wave of positive momentum in the Russia-Egypt partnership that followed the Sochi Summit, Moscow-Cairo relations did not improve in a uniformly linear fashion. While Sisi's threats of military intervention in eastern Libya and frustrations with Russia's Sputnik V vaccine distributions created temporary frictions in the Russia-Egypt relationship, the GERD dispute inflicted more lasting damage. As tensions between Egypt and Ethiopia soared over the GERD, Russia backtracked on its Sochi Summit promise to mediate and instead supported an African-Union-led resolution of the crisis. As Egypt wished to internationalize the GERD dispute by engaging great powers and the UN Security Council, and Ethiopia insisted on an African-led solution, Russia's position aligned more closely with Ethiopia rather than Egypt. Lobbying efforts by Egyptian officials aimed at changing Russia's view on the GERD dispute fell flat. Ahead of Lavrov's April 2021 trip to Cairo, Sameh Shoukry urged Russia to 'play a more influential part' in the GERD dispute and leverage its close relations with Ethiopia to 'reduce tensions caused by them in East Africa and the Horn of Africa'.[72] Sergei Lavrov responded by insisting that Russia was not asked to mediate the GERD dispute and reaffirming Moscow's support for an African-led solution.[73]

Russia's resolute support for an AU-led mediation triggered backlash in Egypt. Emad Eddine Hussein, an Egyptian Senator and editor of *al-Shorouk*, described Russia's position on the GERD as 'very negative' and claimed that Vladimir Putin was 'trying to satisfy Ethiopia on the issue of the dam'.[74] Mamdouh Munir contended that Russia's GERD position showed that it valued its partnership with Ethiopia over Egypt, as backing Addis Ababa would allow Russia to coordinate with China against the United States.[75] In Egypt,

## RUSSIA'S AFRICA POLICY IN THE AGE OF COVID-19

Russia's stance on the GERD and Tigray was viewed as 'negative neutrality', which reflected the unwillingness of great powers to make statements that would weaken Abiy Ahmed's domestic position ahead of the June 2021 elections.[76] Vasily Nebenzia's comments of 8 July, which acknowledged the legitimacy of Egypt and Sudan's concerns about the GERD causing drought, and implicit criticism of Ethiopia's unilateral second filling of the dam,[77] did not assuage Egypt's concerns. The long-term impact of Russia's GERD position on relations with Egypt was more unclear. Mohamed Farid, an Egyptian Senator, noted that the GERD posed an 'existential threat' and could have a more unpredictable impact on Russia-Egypt cooperation than previous areas of disagreement.[78] Another Egyptian analyst suggested that it would not do damage to the Russia-Egypt relationship, as Cairo had been able to work around similar disagreements with China.[79] Notwithstanding these ambiguities, Egypt more aggressively courted US and European support for its position on the GERD, and participated in NATO's Sea Breeze drills. These maneuvers did not result in a whole-sale re-evaluation of the US or EU position on the GERD but signified Egypt's willingness to divest from Russia.

Egypt's concerns about Russia's trustworthiness as a partner were further amplified by its reaction to the Suez Canal blockage in March 2021. On its official Twitter account, Rosatom facetiously quipped that 'You might get stuck in the Suez Canal for days' and advertised the Northern Sea Route as an alternative to the Suez Canal.[80] Rosatom's special representative for Arctic development, Vladimir Panov, claimed that the Suez Canal blockage underscored the fragility of a Europe-Asia trade route and urged Japan, South Korea and China to consider alternatives to the Suez Canal.[81] The Russian Foreign Ministry swiftly augmented Rosatom's attacks on the Suez Canal's viability. On 12 April, Lavrov told Iranian officials that the Suez Canal blockage should expedite the growth of the North-South transit corridor, as land transport routes were more reliable than trans-continental maritime waterways.[82] Mohammed Orabi, who served as Egypt's Foreign Minister in 2011, expressed confidence that Russia's divestment efforts would have minimal impact, as the normal flow on the Suez Canal resumed and

251

alternative projects would take time to implement,[83] but Moscow's efforts to capitalize on Egypt's predicament reinforced scepticism about its reliability.

As tensions between Egypt and Russia grew, Moscow compartmentalized its disagreements with Cairo over the GERD and strengthened its cooperation with Ethiopia as an alternative partner. Russia's delivery of Su-35 jets played a critical role in containing tensions with Egypt. During the spring of 2020, the Su-35 jets were assembled for distribution and on 23 February Secretary of State Anthony Blinken urged Sameh Shoukry to reconsider purchase of these jets. Despite Blinken's cajolery and the threat of US sanctions, Russia announced on 25 February that five of the twenty-four Su-35 jets had arrived in Egypt.[84] After some initial speedbumps, Putin also authorized a restoration of Russian flights to Egyptian resorts on 8 July. Egyptian officials widely praised this move, as Russia shored up Egypt's tourism sector at a time when it was being battered by security concerns and the aftershocks of the COVID-19 pandemic. Egypt's Deputy Minister of Tourism and Antiquities predicted that 300,000 to 400,000 Russian tourists would arrive in Egyptian resorts every month. Elhamy el-Zayat, the former head of the Egyptian Tourism Federation, predicted that it could lead to 1.5 million trips per year.[85]

The El Dabaa nuclear reactor has also helped preserve Russia-Egypt cooperation, despite rumours that dissension over the GERD had stalled Rosatom's dialogue with Egyptian officials.[86] The delay in El Dabaa's expected completion from 2028 to 2030 was also linked to political tensions between Russia and Egypt. On 15 July, a joint Russian-Egyptian delegation inspected the El Dabaa nuclear reactor site and, in early August, Russia began producing core catcher devices 1 and 2 of the plant. Russia and Egypt have both taken steps to showcase their commitment to El Dabaa and have a vested interest in ensuring that it progresses to completion. In March 2021, Russian Ambassador to Egypt Georgy Borisenko described El Dabaa as a project that was comparable to the Aswan High Dam.[87] Egypt believes that the nuclear reactor will benefit the development of Mersa Matruh governorate, which is a priority region for Sisi's economic plans.[88] In January 2018, Mersa Matruh created an

RUSSIA'S AFRICA POLICY IN THE AGE OF COVID-19

'integrated investment project', which spans the hospitality and infrastructure sectors, which is expected to create 20,000 jobs.

As the limits of Russia-Egypt strategic cooperation were exposed, Moscow came to view Ethiopia as an increasingly appealing regional partner. As Trump pivoted strongly towards Egypt's position on the GERD, Russian media outlets accused the US of abandoning its 'former ally' Ethiopia and positioned itself as a reliable alternative partner.[89] The outbreak of the Tigray War in November 2020 gave Russia an opportunity to highlight its reliability as a partner to Ethiopian officials. At the conflict's outset, Russian experts did not anticipate a role for external powers in the Tigray War, as Ethiopia was keen to assert its sovereignty, and criticized Abiy Ahmed's pro-Western orientation and failed economic policies.[90] China spearheaded the campaign within the UN to derail criticism of Ethiopia's conduct in Tigray, and on 5 March, Russia joined China at the last minute to block a UNSC call to end violence in Tigray.[91] Much like the GERD, Russia championed an African Union solution to the Tigray War and reaffirmed this position even as Tigray plunged into famine. On 2 July, Vasily Nebenzia stated that 'the situation in Tigray must remain an internal affair of Ethiopia' and urged the UN Human Rights Council to refrain from publishing a statement on Tigray that unduly blamed Ethiopian officials for the crisis.[92] Nebenzia also placed Ethiopia's unilateral ceasefire announcement in Tigray, which was unveiled on 28 June, as a positive step towards ending the conflict.

The synergistic impact of Russia's conciliatory positions on Tigray and the GERD bolstered its soft power in Ethiopia. On 30 May, 10,000 people attended an anti-US rally in Addis Ababa, which protested the imposition of sanctions against Ethiopian officials, and held placards of Vladimir Putin. Discussions about Ethiopia's 'eastward pivot' gained prominence within the foreign policy establishment and this diplomatic reorientation bolstered Russia's standing as a potential partner.[93] Moreover, Russia's position on Tigray helped abate the generational and religious cleavages, which limited its soft power in Ethiopia. Kalkidan Yibeltal, an Ethiopian journalist who covered the anti-US protests, noted that the Ethiopian Orthodox Christian community was historically pro-Russian, but Russia's soft power

253

in Ethiopia diminished dramatically in the 1990s and early 2000s due to its support for the Derg regime.[94] While cultural contacts, such as the exposure of young Ethiopians to Russian literature during the Derg era, kept Russia's image afloat, Moscow's stance on Tigray now provided a political foundation for it soft power. Russia's support for an AU-led solution to the GERD and Tigray crises, also resonated at a popular level. Within Ethiopia, resentment of Britain's marginalization of 'black African' countries from Nile River access reached new heights and Egypt's contravention of African institutions was viewed as a sign of its 'overall racist views against Black Africa's development'.[95]

Russia's positions on Tigray and GERD could also deepen its security and diplomatic cooperation with Ethiopia. On 9 June, Russia and Ethiopia agreed to strengthen coordination between their respective security services, and to deepen intelligence cooperation. This pact complements a similar agreement struck with Israel in February 2021.[96] Space cooperation, which was formalized by a Russia-Ethiopia agreement in March, and anti-piracy in the Gulf of Aden are additional areas of security cooperation.[97] In April 2021, Ethiopian Foreign Minister Demeke Mekonnen asked Oleg Ozerov for the opportunity to host the second Russia-Africa summit in Addis Ababa in 2022. While Ethiopia's bid faces competition from Djibouti, the connectivity of Ethiopian Airlines in Africa is a significant logistical advantage. The close relationship between Russian Ambassador to Ethiopia Yevgeny Terekhin, who speaks Amharic, and his Ethiopian counterpart Alemayehu Tegenu, who was educated in Tashkent, also boosts Ethiopia's case. Despite these positive developments, Russia's economic ties with Ethiopia continue to lag those with Egypt, and suggest that Moscow will likely opt to balance between Cairo and Addis Ababa in the years ahead.

9

# NEW FRONTIERS OF RUSSIAN SECURITY POLICY IN AFRICA

The COVID-19 pandemic coincided with deepening insecurity and instability in Africa. Civil wars in Libya and Central African Republic persisted, Sudan's democratic transition faced chronic strains and the Sahel was marred with insurgencies and coups. These manifold security crises presented Russia with a mixture of challenges and opportunities, and heralded sweeping changes in Russian policy. As Russia's military intervention on Haftar's behalf in Libya unravelled, Moscow pivoted towards a 'multiple bets' approach that balanced relations with the Government of National Unity (GNU) and anti-systemic actors. Russia's approach to growing political violence in the Central African Republic was starkly different, as Moscow expanded its military intervention on Touadéra's behalf. As civil-military relations in Sudan remain parlous, Russia aligned with the Sudanese military by securing a base agreement in Port Sudan, while keeping an open door to its civilian authorities. Russia has pursued a flexible diplomacy strategy in the Sahel, which has allowed it to partially fill the vaccuum left by France's drawdown and adapt to regime changes in Mali, Chad and Guinea.

The long-term effectiveness of Russia's recalibrated hybrid warfare techniques and balancing strategies are unclear, but

Moscow's actions reaffirm its standing as a continent-wide great power. The remainder of this chapter will examine Russia's policy shifts in Libya, the Central African Republic, Sudan and the Sahel, and provide a window into the future of Moscow's interventions in four of the most unstable countries and regions in Africa.

## Russia Recalibrates Its Strategy in Libya

Despite persistent calls for a pandemic-inspired ceasefire in Libya, the LNA's attacks on residential neighborhoods in Tripoli continued unabated. On 26 March 2020, LNA spokesperson Major General Ahmed al-Mismari stated that his forces had captured the towns of Jumail, Regdalein and Zultun in northwestern Libya, surrounded Tripoli on three sides and killed over one hundred Turkish-aligned Syrian mercenaries in seventy-two hours.[1] Hours later, Fayez al-Sarraj announced Operation Peace Storm to expel the LNA from western Libya. This GNA counteroffensive was a resounding success. On 18 May, GNA forces recaptured the strategic al-Waiya airbase, and on 6 June the GNA moved the battlelines to central Libya by launching a counter-offensive on Sirte and Al Jufra Airbase. Russia responded to the LNA's setbacks by expanding its military intervention and attempting to freeze the conflict through a mixture of clandestine and public outreaches to Speaker of the Libyan House of Representatives Aguila Saleh and Khalifa Haftar.

Due to the GNA's escalating counter-offensive and incoherent pushback from the international community, Russia's military intervention in Libya expanded in the spring of 2020. The Wagner Group increased its military presence and escalated its attacks on Libyan civilians and received greater aerial support from the Russian military. In May 2020, a UN Panel of Experts report on arms embargo violations in Libya concluded that the Wagner Group acts as 'an effective force multiplier' for Haftar and has deployed between 800 and 1,200 forces in Libya. To compensate for the GNA's rapidly growing manpower advantage, the Wagner Group began recruiting Syrian mercenaries from Assad-held areas to fight in Libya. Audio-recordings, which were leaked by a Syrian National Youth Party leader in al-Suwayda in March 2020, revealed that the

## NEW FRONTIERS OF RUSSIAN SECURITY POLICY IN AFRICA

Wagner Group offered Syrians $1,000/month to guard military installations in Libya, $1,500/month to participate in combat operations and extra compensation for families if Syrian troops are killed.[2] These new recruits did not greatly enhance the Wagner Group's efficacy in offensive positions. On 25 May, 1,500–1,600 Russian-aligned mercenaries retreated to Bani Walid, located 150 km from Tripoli, taking heavy equipment, such as Pantsir S-1s, with them. This contingent of Wagner Group PMCs relocated to Jufra, an LNA stronghold.[3]

As the influx of Wagner Group PMCs failed to turn the tide, Russia deployed MiG-29 and Su-24 fighter jets to Libya in May 2020. The entry of Russian aircraft had a negligible impact on the conflict's trajectory and were likely deployed to stall the GNA's counter-offensive while Russian backchannel diplomacy intensified. In an embarrassing setback, two Russian jets crashed in the weeks following their arrival. These crashes were attributed to mechanical failures and potential friendly fire, as Pantsir S-1 air defence systems might have mistakenly shot down unmarked Russian jets.[4] Nevertheless, the appearance of Russian aircraft in Libya alarmed US officials. AFRICOM asserted that these 'fourth-generation fighter jets' had arrived in Libya via Syria, where they were repainted to conceal their Russian origins. Pentagon spokesperson Jonathan Hoffman estimated that Russia had deployed a total of fourteen jets to Libya. Stephen Townsend stated that 'For too long, Russia has denied the full extent of its involvement in the ongoing Libyan conflict. Well, there is no denying it now', and compared Moscow's efforts to 'tip the scales in its favour in Libya' with the Wagner Group's prior actions in Syria.[5]

To dismantle Townsend's accusations, Russian officials insisted that Libya had merely refurbished Soviet-era jets. The Federation Council and State Duma were AFRICOM's most strident critics, as executive branch officials did not acknowledge the accusations. Federation Council Defence Committee and Security Chair Viktor Bondarev stated that 'if there are any airplanes in Libya, they are Soviet not Russian', and called AFRICOM statements on MiG-29 'crazy talk'.[6] Bondarev argued that the MiG-29 was early 1980s Soviet technology and likely arrived in Libya via sales from post-

Soviet republics, such as Ukraine and Moldova, during the 1990s. This statement was immediately greeted with scepticism, as Su-24 jets were not in Libya's arsenal during the Cold War. A September 2020 UN Panel of Experts report discredited Bondarev's claims by providing evidence that a MiG-29A fighter jet began operating at Al-Jufra base on 18 May, while Su-24s were operational from Al-Jufra and Al-Kadim bases later that day.[7] These aircraft arrived alongside a 'main battle tank upgrade', and two armoured personnel carriers designed for use by Wagner Group PMCs. Nevertheless, Bondarev's claims were repeated by other Russian lawmakers, such as State Duma Defence Committee Deputy Chairman Andrei Krasov and Federation Council Foreign Affairs Committee Chairman Vladimir Dzhabarov, who accused AFRICOM of spreading disinformation against Russia.

Although the arrival of Russian aircraft had little military impact, it signified Russia's willingness to use more brazen tactics in Libya. Instead of pursuing an outright LNA victory, the Wagner Group became a spoiler which would weaken the GNA's revenue stream, derail its seizure of military assets and dilute its morale. This spoiler role ensured that Russia's interests at the bargaining table could not be sidestepped and added coercive heft to its bids for oil-related reconstruction contracts. To compound the impact of Haftar's oil blockade, which spanned from January to September 2020, Wagner Group PMCs occupied Libya's major oil fields. In a Al-Ahrar interview of 5 July, Mustafa Sanallah revealed that Wagner Group PMCs had occupied the El-Sharara oil field, tried to smuggle oil from Tobruk's Hariga port and breached the Sidra port, which alongside Ras-Lanuf exports half of Libya's oil.[8] Condemnations from Libya's Mufti, who urged all Muslims to fight against Wagner Group PMCs and resist a Russian 'occupation of Libya', inflamed the GNA's Islamist partners.[9] The US Treasury Department supported the GNA by imposing sanctions on Prigozhin over Wagner's conduct in Libya and threatening sanctions against Haftar. The Wagner Group complemented its control of oil ports by securing positions in Libya's airbases and by 1 July, Wagner Group PMCs were stationed in Al-Jufra, Brak, Ghardabiya, Sabha and Wadden. Through capturing Libya's critical military infrastructure, Wagner Group PMCs could

## NEW FRONTIERS OF RUSSIAN SECURITY POLICY IN AFRICA

advance Russian interests independently and were no longer reliant on Haftar as a proxy.

The Wagner Group also resorted to extreme tactics such as the use of landmines and chemical weapons to advance its interests. AFRICOM also revealed photographic evidence showing Wagner Group PMCs 'indiscriminately placed booby traps and minefields' on the outskirts of Tripoli and Sirte in mid-June. On 13 July, Stéphane Dujarric, Guterres's spokesman, stated that these landmines had killed fifty-two civilians and wounded ninety-six around Tripoli.[10] These landmines aimed to slow the pace of the GNA's counter-offensive by increasing casualties, and bought the LNA time to regroup after Wagner's withdrawal from Tripoli in May.

Stephanie Williams noted that the UN did not act on the chemical weapons allegations, as that was in the purview of the Organisation for the Prohibition of Chemical Weapons (OPCW), and remarked that Libya's UN mission likely did not request a sweeping investigation.[11] The UN Panel of Experts has also failed to take decisive action against the Wagner Group. The May 2020 UN Panel of Expert report's discussion of the Wagner Group contrasted with the December 2019 report, which exclusively referenced mercenaries from Chad and Sudan. However, it did not call for UN sanctions against Prigozhin and António Guterres's description on foreign mercenaries did not mention the Wagner Group by name.[12] In September 2020, Germany attempted to release a UN Panel of Experts report detailing the Wagner Group's arms embargo violations, but this report was blocked by Russia and China.[13]

While the Wagner Group stalled the GNA's counter-offensive and embraced its spoiler role, Russia sought to secure its interests in Libya at the bargaining table. As Russia viewed Haftar's intransigence as a potential liability, it strengthened its relationship with Speaker of the Libyan House of Representatives Aguila Saleh. Andrey Chuprygin stated that Saleh began pursuing his own political ambitions after Haftar's defeats in early 2020. Although Saleh was unlikely to become Prime Minister, Russian officials believed that he could become a ceremonial president, who would also be acceptable to Turkey, Italy and France.[14] Russia's embrace of Saleh became public in April 2020, as Lavrov chastised Haftar and praised Saleh in back-

259

RUSSIA IN AFRICA

to-back statements. On 28 April, Sergei Lavrov stated that Russia disapproved of Haftar's efforts to 'single-handedly decide how the Libyan people should live' and compared his unilateral abrogation of the Skhirat Agreement to al-Sarraj's refusal to speak with Haftar.[15] Three days later, Lavrov praised Saleh's ceasefire initiative as 'exactly what we have been talking about all these years'. Saleh's admission that 'it's no secret that Russians are with us, including in our internal work' fuelled speculation that his ceasefire proposals were drafted in Moscow.[16]

As its alignment with Saleh strengthened and the LNA's military position weakened, Russia tried to freeze the Libyan conflict. A frozen conflict suited Russia's interests, as it could lead to a de facto partition of Libya, which would grant Moscow hegemony over its eastern regions.[17] On 30 April, Haftar made the GNA a ceasefire offer, and Saleh stated that this U-turn was made on the 'command of Russia'.[18] Russian officials privately urged Haftar to acquiesce to the reformation of the Presidency Council, which was formed by the Skhirat Agreement. As the GNA was gaining ground in Tarhuna and LNA refuelling supplies were disrupted, Russian officials convinced Haftar that the military situation in Libya was dire enough to accept a ceasefire. Russia's de-escalation efforts ended in failure. The GNA rejected Haftar's ceasefire on the grounds that it did not trust the LNA chieftain, and on 5 June, GNA forces triumphed in Tarhuna. Haftar's defeat in Tarhuna prompted Sisi to unveil the Cairo Declaration on 6 June, which called for an immediate cessation of hostilities and the institutionalized division of power between Tripoli, Cyrenaica and Fezzan. Bogdanov's endorsement of the Cairo Declaration reflected Russia's satisfaction with the agreement's decentralization of power on regional lines and solidarity with Egypt.

While Russia and Haftar's main Arab sponsors, Egypt and the UAE, presented a united front in public, the true picture of the relationship between these external powers in Libya was more ambiguous. Russia-UAE military cooperation in Libya continued unabated. Flight coordination between Russia and the UAE helped provide supplies to the LNA, as Russian flights moved war materiel from Syria to eastern Libya, while Emirati flights moved weaponry from western Egypt to eastern Libya.[19] A Pentagon report of

260

## NEW FRONTIERS OF RUSSIAN SECURITY POLICY IN AFRICA

November 2020 revealed the persistence of Emirati financing of Wagner Group PMCs in Libya. This military collaboration was diluted by divergent views on the diplomatic process. In April 2020, Egypt and the UAE coordinated with the US in derailing the appointment of Ramtane Lamamra as UN Special Envoy to Libya on the grounds that he had close ties with Russia and the Tripoli authorities.[20] While Egypt and UAE aligned to back Russia's empowerment of Saleh, Stephanie Williams recalled that the UAE was much less convinced by Saleh's leadership qualities.[21]

The main area of disagreement between Russia, Egypt and the UAE pertained to Turkey's diplomatic role in Libya. Russia's consistent engagement with Turkey on Libya, which included regular meetings between Turkish Foreign Minister Mevlüt Çavuşoğlu and Sergei Lavrov, clashed with Cairo and Abu Dhabi's belief that Ankara's military intervention in Libya unacceptably violated the sovereignty of an Arab state. Çavuşoğlu's 16 September statement that Turkey and Russia were on the verge of negotiating a ceasefire agreement sharpened this divide.[22] Russian officials also viewed their engagement with Turkey as an efficient way of marginalizing other stakeholders in Libya, such as Egypt and the UAE.[23] Due to its belief that military confrontation with Turkey in Libya was counter-productive, Russian media outlets criticized Sisi's June 2020 plan to intervene in eastern Libya, which was enthusiastically supported by the UAE and Aguila Saleh. Chuprygin warned that an Egypt-Turkey clash will lead to a 'colossal explosion of military problems throughout the Middle East', while Lavrov's emphasis on negotiations between Egypt and Turkey was interpreted as a critique of Sisi's plan.[24] A V*zyglad* article of 22 June claimed that Egypt's threat to intervene in Libya reflected its insecurity about its diminished status in the Arab world, which was laid bare by Ethiopia's GERD construction.[25]

As prospects for long-term diplomatic cooperation with Egypt and the UAE faded, Russia tried to find common ground with France. During his discussion with Putin on 26 June, Macron expressed optimism about the prospects of Franco-Russian cooperation in Libya. Three days later, Macron called Turkey's military intervention in Libya 'criminal' and chastised Turkey for 'massively importing' jihadists from Syria to Libya but refrained from criticizing Russia's military intervention in similar terms. When pressured about Russia's role, Macron admitted that he had expressed displeasure to Putin about the Wagner Group's conduct in Libya but noted that Putin 'plays on the ambivalence' of Wagner's relationship to the Russian state.[26] Çavuşoğlu responded by claiming that France was trying to increase Russia's role in Libya[27] but Turkey's criticisms, which were shared by other NATO members, did not deter Franco-Russian engagement in Libya. The poisoning of Alexei Navalny on 20 August, which strained EU-Russia relations, did not derail dialogue between France and Russia on Libya. This cooperation contrasted markedly with the stark deterioration of Franco-Russian relations in the Central African Republic and Sahel in the second half of 2020.

### Russia's Involvement in Libya under the Government of National Unity

The 23 October 2020 ceasefire in Libya, which paved the way for the 5+5 talks that created the GNU, caused Russia to thaw its relationship with Tripoli. Although Russia maintained open channels of communication with the GNA throughout Haftar's Tripoli offensive, Russian officials viewed Fayez al-Sarraj as an ineffectual leader. On 21 September, Bogdanov openly questioned Sarraj's authority by stating that 'many issues are controlled by armed groups in Tripoli' and that there are 'different structures that do not really listen to the positions of the official authorities'.[28] Bogdanov attributed the GNA's refusal to release detained Russian nationals, Maxim Shugaley and Samer Seifan, to the influence of these militias. Sarraj's refusal to endorse the September 2020 agreement between GNA Deputy Prime Minister Ahmed Maiteeq and Khalifa Haftar in Sochi, which ended the oil embargo, and obstruction of Maiteeq's visit to Sirte to sign the agreement exposed intra-GNA rifts to Russian officials.[29] Breakthroughs in negotiations on Shugaley and Seifan's release in mid-October resulted in a shift in Russia's rhetoric on the GNA. On 5 November, Bogdanov endorsed Sarraj's decision to rescind his resignation as Libya's Prime Minister, as Russia did not wish to see a power vacuum in Libya.[30] As LNA-aligned media outlets, such as

## NEW FRONTIERS OF RUSSIAN SECURITY POLICY IN AFRICA

*Al-Arabiya*, had accused al-Sarraj of staying due to Turkish pressure, Bogdanov's solidarity with the GNA was especially noteworthy.

When Shugaley and Seifan were released on 10 December, Russia-GNA relations immediately improved. On 30 December, GNA Foreign Minister Mohamed Siyala and Ahmed Maiteeq met Lavrov in Moscow. Unlike the tensions that sullied Siyala's June 2020 visit to Moscow, *Kommersant*'s Marianna Belenkaya noted that 'the atmosphere of the meeting was strikingly different from other negotiations with Tripoli representatives. The interlocutors were clearly pleased with each other.'[31] Despite this goodwill, Siyala and Lavrov disagreed on the reasons for the stalled Libyan peace process. In a veiled reference to France and Russia's support for Haftar, Siyala lamented divisions within the UN Security Council. Lavrov dismissed Siyala's assertions and claimed that the delayed appointment of a UN Special Envoy, which occurred because the US was silencing the African Union's voice, impeded progress towards peace. Russia's support for Libya's elections in December 2021 and calls for a de-escalation between Haftar and Turkey assuaged GNA concerns. Maiteeq's meeting with Russian Minister of Industry and Trade Denis Manturov in January 2021 revived Moscow-Tripoli commercial cooperation, which included discussions about SSJ100 and MS-21 passenger aircraft sales.[32]

The selection of Abdul Hamid al-Dbeibah as Libya's interim Prime Minister and Mohammed Menfi as Presidency Council chairman in February 2021 was an unwelcome surprise for Russian officials. After extensive backchannel negotiations with Turkey and Egypt, Russia was confident that Aguila Saleh and Fathi Bashagha would triumph in the Libyan Political Dialogue Forum (LPDF) vote.[33] While Dbeibah was known to Russian businesspeople, as he oversaw Libya's housing and utilities sectors under Gaddafi, he also used his influence to stymie the activities of the Russia-Libyan Business Council.[34] In spite of their reservations about the GNU, Russia welcomed Dbeibah to Moscow in April 2021 with open arms. After meetings with Putin, Mishustin, Patrushev, Lavrov and Shoigu, Dbeibah called Russia a 'great nation' and called for the revival of Russian energy and infrastructure projects in Libya. Shoigu described the Libyan people as 'Russia-friendly', and claimed that his meeting with Dbeibah rebooted Russia-Libya defence ministry cooperation.[35] This meeting reignited Russia-Libya cooperation in the energy sector. On 27 May, Gazprom announced plans to expand its oil production in Libya from 43,000 to 62,000 BPD, which ended a ten-month hiatus in extraction from its Libyan oil field, and Tatneft has repeatedly announced plans to revive its oil exploration presence in Libya.

While Russia publicly supported the GNU, it also maintained close ties with Tobruk-based officials. Russia's intention to hedge its bets in Libya became apparent just weeks after the 23 October ceasefire. On 20 November, Russia blocked a UNSC resolution advanced by the US and Germany, which would have imposed an asset freeze and travel ban on Haftar-aligned al-Kaniyat militia leader Mohammed al-Kani for massacres in Tarhuna.[36] Despite evidence of al-Kaniyat's perpetration of the September 2019 Tarhuna prison executions and the discovery of four unmarked graves in the summer of 2020, Russia claimed that there was insufficient evidence al-Kani was involved in civilian casualties. Russia's active engagement with Tobruk-based officials, such as Foreign Minister Abdel Hadi al-Huweij and LNA General Heiri al-Tamimi, in the days leading up to Dbeibah's appointment underscored Moscow's desire to maintain its relationships in eastern Libya. On 27 January, Bogdanov told al-Huweij that twenty Russian companies wished to invest in eastern Libya, while al-Huweij insisted that Turkish 'terrorist mercenaries' were Libya's main security threat and denied the existence of Wagner Group PMCs.[37] As tensions between Haftar and Dbeibah escalated, the LNA chieftain thwarted Dbeibah's planned visit to Benghazi in April, and the Wagner Group stealthily deployed 300 additional Syrian mercenaries to strengthen Haftar's position.[38]

Russia's ties with anti-systemic actors have fuelled concerns about its potential interference in Libya's elections, which were scheduled for December 2021 and subsequently delayed. Russian election interference could include smear campaigns against hostile candidates and efforts to elevate the ambitions of Kremlin-friendly figures. Due to his support for a US military base to counter Russian influence in Libya and condemnations of the Wagner Group, Fathi Bashagha is routinely castigated by Prigozhin-aligned media outlets. The Federal News Agency described Bashagha in April 2020 as a

# NEW FRONTIERS OF RUSSIAN SECURITY POLICY IN AFRICA

'clever, cynical and unprincipled son of the Muslim Brotherhood in Misrata', and has repeatedly claimed that Bashagha aligned with al-Qaeda in Misrata.[39] Prigozhin's smear campaign against Bashagha prevented him from meeting Russian officials in January 2021.[40] Russia has refrained from supporting Aguila Saleh, as Libyan lawmakers have refused to legitimize Lavrov's claims that Moscow's military intervention in Libya received HoR approval. Due to uncertainties about its relationship with Saleh and Haftar's mixed signals about running in the elections, Russia could support multiple candidates in the Libyan elections that might advance its interests. Aref Nayed, the Tobruk-based government's ambassador to the UAE from 2011 to 2016, could receive Russian support. On 13 August, Bogdanov met Nayed in Moscow to discuss Libya's election after the LPDF failed to agree to a constitutional procedure.[41] Nayed also published a book entitled *Russian Engagements: On Libyan Politics and Libyan-Russian Relations* in 2019, which reflected favourably on his academic collaboration with Russian institutions.

Russia could also support Saif al-Islam Gaddafi's political aspirations. Prigozhin remains Gaddafi's primary backer, as he issued two films lionizing Shugaley's pro-Gaddafi efforts and paid 18 million rubles to Shugaley and Seifan via Concord in December 2020. Prigozhin's pro-Gaddafi activism could reflect Kremlin support.[42] Bogdanov has repeatedly expressed support for Gaddafi's participation in Libya's elections, and on 15 January he met with Saif al-Islam Gaddafi's representatives. In August 2021, a RIA Novosti article dismissed Haftar as 'not fit for this role', and stated that Gaddafi has no competitors as a unifying figure in Libya. The article stated that Gaddafi could secure 57% support in Libya by earning the loyalty of a broad array of regions and tribes.[43] A Libyan intelligence officer stated that 'If Russia had its way, we would have Saif al-Islam Gaddafi giving his victory speech in Tripoli's famous martyr's square.'[44] However, there are reasons to be sceptical of Russia's pro-Gaddafi stance. Stephanie Williams notes that Gaddafi's ICC warrant harms his reputation, and that his extensive media machine might not translate into support on the ground. Russian experts concur with this view, as estimates of his support run from as low as 1.3% to as high as 7%.[45] Williams also stated that Russia's indifference

265

to Al-Saadi Gaddafi's plight raises doubts about its commitment to supporting Gaddafi loyalists.[46] As Libyan prosecutors announced plans to impose criminal charges against Gaddafi over his collusion with the Wagner Group in August 2021, his political aspirations were called into question. Despite these uncertainties, Bogdanov's threat to withdraw support for the Libyan elections if Gaddafi was not allowed to be a candidate underscored Moscow's enduring belief in his viability as a pro-Kremlin figure.

Russia's efforts to expand its geopolitical influence in Libya could be thwarted by its dearth of partnerships with other external powers. The UAE and Egypt's tentative de-escalation of tensions with Turkey and public embrace of the GNU have ameliorated their main frictions with Russia. While Russia's much-discussed Benghazi-to-Sirte railway project might complement Egypt's proposed Benghazi-to-Marsa-Matrouh rail-line, Moscow is likely to compete with Cairo and Abu Dhabi for reconstruction contracts. Russia's relations with Europe and the US in Libya will likely also remain contentious. Russia has criticized the EU's Naval Force Mediterranean Operation Irini inspections and described Greece's 11 January inspection of a Russian cargo ship off Libya's coast as 'incomprehensible'.[47] US President Joe Biden's appointment of Richard Norland as Special Envoy to Libya in May could also increase US-Russia tensions, as he has praised Turkey's military intervention in Libya while condemning the Wagner Group. If the Biden administration eventually reverses the US's Trump-era disengagement from Libya, tensions between Russia and the US could escalate further.

The prospects of Russia-Turkey cooperation in Libya, which influenced Moscow's calculations during the final stage of Haftar's Tripoli offensive, have also receded. Ferhat Polat, an Istanbul-based expert on Libya, contends that the immediate risk of conflict has receded, but Turkey-Russia relations are likely to remain 'contentious and competitive' rather than cooperative.[48] Despite pressure from France and dialogue at the June 2021 Berlin Conference on the departure of foreign forces, neither Turkey nor Russia wish to unilaterally withdraw its mercenaries from Libya. Turkey insists that its presence in Libya is legal, as it was invited by the UN-recognized GNA, while Russia continues to claim that the Wagner Group is

266

# NEW FRONTIERS OF RUSSIAN SECURITY POLICY IN AFRICA

dissociated from the Russian state. Beyond the mercenary issue, numerous other fault-lines impede Russia-Turkey cooperation. Turkey possesses $13 billion in Gaddafi-era construction contracts and an exclusive economic zone agreement with Libya in the eastern Mediterranean, which gives it a decisive advantage over Russia in the post-conflict reconstruction process.[49] Turkey's engagement with Egypt in Libya is also aimed at diluting Moscow-Cairo cooperation.[50] These factors could prevent Russia and Turkey from compartmentalizing their disagreements in Libya like they have in Syria and Nagorno-Karabakh.

## Russia Consolidates Its Leverage in the Central African Republic

Although Russia's strategy towards the Central African Republic has remained consistent in the post-2018 period, the December 2020 elections tested Moscow's approach to the conflict. The Constitutional Court rejected Touadéra's efforts to postpone the elections over the COVID-19 pandemic in June 2020, and 800 polling stations were shuttered by political violence. Immediately prior to the CAR elections, former President François Bozizé mobilized loyalist forces near Bossembélé with the intention of marching on Bangui. These mobilizations caused the CAR government to warn of a coup attempt, which was emphatically denied by Bozizé, and UN peacekeepers were scrambling to prevent a Bangui blockade by Bozizé loyalists and ex-Seleka rebels, as voters went to the polls.

In response to this heightened state of insecurity, Russia recalibrated its CAR strategy in two ways. First, Russia expanded its military intervention in CAR. On 22 December, Russia deployed 300 military instructors to CAR to counter a 'sharp degradation of security' and answer Touadéra's call for military assistance. The nature of this force deployment was ambiguous, as it triggered contradictory narratives in Russia and CAR.[51] Mikhail Bogdanov insisted that the Russian military was not involved in CAR, and that the instructors were 'not the army nor the special forces'. Touadéra's spokesman Maxime Kazagui claimed that Russia sent 'soldiers and heavy weaponry' to support the CAR Armed Forces, and that Moscow's formal military presence aligned with pre-existing Russia-

CAR bilateral defence agreements. Second, Russia contributed to the CAR conflict's internationalization by militarily aligning with Rwanda to thwart France-Chad security cooperation. Rwanda sent 'several hundred' troops to CAR in a synchronous fashion with Russia and focused its efforts on containing Bozizé's threats against UN peacekeepers.[52]

These measures faced little resistance from the US or the EU, as Western powers concurred with Russia on supporting Touadéra's legitimacy, despite serious doubts about the fairness of the elections.[53] Moreover, Russian officials emphasized the temporary nature of these developments, but Moscow merely reverted to its pre-election tactics and sent a new batch of instructors to CAR in the spring and summer of 2021. On 15 January, Russia withdrew its instructors and three to four transport helicopters from CAR, as Touadéra's election victory was secured. This drawdown showcased the success of the joint Russia-Rwanda military intervention in CAR, which reduced friendly fire from the CAR armed forces and increased the efficiency of the CAR military's targeting of ex-Seleka rebels.[54] The Wagner Group's return to its counterinsurgency support role was apparent on 26 January, as CAR troops with Russian support killed forty-four rebels outside of Bangui.[55]

Russia's growing military intervention in CAR can be explained by a mixture of situational and strategic factors. Russia initially sought to thwart French interference in the CAR elections and capitalize on France's expected disengagement if Touadéra triumphed. During the CAR election campaign, individuals linked with the French military created fake Facebook accounts to counter the activities of Prigozhin's Internet Research Agency, a Russian troll farm in St Petersburg.[56] France's principal allegation was that Russia was seeking to extract resources from CAR, and the slogan 'The main destabilizer in the Central African Republic is Russian mercenaries! They are the real thieves!' featured prominently.[57] These posts assuaged fears of French neocolonialism, which dated back to the Bokassa era, and challenged the anti-colonial rhetoric that undergirded Russian soft power. Russia's social media campaign not only addressed France's 'destabilizing policies' in CAR, but also highlighted other narratives, such as its COVID-19 response to

268

## NEW FRONTIERS OF RUSSIAN SECURITY POLICY IN AFRICA

support Touadéra's counterterrorism efforts. Although this Franco-Russian information war extended to other African countries, such as Algeria, Cameroon, Libya, Mali and Sudan, it had a negligible impact on public opinion in CAR. Russia's on-the-ground activities, which consisted of Maxim Shugaley's pro-Touadéra propaganda and the promotion of Russian culture through ballet performances, might have had a greater impact on its soft power than social media efforts.[58]

France's meek response to the CAR's post-election turmoil, which consisted of a symbolic fly-over on 24 December and a Macron-Touadéra phone call, reassured Russia of its vulnerability. Russian media reports highlighted local backlash against France's efforts to discredit the CAR Armed Forces and Macron's failure to regain 'lost positions' as proof of France's weakness.[59] Russia's anti-French narratives were promoted locally by allies of Prime Minister Henri-Marie Dondra, who contrasted the efficacy of Wagner Group anti-extremist efforts against France's struggles in Mali, Lake Chad and the CAR.[60] French officials responded by claiming that Russia had suspended all cooperation with UN peacekeepers in February 2021, and was coordinating with Britain, Ireland, Estonia and the US on stalling sanctions committee meetings over the arrival of Russian military instructors. These measures were surprisingly followed by France's retrenchment from CAR. On 8 June, France cut €10 million to CAR over its tolerance of Russian disinformation, which included the rumour that France was moving its embassy from Bangui to Cameroon.[61] France's framing of Russian disinformation as a national security threat, as it targeted its military personnel, was followed on 18 June by its condemnation of Russia's 'seizure of power' in CAR.[62] Due to this chain of events, Russia's use of military deployments to expedite a French withdrawal could be framed as a tactical victory.

Beyond outflanking France, Russia used its military instructor deployments to counter human rights allegations against the Wagner Group and consolidate its long-term leverage in CAR. A UN report of March 2021 alleged that the Wagner Group PMCs were involved in mass summary executions, arbitrary detention, torture during interrogation, forced displacement of civilians, forced disappearances

269

and attacks on humanitarian organizations.[63] Russian PMCs were accused of opening fire on a vehicle at a checkpoint in Ouaka prefecture in December 2020, which resulted in three fatalities, and of attacking a mosque in Bambari. These actions triggered retaliatory attacks from the Bozizé-aligned Coalition of Patriots for Change (CPC), which ambushed Wagner Group PMCs in Manga and killed two Russian nationals. The US, Britain and France presented a coordinated condemnation of the Wagner Group's human rights abuses in June 2021.[64] US Deputy Ambassador to the UN Richard Mills noted the Wagner Group's threat against MINUSCA's deputy representative and a UN humanitarian delegation in Bang, which is at the intersection of CAR, Cameroon and Chad. Britain's Deputy UN Ambassador James Roscoe accused the Wagner Group of carrying out sexual violence in CAR. France's UN Ambassador Nicolas de Rivière focused on the Russian threat to Muslim communities and urged MINUSCA to release the names of Prigozhin-aligned figures involved in these crimes.

Russia's response to revelations of Wagner Group misconduct consisted of emphatic denials. Dmitry Polyanskiy discredited these reports by insisting that Russian military instructors were unarmed as they were instructors and insisted that he was unaware of soldier deployments.[65] Dmitry Peskov bluntly stated that 'Russian military advisors could not participate and never took part in murders or robberies, this is another lie.' Alexander Ivanov, director of the Officers Union for International Security (OUIS), which is a PMC that operates in CAR, aided the Kremlin's efforts to silence the story within Russia and manipulate international opinion in Russia's favour. Ivanov threatened to sue *Rosbalt* for reporting on the execution of five men in Bambari by Wagner Group forces These narratives were supported by the Russian media and sympathetic local voices.[66] Ivanov claimed that OUIS instructors were 'professors of military science and other humanitarian sciences', as well as 'specialists in military medicine and the educational sphere', and were not involved in the murders of civilians. Ivanov also stated that 'any success of Russia irritates some countries' and accused the French media of elevating anonymously sourced and unverified accusations of criminal activity by Russian PMCs.[67]

270

## NEW FRONTIERS OF RUSSIAN SECURITY POLICY IN AFRICA

Russian media outlets and sympathetic voices in CAR amplified the Kremlin's counterpoints. *Izvestia* redirected attention towards violence against Russian nationals in CAR, as it highlighted a mine explosion which resulted in the deaths of three Russian citizens.[68] Sputnik described these reports as an 'anti-Russia political hit job', and cited Mankeur N'Diaye's claims that Bozizé-aligned armed groups are responsible for most of CAR's human rights abuses.[69] As CAR rebels were widely viewed as mineral-hungry criminal entities that would not accept a political solution, the Wagner Group's aggressive tactics could be spun effectively in a positive light.[70] A Russian-CAR film called *The Tourist*, which starred Alexander Ivanov, packed Bangui's largest stadium and extolled the stabilizing role of Russian PMCs. Sylvain Nguema, a Bangui-based defence analyst, noted that Russia's December 2020 military intervention 'prevented a large-scale war on Central African soil' and Russian military assistance was still necessary now that the CPC had 'dispersed and changed its tactics'.[71] On 29 June, an article in CAR newspaper *Ndjoni Sango* praised Russia and Rwanda's continued efforts to help the CAR emerge from chronic instability and contrasted them with neocolonial powers that 'tried to tear CAR to a thousand pieces, to take possession of our resources, leaving our people in the dark, misery'.[72] This article mirrored the sentiments of the 3,000 pro-Russian protesters who congregated in Bangui in February 2021 with slogans such as 'Long Live Russia and Rwanda!' and 'No to Dialogue with the Terrorists of the Coalition of Patriots for Change!'

Despite this information counter-offensive, Russian officials were privately alarmed by the reputational damage to the Wagner Group. Russia reportedly considered a Wagner Group withdrawal from Bangui, mulled dismissing Ambassador Vladimir Titorenko and privately hinted to CAR officials that it would temporarily redeploy forces to Nigeria until the story faded.[73] CAR defence minister Marie-Noëlle Koyara, who worked closely with Russia, considered rival training proposals from the United States.[74] Russia-Rwanda coordination in CAR also diminished, as Rwanda pivoted its attention towards the crisis in northern Mozambique. Signals of a potential Russian retrenchment, which fuelled intense speculation in Bangui, proved to be an elaborate feint, as Russia expanded its

271

military presence in CAR. On 2 July, the Russian Foreign Ministry confirmed the arrival of 600 instructors to CAR to train the army, police and national gendarmerie, and notified the UN Security Council of these deployments.[75] These instructor deployments had been negotiated in the preceding months, as Valery Zakharov confirmed on 17 February that Russia-CAR military cooperation would 'expand further'.[76]

Russia has also taken major steps to consolidate its influence within the CAR economy. Russian nationals occupied customs stations in CAR and the CAR Finance Ministry delegated a growing number of responsibilities to its Russian advisors.[77] Russia has also taken steps to secure an advantageous position in the CAR's reconstruction. Pascal Bida Koyagbélé, the minister responsible for major works and investments in CAR, asked for $11 billion in reconstruction investments after an April 2021 meeting with Mikhail Bogdanov in Moscow.[78] These investments would consist of $6 billion for road projects, $3 billion for rail projects and a new city worth $2 billion. While Koyagbélé acknowledged that CAR was considering investment proposals from Britain, Germany and Norway, it would give Russia first rights to reconstruction contracts. Russia's ascension as Kimberley Process chair in 2021, which regulates conflict diamonds, could also complement its efforts to create loopholes in the UN sanctions regime against Touadéra. This would further consolidate Russia's first-mover advantage in the CAR's economic reconstruction and set the stage for more contentious Franco-Russian clashes in the UN Security Council.

## Russia Expands Its Presence on the Red Sea

The year 2020 saw a marked expansion of insecurity on the Red Sea. The November 2019 Riyadh Agreement, which created a coalition between Yemen's President Abd Rabbuh Mansur Hadi's government and the UAE-aligned separatist Southern Transitional Council (STC), raised hopes for a resolution of the Yemeni civil war. The August 2020 agreement between the Sudanese government and the Sudan Revolutionary Front (SRF), an alliance of armed groups in the Blue Nile, Darfur and South Kordofan, increased

272

## NEW FRONTIERS OF RUSSIAN SECURITY POLICY IN AFRICA

optimism about a stable democratic transition in Sudan. By the end of 2020, this mood of cautious optimism had been dashed. A wave of Houthi drone strikes on Saudi Arabia dashed hopes for a ceasefire in Yemen and al-Shabab gained momentum in Somalia, as US forces prepared to withdraw. On 3 November, an armed conflict erupted in Tigray, which saw Ethiopia and Eritrea militarily align against the Tigray People's Liberation Front. The GERD dispute resulted in an escalation of Egypt-Ethiopia tensions, while the historic Sudan-Ethiopia el-Fashaga border dispute reignited in December 2020. This atmosphere of insecurity lingered into 2021, as regional and multilateral diplomatic efforts failed to stabilize the Red Sea region.

In response to growing instability in the Red Sea region, Russia strengthened its security partnerships with Sudan and Ethiopia, while reiterating its support for non-interference and 'African solutions to African problems' in regional crises. Through these outreaches, Russia achieved notable successes, such as a prospective naval base in Port Sudan and an upgraded security agreement with Ethiopia. However, periodic frictions also surfaced in Russia-Egypt relations, which compounded their growing divergences in Libya. Russia was able to mitigate these frictions with Cairo by dangling the prospect of Su-35 jet sales and regular bilateral summits. While Russia's power projection capabilities trail other great powers, Moscow has capitalized on fluctuations in the US and EU commitment to Red Sea security, bolstered its standing as a rising power in the Indian Ocean, and countered the impact of Turkey's growing influence in Somalia and Sudan.

### Russia Consolidates its Security Presence in Sudan

Although Russia officially supported Sudan's democratic transition, Moscow upgraded its partnership with Khartoum through direct engagement with the Sudanese military. In August 2020, Sudan agreed to purchase Russian equipment at the Army-2020 Forum.[79] This deal underscored Sudan's importance as a Russian arms client, as Moscow's only other contract was with Laos, and its outreaches to Serbia and Mongolia did not result in weapons sales. Russia's embrace of the Sudanese military was apparent from its reaction to the October 2021 coup, which resulted in Hamdok's temporary detention and Burhan's seizure of power. Immediately after the coup, Russian state-aligned media outlets expressed concern about Western instigation. In an interview with Interfax, retired Colonel-General Leonid Ivashov warned that external forces, such as the United States, could be behind the coup.[80] Russian officials did not describe Burhan's takeover as a coup and called for non-interference in Sudan. Dmitry Polyanskiy stated that 'It was hard to say whether it's a coup or not. There are situations like this in many parts of the world, and they are not called a coup', and emphasized that the Sudanese people should decide if it is a coup.[81] Sergei Lavrov warned against interference in Sudan, which could destabilize Africa, and reiterated Russia's opposition to US democracy promotion efforts after the secession of South Sudan.[82] Russia emphasized the need for the UN Security Council to call for dialogue and a cessation of violence, but did not steer the body towards normative criticism of Burhan's extra-legal seizure of power. Russia's Ministry of Defence International Cooperation Directorate immediately held talks with Sudanese Chief of Staff General Mohamed Osman el-Hussein and dispatched a defence delegation to Khartoum.

Despite Russia's fluctuating relationships with Sudan's political authorities, it has persistently supported establishing a foothold on its Red Sea coast. On 12 November 2020, Russia unveiled plans to establish a logistical support centre in Port Sudan, which is located on Sudan's Red Sea coast. According to the basing agreement, which was signed by Russian Prime Minister Mikhail Mishustin, Russia's proposed Port Sudan facility would contain 300 military and civilian personnel and four ships, which included nuclear-powered vessels.[83] Russia also agreed to supply Sudan with military equipment required to guard the base for free and announced plans to use the Port Sudan facility as a resupply centre for Russian warships.[84] This basing agreement would last twenty-five years, and unless there were objections raised by Russia or Sudan, it would automatically extend in ten-year intervals. As the agreement had already been signed on 23 July 2019, in Khartoum, which was just six days after Sudan's democratic transition was ratified, it was signed into effect in Moscow on 1 December 2020.[85]

274

## NEW FRONTIERS OF RUSSIAN SECURITY POLICY IN AFRICA

Russia's naval facility agreement with Sudan serves two purposes. First, it allows Russia to preserve its relationship with the Sudanese military in the post-transition period and gives Moscow a foothold in Sudan that is immune to political volatility. Sudanese Foreign Minister Omar Qamar al-Din also admitted that he had not received a copy of the Port Sudan basing agreement prior to its ratification.[86] This suggests that Burhan sidelined Sudan's civilian authorities on Port Sudan, much as he had done with the Israel normalization. Anton Mardasov, an expert at the RIAC, contends that the Port Sudan base allows Russia to 'legalize' its military presence in Sudan and ensures the Russian military can assume responsibilities that were previously allotted to PMCs.[87] Russia's push for a legal military presence in Sudan reflects the Wagner Group's diminishing effectiveness in promoting Russia's interests and declining presence since Bashir's ouster. Cameron Hudson, the former chief of staff of the US Special Envoy to Sudan, notes that the Wagner Group operates outside of Khartoum to avoid public scrutiny and primarily works on guarding the Jabal Amer gold mine.[88] Through this guardianship role, the Wagner Group can capitalize on divisions within Sudan's military and intelligence services by establishing links with key figures in those bodies, but it is unable to project power on Russia's behalf at a national level.[89] As the most consequential aspects of Russia-Sudan bilateral relations are developed via the military and intelligence sectors, instead of the diplomatic sector, the naval base negotiations augmented the partnership between the security institutions of both countries.[90]

Second, Russia views its Port Sudan naval facility as a gateway to expanded power projection in the Red Sea, Eastern Mediterranean and Indian Ocean. After the Port Sudan agreement was announced, Russian security officials, such as RSB Group head Oleg Krinitsyn, highlighted Port Sudan's proximity to the Bab el-Mandeb Strait, which is critical to global oil exports.[91] The base would also allow Russia to challenge unquestioned US hegemony over the rules of navigation in the Red Sea.[92] Securing access to the Red Sea would additionally allow Russia to compete with Turkey, which had $650 million in infrastructure contracts and direct investments in Sudan's Suakin port at the time of Moscow's Port Sudan base

275

announcement.[93] The location of, and responsibilities allotted to, Russia's Port Sudan facility could also strengthen Moscow's presence in the eastern Mediterranean. Russian defence experts, such as Yuri Lyamin, believe that the Port Sudan facility could increase Moscow's access to the Suez Canal and alleviate pressure on Russia's facility in Tartous, Syria, which currently carries out most of the resupply responsibilities.[94] The redistribution of these responsibilities from Syria to Sudan could allow Russia's planned expansion of Tartous, which was announced in May 2020, to be completed more swiftly than expected.

Third, Russia believes that its Port Sudan facility will have reciprocal benefits for its cooperation with China and India on Red Sea security. This engagement will compensate for the near collapse of Russia-West cooperation on anti-piracy, but the escalation of China-India tensions presents Moscow with a difficult balancing act. While Chinese officials have remained silent about the Port Sudan facility, state-aligned media outlets have expressed cautious optimism about Russia's facility construction. Although COVID-19 and the possibility of Russian defence cuts could dilute the Port Sudan base's impact, *The People's Liberation Army Daily* viewed the installation as a key step in Russia's bid to 'break long-term strategic containment by the United States and NATO'.[95] Chinese media outlets also praised Russia's Port Sudan base as a bulwark against a potential 'colour revolution' in Sudan. As China-Russia-Iran trilateral drills in the Indian Ocean become routine and China is content with Russia spearheading their shared efforts to contain US influence in the Red Sea, China's Djibouti base and Russia's Port Sudan facility could cooperate in a harmonized fashion. Russia's Port Sudan base proposal has also earned plaudits in New Delhi. Rajesh Soami, an Associate Fellow at the National Maritime Foundation in New Delhi, contends that Russia's presence in the Indian Ocean is viewed favourably in New Delhi, especially as India seeks to prevent the creation of new Chinese naval bases in eastern Africa.[96] In December 2020, Russia and India held two sets of naval drills in the Eastern Indian Ocean region, while both countries pledged to sign an intra-naval mutual logistics pact. As India's naval power is concentrated in Seychelles, Mauritius, Madagascar

# NEW FRONTIERS OF RUSSIAN SECURITY POLICY IN AFRICA

and Comoros, Russia's Port Sudan base could lead to harmonized security cooperation.[97]

Due to Sudan's elevated importance to Russia's Red Sea strategy, Russian officials placed a high priority on upgrading its relationship with Khartoum. Although Sudan appointed a new Cabinet and internecine turmoil between Burhan and Hamdok prevented a clear green-light for the Port Sudan base, Russia operated under the assumption that the facility would proceed. The Russian MoD sent a delegation to Sudan in February 2021, which carried out reconnaissance on Port Sudan's technical capabilities and calculated the dimensions of the structures that would be erected on the base's site.[98] Russia paired its base construction forays with bilateral outreaches to Sudan.[99] On 30 March, Nikolai Everstov, a representative of Russia's Chamber of Commerce and Industry in Khartoum, announced Russia's plans to train Sudanese agricultural specialists to increase wheat production, provide Sudan with aviation technology like the Sukhoi Superjet, MS-21s and Il-114, and create a telecommunications network. Everstov also called Sudan Russia's 'gateway to Africa' due to its potential for rapid development and pledged to enhance Sudan's 'digital sovereignty' by providing it with modern communication security technologies and high-speed Internet.[100] These development investments allowed Russia to showcase its win-win cooperation with Sudan and commitment to the Red Sea region's economic development.

Despite these strides in the Russia-Sudan bilateral relationship, intra-Sudanese discord put an unexpected wrench in the base's construction. The basing agreement's opacity, which was exemplified by Lieutenant Colonel Hisham Hussein's refusal to take media questions and Hamdok's silence on the deal, exacerbated political frictions.[101] FFC supporters sharply criticized the Port Sudan base. Kamal Bolad, spokesperson for the FFC Central Council, claimed that the army had 'hijacked the position of decision-making', and asserted that 'There is no transparency in the ruling of this country.'[102] FFC supporters also attributed the basing agreement to Burhan's fear of the incoming Biden administration's human rights agenda and warned that Russia was using the base to recreate a Bashir-style tyranny in Sudan.[103] On 29 April, Sudan reportedly

277

suspended Russia's planned naval base and the cessation of 'any new deployment of the Russian military' on its soil. The Russian Embassy in Khartoum swiftly denied these reports, and on 2 May the Russian Navy's Amur class repair ship PM-138 travelled through Port Sudan to work on base construction.[104] In mid-May, Minister for Cabinet Affairs Khaled Omar Youssef informed Russia's Deputy Defence Minister Alexander Fomin of Sudan's unwillingness to extend the base offer.[105] This development was concealed by Russian and Sudanese official statements and state media outlets. On 2 June, Lieutenant-General Mohammed Othman al-Hussein and Mikhail Bogdanov both admitted that the terms of the Port Sudan basing agreement were being renegotiated.[106]

As speculation about a breach in Russia-Sudan relations circulated in Arabic media outlets, such as Qatar's Al-Jazeera and the UAE's *Al-Ain*, as well as the Western press, Russian and Sudanese officials sought to quash speculation about the base. During their 12 July meeting, Lavrov and Sudan's Foreign Minister Mariam al-Sadiq al-Mahdi insisted that the base negotiations would proceed. Nevertheless, doubts persisted. Al-Hussein's assertion that the terms of the basing agreement were 'somewhat harmful' raised questions about the negotiations. Al-Mahdi's contention that the Sudanese legislature would deliberate on the deal were equally dubious, as Sudan's legislature had not yet been set up.[107] To deflect from the Port Sudan base controversy, Russia and Sudan took pains to emphasize the overall progress of their bilateral relationship. Al-Mahdi praised Russia's approach to the GERD dispute, which was a rare departure from Egypt's critical position. This flattery was likely based on Sudan's belief that Russia could leverage its close relations with Ethiopia to delay the GERD filling.[108] Russia responded by condemning UNSC sanctions against Sudan, which were first imposed in 2004, and offering debt relief negotiations that would compound the positive impact of IMF debt forgiveness on the Sudanese economy. Lavrov and al-Mahdi also discussed a wide range of international crises, such as Israel-Palestine, Libya, Chad and CAR, which allowed Russia to elevate Sudan's status as a regional foreign policy actor.

The Port Sudan base construction moratorium provoked disparate reactions in Khartoum and Moscow. Sudanese analysts believed that

## NEW FRONTIERS OF RUSSIAN SECURITY POLICY IN AFRICA

the renegotiation was a temporary disruption to the base agreement and contended that security cooperation with Russia would facilitate Sudan's participation in the multipolar world order. Wasil Ali, the former deputy editor-in-chief of the *Sudan Tribune*, contended that Sudan saw few benefits from the agreement.[109] However, it also did not wish to abandon Russia and cast its lot firmly with the US, as Washington would not provide it with lethal arms or sophisticated military technology. Given these calculations, Ali contended that pressure from Saudi Arabia, which was fearful of the Russia-Iran partnership and did not want a Russian base near its territory, might have been the trigger for Sudan's renegotiation. Waiel Mahboub, a Sudanese engineer and commentator, acknowledged that Sudan was unwilling to engage in a confrontation with any external power during its transition period and that the base would only be rejected if it violated Sudan's sovereignty. As the Russian installation was only designed for the servicing of ships, there were no realistic concerns about state sovereignty in Sudan.[110] This lack of concern about Sudanese sovereignty is a notable triumph for Russia's narratives in Africa. Russia has used the Port Sudan base as proof that its long-term presence will strengthen the sovereignty of African states and not make it a new colonial power.[111]

Russia's analytical community was more pessimistic about the Port Sudan base than their Sudanese counterparts. When asked about the base renegotiations, Sergei Seregichev bluntly stated that 'I think that the Russian military base in the Port Sudan area will not be created.'[112] Boris Dolgov contended that the Russian base in Port Sudan was driven by Bashir's foreign policy orientation and expressed fears that closer US-Sudan relations could potentially derail the basing agreement.[113] Seregichev mused that Sudan was blackmailing the United States into providing it with multibillion-dollar investments in exchange for abandoning the Russian naval base.[114] This zero-sum view of Sudan's relationships with Russia and the US underscores Moscow's doubts about Khartoum's ability to sustain a genuinely multipolar foreign policy. Russia's analytical community is sharply divided on whether Moscow's Red Sea power projection ambitions depend on Sudan. A *Nezavisimaya Gazeta* article of 2 June contended that the cluster of foreign powers in Djibouti

279

RUSSIA IN AFRICA

ensures that Sudan is Russia's only plausible gateway to the Indian Ocean.[115] Sergei Kostelyanets, an expert at the Institute for African Studies, contended that Sudan's status as a recognized UN member state made it a much more desirable base location than eastern Libya or Somaliland.[116] Other experts, such as IMEMO's Ilya Kramnik, disagree, and contend that Eritrea and Somaliland could be realistic alternatives for a Russian naval base.[117]

In February 2021, Eritrean Ambassador to Russia Petros Tsegai revived Lavrov's logistics facility proposal, as he praised Russia's engagement with 'besieged countries'.[118] While US and EU sanctions on Eritrea over its involvement in the Tigray War could strengthen Moscow-Asmara relations, this is unlikely to extend to a naval base. Eritrea's lack of economic connectivity to Ethiopia and the disruption caused by the Tigray War have given Russia pause about long-term investments in Eritrea.[119] Eritrean Information Minister Yemane Meskel described the prospect of a Russian naval base as a 'wild assertion', which was 'not on Eritrea's radar screen'.[120] Despite the risk of violating Somalia's sovereignty and the potential for competition with Turkey, Somaliland is viewed as a more promising back-up location for a Russian naval base. A RIAC report in June 2021 speculated that Russia would likely pursue a logistics pact with Somaliland, which would partially recognize its sovereignty without providing Hargeisa with any security guarantees.[121] The prospect of Russia constructing a base in Somaliland is viewed with scepticism in Hargeisa. Abdirisak Mohamed, a Somaliland political analyst, stated that support for a base in Moscow is limited to some Muslim State Duma representatives and countervailing pressure from the US and Britain caused Russia to abandon its basing ambitions by 2015.[122]

Given the implausibility of these alternatives, the future of Russia's security presence on the Red Sea will likely revolve around the Port Sudan naval base for the foreseeable future. Although Burhan conceded in a November 2021 interview with Sputnik that there were some faults to be remedied', he insisted that the coup would not jeopardize the Port Sudan base's construction. The long-term future of the Port Sudan base could hinge on the acceptability of Russia's concessions to Sudan. While Sudan initially requested S-400 anti-aircraft systems, Su-30 and Su-35 jets and a 1,200 MW power plant on the Nile River, Russia is reportedly prepared to offer Sudan complimentary arms shipments and information about the hydrometeorological situation in the Red Sea.[123] Abdalla Hamdok's resignation in January 2022 could remove pressure from the Sudanese civilian authorities for a tougher bargain and allow Khartoum to accept Moscow's middle-ground offer.

## Russia Capitalizes on Growing Instability in the Sahel

During the first half of 2020, the security crisis in the Sahel intensified. According to the Armed Conflict Location and Event Data Project, political violence killed 4,660 people in Burkina Faso, Mali and Niger from January to June 2020, and more than 1 million people were displaced in the preceding year.[124] This upsurge of violence was followed by an alarming deterioration of regional governance, which manifested itself in a series of coups. In August 2020, Mali's President Ibrahim Boubacar Keïta was overthrown by Assimi Goïta in a coup d'état, which was followed by a pledged eighteen-month transition to civilian rule. On 20 April, Idriss Déby was assassinated immediately after his re-election by Front for Change and Concord in Chad (FACT) rebels, and Chad fell under the rule of the Transitional Military Council headed by his son Lieutenant-General Mahamat Déby. On 24 May, Mali's military-brokered transition was derailed by a second coup led by Assimi Goïta, which resulted in its expulsion from the African Union and France's suspension of military cooperation with Mali's army. On 5 September, Guinea's Armed Forces overthrew Alpha Condé, and installed Colonel Mamady Doumbouya as president. While the Guinea coup posed a threat to its economic interests, Russia saw the developments in Mali and Chad as opportunities to deepen its security involvement in the Sahel.

## Mali: The Newest Theatre of Russian Security Involvement in Africa

The Russian Foreign Ministry's reaction to the August 2020 Mali coup aligned firmly with the international consensus, as it called for Malians to peacefully resolve the crisis at the negotiating table.[125]

Despite this blandly predictable statement, Russia established cordial relations with Mali's transitional government and opposed a France-led effort to isolate Goïta's coup regime. On 21 August, Russian ambassador to Mali Igor Gromyko became one of the first foreign diplomats to meet with Mali's coup plotters.[126] While the meeting between Gromyko and the Malian military was officially about securing the Russian embassy in Bamako, it also reflected Moscow's belief that a democratic transition was unlikely, and that the coup needed to be normalized for Mali's political stability to be upheld. Citing prominent Africanists from the Center for Russian-African Relations Studies, RAS Institute for African Studies, such as former Russian ambassador to Mali Evgeny Korendyasov and Nikolai Scherbakov, *Izvestia* warned on 19 August that elections in Mali were unlikely to follow soon, and cautioned that jihadists would weaken Mali's central government.[127]

While Russia's embrace of Mali's coup plotters dovetailed with its strong-state approach to counterinsurgency, Moscow's welcoming response to the coup can also be explained by its close ties with Goïta's coalition. Colonel Malick Diaw, the Vice-President of Mali's National Committee for the Salvation of the People (NCSP) and the lead coordinator of the Mali coup, and his partner Colonel Sadio Camara, had attended a training course in Moscow from January to August 2020 and launched a coup d'état just days after returning to Bamako.[128] This fuelled speculation that Russia played a role in instigating the Mali coup. Malian army sources contended that Diaw and Camara had plotted the coup from Russia and might have received protective cover from the Kremlin as they planned Keïta's overthrow.[129] These allegations were denied by the Kremlin and were ultimately subsumed by ambiguous evidence. Oleg Morozov, a prominent member of Russia's Federation Council, refuted this speculation by saying that 'any talk that Russia is somehow involved in the August military coup looks ridiculous'.[130] Moreover, AFRICOM revealed that Goïta had participated in US Africa Command Flintlock Training exercises, and that Malian military personnel who received foreign training were typically a self-selected pool of ambitious cadres.[131] Therefore, it appears more likely that Russia pragmatically embraced Goïta's coterie

## NEW FRONTIERS OF RUSSIAN SECURITY POLICY IN AFRICA

as they were known quantities and anti-French, not because of Moscow's involvement in the coup.

Despite the promising start to Russia's relationship with Goïta, Moscow's subsequent engagement with Mali was largely inconsequential. The enthusiastic reaction of Kremlin-aligned media outlets to Malian demonstrators carrying Russian flags in March 2021, which was also observed after the August 2020 coup, encapsulated Moscow's focus on symbolism over substance. In response to these pro-Russian demonstrations in Mali, *Krasnaya Vesda* praised the contrast between Russia's effective establishment of order in Syria and the Central African Republic with 'the obvious failure of a number of Western countries in the Middle East and Africa in the fight against terrorism'.[132] France's information warfare machinery emphatically rebutted this narrative, as the slogan 'The Russian imperialists are a gangrene on Mali! Watch out for the Tsarist Lobotomy!' circulated on Facebook.[133] Russia did not offer meaningful military support or try to pry the Malian authorities away from France after Operation Barkhane was implicated in civilian casualties.

The May 2021 coup has fuelled optimism in Moscow about a more substantive expansion of Russia-Mali cooperation, as it corresponded with a reduction of France's commitment to counterterrorism operations in Mali. On 31 May, Emmanuel Macron warned that France would withdraw from Mali if the country was overwhelmed by 'radical Islamism', and on 3 June, France suspended its cooperation with the Malian authorities. Anticipating a disruption of France-Mali security cooperation, Russia did not emulate Paris's criticisms of the coup and instead presented an optimistic picture of the military takeover. Immediately after the coup, Russian officials appealed to Goïta by downplaying its potential to result in political violence and reaffirming their ties with the Malian military. Lev Matoshin, the press attaché of the Russian embassy in Mali, claimed that 'the situation in the capital of Mali and its environs after the military coup is calm'.[134] The Russian Foreign Ministry also praised Goïta's release of Mali's interim President Bah Ndaw and acting Prime Minister Moctar Ouane as positive steps, while still calling for a democratic transition.[135]

283

Russia has also bolstered its soft power in Mali by using the local reach of its media outlets to promote itself as a counterinsurgency partner and criticize French policy. A Federal News Agency article contended that Goïta would view Russia as a priority partner based on the success of their counterinsurgency efforts in CAR and highlighted slogans carried by the pro-coup demonstrators, such as 'France out', 'Putin help' and 'The Malian people demand a defence treaty with Russia'.[136] These slogans were paired with Cold War-symbolism, such as portraits of Che Guevara. While the demonstrations outside of Russia's embassy in Bamako consisted of only seventy to eighty people, Russian media outlets suggested that there was a groundswell of pro-Russian sentiments in Mali. Evgeny Korendyasov claimed that Malians were infuriated by France's decision to 'cut off the supply of food to Mali', which included replacing cane sugar with beet sugar, and claimed that polls showed that 2 million Malians wanted Russian support against Islamic extremism.[137] Despite these bold pronouncements, Russian officials acknowledged that Mali's initial focus is on repairing its relationships with its West African neighbors but believed that Mali will choose it over France as a partner.[138]

Russia's confidence in the prospective strength of its partnership in Mali facilitated its much-discussed Wagner Group PMC deal with Bamako in September 2021. A report on 13 September revealed that up to 1,000 Wagner Group PMCs could be involved, and that these mercenaries could cost the Malian authorities $10.8 million a month. While these figures are disputed, the Wagner Group PMCs would likely participate in military training and protecting senior Malian officials.[139] Russia and Mali's reactions to these reports were conflicting and did not dampen speculation about mercenary deployments. Dmitry Peskov immediately suppressed these reports by stating that no Russian mercenaries were present in Mali and no negotiations were taking place. Evgeny Korendyasov stated that reports about Russian mercenaries in Mali were 'wrong' and insisted that Malian civil society pressured the authorities to engage in talks with Russia about military aid, which had an uncertain outcome.[140] Sergei Lavrov was more candid about the negotiations, as he stated that Mali reached out to 'private Russian companies'

## NEW FRONTIERS OF RUSSIAN SECURITY POLICY IN AFRICA

for assistance as it was concerned by France's drawdown from the counterterrorism struggle.[141]

The Malian Defence Ministry's response was similarly ambiguous, as it refused to confirm or deny rumours about the Wagner Group's arrival. On 1 October, Russia delivered a cargo plane to Mali consisting of Mi-171Sh and M-17V5 helicopters, weapons and ammunition, which the Sadio Camara claimed were 'gifts' pledged in a December 2020 Moscow-Bamako defence deal.[142] During his 26 September UNGA speech, Malian Prime Minister Choguel Kokalla Maïga hinted at stronger defence cooperation with alternative partners, such as Russia, as he blamed France for unilaterally withdrawing from Mali and not discussing the future of Operation Barkhane with the Malian authorities.[143] While the exact nature of Moscow's security negotiations with Mali remained unclear, Russia deployed 500 PMCs to Bamako in late December 2021. The Malian authorities claimed that their recruitment of the Wagner Group was 'baseless' and insisted that 'Russian trainers' were recruited to strengthen Mali's security forces.[144] The junta justified Russia's entry into Mali on cost grounds, as it would be more financially efficient to have Russian trainers work in Mali than to send Malian officers to Moscow. On 7 January, Wagner Group PMCs surfaced in Timbuktu and were officially tasked with training Malian forces. These Russian PMCs occupied bases that were evacuated by France following the conclusion of Operation Barkhane in northern Mali.

As speculation about Russian PMC deployments in Mali intensified, the EU presented a united front against the expansion of Moscow's presence in the Sahel. France predictably led the chorus of condemnations, as French Minister for Europe and Foreign Affairs Jean-Yves Le Drian reminded the international community of the Wagner Group's human rights abuses in CAR, while French Minister of the Armed Forces Florence Parly said she was 'extremely concerned' by Russia's plans.[145] The Czech Republic warned that the Wagner Group PMC deployments were part of Russia's broader plan to 'convince Malians that the EU occupies Mali', while Germany framed Moscow's PMC deployments as an unambiguous anti-French or anti-EU gesture. Anna Fotyga presented a message of EU solidarity against Russian PMCs, stating that 'Many initiatives

285

RUSSIA IN AFRICA

have been taken to limit the detrimental impact of the Wagner Group on vulnerable states. Mali is just another example that we still have to do more.'[146] This EU solidarity spiked further after the arrival of Wagner Group PMCs was confirmed in December 2021, and was joined by condemnations from Canada, US Secretary of State Anthony Blinken and Turkey. AFRICOM raised concerns that the Wagner Group would seek to establish a permanent presence in Mali and argued that its deployments could pose a spillover threat to Mali's neighbours.[147] As Mali bolstered its reliance on Russian PMCs, participants in the EU's Takuba peacekeeping force exited through a mixture of voluntary withdrawals and forced expulsions. After Mali expelled the French ambassador over Le Drian's 31 January comments that the junta was 'illegitimate', France withdrew its remaining 2,400 counterterrorism forces. In a parting shot to Mali's military rulers, Macron blasted the Wagner Group of arriving with 'predatory intentions' and argued that the junta chose the Wagner Group because it wanted a partner to help 'protect its power, not to fight against terrorism'.[148]

The US and Europe's dire warnings about the Wagner Group's malign intentions in Mali ultimately came to fruition. Russia's counter-terrorism efforts and economic infiltration of Mali have failed to gain traction. On 19 December 2021, a Wagner Group-linked Tu-154 jet travelled from Russia to Bamako with stopovers in Syria and Libya, and French officials noted frequent visits by Wagner Group executives and affiliated geologists to Mali.[149] On 6 January 2022, the Malian army confirmed that Wagner Group PMCs had arrived in Timbuktu, and locals witnessed 'uniformed Russian men' driving across the city.[150] Wagner Group PMCs also moved to central Mali to combat al-Qaeda-linked Jama'at Nasr al-Islam wal Muslimin (JNIM) fighters and communal militias. The Soviet Union poured extensive capital into the Kalana gold project in southwestern Mali but Moscow's presence in Malian gold mines diminished after 1991 and was supplanted by the London-based Nelson Gold Corporation in 1997.[151] Russia was determined to overcome this trend. The Wagner Group struggled to secure profits from gold mines due to stricter government regulations than CAR and anti-Russian sentiments from non-state actors that control

286

## NEW FRONTIERS OF RUSSIAN SECURITY POLICY IN AFRICA

mines in northern Mali, such as Coordination des Mouvements de L'Azwad.[152] Grigory Lukyanov also noted that, until mid-February, Russia used the 'Malian card' as a bargaining chip in negotiations with France over security guarantees.[153] The Malian junta saw Russia as its most effective partner for authoritarian consolidation, as it was sanctioned by ECOWAS in January for its five-year plan for democratic transition.

Despite these failures and the Ukraine war, Russia has taken decisive steps towards establishing a long-term presence in Mali. Russia has also highlighted popular support for its counter-insurgency campaign in Mali to justify a long-term presence. Prigozhin-aligned entities used 'sociological research', planted interviews and disinformation to bolster Russian soft power. The Foundation for the Protection of National Values claimed that 87% of Malians backed Goïta's request for Russian counterterrorism assistance and hailed the increase in support for the junta from 62.9% to 72.5% in September 2021.[154] Alexander Ivanov framed the Wagner Group as an entity that works within existing legal frameworks and hailed its successes on a variety of terrains, such as the Syrian desert and the CAR jungle.[155] This triumphalist propaganda was supplemented with disinformation, which showed fake photos of Russian technical advisors training Malians when they were near Emperor Bokassa's palace in CAR, and the use of troll Facebook accounts like Moussa Dembélé, which praised Russia and criticized France.[156] Russia promoted contradictory narratives of France's unreliability and propensity to overstay its welcome. HSE academic Grigory Lukyanov argued that France's withdrawal from Mali when terrorism still posed a security threat highlighted its unreliability as a partner to states in West and North Africa.[157] A Federal News Agency article of 10 January blasted France's 'dreams of creating a new colonial empire' and accused Paris of not suppressing radical groups in Mali when it had a chance in 2013, as it preferred to assassinate figures like Gaddafi and Déby 'to continue the plunder of Africa'.[158] Lukyanov's HSE colleague Ivan Timofeev admitted that Macron's efforts to overhaul the notion that Mali was France's backyard failed, as the EU did not step up its role, and claimed without evidence that the French military would continue operations until June 2022.[159] The outbreak of the Ukraine

RUSSIA IN AFRICA

war saw Russia amplify these narratives, as Macron vacillated from being a voice of de-escalation with Russia to a strong supporter of EU efforts to punish Moscow for its aggression.

## Russia's Pursuit of Influence in Chad and Guinea

Russia's efforts to expand its influence in Chad and mitigate the risks associated with the Guinea coup underscore its desire to engage in a Sahel-wide competition with France. In contrast to its pragmatic accommodation of Mali's ruling authorities, Russia's influence in Chad hinges on its alignment with the FACT rebels. Russia's decision to centre its policy in Chad around an anti-systemic actor mirrored its alignment with Haftar in Libya and suggests that Moscow is exporting both its Libyan and CAR models of power projection to the Sahel. Although Russia and Chad signed a judicial cooperation agreement in October 2020, which would strengthen bilateral relations, tensions soon flared between the two countries over CAR. In December 2020, Russia and CAR were informed of Chad's alignment with Frederic Bozizé, and both countries believed that Chad was helping France expel Russia from CAR.[160] On 29 March, Vladimir Titorenko claimed that Chad was not helping CAR secure its shared border and noted that Chad's detachment caused weapons to flow into the hands of rebel groups. Chadian journalists and officials interpreted Titorenko's comments as a Russian accusation of arms trafficking. On 7 April, the Russian embassy in CAR tried to de-escalate tensions by denying that Titorenko had accused Chad of arms trafficking and praised Chad as a partner that works with Russia on regional stability.[161] This statement did not ameliorate Russia-Chad tensions, as they were swiftly subsumed by reports that the Wagner Group had trained the FACT rebels in Libya.[162] This training was the product of a non-aggression pact that the Chadian rebel group signed with Haftar in 2017.[163]

Although the Wagner Group did not train the FACT rebels for combat outside Libya, its arms provisions to FACT indirectly threatened Chad's security, as FACT rebels streamed into Chad from Libya in early 2021. Chad's Deputy Foreign Minister Oumar Ibn Daoud highlighted this security threat at the UN Security Council in

288

## NEW FRONTIERS OF RUSSIAN SECURITY POLICY IN AFRICA

March 2021 and Kenya, Tunisia and Niger requested that this threat be discussed in a closed-door UNSC meeting. Chad's criticisms of Russia's security policy became more strident, as Wagner Group PMCs arrived in Mali. In an explosive September 2021 interview with AFP, Chad's Foreign Minister Chérif Mahamat Zene decried Russia's external interference as posing a 'very serious problem for the stability and security of my country'. While Zene was unwilling to contradict Mali's claims that the Wagner Group was present, he highlighted threatening telephone conversations between Wagner Group operatives in Libya and CAR and accused Russia of carrying out an attack on 30 May on the Chad-CAR border.[164] Russian media outlets did not engage in escalatory rhetoric towards Chad, but aggressively countered the link between the Wagner Group and Déby's assassination. An article in *Krasnya Vesna* accused France of orchestrating his assassination, as France had a history of abandoning its allies in CAR through armed coups.[165]

Despite the Wagner Group's cordial links with FACT, Russia is keeping the door open to cooperation with Mahamat Déby's regime. After Idriss Deby's death, a Lenta.ru article noted Russia's close relationship with Sudan, which could spill-over to Chad, and argued that Moscow could make Chad its entry point to the Sahel if it could overcome its Deby-era disagreement over CAR.[166] Sergei Lavrov's meeting with Zene on 7 December was cordial, and resulted in Russia's pledge to provide weapons to and offer training of peacekeepers from the G5 Sahel bloc.[167] Russia and Chad could eventually see instability on the Chad-CAR border as a common threat. A June 2021 attack, which killed six Chadian troops and three Russian technical advisors, caused Chad and CAR to temporarily shelve their disagreements and call for an African Union and UN joint investigation.[168] This suggests that Russia could balance between FACT and Déby to maximize its influence in Chad.

Although Russia capitalized on instability in Mali and Chad, it viewed Alpha Condé's September 2021 overthrow in Guinea as a concerning development. The coup immediately preceded a scheduled meeting by Guinean Foreign Ministry officials in Moscow, which would have led to an upgrade in bilateral relations. On 6 September, the Russian Foreign Ministry condemned Condé's 'anti-

289

constitutional' overthrow and urged Guinea's competing parties to resolve their dispute through dialogue. As 42% of its bauxite production originates from three mines and one aluminium refinery in Guinea, Rusal viewed the coup as a direct threat to its commercial interests and devised contingency plans to evacuate its personnel.[169] As already-soaring aluminium prices reached a ten-year high and Rusal's stock rose by 9%, Oleg Deripaska warned that 'the aluminum market can be seriously shaken up' by the Guinea coup.[170] While Rusal scrambled to protect its investments, Russian commentators were less surprised by the developments that unfolded in Guinea. Alexey Tselunov, who runs the Zangaro Today Telegram channel, contended that the weak international response to coups in Mali and Chad was inspiring 'putschists' across West Africa. Guinea was a prime candidate for a coup or potential civil war, as its lack of military cohesion meant that a lieutenant colonel could have more power than generals.[171] Irina Filatova, an academic at the Higher School of Economics, argued that the Guinea coup was expected, as Condé was a 'very old man' and 'the people are tired of him'.[172]

Deripaska's alarmism about the coup caused Russia to accommodate Guinea's new authorities. On 8 September, rebel leader Mamadi Dumbuya met with the Russian ambassador to Guinea to discuss bilateral relations. Despite these outreaches, the long-term future of Russia-Guinea relations remains murky. Russian State Duma MP Gennady Onishchenko expressed optimism about Guinea's coup plotters, as he stated that their decision to put Condé under house arrest rather than assassinate him was a 'definitive democratic step'.[173] He predicted that Dumbuya was 'preparing for positive changes in a democratic manner, albeit with machine guns'. Tatyana Denisova, an expert at the Institute for African Studies, noted that the 1984 and 2008 coups did not disrupt Russia-Guinea relations, and argued that a coup triggered by socioeconomic conditions or Condé's unpopularity would have a negligible effect. Denisova argued that foreign interference in the coup would inevitably strain Russia-Guinea relations.[174]

As Guinean mutineers were US trained, conspiracies about Western orchestration of the Guinea coup spread widely in Kremlin-aligned media outlets. A 7 September RT article called France an

## NEW FRONTIERS OF RUSSIAN SECURITY POLICY IN AFRICA

'invisible hegemon' with unique military and fiscal power over its former African colonies and framed the Guinea coup as a front in the US-China competition for strategically valuable commodities.[175] Sputnik Radio aired a broadcast entitled 'Examining Neocolonial Interests in the Guinea coup' on 9 September. In this broadcast, Kinshasa-based analyst Kambale Musavuli exposed Dumbuya's 'history with imperialist countries'.[176] Onishchenko expressed concern about the role of French business interests in instigating the coup and compared France's interference in Guinean affairs to alleged US interference in Russia's elections.[177] As Dumbuya consolidates power, Russia will balance between using Guinea as a theatre in its information war with France in Africa, and ensuring that its conspiratorial rhetoric about Western interference does not sully Moscow-Conakry relations.

# 10

## THE UKRAINE WAR AND RUSSIA'S AFRICA STRATEGY

On 24 February 2022, Vladimir Putin announced the start of a Russian special military operation to 'demilitarize and denazify Ukraine'. This speech was swiftly followed by a full-fledged Russian invasion of Ukraine, as Putin sought to overthrow President Volodymyr Zelensky and install a pro-Kremlin president in Kyiv. While Russia was initially confident that it would achieve its objectives in Ukraine within days, its military progress was uneven and Western sanctions have threatened to cripple the Russian economy. Despite Russia's appalling war crimes in Ukraine and the gravity of Moscow's violations of international law, the Global South has not mirrored the West's policies to counter Russian aggression. In keeping with the Global South perspective, no African countries have sanctioned Russia, and condemnations of the Russian invasion, especially outside of the UN General Assembly, are sporadic. This chapter will lay out Africa's response to the Ukraine war and how Russia's growing isolation will impact its great power ambitions in Africa. Overall, African countries have engaged with Russia in a business-as-usual fashion and the Kremlin views Africa as more important for its global strategy, but the long-term sustainability of Russia's hard-won resurgence is less clear.

293

## How Africa Reacted to Russia's Invasion of Ukraine

Much like the rest of the Global South, African countries responded to Russia's invasion of Ukraine in a highly polarized fashion. In line with the response of African states to the Crimea annexation, few countries expressed explicit support for Russian aggression in Ukraine. During the 2 March UN General Assembly vote, Eritrea was the only African country that sided with Russia and joined Belarus, Syria and North Korea in opposing a resolution condemning Russia's invasion of Ukraine. Russia's decision on 21 February to recognize the Donetsk and Luhansk People's Republics as independent countries, which presaged its invasion, also received little support. The Central African Republic stated that recognizing these republics 'will undoubtedly save lives and prevent a lot of violence', but no other African country followed suit. Amongst African officials, Yoweri Museveni's son Lieutenant General Muhoozi Kainerugaba, who serves as Uganda People's Defence Forces chief, was a rare supporter of the Russian invasion. In a much-publicized tweet, Kainerugaba stated that 'The majority of mankind that are non-white support Russia's stand in Ukraine. Putin is absolutely right!' and compared NATO's alleged provocations against Russia to the Cuban Missile Crisis.[1] Expressing sympathy with Kremlin narratives on Ukraine, while stopping short of backing the invasion, was a much more common response from African leaders. While Museveni called his son's pro-Putin stance a personal view, he chastised Western double standards, repeated Kremlin narratives about the destruction of Libya in 2011 and implicitly recognized Russia's right to a sphere of influence by calling it a 'center of gravity' in Eastern Europe.[2] Although South Africa indirectly criticized Russia's use of force and violations of international law, Cyril Ramaphosa stated on 18 March that the Ukraine war could have been avoided if NATO had refrained from eastward expansion.[3]

These pro-Kremlin narratives have not been universally accepted by African leaders. During their 24 May joint statement in Accra, the presidents of Ghana and Mozambique condemned the Russian invasion's devastating impact on Africa and global security. In the UN General Assembly, Russia's invasion of Ukraine received

# THE UKRAINE WAR AND RUSSIA'S AFRICA STRATEGY

substantial backlash. Twenty-eight African countries voted in favour of condemning Russia, including regional powers like Nigeria, Egypt and Kenya; seventeen countries abstained, including South Africa and Algeria; and eight countries refrained from voting altogether.[4] These polarizations extended to the 7 April vote on suspending Russia from the UN Human Rights Council. African countries that hired Russian PMCs, such as Burundi, Congo, CAR and Mali, opposed Russia's removal from the council, as did Algeria, Eritrea, Ethiopia, Gabon and Zimbabwe. Most African countries either acquiesced to its suspension through abstention or overtly voted for Russia's removal. To contextualize the distinctions in African voting patterns in the UN, a CSIS report of March 2022 categorized Africa's responses to the Ukraine war in four ways: Understanding Russia's Concerns, Abstained for Neutrality, Abstained to Push Mediation and Dialogue and Concerned for Ukraine's Self-Determination.[5]

While this framing is useful, it neglects four consistent themes in Africa's response to the Russian invasion of Ukraine that are not readily apparent from merely listing the voting records of individual countries. The first gap is the distinction between expressing solidarity with Ukraine and supporting international law. Kenyan UN Ambassador Martin Kimani's powerful 22 February speech was widely interpreted in the West as a display of solidarity with Ukraine but could be more accurately depicted as an emphatic defence of international law.[6] Kimani accused Vladimir Putin's pursuit of military solutions as putting multilateralism on its 'deathbed' and stated his opposition to 'irredentism and expansionism on any basis'. Kimani's words are deeply rooted in Kenya's historical experience, as he stated that Kenya chose to respect its British colonial borders because of its commitment to the UN Charter and desire to prevent an endless succession of internecine civil wars. Kimani's speech sparked controversy in Africa, as Nairobi-based author Patrick Gathara wrote a widely shared article for Al Jazeera that chastised Kimani's implicit resignation to colonial legacies,[7] but Kenya's position gained traction on the continent. Nigeria's opposition to the Russian invasion was premised not on support for Ukraine but on the need to respect international law and its experience addressing

295

its border dispute with Cameroon over Bakassi heavily influenced its position.[8]

The second gap is the prevailing belief that Russia's invasion of Ukraine is not Africa's problem. This perspective mirrors the responses of other Global South countries, such as India, which has argued that Afghanistan's proximity to its borders makes it a higher priority crisis than Ukraine. Johannesburg-based commentator Tafi Mhaka urged African leaders to apply the same conviction in support for Palestine to Ukraine, but Gathara acknowledged that the contrary view, which equated Ukrainians with 'their benefactors from Western Europe', fuelled apathy towards their plight.[9] These sentiments, which are regularly accompanied by whataboutisms, highlighted the perceived racially motivated contrast between Western aid to Ukraine and indifference to African conflicts, have been amplified by print and social media. Guinea's Prime Minister Mohamed Béavogui was one of the few African leaders to express this position publicly. At the 30 March Dubai Forum, Béavogui said 'For years people said don't worry about war "it's only in Africa". Now it is in the middle of Europe, and we are suddenly asked to choose.'[10] Due to surging food and fuel prices, the Ukraine war's relevance for African countries has become more tangible, as the conflict has compounded the impact of COVID-19 and climate change. On 25 May, in a statement commemorating the anniversary of the Organization of African Unity's formation, African Union Commission chairperson Moussa Faki Mahamat described Africa as a 'collateral victim' of the Ukraine war and warned that the conflict would increase the structural fragility of African economies.[11] Senegalese President Macky Sall, who chairs the African Union, reiterated this point to Vladimir Putin during his 3 June trip to Sochi while praising Russia's willingness to constructively address the grain export impasse.

The third gap is Africa's consistent opposition to Russia's isolation from the international system or the imposition of punitive measures against the Russian economy. This trend is reflected in Russia's business-as-usual engagements with African countries and the unwillingness of African countries to impose sanctions on Russia. In the first month after Russia's invasion of Ukraine, Mikhail Bogdanov held bilateral discussions with ambassadors from

THE UKRAINE WAR AND RUSSIA'S AFRICA STRATEGY

Benin, Djibouti, Egypt, Libya, Nigeria, Somalia, South Africa and Tanzania.[12] The unwillingness of African countries to disrupt their relations with Russia aligns with public opinion. In March 2022, Mali was the only nation with plurality support for its conduct in Ukraine, and Côte d'Ivoire registered sizeable minority support. Elsewhere on the continent, perceptions of Russia's conduct in Ukraine were overwhelmingly negative, but this antipathy and Moscow's military travails did not drastically diminish support for Russia as an economic partner.[13] As Russia is viewed as an important economic partner, opinion towards sanctions is largely negative. Sall has condemned SWIFT sanctions on Russia for restricting the ability of African countries to purchase agricultural products. Cyril Ramaphosa similarly warned that Western sanctions on Russia hurt 'countries that are either bystanders or not part of the conflict'.[14] Aggressive counter-programming from Western officials that Russia's blockade of Ukraine's Black Sea ports are the cause of sanctions has so far not eviscerated Russia's narratives on sanctions. Zelensky's much-anticipated 21 June address to the AU, which occurred ten weeks after his initial speaking request, poignantly warned that Africa was a 'hostage' of the Ukraine war but was received by only four African heads of state, as the remaining countries sent lower-level representatives.

The fourth theme is widespread support for a diplomatic solution to the war in Ukraine. During his 22 May press conference with German Chancellor Olaf Scholz, Sall declared that the AU wanted 'peace through dialogue', and although he condemned Russia's invasion, the AU wanted a 'ceasefire' and 'dialogue'. Sall's argument has been backed by African officials, such as Tanzania's Vice President Philip Mpango and Uganda's Prime Minister Robinah Nabbanja, who equated abstentions in the UN with diplomacy.[15] South Africa's repeated mediation offers in the Ukraine war and the participation of Egypt, Algeria and Sudan in Arab League diplomatic efforts underscores Africa's desire to assert itself as a discrete pole in the international system. Nairobi-based expert Mark Kapchanga rebuked Western claims that Russia's 'colonization' of Africa explained its position, and framed Africa's support for diplomacy as proof of its foreign policy independence.[16] The sincerity of the AU's

297

commitment to neutrality has been disputed. The AU's rejection of Ukrainian President Volodymyr Zelensky's proposal to address the body on two occasions and Sall's implicit acknowledgement that some African leaders would be unwilling to meet with Zelensky fanned the flames of scepticism.[17] South Africa's efforts to frame Russia and Ukraine as 'two belligerent entities', Ukrainian Ambassador Liubov Abravitova's lack of access to ANC officials and Cyril Ramaphosa's decision to call Zelensky seven weeks after engaging with Putin has augmented these concerns.[18] This suggests that African mediation efforts might simply be a smokescreen for a pro-Kremlin agenda.

*The Ukraine War and Russia's Vision for Great Power Projection in Africa*

As African countries are broadly opposed to breaking off cooperation with Russia, despite their contrasting positions on the invasion, the Kremlin views Africa as an increasingly important power projection theatre, as it pivots to a post-Western foreign policy. Sergei Lavrov views Russian engagement with Africa as a shield against the West's policy of 'total hybrid war', and African issues occupied a prominent position in the June 2022 St Petersburg Economic Forum. During Sall's visit to Sochi, State University of Management Professor Yevgeny Smirnov declared that Russia needs to synthesize unilateral cooperation with African countries with deeper coordination via the BRICS and African Union formats.[19] Russia also believes that its soft power will survive the Ukraine invasion. In a January 2022 *Russia in Global Affairs* article, Andrey Maslov and Dmitry Suslov expressed similar optimism and predicted breakthroughs for Russian policy in Africa, as 'none of the African countries perceives Russia as an enemy, a former colonialist or a potential hegemon'.[20]

Despite these grand pronouncements, there are growing concerns that Russia's resurgence in Africa might not be smooth or linear. Journalist Yuri Sigov acknowledges that Russia has a historic opportunity to crystallize its resurgence in Africa and concurs with Suslov and Maslov on the power of historical legacies by saying 'without the existence of the USSR, there would not be a single independent state on the modern map of the continent'.[21] However,

# THE UKRAINE WAR AND RUSSIA'S AFRICA STRATEGY

Sigov warns that Russian officials are not doing enough to facilitate a full-scale 'turn towards Africa', as military ties progress unevenly, Russian language instruction lags and education is focused on training professionals instead of future leaders. Sigov also acknowledged the difficulties that Russia faces doing business in Africa, as he stated that African countries want to 'get everything for nothing' from Russia, play international rivals off each other and 'swindle visiting foreign businessmen for money'. Nonetheless, Sigov believes that Africa should be an integral component of Russian foreign policy, and the Ukraine war's outcome is the primary factor that will determine the success of Moscow's outreach. Sigov says that military success in Ukraine will encourage African countries to resist countervailing Western pressures, but concedes that military failure will lead to less than half of African leaders attending the fall 2022 Russia-Africa Summit in St Petersburg. Despite these uncertainties, Russia's trade trajectory with Africa is increasingly positive. During the first five months of 2022, Russia's trade with Africa increased by 34% from 2021 levels. On 25 May, Mikhail Bogdanov announced that many of Russia's key partners in Africa would switch to trading in national currencies, which would counter the impact of SWIFT sanctions.[22]

Beyond this trade expansion, a *Vzglyad* article of 4 June laid out new frontiers of Russian cooperation with African countries.[23] The article expressed optimism about Africa's ability to help Russia weather sanctions, as key economies like Ethiopia showed 5–10% economic growth before COVID-19. African countries could import Russian wheat to compensate for sagging local agricultural production and the seizure of Kherson Region, which supplied Ukrainian wheat via the Black Sea, would enable agricultural trade via Crimea and the Sea of Azov. This is unsurprising, as Russia has seized an estimated 500,000 tons of grain from Kherson, Zaporizhzhia, Donetsk and Luhansk, and could net $100 million in revenues from illicit exports. Acknowledging this threat, the US warned fourteen African countries on 5 June about the possibility of Russia marketing 'stolen Ukrainian grain' in Africa. These warnings were largely ignored in Africa, as the severity of the food insecurity crisis trumped concerns about theft from Ukraine. Hassan Khannenje, the director of HORN International Institute for Strategic Studies in Nairobi,

299

said that 'Africans don't care where they get their food from, and if someone is going to moralize about that, they are mistaken.'[24]

The Ukraine war will also aid Russia's repositioning vis-à-vis other great powers in Africa. *Vzglyad* argued that Russia could capitalize on opposition to Chinese neocolonialism and leverage ties with countries, such as Turkey, which acted as conduits for Russian products in African markets. Despite Russia's near-complete isolation from the West, Suslov and Maslov warns against replicating the Soviet-style Cold War playbook and linking engagement with African countries to geopolitical rivalries. In effect, they argue that staying above the fray of geopolitical rivalries will allow Russia to win the competition for influence amongst great powers in Africa. Instead, Suslov and Maslov contend that Russia should engage independently with African countries on areas of common interest, such as climate change and strengthening peacekeeping infrastructure, and extend beyond open-ended cultural diplomacy to civil society and academic cooperation. Suslov and Maslov also urged the Kremlin to shift responsibility for Russian development assistance from the Finance Ministry to the Foreign Ministry to maximize its geopolitical impact. While these recommendations have not been concretely incorporated into Russia's official vision for Africa, they could occupy a larger part of Moscow's heightened attention to the continent in the months ahead.

### The Ukraine War's Impact on Russia's Continent-Wide Power Projection in Africa

Although general trends point to expanded Russian engagement with African countries and limited disruption to Russia's current influence in Africa, the Ukraine war could profoundly influence Moscow's individual bilateral relationships on the continent. The most likely frontiers for expanded Russian influence are the Sahel and the Horn of Africa, and Moscow's pursuit of leverage in these regions will be complemented by shoring up its core partnerships and perpetuating its existing array of informal military interventions. Food insecurity, extra-legal regime changes, shifting patterns of Western counterterrorism engagement and the efficacy of secondary

## THE UKRAINE WAR AND RUSSIA'S AFRICA STRATEGY

sanctions are key variables that could present Russia with risks and opportunities in Africa. The remainder of this chapter will present a region-by-region breakdown of the Ukraine war's impact on Russia's influence in Africa and serve as a gateway for the conclusion's future-looking examination of Moscow's presence on the continent.

### The Resilience of Russian Influence in North Africa

Despite countervailing pressure from the West and Russia's manpower shortages in Ukraine, Russia's two-decades-long expansion of influence in North Africa has not been reversed. Egypt's calls for Russia-Ukraine dialogue after the invasion mirrored its position after the Crimea annexation in 2014, but intense pressure from the G7 and the EU caused Cairo to eventually take a more definitive pro-Ukrainian stance. Egypt voted to condemn Russia's invasion in the UN General Assembly on 2 March, and Sisi held talks with Zelensky on 24 March. Nevertheless, Egypt's discourse and policies more closely mirrored Russian than Western objectives. Ukrainian charge d'affaires Ruslan Nechai's 8 March plea for Egyptian assistance was largely ignored in Cairo, and a Russian delegation visited the El Dabaa nuclear plant on 17 April to discuss next steps on the project.[25] Egyptian experts, such as Al-Ahram Center for Political and Strategic Studies researcher Ahmed Aliba, rejected the notion that Russia's invasion of Ukraine was an act of unprovoked aggression, and highlighted NATO's failure to create a neutral buffer with Russia as a driver of conflict.[26] In contrast to US alarmism about potential Chinese military support for Russia, the Egyptian foreign policy community was inclined to view China as a potential mediator that could prevent World War III between Russia and NATO. Egypt's Permanent UN Representative Osama Abdel-Khalek also decried Western sanctions on Russia, as he stated that Egypt opposed sanctions that were not imposed by the multilateral international system and highlighted supply chain and air traffic disruptions that could create economic shocks.[27]

While Sisi's delicate balance between Russia and the West will advance Egypt's geopolitical interests, the Ukraine war could exacerbate Egypt's economic woes. Immediately after the war began,

301

concerns about rising food prices and decreased tourism revenues caused foreign investors to sell $1.19 billion in Egyptian bonds. Egypt responded to these economic shocks by raising interest rates by 1%, devaluing the pound by 14%, requesting a new IMF loan and securing $5 billion in capital deposits from Saudi Arabia.[28] As 70% of Egypt's wheat imports are sourced from Russia and 11% come from Ukraine, Egypt has been forced to engage with alternative suppliers, such as India, to stem price hikes, and has also weathered the potential loss of 1.6 million Ukrainian tourists. If the US eventually imposes sanctions on Rosatom, the July 2022 start date for El Dabaa will be indefinitely postponed and Ethiopia's concomitant GERD filling could exacerbate Egypt's electricity shortages. One rare bright spot for the Egyptian economy is the expansion of Suez Canal revenues. The Suez Canal Authority has embraced a policy of strict neutrality, as it allows Russian and Ukrainian vessels to pass through its waters, and in April 2022, it secured its highest-ever monthly revenue at $629 million.[29] This was directly linked to Europe and Canada's energy divestments from Russia and pivot towards imports from the Gulf monarchies. Egyptian economists, such as the Al-Ahram Center's Hossein Solaiman, expect this to be a temporary boon, as the overall economic impact of the Ukraine war on Egypt remains negative.

The Ukraine war has also not undermined Algeria's historical partnership with Russia. On 28 March, Nikolay Patrushev met with his Algerian counterpart Noureddine Makri to discuss cybersecurity cooperation and Sergei Lavrov travelled to Algiers on 10 May to strengthen bilateral ties. This dialogue persisted despite Anthony Blinken's emphasis on Russian aggression during his 31 March trip to Algiers and Ukrainian Foreign Minister Dmytro Kuleba's dialogue with Algeria on food insecurity. Despite its continued cooperation with Moscow, Algeria's growing profile as an alternative gas supplier to Europe ensures that it is a beneficiary from sanctions on Russia. Due to its deal with Eni on 11 April, Algeria will export 30 billion cubic meters of gas to Italy, which eclipses the 29 billion cubic meters shipped by Russia.[30] Much like previous tensions over gas exports, Algeria's energy deals with Europe are unlikely to severely undermine cooperation with Russia. Due to its pressing need for

# THE UKRAINE WAR AND RUSSIA'S AFRICA STRATEGY

hard currency and leverage as an arms purchaser, Algeria is unlikely to appease Russia by restricting gas exports to Europe.[31] Regardless of its intentions, rising domestic consumption, underinvestment in production, political instability and disputes with Europe over the Western Sahara limit Algeria's ability to supplant Russia as a gas supplier.[32] Russian experts, such as Sergei Balsamov and Igor Yushkov, have acknowledged similar risks and noted that Algeria could choose to expand LNG sales to Asia instead of dispatching excess gas reserves to European markets.[33] This move, which would limit inflation-related Hirak protests, will preserve Russia-Algeria relations.

Although Biden has not reversed Trump's recognition of Western Sahara as Moroccan territory, Morocco treaded cautiously on Russia's invasion of Ukraine. Morocco's neutrality stemmed from its desire to avoid economic shocks, as it imports $286 million of Ukrainian grain and $110 million of Russian grain each year, and relies heavily on Russian mineral, chemical and energy resources to power its industries.[34] On 31 March, Zelensky recalled Ukraine's ambassador to Morocco over Rabat's inadequate support for Kyiv and pressure from Blinken to join the sanctions regime proved futile. Due to airspace closures, Moroccan airports witnessed an uptick in Russian flights and Agadir International Airport became a key stopover point for Morocco's flights to Latin America. Morocco's refusal to punish Russia reflected public opinion, as 37% of Moroccans wanted to keep economic ties with Russia, while 14% opposed ties with Russia and 30% viewed Russia positively, compared to 26% who viewed it negatively.[35] Despite these policies, Russia's engagement with Morocco has been much less pronounced than with Algeria, and there are signs that Rabat's future policy might be less conciliatory towards Moscow. Along with Kenya and Liberia, Morocco joined Tunisia as a non-NATO country invited to a high-level military summit about Ukraine on 27 April. The imposition of a death sentence by the Donetsk People's Republic on a Moroccan national fighting for Ukraine could also create tensions, even though Morocco's reaction has been much more muted than Britain's. Given these risk factors, it is likely that Russia's North Africa strategy will run through Algeria and Egypt, while its partnerships with Tunisia and Morocco will continue to lag.

303

Despite manpower depletion within its battalion tactical groups (BTGs) in Ukraine, Russia's informal military presence and diplomatic influence in Libya has weathered conflict-related pressures. Jalel Harchaoui notes that there were no signs of a clandestine Russian withdrawal from Libya before the 24 February invasion, and states that Wagner Group control over key facilities is so pervasive that LNA forces need to ask permission for entry.[36] Russia's aerial access to Benghazi remains a crucial trans-shipment point for war materiel between Syria and Mali. As Libya's planned elections atrophied, Prigozhin-aligned figures, such as Maxim Shugaley, continued to highlight Haftar's popularity and claimed that US collusion with returning UN envoy Stephanie Williams delayed elections that Haftar would inevitably win.[37] Russia's continued loyalty to Haftar could also translate into military support, as the Kremlin aggressively recruited Middle Eastern foreign fighters to serve in Ukraine. The Ukrainian Defence Ministry asserted that Russia had a clandestine agreement with Khalifa Haftar to send Libyan mercenaries to Donbas, and a European official claimed on 20 April that Libyans were represented amongst the 10,000 to 20,000 foreign fighters in Ukraine. Despite these reports and anecdotal claims about Libyan casualties, LNA Major General Khaled Mahjoub says that the army 'has nothing to do whatsoever with the Ukrainian war'.[38]

Although the LNA has not been dragged into the Ukraine War, the Wagner Group's presence remains problematic for Europe, human rights in Libya and the U.S. As Libya is the only African country, aside from Algeria, which has a gas pipeline linkage to Europe, it could be very helpful in the EU's quest to divest from Russian energy. The Wagner Group and LNA's control of the al-Wafa field near the Libya-Algeria border and al-Fargh field in Ajbadiya, which is Libya's largest gas field for domestic consumption, has diminished Libya's ability to export gas to the EU.[39] In May 2022, a UN Panel of Experts report authenticated a Samsung electronic tablet that was left by the Wagner Group in Libya and obtained by the BBC in early 2021. This tablet revealed 35 unmarked anti-personnel mines in Ain Zara of southern Tripoli, which was under LNA control, and raised pressure on Russia to suspend anti-personnel landmine use.[40] On July 29, Polyanskiy announced that Russia would only extend the UN mission by three months, as Stephanie Williams's departure meant that a new special representative needed to be appointed.[41] Russia's alleged involvement in the shooting down of a US drone over Benghazi also points to a potentially more provocative policy in Libya, even as Moscow's current strategy appears to be principally geared at using its 2,000 PMCs to keep the status quo.[42]

Although Russia's relationship with Haftar remains its primary path to leverage in Libya, Moscow has also established a close partnership with Fathi Bashagha. In stark contrast to his prior circulation of terrorism allegations against Bashagha, Prigozhin praised Bashagha as the only western Libyan politician who could rein in militias near Tripoli, and called him a 'true patriot'.[43] Prigozhin's words were swiftly incorporated into Russian official policy, as the Kremlin viewed Bashagha's tacit alignment with Haftar in a favourable light. In a statement on 10 February, the Russian Foreign Ministry expressed hope that Bashagha would unify Libyan society and steer Libya towards national elections, and Russia was the first major world power to explicitly support Bashagha over his political rivals.[44] Despite these displays of solidarity, Bashagha did not support Russia's invasion of Ukraine. Channeling rhetoric from Dbeibah's foreign minister Najla Mangoush, Bashagha called Russia's invasion a 'clear violation of international law and the sovereignty of a democratic Ukraine', and Libya voted to suspend Russia from the UN Human Rights Council on 7 April. Food insecurity could have played a part in Bashagha's rhetoric. As Libya was the world's tenth largest purchaser of Ukrainian wheat in 2020, it was exceptionally impacted by war-related agricultural supply disruptions, and was forced to procure more expensive wheat from the US, Canada, Australia and Argentina.[45] Despite these condemnations, Bashagha has yet to act on his June 2020 vow that the Qardabiyah base will cease to be a Russian facility, which has prevented an escalation with Russia.

*Russia Consolidates its Foothold in the Red Sea and Horn of Africa*

Despite mounting concerns about the sustainability of its global influence, Russia continues to view the Indian Ocean and, by extension, the Red Sea and Horn of Africa as critical theatres for its great power ambitions. Hemedti's controversial trip to Moscow on 23 February underscored Russia's enduring aspirations in the Red Sea region, but also highlighted the limits of Russian influence in Sudan. Although Hemedti insisted that the Ukraine war would not scupper Russia's basing agreement in Port Sudan, his statement left the door open for rival powers to open a facility on Sudan's 730 km Red Sea coast.[46] In Washington, DC, Hemedti's courtship of Moscow was widely seen as an attempt at a bidding war with the US, and US officials, such as Stephen Townsend, regarded the Port Sudan base as a strategic threat akin to Russia's involvement in Libya or China's facility in Djibouti. Hemedti's public support for the Port Sudan facility also stoked rumours in the US that Russia had played a role in instigating the October 2021 coup.[47] In addition to countervailing US pressure, the Port Sudan base faces the prospect of local backlash. Hemedti's courtship of Russian security assistance prompted concerns that he was seeking Moscow's covert support for a coup that would undermine Burhan.[48] During Hemedti's 16 March visit to the installation site, widespread protests erupted.[49] Speculation about a privatization agreement between the UAE and Sudan stoked the demonstrations, but concerns about the sovereignty of Sudanese port facilities could create backlash against other external players such as Russia.

Beyond the uncertainties about the Port Sudan base, Russia's influence in Sudan is undercut by severe macroeconomic risks. Sudan depends on Russia and Ukraine for one-third of its wheat supply, and Hemedti's request for subsidized Russian wheat has not eased food insecurity.[50] WFP estimates reveal that the coup, poor harvests and the Ukraine war could tip 20 million Sudanese into food insecurity, which might lead to new street protests that undermine Moscow's partners within Sudan's military. Secondary sanctions also pose a growing risk to Russia's economic interests in Sudan. A *New York Times* report of 5 June revealed the existence of 'The Russian Company', a tightly guarded gold-processing plant 200 miles north of Khartoum that is operated by the Wagner Group.[51] Although Prigozhin denies operating a gold-mining company, his close associate from the Internet Research Agency Mikhail Potepkin

## THE UKRAINE WAR AND RUSSIA'S AFRICA STRATEGY

reportedly operates Meroe Gold, which transported construction equipment for gold mining into Sudan.[52]

The Wagner Group's continued presence, which was denied by the Sudanese Foreign Ministry as an attempt to drag Sudan arbitrarily into the Ukraine conflict, is especially vulnerable to sanctions.[53] In December 2021, an ECFR report urged the EU to impose sanctions on up to 250 Sudanese military-aligned companies that conduct business with the Wagner Group.[54] The Wagner Group's egregious human rights abuses in the Sudan-Central African Republic border region strengthens the case for sanctions, as dozens of miners perished in three major Wagner Group attacks and concomitant offensives on six mines in CAR. Sudanese eyewitness accounts reveal that the Wagner Group swept through encampments with Sudanese and Chadian migrant miners in Am Daga over a six-week period.[55] Wagner Group PMCs and aligned CAR forces used automatic weapons to create a mass grave of at least twenty Sudanese miners, and one account given to *The Guardian* from March 2022 revealed that up to seventy miners could have perished in these assaults.[56] The destruction of mining equipment, demolition of buildings and theft of motorcycles underscores the Wagner Group's kleptocratic intention of destroying local mining infrastructure and placing gold assets into Russian control. Calls for sanctions on Sudanese businesses that cooperate with Russia have intensified, as Moscow's smuggling of 30 tons of illicit Sudanese gold per year via Dubai has helped counter punitive measures against the Russian Central Bank.

While the long-term future of Russian influence in Sudan is unclear, Russia's partnerships with Ethiopia and Eritrea are set to strengthen. Abiy Ahmed has called for restraint in Ukraine and justified Addis Ababa's neutrality by highlighting the Tigray War's devastating impact on Ethiopia's stability.[57] Pro-Russian sentiments in Ethiopia, which spiked following Moscow's support for non-interference in Tigray, fuelled line-ups of Ethiopian men seeking to participate in Russia's war effort in Ukraine and secure emigration to Russia.[58] This display of Russian soft power has not translated into Ethiopian participation in the Ukraine war, as Russia insists that it has sufficient manpower for its military operations. On 27

April, Lavrov held talks with Eritrean Foreign Minister Osman Saleh, which reflected Russia's appreciation for Eritrea's support for its war in Ukraine. As Eritrea has tense relations with its neighbors and remains a belligerent in the Tigray War, the absence of a UN arms embargo could allow Eritrea to procure Russian weapons that amplify its ability to destabilize the Horn of Africa.[59]

Although Russia's post-Cold War cooperation with Kenya is limited, the Ukraine war could further restrict Moscow's ability to constructively engage with one of East Africa's leading regional powers. Sanctions halted millions of dollars of trade in non-essential goods between Russia and Kenya, such as tea and flower exports. Russia's Ambassador to Kenya Dmitry Maksimychev has been vocal about linking SWIFT sanctions to commodity-induced humanitarian crises.[60] Despite Maksimychev's outspokenness, Kenya is an outlier in Sub-Saharan Africa, as it is one of the few countries with an intense debate on sanctions policy. During his presidential campaign, Raila Odinga deplored Russia's 'senseless conflict' in Ukraine, and supported sanctioning Russia even if it would cost Kenya $100 million in export revenues.[61] Even though Tanzania has been more conciliatory towards Russia than Kenya, it is similarly unlikely to serve as Russia's gateway to East Africa. Due to soaring import costs of white petroleum products, Tanzania registered a current account deficit of $1.31 billion in first quarter of 2022 compared to $352 million a year earlier.[62] A Russian disinformation campaign, which featured doctored images of Vladimir Putin with Mozambique's Samora Machel and Zimbabwe's Emmerson Mnangagwa at a Tanzanian military training camp in 1973, and falsely took credit for Chinese military training caused controversy.[63] Due to Rwanda's energy ties to the Middle East and Indo-Pacific region, and Uganda's conciliatory position towards Russia, Moscow will likely rely on these partnerships to provide it with an East African foothold.

### Russia's Security and Diplomatic Forays in Central and West Africa

Russia's military interventions in CAR and Mali continue to underpin its power projection in Central and West Africa, but sanctions have

# THE UKRAINE WAR AND RUSSIA'S AFRICA STRATEGY

not deterred Moscow from courting new regional partners. Despite highly publicized reports about Russia transferring Wagner Group PMCs from CAR to Ukraine in the weeks leading up to the invasion, Moscow's influence in the CAR has remained intact. The Touadéra government has taken several steps to expand Russia's economic influence and soft power in CAR. Even though 90% of CAR's population lacks Internet access, CAR became the second country in the world after El Salvador to legalize Bitcoin. This measure, which sparked an unusual amount of internal dissent in CAR, was widely attributed to Touadéra's desire to circumvent sanctions on Russia.[64] Notwithstanding concerns about state capture and the Wagner Group's botched counterinsurgency campaigns outside Bangui, Russia's soft power in CAR has continued to expand. This expansion has been attributed by the unwillingness of CAR civil society groups to criticize Russia, even as discontent with Russian seizures of mining assets mounted after the April 2022 assault on Kouki.[65] Touadéra also announced that Russian would be CAR's third official language after Sango and French, and would be mandatory in universities from the 2022–23 academic year and in lower education levels in subsequent years. On 3 February, Touadéra held a ceremony commemorating the first anniversary of the formation of the 7th Territorial Infantry Battalion, which was accompanied by local media portrayals of the Wagner Group's contributions to the security of CAR.[66]

While Russia is unlikely to be dislodged by local backlash or rival great powers from CAR, its war crimes have attracted severe criticisms. From 16–17 January, Wagner Group PMCs redeployed from Bria to Aïgbado, which was near a hub for Union for Peace in the Central African Republic rebels. Upon their arrival in Aïgbado, Wagner Group forces allegedly shot indiscriminately at civilians, killing sixty-five people, burned a dozen homes, established a base in the village and deployed landmines to block the entry of peacekeepers. The Wagner Group blocked exit paths for residents of Aïgbado and the neighboring Yanga village, and residents feared being killed if they tried to escape.[67] On 11–12 April, the Wagner Group and the CAR armed forces killed between ten and fifteen civilians in Gordile and Ndah villages, which precipitated the launch of a UN investigation on 15 April.[68] These war crimes followed a

309

series of alleged prior abuses documented since 2019, such as the July 2021 Bossangoa massacre that killed twelve unarmed men, and prompted the AU to call for the complete removal of mercenaries from African soil. Human Rights Watch has also called for judicial institutions, such as the Bangui-based Special Criminal Court and the ICC to hold Russian forces to account, and has collected eyewitness accounts of assaults, extra-judicial killings and the use of unmarked graves.[69] While these revelations might not weaken CAR's dependence on Russia, the coincidental timing between these allegations and Russian war crimes in Ukraine and Mali could erode its appeal as a security partner for African countries.

Elsewhere in Central Africa, Russia has accrued influence in a modest but symbolically significant fashion. On 12 April, Russia and Cameroon signed a new military cooperation agreement. This pact was ambiguously drafted as it did not reference the Anglophone crisis or Cameroon's struggle against Boko Haram, but it nonetheless fuelled speculation that Cameroon sought out low-cost Russian equipment for use in Ambazonia.[70] In stark contrast to its condemnations of Russian involvement in Mali and CAR, France did not respond publicly to the expansion of Russia-Cameroon security cooperation. However, Macron's decision to dispatch the principal influencer of French foreign policy in Africa Christophe Bigot to Yaoundé in early May was likely linked to France's desire to contain Russian influence in Cameroon.[71] Russia has also recruited a small but growing contingent of fighters from the Democratic Republic Congo to staff its offensive in Donbas. Based on testimony from Congolese soldier Jean-Claude Sangwa, some fighters arrived in Luhansk as early as August 2021 and were incorporated into the Luhansk People's Republic militias after Russia invaded Ukraine.[72] Sangwa, who studied the Russian language and economics in Luhansk, claims that he serves alongside three Congolese fighters who are meshed with volunteers from Arab countries, Belarus and California. While the DRC is unlikely to contribute substantial manpower to the Ukraine war, the case of Congolese volunteers reveals Russia's enduring soft power in Central Africa.

While Russia's military interventions in Libya and CAR have remained stable, the Ukraine war has interestingly coincided with

# THE UKRAINE WAR AND RUSSIA'S AFRICA STRATEGY

an intensification of Moscow's counterinsurgency operations in Mali. The expansion of Russia's involvement in Mali is evidenced by military equipment transfers. On 30 March, Russia transferred two Mi-35M attack helicopters and an advanced radar system to Mali, and the Kremlin claims that 200 Malian service members and nine police officers are already being trained in Moscow.[73] These arms transfers, which were followed by a second identical weapons tranche on 18 April, fulfilled a Keïta-era contract between Russia and Mali, which the junta accepted.[74] Despite these arms transfers, Russia has been unable to improve Mali's security situation, and has instead attracted widespread criticism for its perpetration of massacres against civilians. Between 27 and 31 March, the Malian Armed Forces and Wagner Group PMCs allegedly killed 300 civilian men in the central Malian town of Moura. This massacre, which Human Rights Watch described as the worst single atrocity of Mali's decade-long armed conflict, was precipitated by concerns of collaboration between Moura residents and armed Islamists. Victims of the massacre were mostly from the Fulani ethnic group, which were key recruitment targets for Al-Qaeda in the Islamic Maghreb (AQIM) and the Islamic State in the Greater Sahara (ISGS), and Sharia law had been imposed by these extremist groups on the residents of Moura.

The indiscriminate nature of the Wagner Group's alleged killings in Moura, which coincided in timing with the Bucha Massacre on the outskirts of Kyiv, was fiercely condemned in Western capitals. Britain's Minister for Africa Vicky Ford stated that she was 'horrified' by the killings and urged the Malian government to suspend all ties with the Wagner Group.[75] German Foreign Minister Annalena Baerbock visited Bamako on 13 April and urged Mali to suspend ties with Russia over 'massive war crimes', which mirrored Moscow's conduct in Syria and Ukraine.[76] The Federal News Agency strongly rebutted Western allegations of Wagner Group misconduct, and claimed that France was accusing the Malian government of 'genocide' because it could not reconcile itself with its loss of influence in Mali.[77] Despite the Russian media's insistence that Mali was merely combatting terrorism in Moura, evidence mounted of additional massacres with Wagner Group involvement. Data compiled by the Armed Conflict Location and Event Data Project

311

(ACLED) revealed that as many as 456 civilians were killed in Mali from January to mid-April. These killings occurred in March in Nioni, through a joint Wagner-junta patrol in Hombori on 19 April, and in Mondoro and Boni on 23 April.[78] Internal Malian documents revealed an injury to a Russian instructor at the crowded marketplace massacre site in Hombori and the deaths of four Russian military personnel during the 23 April killings.

In response to mounting evidence of Russian war crimes in Mali, the Kremlin attempted to turn the tables and falsely accused France of carrying out a massacre in Gossi. On 19 April, France handed over the Gossi base to the Malian junta, and less than twenty-four hours later, the French army caught 'Caucasians suspected of belonging to the Wagner Group' unloading equipment in Gossi. Citing a self-described 'retired soldier, Malian patriot and political analyst', France asserted that Wagner Group PMCs had disposed of corpses in Gossi, and on 21 April, French satellite imagery revealed the same group of 'Caucasian individuals' standing next to ten corpses.[79] Russian social media accounts retaliated by accusing France of covering its tracks in Gossi. One prominent pro-Russian supporter of the Malian junta Dia Darra spread images of corpses buried in the sand and VK amplified images from pro-Kremlin accounts located as far afield as Colombia.[80] While the trendlines in Russian media coverage of the Malian junta are overwhelmingly positive, there is still uncharacteristic room for expert community dissent from the Kremlin position. Alexei Tselunov, a prominent Russian commentator on African affairs, warned that aggressive nationalist rhetoric was on the rise in Mali, cautioned against the junta priming public opinion for a war with northern Malian Tuaregs and criticized the Malian junta's opacity towards the MINUSMA mission.[81] These sentiments are in the minority, especially outside of the Russian-language media space, as Kremlin disinformation is the most potent driver of local and international support for the Malian junta's conduct.

Countering Russian disinformation about the Gossi massacre was problematic, as Prigozhin-aligned social media networks relied increasingly on real people instead of inauthentic bots and were able to effectively skirt Facebook's content moderation policies.[82] This

# THE UKRAINE WAR AND RUSSIA'S AFRICA STRATEGY

reflected a substantial upgrade in Russia's disinformation in Mali, which began after the May 2021 coup and accelerated into a full-blown pro-Wagner Group social media campaign after the junta began negotiating with the group in September 2021. The narrative war between Russia and the West over the Wagner Group's conduct in Mali moved to the floor of the UN on 19 June. Breaking with the African Union's public criticisms of mercenaries, Russian Deputy UN Ambassador Anna Evstigneeva told the UN Security Council that African nations had every right to hire foreign soldiers and blasted criticisms of Russia's policy in Mali as 'neocolonialist approaches and double standards'.[83] This narrative war is set to intensify as the Malians try to prevent their country from becoming a great power battleground and discontent with the increasingly Niger-centric Operation Barkhane persists.

Despite Russia's dismal track record in the counterinsurgency arena, its appeal as a security partner for countries in the Sahel has endured. Despite the frosty relationship between the Chadian transitional military government and the Kremlin, opposition demonstrations routinely feature burnings of French flags and the waving of Russian flags.[84] Pro-Russian sentiments are even more pronounced in Burkina Faso, which is the Wagner Group's most plausible new frontier. On 23 January 2022, Burkina Faso's President Roch Marc Christian Kaboré was overthrown in a coup d'état. Like in Mali, anti-French sentiments, and a desire for stability after major terrorist attacks, such as the northern Inata military base attack in November 2021 that killed fifty people, ensconced support for the coup plotters. Russian media outlets praised the coup and highlighted Assimi Goïta as a leader of an 'African protest movement' against neocolonialism, which spread to Burkina Faso. As the US cut off aid to Burkina Faso, the military regime courted Russian assistance. Colonel Paul-Henri Damiba, who led the coup, is a strong supporter of a Russian security presence in Burkina Faso. Damiba pressured Kaboré to accept Russian help in the months leading up to the coup and Russian newspaper *Vzyglad* claimed that Kaboré's refusal to accept Russian assistance contributed to his demise.[85]

Pro-coup demonstrators in Burkina Faso stridently condemned France's counterterrorism efforts, requested Russian security

313

assistance and waved Russian flags in Ouagadougou.[86] Alexander Ivanov, a Prigozhin-aligned Russian operative who was honored by CAR for fighting 'armed bandits', capitalized on these sentiments by highlighting Burkina Faso's historical relationship with the Soviet Union.[87] Ivanov's praise of Thomas Sankara, who served as military dictator of Burkina Faso from 1983 to 1987 and was described as 'Africa's Che Guevara', raised eyebrows as Sankara opposed the Soviet-Afghan War, criticized Soviet aid as a form of imperialism and purged the pro-Soviet Patriotic League of Development. Nevertheless, he described the coup plotters, who were frustrated with France's failed counterterrorism campaign, as Africa's new Che Guevaras, and claimed 'I think that if Russian instructors are invited to form a new Burkina Faso army, they will do it effectively.'[88] French officials dismissed these claims, as it believed Damiba's training in Paris would cause Burkina Faso to back it over Russia, but the impending end of Operation Barkhane could give Moscow another opportunity for power projection.

On 30 September 2022, the coup in Burkina Faso which replaced Damiba with 34-year old Captain Ibrahim Traore sparked jubilation in Moscow and alarm in Paris. Russian defence analyst Boris Rozhin stated that he was hopeful that Niger and Burkina Faso would be vulnerable to anti-colonial coups, and predicted that if Burkina Faso followed Mali's lead, France would lose 'three dependent countries' and its neo-colonial empire in northwest Africa.[89] Building on Prigozhin's praise for Traore's takeover, RIAFAN also expressed confidence that Burkina Faso would welcome Wagner Group PMCs.[90] Former Kremlin advisor Sergei Markov added fuel to these predictions by claiming that 'our people' helped Traore to take power and predicted that after a Russian triumph in Ukraine, Wagner Group PMCs would stream into Africa.[91] As the Burkina Faso coup coincided with anti-French protests in Niger brandishing Russian flags, France has stepped up its efforts to counter Russian disinformation and highlight Wagner Group human rights abuses in Africa. By keeping its military operations that have failed to dislodge insurgents under wraps and highlighting French development assistance, France hopes to bolster its soft power at Russia's expense.[92]

# THE UKRAINE WAR AND RUSSIA'S AFRICA STRATEGY

While Russia remains well-placed to act as a spoiler to French and American interests in the G5 Sahel bloc, its ability to constructively engage with key West African regional partners, such as Niger, Nigeria and Senegal, are unclear. Niger has mirrored Chad's opposition to the Wagner Group's deployments in Mali, and to court Western support, Nigerien President Mohamed Bazoum attacked the dire consequences of the Ukraine war for the Global South.[93] Due to Russia's aggressive efforts to curb foreign fighter recruitment for Ukraine, Moscow positively greeted Senegal and Nigeria's strident opposition to Ukrainian efforts to recruit combatants in early March. However, it was swiftly apparent that Nigeria and Senegal's economic interests would be harmed by continued engagement with Russia. The Ajaokuta steel plant is especially vulnerable to delays due to suspended communication between Nigerian and Russian business figures, and some Nigerian business elites feared that the repeated postponements of this project will diminish their country's industrial capacity. Although Buhari had released $2 billion in funds to Russia since 2020, the Nigerian government has reportedly negotiated a fresh contract with a British company to oversee the project.[94] To compound the loss of Ajaokuta, Nigeria's condemnation of the Ukraine war, which contrasted markedly with its time-tested neutrality policy, jeopardized the $2.3 billion in trade volumes with Russia. Rising oil prices were also a double-edged sword for the Nigerian economy, as rising export revenues corresponded with soaring petrol import and subsidy costs for Nigerian consumers.

This decline in economic engagement could grow further if both countries became rivals for natural resources.[95] On 25 March, Nigeria's Minister for State Petroleum Resources Timipre Sylva expressed interest in becoming an alternative gas supplier to Europe and urged Shell, Eni and Total to expand energy investments in the Nigerian energy sector.[96] The Algeria-Niger-Nigeria gas pipeline, which stretches across 4,128 km of Sahara Desert territory, would also weaken Europe's reliance on Russian gas. Russia has sought to pre-empt this pipeline's construction by proposing an alternative Morocco-to-Nigeria pipeline. Sylva confirmed that Russia was one of many foreign stakeholders interested in constructing pipelines of this nature.[97] Despite Macky Sall's congenial comments towards

315

Putin and reiterations of Russian narratives, Senegal could also compete with Russia for gas supply to Europe. On 23 May, German Chancellor Olaf Scholz initiated talks with Senegal about liquefied natural gas exports and underscored Senegal's strategic significance by making it the first stopover point on his African tour.

## Russia Maintains its Geopolitical Foothold in Southern Africa

Despite the plethora of leadership changes in southern Africa in the years following the Crimea annexation, the region's response to Russian aggression in Ukraine did not deviate markedly from the events of 2014. Southern Africa broadly refrained from criticizing Russia's invasion of Ukraine with the notable exception of Zambia, which voted to condemn the war in the UN General Assembly. Due to its historically non-aligned foreign policy, Zambia's anti-Russian stance was harshly criticized by the Democratic Party and Patriotic Front who feared that condemning Russia would disrupt military equipment transfers and fertilizer exports.[98] The Patriots for Economic Progress Party supported Zambia's condemnation of the Ukraine war and taunted Russia by stating that it 'should go ahead' and close its embassy in Lusaka if it was displeased with the Zambian position. South Africa's officially neutral position on the Ukraine war has created considerable domestic polarizations. The Economic Freedom Fighters (EFF) Party, which is led by long-time ANC critic Julius Malema, supports Ramaphosa's efforts to shift the blame from Russia to NATO for the Ukraine war. Citing Moscow's support for anti-apartheid movements, Malema stated 'We are with Russia', urged Russia to teach the US and NATO a lesson and vowed that 'We will never denounce Russia.'[99] Jacob Zuma aligned with Malema by claiming that Russia was provoked into war, expressing solidarity between two BRICS countries, and praising Vladimir Putin as a 'man of peace'.[100] South Africa's Deputy Minister of International Relations and Cooperation Alvin Botes trod a more cautious line, as he did not absolve Russia, but insisted that wars of aggression motivated by conservative nationalism were no more heinous than those inspired by liberal imperialism like Iraq, Afghanistan or Yugoslavia.[101] Botes framed South Africa's policy

## THE UKRAINE WAR AND RUSSIA'S AFRICA STRATEGY

as a generic opposition to military solutions and accused Western countries of engaging in racist double standards.

Opposition to the Russian invasion of Ukraine also mirrored the trend-lines established by Crimea in 2014. An initial source of opposition to the war came from within the ANC government, as the Department of International Relations and Cooperation urged Russia to militarily withdraw from Ukraine. Ramaphosa swiftly lobbied for a retraction of this statement, reassured Russia that it did not represent ANC policy and proceeded to call Russia's invasion a 'military operation' instead of a war.[102] Opposition to the war was largely concentrated amongst opposition parties and ANC-aligned apolitical organizations. The Democratic Alliance Party stridently criticized the Russian invasion of Ukraine. The DA-led Cape Town government lit up the City Hall in the Ukrainian flag's yellow and blue colours and its leader John Steenhuisen blasted South Africa's 'shameful foreign policy decisions' and 'cowardly and immoral' position on Ukraine.[103] Within the ANC's traditional support base, the most strident criticisms came from South Africa's clerical establishment. Anglican Bishop of Cape Town Thabo Makgoba, who replaced Desmond Tutu, deplored South Africa's silence on the bombing of civilians and health care facilities in Ukraine, and asked 'Where is our ubuntu, our humanity.'[104] The General Industrial Workers Union scheduled a march on the Russian Embassy in Pretoria, which called for the immediate release of 15,000 Russian anti-war activists who were detained by Putin's regime.[105] This contrasted with the South African Communist Party's full-throated defence of the narrative that US imperialism caused the Ukraine war.

Beyond its offers to facilitate a diplomatic settlement in Ukraine, South Africa has embraced business-as-usual economic relations with Russia. South Africa's Central Energy Fund is looking for a gas aggregator to secure LNG for gas-to-power projects in Eastern Cape's Coega special economic zone and has turned to Gazprombank as a potential supplier.[106] Although Gazprom is competing for this contract with Azerbaijan's SOCAR company and South Africa has also secured gas supplies from Mozambique, *The Daily Maverick* expressed concern that South Africa's gas interests were colouring its perspectives on the Ukraine war. These trepidations have spilt

317

over into political debates in South Africa. National Freedom Party MP Shaik Emam raised suspicions about South Africa's gas purchases from Russia, while Deputy President David Mabuza insisted that there was 'nothing sinister' about these deals.[107] Despite the negative precedent of Zuma's efforts to tie solidarity with Russia with nuclear energy, soaring fuel prices will likely ensure that the ANC's courtship of gas receives limited popular backlash in the months ahead. South Africa's growing importance as an alternative coal supplier to Europe, which was evidenced by the 40% uptick in exports from Richards Bay Coal Facility from January to May, will also mellow Western backlash over its Russia policy.

Zimbabwe mirrored South Africa's reluctance to suspend cooperation with Russia but are vigilant about the Ukraine war's economic fallout. Tawanda Zinyama, an academic at the University of Zimbabwe, described Zimbabwe's position as a 'loyalty vote' that would not derail Harare's re-engagement with the West.[108] Zimbabwe emulated China's implicit display of solidarity with Russia without receiving backlash from Western countries that outright supporters of the invasion like Belarus gained. On 11 April, Mnagagwa stated that Zimbabwe's negative experience with Western unilateralism caused it to sympathize with Russia's fears of NATO encirclement and eastward expansion. Mnagagwa also praised Russia's insistence on local currency payment for gas as a complement to China's challenge against US dollar hegemony.[109] Persistence Gwanyanya, a Harare-based economist and member of the Reserve Bank of Zimbabwe's Monetary Policy Committee, stated that Zimbabwe was learning lessons from Russia as it sought to divest from the US dollar and revive the value of its currency.[110] Zimbabwe's parlous fiscal situation, which includes a $1.2 billion trade deficit that contrasts with Russia's $203 billion trade surplus, has raised doubts about Zimbabwe's ability to emulate Russia's response to Western sanctions. While Zimbabwean precious metal producers believed that the Ukraine war would boost their profits, Zimbabwe's dependency on Russia for at least 50% of its wheat and soaring fuel prices create a murkier picture.

Angola has emulated South Africa and Zimbabwe's neutrality policies towards the Ukraine war but has been more circumspect

## THE UKRAINE WAR AND RUSSIA'S AFRICA STRATEGY

about endorsing pro-Russian narratives. On 28 April, João Lourenço and Vladimir Putin held talks about the Ukraine war and emphasized their shared commitment to normal bilateral relations.[111] Western sanctions on Russia pose economic risks to Angola's mining sector but could create opportunities in the oil and gas arena. On 9 May, Angola's state-run Endiama diamond manufacturer claimed that sanctions on Russia would delay the supply of parts and machinery and projected a decline in diamond output from 13.8 million to 10.05 million carats.[112] To counteract its reliance on Alrosa Diamond, Angola has successfully negotiated a return of De Beers for the first time since 2012 and has engaged with Rio Tinto on exploration in Luanda Norte's Chiri mine. Italian Prime Minister Mario Draghi has targeted Angola and the Republic of Congo as key alternative gas suppliers to Europe, and on 21 April, Italy and Angola signed a declaration of intent to develop new natural gas ventures.[113] The sustainability of Angola's purchases of Russian military equipment is a significant wildcard in the bilateral relationship, and Luanda's $85 million authorization to purchase Chinese military equipment in July 2021 could pave the way for tighter China-Angola cooperation. Russia's preservation of its partnerships in Africa against competition from China and Europe in an era of sanctions will play an indispensable role in shaping the success of its continental strategy.

# EPILOGUE TO THE PAPERBACK EDITION
## RUSSIA'S AFRICA POLICY IN 2023—SEISMIC SHOCKS, SMALL TRANSFORMATIONS

On 27 July 2023, delegations from forty-nine African countries arrived in St Petersburg's Expoforum for the second Russia-Africa Summit. The Summit, which was co-hosted by Comoros President Azali Assoumani and Vladimir Putin, swiftly devolved into a propaganda festival. Putin described Africa as a 'new centre of power' and declared that 'Russia's attention to Africa is steadily growing'. After hailing Russia's forgiveness of $23 billion in Soviet-era debt and offering free grain to six African countries, Putin depicted Russia and Africa as ideological allies against neocolonialism, sanctions and non-traditional values.[1] Conference attendees enthusiastically embraced Putin's propaganda. Yoweri Museveni declared that Uganda was an 'island of stability' because of its reliance on Russian weaponry.[2] Guinean diplomat Lama Jacques Sevoba entered the Summit with a Putin T-shirt and told *Izvestia* that 'This is my soul—the person who is on the T-shirt.'[3]

Pageantry reigned at the Expoforum, but was it just a mirage? Only seventeen African heads of state were in attendance, compared to the forty-three who participated in the Sochi Summit four years earlier. Ten days before the Summit, Russia refused to renew the Black Sea Grain Initiative. The Kremlin's decision received stinging criticisms in Africa. Kenya's Principal Secretary for Foreign Affairs Korir Sing'Oei described Russia's move as a 'stab [in] the back at global food security prices' and argued that it disproportionately hurt drought-afflicted countries in the Horn of Africa.[4] General Abdel Fattah el-Sisi used his plenary speech at the St Petersburg Summit to call for the deal's revival. Yevgeny Prigozhin's meeting with a CAR delegate at his family-owned Trezine Hotel spotlighted divisions within the Russian leadership. Scarcely a month earlier, Prigozhin had led an abortive mutiny against the Russian Defence Ministry and was branded by Putin as a traitor.

As the Ukraine War enters its third year, Russia has never been more determined to expand its influence in Africa. But Russia's power projection capacity is hampered by economic struggles, dwindling soft power, internal discord and a strategy that relies on exploiting chaos. The split-screen between the Expoforum's pageantry and dire geopolitical realities is an allegory of Russian policy towards Africa.

## Russia Struggles to Deepen Partnerships in Africa

Ahead of the St Petersburg Summit, Sergei Lavrov embarked on a series of continent-wide tours to shore up Russia's partnerships in Africa and promote the Kremlin's narratives on the Ukraine War. Immediately after the Black Sea grain deal was signed, Lavrov visited Egypt, Ethiopia, the Republic of Congo and Uganda from 24 to 28 July 2022. Ahead of his tour, Lavrov primed public opinion in his direction by articulating the Kremlin's official line to African media outlets. Lavrov's comments highlighted the Soviet Union's investment in African companies, Russia's efforts to help African countries pursue independent development paths and Russia's support for the rules-based international order.[5] This preserved Russia's first-mover information warfare advantage over the West and pre-empted Emmanuel Macron's castigation of Russia as 'one of the last imperial colonial powers' during his 27 July visit to Benin.[6]

During his trip, Lavrov unabashedly promoted Russia's war in Ukraine and commitment to abating food insecurity. At the 25 July Arab League Summit in Cairo, Lavrov described the war as an effort to liberate the people of eastern Ukraine from an 'absolutely unacceptable regime' and vowed to overthrow Zelensky's 'anti-people and anti-historical' government.[7] While African leaders

## EPILOGUE TO THE PAPERBACK EDITION

did not explicitly reiterate Moscow's position on Ukraine, they continued to insist that Russia was not on the wrong side of history. Museveni claimed during Lavrov's July 2022 visit to Uganda that he would criticize Russia if it erred—as he had demonstrated against the 1968 Prague Spring crackdown—but declared, 'when they have not made a mistake, we cannot be against them'.[8]

Although Russia struck Odesa port immediately after the grain deal was signed, Lavrov claimed that COVID-19 and Western sanctions exacerbated food insecurity in Africa and confirmed the endurance of Russia's grain export supply chain to Uganda and Ethiopia. Lavrov considered Ethiopia's offer to purchase additional Russian grain to compensate for the 50% of its grain that originated from Ukraine.[9] The receptivity of African countries to Lavrov's narratives caused *Vzyglad* to declare, 'Russia wins against the West in the fight for Africa'.[10] Yet the trip did not result in any breakthrough contracts for Russia. The Ugandan president's assertion that he is neither pro-West nor pro-East but 'pro-Myself' also underscored the wariness of even Kremlin-friendly countries to forge a hard anti-Western alignment with Moscow.[11]

Lavrov reiterated similar themes during his January 2023 visits to Angola, Eswatini, Eritrea and South Africa, and February 2023 trips to Mali, Mauritania and Sudan. Upon his return to Moscow on 10 February, Lavrov triumphantly proclaimed, 'Today we can affirm that the West's plans to isolate Russia by surrounding us with a sanitary cordon have been a fiasco.'[12] These trips and their aftermath underscored the polarization surrounding Russia's role in Africa, its limited ability to court countries with viable Western foreign policy vectors, and the concentration of its partnerships in isolated countries. Lavrov's trip to South Africa highlighted the split-screen reactions between elites and civil society that limit Russian influence in Africa. South African Minister of International Relations and Cooperation Naledi Pandor hailed her 'most wonderful meeting' with Lavrov, which presaged South Africa's controversial 17 to 27 February Mosi II naval exercises with Russia and China.[13] Yet Pandor's embrace of Lavrov was greeted with derision by the opposition, the Democratic Alliance Party, and by Ukrainian protesters chanting 'Go Home Lavrov!' and 'Stop the Lies! Stop the War'.

323

The controversies, which accompanied the Lavrov-Pandor meeting, endured in the months that followed. The Mosi II exercises ended up being an underwhelming spectacle, which strained US-South Africa relations. The South African Navy only deployed the frigate *Mendi* for the drills, while the much-hyped Russian Zircon hypersonic missile test did not take place.[14] Russia's *Admiral Gorshkov* frigate called at Cape Town port from 14 to 15 February and Durban on 19 February. The US Department of State expressed 'concern' about the Mosi drills and urged South Africa to pursue military cooperation with fellow democracies.[15] Michigan Republican Congressman John James expressed sharper opposition to the ANC's actions, as he advanced Bill Resolution 145 calling for a 'thorough review' of US-South Africa relations.[16]

The Mosi II drills were followed by a controversy around the ICC's March 2023 issuance of an arrest warrant for Putin. As the August 2023 BRICS Summit was being hosted in Johannesburg, South Africa had a legal obligation to arrest Putin if he attended. South Africa's official response was marred by incoherence. During the author's March 2023 trip to Pretoria, a Department of International Relations and Cooperation (DIRCO) official claimed that South Africa would uphold its ICC commitments but was undecided on whether Putin would be invited. On 25 April, Cyril Ramaphosa declared that the ANC would pull out from the ICC over the way in which it deals 'with these types of problems'. Hours later, Ramaphosa's office confirmed that South Africa remained a signatory to the ICC.[17] Yet the ANC continued to exploit loopholes that could allow Putin to attend the BRICS Summit with impunity. On 18 July, Ramaphosa asked the ICC to exempt it from arresting Putin, as doing so would amount to South Africa declaring war on Russia.[18] As the ICC refused to waver, Putin decided not to attend the BRICS Summit and released a pre-recorded speech to attendees on 22 August. Had Putin attended, Steve Gruzd, head of African Governance and Diplomacy Programme at the South African Institute of International Affairs, contends that South Africa would have whisked Putin in and out of the Summit under heavy security, much like they had done with then Sudanese president Omar al-Bashir. Nevertheless, Gruzd argues that Ramaphosa dissuaded Putin from attending after the Russia-Africa

## EPILOGUE TO THE PAPERBACK EDITION

Summit as he feared handing Russia a huge propaganda victory and did not want to appear like a 'serial ignorer' of ICC mandates.[19]

In tandem with its deliberations on the ICC warrant, South Africa faced a scandal pertaining to alleged arms deliveries to Russia. On 11 May, US Ambassador to South Africa Reuben Brigety accused South Africa of arming Russia and urged South Africa to start 'practicing its non-alignment policy'. Brigety's comments referred to the alleged transfer of weapons and ammunition from the *Lady R* cargo ship in Simon's Town Naval Base to Russia in December 2022.[20] Ramaphosa denied these assertions and launched an investigation into *Lady R*'s activities. The controversy resulted in a spike in anti-American sentiments in South Africa, which included an alleged dressing down of Brigety by DIRCO and fuelled reciprocal calls from US lawmakers to move the 2023 AGOA Forum from Johannesburg.[21] The final report, which was published in September 2023 to cover the findings of Ramaphosa's investigation, exonerated South Africa. The *Lady R* ship was transporting goods intended for the South African military, which were ordered from a UAE-based company. The South African authorities had no sway over the use of a sanctions-designated ship and *Lady R* docked in Simon's Town because Ngqura-Port Elizabeth port denied it service.[22]

Lavrov's trip to Angola was a damage-control mission. After voting against Russia's illegal annexation of Ukraine's Donetsk, Kherson, Luhansk and Zaporizhzhia regions in September 2022, Angola called for a Russian unilateral ceasefire.[23] Lavrov's reminders of Soviet support for the MPLA during the Angolan Civil War and entreaties did not thwart Angola's embrace of strategic ties with the US. Lavrov's February 2023 visit to Mauritania, which was the first by any Russian foreign minister, was similarly unsuccessful. Lavrov offered to 'help' Mauritania contain terrorist threats in the Sahara-Sahel region and the spill-over of Algeria-Morocco tensions over the Western Sahara.[24] These oblique security offers did not dissuade Mauritania from pursuing a potential NATO military installation on its coast.

Russia's greatest diplomatic successes came from largely isolated autocracies. Aside from expected visits to Mali and Sudan, Lavrov made a surprise trip to Eritrea to discuss the development of the

325

Massawa port on its Red Sea coast. Lavrov also oversaw a historic breakthrough in Russia's partnership with Eswatini. Days after the assassination of Thulani Maseko, a leading opposition politician and human rights activist, Lavrov offered security training to Eswatini's absolute monarchy.[25] As Eswatini had only fifty security personnel enrolled in Russian defence universities, Lavrov's trip reflected the meagre results of Russia's educational diplomacy in Africa.

Despite these mixed results, Russia's diplomatic courtship of Africa continued. The 19 March Second International Parliamentary Conference 'Russia-Africa' featured diatribes against neocolonialism from Putin and Chairman of the State Duma Vyacheslav Volodin. Cipriano Cassamá, the president of Guinea-Bissau's National People's Assembly declared that 'Russia has a great president and statesman. We are always on his side; we stand with him.'[26] Cassamá's effusive comments reflected vested interests, as Russia had forgiven Guinea-Bissau's Soviet-era debt in January 2023. Lavrov also met with Kenya's President William Ruto in Nairobi in May 2023, which resulted in plans to strike a trade pact by the end of the year. An optimistic conclusion to Lavrov's pre-St Petersburg Summit diplomatic blitz.

### Russia Fights to Preserve its Soft Power in Africa

Nearly two years into the Ukraine War, Russia's soft power in Africa looks increasingly fragile. A June 2023 Ipsos poll revealed a marked pro-Ukraine tilt in African public opinion.[27] The majority of those surveyed in Kenya, Nigeria, Senegal, South Africa, Uganda and Zambia believed that Russia's invasion of Ukraine was illegal, and that Russia had committed war crimes in Ukraine. Except for Senegal, where apathy predominated, a majority of those surveyed believed that their government should care about Russia's territorial occupations and urge Russian troops to leave Ukraine. Ipsos's findings mirrored those of other surveys. A July 2023 Pew Research Survey showed that Russia's favourability ratings stood at just 28% in South Africa, 40% in Kenya and 42% in Nigeria.[28]

The erosion of Russia's image can be partially explained by louder calls for peace in Ukraine from African leaders and the surprising efficacy of Ukraine's diplomatic outreaches. On 17

## EPILOGUE TO THE PAPERBACK EDITION

May, Ramaphosa inaugurated an 'African leaders peace mission' that would visit Moscow and Kyiv in mid-to-late June.[29] The South African-led peace mission also consisted of the leaders of Egypt, the Republic of Congo, Senegal, Uganda and Zambia. Jean-Yves Ollivier, an Algerian-born French diplomat who helped facilitate talks to end apartheid in the late 1980s, oversaw the peace mission and boasted of its broad international support. Yet even Ollivier was circumspect about the prospects of a decisive breakthrough, claiming that 'We are not dreamers' and that 'unless something happens, I don't think we are going to finish this mission with a ceasefire.'[30]

Ollivier's pessimistic outlook was sharply attuned to geopolitical realities. African diplomats initially pushed for a temporary ceasefire and second referendum in Donbas and claimed that these actions needed to be implemented before they would visit Kyiv or Moscow. As the Kremlin's baseline negotiating position is Ukraine's surrender of all the regions illegally annexed by Russia, it rejected this proposal.[31] Ultranationalist firebrand Igor Girkin, the perpetrator of the July 2014 shootdown of a MH-17 jet over Ukraine, facetiously called for 'the relocation of all employees of the African Peace Mission in Ukraine to one of the abandoned Soviet Antarctic stations.'[32]

While the African peace mission ultimately visited Kyiv and Moscow in mid-June, its diplomatic efforts were a resounding failure. The AU did not officially endorse the peace mission and Sisi, Museveni and Nguesso cancelled their participation days before the delegation was set to leave for Kyiv. Nguesso's absence was a humiliating blow to Ollivier, as he was a long-time associate of the Congolese president. When the African peace mission arrived in Kyiv on 16 June, it was greeted by a barrage of Russian missiles and warnings from Ukraine's top officials not to request territorial concessions. Ramaphosa was mocked by South Africa's opposition parties for crossing the Ukrainian border without receiving adequate security protocols from the Polish authorities.

For attendees and would-be participants, the peace mission helped counter Western perceptions of pro-Russian sympathies. Gruzd believes that Ramaphosa kept the idea of launching an African peace initiative on the backburner for a long time and only decided to implement it after the US's scrutiny of *Lady R*'s arms shipments.[33] Sisi's approach to the peace mission reflected similar calculations. During the second half of 2022, Egypt earned goodwill in the US by forcing Russia to redirect Cairo-bound Su-35 jets to Iran and rejecting the use of Russian Mir credit cards. After the US withheld $130 million in foreign military aid to Cairo over human rights concerns, Egypt stealthily strengthened security ties with Russia. US officials were especially critical of Egypt's alleged plan to export 40,000 rockets to Russia in February 2023.[34] Although Egypt assuaged the US by agreeing to supply ammunition to Ukraine in April 2023, mulling participation in the peace mission was a useful way for it to highlight its 'constructive engagement' with Russia.

Ukraine's diplomatic engagement efforts with Africa have also intensified over the past eighteen months. These overtures began inauspiciously. After seeing his offer to address the African Union fall flat, Zelensky's June 2022 Zoom call with African leaders only attracted the heads of state of Côte d'Ivoire, the Republic of Congo and Senegal.[35] Despite these setbacks, Ukraine incrementally expanded its media outreaches in Africa. Ukrainian Minister of Foreign Affairs Dmytro Kuleba's warning about Russia's contributions to food insecurity reached Nigeria's *Premium Times*. In a briefing to African journalists, Zelensky highlighted Russia's dearth of investment in Africa as proof of its self-serving policies.[36] But these endeavours were similarly fraught with challenges. In August 2022, the *Premium Times* condemned Zelensky as a 'divisive figure and a warmonger' and castigated Ukraine for its poor treatment of African students.[37]

Despite these controversies, Kuleba assumed that Africa's accommodation of Russia was triggered by unfamiliarity with Ukraine, which only possessed ten embassies in Africa and negligible trade relations with the continent outside the agricultural sphere. Upon his arrival in Senegal in October 2022, Kuleba declared, 'Russia's narrative has been very present here. Now it's time for Ukrainian truths.'[38] While Kuleba's African tour was unexpectedly cut short by Russia's barrages on critical infrastructure in Ukraine, it set the tone for deeper Ukrainian engagement with Africa. Zelensky unveiled the Grain from Ukraine initiative in November 2022, which directly delivered grain to Sudan and Somalia. One month later, he called for the construction of ten new Ukrainian embassies

328

EPILOGUE TO THE PAPERBACK EDITION

in Africa. Kuleba's August 2023 trip revealed the scale of Ukraine's ambitions, as it featured calls for a 'diplomatic counteroffensive' against Russia in Africa and his pledge to 'free Africa from Russia's grip'.[39] By selling win-win cooperation and shared experiences of colonial oppression, Ukraine hopes to undo the impact of decades of assiduous Russian outreaches towards Africa's elites.

While Africa's calls for peace in Ukraine and Ukrainian diplomacy fuelled perceptions of Russia as an aggressor country, Moscow's naked subversion of the Black Sea grain deal had a surprisingly less potent negative impact. Russia responded to these concerns with high-profile offers of free grain and fertilizer. Putin's St Petersburg Summit pledge of 25,000 to 50,000 tons of free grain to Burkina Faso, Zimbabwe, Mali, Somalia, CAR and Eritrea gained particular attention. Russia's choice of countries for free grain deliveries underscored its desire to use agricultural exports to shore up its core partnerships. Somalia was the sole exception. After his address to RUSI in November 2023, Somalia's President Hassan Sheikh Mohamud reaffirmed to the author that he disapproved of Russia's invasion of Ukraine regardless of these grain deliveries.[40] After a months-long delivery delay, Russian Minister of Agriculture Dmitry Patrushev confirmed on 17 November that the first tranche of grain would arrive in Burkina Faso and Somalia by early December at the latest.[41]

Although Russia's free grain deliveries aided its allies, Russian manufacturer Uralchem-Uralkali's pledge of 260,000 tons of fertilizer to Africa appeased Moscow's critics. Although Malawi consistently voted against Russia in the UNGA, it received 20,000 tons of Russian fertilizer in March 2023. Uralchem-Uralkali claimed that it was a gift to Malawi, but its delivery was politically charged. Russia framed it as a critique of the EU sanctions regime. The Netherlands had previously held up Russian fertilizer shipments, and even after they were finally released from Dutch custody in January 2023, the fertilizer was forced to travel by truck from Mozambique (where it had experienced further delays) to Malawi.[42] When the fertilizer arrived in Malawi, Russia got a PR bonanza. Malawi's Minister of Agriculture Samuel Kawale told Russia's Ambassador Nikolay Krasilnikov that 'You came to our rescue when we needed you

329

the most' and described Russia as a 'true friend'. Kawale also hailed the potential for Russia's fertilizer deliveries to ease food insecurity amongst 400,000 Malawian households. Russia's 1 June delivery of 34,000 tons of fertilizer to Mombasa, which was previously stored in Latvia, similarly boosted its relations with Kenya and aided small farmers.[43]

Russia has also presented itself as part of the solution to Africa's food security challenges. This consisted of bilateral agricultural deals with African countries, such as its September 2023 agreement to ship 480,000 tons of wheat to Egypt at the discounted price of $270 a ton.[44] It also consisted of a more sweeping challenge to Western-backed mechanisms to combat food insecurity in Africa. In his pre-St Petersburg Summit article on Russia's Africa policy, Putin claimed that the Black Sea grain deal was 'shamelessly used solely for the enrichment of large US and European businesses that exported and resold grain from Ukraine.'[45] Putin asserted that the world's most food insecure countries, such as Ethiopia, Sudan and Somalia, received just 3% of the grain allotted through the scheme, or one million tons. He claimed that Russia was making up the shortfall despite Western sanctions, as it exported nearly 10 million tons to Africa in the first half of 2023, compared to 11.5 million tons in all of 2022.

Russia also called for the direct transfer of grain to African countries via third party intermediaries Turkey and Qatar. In early September 2023, Putin and the Deputy Minister of Foreign Affairs Alexander Grushko confirmed that one million tons of grain would be directly transferred through Turkey to the world's poorest countries. This assertion was greeted with scepticism, even in Russia's tightly controlled media space. Citing Grushko, RBC highlighted unresolved questions about logistics, financing and destination countries.[46] Former State Duma Deputy Elena Panina expressed scepticism about Turkey's trustworthiness and claimed that Russia would ultimately coordinate with Qatar on grain exports.[47] A Qatari diplomat told the author that Qatar had never seriously considered or agreed to take part in Russia's grain delivery scheme.[48] These uncertainties, combined with the low quantity

## EPILOGUE TO THE PAPERBACK EDITION

of exportable grain, suggest that Russia's claims to be part of the solution to food insecurity are dubious.

The Gaza War might also provide Russia with an opportunity to strengthen its partnerships in North Africa. Since Israel initiated its campaign to eradicate Hamas from the Gaza Strip in October 2023, Russia has leveraged its pro-Palestinian rhetoric in its outreaches to Egypt and Algeria. In a November 2023 RT interview, Lavrov highlighted Egypt's commitment to peace in Gaza, which included hosting a regional summit in Cairo on 21 October, and hailed Egypt as a 'global player'.[49] Mohamed Hassan, a prominent Egyptian commentator, contends that Egypt's coordination with Russia furthers its goal of creating a campaign of 'massive international pressure' against Israel's military operations.[50] As Algeria will become a non-permanent UNSC member in 2024–5, Putin has praised its rising diplomatic profile. Russia's *Mercury-734* missile corvette and *Admiral Grigorovich* frigate have docked in Algiers port for western Mediterranean drills.[51]

These outreaches have not created substantive breakthroughs. Egypt coordinated with the US and Qatar on the release of 110 Israeli hostages and Algeria campaigned for new US arms deliveries. At a popular level, Russia's rhetoric has bolstered its image. Egyptian political scientist Ahmed Dahshan argues that the Gaza War has eroded US soft power in Egypt more than any other post-Cold War event and notes that many young Egyptians, who previously sympathized with Ukraine, see Zelensky as unprincipled for his pro-Israel stance.[52] These sentiments will likely intensify, as Russia leverages its Arabic-language state media machinery to portray itself to vast audiences as a peacemaker and the US as a warmongering aggressor.

### Russia's Post-Wagner Security Policy in Africa

By early 2023, Yevgeny Prigozhin's business empire in Africa had withstood sanctions and was ripe for expansion. To bolster his 'people's oligarch' brand, Prigozhin declared he 'spit on sanctions', but did not enrich himself from Africa's resources. A February 2023 *Financial Times* investigation suggested otherwise.[53] It revealed that Prigozhin had received $250 million in natural resource payments from 2018 to 2022, underscoring his ability to skirt sanctions. M-Invest generated $2.6 million in revenues from Sudan's gold mines in the twelve months after the US sanctioned it in July 2020. Two companies that export industrial equipment to Wagner-linked entities in Sudan and CAR received $6 million in revenues by late 2021.

Prigozhin was increasingly brazen about his desire to expand Wagner's presence in coastal West Africa. This pivot followed abortive Wagner-linked attempts at regime change in Chad, which were exposed by US intelligence in February 2023. Russia's Ambassador to Ghana, Sergei Berdnikov, aided these efforts, as he appointed an American ex-convict Melee Kermue as Russia's honorary consul-general in Liberia. Kermue allowed Wagner experts to enter Liberia under the guise of businessmen.[54] In November 2022, the Neo-Nazi Rusich Battalion sent a delegation to Sierra Leone. A popular Prigozhin-linked animated video depicted Wagner forces as heroes that crushed French forces in Mali and Burkina Faso, and warned of its future arrival in Côte d'Ivoire.[55]

As Prigozhin's conflict with the Russian Defence Ministry sharpened over war materiel supplies and frontline tactics, he became increasingly critical of the Kremlin's policy in Africa. On 7 April, Prigozhin published an explosive Telegram critique of the Kremlin's Africa strategy. Prigozhin declared that in African countries like Libya where he is 'well immersed', we do 'absolutely nothing'. Prigozhin assailed the bureaucratic nature of Russian foreign policy and the difficulties of communications with Russian ministries, which placed Russia at a disadvantage to the US and France. Prigozhin claimed that an anti-Russian lobby existed within the Kremlin, which deprived Wagner fighters of aircraft and aimed to restrict the potential for Russia to extend its influence in Africa.[56] The Russian Foreign Ministry responded by highlighting its UNSC meetings on Africa. Prigozhin remained dissatisfied and released an alternative fifteen-point UNSC agenda, which devoted significant attention to Africa.[57]

These bombastic criticisms were small steps in the long road to the 23 June Wagner mutiny. Prigozhin's failed coup attempt imperilled Wagner's future in Africa. Lavrov tried to assuage anxiety

## EPILOGUE TO THE PAPERBACK EDITION

by claiming that Wagner contracts would not concern the Russian state, as they were signed without Kremlin oversight.[58] The Russia-Africa Summit added to this business-as-usual feeling. Aside from Prigozhin's much-discussed attendance, his lieutenant Maxim Shugaley met with Viktor Bout, who was released from US prison in December 2022. Shugaley discussed aircraft and SUV production in Ulyanovsk with Bout and argued that Russia should aggressively market these products to Africa before China stepped in.[59]

This illusion of stability was shattered by the 23 August plane crash over Kuzhenkino, which saw Prigozhin, Dmitry Utkin and Wagner logistics chief Valery Chekalov meet a grisly demise. Russian Deputy Defence Minister Yunus-Bek Yevkurov embarked on an African tour to promote the nationalization of Wagner's assets, but no major changes were observed on the ground. On 24 September, a US defence official confirmed that Wagner had not withdrawn from Africa 'in any substantial or meaningful numbers' and there was no 'decisive shift' in Wagner's relationship with the Kremlin.[60] By early November, the status quo appeared to have changed. Konstantin Mirzayants, a commander of Redoubt PMC, formed in 2008 and deployed to Ukraine, appeared in Africa. A high-ranking GRU officer Andrei Averyanov, who was notorious for his repression of Russian dissidents and attended the Russia-Africa Summit, was deemed to be the leader of Wagner's operations.[61]

While it does not appear that Wagner PMCs have been largely replaced by their Redoubt counterparts, the Russian Defence Ministry is trying to create an umbrella organization called Africa Corps. Yevkurov reportedly initiated the concept of Africa Corps during his 22 August meeting with Haftar, and Africa Corps has since posted recruitment advertisements with a starting salary of $3,160 per month.[62] This is a substantially higher pay rate than the Russian Defence Ministry offered PMCs after the Wagner mutiny, and exceeds what Prigozhin paid Wagner PMCs before his death.

The viability of Africa Corps remains a subject of intense debate. Andrey Chuprygin, a professor at the Faculty of World Economy and International Affairs at the Higher School of Economics in Moscow, contends that Africa Corps will include both Wagner and Redoubt, as 'the money is too attractive to be outside official control' and the

Kremlin is 'afraid of a Prigozhin 2.0'. Chuprygin does not believe that Wagner can exist autonomously, stating, 'We can forget the Wagner name when we are not talking about the famous composer.'[63] The Institute for the Study of War takes a more sceptical view, as it sees public advertisements for Africa Corps as proof that the Russian Defence Ministry is struggling to recruit ex-Wagner fighters.[64] The future of Russia's military interventions in Libya, CAR, Sudan and Mali will be outlined below, as will its prospects of deploying forces to Burkina Faso and Niger.

## Russia's Military Presence in Libya: A Possible Rebrand?

As Libya's election impasse continued, the US viewed the Wagner Group's presence as a major impediment to its long-term stability. In February 2023, CIA Director William J. Burns met with Haftar at the Al-Rajma military complex near Benghazi and discussed the Wagner Group's potential ouster.[65] Haftar did not offer Burns any promises about Wagner and asked for reassurances that Turkish-aligned militias in western Libya would not attack LNA forces in Sirte or central Libya. Parallel talks with Egypt were similarly inconclusive, even though Sisi opposes Wagner's deployment near the Egypt-Libya border.

Despite the failure of US outreaches, Haftar's attitude towards Wagner was souring. Prigozhin's suspicions about Haftar's ties to France and crude pressure tactics to pry $200 million from him in October 2022 intensified latent frictions between Wagner and the LNA.[66] When he met Haftar to collect the funds, Prigozhin was so fearful of French and US intelligence infiltration of LNA bases that he donned a fake beard and Libyan military outfit. One Libyan observer quipped that 'everyone who saw him thought he was a Salafist'.[67]

Haftar's confidence in Wagner's security umbrella was further shaken on 30 June, as a drone was fired on the al-Kharruba air base, located 150 km southwest of Benghazi. Although Prigozhin planned to deploy Wagner's elite 5th Special Operations Forces to Libya, Haftar was already planning for a post-Wagner future.[68] Yevkurov spoke with eastern Libya officials at the August 2023 Moscow Security Conference and met with Haftar in Benghazi a week later. The Russian Defence Ministry described its 22 August trip as 'the

## EPILOGUE TO THE PAPERBACK EDITION

first official visit of a Russian military delegation' and pledged to cooperate with the LNA against 'international terrorism'.[69]

After Prigozhin's death, the Russian Defence Ministry's outreaches to Libya intensified further. After the collapse of two dams flooded the city of Derna in September 2023, killing thousands of Libyans, an Ilyushin Il-76 jet with search and rescue equipment touched down in Benghazi. A military truck brandishing Russian and Libyan flags simultaneously appeared on the tarmac of Benghazi's Benina Airport. These aid deliveries paved the way for Yevkurov's second post-mutiny meeting with Haftar on 17 September and Haftar's meeting with Putin in Moscow on 28 September.

The US watched these trips with alarm, as it feared that Haftar had struck an agreement with Putin to revive Russia's naval base plan in Tobruk. In exchange for basing rights, Haftar would receive Russian air defence systems and training assistance for LNA pilots and special forces.[70] These reports were greeted with scepticism in Moscow. Russian defence expert Yuri Lyamin noted that rumours of this kind had swirled for five to six years and insisted Libya's division between different governments, which restrained base construction in the past, would impede Russia's efforts.[71] Lyamin's concerns have validity, as Russia continues to seek out economic cooperation opportunities with the Tripoli authorities. Tatneft announced the discovery of major oil fields in the Ghadames Basin in May 2023, and has coordinated with the NOC on oil exploration efforts.[72]

While Russia's post-Wagner strategy in Libya closely resembles its prior approach, uncertainties lie ahead. Jalel Harchaoui notes that any agreement between the Russian Defence Ministry and LNA would require approval from the House of Representatives (HoR), which gives Egypt sway over the deal's implementation.[73] HoR approval will likely be a prerequisite for the deployment of Russian warships off Libya's coast. This would further antagonize the US, even though its retaliatory options are limited. As Russia's strategic commitment to Libya endures, Wagner will likely survive in a rebranded form. Harchaoui predicts that Russia could return to Redoubt PMC if it needs additional forces, as it does not want regular forces to be linked to criminal activities in southern Libya.[74]

335

### Russia's Enduring State Capture of the Central African Republic

Much like Libya, Russian policy in CAR will likely be defined by continuities. In February 2023, hostilities flared between Wagner forces and rebel groups on CAR's porous borders with Chad, Cameroon and Sudan. According to Ahmadou Ali, a senior leader in the Coalition of Patriots for Change movement, rebels staged a successful ambush against Wagner forces.[75] This ambush resulted in the deaths of between seven and seventeen Wagner fighters. As Wagner fighters carried out operations without CAR military support, the scale of Russia's state capture was laid bare. One figure close to the CAR military lamented, 'The Russians have taken all over the country' and declared 'They stole all our resources.'[76]

Due to growing discontent with Russia's policies, Prigozhin redirected attention towards French misconduct with incendiary conspiracy theories. After accusing France of state-sponsored terrorism and allegedly trying to assassinate Dmitry Sytii with a mail bomb in December 2022, Prigozhin accused French forces of organ-harvesting and raping twelve-year-old girls in CAR.[77] This rhetoric clashed with CAR President Faustin-Archange Touadéra's March 2023 meeting with Macron in Gabon, which was criticized by Wagner-aligned Telegram channels.[78] The March 2023 killing of nine Chinese gold miners in CAR, which rebel groups and Western officials alleged was linked to Wagner, created further frictions between Prigozhin and Touadéra.

Despite these controversies, Touadéra needed Wagner's full support to ensure that his contentious July 2023 term extension referendum would proceed without incident. Although 100 Wagner PMCs reportedly fled CAR for Entebbe, Uganda, after Prigozhin's mutiny, this was swiftly determined to be a routine troop rotation and hundreds of reinforcements streamed into CAR in mid-July. At the Russia-Africa Summit, Touadéra praised Russia for saving democracy in CAR and his re-election in early August was not accompanied by political violence. Nevertheless, Touadéra was already looking beyond Wagner. Shortly after the mutiny, Touadéra's special advisor Fidèle Gouandjika quipped, 'Russia gave us Wagner, the rest isn't our business. If it's not Wagner anymore and they send

## EPILOGUE TO THE PAPERBACK EDITION

Beethoven or Mozart, it doesn't matter, we'll take them.'[79] On Putin's recommendation, Touadéra did not meet with Prigozhin at the Russia-Africa Summit.[80]

After Gouandjika mourned Prigozhin's death by wearing an 'I am Wagner' T-shirt, and bagpipe ceremonies for Wagner's leadership were held, Yevkurov visited Bangui in September 2023. The Russian Defence Ministry tried to nationalize Wagner's assets, but it was unclear whether it would be able to take over Prigozhin's networks. Due to this uncertainty and growing discontent in CAR with Russia's misleading 'win-win partnership' offer, Western powers see opportunities to make diplomatic inroads in CAR. In November 2023, Gouandjika admitted that CAR had one month left to decide on accepting security assistance from the US. These overtures have not been a source of major concern in Moscow. Retired Russian military officer and Africa expert Sergey Eledinov remarked that 'Touadéra is like a disabled man walking with a cane and that cane is Wagner.'[81] As Touadéra plans to run for president again in 2025, his regime security concerns could take precedence over the CAR's foreign policy diversification plans.

## Russia's Balancing Strategy in Sudan's Intra-Military Civil War

On 15 April 2023, festering tensions between Hemedti's RSF and Burhan's SAF escalated into a full-scale civil war. Russian officials responded to Sudan's intra-military conflict by highlighting Western policy failures and extolling the virtues of authoritarian rule. On 25 April, Lavrov accused the US of 'geopolitical engineering', as it pressured al-Bashir into letting South Sudan secede and sanctioned both Sudan and South Sudan, instead of encouraging their peaceful development.[82] Anna Evstigneeva blamed the conflict on the December 2022 democratic transition framework, which she called insufficiently inclusive.[83] Russian Telegram channels promoted synergistic narratives. The 'Militarist' Telegram channel blamed Under Secretary of State for Political Affairs Victoria Nuland's democracy promotion efforts for the Burhan-Hemedti conflict.[84] Sergei Markov lionized al-Bashir as a Leonid Brezhnev-style stabilizing figure and compared the SAF-RSF conflict to the rivalry

337

# RUSSIA IN AFRICA

between Mikhail Gorbachev and Boris Yeltsin which destroyed the Soviet Union.[85]

As civil war persisted, Russian experts supported a swift return to authoritarian stability in Sudan and did not believe that Moscow's interests would be advanced by aligning with either Burhan or Hemedti. Sergei Seregichev argued that Russia wanted to 'avoid the scenario of Somalization' as it would impede effective cooperation with Sudan and warned against Sudan becoming an 'eternal battlefield' between different forces.[86] A long war would also be detrimental to Russia's Red Sea naval base plan. On 9 February, Lavrov had visited Khartoum and announced that Russia had finalized the terms for the Port Sudan facility's construction.[87] All that stood in its way was approval by a Sudanese civilian parliament, which was further delayed by the outbreak of war.

Despite the Kremlin's official neutrality, Prigozhin forged a clandestine military alliance with Hemedti. The US unsuccessfully tried to thwart this alliance from forming in early 2023 by encouraging Egypt's intelligence chief Abbas Kamel to pressure Burhan over Wagner using Sudanese territory to launch operations in CAR. While Wagner forces were not directly involved in frontline combat, as they were primarily stationed in Am Dafok near the Sudan-CAR border, they provided the RSF with valuable military supplies.

As the RSF prepared to strike SAF facilities, Russian Ilyushin Il-76 jets shuttled between the Haftar-controlled Khadim and Jufra air bases, and Russia's base in Latakia, Syria. These trips caused the Il-76 to airdrop surface-to-air missiles to RSF positions in northwestern Sudan on 16 April.[88] Prigozhin subsequently offered Hemedti surface-to-air missiles from Wagner's stockpiles in CAR. While it was initially unclear whether Hemedti accepted the offer, a Sudanese official confirmed that five RSF commanders travelled from Darfur's Songo mine to CAR in August 2023 to pay Prigozhin for these missiles. Prigozhin allegedly responded 'I need more gold' and vowed to help the RSF triumph.[89]

As evidence of their collaboration mounted, Prigozhin and Hemedti went to great lengths to obscure their alliance. On 20 April, the Wagner Group blasted media speculation about its pro-RSF

338

## EPILOGUE TO THE PAPERBACK EDITION

activities as 'provocative' and claimed that it had exited Sudan more than two years earlier. Prigozhin even offered to mediate in Sudan's intra-military conflict, as he had received an Order of the Republic of Sudan award in 2018 and Order of the Two Niles in 2020.[90] Building on Prigozhin's denials, Seregichev claimed that Ukrainian special forces are 'working' in Sudan under the flag of the Wagner Group to accuse Russia of destabilization.[91] Hemedti simultaneously declared that the RSF had suspended military training with Wagner. These cover-up efforts were unconvincing to Western audiences but allowed the Kremlin to distance itself from Prigozhin's policies.

Prigozhin's death has not disrupted the foundations of Russia's approach to Sudan. However, the Kremlin watched Ukraine's strengthening ties with Burhan with suspicion. On 23 September, Zelensky discussed Russia-funded illegal armed groups with Burhan at an impromptu meeting in Ireland's Shannon Airport.[92] This followed speculation about a possible Ukrainian drone attack on RSF facilities near Omdurman.[93] At least eight of the drone strikes were carried out by UAVs used by the Ukrainian military and Ukrainian-language text was observed on the drone controller. The drone attacks swooped down on their intended target, which aligns much more closely with Ukrainian military tactics than Sudanese ones. While this attack was an isolated incident, US officials believe that it could serve as a pretext for the expansion of Russian military assistance to the RSF.[94]

### Russia's Strengthening Partnership with Mali

As the Wagner Group's military intervention in Mali approached its eighteen-month anniversary, it was undeniably a mission in crisis. From late 2022 to August 2023, Islamic State in the Greater Sahara (ISGS) has more than doubled its territorial control, and the militant jihadist JNIM (Jama'at Nasr al-Islam wal Muslimin, Support Group for Islam and Muslims) has positioned itself as the sole bulwark against its further expansion. A December 2022 West Point Combating Terrorism Center report partially attributes these failures to Ukraine War-induced military resupply difficulties.[95] Although AFRICOM has not noticed force drawdowns from Mali to Ukraine, Wagner PMCs suffered from a loss of Russian logistical support.

339

As the Battle of Bakhmut intensified, war materiel shipments were confined to guns, ammunition and rations.

These equipment shortages limited Wagner's ability to combat ISGS. In June 2022, a legion of pro-junta Tuareg forces, which included a commander donning Russian military fatigues, tried to evict ISGS from Ménaka. Wagner provided no aerial support for these forces, which were lured by ISGS into a trap 40 km away from the town. This aligned with a broader trend, as Wagner only engaged once with ISGS in Ansongo in September 2022. This mission failed and according to ISGS, fifteen Wagner PMCs perished. Wagner desperately tried to conceal these failures with propaganda. The Wagner-aligned Reverse Side of the Medal Telegram channel boasted that ISGS dropped their ammunition and fled when Wagner PMCs arrived 'somewhere nearby' in January 2023.[96]

Despite Wagner's woeful counterterrorism record, it prolifically targeted Malian civilians. The US Department of State estimates that civilian deaths in Mali have increased by 278% since Wagner's arrival.[97] While UN experts have not verified this figure, they have pointed to alleged Wagner war crimes in Mali. A January 2023 UN Working Group on mercenary use linked Wagner to atrocities in Mali and accused it, along with the Malian Armed Forces, of targeting the Fulani. While the ICC's track record of trying individuals instead of mercenary organizations likely leaves Wagner immune from prosecution, it dealt a reputational blow to its mission in Mali.[98] The Wagner Group's alleged atrocities have also aided terrorist recruitment campaigns. As early as August 2021, the ethnic Tuareg JNIM leader Iyad Ag Ghali listed Russia as an enemy, and by late 2022, JNIM was stepping up recruitment in markets and mosques.[99]

Despite Wagner's inefficacy as a counterterrorism force and disregard for civilian lives, Russia's partnership with Mali's junta remains unshakeably strong. On 6 February, Lavrov arrived in Bamako for a two-day trip aimed at strengthening Russia-Mali defence cooperation. During his visit, Lavrov expanded Malian officer training in Russian universities and increased the number of state-funded civilian higher education spots for Malians from thirty-five to 290.[100] The Malian junta responded by aggressively defending its partnership with Wagner and disputing accusations of war crimes.

340

## EPILOGUE TO THE PAPERBACK EDITION

Prime Minister Choguel Kokalla Maïga even called himself a 'Malian Muscovite' due to his past Russian-language training.[101]

Russia returned the favour by expanding its economic, diplomatic and military support for Mali's junta. From June to July 2023, Russia supplied Mali with 50,000 tons of wheat at a heavily discounted price of $220/ton.[102] Goïta's eighty-person delegation at the St Petersburg Summit focused on sanctions-proof economic cooperation. On 31 August, Russia vetoed a joint France-UAE proposal to extend UN sanctions on Mali for an additional year.[103] This unilateral veto was unsurprising, as Russia's conditions for a one-year extension revolved around the end of the independent UN monitoring team. Vasily Nebenzia justified this decision by declaring that sanctions should not be used as a tool of 'foreign influence' in Mali, and implicitly criticized their inefficacy in facilitating a peace agreement.

Prigozhin's mutiny initially sparked concerns in Mali about a disruption to Wagner military activities. Malian political analyst Bassirou Doumbia argued that Wagner's conflict with the Kremlin would cause Mali to 'suffer consequences on the security front'.[104] These fears were amplified by the concurrent withdrawal of MINUSMA from Mali. MAXAR satellite imagery swiftly raised concerns about a Wagner drawdown. The construction of an expanded storage area in Wagner's Malian base, which began in March 2023, continued after the mutiny, and paved the way for the arrival of additional Russian military equipment.[105] Russian and Malian forces swiftly replaced their MINUSMA counterparts and by mid-October, they had established a beachhead in the rural north-eastern town of Tessalit.[106]

Since Prigozhin's death, the efficacy of Wagner's military operations in Mali has arguably improved. On 14 November, the Wagner flag was planted over Kidal, a strategic town that had been controlled by Tuareg Coordination of Azawad Movements (CMA) rebels since 2013.[107] This military success generated swift economic rewards. Goïta implemented legislation in August 2023 that would increase the scope of nationalized gold mines. Russia was the primary beneficiary, as it struck a four-year MOU with Mali to create a new gold refinery. This refinery, if constructed, would produce 200 tons

# RUSSIA IN AFRICA

of gold per year, and would increase Wagner's revenues from its current $10.8 million per month payments.[108]

## Russia's Ambiguous Security Alliance with Burkina Faso

At the December 2022 US-Africa Summit in Washington, DC, Ghana's President Nana Akufo-Addo made a bombshell allegation about the Burkina Faso junta's relationship with Russia. Akufo-Addo claimed that Wagner entered Burkina Faso and received Yimiougo mine access as payment.[109] Burkina Faso reacted furiously to Akufo-Addo's assertions and summoned Ghana's envoy. Doubts were swiftly raised about Ghana's claims and Russia's expert community was unconvinced by Wagner's ability to enter Burkina Faso. Vasily Filippov, an expert at Moscow's Institute of African Studies, argued he would not be surprised by Wagner's arrival, but noted that Wagner's commitments in Ukraine could impede its entry into Burkina Faso.[110] A December 2022 IMEMO RAN report cited Traoré's uncertain hold on power as a reason why Wagner might not enter Burkina Faso, as Damiba and Campaore loyalists were still active.[111]

These calculations prevented Wagner from entering Burkina Faso, even after France officially ended its military operations in the country on 20 February. Nevertheless, the Russia-Burkina Faso partnership continued to strengthen. On 5 May, Traoré described Russia as a 'strategic ally' and declared, 'I am satisfied with the cooperation with Russia. It's frank.'[112] Traoré also asserted that Russia had provided large quantities of weapons to Burkina Faso. Yevkurov discussed training programs for Burkinabe officers during his September 2023 visit to Ouagadougou, and Burkina Faso joined Mali in striking a cooperation agreement with Rosatom a month later. Traoré sees the Rosatom deal as crucial for his development goals, which have a 95% electricity access target in urban areas and 50% access target in rural areas by 2030, and in making Burkina Faso a regional energy export hub.[113]

Despite this cooperation, Burkina Faso's junta chafed at the notion that it is a client state of Russia. At the St Petersburg Summit, Traoré accused African countries of 'beggary' and claimed that Burkina Faso would engage with Russia and the US in a similar fashion.[114]

342

EPILOGUE TO THE PAPERBACK EDITION

Traoré also expressed optimism that Burkina Faso would become agriculturally self-sufficient, even as he thanked Russia for its free grain initiative. A tall order given the steady stream of terrorist attacks and Burkina Faso's diminishing economic ties with the West.

## Niger's Military Dictatorship: Russia's Next Frontier?

As African leaders gathered in St Petersburg, Nigerien General Abdourahamane Tchiani staged a bloodless coup against President Bazoum. After two days of uncertainty, the Tchiani-led National Council for the Safeguard of the Homeland (CNSP) military junta consolidated power in Niger. While the US and EU condemned Tchiani's power grab, Russia struck a different tune. Lavrov released an ambiguous statement calling for a restoration of 'constitutional order' in Niger, while Maria Zakharova, spokesperson for Russia's Ministry of Foreign Affairs, insisted on Bazoum's immediate release.[115] Russian ultranationalists celebrated the coup. Dugin declared, 'Niger is Ours! The last puppet of France-Afrique is overthrown during the Russia-Africa Forum. Niger to Nigeriens!'[116]

Prigozhin was an especially brazen cheerleader of Tchiani's coup. In an explosive 28 July Telegram audio message, Prigozhin accused Western colonizers of filling African countries with 'terrorists and various bandit formations' and claimed that 1,000 Wagner Group PMCs would be sufficient to restore order.[117] On 5 August, Prigozhin elaborated on these allegations by claiming that France sold Nigerien uranium for $218 on the market and handed Niger $11 back.[118] Russian commentators enthusiastically backed these contentions and predicted the Wagner Group's imminent entry into Niger. Sergey Savchuk praised Niger's decision to stop selling gold and uranium to France by claiming, 'Paris is sucking all the juice out of Niger, giving in return shredded paper to fill its meager budget.'[119]

At first, Western officials took Russia's statements of intent in Niger at face value. Rumours swirled that Modi had made a formal request for Wagner assistance during his trip to Mali.[120] Zelensky advisor Mykhailo Podolyak accused Russia of instigating the Niger coup, as it seeks to promote instability across the globe and wishes to create a diversion from the Ukraine War.[121] These allegations were implausible. Tchiani had loyally backed Bazoum's pro-French

343

## RUSSIA IN AFRICA

agenda and helped thwart a coup attempt against him in March 2021. Tchiani's turn against Bazoum was triggered by fears of his demotion and concerns within Bazoum's inner circle about his loyalty to ex-President Mahamadou Issoufou. With these factors in mind, the US dismissed allegations that Russia masterminded Tchiani's coup but warned that Wagner could 'take advantage' of instability in Niger.[122]

As the dust settled on Tchiani's coup, it became apparent that Russia was not serious about military intervention in Niger. The Wagner Group's capacity to enter Niger was hamstrung by a virtually non-existent bilateral partnership, historical mistrusts and lack of a credible financing source. Russia did not have an embassy in Niamey, as its diplomatic relations with Niger were handled by the Russian Embassy in Mali. Russia's most significant arms deal with Niger in recent times was marred by a corruption scandal. Nigerien arms dealer Aboubacar Hima facilitated the purchase of two Mi-17Sh military transport and assault helicopters from Rosoboronexport for $54.8 million in 2016. This was an overpayment of $19.7 million. When Nigerien auditors probed the transaction, Rosoboronexport refused to cooperate and insisted the arms deal records were 'confidential'.[123] HSE academic Andrey Maslov argued that Russia had never tried to compete with China and France for Niger's uranium reserves and would not wish to 'destabilize its fragile uranium market'.[124]

While Russia decided not to deploy Wagner to Niger, it vigorously rallied its regional partners against ECOWAS's regime change ambitions and stepped up its anti-Western information warfare. The Russian Foreign Ministry backed ECOWAS's mediation efforts but warned that using military force would lead to a 'protracted confrontation' in Niger and destabilize the Sahara-Sahel region.[125] While Putin's 15 August and 10 September phone calls with Goïta made headlines, Russia also leveraged Algeria's opposition to an ECOWAS intervention. Russia exploited the coup-induced freezing of construction on the Trans-Sahara pipeline, which crossed the Algeria-Niger border. Shoigu's post-coup meeting with Algeria's People's Army Chief of Staff Saïd Chengriha raised eyebrows, ˒ even though RIA Novosti denied that it was linked to the Niger

344

## EPILOGUE TO THE PAPERBACK EDITION

developments.[126] General Sergei Surovikin's 15 September trip to Algiers, which followed his release from detention for his alleged role in the Wagner mutiny, fuelled speculation that a Russia-Algeria bloc was forming in the Sahel.

Russia's disinformation efforts intensified after Bazoum's April 2022 approval of additional European force deployments to Niger. The M62 movement, which was formed in August 2022, was Russia's primary disinformation surrogate against French influence in Niger. Seydou Abdoulaye, a M62 coordinator, organized rallies in Niamey with the slogans 'Barkhane Out!', 'Down with France' and 'Long Live Putin and Russia'.[127] M62's actions were part of a broader Russian disinformation campaign, which glorified Wagner's intervention in Mali and spread incendiary fabricated imagery. During Bazoum's February 2023 meeting with Macron in Paris, Russian-linked Tik Tok and Facebook accounts shared videos of the March 2021 coup attempt as new footage and fake images of a French attack on a Nigerien military convoy.[128] These efforts proved effective. An August 2023 Premise Data poll showed that over 60% of Nigeriens saw Russia as their most reliable partner and half of supporters of foreign intervention in Niger wanted Russia to lead it.[129]

In spite of the efficacy of Russian disinformation, Wagner's deployment did not transpire. ECOWAS's decision not to intervene in Niger played a part. In Moscow, it is widely believed that the US and Niger's junta struck a deal to prevent Tchiani from accepting Wagner PMCs.[130] This agreement ensured the US' junta preserved its military bases and 1,000-troop force contingent in Niger, which would allow it to monitor the activities of Mali and Burkina Faso's juntas.[131] In exchange, the US talked ECOWAS out of a costly intervention, which would have risked a regional war and humanitarian crisis.[132] This deal started to unravel in March 2024. Pressure from Washington over Niger's strengthening ties with Russia caused the junta to call for the expulsion of US forces. The US has resisted pressure to withdraw. Nevertheless, the 12 April arrival of 100 Russian instructors for air defence training in Niger underscores Tchiani's desire to strengthen ties with Moscow.

## RUSSIA IN AFRICA

*Russia's Endurance as a Virtual Great Power in Africa*

While 2023 was arguably the most dramatic year in Russia-Africa relations in the post-Cold War period, it ended largely as it began. Russia remains a virtual great power with outsized ambitions and limited material capabilities. The St Petersburg Summit featured flashy MOUs, such as the tripling of Ethiopia's state-funded places in Russian university and a common declaration on information security with African countries. But these MOUs paper over the two largest cracks in Russia's Africa strategy. These are its trade volumes and foreign investment levels in Africa, which stubbornly hang around $400 million. Commercial deals, such as Zimbabwe's May 2023 purchase of eighteen helicopters at inflated prices, are often more effective in providing regime security for dictators than at counterterrorism. Russia sells win-win partnerships in Africa, but the wins for Africans seem less convincing than those for the Kremlin.

Despite these shortcomings, Putin's commitment to Primakov's foreign policy playbook and tenacious desire to recreate the illusion of Soviet-era superpower status in Africa endures. The Ukraine War's continuation is a double-edged sword. War materiel demands constrain Russia's ability to extend its security presence to theatres in Africa, but sanctions require it to rely more heavily on minerals from fragile states. Russia frames itself as an opponent of neo-imperialism, while pursuing the largest colonial war of the twenty-first century on European soil. It remains to be seen whether those contradictions relegate Russia to a spoiler role in Africa or prove surmountable through Russia's cynical synthesis of frenetic disinformation and artful diplomacy.

## NOTES

### INTRODUCTION

1. Paul Stronski, 'Late to the Party: Russia's Return to Africa', Carnegie Endowment for International Peace, 16 October 2019, https://carnegieendowment.org/2019/10/16/late-to-party-russia-s-return-to-africa-pub-80056

2. Kimberly Marten, 'Russia's Back in Africa: Is the Cold War Returning?', *The Washington Quarterly*, Volume 42, Issue 4, 2019, pp. 155–70.

3. Anne Clunan, 'The Social Construction of Russia's Resurgence: Aspirations, Identity and Security Interests', 2009.

4. Joseph Siegle, 'Russia's Asymmetric Strategy for Expanding Influence in Africa', LSE, 17 September 2021, https://blogs.lse.ac.uk/africaatlse/2021/09/17/russia-asymmetric-strategy-expanding-influence-in-africa-security-moscow/

5. 'Gems, Warlords and Mercenaries: Russia's Playbook in Central African Republic', *New York Times*, 30 September 2019, https://www.nytimes.com/2019/09/30/world/russia-diamonds-africa-prigozhin.html

6. Jamie Dettmer, 'Guns, Mercenaries and Minerals', Voice of America, 21 October 2019, https://www.voanews.com/a/europe_guns-mercenaries-minerals-russia-embraces-africa/6177907.html

7. The concept of multipolarity has Soviet-era antecedents and numerous associated terminologies, such as polycentric world order. In the contemporary Russian context, it refers to Moscow's resistance to US unilateralism and hegemony. It also depicts a world order where decisions are made by a great power consensus and where non-Western powers, such as Russia, India and China, have a seat at the table. To understand multipolarity from the vantage point of Russian policymakers, Fyodor Lukyanov, 'Russian Dilemmas in a Multipolar World', *Journal of International Affairs*, Volume 63, Number 2, Rethinking Russia (Spring/Summer 2010), pp. 19–32 and

347

# NOTES

pp. [7–10]

Andrei Kortunov, 'Between Polycentrism and Bipolarity', *Russia in Global Affairs*, Number 1, 2019, January/March are helpful articles to reference.

8. Status is a concept in international relations, which refers to the hierarchy of states within the international system and their pursuit of external recognition. This book presents a broad-brush definition of status, which includes Russia's quest for recognition by the US, Europe and China as a great power, and domestic perceptions of Russia's place in the world. Key dimensions of Russia's status-seeking behaviour include its consolidation of a sphere of influence in the post-Soviet space, efforts to challenge the Western-led international legal order and pursuit of great power ambitions in the Global South. T.V. Paul, Deborah Welch-Larson and William Wohlforth, *Status in World Politics*, Cambridge: Cambridge University Press, 2014 is an excellent primer on status as an international relations concept. Anne Clunan, *The Social Construction of Russia's Resurgence*, Baltimore: Johns Hopkins University Press, 2009 highlights the domestic forces that drive Russia's pursuit of great power status and the impact of status recognition by the West on Russian foreign policy.

9. Apollon Davidson, *Russia and Africa*, Moscow: Nauka Publishing House, 1966, p. 159

10. Elena Studneva, 'Vizit tsesarevicha Nikolaya Romanova v Yegipet glazami sovremennikov' (Tsar Nicholas II's Visit to Egypt Through the Eyes of his Contemporaries), *International Affairs*, 4 April 2017, https://interaffairs.ru/news/show/17252; Paul De Quenoy, 'The Russian Empire and Egypt, 1900–1915: A Case for Public Diplomacy', *Journal of World History*, 2008, pp. 213–22 presents a thorough examination of the relationship between Egypt and Tsarist Russia.

11. Kurt Campbell, *The Heritage of Russian Involvement in South Africa: The Anglo-Boer War in Kurt Campbell, Soviet Policy Towards South Africa*, London: Palgrave Macmillan, 1986, pp. 8–22.

12. Paul de Quenoy, 'Tidings from a Faraway East: The Russian Empire and Morocco', *International History Review*, 2011, pp. 185–203.

13. Getachew Metaferia, *Ethiopia and the United States: History, Diplomacy and Analysis*, Algora Publishing, p. 12.

14. Rashed Chowdhury, 'Russian Medical Diplomacy in Ethiopia, 1896–1913', Anna Winterbottom and Facil Tesfaye, *Histories of Medicine and Healing in the Indian Ocean World*, London: Palgrave Macmillan, 2016, pp. 115–45.

15. Interview with Ethiopian Analyst Zerihun Adebe, April 2021.

16. Apollon Davidson and Irina Filatova, *The Russians and the Anglo-Boer War*, Cape Town: Human and Rousseau Publishers, 1998.

17. Campbell, 1986.

18. R.W. Johnson, 'Rogue's Paradise', *London Review of Books*, Volume 20, Number 14, July 1998, https://www.lrb.co.uk/the-paper/v20/n14/r.w.-johnson/rogue-s-paradise

19. Campbell, 1986.

pp. [10–15]  NOTES

20. Davidson and Filatova, 1998.
21. 'Stalinskaya afrikanskaya igra' (Stalin's African Game), *Kommersant*, 3 October 2020, https://www.kommersant.ru/doc/4518596
22. John Barratt, 'The Soviet Union and Southern Africa', South Africa Institute of International Affairs, May 1981, p. 3, https://media.africaportal. org/documents/SAIIA_THE_SOVIET_UNION_AND_SOUTHERN_ AFRICA.pdf
23. Elizabeth Schmidt, *Foreign Intervention in Africa: From the Cold War to the War on Terror*, Cambridge: Cambridge University Press, p. 25. Robert Legvold, *Soviet Policy in West Africa*, Cambridge: Harvard University Press, 1970 provides more details on the Soviet Union-Ghana partnership.
24. Gu Guan-Fu, 'Soviet Aid to the Third World: An Analysis of its Strategy', *Soviet Studies*, Volume 35, Number 1, 1985, pp. 71–72.
25. Julius Nyerere, *Ujamaa: Essays on Socialism*, Dar-es-Salam: 1968, pp. 12–17.
26. Ebere Nwaubani, *The United States and the Decolonization of West Africa: 1950– 60*, Rochester: University of Rochester Press, 2001, p. 126.
27. Yahia Zoubir, 'The United States, the Soviet Union, and Decolonization of the Maghreb, 1945–62', *Middle Eastern Studies*, Volume 31, Issue 1, 1995, pp. 58–59.
28. E.D. Modrzhinskaia, *Ideologia Sovremennogo Kolonializma*, Moscow: 196.
29. Speech by Mr Khrushchev, Chairman of the Council of Ministers of the Union of Soviet Socialist Republics, at the 869th Plenary Meeting of the 15th Session of the United Nations General Assembly, Wilson Center, 23 September 1960.
30. Alessadnro Iandolo, 'Imbalance of Power: The Soviet Union and the Congo Crisis, 1960–61', *Journal of Cold War Studies*, Volume 16, Number 2, Spring 2014, p. 33.
31. Ibid.
32. Sergey Mazov, 'SSSR I Kongolezskiy Krizis, 1960–63' (USSR and the Congolezian Crisis, 1960–63), *Asia and Africa Today*, Issue 4, pp. 53–59.
33. Nikolai Federenko, 'The Soviet Union and African Countries', *Africa in Motion*, July 1964, pp. 1–8.
34. Schmidt, p. 26.
35. Colin Lawson, 'Soviet Economic Aid in Africa', *African Affairs*, Volume 87, Number 349, 1988, pp. 501–02.
36. Angela Stent, 'The Soviet Union and the Nigerian Civil War: A Triumph of Realism', *Issue: A Journal of Opinion*, Volume 3, Issue 2, Summer 1973, p. 44.
37. Isabel Ginor and Gideon Remez, *The Soviet-Israeli War 1967–73: The USSR's Military Intervention in the Egyptian-Israeli Conflict*, New York: Oxford University Press, 2017.
38. Lorenz Luthi, *The Sino-Soviet Split: Cold War in the Communist World*, Princeton: Princeton University Press, 2008, p. 221.
39. Robert Scalapino, *On the Trail of Chou en-Lai*, RAND Corporation, April 1964.

## NOTES

40. Robert Scalapino, 'Sino-Soviet Competition in Africa', *Foreign Affairs*, Volume 42, Number 4, July 1964, p. 640.
41. Ibid.
42. Seweryn Bialer, *The Soviet Paradox: External Expansion, Internal Decline*, Knopf, 1986.
43. Robbin Laird, 'Soviet Arms Trade with the Noncommunist Third World', *Proceedings from the Academy of Political Science*, 1984, p. 197.
44. Lawson, 1988.
45. George Glass, 'East Germany in Black Africa: A New Special Role', *The World Today*, Volume 36, Number 8, August 1980, pp. 305–12.
46. Radoslav Yordanov, *The Soviet Union and the Horn of Africa During the Cold War: Between Ideology and Pragmatism*, Lanham: Lexington Books, 2016.
47. Ibid.
48. Robert Patman, *Soviet-Ethiopian Relations: The Horn of Dilemma in Margot Light, Troubled Friendships: Moscow's Third World Ventures*, London: British Academic Press.
49. Interview with author, March 2021.
50. Federica Saini Fasanotti, 'Russia and Libya: A Brief History of an On-Again Off-Again Friendship', Brookings Institution, 1 September 2016, https://www.brookings.edu/blog/order-from-chaos/2016/09/01/russia-and-libya-a-brief-history-of-an-on-again-off-again-friendship/
51. Hella Pick, from the Archive, 8 September 1973: 'Gaddafi and Castro clash over Soviet Union', *The Guardian*, 8 September 2015, https://www.theguardian.com/world/2015/sep/08/gaddafi-castro-soviet-union-communism-1973
52. Robert Grey, 'The Soviet Presence in Africa: An Analysis of Goals', *The Journal of Modern African Studies*, Volume 22, Number 3, September 1984, pp. 511–27.
53. Neil MacFarlane, 'Soviet-Angolan Relations, 1975–90', National Council for Soviet and East European Research Occasional Paper, 15 March 1992.
54. Interview with author, April 2021.
55. Peter Shearman, 'Gorbachev and the Third World: An Era of Reform?', *Third World Quarterly*, October 1987, Volume 9, Issue 4, pp. 1,083–87.
56. Michael Dobbs, 'Algerian to Seek Arms in Visit Here', *The Washington Post*, 14 April 1985, https://www.washingtonpost.com/archive/politics/1985/04/14/algerian-to-seek-arms-in-visit-here/a3dd1e38-69ba-455e-8231-ebcad40b0fde/
57. 'Kto yest kto Sivar ad-Dakhab' (Who's Who: Siwar al-Dahab), *Izvestiya*, 5 May 1985.
58. Diana Ohlbaum, 'Ethiopia and the Construction of Soviet Identity: 1974–91', *Northeast African Studies*, Volume 1, Number 1, 1994, p. 68.
59. Galina Krylova, 'Otkryte Voprosy Revoliutsii' (Open the Question of Revolution), *Asia and Africa Today*, Issue 11, November 1988.
60. 'Soviet Policy Towards Individual States', *The Adelphi Papers*, Volume 28, Issue 227: Southern Africa in Soviet Foreign Policy, 1987.

## pp. [21–29]     NOTES

61. Michael McFaul, 'Soviet-Angolan Relations under Gorbachev', *Journal of Southern African Studies*, Volume 16, Number 1, March 1990, pp. 165–89.
62. W. Raymond Duncan, *Moscow and the Third World under Gorbachev*, Abingdon: Routledge, 2019.
63. Wayne Limberg in Mark Katz, *The USSR and Marxist Revolutions in the Third World*, Cambridge: Cambridge University Press, 1990, p. 84.
64. 'Dobrykh Serdets Sovetskiye Vrachi Prikhodyat na Pomoshch Zhertvam Zasukhi Efiopii' (Kind Hearts: Soviet Doctors Come to the Rescue of Drought Victims in Ethiopia), *Pravda*, 21 January 1985.
65. 'Soviet Relations with African Countries Examined', Moscow, 15 March 1985 (FBIS-SOV-85-053).

## 1.   THE TUMULTUOUS 1990s

1. 'As Soviet Debt Grows, So Do Western Worries', *New York Times*, 12 July 1991, https://www.nytimes.com/1991/07/12/world/as-soviet-debt-grows-so-do-western-worries.html
2. 'Dumaya o svoikh interesakh. Obozrevatel' "Izvestiy" A. Bovin beseduyet s glavoy MID RSFSR A.V. Kozyrev' (Thinking About Our Own Interests. Izvestiya Political Observer A. Bovin Converses with RSFSR Foreign Minister A.V. Kozyrev), *Izvestiya*, 7 October 1991.
3. 'Program Reviews International Role, Events, 3 November 1991', Daily Report, Soviet Union (FBIS-SOV-91-213).
4. Alexander Golts, 'Mir Segodnya Problemy i Vzglyady' (World Today: Problems and Views), *Krasnaya Zvesda*, 13 September 1991.
5. 'Al-Qadhafi Lauds Yanayev's "Brave" Action, Tripoli Great Jamahiriyah Radio Network', Daily Report, Near East and South Asia (FBIS-NES-91-161).
6. 'Bush's "Blatant Interference" in USSR Assailed, Tripoli Libyan Television Network', Daily Report Near East and South Asia, 21 August 1991 (FBIS-NES-91-162).
7. 'USSR Official Praises Libya, Departs, Tripoli', JANA, Daily Report-Near East and South Asia, 17 May 1991 (FBIS-NES-91-096).
8. Alexander Makhov, 'Interview with Andrey Kozyrev, Russian Soviet Federated Socialist Republic Foreign Minister', *The Moscow News*, 6 November 1990.
9. Tommie Cromwell Anderson-Jacquet, *Restructuring the Soviet-Ethiopian Relationship: A Case Study in Asymmetric Exchange*, London School of Economics and Political Science, May 2002, p. 90.
10. Viktor Zheltov and Maxim Zheltov, 'Alzhir: Reformy Kak Proyavleniye Arabskoy Vesny' (Algeria: Reforming as a Manifestation of the Arab Spring), *Bulletin of Kemerovo State University*, 2015.
11. Tomas Kolesnichenko, 'Posmotrite Na Sebya' (Look at Yourself), *Pravda*, 15 February 1992.
12. Igor Tarutin, 'Vid iz Kharare: pochemu Flagshtok bez flaga' (View from Harare: Why is the Flagstaff without the Flag), *Pravda*, 18 January 1992.

## NOTES

13. 'Committees Reviewing Foreign Policy Priorities', Interfax, 21 February 1992.
14. 'Kozyrev Plans to Preserve "Positive" Diplomacy', Interfax, 25 February 1992.
15. 'Foreign Minister on Relations with Former USSR', Luanda Radio Nacional Network, 1 January 1992 (FBIS-AFR-92-001).
16. 'Angolan Visit Viewed', Moscow Radio Moscow, 29 February 1992 (FBIS-SOV-92-041).
17. Robert Patman in Peter Shearman, *Russian Foreign Policy Since 1990*, Abingdon: Routledge, 2018.
18. 'Russian Delegation on Possible Trade Expansion', *Johannesburg Business Day*, 14 February 1991 (FBIS-AFR-91-039).
19. 'Bez Posrednikov' (Without Middlemen), TASS, 23 July 1991.
20. Vladimir Mikhaylov, 'Dlya Rulofa Boty tozhe yest biznes v Moskve' (There is Business in Moscow for Roloef Botha Too), *Rabochaya Tribuna*, 9 November 1991.
21. Vladimir Shubin, 'The Soviet Union/Russian Federation's Relations with South Africa, with Special Reference to the Period Since 1980', *African Affairs*, Volume 95, Number 378, pp. 27–28.
22. Mikhail Bogdanov, 'Transformatsiya Otnosheniy Mezhdu Rossiyey I Yegiptom: 1991–2011' (Transformation of Relations Between Russia and Egypt: 1991–2011), Institute for African Studies, at the Russian Academy of Sciences, 2017, pp. 22–23.
23. A. Yegorin, 'Blizhniy Vostok v Tsentre Vnimaniya Madrida: Tuzy Yeshche Ne Razygrany' (Near East in the Focus of Madrid: The Aces Have Not Yet Been Played), *Pravda*, 14 November 1991, p. 5.
24. 'Holds Talks with Mubarak', Cairo MENA, 1 March 1992 (FBIS-NES-92-041).
25. 'Kozyrev Meets Libyan Official', Tripoli Voice of the Greater Arab Homeland, 1 March 1992 (FBIS-NES-92-041).
26. Robert Donaldson and Joseph Nogee, *Russian Foreign Policy: Changing Systems, Enduring Interests*, Abingdon: Routledge, 1998, p. 332.
27. 'B. Yeltsin Zakryl Desyat Posolstv' (B. Yeltsin Closes Ten Embassies), *Izvestiya*, 29 April 1992.
28. 'Prezident Rossii Pokoril Ameriku' (Russian President Conquered America), *Nezavisimaya Gazeta*, 18 June 1992.
29. 'Opening Speech Broadcast', Tripoli Libyan Television Network, 13 June 1992 (FBIS-NES-92-115).
30. 'US Funding ANC, "New World Order" Viewed', *Pretoria Patriot*, 10 April 1992 (FBIS-AFR-92-077).
31. 'Moscow to Reduce Diplomatic Personnel in Africa', Interfax, 16 November 1992.
32. 'Vy Ne Mozhete Voyti v Odnu i Tu Zhe Afriku Dvazhdy' (You Cannot Enter Africa the Same Way Twice), *Kommersant*, 23 October 2019, https://www.kommersant.ru/doc/4134125

pp. [35–38]                NOTES

33. Margarita Obraztsova, 'Sotrudnichestvo Rossii i YUAR: ot upushchennykh Vozmozhnostey k Potentsialu Rosta' (Russia-South Africa Cooperation: From Missed Opportunities to Growth Potential), *Asia and Africa Today*, Issue Number 4, pp. 64–69.

34. Richard Grimmett, 'Conventional Arms Transfers to the Third World: 1984–1991', Congressional Research Service, 20 July 1992.

35. Richard Grimmett, 'Conventional Arms Transfers to Developing Nations, 1988–1995', pp. 50–51.

36. Leonid Fituni, 'Russia's Arms Sales to Africa: Past, Present and Future', *CSIS Africa Notes*, Number 140, Summer 1992, p. 5.

37. The exact military debt figures to the Soviet Union in thousands of millions were Ethiopia (2,630), Algeria (2,477.5), Angola (2,100), Egypt (1,682) and Libya (1,598). Original Source: *The Moscow News*, No. 48, 1991.

38. Interfax, 16 November 1992.

39. Anthony Cordesman, *A Tragedy of Arms: Military and Security Developments in the Maghreb*, Westport: Praeger Publishers, 2002, p. 33.

40. Interview with Algerian Political Scientist Yahia Zoubir, 25 November 2020 (Skype).

41. Interview with Algerian Political Analyst Akram Kharief, 27 November 2020 (Telephone).

42. Tamsin Page, *Petulant and Contrary: Approaches by the Permanent Five Members of the UN Security Council to the Concept of Threat to Peace Under Article 39 of the UN Charter*, Leiden: Brill, 2019, pp. 128–29.

43. Alexey Vasiliev, *Russian Policy in the Middle East: From Messianism to Pragmatism*, Ithaca: Ithaca Press, 1993, p. 301.

44. Cordesman 2002, p. 33.

45. Ian Anthony, *Russia and the Arms Trade*, p. 84.

46. Interview with Veniamin Popov, 11 September 2017 (In-Person).

47. Interview with Alexey Podtserob, 26 November 2020 (Email).

48. 'Sanktsii Protiv Livii: Osoboye Mneniye Moskvy' (Sanctions Against Libya: Moscow's Dissenting Opinion), *Rossiyskaya Gazeta*, 3 November 1993.

49. 'Sovmestima li Poyezdka Ministra Davydova s Sanktsiyami Protiv Livii?' (Is Minister Davydov's Trip Compatible with Sanctions against Libya?), *Izvestiya*, 17 November 1993.

50. 'Perspektivy Torgovli s Yuzhnaya Afrika Otsenen' (Prospects for Trade with South Africa Assessed), *Kommersant*, 6 December 1993.

51. Brian Frederking, *Resolving Security Dilemmas: A Constructivist Explanation of the INF Treaty*, Abingdon: Routledge, 2007, p. 49.

52. Robert Patman, *Globalization and Conflict: National Security in a 'New' Strategic Era*, Abingdon: Routledge, 2006, pp. 12–13.

53. Alexei Bogaturov, 'Tri Pokoleniya Rossiyskoy Vneshney Politicheskoy Doktriny' (Three Generations of Russian Political Doctrines), *International Trends*, 2008, http://www.intertrends.ru/old/thirteen/005.htm

353

NOTES pp. [38–45]

54. Dina Malysheva, 'Konflikty v razvivayushchikhsya stranakh, Rossii i Sodruzhestve Nezavisimykh Gosudarstv' (Conflict in the Developing World, Russia and the Commonwealth of Independent States), Russian Academy of Sciences, 1997, p. 88.
55. *Kommersant*, 6 December 1993.
56. Interview with author, April 2021.
57. 'Kolokolov Sums up Results of South Africa Trip', TASS, 5 May 1993.
58. Irina Filotova, 'Rossiya i Yuzhnaya Afrika' Tri veka Otnosheniy' (Russia and South Africa: Three Centuries of Relations), Moscow: Higher School of Economics, 2012.
59. Interview with author, April 2021.
60. Bahaa Elkoussy, 'Russia, Egypt End Upbeat Nuclear Talks', UPI, 29 March 1995, https://www.upi.com/Archives/1995/03/29/Russia-Egypt-end-upbeat-nuclear-talks/9547796453200/
61. 'Rossiysko-yegipetskiye ekonomicheskiye otnosheniya. Dos'ye' (Russian-Egyptian Economic Relations: Dossier), TASS, 24 May 2015, https://tass.ru/info/1754021
62. 'Spokesman Karasin on Nigerian Transfer of Power', TASS, 10 October 1995.
63. 'Nigeria Receives Condemnation over Executions', TASS, 13 November 1995.
64. 'Russia Intensifies African Direction of its Foreign Policy', TASS, 9 April 1998.
65. Andranik Migranyan, 'Konets Rossii?' (End of Russia), *Free Thought*, 2002, Issue 7, p. 156.
66. Sergei Karaganov, 'Oslableniye Zapada udarit po Rossii' (Weakening of the West will Hit Russia), *Vedomosti*, 15 January 2013.
67. Vladimir Lopatov, 'Rossiya i Afrika: ploshchadki dlya sotrudnichestva' (Russia and Africa: Venues for Cooperation), *International Affairs*, Volume 42, Number 5, 1996, pp. 80–86.
68. Boris Bruk, 'Russia's Murky Angola Debt Deal', Institute of Modern Russia, 20 August 2013, https://imrussia.org/en/economy/535-angolagate-and-the-russian-debt-deal
69. Peter Orekhin, 'Tochka Proshcheniya' (Point Forgiveness), *Nezavisimaya Gazeta*, 14 January 2004, https://www.ng.ru/economics/2004-01-14/1_dolg.html
70. 'Mozambique Foreign Policy and Government Guide Volume 1', International Business Association, October 1999, p. 161.
71. 'Kak Rossiya spisyvala dolgi afrikanskim stranam' (How Russia Wrote off Debts to African Countries), TASS, 23 October 2019, https://tass.ru/info/7037257
72. Igor Shchogolev, 'Russia wants to Promote Trade with Egypt, Nemtsov says', TASS, 23 September 1997.
73. 'Nigeria: Yeltsin Reportedly Expresses Support for Civil Rule Program', Lagos NTA Television Network, 23 February 1996 (FBIS-AFR-96-038).

## NOTES

74. Paul Lewis, 'US Seeking Tougher Sanctions to Press Nigeria for Democracy', *New York Times*, 12 March 1996, https://www.nytimes.com/1996/03/12/world/us-seeking-tougher-sanctions-to-press-nigeria-for-democracy.html
75. Russia, 'Nigeria to Pool Oil and Gas Interests', Interfax, 4 December 1998.
76. Richard F. Grimmett, 'Conventional Arms Transfers to Developing Nations', Congressional Research Service 1998–2005.
77. 'Voyenno-tekhnicheskoye sotrudnichestvo Rossii i Yegipta' (Military-Technical Cooperation Between Russia and Egypt), *Kommersant*, 29 May 2017, https://www.kommersant.ru/doc/3311195
78. 'Rossiysko-angolskiye otnosheniya. Kak mozhno koroche' (Russian-Angolan Relations: As Short as Possible), TASS, 4 April 2019, https://tass.ru/mezhdunarodnaya-panorama/6291849
79. 'Arms Trade and Embargo Violations', Human Rights Watch, 1999, https://www.hrw.org/reports/1999/angola/Angl998-09.htm
80. Igor Tarutin, 'UNITA snova govorit o mire' (UNITA Talks About Peace Again), *Nezavisimaya Gazeta*, 30 October 1999, https://www.ng.ru/world/1999-10-30/6_unita.html
81. Human Rights Watch, 1999.
82. 'Vsem sestram na stvolakh Rossiya uvazhayet: Eritreyu ne menshe Efiopii' (To all Sisters on the Trunks: Russia Respects Eritrea no Less than Ethiopia), *Kommersant*, 15 April 2005, https://www.kommersant.ru/doc/570344
83. Bayo Lamin, 'Grazhdanskaya voyna v Respublike Syerra-Leone i Rol Mezhdunarodnogo Soobshchestva v Uregulirovanii Vooruzhennogo Konflikta' (Civil War in the Republic of Sierra Leone and the Role of the International Communtiy in the Settlement of Armed Conflict), 2001.
84. Interview with Charles Ray, 17 March 2021 (Email).
85. 'Minister Denies Airlifting Arms to Rwandans', Accra Ghana Broadcasting Network, 15 June 1995 (FBIS-AFR-95-116).
86. Interview with senior US official, March 2021.
87. 'Zimbabwe Government Orders Military Hardware', *Zimbabwe Independent*, 18 December 1998.
88. 'Security Council Demands Sudan Act to Extradite Suspects in Assassination Attempt of Egyptian President by 10 May, or Face Limited Sanctions', Press Release SC/6214, 26 April 1996, https://www.un.org/press/en/1996/19960426.sc6214.html
89. 'Security Council Discusses Sanctions Imposed on Libya Following Bombing of Pan Am Flight 103, UTA Flight 722', United Nations, 20 March 1998, https://www.un.org/press/en/1998/19980320.SC6490.html
90. V.P. Yurchenko, 'O snyatii mezhdunarodnykh sanktsiy s Livii' (On Lifting International Sanctions on Libya), Institute of the Near East, 29 September 2003, http://www.iimes.ru/?p=3011
91. 'Zyuganov provel peregovory v Tunise, 13 dekabrya vyletayet v Liviyu' (Zyuganov Holds Talks in Tunis, Departs for Libya on December 13), *TASS*, 11 December 1998

# NOTES

92. 'Russian Foreign Ministry Statement Says US Air Strikes Set "Dangerous Precedent"', Interfax, 21 August 1998.
93. 'Russian Communist Leader Likens US Air Strikes to "State Terrorism"', Interfax, 21 August 1998
94. 'Ultranationalist Leader Zhirinovsky Addresses Duma Session, Rossiya 1', 21 August 1998 BBC Monitoring Report.
95. 'Russia's Union of Muslims Denounce US Airstrikes in Afghanistan and Sudan', TASS, 21 August 1998.
96. 'US Attacks are "Dangerous Precedent" – Chechen Minister', Interfax, 21 August 1998.
97. 'Russia, Egypt Oppose Use of Force Against Iraq', TASS, 18 December 1998.
98. 'Russia Backs Egypt's Initiatives, Seleznyov Says', TASS, 14 September 1997.
99. Thomas Ambrosio, *Challenging America's Global Pre-Eminence: Russia's Quest for Multipolarity*, Abingdon: Routledge, 2017, p.116.
100. 'Russian MPs, Sudanese Leaders Condemn NATO Airstrikes Against Yugoslavia', TASS, 5 April 1999.
101. 'Yeltsin prinyal Mandelu i Annana i pogovoril s nimi o Yugoslavii' (Yeltsin Received Mandela and Annan and Talked to Them About Yugoslavia), *Kommersant*, 30 April 1999, https://www.kommersant.ru/doc/217827
102. John Stremlau, 'The 1999 Kosovo War Through a South African Lens', *South African Journal of International Affairs*, Volume 7, Issue 1, 2000, pp. 131–32.
103. 'People Begin to See Dangers of the Unipolar World, says Russian Foreign Minister', TASS, 3 September 1999.


## 2. THE DAWN OF RUSSIA'S RESURGENCE IN AFRICA

1. 'The Foreign Policy Concept of the Russian Federation', 28 June 2000, https://fas.org/nuke/guide/russia/doctrine/econcept.htm
2. Interview with author, 26 April 2021.
3. T.L. Deich and D.V. Polikanov, 'Rossiya i Afrika politicheskiye otnosheniya sovremennoye sostoyaniye i perspektivy' (Russia-African Political Relations: Contemporary State and Prospects), Moscow: Institute of African Studies, 2003.
4. Vasilii Sredin, 'Rossiya i Afrika' (Russia in Africa), *International Affairs*, Volume 47, Number 5, 2001, pp. 23–29.
5. Alexander Saltanov, 'Mai v afrike' (May in Africa), *International Affairs*, Volume 50, Number 3, 2004, pp. 15–21.
6. 'Russia Vows to Forgive Ethiopia's Debts Amid Growing Push for Influence in Africa', *The Moscow Times*, 22 October 2019, https://www.themoscowtimes.com/2019/10/22/russia-vows-to-forgive-ethiopias-debts-amid-growing-push-for-influence-in-africa-a67851
7. Alexandra Archangelskaya and Vladimir Shubin, 'Russia's Africa Policy', South African Institute of International Affairs, Occasional Paper Number 157, p. 20.

pp. [57–61]                     NOTES

8. Stronski, 2019.
9. Hakan Fidan and Bulent Aras, 'The Return of Russia-Africa Relations', 2010.
10. 'Josselin to Attend Igad Meet on Somalia, Sudan in Rome', Relief Web International, 19 March 2001, https://reliefweb.int/report/eritrea/josselin-attend-igad-meet-somalia-sudan-rome
11. Interview with IGAD official, July 2021.
12. Téte António, 'Angola i Rossiya: 45 let druzhby i sotrudnichestva' (Angola and Russia: 45 Years of Friendship and Cooperation), International Affairs, 23 November 2020, https://interaffairs.ru/news/show/28195
13. Vladimir Lopatov, 'Rossiya I Afrika: Kto Nuzhen Kto Bolshe' (Russia and Africa: Who Needs Who More?), Asia and Africa Today, pp. 45–58.
14. Vladimir Lopatov, 'Obraz Rossii v Afrike: Economicheskiye Aspekty' (Image of Russia in Africa: Economic Aspects), Asia and Africa Today, 2007, pp. 34–40.
15. Fidan and Aras, 2010.
16. Edgar Agubamah, 'Nigeria-Russia Relations: After and Now', European Scientific Journal, 2014, p. 195.
17. 'Po slovam prezidenta Obasandzho, Rossiya i Nigeriya ochen' pokhozhi' (According to President Obasanjo, Russia and Nigeria are very Similar), Lenta.ru, 7 March 2001, https://lenta.ru/news/2001/03/07/nigeria
18. 'Prezidenty Nigerii i Rossii dogovorilis' o partnerstve' (Presidents of Nigeria and Russia Agree on Partnership), Kommersant, 7 March 2001, https://www.kommersant.ru/doc/171043
19. Interview with author, April 2021.
20. Ibid.
21. Michael Stuermer, Putin and the Rise of Russia, Paris: Hachette, 2008.
22. Agumabah, 2014.
23. 'Andrey Ivanov and Ivan Safronov, Efiopiya vyplatit dolg Rossii' (Ethiopia Will Repay the Debt to Russia), Kommersant, 4 December 2001, https://www.kommersant.ru/doc/300353
24. Gennady Charodeev, 'Rog izobiliya' (Cornucopia), Izvestia, 4 December 2001, https://iz.ru/news/255485
25. 'Vladimir Putin v ponedel'nik provedet peregovory s Prem'yer-ministrom Efiopii Melesom Zenaui' (Vladimir Putin Will Hold Talks on Monday with Prime Minister of Ethiopia Meles Zenawi), RIA Novosti, 3 December 2001, https://ria.ru/20011203/27430.html
26. Charodeev, 2001.
27. Evgeny Korendyasov, 'Rossiya Atakuyet Rynki Vooruzheniy i Voyennoy Tekhniki v Afrike' (Russia Attacks Arms And Military Equipment Markets in Africa), Russian International Affairs Council, 11 May 2017, https://russiancouncil.ru/analytics-and-comments/analytics/rossiya-nastupaet-na-rynki-vooruzheniy-i-voennoy-tekhniki-v-afrike/
28. 'Rossiya spisala 1,1 milliarda dollarov iz dolga Efiopii na 1,26 milliarda dollarov' (Russia Wrote Off $1.1 Billion of Ethiopia's $1.26 billion of

NOTES pp. [61–64]

Debt), *Vedomosti*, 31 March 2005, https://www.vedomosti.ru/library/news/2005/03/31/rossiya-spisala-jefiopii-11-mlrd-iz-126-mlrd-dolga

29. Grigorieva Valerevna, 'Rossiysko-efiopskiye otnosheniya v kontse 1990-kh nachale 2000-kh godov' (Russian-Ethiopian Relations in the late 1990s and early 2000s), Bulletin of the Nizhny Novgorod University Lobachevsky, 2012.

30. Andrew Weiss and Eugene Rumer, 'Nuclear Enrichment: Russia's Ill-fated Influence Campaign in South Africa', Carnegie Endowment for International Peace, 16 December 2019, https://carnegieendowment.org/2019/12/16/nuclear-enrichment-russia-s-ill-fated-influence-campaign-in-south-africa-pub-80597

31. Mark Gevisser, *Thabo Mbeki: The Dream Deferred*, Johannesburg: Jonathan Ball Publishers, 2007, pp. 483–84.

32. Weiss and Rumer, 2019.

33. Interview with author, May 2021.

34. Alexandra Archangelskaya and Vladimir Shubin, 'Russia-South Africa Relations: Beyond Revival', South African Institute of International Affairs, July 2013.

35. 'Putin in Historic South Africa Visit', Al Jazeera English, 5 September 2006, https://www.aljazeera.com/news/2006/9/5/putin-in-historic-south-africa-visit

36. 'Rossiya i YUAR budut vmeste borot'sya s terrorizmom i sotrudnichat' v kosmose' (Russia and South Africa will Fight Terrorism Together and Cooperate in Space), *Vesti*, 5 September 2006, https://www.vesti.ru/amp/article/2313466

37. 'P. Mlambo-Ngucka on Meeting Russian Prime Minister M. Fradkov', Government of South Africa, 19 March 2007, https://www.gov.za/p-mlambo-ngcuka-meeting-russian-prime-minister-m-fradkov

38. 'Kaddafi priglasil Putina' (Gaddafi Invited Putin), *Trud*, 2 August 2000, https://www.trud.ru/article/02-08-2000/9776_kaddafi_priglasil_putina.html

39. Andrew McGregor, 'Russia's Arms Sales to Sudan a First Step in Return to Africa: Part Two', *Jamestown Foundation Eurasia Daily Monitor*, Volume 6, Issue 29, 12 February 2009, https://jamestown.org/program/russias-arms-sales-to-sudan-a-first-step-in-return-to-africa-part-two/

40. 'Sudan: UNSC Imposes Travel Ban, Assets Freeze on Those Impeding Peace Process in Darfur, Adopting Resolution 1591' (2005) by 12-0-3, Relief Web International, 29 March 2005, https://reliefweb.int/report/sudan/sudan-un-sc-imposes-travel-ban-assets-freeze-those-impeding-peace-process-darfur

41. 'Sudan vstupayet v voyennuyu sluzhbu' (Sudan Gets into Military Duty), *Kommersant*, 20 October 2006, https://www.kommersant.ru/doc/714849

42. Ibid.

pp. [64–68]    NOTES

43. Vadim Kozyulin, 'Sudan Mezhdu Mirom I Voynoy' (Sudan Between Peace and War), PIR Center, 2009, p. 40, http://www.pircenter.org/media/content/files/11/13656800100.pdf

44. 'Russian Humanitarian Aid to Population of Darfur, Sudan', Relief Web, 12 July 2006, https://reliefweb.int/report/sudan/russian-humanitarian-aid-population-darfur-sudan

45. 'Belykh fermerov gromyat v Zimbabve' (White Farmers are Being Smashed in Zimbabwe), *Kommersant*, 20 April 2000, https://www.kommersant.ru/doc/145923#id2118238

46. Vladimir Kara-Murza and Mikhail Zygar, 'Vybory v Zimbabve proshli bez izbirateley' (Elections in Zimbabwe Passed without Voters), *Kommersant*, 11 March 2002, https://www.kommersant.ru/doc/313669

47. Arkady Khantsevich, 'Robert Mugabe: "Toni Bler – lzhets"' (Robert Mugabe: Tony Blair is a Liar), *Nezavisimaya Gazeta*, 14 May 2004, https://www.ng.ru/world/2004-05-14/1_zimbabve.html

48. 'Bauxite Deal Signals Stronger Guinea-Russia Ties', Stratfor, 20 August 2001, https://worldview.stratfor.com/article/bauxite-deal-signals-stronger-russia-guinea-ties

49. Ibid.

50. 'Prezident Omar Bongo poobeshchal sotrudnichat" (President Omar Bongo Pledged Cooperation), *Kommersant*, 24 April 2001, https://www.kommersant.ru/doc/255026#id2123318

51. Ibid.

52. 'Russia-Gabon Agreement', BBC, 24 April 2001, http://news.bbc.co.uk/1/hi/world/europe/1294171.stm

53. Interview with author, September 2017.

54. Mikhail Kamynin, 'V svyazi s vizitom Sergeya Lavrova v strany Severnoy Afriki' (In Connection with Sergei Lavrov's Visit to North Africa), RIA Novosti, 20 November 2005, https://ria.ru/20051120/42151455.html

55. 'Putin Meets Morocco's King', RFE/RL, 7 September 2006, https://www.rferl.org/a/1071146.html

56. Shireen Hunter, Jeffrey Thomas and Alexander Melikshvili, *Islam in Russia: The Politics of Identity and Security*, Amonk, New York: ME Sharpe, 2004, p. 388.

57. Alexei Vassiliev, *Russia's Middle East Policy*, Abingdon: Routledge, p. 310.

58. Ibid.

59. Bogdanov, p. 32.

60. Vladislav Vorobiev, 'V Yegipet po rabote' (To Egypt for Work), *Rossiyskaya Gazeta*, 27 April 2005, https://rg.ru/2005/04/27/egipet.html

61. Svetlana Ofitova, 'Moskva ne neset otvetstvennosti za sud'bu Khuseyna' (Moscow is Not Responsible for Fate of Hussein), *Nezavisimaya Gazeta*, 30 January 2003, https://www.ng.ru/politics/2003-01-30/2_iraq.html

62. Alexander Ignatenko, 'Voyna fetv' (War of Fatwas), *Nezavisimaya Gazeta*, 4 February 2003, https://www.ng.ru/ng_religii/2003-04-02/7_iraq.html

359

## NOTES pp. [68–72]

63. 'Joint Press Conference with President Hosni Mubarak of Egypt', President of Russia, 28 May 2004, http://en.kremlin.ru/events/president/transcripts/page/395

64. 'Pervoye prishestviye' (First Coming), *Kommersant*, 26 April 2005, https://www.kommersant.ru/doc/573420

65. Ibid.

66. Ibid.

67. Vasiliev, 2005.

68. 'Putin and Mubarak Discuss Trade, Middle East', RFE/RL, 2 November 2006, https://www.rferl.org/a/1072469.html

69. Issaev, 2017.

70. Interview with author, May 2021.

71. E.M. Bogucharsky, 'Rossiysko-alzhirskoye sotrudnichestvo na rubezhe vekov' (Russian-Algerian Cooperation at the Turn of the Century), Institute of African Studies, 2007, pp. 108–25.

72. Boris Dolgov, 'Radikal'nyy islamizm v Alzhire' (Radical Islamism in Algeria), *Russia and the Muslim World*, 2003.

73. Mark Katz, 'Russia and Algeria: Partners or Competitiors?', *Middle East Policy*, 2006.

74. Interview with author, May 2021. See R.G. Landa, 'Rossiya I Alzhir Obshchiye Osobennosti Perekhodnogo Perioda' (Russia and Algeria: General Features of the Transition Period), *East Afro-Asian Societies: History and Modernity*, 2008, pp. 140–46 for more details.

75. Ibid.

76. Bogucharskiy, 2007.

77. Katz, 2006.

78. Vladimir Titorenko, 'Rossiya vozvrashchayetsya v Alzhir' (Russia Comes Back to Algeria), *International Affairs*, Volume 52, Number 4, 2006, pp. 163–64.

79. Gennady Charodeyev, 'Pora podschitat', skol'ko nam dolzhen nash byvshiy soyuznik' (Time to Count How Much Our Former Ally Owes Us), *Izvestia*, 6 April 2001, p. 6.

80. Antonio Sanchez Andres, 'Political-Economic Relations Between Russia and North Africa', Real Instituto Elcano, 11 July 2006, p. 3.

81. Katz, pp. 155–56.

82. Alexander Babakin, 'Byudzhet teryayetsya, a Rosoboroneksport nabirayet oboroty' (The Budget is Losing, and Rosoboronexport is Picking Up), *Nezavisimaya Gazeta*, 26 January 2006, https://www.ng.ru/economics/2006-01-26/1_budget.html

83. Ibid.

84. Natalia Melikova, 'Spisat' dolgi po russki' (To Write off Debts in Russian), *Nezavisimaya Gazeta*, 13 March 2006, https://www.ng.ru/politics/2006-03-13/2_price.html

85. Victor Yassman, 'Russia: Energy, Weapons Bring Moscow Closer to Algiers', RFE/RL, 10 March 2006, https://www.rferl.org/a/1066581.html

pp. [72–79]                    NOTES

86. Melikova, 2006.
87. Katz, 2006.
88. 'Algeria's Bouteflika in Moscow to Strengthen Ties', France-24, 19 February 2008, https://www.france24.com/en/20080219-algerias-bouteflika-moscow-strengthen-ties-algeria-russia
89. 'Putin prinyal priglasheniye Kaddafi posetit' Tripoli' (Putin Accepted Gaddafi's Invitation to Visit Tripoli), Lenta.ru, 31 July 2000, https://lenta.ru/news/2000/07/31/livan/
90. *Trud*, 2 August 2000.
91. Ibid.
92. Mark Katz, 'The Russian-Libyan Rapprochement. What Has Moscow Gained?', *Middle East Policy*, 2008, p. 65.
93. Georgy Bovt, 'Liviya stavit SSHA ul'timatum i ne vspominayet o Rossii' (Libya Puts an Ultimatum to the United States and Does not Remember Russia), *Izvestia*, 22 April 2004.
94. V.P. Yurchenko, 'O snyatii mezhdunarodnykh sanktsiy s Livii' (On Lifting International Sanctions from Libya), IIMES, 29 September 2003, http://www.iimes.ru/?p=3011
95. Ibid.
96. Ibid.
97. Bovt, 2004.
98. Elam Kasaev, 'Vnutrennyaya Situatsiya v Livii: Problemy I Perspektivy Razvitiya' (Domestic Sitaution in Libya: Problems and Prospects for Development), *East Afro-Asian Societies: History and Modernity*, 2008, pp. 92–97.
99. Katz, p. 66.
100. 'Russia Cancels Libya's Debt, Eyes Arms Deals', France-24, 17 April 2008, https://www.france24.com/en/20080417-russia-cancels-libyan-debt-eyes-arms-deals-tripoli
101. Alexey Malashenko, 'Rossiya i musul'manskiy mir' (Russia and the Muslim World), Carnegie Endowment for International Peace, 2008, p. 6.
102. Aliya Samigullina, 'Palatochnaya diplomatiya' (Tent Diplomacy), Gazeta.ru, 17 April 2008, https://www.gazeta.ru/politics/2008/04/17_a_2697458.shtml
103. Katz, 2008.
104. Ibid.
105. Vladimir Kuzmin, 'Dvoye v Tripoli' (Two in Tripoli), *Rossiyskaya Gazeta*, 18 April 2008, https://rg.ru/2008/04/18/putin-livija.html

3.   THE MEDVEDEV INTERREGNUM

1.   Polina Matveeva, 'Diktator vytashchil vtoroy raund' (The Dictator Pulled out of the Second Round), Gazeta.ru, 5 April 2008, https://www.gazeta.ru/politics/2008/05/04_a_2714691.shtml

361

NOTES                                    pp. [79–82]

2. Alexander Artemiev, 'Moskva perebralas' v Zimbabve' (Moscow Made a Move to Zimbabwe), Gazeta.ru, 12 July 2008, https://www.gazeta.ru/politics/2008/07/12_a_2781029.shtml

3. 'Miliband Says Veto of Zimbabwe Sanctions "Incomprehensible"', Reuters, 12 July 2008, https://www.reuters.com/article/uk-zimbabwe-crisis-britain-idUKL1244764220080712

4. Louis Charbonneau, 'UN May Want to Suspend ICC Action on Bashir: Russia', Reuters, 22 July 2008, https://www.reuters.com/article/us-warcrimes-sudan-russia-idUSN2144665520080722

5. 'Sudan Voices Support to Russian Military Campaign in Georgia', *Sudan Tribune*, 15 August 2008, https://sudantribune.com/Sudan-voices-support-to-Russian,28295

6. One study on Russia-Sudan relations was 'Gerasimov Vyacheslovich, Rossiya – Sudan: iz istorii vzaimootnosheniy: Po knige E. P. Kovalevskogo "Puteshestviye vo Vnutrennyuyu Afriku"' (Russia-Sudan: The History of Relations based on the book by E.P. Kovalevsky, 'A Journey to Inner in Africa'), Bulletin of St Petersburg University Oriental and African Studies, 2009.

7. Kozyulin, p. 43.

8. 'Margelov: Resheniye MUS ob areste prezidenta Sudana – opasnyy pretsedent' (Margelov: ICC's Decision to Arrest the President of Sudan is a Dangerous Precedent), RIA Novosti, 4 March 2009, https://ria.ru/20090304/163847909.html

9. Elena Mazneva, 'Nigeriya snova zvonit v Gazprom' (Nigeria Calls Gazprom Again), *Vedomosti*, 19 February 2008, https://www.vedomosti.ru/library/articles/2008/02/19/nigeriya-snova-zovet-gazprom

10. 'EU and Russia in Scramble for Nigerian Gas', Euractiv, 18 September 2008, https://www.euractiv.com/section/energy/news/eu-and-russia-in-scramble-for-nigerian-gas/

11. 'Russia Wants to Fight Pirates in Somalia's Waters', Reuters, 23 October 2008, https://www.reuters.com/article/us-russia-somalia-piracy-idUSTRE49M3YJ20081023

12. 'Net Inoplanetnykh Piratov' (There are No Alien Pirates), Lenta.ru, 20 November 2008, https://lenta.ru/articles/2008/11/20/pirates/

13. 'Pyatnadtsat Sostoyaniy Na Sunduk Mertvetsa' (Fifteen States per Dead Man's Chest), Lenta.ru, 3 June 2008, https://lenta.ru/articles/2008/06/03/pirat/

14. Alexander Artemiev, 'Litsenziya Na Piratskoye Unichtozheniye' (Pirate Destruction License), Gazeta.ru, 3 June 2008, https://www.gazeta.ru/politics/2008/06/03_a_2742804.shtml

15. Reuters, 23 October 2008.

16. 'Russia Call to Halt Somali Piracy', BBC, 3 October 2008, http://news.bbc.co.uk/1/hi/world/africa/7651329.stm

17. Lenta.ru, 20 November 2008.

362

## NOTES

18. James Kilner, 'Russian Warship Seizes 3 Pirate Ships off Somalia', Reuters, 13 February 2009, https://www.reuters.com/article/us-russia-pirates-idUSTRE51C2QZ20090213

19. Peter Walker, 'British and Russian Ships Fight Off Somali Pirates', *The Guardian*, 12 November 2008, https://www.theguardian.com/world/2008/nov/12/somalia-russia

20. 'Sovet Bezopasnosti OON sanktsioniruyet primeneniye sily protiv piratov na zemle i v vozdukhe' (UN Security Council Authorizes Use of Force Against Pirates on the Ground and from the Air), RIA Novosti, 17 December 2008, https://ria.ru/20081217/157402820.html

21. Simon Sardhazyan, 'The Dynamics of Russia's Response to the Piracy Threat', *Connections*, Volume 9 Number 3, Summer 2010, p. 21.

22. Interview with author, 16 December 2020.

23. 'Somalia Says Relations with Russia May be Harmed over Pirates'Treatment', Voice of America, 20 May 2010, https://www.voanews.com/africa/somalia-says-relations-russia-may-be-harmed-over-pirates-treatment

24. Interview with author, December 2020.

25. Vladislav Vorobiev, 'S Lavrovym bez protokola' (With Lavrov without Protocol), *Rossiyskaya Gazeta*, 18 February 2009, https://rg.ru/2009/02/18/hamas.html

26. 'Itogi afrikanskogo turne prezidenta Dmitriya Medvedeva: Rossiya vozvrashchayetsya v Afriku' (The Outcome of the African Tour of Dmitry Medvedev: Russia Returns to Africa), TV1, 28 June 2009, https://www.1tv.ru/news/2009-06-28/169692-itog_afrikanskogo_turne_prezidenta_dmitriya_medvedeva_rossiya_vozvraschaetsya_v_afriku

27. Vladimir Kuzmin, 'I aravan idet' (And the Caravan Goes), *Rossiyskaya Gazeta*, 26 June 2009, https://rg.ru/2009/06/26/medvedev-namibia.html

28. 'Russia and Egypt Raised their Bilateral Relations to a Strategic Partnership', President of Russia, 23 June 2009, http://www.en.kremlin.ru/events/president/news/44999

29. 'Oleg Shchedrov, Russia Eyes Nuclear Power Deals with Egypt, Nigeria', Reuters, 24 June 2009, https://www.reuters.com/article/russia-africa-nuclear-idUKLO90021520090624

30. 'Medvedev pribyl s ofitsialnym vizitom v Yegipet' (Medvedev Arrives on an Official Visit to Egypt), RIA Novosti, 23 June 2009, https://ria.ru/20090623/175162441.html

31. TV-1, 28 June 2009.

32. Jana Borisova, 'Al-Islam Bayn Uwbama Wamydfydif fi Alqahira Almsd' (Islam Between Obama and Medvedev in Cairo), *Al-Bayan*, 29 June 2009, https://www.albayan.ae/opinions/2009-06-29-1.448390

33. 'Medvedev Visit to Nigeria Marred by Attacks', RT, 27 June 2009, https://www.rt.com/news/medvedev-visit-to-nigeria-marred-by-attacks/

34. 'Medvedev Advances Further into Africa', RT, 24 June 2009, https://www.rt.com/news/medvedev-advances-further-into-africa/

NOTES pp. [87–91]

35. 'Joint News Conference with President of Nigeria Umaru Yar'Adua Following Russian-Nigerian Talks', President of Russia, 25 June 2009, http://en.kremlin.ru/events/president/news/page/781
36. 'Gazprom Seals \$2.5bn Nigeria Deal', BBC, 25 June 2009, http://news.bbc.co.uk/1/hi/business/8118721.stm
37. 'Gazprom Nigeria Venture, Nigaz, Stirs Racism Debate', Reuters, 1 July 2009, https://www.reuters.com/article/ozabs-russia-nigeria-nigaz-20090701-idAFJOE5600C020090701
38. 'Nigeria to Press for Reform of Security Council, its President Says', UN News, 24 September 2007, https://news.un.org/en/story/2007/09/233072-nigeria-press-reform-security-council-its-president-says
39. 'Medvedev soglasilsya rasshirit' rossiyskiye investitsii v ekonomiku Namibii' (Medvedev Agreed to Expand Russian investments in the Economy of Namibia), RIA Novosti, 26 June 2009, https://ria.ru/20090626/175455668.html
40. TV-1, 28 June 2009.
41. 'Oleg Shchedrov, Russia's Medvedev Seeks Uranium Deals with Namibia', Reuters, 25 June 2009, https://www.reuters.com/article/ozatp-russia-namibia-medvedev-20090625-idAFJOE55O0N620090625
42. 'Medvedev to Discuss Russian Investment in Namibia', 24 June 2009, https://russianpartner.biz/news/1874.html
43. 'Gazprom Strikes Billion-Dollar Namibia Deal', France-24, 26 June 2009, https://www.france24.com/en/20090626-russia-gazprom-billion-dollar-namibia-deal-south-africa
44. BBC, 25 June 2009.
45. Xu Guoqing, 'Èluósī duì fēizhōu zhèngcè de yǎnbiàn jí qí zhī jiān de hézuò. Yǔ fēizhōu guānxì lǐngyù de zhōng é' (The Evolution of Russian Policy Towards Africa and Cooperation Between Russia and China in the Field of Relations with Africa), 2017.
46. Leonid Issaev, 'Russia and Egypt: Opportunities in Bilateral Relations and the Limits of Cooperation', Al-Sharq Forum, January 2017, p. 10.
47. 'Yegipet podtverdil status samoy opasnoy strany dlya rossiyskikh turistov' (Egypt has Confirmed its Status as the Most Dangerous Country for Russian Tourists), Prime, 22 November 2010, https://1prime.ru/Politics/20101122/754477903.html
48. 'Nigeria Launches Two Satellites', BBC, 17 August 2011, https://www.bbc.co.uk/news/science-environment-14563647
49. 'Joint News Conference with President of South Africa Jacob Zuma', President of Russia, 5 August 2010, http://www.en.kremlin.ru/events/president/transcripts/page/259
50. Vladimir Shubin, 'Yuzhnaya Afrika v BRIKS: posledneye, no ne meneye vazhnoye' (South Africa to BRICS: Last but Not Least), 2015.
51. Vladimir Shubin, 'Pochemu Yuzhnaya Afrika nuzhen BRIKS i zachem BRIKS Yuzhnaya Afrika' (Why does South Africa need BRICS and why does BRICS need South Africa), PIR Center Security Index, 2013.

364

pp. [91–94]  NOTES

52. Shubin, 2013.

53. Gregory Shin and Anton Malkin, 'Russia as a Re-Emerging Donor: Catching up Africa', Center for International Governance Innovation, 8 March 2012, https://www.cigionline.org/publications/russia-re-emerging-donor-catching-africa

54. Shin and Malkin, 2012.

55. 'Rossiyskaya Federatsiya prinyala resheniye ob okazanii srochnoy gumanitarnoy pomoshchi Zimbabve – MID Rossii' (Russian Federation Decided to Provide Urgent Humanitarian Aid to Zimbabwe-Russian Foreign Ministry), RIA Novosti, 27 February 2009, https://ria.ru/20090227/163380127.html

56. 'Rossiya spaset Zimbabve' (Russia will Save Zimbabwe), Gazeta.ru, 27 February 2009, https://www.gazeta.ru/politics/2009/02/27_kz_2950024.shtml

57. 'Rossiya okazyvayet Efiopii prodovol'stvennuyu pomoshch' na 2 milliona dollarov' (Russia provided Ethiopia with food aid for $2 million), Prime, 26 July 2010, https://1prime.ru/politics_economy/20100726/758721543.html

58. Petr Troilo, 'For Russian Foreign Aid, a Second Act', Devex, 19 March 2012, https://www.devex.com/news/for-russian-foreign-aid-a-second-act-77769

59. Troilo, 2012.

60. Interview with author, November 2020.

61. Bogdanov, 2017, p. 24.

62. Interview with author, September 2017.

63. Interview with author, September 2018.

64. 'Dmitri Medvedev Addressed the World Economic Forum in Davos', President of Russia, 26 January 2011, http://en.kremlin.ru/events/president/news/10163

65. 'Tunisia Riots Because it Lacks Jobs and Opportunities – Analysts', RT, 18 January 2011, https://www.rt.com/news/tunisia-riots-economy/

66. 'Zhasminovaya revolyutsiya v Tunise' (Jasmine Revolution in Tunisia), Interfax, 19 January 2011, https://www.interfax.ru/russia/173530

67. 'Medvedev Calls Egyptian President as Russians Flee', *The Moscow Times*, 3 February 2011, https://www.themoscowtimes.com/2011/02/03/medvedev-calls-egyptian-president-as-russians-flee-a4752

68. Dmitri Trenin, 'Russia and Egypt: An Old Relationship', Carnegie Moscow Center, 11 February 2011, https://carnegie.ru/2011/02/11/russia-and-egypt-old-relationship-pub-42598

69. 'Statement by the President of Russia on the Situation in Egypt', 12 February 2011, http://en.kremlin.ru/events/president/news/10321

70. 'Medvedev Warns Arabs of "Extremism"', Al Jazeera English, 22 February 2011, https://www.aljazeera.com/news/2011/2/22/medvedev-warns-arabs-of-extremism

NOTES                                                pp. [94–98]

71. Mark Katz, 'Russia and the Arab Uprisings of 2011', Middle East Policy Council, https://mepc.org/commentary/russia-and-arab-uprisings-2011

72. Alexander Ignatenko, 'Zakat politicheskogo islama' (The Decline of Political Islam), *Nezavisimaya Gazeta*, 16 February 2011, https://www.ng.ru/ng_religii/2011-02-16/1_islam.html

73. Vasily Lyov, 'Revolyutsiya v Yegipte – vzglyad iz Rossii' (Revolution in Russia- A View from Russia), 31 January 2011, https://www.golosameriki.com/a/bl-egypt-russian-perspective-2011-01-31-114964074/192849.html

74. Lyov, 31 January 2011.

75. Alexey Malashenko, 'Russia and the Arab Spring', Carnegie Moscow Center, October 2013, https://carnegieendowment.org/files/russia_arab_spring 2013.pdf

76. 'S chuvstvom neizbezhnogo dolga' (With a Sense of Escapable Duty), *Kommersant*, 31 October 2008, https://www.kommersant.ru/doc/1049923

77. 'Kaddafi predlozhil Rossii sovmestno razvivat' deyatel'nost' v Afrike' (Gaddafi Invited Russia to Jointly Develop Activities in Africa), RIA Novosti, 1 November 2008, https://ria.ru/20081101/154278960.html

78. 'Libya, Russia Agree $1.8 Billion Arms Deal: Putin', Reuters, 30 January 2010, https://www.reuters.com/article/us-russia-libya-arms-idUSTRE60 T1ED20100130

79. 'Do posledney puli' (Until the Last Bullet), Lenta.ru, 21 February 2011, https://lenta.ru/articles/2011/02/21/muammar/

80. Alexander Ignatenko, 'Arabskiy mir zakhlestnuli revolyutsii Maydana' (Arab World Overwhelmed by Maidan Revolutions), *Nezavisimaya Gazeta*, 27 April 2011, https://www.ng.ru/scenario/2011-04-27/12_revolution. html

81. 'Zhirinovsky Invites Gaddafi to Move to Moscow', RT, 21 February 2011, https://www.rt.com/russia/gaddafi-zhirinovsky-libya-unrest/

82. 'Medvedev skazal, chto Liviya nuzhdayetsya v izmeneniyakh k 2011 godu' (Libya Needed Changes by 2011, Medvedev said), RIA Novosti, 13 November 2018, https://ria.ru/20181113/1532705323.html

83. Colum Lynch, 'UN Votes to Impose Sanctions on Gaddafi', *The Washington Post*, 26 February 2011, https://www.washingtonpost.com/wp-dyn/content/article/2011/02/26/AR2011022603386.html

84. 'Airstrikes in Libya did not Take Place – Russian Military', RT, 1 March 2011, https://www.rt.com/news/airstrikes-libya-russian-military/

85. 'Medvedev: Rossiya soznatel'no ne nalozhila veto na rezolyutsiyu SB OON po Livii' (Medvedev: Russia Deliberately did not Veto UN Security Council Resolution on Libya), RIA Novosti, 21 March 2011, https://ria. ru/20110321/356344423.html

86. 'Security Council Approves "No-Fly Zone" over Libya, Authorizing All Necessary Measures to Protect Civilians by Vote of 10 in Favour with 5

pp. [98–101]  NOTES

Abstentions', United Nations, 17 March 2011, https://www.un.org/press/en/2011/sc10200.doc.htm

87. Alexei Anishchuk, 'Russia's Medvedev Raps Putin's Libya "Crusade" Jibe', Reuters, 21 March 2011. https://www.reuters.com/article/us-libya-russia-idUSTRE72K5AJ20110321

88. 'Obama Tarnishes Nobel Peace Prize with "Indiscriminate" Military Action in Libya', RT, 20 March 2011, https://www.rt.com/russia/libya-russia-military-force/

89. 'Sergey Ivanov: NATO vmeshivayetsya vo vnutrenniy konflikt v Livii' (Sergei Ivanov: NATO Intervenes in the Internal Conflict in Libya), RBC, 5 June 2011, https://www.rbc.ru/politics/05/06/2011/5703e81c9a79477633d33b5a

90. Marzia Cimmino, 'Moscow's Perspectives on War in Libya', Carnegie Endowment for International Peace 31 March 2011, https://carnegieindia.org/2011/03/31/moscow-s-perspectives-on-war-in-libya-pub-43371

91. Interview with author, September 2017.

92. Steve Gutterman, 'Sacked Libyan Envoy Criticizes Russian "Betrayal"', Reuters, 24 March 2011, https://www.reuters.com/article/libya-russia-ambassador-idAFLDE72N04D20110324

93. Alexei Anishchuk, 'Medvedev Says Gaddafi Must Go, Sends Envoy to Benghazi', Reuters, 27 May 2011, https://www.reuters.com/article/uk-libya-russia-medvedev-idUKTRE74Q4VR20110527

94. 'NATO will use Gaddafi Arrest Warrant as Excuse to Intensify Military Operations – Envoy', RT, 27 June 2011, https://www.rt.com/russia/gaddafi-warrant-arrest-nato/

95. Roy Allison, *Russia, the West and Military Intervention*, Oxford: Oxford University Press, 2013, p. 173.

96. Mikhail Budaragin, 'Urok Indiyskogo Yazyka' (Indian Lesson), *Vzglyad*, 1 February 2011, https://vz.ru/columns/2011/2/1/465371.html

97. Stephen Blank and Carl Saivetz, 'Russia Watches the Arab Spring', RFE/RL, 24 June 2011, https://www.rferl.org/a/commentary_russia_watches_arab_spring/24245990.html

98. Roland Dannreuther, 'Russia and the Arab Spring: Supporting the Counter-Revolution', *Journal of European Integration*, Volume 37, 2015.

99. 'Rossiya zanyala dvoyakuyu pozitsiyu po otnosheniyu k Livii' (Russia Took a Double Stance Towards Libya), *Vedomosti*, 21 March 2011, https://www.vedomosti.ru/politics/articles/2011/03/21/udar_po_livii

100. 'Russia and China Urge Adherence to Libya Resolutions', Reuters, 16 June 2011, https://www.reuters.com/article/libya-russia-china-idAFLDE75F13V20110616

101. Zhong Shi, 'Xīfāng wéi hé xíjí lìbǐyǎ' (Why is the West attacking Libya), 2011.

102. 'Aleksey Pushkov: Pozornaya voyna' (Alexey Pushkov: A Shameful War), AIF, 7 June 2011, https://aif.ru/politics/world/26431

367

## NOTES pp. [101–106]

103. Shaun Walker, 'Gaddafi's Death Breached the Law', *Independent*, 21 December 2011, https://www.independent.co.uk/news/world/europe/gaddafi-s-death-breached-law-says-russia-2374250.html

104. 'Russia's Putin Disgusted by Gaddafi Death Images', Reuters, 26 October 2011, https://www.reuters.com/article/idINIndia-60139820111026

105. 'Gaddafi's Death: Envoy Slams "Sadistic" Triumphalism', RT, 21 October 2011, https://www.rt.com/russia/blasts-western-leaders-gaddafis-417/

106. Ahmed Eleiba, 'Arab League Amr Moussa Defends its Support for UN No-Fly Zone Resolution', *Al-Ahram*, 21 March 2011, https://english.ahram.org.eg/NewsAFCON/2019/8259.aspx

107. 'Sobytiya v Livii mogut usilit' mezhdunarodnyy terrorizm – Lavrov' (Events in Libya May Intensify International Terrorism- Lavrov), RIA Novosti, 22 March 2011, https://ria.ru/20110322/356677515.html

108. Alexey Bogustavsky, 'Afrikanskiy soyuz i liviyskiy krizis: kto slyshal golos Afriki?' (African Union and the Libyan Crisis: Who Heard Africa's Voice?), *International Affairs*, Issue 11, 2011, https://interaffairs.ru/jauthor/material/559

109. Andrey Urnov, 'Afrika I OON' (Africa and the UN), Moscow: Institute of African Studies, 2009.

110. Bogustavksy, 2011.

111. Vladimir Shubin, '2011: Africa, Libya, NATO and the R2P as a Projection of Power', *Journal of African Union Studies*, Volume 2, Issue 3–4, 2011, p. 141.

112. David Brunnstrom and Denis Dyomkin, 'Libya Dominates Russian Meetings with NATO, Zuma', Reuters, 4 July 2011, https://www.reuters.com/article/us-russia-nato-libya/libya-dominates-russian-meetings-with-nato-zuma-idUSTRE76326J20110704

113. John Campbell, 'Russia Delays UNSC Vote on Cote d'Ivoire', Council on Foreign Relations, 18 January 2011, https://www.cfr.org/blog/russia-delays-unsc-vote-cote-divoire

114. 'Lavrov Questions Use of Force in Cote d'Ivoire', *The Moscow Times*, 5 April 2011, https://www.themoscowtimes.com/2011/04/05/lavrov-questions-use-of-force-in-ivory-coast-a6104

115. 'Russia Lashes out at UN Military Action in Cote d'Ivoire', RT, 5 April 2011, https://www.rt.com/news/cote-ivoire-gbagbo-un/

116. Igor Ivvanikov and Konstantin Pahorukov, 'Problemy mirotvorchestva OON i rol' Frantsii v uregulirovanii konflikta v Kot-d'Ivuare' (Problems of UN Peacekeeping and the role of France in Resolving the Conflict in Cote d'Ivoire), POLITEX, 2013.

## 4. RUSSIA'S ANTI-WESTERN TILT IN AFRICA

1. Interview with author, November 2020.
2. Interview with author, 3 May 2021.

368

pp. [107–110]  NOTES

3. I.O. Abramova and L.L. Fituni, 'Otsenka perspektivy ekonomicheskoy ekspansii v subsakharskuyu Afriku i investitsionnogo potentsiala regiona s tochki zreniya strategicheskikh interesov' (Assessment of the Prospects for Economic Expansion in Sub-Saharan Africa and the Investment Potential of the Region from the Vantage Point of Strategic Interests), Moscow: Institute of African Studies, 2016.

4. 'Strana pyati baz' (Country of Five Bases), *Kommersant*, 13 February 2017, https://www.kommersant.ru/doc/3217935

5. Eugene Steinberg, 'Putin's Russia and Africa, Council on Foreign Relations', CFR, 13 August 2015, https://www.cfr.org/blog/putins-russia-and-africa

6. 'Factbox: Russian Military Cooperation Deals with African Countries', Reuters, 17 October 2018, https://www.reuters.com/article/us-africa-russia-factbox-idUSKCN1MR0KH

7. 'An example of the neocolonialism narratives that were regularly promoted by RT and Sputnik during this period is Dan Glazebrook, West Eyes Recolonization of Africa by Endless War; Removing Gaddafi was Just First Step', RT, 20 October 2017, https://www.rt.com/op-ed/407332-gaddafi-west-sirte-recolonization/

8. Alimov and Nesterova, 2017.

9. Interview with Jonathan Winer, November 2020.

10. Eric Maurice, Nikolaj Nielsen and Andrew Rettman, 'Malta Raises Alarm on Russia in Libya', *EU Observer*, 13 January 2017, https://euobserver.com/foreign/136537

11. Interview with author, April 2021.

12. See Alexandra Lomonova, 'Perspektivy razvitiya kitaysko-afrikanskikh otnosheniy (po materialam Shestogo foruma kitaysko-afrikanskogo sotrudnichestva)' (Prospects for the Development of China-Africa Relations (Based on the Materials of the Sixth China-Africa Cooperation Forum), Power, 2017 and P. Sinukhina, S. Sebeldina and Ch. Chen, 'Tendentsii Razvitiya Kitaysko-Afrikansko Sotrudinestva Po Linii "Yug-Yug" v Ramakh Foruma Sotrudnichestva Kitay Afrika' (Development Trends of Chinese-African Cooperation on the 'South-South' Line in the Framework of the China-Africa Cooperation Forum), MGIMO, 2017.

13. Lomonova, 2017.

14. 'Kitay i Afrika: itogi ekonomicheskogo sotrudnichestva za posledniye gody' (China and Africa: The Results of Economic Cooperation in Recent Years), Institute of African Studies, 28 November 2017, https://www.inafran.ru/node/1548

15. 'Russia's Kamaz Trucks Donated to Support WFP Operations in DRC', World Food Programme, 25 November 2015, https://reliefweb.int/report/democratic-republic-congo/russia-s-kamaz-trucks-donated-support-wfp-operations-drc

NOTES                                      pp. [110–113]

16. 'A Friend in Deed: Russia Writes Off Over $20Bln for African Countries', Sputnik, 29 September 2017, https://sputniknews.com/russia/201709281057784610-russia-africa-debt/
17. 'Rossiya potratit 2 mlrd dollarov na pomoshch' Afrike' (Russia Will Spend $2 Billion on Aid to Africa), Finanz.ru, 30 October 2017, https://www.finanz.ru/novosti/aktsii/rossiya-potratit-%242-mlrd-na-pomoshch-afrike-1006159460
18. Margaret Vice, 'Publics Worldwide Unfavourable Towards Russia, Putin', Pew Research, 16 August 2017, https://www.pewresearch.org/global/2017/08/16/publics-worldwide-unfavorable-toward-putin-russia/
19. Michelle Nichols, 'Burundi: UN Security Council Should Stay out of the Burundi Dispute', Reuters, 16 October 2015, https://www.reuters.com/article/us-burundi-politics-un-idUSKBN0NM49120150501
20. 'Burundi / Russie : S.E. Vladimir Putin félicite la réélection de S.E. Pierre Nkurunziza' (Burundi/Russia: H.E. Vladimir Putin Congratulates Pierre Nkurunziza on Re-election), AG News, 4 August 2015, https://burundi-agnews.org/politique/burundi-russie-s-e-vladimir-putin-felicite-la-reelection-de-s-e-pierre-nkurunziza/
21. 'Military Cooperation with Russia Reinforced', Economist Intelligence Unit, 14 September 2016, http://country.eiu.com/article.aspx?articleid=1814603165&Country=Gambia&topic=Politics&subtopic=F_7
22. 'Rights Defenders Raise Alarm over Russia-Gambia Military Cooperation', Vanguard Africa Foundation, 1 October 2016, http://www.vanguardafrica.com/news/2016/10/1/rights-defenders-raise-alarm-over-russia-gambia-military-cooperation-smbc-news-october-1
23. S. Zhdanov, 'Sudan bolshiye Peremeny' (Sudan: Great Changes), World and National Economy, No. 3(30), 2014), https://mirec.mgimo.ru/2014/2014-03/sudan-bolsie-izmenenia
24. 'South Sudan Official Says Russia will Block UN Sanctions', Voice of America, 29 May 2014, https://www.voanews.com/africa/south-sudan-official-says-russia-will-block-un-sanctions
25. Somini Sengupta, 'UN Report Details Flow of Foreign Weapons into South Sudan', New York Times, 25 August 2015, https://www.nytimes.com/2015/08/26/world/africa/un-report-details-flow-of-foreign-weapons-into-south-sudan.html
26. 'Rossiya ne podderzhala embargo na postavki oruzhiya v Yuzhnyy Sudan' (Russia Did Not Support the Embargo on Arms Supplies to South Sudan), Bfm.ru, 18 November 2016, https://www.bfm.ru/news/339160
27. 'Uganda Picks Russia's RT Global Resources to Build Refinery', Reuters, 17 February 2015, https://www.reuters.com/article/uganda-energy-idUKL5N0VR1JT20150217
28. 'US Cautions Uganda over Russia Refinery Deal', Argus, 26 February 2015, https://www.argusmedia.com/en/news/999080-us-cautions-uganda-over-russia-refinery-deal

370

pp. [113–116]                    NOTES

29. 'Vseobshchiye vybory v Ugande' (General Elections in Uganda), Ministry of Foreign Affairs of the Russian Federation, 21 February 2016, https://www.mid.ru/foreign_policy/news/-/asset_publisher/cKNonkJE02Bw/content/id/2105587

30. David Rogers, 'Russian Consortium Pulls Out of $4bn Uganda Refinery Contract', *Global Construction Review*, 8 July 2016, https://www.global-constructionreview.com/sectors/russian-consortium-p7ulls-o7ut-4bn-ugan7da/

31. 'Russia's Putin Invites Uganda's Museveni to Kremlin – Envoy', Africanews, 25 November 2016, https://www.africanews.com/2016/11/25/russia-s-putin-invites-uganda-s-museveni-to-kremlin-envoy//

32. 'Russia, Uganda Sign Agreement on Use of Atomic Energy', Xinhua, 21 June 2017, http://www.xinhuanet.com/english/2017-06/21/c_136381745.htm

33. Nuclear Engineering International, 9 November 2016.

34. 'Ugandan President Calls for Russia-Africa Summit', Xinhua, 18 October 2017, http://www.xinhuanet.com/english/2017-10/18/c_136689670.htm

35. Alexandra Archangelskaya, Vladimir Shubin and Ana Cristina Alves, 'Russia and Angola: The Rebirth of a Strategic Partnership?', South African Institute for International Affairs, October 2013, p. 12.

36. Janet Shoko, 'Zimbabwe to Swap Mineral Reserves for Russian Military Hardware', *The Africa Report*, 28 June 2012, https://www.theafricareport.com/6983/zimbabwe-to-swap-mineral-reserves-for-russian-military-hardware/

37. Andrey Maslov and Vadim Zaytsev, 'What's Behind Russia's Newfound Interest in Zimbabwe', Carnegie Moscow Center, 14 November 2018, https://carnegiemoscow.org/commentary/77707

38. 'Nqobile Bhebhe, Russia and Zimbabwe in $3bn Mining Deal Negotiations', *The Africa Report*, 16 September 2014, https://www.theafricareport.com/3982/russia-and-zimbabwe-in-3bn-mining-deal-negotiations/

39. 'Ukraine Angry as Zimbabwe Minister visits Crimea', *Kyiv Post*, 22 December 2014, https://www.kyivpost.com/article/content/war-against-ukraine/ukraine-angry-as-zimbabwe-minister-visits-crimea-375889.html

40. 'Russia's Lavrov Signs Deal, Lauds Zimbabwe's Mugabe', RFE/RL, 17 September 2014, https://www.rferl.org/a/mugabe-russia-economic-signing/26589588.html

41. Jason Moyo, 'Zim: Now the Russians are Coming Too', *Mail and Guardian*, 18 September 2014, https://mg.co.za/article/2014-09-18-zim-now-the-russians-are-coming-too/

42. 'Vernut'sya v Afriku' (Return to Africa), Lenta.ru, 20 September 2014, https://lenta.ru/articles/2014/09/19/lavrov/

43. Godfrey Marawanyika and Brian Latham, 'Russia, Zimbabwe to Develop Nation's Biggest Platnium Mine', Bloomberg, 15 September 2014, https://

371

NOTES pp. [116–120]

www.bloomberg.com/news/articles/2014-09-15/russia-zimbabwe-to-jointly-operate-platinum-mine-in-darwendale

44. 'Lavrov v Zimbabve pristupit k dobyche platiny' (Lavrov in Zimbabwe to Launch Platinum Mining), RIA Novosti, 16 September 2014, https://ria.ru/20140916/1024246932.html

45. Interview with author, May 2021.

46. 'Meeting with President of Zimbabwe Robert Mugabe', President of Russia, 10 May 2015, http://en.kremlin.ru/events/president/news/49451

47. Dzvinka Kachur, 'Russia's Resurgence in Africa: Zimbabwe and Mozambique', South African Institute of International Affairs, p. 24.

48. V.G. Shubin, A.A. Tokarev and E.R. Salakhetdinov, 'Politicheskiy krizis v Zimbabve: otsenka i prognoz razvitiya situatsii' (Political Crisis in Zimbabwe: Assessment and Forecast of the Development of the Situation), Institute of African Studies, November 2017, https://www.inafran.ru/node/1518

49. 'Mugabe's Removal Likely Fits China's Interests in Economic Stability in Zimbabwe', Sputnik, 21 November 2017, https://sputniknews.com/analysis/201711211059309845-china-zimbabwe-military-coup/

50. Andrew Korybko, 'Zimbabwe: Saying Bye-Bye to Bob', Sputnik, 25 November 2017, https://sputniknews.com/radio_trendstorm/201711251059403891-zimbabwe-saying-bye-bye-to-bob/

51. 'Russia Hopes for Constructive Cooperation with Zimbabwe under New Authorities', TASS, 23 November 2017, https://tass.com/politics/977178

52. 'Sudan Votes Again Resolution on "Invalid" Crimean Referendum', Sudan Tribune, 27 March 2014, https://sudantribune.com/spip.php?article50458

53. 'Lavrov obsudit v Khartume otnosheniya Rossii i Sudana' (Lavrov in Khartoum to Discuss Relations Between Russia and Sudan), RIA Novosti, 3 December 2014, https://ria.ru/20141203/1036267221.html

54. 'Sudan Speaks of Disagreements with Russia over Syria', Sudan Tribune, 11 October 2015, https://sudantribune.com/spip.php?iframe&page=imprimable&id_article=56690

55. Sergey Kostelyanets, 'Rossiysko-sudanskiye otnosheniya v nachale XXI veka: upushchennaya vozmozhnost' ili osnova dlya novogo nachala?' (Russia-Sudan Relations in the Early Twenty-First Century: A Lost Opportunity or Foundation for a New Beginning?), Asia and Africa Today, Issue 9, pp. 56–62.

56. 'Russia-Sudan Talks', President of Russia, 23 November 2017, http://en.kremlin.ru/events/president/news/page/232

57. 'Rossiya mozhet sozdat' voyenno-morskuyu bazu v Sudane' (Russia May Create a Military Base in Sudan), Gazeta.ru, 25 November 2017, https://www.gazeta.ru/army/2017/11/25/11006558.shtml

58. 'Spasite Afriku ot SSHA: prezident Sudana pribyl v Sochi za pomoshch'yu' (Save Africa from the United States: Sudanese President Arrives in Sochi for Help), Sputnik Radio, 23 November 2017, https://radiosputnik.ria.ru/20171123/1509448810.html?in=t

372

pp. [120–123]  NOTES

59. Amalia Zatari, 'Rossiyskaya baza v Sudane: eto chudovishchnyye raskhody' (Russian Base in Sudan: These are Monstrous Expenses), Gazeta.ru, 1 December 2017, https://www.gazeta.ru/army/2017/12/01/11024036.shtml?updated

60. Alexei Vasiliev, 'Rossii nuzhna Afrika. Afrike nuzhna Rossiya // Afrika i vyzovy XXI veka' (Russia Needs Africa. Africa Needs Russia. Challenges of the 21st Century), 2012, pp. 140–45.

61. Andrey Urnov, 'Rossiya i Afrika' (Russia in Africa), Institute of African Studies, 2012.

62. 'Renova Puts up $400mln in South Africa Manganese Business', Interfax, 23 August 2012, https://interfax.com/newsroom/top-stories/54731/

63. 'Putin Looks to do Business with South Africa's Zuma', *The Moscow Times*, 16 May 2013, https://www.themoscowtimes.com/2013/05/16/putin-looks-to-do-business-with-south-africas-zuma-a24053

64. Simon Allison, 'South Africa: Treading a Fine Line', in Felix Hett and Moshe Wien, *Between Principles and Pragmatism: Perspectives on the Ukraine Crisis from Brazil, India, China and South Africa*, Friedrich Ebert Stiftung, May 2015, pp. 11–12.

65. Elizabeth Sidiropoulos, 'South Africa's Response to the Ukrainian Crisis', Norwegian Peacebuilding Resource Center, June 2014, https://www.files.ethz.ch/isn/181295/1d676013a28a2c93f0abf4a5dfc4567b.pdf

66. Allison, 2015, 12.

67. Garth Abraham, 'Crimea Raises Old Questions of Statehood', *Sunday Independent*, 23 March 2014, https://www.iol.co.za/sundayindependent/crimea-raises-old-question-of-statehood-1664991

68. Seumas Milne, 'It's NATO, not Russia, Provoking the Ukraine Crisis', *Mail and Guardian*, 4 September 2014, https://mg.co.za/article/2014-09-04-its-nato-not-russia-provoking-the-ukraine-crisis/

69. Simon Allison, 'South Africa's Strange Bedfellows at the Human Rights Council', *Daily Maverick*, 22 May 2014, https://www.dailymaverick.co.za/article/2014-05-22-analysis-south-africas-strange-bedfellows-at-the-human-rights-council/

70. Elizabeth Sidiropoulos, 'South African Response to Conflict Must be Astute', SIIA, 7 September 2014, https://saiia.org.za/research/sa-response-to-conflict-must-be-astute/

71. S'Thembiso Msomi, 'The Big Read: The Zuma-Putin Bromance', *Sunday Times*, 28 August 2014, https://www.timeslive.co.za/news/south-africa/2014-08-28-the-big-read-the-zuma-putin-bromance/

72. Ibid.

73. Ibid.

74. 'Valyutnaya korzina BRIKS' (BRICS Currency Basket), *Kommersant*, 16 July 2014, https://www.kommersant.ru/doc/2525874

75. Philip De Wet and Qaanitah Hunter, 'Nuke Deal: Russians Push Charm Button', 2 October 2014, https://mg.co.za/article/2014-10-02-nuke-deal-russians-push-charm-button/

NOTES pp. [123–127]

76. 'Putin Offers Help to South African Nuclear Industry', World Nuclear Industry, 28 March 2013, https://www.world-nuclear-news.org/Articles/Putin-offers-help-to-South-African-nuclear-industr
77. DeWet and Hunter, 2014.
78. 'SA, Russia Agree to $50-Billion Nuclear Deal', Mail and Guardian, 23 September 2014, https://mg.co.za/article/2014-09-23-sa-russia-agree-to-50-billion-nuclear-deal/
79. Alexandra Archangelskaya, 'Rossiya – YUAR: nalazhivaniye partnerskikh otnosheniy' (Russia and South Africa: Forging Partnerships), International Affairs, 2014, https://interaffairs.ru/jauthor/material/1331
80. Mail and Guardian, 2014.
81. 'South Africa Signs $10 Billion Nuclear Deal with Russia', World Nuclear News, 22 September 2014, https://www.world-nuclear-news.org/NN-South-Africa-signs-10-billion-nuclear-agreement-with-Russia-23092014.html
82. DeWet and Hunter, 2014.
83. Ibid.
84. Interview with author, June 2021.
85. 'Russia's Global Image Negative Amid Crisis in Ukraine', Pew Research Center, 9 July 2014, https://www.pewresearch.org/global/2014/07/09/russias-global-image-negative-amid-crisis-in-ukraine/
86. Interview with author, April 2021.
87. Weiss and Rumer, 2019.
88. Andrey Alimov and Irina Nesterova, 'Interesy SSHA v sovremennykh afrikanskikh gosudarstvakh' (US Interests in Modern African States), Terra Humana, 2017.
89. Geert de Clercq, 'South Africa Nuclear Tender Open to All, Rosatom not Frontrunner', Reuters, 15 September 2016, https://www.reuters.com/article/us-safrica-nuclear-idUSKCN11L1SM
90. Wendell Roelf, 'South African Court Declares Nuclear Plan with Russia Unlawful', Reuters, 26 April 2017, https://www.reuters.com/article/us-safrica-nuclear-court-idUSKBN17S25R
91. Alexander Winning, 'Russia's Putin Raises Nuclear Deal at Ramaphosa Meeting During BRICS', Reuters, 30 July 2018, https://www.reuters.com/article/us-safrica-nuclear-idUSKBN1KG0S5
92. Mfuneko Toyana, 'South Africa's Zuma Fired Me for Blocking Russian Nuclear Power Deal: Nene', Reuters, 3 October 2018, https://www.reuters.com/article/us-safrica-politics-finmin-idUSKCN1MD0TJ
93. 'Arc of Instability May Turn into Battlefield- Moscow's Envoy', RT, 27 March 2012, https://www.rt.com/russia/mali-africa-arab-spring-538/
94. 'Rossiya podderzhivayet vosstanovleniye tselostnosti Mali' (Russia Supports the Restoration of the Integrity of Mali), RIA Novosti, 29 May 2012, https://ria.ru/20120529/659903611.html

374

pp. [127–129]  NOTES

95. Sergey Smirnov and Alexander Artemiev, 'Liviya prishla v Mali' (Libya came to Mali), Gazeta.ru, 23 March 2012, https://www.gazeta.ru/politics/2012/03/23_a_4102809.shtml

96. Maria Sapronova, 'Krizis v Mali kak prodolzheniye "arabskoy vesny"' (Crisis in Mali as a Continuation of the Arab Spring), MGIMO, 30 January 2013, https://mgimo.ru/about/news/experts/234989/

97. Lance Davies, *Russian Conflict Management and European Security Governance: Policy and Practice*, Lanham: Rowman and Littlefield, 2020, p. 58.

98. Neil MacFarqhuar, 'UN Votes to Establish Peacekeeping force for Mali', *New York Times*, 25 April 2013, https://www.nytimes.com/2013/04/26/world/africa/un-security-council-establishes-peacekeeping-force-in-mali.html?_r=0

99. John Campbell, 'UN Security Council Unanimously Authorizes UN Mission in Mali', Council on Foreign Relations, 26 April 2013, https://www.cfr.org/blog/un-security-council-unanimously-authorizes-un-mission-mali

100. Nile Bowie, 'Elections in Mali: Francophile A vs. Francophile B', RT, 6 August 2013, https://www.rt.com/op-ed/presidential-elections-mali-france-104/

101. Mali Gold, 'Splendor for Foreign Firms, Misery for Malian Miners', RT, 10 June 2013, https://www.rt.com/news/mali-gold-foreign-corporations-450/

102. 'Russia Sends Aid to Mali, Worried by Militant Islam', Reuters, 22 February 2013.

103. 'Nigeria Arrests 15 Russian Sailors Carrying Arms', Reuters, 29 October 2012, https://www.reuters.com/article/us-nigeria-arrests-idUSBRE89M0KC20121023

104. 'Nigeria Charges Russian "Gun Dealers"', BBC, 19 February 2013, https://www.bbc.co.uk/news/world-africa-21509535

105. Kimberly Marten, 'Russia's Use of Semi-State Security Forces: The Case of the Wagner Group', *Post-Soviet Affairs*, Volume 35, Issue 3, 2019, pp. 181–204.

106. 'No Oil, No "Protection"? Boko Haram Massacre in Nigeria Sees Little Reaction from the US', RT, 17 January 2015, https://www.rt.com/news/223575-boko-haram-nigeria-usa/

107. Andrew Korybko, 'While Syria and Chad Both Fight Terrorists, US Plays Favorites', Sputnik, 9 February 2015, https://sputniknews.com/columnists/201502091018017013/

108. 'Terrorism: 1,200 Nigerian Security Personnel Leave for Russia', *Vanguard*, 27 September 2014, https://www.vanguardngr.com/2014/09/terrorism-1200-nigerian-security-personnel-leave-russia/

109. 'Russian Army Starts Training 1,200 Nigerian Personnel in Counterinsurgency Warfare', Defence Web, 23 October 2014, https://www.defenceweb.co.za/security/national-security/russian-army-starts-training-1-200-nigerian-personnel-in-counter-insurgency-warfare/

110. Sunday Omotuyi, 'Russo/Nigerian Relations in the Context of Counterinsurgency Operation in Nigeria', Jadavpur Journal of International Relations, 19 November 2018.

NOTES pp. [129–132]

111. John Campbell, 'Nigeria Turns to Russia, Czech Republic and Belarus for Military Training and Materiel', Council on Foreign Relations, 29 October 2014, https://www.cfr.org/blog/nigeria-turns-russia-czech-republic-and-belarus-military-training-and-materiel

112. Interview with author, April 2021.

113. Interview with Nigerian defence expert, April 2021.

114. Ibid.

115. Joe DeCapua, 'Analysts Weigh Nigeria-Russia Arms Deal', Voice of America, 10 December 2014, https://www.voanews.com/africa/analysts-weigh-nigeria-russia-arms-deal

116. Ibid.

117. 'Nigeriya gotovitsya pokupat' rossiyskoye oruzhiye dlya bor'by s Boko Kharam' (Russia Prepares to Buy Russian Weapons to Counter Boko Haram), Topwar, 3 December 2014, https://topwar.ru/63931-nigeriya-gotovitsya-zakupat-rossiyskoe-oruzhie-dlya-protivostoyaniya-boko-haram.html

118. Interview with former US official, April 2021.

119. 'Rossiya otkrestilas' ot zaderzhannogo v Nigerii samoleta s oruzhiyem' (Russia Disowns a Plane with Weapons Detained in Nigeria), RBC, 7 December 2014, https://www.rbc.ru/politics/07/12/2014/54836c87cbb20f5a946bd2d7

120. 'France: No Weapons on Russian Cargo Plane Held in Nigeria', Voice of America, 8 December 2014, https://www.voanews.com/africa/france-no-weapons-russian-cargo-plane-held-nigeria

121. Conor Gaffey, 'Buhari: Nigeria Feels Syria's Pain', Newsweek, 5 February 2016, https://www.newsweek.com/muhammadu-buhari-nigeria-feels-syrias-pain-423441

122. 'Somalia Seeks Russia's Help in Fighting Al-Shabaab Terrorists, Strengthening Economy', Mogadishu Center for Research and Studies, 20 April 2016, http://mogadishucenter.com/English/2016/04/20/somalia-seeks-russias-help-in-fighting-al-shabaab-terrorists-strengthening-economy/

123. 'Russia, China Block Central African Republic Blacklist at the UN', Reuters, 23 April 2014, https://www.reuters.com/article/us-centralafrica-un-sanctions-idUSBREA3M1GA20140423

124. 'CAR is the Victim of West vs. China Fight for Influence in Africa, RT', 27 February 2014, https://www.rt.com/op-ed/central-african-republic-intervention-996/

125. 'Marshall Comins and Dmitry Yermolaev, Russia has the Ability to Help the Democratic Republic of Congo Reach its Potential', 23 October 2015, http://www.foreignpolicy.ru/en/analyses/russia-has-the-ability-to-help-democratic-republic-of-congo-reach-its-potential/

126. 'Treasury Increases Pressure on Russian Financier', US Department of the Treasury, 23 September 2020, https://home.treasury.gov/news/press-releases/sm1133

127. 'Press Release on Foreign Minister Sergey Lavrov's Meeting with President of the Central African Republic Fausatin-Archange Touadéra', Ministry

376

pp. [133–137]                    NOTES

of Foreign Affairs of the Russian Federation, 9 October 2017, https://www.mid.ru/en/maps/cf/-/asset_publisher/obfEMxF2i9RB/content/id/2894441

128. Interview with author, April 2021.
129. Interview with author, April 2021.
130. Ibid.
131. Interview with Beatriz Lockhart, a defence consultant with experience in CAR, January 2021.
132. Aaron Ross, 'How Russia Moved into Central Africa', Reuters, 17 October 2018, https://www.reuters.com/article/us-africa-russia-insight-idUSKCN1MR0KA
133. Anatoly Isaenko, 'Vesennyaya kampaniya na Mirnom fronte' (Spring Campaign on the Peace Front), 16 June 2017, https://nvo.ng.ru/forces/2017-06-16/9_952_oon.html


5.    RUSSIA REBUILDS ITS INFLUENCE IN NORTH AFRICA

1.    '"Bratya-musulmane" Ne Veli Sebya Kak Bratya' (Muslim Brothers did not Behave like Brothers), *Kommersant*, 7 December 2012, https://www.kommersant.ru/doc/2084267
2.    'Vybory v Yegipte: vozmozhno vozvrashcheniye shariata' (Elections in Egypt: Sharia Return Possible), RBC, 23 May 2012, https://www.rbc.ru/politics/23/05/2012/5703f7ea9a7947ac81a683a5
3.    Gevorg Mirazayan, 'Zelenoye budushcheye Yegipta' (Egypt's Green Future), *Russia in Global Affairs*, 5 September 2012, https://globalaffairs.ru/articles/zelenoe-budushhee-egipta/
4.    'Islamist Constitution Spurs Controversy in Egypt as Protests Grow', RT, 30 November 2012, https://www.rt.com/news/egypt-approves-constitution-941/
5.    'US is OK with Al-Qaeda in Syria, Libya- Egypt's Islamists won't be Problem, either', RT, 16 July 2012, https://www.rt.com/news/usa-egypt-muslim-military-233/
6.    'Levada Center data ranked Chechen militants as the most hostile group towards Russia in 2011 (48%) and second most hostile group after the United States in 2012 (39%)', Levada Center, Table 22.5, 2012–13, https://www.levada.ru/sites/default/files/2012_eng.pdf
7.    'Russia Supplying Arms to Syria Under Old Contracts: Lavrov', Reuters, 5 November 2012, https://www.reuters.com/article/us-syria-crisis-russia-arms/russia-supplying-arms-to-syria-under-old-contracts-lavrov-idUKBRE8A40BE20121105
8.    'Telephone Conversation with President of Egypt Mohammed Morsi', UNISPAL, 15 November 2012, https://unispal.un.org/DPA/DPR/UNISPAL.NSF/bc8b0c56b7bf621185256cbf005ac05f/88babec1d82c62c285257ab8004f1da7?OpenDocument

377

## NOTES

pp. [137–140]

9. 'Meeting with President of Egypt Mohammed Morsi', President of Russia, 27 March 2013, http://en.kremlin.ru/events/president/news/page/508

10. 'Putin vstretitsya s prezidentom Yegipta Morsi 19 aprelya v Sochi' (Putin will Meet with Egyptian President Morsi on April 19 in Sochi), RIA Novosti, 18 April 2013, https://ria.ru/20130418/933209665.html

11. 'Russian-Egyptian Talks', President of Russia, 19 April 2013, http://www.en.kremlin.ru/events/president/news/page/495

12. 'Egypt Invites Russia to Mine Uranium, Build Nuclear Power Plants', RT, 20 April 2013, https://www.rt.com/news/putin-morsi-nuclear-uranium-132/

13. Gabriela Baczynska, 'Russia may Ease Muslim Brotherhood Ban to Boost Egypt Ties', Reuters, 18 December 2012, https://www.reuters.com/article/us-egypt-politics-russia-idUSBRE8BH0VD20121218

14. Stephen Roll, 'Managing Change: How Egypt's Military Leadership Shaped the Transformation', *Mediterranean Politics*, Volume 21, 2016, pp. 23–43 provides an instructive explanation of the buildup to the 2013 coup and Sisi's consolidation of power. More recent assessments, such as Neil Ketchley, 'How Egypt's Generals Used Street Protests to Stage a Coup', *The Washington Post*, 3 July 2017, dispute the military's official statistics on the mass protests and claim that only 1 million Egyptians rallied against Morsi.

15. 'Russia Urges Political Forces in Egypt to Show Restraint', Xinhua, 4 July 2013, http://en.people.cn/90777/8311762.html

16. 'Sobytiya v Yegipte – revolyutsiya novogo tipa, a ne voyennyy perevorot: mneniye' (Events in Egypt: A Revolution of a New Type: Not a Military Coup), Regnum, 5 July 2013, https://regnum.ru/news/accidents/1680597.html

17. 'Politicheskaya Revolutsiya v Egipte: Etap Vtoroy Akualnyy Kommentariy' (Political Revolution in Egypt: Stage 2), IMEMO-RAN, 12 July 2013, http://old.imemo.ru/ru/publ/comments/2013/comm_2013_020.pdf

18. Yuri Matsarsky, 'Islamisty Yegipta prizyvayut 'borot'sya i umeret' za demokratiyu" (Egypt's Islamists Call to 'Fight and Die for Demcoracy'), *Izvestia*, 7 July 2013, https://iz.ru/news/553240

19. Michel Choussudovsky, 'Was Washington Behind Egypt's Coup d'État?', RT, 6 July 2013, https://www.rt.com/op-ed/us-egypt-muslim-brotherhood-704/

20. Denis Primakov, 'Padeniye Mursi' (The Fall of Morsi), Russian International Affairs Council, 22 August 2013, https://russiancouncil.ru/analytics-and-comments/analytics/padenie-mursi/

21. Pepe Escobar, "Bloodbath that is not Bloodbath': Why Egypt is Doomed', RT, 15 August 2013, https://www.rt.com/op-ed/egypt-protests-terror-muslim-brotherhood-526/

22. S.N. Volkov, 'Novyy etap v otnosheniyakh SSHA I Yegipta' (A New Stage in the Relationship Between the United States and Egypt), Institute of African Studies https://www.inafran.ru/node/1414

378

pp. [140–143]    NOTES

23. Mahdi Nazemroaya, 'Russian Bear Steps in as American Empire Unravels in the Middle East', RT, 5 December 2013, https://www.rt.com/op-ed/us-middle-east-russia-757/

24. 'Egypt Says Improving Ties with Russia is not a Snub to the US', *The Guardian*, 14 November 2013, https://www.theguardian.com/world/2013/nov/14/egypt-russia-us-relations-ally

25. 'Egypt and Syria to Keep Consulate Relations: FM Spokesperson', *Al-Ahram*, 7 July 2013, https://english.ahram.org.eg/NewsContent/1/64/75951/Egypt/Politics-/Egypt-and-Syria-to-keep-consulate-relations-FM-spo.aspx

26. 'Rossiya i Yegipet podpisali voyennyye kontrakty na 3 milliarda dollarov' (Russia and Egypt Signed Military Contracts for $3 Billion), *Aviation Express*, 14 February 2014, https://www.aex.ru/news/2014/2/14/116928/

27. 'Budushchiy prezident Yegipta posetil Rossiyu' (Future Egyptian President Paid Visit to Russia), *Kommersant*, 13 February 2014, https://www.kommersant.ru/doc/2407255

28. 'Ministr oborony Yegipta stremitsya k oruzheynoy sdelke s Rossiyey pered prezidentskimi vyborami' (Egyptian Defence Minister Seeks Arms Deal with Russia Before Presidential Election), Topwar.ru, 19 February 2014, https://topwar.ru/39981-ministr-oborony-egipta-stremitsya-zaklyuchit-oruzheynuyu-sdelku-s-rossiey-do-prezidentskih-vyborov.html

29. Irina Mokhova, 'Novyye vekhi vo vneshney politike Yegipta' (New Landmarks for Egyptian Foreign Policy), *Nezavisimaya Gazeta*, 3 March 2014, https://www.ng.ru/courier/2014-03-03/9_egypt.html

30. Ibid.

31. 'An Egyptian-Russian Rapprochement', Middle East Policy Council, 2013, https://mepc.org/commentary/egyptian-russian-rapprochement

32. Mahmoud Salem, 'Egypt Caught Between Saudi Arabia, Russia', Al-Monitor, 11 March 2014, https://www.al-monitor.com/originals/2014/03/egypt-russia-saudi-arabia-leverage-ties.html

33. Ibid.

34. Paul Saunders, 'Gazprom Deal Boosts Russia-Egypt Ties', Al-Monitor, 19 May 2014, hhttps://www.al-monitor.com/originals/2014/05/gazprom-russia-egypt-obama-ties-gas-export.html

35. 'Egypt Obtains Russian Gas at Lower Price', *Daily News Egypt*, 13 May 2014, https://dailynewsegypt.com/2014/05/13/egypt-obtains-russian-gas-lower-prices/

36. Michelle Dunne and Andrew Miller, 'Losing Egypt to Russia Isn't the Real Problem – But the Collapse Is', Carnegie Endowment for International Peace, 20 July 2018, https://carnegieendowment.org/2018/07/20/losing-egypt-to-russia-isn-t-real-problem-but-collapse-is-pub-76918

37. Mark Katz, 'Sisi and Russia: No Replacement for the United States', Atlantic Council, 5 June 2014, https://www.atlanticcouncil.org/blogs/menasource/sisi-and-russia-no-replacement-for-the-united-states/

379

NOTES pp. [143–146]

38. 'Russia to Lend Egypt $25 Billion to Build Nuclear Power Plant', Reuters, 19 May 2016, https://www.reuters.com/article/us-egypt-russia-nuclear-idUSKCN0YA1G5
39. Anna Borschevskaya, 'Free Trade Zone in Context of Growing Russia-Egypt Ties', *Forbes*, 25 August 2017, https://www.forbes.com/sites/annaborshchevskaya/2017/08/25/free-trade-zone-in-context-of-growing-russia-egypt-ties/?sh=24e4d7af7911
40. Ibid.
41. 'Egypt Says Russia's Intervention in Syria Will Counter Terrorism', Reuters, 3 October 2015, https://www.reuters.com/article/mideast-crisis-syria-egypt-idAFL3N1230CF20151003
42. May Ghaith, 'altadakhul alruwsiu fi suria 'abeaduh wasinariuhatih' (Russian Intervention in Syria: Dimensions and Scenarios), Egyptian Institute for Political and Strategic Studies, 25 November 2015, https://eipss-eg.org/التدخل_الروسي_في_سوريا_الأبعاد_والسيناريوهات/
43. Interview with Ahmed Dahshan, April 2021.
44. Ibid.
45. Ibid.
46. Muhammad Mansour, 'Arab Countries' Conflicting Views on Russian Intervention in Syria', The Washington Institute, 4 November 2015, https://www.washingtoninstitute.org/policy-analysis/arab-countries-conflicting-views-russian-intervention-syria-0
47. 'Rossiya gotova priglasit' Yegipet prisoyedinit'sya k dogovorennostyam po Sirii' (Russia is Ready to Invite Egypt to Join the Agreements on Syria), RIA Novosti, 29 December 2016, https://ria.ru/20161229/1484904500.html
48. 'Egypt Refutes Media Report on Participation in Astana Talks', *Egypt Today*, 27 October 2017, https://www.egypttoday.com/Article/1/29765/Egypt-refutes-media-report-on-participation-in-Astana-talks
49. Interview with Mohammed Orabi, June 2021.
50. Ahmed Megahid, 'Grozny Conference Stirs Criticism of Al-Azhar', *The Arab Weekly*, 18 September 2016, https://thearabweekly.com/grozny-conference-stirs-criticism-al-azhar
51. Sergey Balmasov, 'Algeria: Russia's Crisis-Proof Partner in the Arab World', Russian International Affairs Council, 1 June 2016, https://russiancouncil.ru/en/analytics-and-comments/analytics/alzhir-antikrizisnyy-partner-rossii-v-arabskom-mire/
52. Boris Dolgov, 'Arabskiy Magrib i interesy Rossii' (Arab Maghreb and Russian Interests), *Russia and the Muslim World*, 2012, pp. 174–86.
53. Alexei Anishchuk, 'Russia's Putin Says Regional Revolts Led to Algeria Attack', Reuters, 24 January 2013, https://www.reuters.com/article/uk-sahara-crisis-russia/russias-putin-says-regional-revolts-led-to-algeria-attack-idUKBRE90N0NE20130124
54. Interview with Dalia Ghanem, December 2020.

380

pp. [147–149]   NOTES

55. 'aikhtilaf fi tafsir mawqif aljazayir min altadakhul alruwsii fi suria' (A Difference in Interpretation of Algeria's Position on the Russian Intervention in Syria), Quds Press International News Agency, 26 October 2015, http://www.qudspress.com/index.php?page=show&id=11678

56. Tawfik Rebbakhi, 'Masirat rusia fi suria' (Russia's Walk in Syria), Al-Quds Al-Arabi, 5 October 2015, https://www.alquds.co.uk/%EF%BB%BF نزهة-روسية-في-سوريا/

57. Quds Press International News Agency, 26 October 2015.

58. 'Naryshkin: vmeshatel'stvo SSHA i NATO v zhizn' Livii, Sirii, Iraka ne mozhet byt' opravdano' (Naryshkin: US and NATO Intervention in the Life of Libya, Syria and Iraq Cannot be Justified), TASS, 4 November 2015, https://tass.ru/politika/2407681

59. 'Eksport mira' (Exporting the World), *Rossiyskaya Gazeta*, 5 November 2015, provides a detailed account of Naryshkin's trips to Algeria and Tunisia, https://rg.ru/2015/11/06/naryshkin.html

60. Sergey Balsamov, 'Alzhir pytayetsya razreshit' konflikt mezhdu Rossiyey I Turtsiyey' (Algeria Tries to Resolve Conflict Between Russia and Turkey), The Institute of the Middle East, 10 April 2016, http://www.iimes.ru/?p=28000

61. Ibid.

62. Alexey Nikolsky, 'Poltory sotni tankov T-90S postavyat v Alzhir i Turkmenistan' (One and a Half Hundred T-90S Tanks will be Delivered to Algeria and Turkmenistan), *Vedomosti*, 14 February 2012, https://www.vedomosti.ru/politics/articles/2012/02/14/500_mln_na_tankah

63. Anna Borschevskaya, 'The Tactical Side of Russia's Arms Sales to the Middle East', Jamestown Foundation, 9.

64. 'Algeria Orders Two Kilo Submarines from Russia', Defence Web, 27 June 2014, https://www.defenceweb.co.za/sea/sea-sea/algeria-orders-two-kilo-submarines-from-russia/

65. Alexey Nikolsky, 'Podpisan kontrakt na litsenzionnoye proizvodstvo tankov T-90 v Alzhire' (A Contract was Signed for the Licensed Production of T-90 Tanks in Algeria), *Vedomosti*, 20 February 2015, https://www.vedomosti.ru/newspaper/articles/2015/02/20/tank-alzhirskoi-sborki

66. Peter Wezeman, et al, 'Trends in International Arms Transfers', SIPRI, 2019, sites/default/files/2020-03/fs_2003_at_2019_0.pdf

67. Alec Luhn, 'Russia's Campaign in Syria Leads to Arms Sale Windfall', *The Guardian*, 29 March 2016, https://www.theguardian.com/world/2016/mar/29/russias-campaign-in-syria-leads-to-arms-sale-windfall

68. Mansur Mirovalev, 'Syria's War: A Showroom for Russian Arms Sales', Al Jazeera, 6 April 2016, https://www.aljazeera.com/news/2016/4/6/syrias-war-a-showroom-for-russian-arms-sales

69. 'Russia Delivered Jets, Tanks and Missiles to Africa in 2017', Defence Web, 14 March 2018, https://www.defenceweb.co.za/industry/industry-

381

NOTES                              pp. [149–151]

industry/russia-delivered-jets-tanks-and-missiles-to-africa-in-2017/?catid
=7%3AIndustry&Itemid=116

70. 'Russia-Algeria: An Effective Strategic Partnership', St Petersburg International Economic Forum, 2016, https://forumspb.com/en/news/news/rossiya-alzhir-effektivnoe-strategicheskoe-partnerstvo/

71. 'Russia and Algeria Have Signed an Agreement Concerning the Cooperation in the Peaceful Uses of Atomic Energy', Rosatom, 4 September 2014, https://rosatom-easteurope.com/en/press-centre/highlights/russia-and-algeria-have-signed-an-agreement-concerning-the-cooperation-in-the-peaceful-uses-of-atomic-energy-12/

72. 'Rossiyskiye atomshchiki gotovy ostriot' pervuyu atomnuyu elektrostantsiyu v Alzhire' (Russian Nuclear Scientists are Ready to Build the First Nuclear Power Plant in Algeria), RIA Novosti, 3 September 2014, https://ria.ru/20140903/1022621373.html

73. 'Rosatom to Help Algeria in the Race to Build Africa's First Modern Nuclear Power Plant', *Global Construction Review*, 2 March 2016, https://www.globalconstructionreview.com/news/rosatom-help-algeria-race-b7uild-afric7as-fir7st/

74. Paul Saunders, 'Algeria Buys Russian Arms but Keeps Moscow at Arms Length', Al-Monitor, 25 March 2015, https://www.al-monitor.com/originals/2015/03/russia-algeria-weapons-gas-bouteflika-putin.html

75. 'Sergey Balmasov: Padeniye dobychi gaza v Alzhire vyzvano politicheskimi problemami' (Sergey Balsamov: The Drop in Gas Production in Algeria is Caused by Political Problems), ProGas, 19 February 2015, http://www.pro-gas.ru/news_interview/25.htm

76. Saunders, 2015.

77. *Rossiyskaya Gazeta*, 6 November 2015.

78. 'Full Text of the Throne Day Speech Delivered by King Mohammed VI', 30 July 2014, https://www.moroccoworldnews.com/2014/07/135688/full-text-of-the-throne-day-speech-delivered-by-king-mohammed-vi

79. 'Hamid Ait El Gaid, Morocco-Russia Relations: Who is More in Need of the Other?', *Morocco World News*, 27 December 2014, https://www.moroccoworldnews.com/2014/12/148258/morocco-russia-relations-who-is-in-more-need-of-the-other

80. 'Khaddad: Zapadnaya Sakhara rasschityvayet na Rossiyu v razreshenii krizisa' (Khaddad: Western Sahara Counts on Russia to Solve this Crisis), RIA Novosti, 27 February 2015, https://ria.ru/20150227/1050003421.html

81. 'alsahra' algharbiat turahib bialtaeawun mae alsharikat alruwsiat libina' ealaqat mustaqbalia' (Western Sahara Welcomes Cooperation with Russian Companies to Build Future Relations), Sputnik Arabic, 27 February 2015, https://arabic.sputniknews.com/business/201502271013595116/

82. 'Vitaly Naumkin, Russia Shows Interest in Western Sahara', Al-Monitor, 1 April 2015, https://www.al-monitor.com/originals/2015/04/russia-western-sahara-interest-polisario-active-role.html

pp. [152–154]  NOTES

83. Ekaterina Stepanova, 'Russia's Approach to the Conflict in Libya, the West-West Dimension and the role of the OSCE', p. 93, http://www.estepanova.net/Stepanova_Russia_Libya.pdf

84. 'Liviyskaya revolyutsiya pozhirayet svoikh ottsov' (Libyan Revolution Devours its Fathers), *Kommersant*, 13 September 2012, https://www.kommersant.ru/doc/2020715

85. 'Benghazi Attack Resulted from US "Allowing Arms Deliveries" to Militants', RT, 23 April 2014, https://www.rt.com/news/154316-benghazi-attack-us-fault/

86. Vladislav Senkovich, 'Is There an Alternative to the Western Patronage of Libya?', Russian International Affairs Council, 7 February 2012, https://russiancouncil.ru/en/analytics-and-comments/analytics/is-there-an-alternative-to-the-western-patronage-of-libya/

87. 'Rossiya postavit Livii vooruzheniye i lichnyy sostav' (Russia will Supply Libya with Weapons and Personnel), *Kommersant*, 10 September 2013, https://www.kommersant.ru/doc/2275806

88. 'Ghaith Shennib and Thomas Grove, Russian Embassy in Libya Comes under Fire, Attack Repelled', Reuters, 2 October 2013, https://www.reuters.com/article/uk-libya-embassy-attack-idUKBRE99112E20131002

89. 'Foreign Ministry Denies Russian Diplomats Were Advised to Quit Libya', *The Libya Herald*, 4 October 2013, https://www.libyaherald.com/2013/10/04/foreign-minister-denies-russian-diplomats-were-advised-to-quit-libya/#axzz2g2c4kUTL

90. Interview with Russian academic, 2018.

91. 'Libya's Ongoing Violence is "NATO-Exported Democracy"', RT, 18 May 2014, https://www.rt.com/op-ed/159836-libya-nato-exported-democracy/

92. 'General vygnal politikov' (General Kicked out Politicians), *Rossiyskaya Gazeta*, 20 May 2014, https://rg.ru/2014/05/20/perevorot.html

93. Vitaly Naumkin, 'Are there Any Prospects for Moscow-Libya Cooperation', Al-Monitor, 13 January 2015, https://www.al-monitor.com/originals/2015/01/russia-libya-cooperation-militia-islamists-egypt.html

94. 'liqa' siriyun fi alqahirat yumahid altariq limaerakat banghazi' (A Secret Meeting in Cairo Paves the Way for the Battle of Benghazi), Al-Araby Al-Jadeed, 14 February 2015, https://www.alaraby.co.uk/لقاء-سرّي-في-القاهرة-يمهد-لمعركة-بنغازي

95. Ayah Aman, 'Egypt Acts as Middleman for Russia-Libya Arms Deal', Al-Monitor, 19 February 2015, https://www.al-monitor.com/originals/2015/02/egypt-efforts-libya-army-russia-weapons.html

96. 'Cairo to Hail Russian Warships' Possible Help in Libya's Naval Blockade – Egyptian FM', TASS, 26 February 2015, https://tass.com/world/779784

97. Paul Saunders, 'Russia Indicates it Might Take Anti-IS Action in Libya', Al-Monitor, 11 March 2015, https://www.al-monitor.com/originals/2015/03/russai-naval-blockade-arms-libya-militas.html

383

NOTES pp. [154–157]

98. Alexander Bratersky, 'Vmeste protiv IGIL' (Together Against ISIS), Gazeta.ru, 19 February 2015, https://www.gazeta.ru/politics/2015/02/19_a_6418217.shtml
99. Ibid.
100. 'Renzi Appeals to Putin for Russian Help to Stabilize Libya', *Financial Times*, 5 March 2015, https://www.ft.com/content/c1ef0ec4-c35e-11e4-9c27-00144feab7de
101. 'Neskol'ko slov o prekrasnom, Putin i Rentsi obsudili Ukrainu, Liviyu i ital'yanskikh zhenshchin v Kremle' (A Few Words about the Beautiful: Putin and Renzi Discussed Ukraine, Libya and Italian Women in the Kremlin), Lenta.ru, 5 March 2015, https://lenta.ru/articles/2015/03/05/putin_renzi/
102. Interview with Deputy Director of the Faculty of World Economy and International Affairs at the Higher School of Economics, Dmitry Suslov, September 2018.
103. 'His Holiness Patriarch Kirill's Condolences over the Mass Killings of Christians in Libya', The Russian Orthodox Church, 17 February 2015, https://mospat.ru/en/news/50633/
104. 'Predstavitel' Russkoy Pravoslavnoy Tserkvi: kazn' yegipetskikh khristian – kul'minatsiya bezbozhiya' (Representative of the Russian Orthodox Church: The Execution of Egyptian Christians is the Culmination of Godlessness), RIA Novosti, 17 February 2015, https://ria.ru/20150217/1048239761.html?in=t
105. 'Lavrov: IS is Committing "Genocide" Against Christians', RFE/RL, 3 March 2015, https://www.rferl.org/a/russia-genocide-accusation-isis-christians-egypt/26879905.html
106. TASS, 26 February 2015.
107. Saunders, 11 March 2015.
108. Naumkin, 13 January 2015.
109. 'althaniu fi muqabalat khasat li RT: turkia tadeam al'iirhab fi ibya bi'amwal qataria' (Al-Thinni in an Exclusive Interview with RT: Turkey Supports Terrorism in Libya with Qatari Money), RT Arabic, 16 April 2015, https://arabic.rt.com/news/780235-الثني-نسعى-لتفعيل-الاتفاقيات-العسكرية-مع-روسيا-في-ظل-الظروف-التي-تعيشها-ليبيا/
110. Mustafa Fetouri, 'Libya Looks to Russia for Arms', Al-Monitor, 20 April 2015, https://www.al-monitor.com/originals/2015/04/libya-us-uk-france-russia-uneast-west-armament-deal-morocco.html
111. Patrick Wintour, 'Distribution of New Banknotes Raises Fears for Libyan Unity', *The Guardian*, 1 June 2016, https://www.theguardian.com/world/2016/jun/01/distribution-of-new-banknotes-raises-fears-for-libyan-unity
112. 'jadal hawl tibaeat milyarat dinar libiin fi rusia' (Controversy over Printing Billions of Libyan Dinars in Russia), Al Jazeera, 2 June 2016, https://www.aljazeera.net/ebusiness/2016/6/3/جدل-حول-طباعة-مليارات-الدنانير/

pp. [157–160]  NOTES

113. 'Remarks with Russian Foreign Minister Sergei Lavrov', 24 March 2016, https://2009-2017.state.gov/secretary/remarks/2016/03/255138.htm

114. 'The Special Role of Russia in Libya Re-Emerges', Menas Associates, 7 June 2016, https://sputniknews.com/world/201611301047994326-libya-russia-weapons-supplies/

115. Ravil Mustafin, 'Nuzhny li Rossii voyennyye bazy v Livii' (Does Russia Need Military Bases in Libya), *Nezavisimaya Gazeta*, 19 January 2017, https://www.ng.ru/world/2017-01-19/1_6906_2livia.html

116. 'Ekspert: Rossiyu prosyat pomoch' v stabilizatsii Livii? U kogo yeshche sprosit'?' (Expert: Russia is Being Asked to Stabilize Libya? Who Else to Ask), Sputnik Radio, 9 February 2017, https://radiosputnik.ria.ru/20170209/1487515145.html?in=t

117. Timur Khayrullin, 'Islamistskiye Proyekty Kak Instrument Borby Za Liderstvo v Arabskom Regione' (Islamist Projects as a Tool of Struggle for Leadership in the Arab Region), Institute of African Studies, 2018.

118. 'Libyan National Army to Require Russian Assistance When UN Arms Embargo Lifted', Sputnik, 30 November 2016, https://sputniknews.com/world/201611301047994326-libya-russia-weapons-supplies/

119. Interview with author, March 2021.

120. 'Russia "To Arm Libya's Haftar in $2bn Arms Deal"', *The New Arab*, 25 January 2017, https://english.alaraby.co.uk/news/russia-arm-libyas-haftar-2bn-weapons-deal

121. Mustafin, 2017.

122. Natalia Raibman and Alexey Nikolsky, 'Rossiyskiy spetsnaz i drony zamecheny u granitsy s Liviyey v Yegipte' (Russian Special Forces and Drones Spotted in Egypt Near the Border with Libya), *Vedomosti*, https://www.vedomosti.ru/politics/articles/2017/03/14/681051-liviei-egipte-spetsnaz

123. 'Malta Raises Alarm on Russia in Libya', *EUobserver*, 13 January 2017, https://euobserver.com/foreign/136537

124. 'Russia Constructing No Talks on Creating Military Bases in Libya', Sputnik, 22 January 2017, https://sputniknews.com/military/201701221049872087-russia-military-bases-libya/

125. Mustafin, 2017.

126. Interview with author, December 2020.

127. 'hal bada'at rusia altakhtit liqaeidat easkariat fi libia' (Has Russia Started Planning a Military Base in Libya?), Al-Araby Al-Jadeed, 14 December 2017, https://www.alaraby.co.uk/هل-بدأت-روسيا-تخطط-لقاعدة-عسكرية-في-ليبيا؟

128. Phil Stewart, 'Idrees Ali and Lin Noueihed, Exclusive: Russia Appears to Deploy Forces in Egypt, Eyes on Libya Role- Source', Reuters, 13 March 2017, https://www.reuters.com/article/us-usa-russia-libya-exclusive-idUSKBN16K2RY

129. Mattia Toaldo, 'Russia in Libya: War or Peace?', European Council on Foreign Relations, 2 August 2017, https://ecfr.eu/article/commentary_russia_in_libya_war_or_peace_7223/

385

## NOTES pp. [160–165]

130. 'V Sovfede oprovergli poyavleniye spetsnaza RF u granitsy s Liviyey' (The Federation Council Denied the Emergence of Special Forces of the Russian Federation Near the Border with Libya), Interfax, 14 March 2017, https://www.interfax.ru/world/553456

131. Mark Katz, 'Russian Policy Towards Libya: The Egyptian Factor', Atlantic Council, 22 March 2017, https://www.atlanticcouncil.org/blogs/menasource/russian-policy-toward-libya-the-egyptian-factor/

132. Interview with Senior Fellow at the Global Initiative Against Transnational Organized Crime Jalel Harchaoui, March 2019.

133. 'Exclusive: Russia's Secret Plan to Back Haftar in Libya', *Middle East Eye*, 30 January 2017, https://www.middleeasteye.net/news/exclusive-russias-secret-plan-back-haftar-libya

134. Yury Barmin, 'Russia Enters Libya's Conflict', Middle East Institute, 2 May 2017, https://www.mei.edu/publications/russia-enters-libyas-conflict

135. 'Libya: Moscow's Diplomatic Offensive', The Warsaw Institute, 13 October 2017, https://warsawinstitute.org/libya-moscows-diplomatic-offensive/

136. 'Den'gov: my ne vstretili nikogo, kto skazal by, chto Rossiya ne nuzhna Livii' (Dengov: We have not Met Anyone who Would Say that Russia is not Needed in Libya), Radio Sputnik, 6 March 2017, https://radiosputnik.ria.ru/20170306/1489400333.html

137. 'Libyan Settlement: Russian Diplomacy 2.0. Panel Discussion', Valdai Discussion Club, 12 December 2017, https://valdaiclub.com/multimedia/video/libyan-russian-diplomacy-

6. RUSSIA BECOMES A CONTINENT-WIDE GREAT POWER

1. 'V Sochi nachalsya pervyy sammit Rossiya-Afrika' (The First Russia-Africa Summit Has Begun in Sochi), RIA Novosti, 23 October 2019, https://ria.ru/20191023/1560100917.html

2. 'Sochi to Host First Russia-Africa Summit on 24 October', 28 May 2019, https://english.ahram.org.eg/NewsContent/1/0/335366/Egypt/0/Sochi-to-host-first-RussiaAfrica-Summit-on--Octobe.aspx

3. 'Interview: Isabel dos Santos "It's Not Africans Who are Taking Money Out of Africa"', RAVision, 16 July 2019, http://en.ravision2030.com/page6587224.html

4. 'Vladimir Putin vystupil na amite Rossiya – Afrika' (Vladimir Putin Spoke at the Russia-Africa Summit), The State Duma, 24 October 2019, http://duma.gov.ru/news/46708/

5. 'First Russia-Africa Summit Sirus Park of Science and Art in Sochi, Russia', African Union, 24 October 2019, https://au.int/ar/node/37574

6. Lorenzo Simoncelli, 'Russia-Africa: What has been Agreed at the Sochi Summit', ISPI, 15 November 2019, https://www.ispionline.it/it/pubblicazione/russia-africa-what-has-been-agreed-sochi-summit-24401

pp. [165–168]          NOTES

7.  Sergei Sukhankin, 'The Kremlin's Controversial Soft Power in Africa (Part One)', Jamestown Foundation, 4 December 2019, https://jamestown.org/program/the-kremlins-controversial-soft-power-in-africa-part-one/

8.  'Prezident Malavi prizyvayet polozhit' konets ekspluatatsii Afriki' (Malawi's President Calls for End of Exploitation of Africa), TASS, 24 October 2019, https://tass.ru/mezhdunarodnaya-panorama/7040579

9.  Julian Borger, 'US Unveils New Africa Policy to Counter 'Predatory' Russia and China', *The Guardian*, 13 December 2018, https://www.theguardian.com/us-news/2018/dec/13/us-john-bolton-africa-policy-russia-china

10.  Salem Solomon, 'Russia Seeks Stronger, More Positive Ties to Africa at Sochi Summit', Voice of America, 23 October 2019, https://www.voanews.com/europe/russia-seeks-stronger-more-positive-ties-africa-sochi-summit

11.  Diana Stacey Correll, 'How AFRICOM Plans to Counter Rusisan, Chinese Influence in Africa', *Military Times*, 20 January 2020, https://www.militarytimes.com/news/your-military/2020/01/20/how-africom-plans-to-counter-russian-chinese-influence-in-africa/

12.  Interview with author, October 2021.

13.  Ibid.

14.  Ibid.

15.  'Putin Informs Macron of the Results of Russia-Africa Summit Held in Sochi', TASS, 26 October 2019, https://tass.com/politics/1085468

16.  Alexandra Archangelskaya, 'Russia-Africa: Dilemmas and Opportunities for the EU', January 2020, http://eu-russia-expertnetwork.eu/en/analytics/euren-brief-14

17.  Andrei Kortunov, 'We Should Exempt Africa from Russia-UK Geopolitical Confrontation', Russian International Affairs Council, 28 October 2019, https://russiancouncil.ru/en/analytics-and-comments/analytics/we-should-exempt-africa-from-the-russia-uk-geopolitical-confrontation/?sphrase_id=31993820

18.  Barnaby Fletcher, 'Britain and Russia in Africa: Not Necessarily at Loggerheads', RUSI, 31 October 2019, https://rusi.org/explore-our-research/publications/commentary/britain-and-russia-africa-not-necessarily-loggerheads

19.  Cui Heng, 'Russia Seeks to Spread Footprint in Africa', *Global Times*, 8 November 2019, https://www.globaltimes.cn/content/1169421.shtml

20.  Liu Naiya, 'É fēi suǒ qì fēnghuì jí qí duì zhōng fēi guānxì de jièjiàn' (The Russia-Africa Sochi Summit and its Reference to Sino-African Relations), Chinese Academy of Social Sciences, Number 24, 2019.

21.  Qing Xiaoyun, 'Duìchōng shìjiǎo xià de èluósī duì fēi zhèngcè' (Russia's African Policy from the Perspective of Hedging), Shanghai Institute of International Studies, 2019.

22.  Wang Jiahao and Luo Jinyi, 'Èluósī zài fēizhōu de 'fǎn zhímín kǎ' hé 'zǐdàn' shìfǒu zúgòu?' (Are Russia's Anti-Colonial Cards and Bullets Sufficient),

387

## NOTES pp. [168–171]

*The New Lens*, 20 November 2019, https://www.thenewslens.com/article/127712

23. 'Talks with President of Egypt Abdelfattah el-Sisi', President of Russia, 17 October 2018, http://kremlin.ru/events/president/news/page/157

24. Menna Farouk, 'Egypt-Russia Partnership Deal Takes Bilateral Ties to New Heights', Al-Monitor, 25 October 2018, https://www.al-monitor.com/originals/2018/10/egypt-russia-cooperation-agreement-economic-relations.html

25. Dunne and Miller, 2018.

26. Marianna Belenkaya, 'Vsestoronniy visit' (A Well-Rounded Visit), *Kommersant*, 16 October 2018, https://www.kommersant.ru/doc/3772302

27. 'Transmashkholding ob'yavil planovuyu datu nachala postavok vagonov v Yegipet' (Transmashholding Announced the Planned Date of the Start of Deliveries of Wagons to Egypt), RIA Novosti, 9 April 2019, https://ria.ru/20190904/1558284454.html

28. Kirill Aleshin, 'Mesto I Rol Yegipta I Alzhira v Vneshney Ekonomicheskoy Politike Rossii' (Place and Role of Algeria and Egypt in Russian Foreign Economic Policy), *Afro-Asian Societies: History and Modernity*, Issue 4, 2018, pp. 131–43.

29. 'Meeting with President of Egypt President Abdelfattah el-Sisi', President of Russia, 23 October 2019, http://en.kremlin.ru/events/president/news/page/138

30. Marianna Belenkaya, 'Yegipetskiy samolet vstretila vodyanaya arka' (Egyptian Plane was Greeted by a Water Arch), Kommersant, December, 12 April 2018, https://www.kommersant.ru/doc/3600743

31. 'Putin Says UAE Interested in Participating in Joint Projects Between Russia and Egypt', TASS, 23 October 2019, https://tass.com/economy/1084703

32. Belenkaya, 2018.

33. 'bihudur eabd almuhsin salamat aitifaqiat taeawun bayn bawaabat alahram wasbutnik alruwsia' (In the Presence of Abdel Mohsen Salama, A Cooperation Protocol Between Al-Ahram Gate and Russian Sputnik), 19 September 2018, https://gate.ahram.org.eg/News/2013679.aspx

34. 'Muslim Brotherhood Trying to Organize Mass Protests in Egypt – Reports', Sputnik, 21 September 2019, https://sputniknews.com/20190921/muslim-brotherhood-trying-to-organise-mass-protests-in-egypt--reports-1076855886.html

35. Igor Subbotin, 'Yegiptyane prizvali svergnut' as-Sissi' (Egyptians Urged to Overthrow Al-Sissi), *Nezavisimaya Gazeta*, 24 September 2019, https://www.ng.ru/world/2019-09-24/1_2_7684_egypt.html

36. 'Pochemu Putin sobral v Sochi vsyu Afriku' (Why Putin Gathered All of Africa in Sochi), RIA Novosti, 23 October 2019, https://ria.ru/20191023/1560080503.html

37. 'bimusharakat misriat, qimat sutshi tueid siaghat 'utur jadidat lilshirakat al'afriqiat alruwsia' (With Egyptian Participation, the Sochi Summit

388

pp. [171–174]                    NOTES

Redrafts New Frameworks for the Africa-Russia Partnership), *Al-Shorouk*, 19 October 2019, https://www.shorouknews.com/news/view.aspx?cdate=19102019&id=52dfbd94-f947-4534-ba21-f84ee06dc7e9

38. 'khubara' yashrahun almakasib alaiqtisadiat alati haqaqatha misr wa'afriqia min qimat sutshi wa'abraz natayijiha' (Experts Explain the Economic Gains for Egypt and Africa from the Sochi Summit and its Most Prominent Results), *Al-Ahram*, 24 October 2019, https://gate.ahram.org.eg/News/2317062.aspx

39. Interview with Egyptian commentator Mohammed Magdy, April 2021.

40. 'Algerian Navy Commissions Additional Two Kilo-Class Submarines', *Naval Today*, 10 January 2019, https://www.navaltoday.com/2019/01/10/algerian-navy-commissions-additional-two-kilo-class-submarines/

41. V.V. Kudelev, 'iya v Alzhire: yanvar' 2019' (Situation in Algeria: January 2019), IIMES, 17 February 2019, http://www.iimes.ru/?p=53398

42. N. Zherlistsyna, 'Krizis Preyemstvennosti v Alzhire' (Continuing Crisis in Algeria), *Asia and Africa Today*, 2019, Issue 6, pp. 19–23.

43. Marianna Belenkaya, 'Russia Expects to Maintain Footprint in Algeria Despite Unrest', Al-Monitor, 21 March 2019, https://www.al-monitor.com/originals/2019/03/russia-algeria-cooperation-protests.html

44. Oleg Barabanov, 'Algeria: A Belated Arab Spring', Valdai Discussion Club, 4 March 2019, https://valdaiclub.com/a/highlights/algeria-arab-spring/

45. Levon Harutyunyan, 'Mest' islamistov: radikaly zakhvatili mirnyy protest v Alzhire' (Revenge of Islamists: Radicals Seize Peaceful Protests in Algeria), Gazeta.ru, 16 April 2021, https://www.gazeta.ru/politics/2021/04/16_a_13561550.shtml

46. Tatiana Shumeleva, 'Arabskaya vesna v Alzhire' (Arab Spring in Algeria), Russian International Affairs Council, 11 March 2019, https://russiancouncil.ru/analytics-and-comments/analytics/arabskaya-vesna-po-alzhirski/

47. Belenkaya, 2019.

48. Vasily Kuznetsov, 'Moscow Monitors Situation in Algeria as Protests Continue', Al-Monitor, 13 March 2019, https://www.al-monitor.com/originals/2019/03/russia-algeria-protests.html

49. Marianna Belenkaya, 'Revolyutsiya ili elitnaya sdelka. Kak uyezzhayet prezident Alzhira' (A Revolution or an Elite Bargain: How the President of Algeria Leaves), Carnegie Moscow Center, 4 April 2019, https://carnegie.ru/commentary/78781

50. Interview with Algerian analyst, December 2020.

51. Belenkaya, 21 March 2019.

52. Interview with author, November 2020.

53. Francis Ghiles, 'Russia and France Wary of Algeria's Hirak Six Months After Onset', *The Arab Weekly*, 24 August 2019, https://thearabweekly.com/russia-and-france-wary-algerias-hirak-six-months-after-onset

54. 'Algeria Seeks to Avoid US Sanctions over Russian Arms Purchases', *The Arab Weekly*, 5 October 2018, https://thearabweekly.com/algeria-seeks-avoid-us-sanctions-over-russian-arms-purchases

NOTES pp. [174–177]

55. Interview with Algerian political analyst Bouda Brahim, August 2021.
56. 'Sergey Lavrov poshel po almaznomu sledu' (Sergey Lavrov Followed the Diamond Trail), *Kommersant*, 6 March 2018, https://www.kommersant.ru/doc/3566668
57. Katya Golubkova and Dmitry Antonov, 'VTB Says in Talks to Prolong Angola's $1.5 Billion Loan to 10 Years', Reuters, 22 January 2018, https://www.reuters.com/article/us-russia-vtb-angola-idUSKBN1FB0YC
58. 'Russia Loses Contact with Angolan Satellite After Launch', RFE/RL, 28 December 2017, https://www.rferl.org/a/russia-launches-first-angola-telecom-satellite-using-ukrainian-rocket-/28940993.html
59. 'Angola Satellite Inoperative, Russia to Build Another One', Reuters, 23 April 2018, https://www.reuters.com/article/us-space-angola-russia-idUSKBN1HU26Q
60. 'Russia and Angola Sign Agreement on Space Research, Space in Africa', 23 April 2019, https://africanews.space/russia-and-angola-sign-agreement-on-space-research/
61. Elena Teslova, 'Russia, Angola Sign Cooperation Deals in Moscow', Anadolu Agency, 4 April 2019, https://www.aa.com.tr/en/africa/russia-angola-sign-cooperation-deals-in-moscow/1442652
62. Dadayan Stepanovich and Anikeev Vladimirovich, 'Voyenno-Tekhnicheskoye Sotrudnichestvo Rossiyskoy Federatsii I Respubliki Angola' (Military-Technical Cooperation of the Russian Federation and Republic of Angola), Moscow University for the Humanities and Economics, 2019, pp. 37–47.
63. 'Alrosa and Endiama Signed a Memorandum of Understanding', Alrosa, 4 April 2019, http://eng.alrosa.ru/alrosa-and-endiama-signed-a-memorandum-of-understanding/
64. 'João Lourenço: Angola has Always Received Maximum Support from Russia', The State Duma, 3 April 2019, http://duma.gov.ru/en/news/30236/
65. Rui Santos Verde, *Angola at the Crossroads: Between Kleptocracy and Development*, London: Bloomsbury, 2021.
66. 'Vlasti Angoly khotyat, chtoby Rossiya razvivala otnosheniya so stranami Afriki' (Angolan Authorities Want Russia to Develop Relations with African Countries), RIA Novosti, 24 October 2019, https://ria.ru/20191024/1560186831.html?in=t
67. 'Na ekonomicheskom forume 'Rossiya-Afrika' v Sochi podpisan memorandum o vzaimoponimanii mezhdu OOO "LEONARDA-SERVIS" i kompaniyey: Gruppo PITABEL Angola' (At the Economic Forum 'Russia-Africa' in Sochi, a memorandum of understanding was signed between LLC Leonarda Service and Company Gruppo Pitabel), TASS, 23 October 2019, https://www.exportcenter.ru/press_center/news/na-ekonomicheskom-forume-rossiya-afrika-v-sochi-sostoyalos-podpisanie-memoranduma-o-vzaimoponimanii-/

pp. [178–182]

NOTES

68. Estelle Maussion, 'Life After Power: The Bitter Exile of Angola's Ex-President Dos Santos', 30 August 2019, https://www.theafricareport.com/16712/life-after-power-the-bitter-exile-of-angolas-ex-president-dos-santos/

69. 'First Diamonds from Angola's New Pipe to Arrive Mid-2020: Alrosa', Reuters, 11 December 2019, https://www.reuters.com/article/us-alrosa-africa-idUSKBN1YF1PP

70. Maslov and Zaytsev, 2018.

71. Blessing Zulu, 'Zimbabwe Hopeful of Better Deals from Russia-Africa Summit Amid Opposition Skepticism', Voice of America, 23 October 2019, https://www.voazimbabwe.com/a/russia-africa-summit-skepticism/5135089.html

72. 'Sochi Summit Breaks New Ground', *Zimbabwe Herald*, 19 October 2019. https://www.herald.co.zw/sochi-summit-breaks-new-ground/

73. 'Russian Consortium to Invest over $500bln into PGM Deposit in Zimbabwe', TASS, 24 October 2019, https://tass.com/economy/1085093

74. 'Alrosa and ZCDC Joint Venture Starts Prospecting for Diamonds in Zimbabwe', Alrosa, 21 July 2020, http://eng.alrosa.ru/alrosa-and-zcdc-joint-venture-starts-prospecting-for-diamonds-in-zimbabwe/

75. Tinashe Karizia, 'Russian-Made Fighter Jets for Zim's Military', *Zimbabwe Independent*, 10 January 2020, https://www.theindependent.co.zw/2020/01/10/russian-made-fighter-jets-for-zims-military/

76. Tinashe Karizia, 'Zim Diamonds for Russian Fuel', 30 January 2020, https://allafrica.com/stories/202001310661.html

77. Vladimir Shubin, 'O smene top-menedzhmenta v YUAR' (On the Change of Top Management in South Africa), IMEMO, 2019, https://www.imemo.ru/news/events/text/o-smene-visshego-rukovodstva-v-yuar?p=4

78. 'South Africa's Economic and Social Decline the Worst of Nations not at War', RT, 17 April 2019, https://www.rt.com/business/456816-south-africa-worst-decline/

79. 'As it re-elects hopeless ANC again, do we finally admit that post-apartheid South Africa has failed?', RT, 11 May 2019, https://www.rt.com/news/459023-south-africa-anc-failure-apartheid/

80. Ibid.

81. "Don't Ever Vote for White Person': South African ANC Leader's Race-Based Call Discussed on RT', RT, 18 April 2019, https://www.rt.com/news/456897-south-africa-race-voting/

82. "A Matter of Life and Death': 15,000 White South African Farmers Seek Refuge in Russia, Report Says', RT, 9 July 2018, https://www.rt.com/business/432375-russia-south-africa-farmers/

83. 'First 50 Families of Farmers from South Africa May Soon Resettle in Russia', RT, 20 July 2018, https://www.rt.com/business/433772-boers-sa-russia-resettlement/

84. Amie Ferris-Rotman, 'Why Russia is Wooing South Africa's White Farmers?', *The Washington Post*, 23 September 2018, https://www.washingtonpost.com/world/europe/why-russia-is-wooing-south-africas-white-

NOTES    pp. [182–184]

farmers/2018/09/23/3308a7c4-b6a3-11e8-ae4f-2c1439c96d79_story.
html

85. 'Pochemu afrikanskiye fermery khotyat pereyekhat' v Rossiyu' (Why African Farmers Want to Move to Russia), *Vzglyad*, 5 July 2018.

86. 'New Home in Russia: White South African Farmer Seeks Safety as Land Seizure Looms', RT, 12 September 2018, https://www.rt.com/news/438318-south-african-farmer-russia-refuge/

87. 'South African Farmers Seek Refuge in Russia's Crimea', RT, 4 August 2018, https://www.rt.com/business/435085-south-african-boers-refuge-russia/

88. 'South African Farmers to Visit Russia's Crimea to Boost Ties while Facing Land Expropriation at Home', RT, 20 October 2018, https://www.rt.com/business/441815-south-african-farmers-crimea/

89. 'Boer Lives Matter: South African Farmers Storm Court Where Two Men Held Over Murder of White Farm Worker', RT, 6 October 2020, https://www.rt.com/news/502738-south-african-farmers-protest-killings/

90. Interview with Senior Fellow at the Global Initiative Against Transnational Organized Crime Gustavo de Carvalho, June 2021.

91. Interview with Professor of Political Science at University of the Free State Theo Neethling, June 2021

92. 'South Africa Scraps Russian Nuclear Plant Plans', RFI, 24 August 2019, https://www.rfi.fr/en/africa/20190824-south-africa-cancel-russia-nuclear-plant-order-economy-ramaphosa

93. Kevin Bloom, From Russia to Mantashe with Love: Chernobyl and the Culture of Climate Meltdown, *Daily Maverick*, 29 July 2019, https://www.dailymaverick.co.za/article/2019-07-29-from-russia-to-mantashe-with-love-chernobyl-and-the-culture-of-climate-meltdown/

94. Peter Fabricius, 'Naledi Pandor Urges SA Businesses to Seize Opportunities Russia Presents', *Daily Maverick*, 23 October 2019, https://www.dailymaverick.co.za/article/2019-10-23-naledi-pandor-urges-sa-business-to-seize-opportunities-russia-presents/

95. 'Russia Sends Nuclear Bombers to South Africa in "Friendly" Visit', *The Moscow Times*, 23 October 2019, https://www.themoscowtimes.com/2019/10/23/russia-sends-nuclear-bombers-south-africa-friendly-visit-a67838

96. 'Gromkiy signal: na Zapade otsenili vizit Tu-160 v YUAR' (A Loud Signal: the West Appreciated the Visit of Tu-160 to South Africa), *Rossiyskaya Gazeta*, 24 October 2019, https://rg.ru/2019/10/24/gromkij-signal-na-zapade-ocenili-vizit-tu-160-v-iuar.html

97. Lydia Misnik, "Prem'yera dlya vsey Afriki': rossiyskiye Tu-160 prizemlilis' v YUAR' ('Premiere for All Africa:' Russian Tu-160s Landed in South Africa), Gazeta.ru, 24 October 2019, https://www.gazeta.ru/army/2019/10/24/12774338.shtml

98. Shile Mayuso, "Shame on You': Ramaphosa Roasted for Sleeping at Russia-Africa Summit', *Sunday Independent*, 24 October 2019, https://www.iol.

pp. [184–187]  NOTES

co.za/news/eish/shame-on-you-ramaphosa-roasted-for-sleeping-at-russia-africa-summit-35820290

99. 'Ramaphosa Pleads Poverty as Putin – Again – Pitches that Big Nuke Deal', *Daily Maverick*, 25 October 2019, https://www.dailymaverick.co.za/article/2019-10-25-ramaphosa-pleads-poverty-as-putin-again-pitches-that-big-nuke-deal/

100. 'Joint Drills of China, Russia, South Africa Aimed to Ensure Stability – Spokesperson', TASS, 28 November 2019, https://tass.com/defense/1093747

101. Peter Fabricius, 'South Africa's Military Drills with Russia and China Raise Eyebrows', ISS Africa, 29 November 2019, https://issafrica.org/iss-today/south-africas-military-drills-with-russia-and-china-raise-eyebrows

102. 'Shoygu poslal signal na Zapad, otpraviv korabli VMF Rossii v YUAR' (Shoigu Sent a Signal to the West by Sending Ships of the Russian Navy to South Africa), Federal News Agency, 24 November 2019, https://riafan.ru/1229601-shoigu-napravil-zapadu-signal-poslav-korabli-vmf-rf-v-yuar

103. Fabricius, ISS Africa, 2019.

104. Interview with author, June 2021.

105. 'Nigeria Looks to Sign Military Cooperation Deal with Russia This Month', Reuters, 11 October 2019, https://www.reuters.com/article/us-russia-nigeria-military-idUSKBN1WQ20W

106. 'Russia-Africa Economic Conference Associated to the 26th Afreximbank Annual Meeting Took Place in Moscow', RAVision, 29 June 2019, http://en.ravision2030.com/page6612509.html

107. 'Prezident Nigerii rasskazal Putinu o zhelanii uchit'sya u Rossii' (The President of Nigeria Told Putin About the Desire to Learn from Russia), *Rossiyskaya Gazeta*, 23 October 2019, https://rg.ru/2019/10/23/reg-ufo/prezident-nigerii-zaiavil-putinu-o-zhelanii-uchitsia-u-rossii.html

108. 'Scepticism Follows Russia-Nigeria Deal Announcements', *African Business*, 9 December 2019, https://african.business/2019/12/economy/scepticism-follows-russia-nigeria-deal-announcements/

109. 'Lukoil Signs MoU with Nigeria's NNPC', *Russia Business Today*, 25 October 2019, https://russiabusinesstoday.com/energy/lukoil-signs-mou-with-nigerias-nnpc/

110. Interview with author, May 2021.

111. Ruth Olurounbi, 'Back to the Future as Nigeria Turns to Russia on Ajaokuta Steel Project', *The Africa Report*, 30 October 2019, https://www.theafricareport.com/19380/back-to-the-future-as-nigeria-turns-to-russia-on-ajaokuta-steel-project/

112. 'Nigeria: Senate Calls for Inclusion of Nuclear in Energy Mix', AFRCSIS, 23 November 2019, https://africsis.org/nigeria-senate-calls-for-inclusion-of-nuclear-in-energy-mix/

113. 'Russia and Cote d'Ivoire Discuss Business Relations and Participation in Russia-Africa Summit', SPIEF, 17 June 2019, https://forumspb.com/en/news/news/rossija-i-respublika-kot-divuar-obsudili-razvitie-torgovo-

393

NOTES pp. [188–191]

ekonomicheskih-otnoshenij-i-uchastie-v-sammite-%C2%ABrossija-afrika%C2%BB/

114. 'Rossiyskiye voyennyye voz'mut pod strazhu odnu iz samykh dikikh stran Afriki' (Russian Military Will Take Custody of One of the Wildest Countries in Africa), *Vzyglad*, 27 June 2019, https://vz.ru/world/2019/6/27/984338.html

115. 'Mali and Russia Strengthen Defence Ties', Defence Web, 16 January 2020, https://www.defenceweb.co.za/joint/diplomacy-a-peace/mali-and-russia-strengthen-defence-ties/

116. 'SMI soobshchili o planakh Rossii po sozdaniyu voyennoy bazy v Somali' (The Media Reported on Russia's Plans to Arrange a Military Base in Somalia), Lenta.ru, 9 April 2018, https://lenta.ru/news/2018/04/09/somalilend/

117. Stephen Blank, 'Sergei Lavrov's Africa Trip: Regional Promises and Global Ambitions', Jamestown Foundation, Volume 15, Issue 53, 9 April 2018, https://jamestown.org/program/sergei-lavrovs-africa-trip-regional-promises-and-global-ambitions/

118. 'Russia to Help Ethiopia's Nuclear Energy Ambitions', Xinhua, 10 March 2018, http://www.xinhuanet.com/english/2018-03/10/c_137028152.htm

119. Sebastien Malo, 'Russia, China Back Nuclear as Clean-Power Fix for Africa', Reuters, 7 February 2019, https://www.reuters.com/article/us-africa-energy-nuclearpower-idUSKCN1PW0KV

120. Arnaud Lefevre, 'Rosatom Will Prepare Ethiopian Specialists to Work in Nuclear Power', NBN, 8 March 2018, https://nbn.business/rosatom-will-prepare-ethiopian-specialists-work-nuclear-power/

121. 'Russian Oil Firm Signs Initial Exploration Deal with South Sudan: Minister', Reuters, 20 November 2018, https://www.reuters.com/article/us-southsudan-gazprom-neft-idUSKCN1NP1ZS

122. 'Russia Accuses US of Undermining South Sudan Peace Deal', *Africa News*, 16 March 2019, https://www.africanews.com/2019/03/16/russia-accuses-us-of-undermining-south-sudan-peace-deal//

123. 'Rossiya ne podderzhala rezolyutsiyu SB OON o prodlenii sanktsiy protiv Eritrei' (Russia did not Support UN Security Council Resolution on the Extension of Sanctions against Eritrea), TASS, 14 November 2017, https://tass.ru/politika/4728663

124. Interview with author, July 2021.

125. 'Rossiya vedet peregovory o sozdanii logisticheskogo tsentra v portu Eritrei' (Russia is Negotiating the Creation of a Logistics Center in the Port of Eritrea), RIA Novosti, 31 August 2018, https://ria.ru/20180831/1527595506.html

126. 'Efiopiya i Eritreya podpisali mirnyy dogovor posle 20 let konflikta' (Ethiopia and Eritrea Sign Peace Treaty After 20 Years of Conflict), *Kommersant*, 17 September 2018, https://www.kommersant.ru/doc/3744538

127. Salem Solomon, 'Russia-Eritrea Relations Grow with Planned Logistics Center', 2 September 2018, https://www.voanews.com/africa/russia-eritrea-relations-grow-planned-logistics-center

394

pp. [191–194]     NOTES

128. Kristiana Denisenko, 'Ukradennyy Nil: Velikoye Vozrozhdeniye Efiopii' (The Stolen Nile: Ethiopia's Great Renaissance), Russian International Affairs Council, 27 October 2017, https://russiancouncil.ru/blogs/dkristiana/ukradennyy-nil-velikoe-vozrozhdenie-efiopii/

129. 'qimat sutshi hi khutwat astiratijiat litatwir alealaqat bayn rusia wamisr wa'afriqia' (Sochi Summit is a Strategic Step for Developing Relations Between Russia, Egypt and Africa), Al-Wafd, 21 October 2019, https://alwafd.news/أخبار-وتقارير/2602205-خبر-باء-قمة-سوتشي-خطوة-استراتيجية-لتطوير-العلاقات-بين-روسيا-ومصر-وإفريقيا

130. 'Russia's Kamaz Trucks Support WFP Operations in East and Central Africa', Relief Web, 18 June 2019, https://reliefweb.int/report/uganda/russias-kamaz-trucks-support-wfp-operations-east-and-central-africa

131. 'Tanzania Could Serve as Springboard for Russia's Expansion in East Africa, Minister Says', *Tanzania Invest*, 4 May 2016, https://www.tanzaniainvest.com/economy/trade/tanzania-could-serve-as-springboard-for-russias-expansion-in-east-africa

132. 'Russia Signs Deals with Tanzania, Uganda', *Nuclear Engineering International*, 9 November 2016, https://www.neimagazine.com/news/newsrussia-signs-deal-with-tanzania-and-uganda-5663831

133. 'Informal Session of the UN Security Council: China, Russia Reaffirm Support for Cameroon', *Cameroon Tribune*, 16 May 2019, https://www.cameroon-tribune.cm/article.html/25705/en.html/informal-session-of-un-security-council-china-russia-reaffirm-support-for-cameroon

134. 'Russian Lukoil in Cameroon to Negotiate the Reconstruction of Sonara', *Business in Cameroon*, 7 February 2020, https://www.businessincameroon.com/economy/0702-9948-russian-lukoil-in-cameroon-to-negotiate-the-reconstruction-of-sonara

135. 'Putin rasschityvayet na aktivizatsiyu sotrudnichestva mezhdu Rossiyey i DR Kongo' (Putin Expects to Intensify Cooperation between Russia and DR Congo), RIA Novosti, 23 October 2019, https://ria.ru/20191023/1560131398.html

136. 'Posol v Kinshase zayavil, chto dostovernoy informatsii o Rossii v DRK net' (There is No Reliable Information about Russia in the DRC, the Ambassador to Kinshasa Said), RIA Novosti, 8 February 2020, https://ria.ru/20200208/1564430324.html

137. Lydia Misnik, "Yest' chto zashchishchat": rossiyskikh voyennykh otpravyat v Kongo' (There is Something to Protect: The Russian Military will be Sent to Congo), Gazeta.ru, 23 May 2019, https://www.gazeta.ru/army/2019/05/23/12372901.shtml

138. 'Putin's Indicted Chef Descends on Africa, Mercenaries in Tow', *The Moscow Times*, 20 November 2018, https://www.themoscowtimes.com/2018/11/20/putin-indicted-chief-descends-on-africa-mercenaries-in-tow-a63541

395

139. Sergei Sukhankin, 'Russian Inroads into Central Africa', Jamestown Foundation, 23 April 2020, https://jamestown.org/program/russia-looks-for-inroads-into-central-africa-part-one/
140. Ibid.
141. Dmitry Lara and Elnar Bainazarov, 'My prizyvayem rossiyskiy biznes investirovat' v Kongo' (We Call on Russian Businesses to Invest in Congo), *Izvestia*, 19 April 2019, https://iz.ru/869621/dmitrii-laru-elnar-bainazarov/my-prizyvaem-rossiiskii-biznes-investirovat-v-kongo
142. Sukhankin, 23 April 2020.
143. Lara and Bainazarov, 2019.
144. O. Ndayisaba, 'Ugroza "Balkanizatsii" Demokraticheskoy Respubliki Kongo I Polozheniye Gosudarstv Velikogozernogo Regiona Afriki' (The Threat of the Balkanization of the Democratic Republic of the Congo and the Positions of States of the Great Lakes Region of Africa), *South Russian Journal of Social Sciences*, 2019.
145. *The Moscow Times*, 20 November 2018.
146. 'Rossiya schitayet vybory vekhoy v normalizatsii situatsii v DR Kongo' (Russia Considers the Elections a Milestone in the Normalization of the Situation in DR Congo), RIA Novosti, 22 January 2019, https://ria.ru/20190122/1549732624.html?in=t
147. Sukhankin, 23 April 2020.
148. Ibid.
149. Galina Dudina, 'Sovmestnaya rabota skrytaya i otkrytaya' (Collaboration Hidden and Open), *Kommersant*, 4 June 2018, https://www.kommersant.ru/doc/3649399#id2121503
150. Ibid.
151. 'Russia's Rosatom, Rwanda Sign Deal to Build Nuclear Science Center', Reuters, 24 October 2019, https://www.reuters.com/article/us-russia-rwanda-nuclear-idUSKBN1X32DV
152. 'Mezhgosudarstvennyye otnosheniya mezhdu Rossiyey i Respublikoy Kongo' (Interstate Relations between Russia and the Republic of Congo), RIA Novosti, 23 May 2019, https://ria.ru/20190523/1554818142.html
153. 'Congo Republic-Russia Deepen Military Cooperation as Sassou Visits', *Africa News*, 25 May 2019, https://www.africanews.com/2019/05/25/congo-republic-russia-deepen-military-cooperation-as-sassou-visits//
154. 'Russia's VEB May Invest in Moroccan Refinery', Congo Pipeline Projects, S & P Global Platts, 24 October 2019, https://www.spglobal.com/platts/en/market-insights/latest-news/oil/102419-russias-veb-may-invest-in-moroccan-refinery-congo-pipeline-projects
155. 'Russia Hopes to Sign Congo Oil Pipeline Deal Soon – Dep Energy Minister', Reuters, 17 December 2019, https://www.reuters.com/article/ozabs-uk-russia-congo-trade-idAFKBN1YL0RZ-OZABS

pp. [197–202]  NOTES

156. 'Russia Beats China to Uganda Energy Deal', *Energy Reporters*, 20 September 2019, https://www.energy-reporters.com/production/russia-beats-china-to-uganda-nuclear-deal/
157. 'Uganda Says Russia to Help it Develop Nuclear Energy', *The Moscow Times*, 19 September 2019, https://www.themoscowtimes.com/2019/09/19/uganda-says-russia-to-help-it-develop-nuclear-energy-a67338
158. 'Russia Delivers First Weapons to Central Africa's Gabon', *The Moscow Times*, 29 November 2019, https://www.themoscowtimes.com/2019/11/29/russia-delivers-first-weapons-to-central-africas-gabon-a68396

7. RUSSIA'S NEW POWER PROJECTION TACTICS IN AFRICA

1. Ruth Maclean, "Russians Have Special Status': Politics and Mining Mix in Guinea', *The Guardian*, 27 August 2019, https://www.theguardian.com/world/2019/aug/27/russians-have-special-status-politics-and-mining-mix-in-guinea
2. Ibid.
3. 'Rusal Starts Shipping Bauxite from Guinea's Dian-Dian Mine', Reuters, 19 June 2018, https://www.reuters.com/article/us-rusal-guinea-bauxite-idUSKBN1JF1UB
4. Polina Trifonova, 'Popavshaya pod sanktsii UC Rusal nachala dobychu na gigantskom mestorozhdenii v Gvineye' (UC Rusal, Which Fell Under Sanctions, Began Production at a Giant Field in Guinea), *Vedomosti*, 20 June 2018, https://www.vedomosti.ru/business/articles/2018/06/20/773257-rusal-gvinee
5. 'Gvineya obsuzhdayet peredachu Rusalu mestorozhdeniya, kotoroye mozhet stat' "gigantskim proyektom"' (Guinea is Discussing Transferring a Field to Rusal that Could Become a 'Giant Project'), TASS, 3 June 2018, https://tass.ru/ekonomika/5258926
6. 'Nordgold Increases Lefa Mine Investment Programme', 29 April 2019, https://www.nordgold.com/investors-and-media/news/nordgold-increases-lefa-mine-investment-programme/
7. 'Russian Ambassador Sparks Backlash with Suggestion Guinea Change Constitution', Reuters, 11 January 2019, https://www.reuters.com/article/us-guinea-russia-idUSKCN1P51SO
8. 'Guinée: la société civile prévoit un sit-in devant l'ambassade de Russie lundi 14 janvier' (Guinea: Civil Society Plans a Sit-in in Front of the Russian Embassy on Monday, January 14), Aminata, 11 January 2019, https://aminata.com/guinee-la-societe-civile-prevoie-un-sit-in-devant-lambassade-de-la-russie-lundi-14-janvier/
9. A.V. Andreev, 'Vneshnyaya politika prezidenta Gvinei Al'fa Konde' (Foreign Policy of the President Alpha Conde), *Problems of the National Strategy*, Number 3 (60), 2020, https://riss.ru/documents/881/65fdb6a5d1e2477e9925a92ab003c54a.pdf

NOTES pp. [203–205]

10. Florian Elabdi, 'Putin's Man in the Central African Republic: Is Valery Zakharov at the Heart of Russian Skulduggery?', *The Daily Beast*, 17 December 2018, https://www.thedailybeast.com/putins-man-in-the-central-african-republic-is-valery-zakharov-at-the-heart-of-russian-skulduggery

11. 'Russia Pledges Continued Support for Central African Republic Security Envoy', Sputnik, 24 October 2018, https://sputniknews.com/20181024/russia-car-security-support-1069157151.html

12. Alexander Gostev, 'Kreml' 'Bitva za Afriku'. Prigozhinskiye nayemniki teper' v dzhunglyakh' (Kremlin 'Fight for Africa': Prigozhin's Mercenaries are Now in the Jungle), Radio Svoboda, 25 April 2018, https://www.svoboda.org/a/29192123.html

13. Tim Lister, Clarissa Ward and Sebastian Shukla, 'More Questions than Answers in Murders of Russian Journalists in Africa', CNN, 16 August 2018, https://edition.cnn.com/2018/08/14/africa/russian-journalists-killed-khodorkovsky/index.html

14. Denis Korotkov, 'Khronika khorosho podgotovlennoy smerti' (Chronicle of Well-Prepared Death), *Novaya Gazeta*, 11 January 2019, https://novayagazeta.ru/articles/2019/01/10/79135-hronika-horosho-podgotovlennoy-smerti

15. 'No Signs of Torture on Bodies of Russian Journalists Killed in CAR – Moscow', Sputnik, 2 August 2018, https://sputniknews.com/20180802/russian-journalists-killing-central-african-republic-1066886887.html

16. Andrew Roth, 'Russian Journalists Killed in CAR Were Researching Military Firm', *The Guardian*, 1 August 2018, https://www.theguardian.com/world/2018/aug/01/russian-journalists-killed-central-african-republic-investigating-military-firm-kremlin-links

17. 'Things to Know About the Russian Mission in Central African Republic', Sputnik, 31 July 2018, https://sputniknews.com/20180731/russian-mission-car-1066832279.html

18. Vadim Zaitsev, Andrey Maslov and Yulia Timofeeva, 'Chto Rossiya delayet v Tsentral'noy Afrike' (What is Russia Doing in Central Africa, Carnegie Moscow Center, 8 October 2018, https://carnegie.ru/commentary/77022

19. Sputnik, 31 July 2018.

20. Interview with author, April 2021.

21. Irek Murtazin, 'Tsentral'noafrikanskaya figura' (Central African Figure), *Novaya Gazeta*, 17 December 2018, https://novayagazeta.ru/articles/2018/12/17/78964-tsentralnaya-afrikanskaya-figura

22. Christophe Chatelot, Isabelle Mandraud and Marie Borreau, 'A République centrafricaine, un pion sur l'échiquier russe' (The Central African Republic, A Pawn on the Russian Chessboard), *Le Monde*, 7 December 2018, https://www.lemonde.fr/international/article/2018/12/07/la-centrafrique-un-pion-sur-l-echiquier-russe_5394051_3210.html

23. 'Russia not Helping to Stabilise Central African Republic – France', Reuters, 28 October 2018, https://www.reuters.com/article/africa-russia-france-idINKCN1N20JJ

pp. [205–208]      NOTES

24. Patricia Huon and Simon Ostrovsky, 'Russia: The New Power in Central Africa', Coda Story, 19 December 2018, https://www.codastory.com/disinformation/russia-new-power-central-africa/
25. 'TSAR poprosil OON otmenit' embargo na postavki oruzhiya' (CAR Asked UN to Lift Arms Embargo), RIA Novosti, 23 October 2019, https://ria.ru/20191023/1560116736.html?in=t
26. 'Prezident TSAR nadeyetsya, chto Rossiya i dal'she budet postavlyat' v respubliku vooruzheniye' (CAR President Hopes that Russia will Continue to Supply Arms to Republic), RIA Novosti, 23 October 2019, https://ria.ru/20191023/1560117504.html?in=t
27. 'Russian Military Base May Appear in CAR – Defence Minister', Sputnik, 10 January 2019, https://sputniknews.com/20190110/russian-military-base-car-1071353197.html
28. Interview with author, April 2021.
29. 'Chto dast Rossii voyennaya baza v Tsentral'noy Afrike' (What will a Military Base in Central Africa Give Russia), Vzyglad, 25 October 2019, https://vz.ru/world/2019/10/25/1004996.html
30. Mieczyslaw Boduszynski and Christopher Lamont, 'Trump Changed US Policy Towards Libya. Here's Why it Matters', The Washington Post, 3 May 2019, https://www.washingtonpost.com/politics/2019/05/03/trump-changed-us-policy-towards-libya-this-is-why-it-matters/
31. 'Safir Libiun Sabq: Hadha Hu Hadaf Altadakhul Al Amrikii Fi Libia' (Former Libyan Ambassador: This is the Aim of the American Intervention in Libya), Sputnik Arabic, 23 February 2018, https://arabic.sputniknews.com/arab_world/201802231030291476-
32. Interview with Stephanie Williams, April 2021.
33. 'Povar i povar. Chast' chetvertaya. Rassledovaniye togo, kak Rossiya uchastvuyet v grazhdanskoy voyne v Livii' (Chef and Cook, Part Four: The Investigation of Russia's Involvement in the Libyan Civil War), Proekt, 12 September 2019, https://www.proekt.media/investigation/prigozhin-libya/
34. Interview with Moscow-based academic, 2018.
35. Maxim Suchkov, 'Russia's "Mulit-layered Pie" Policy on Libya', Al-Monitor, 9 December 2019, https://www.al-monitor.com/originals/2019/12/russia-libya-mercenaries-mfa.html
36. Tom Newton-Dunn, 'Russia Sends Troops and Missiles into Libya in Bid to Enforce Stranglehold on the West', The Sun, 8 October 2018, https://www.thesun.co.uk/news/7448072/russia-missiles-libya-warlord/
37. 'Novyy platsdarm: chto izvestno o perebroske rossiyskikh voyennykh v Liviyu' (New Foothold: What is Known about Transfer of Russian Military to Libya), 9 October 2018, https://www.rbc.ru/politics/09/10/2018/5bbc8efa9a7947544a676112
38. 'Libya Commander Haftar Visits Russia Ahead of Conference', Reuters, 7 November 2018, https://www.reuters.com/article/us-russia-libya-haftar-idUSKCN1NC2OB

399

NOTES pp. [208–211]

39. Kimberly Marten, 'Russia's Use of Semi-State Security Forces: The Case of the Wagner Group', *Post-Soviet Affairs*, Volume 35, 2019, p. 190.

40. Alec Luhn, 'Russian Mercenaries Back Libyan Rebel Leader as Moscow Seeks Influence in Africa', *The Telegraph*, 3 March 2019, https://www.telegraph.co.uk/news/2019/03/03/russian-mercenaries-back-libyan-rebel-leader-moscow-seeks-influence/

41. Interview with author, November 2020.

42. Interview with author, December 2020.

43. 'Russia Blocks UN Statement Singling Out Haftar's Forces', *The New Arab*, 8 April 2019, https://english.alaraby.co.uk/news/russia-blocks-un-statement-singling-out-haftar-forces

44. Igor Sledzevsky and Andrey Korotaev, 'Perspektivy stabilizatsii/destabilizatsii politicheskoy situatsii na Blizhnem Vostoke i Severnoy Afrike' (Prospects for Stabilization and Destabilization of the Political Situation in the Middle East and North Africa), p. 13.

45. 'Masdar Eskry: Qadat Alqaeidat Yasilun Min Suria Iilaa Gharb Libia' (A Military Source: The Arrival of Al-Qaeda Leaders from Syria to Western Libya), RT Arabic, 4 April 2019.

46. 'Rwytrz: Majmueat Musalahat Min Misratat Alliybiat Tatajih Iilaa Tarabulus Limuajahat Quwwat Hiftar' (Reuters: Armed Groups from Misrata, Libya, head to Tripoli to Confront Haftar's Forces), RT Arabic, 4 April 2019, https://arabic.rt.com/middle_east/1011396

47. Vitaly Naumkin and Vasily Kuznetsov, 'Dezhavyu: srednevekovyye motivy v sovremennoy arabskoy politicheskoy zhizni' (Déjà vu: Medieval Motives in Contemporary Arab Political Life, MGIMO University Bulletin, 2020.

48. Barbara Podrugina, 'Liviyskiy Feldmarshal Haftar Obyavil Sebya Glavoy Livii' (Libyan Field Marshal Haftar Declared Himself Head of Libya), *Vedomosti*, 28 April 2020, https://www.vedomosti.ru/politics/articles/2020/04/28/829227-liviiskii-feldmarshal

49. Kamran Hasanov, 'Budet Tam Baza Russkoy Pochemu Voyennye Napravlyavut Silu v Livii' (Will There Be a Russian There? Why the Military is Taking Power in Libya), Tsargrad, 5 April 2019, https://tsargrad.tv/articles/tam-budet-rossijskaja-baza-dlja-chego-voennye-berut-vlast-v-livii_193092

50. Sledvezsky and Korotayev, 2020.

51. 'Foreign Minister Siyala in Russia to Strengthen Cooperation Between the Two Countries', *Libya Observer*, 26 May 2018, https://www.libyaobserver.ly/inbrief/foreign-minister-siyala-russia-strengthen-cooperation-between-two-countries

52. Interview with Egyptian Foreign Ministry official, June 2021.

53. Interview with Egyptian journalist Mohamed Sabry, June 2021.

54. Ibid.

55. 'Russia Makes Move on Libya Peace as Clashes Rage Near Tripoli', *The Moscow Times*, 9 April 2019, https://www.themoscowtimes.com/2019/04/09/russia-makes-move-on-libya-peace-as-clashes-rage-near-tripoli-a65149

## NOTES

56. Interview with Jordanian journalist Osama al-Sharif, April 2021.
57. Interview with author, June 2020.
58. Ibid.
59. Gennady Koslov and Ruslan Shangarayev, 'Strategicheskye Interesy Rossii I Turtsii v Severnoy Afrike Na Primere Liviyskogo Konflikta' (Strategic Interests of Russia and Turkey in North Africa: The Example of the Libya Conflict), *Modern Science and Innovation*, 2020.
60. Interview with author, November 2020.
61. Ibid.
62. Interview with British Ambassador to Libya Peter Millett from 2015 to 2018, March 2021.
63. 'Zaderzhannyye v Livii rossiyane zanyalis' sotsiologicheskim issledovaniyem' (Russians Detained in Libya were Engaged in Sociological Research), Interfax, 5 July 2019, https://www.interfax.ru/world/668096
64. Irek Murtazin, 'Russkiy khunguz' (Russian Hunguz), *Novaya Gazeta*, 24 May 2020, https://novayagazeta.ru/articles/2020/05/24/85513-rossiyskie-hunguzy
65. Kirill Semenov, 'New Challenges for Moscow with Arrest of "Russian Trolls" in Libya', Al-Monitor, 11 July 2019, https://www.al-monitor.com/originals/2019/07/russia-libya-troll-factory-prigozhin-hifter.html
66. Interview with Moscow-based academic, 2018.
67. 'Sarraj not Interfering in Investigation of Cases Against Russians – Libyan Foreign Minister', Sputnik, 31 January 2020, https://sputniknews.com/world/202001311078193484-sarraj-not-interfering-in-investigation-of-cases-against-russians---libyan-foreign-minister/
68. 'A Small Price to Pay for Tripoli', Meduza, 2 October 2019, https://meduza.io/en/feature/2019/10/02/a-small-price-to-pay-for-tripoli
69. Ibid.
70. Marianna Belenkaya, 'Liviya zakupit u Rossii million tonn pshenitsy' (Libya Will Buy A Million Tons of Wheat from Russia), *Kommersant*, 23 October 2019, https://www.kommersant.ru/doc/4134519
71. Kirill Semenov, 'Sarraj Visit to Sochi Exposes Rival Russian Factions on Libya Policy', Al-Monitor, 26 October 2019, https://www.al-monitor.com/originals/2019/10/russia-libya-sarraj-hifter-tripoli-pmcs.html
72. Ibid.
73. Ibid.
74. 'Gosduma vystupila protiv uchastiya terroristov iz Livii v forume Rossiya-Afrika' (The State Duma Opposed the Participation of Terrorists from Libya at the Russia-Africa Forum), Federal News Agency, 17 October 2019, https://riafan.ru/1220470-v-gosdume-vystupili-protiv-uchastiya-terroristov-iz-livii-na-forume-rossiya-afrika
75. Murtazin, 2020.
76. Interview with author, September 2021.
77. Ibid.

NOTES pp. [216–217]

78. Irina Alksnis, 'Erdoğan khochet povtorit' siriyskiy uspekh Moskvy v Livii' (Erdoğan Wants to Repeat Moscow's Syria Success in Libya), RIA Novosti, 30 December 2019, https://ria.ru/20191230/1562995771.html?in=t

79. 'Ekspert: Turtsiya ne smozhet pozvolit' sebe masshtabnuyu operatsiyu v Livii' (Expert: Turkey Will Not be able to Afford a Large-Scale Operation in Libya), RIA Novosti, 27 December 2019, https://ria.ru/20191227/1562943632.html?in=t

80. Danielle Ryan, 'Imperial Delusion: Turkey Sending Troops to Libya Would be No Solution to the Chaos Caused by the 2011 NATO Intervention', RT, 2 January 2020, https://www.rt.com/news/477343-turkey-libya-erdogan-imperial-ambitions/

81. 'Turkish Troops Start Moving Towards Libya', RT, 6 January 2020, https://www.rt.com/news/477531-turkish-troops-moving-libya/

82. Hakki Ocal, 'Russia is Playing with Fire in Libya', *Daily Sabah*, 23 December 2019, https://www.dailysabah.com/columns/hakki-ocal/2019/12/23/russia-playing-with-fire-in-libya

83. 'Russia Opposes Meddling in Libyan Affairs as Turkey Vows to Send Troops to Conflict-Torn Country', Sputnik, 26 December 2019, https://sputniknews.com/20191226/turkish-president-erdogan-joins-tunisia-in-backing-sarraj-government-in-libya-1077868706.html

84. 'Libya's Haftar Leaves Moscow Without Signing Ceasefire Agreement', Al Jazeera, 14 January 2020, https://www.aljazeera.com/news/2020/1/14/libyas-haftar-leaves-moscow-without-signing-ceasefire-agreement

85. Gennady Petrov, 'Khaftar i Saradzh razgovarivali cherez posrednikov' (Haftar and Serraj Talked Through Intermediaries), *Nezavisimaya Gazeta*, 13 January 2020, https://www.ng.ru/world/2020-01-13/6_7766_libya.html

86. 'UAE Embassy in Moscow Obstructed Libya Ceasefire', Anadolu Agency, 15 January 2020, https://www.aa.com.tr/en/middle-east/uae-embassy-in-moscow-obstructed-libya-cease-fire/1703346

87. 'Russia and Turkey Set Perfect Example in Libya, Other Countries Should Join the Initiative- Observers', Sputnik, 15 January 2020, https://sputniknews.com/20200115/russia--turkey-set-perfect-example-in-libya-other-countries-should-join-the-initiative--observers-1078037722.html

88. 'With their Statehood Destroyed by NATO, Libya's Warring Sides Should Come to Terms, Not Fight Each Other – Lavrov', RT, 14 January 2020, https://www.rt.com/news/478196-nato-destroyed-libya-statehood/

89. Sputnik, 15 January 2020.

90. 'Russia Managing Libya Conflict "At Highest Level", Turkey's Erdoğan Says', *The Moscow Times*, 17 February 2020, https://www.themoscowtimes.com/2020/02/17/russia-managing-libya-conflict-at-highest-level-turkeys-erdogan-says-a69315

91. 'Afrikanskiy tur: pochemu Turtsiya terpit ubytki v Livii' (African Tour: Why Turkey is Suffering Losses in Libya), *Izvestia*, 2 March 2020, https://

pp. [218–220]  NOTES

iz.ru/982284/anton-lavrov-bogdan-stepovoi/afrikanskie-gastroli-pochemu-turtciia-neset-poteri-v-livii

92. Ibid.

93. 'Meeting with President of Sudan Omar al-Bashir', President of Russia, 14 July 2018, http://en.kremlin.ru/events/president/news/page/194

94. 'Peskov napravil v Minoborony vopros o pribytii prezidenta Sudana v Siriyu na Tu-154' (Peskov Forwarded to the Ministry of Defense the Question of the Arrival of the President of Sudan to Syria on the Tu-154), Interfax, 17 December 2018, https://www.interfax.ru/russia/642702

95. President of Russia, 14 July 2018.

96. 'Russian Military Firm Working with Sudan Security Service: Sources', *Sudan Tribune*, 7 January 2018, https://www.sudantribune.com/spip.php?article66883

97. Andrew McGregor, 'Russian Mercenaries and the Survival of the Sudanese Regime', Jamestown Foundation, 6 February 2019, https://jamestown.org/program/russian-mercenaries-and-the-survival-of-the-sudanese-regime/

98. Tim Lister, 'Sebastian Shukla and Nima Elbagir, Fake News and Public Executions: Documents Show a Russian Company's Plan for Quelling Protests in Sudan', CNN, 25 April 2019, https://edition.cnn.com/2019/04/25/africa/russia-sudan-minvest-plan-to-quell-protests-intl/index.html?utm_source=Media+Review+for+April+25%2C+2019&utm_campaign=Media+Review+for+April+25%2C+2019&utm_medium=email

99. 'Sudan Says Russia Could Set Up Military Base on Red Sea', *Sudan Tribune*, 13 January 2019, https://www.sudantribune.com/spip.php?article66908

100. 'Druz'ya Omara al'-Bashira spasli stranu ot krizisa' (Friends of Omar al-Bashir Saved the Country from Crisis), Federal News Agency, 27 December 2018, https://riafan.ru/1136256-druzya-omara-al-bashira-spasli-stranu-ot-krizisa

101. 'Zapad ne mozhet slomit' Sudan: Omar al'-Bashir zashchitit stranu ot provokatsiy' (West Cannot Break Sudan: Omar al-Bashir will Protect Country from Provocations), Federal News Agency, 27 February 2019, https://riafan.ru/1155384-zapadu-ne-slomit-sudan-omar-al-bashir-zashitit-stranu-ot-provokacii

102. Luke Harding and Jason Burke, 'Leaked Documents Reveal Russain Effort to Exert Influence in Africa', *The Guardian*, 11 June 2019, https://www.theguardian.com/world/2019/jun/11/leaked-documents-reveal-russian-effort-to-exert-influence-in-africa

103. '"Dosye': polittekhnologi Yevgeniya Prigozhina pomogli eks-prezidentu Sudana sokhranit' diktatorskiy rezhim' ('Dossier:' Yevgeny Prigozhin's Political Strategists Helped the Ex-President of Sudan to Preserve the Dictatorial Regime), *Novaya Gazeta*, 25 April 2019, https://novayagazeta.ru/news/2019/04/25/151199-dosie-polittehnologi-evgeniya-prigozhina-pomogali-sohranit-diktatorskiy-rezhim-eks-prezidentu-sudana

NOTES pp. [220–222]

104. 'safir alsuwdan fi suria: ziarat albashir lidimashq safeatan qatilatan lishayieat altaqarub mae 'iisrayiyl' (Sudanese Ambassador to Syria: Al-Bashir's Visit to Damascus is a Fatal Blow to Rumors of Rapprochement with Israel), RT Arabic, 18 December 2018, https://arabic.rt.com/middle_east/989549-السفير-السوداني-في-دمشق-يعلق-على-سفر-البشير-بطائرة-روسية-لسوريا/

105. Kirill Semenov, 'Top Russian Security Officials Tour Egypt, Gulf to Discuss Syria, Libya', Al-Monitor, 4 February 2019, https://www.al-monitor.com/originals/2019/02/russia-patrushev-ksa-uae-egypt-syria-libya.html

106. Anna Borschevskaya and Catherine Cleveland, 'Russia's Arabic Propaganda: What it is, Why it Matters', Washington Institute for Near East Policy, 19 December 2018, notes that RT Arabic was ranked as Sudan's 104th most viewed website, while Al-Arabiya ranked 116th.

107. 'Abandoned by the UAE, Sudan's Bashir was Destined to Fall', Reuters, 3 July 2019, https://www.reuters.com/investigates/special-report/sudan-bashir-fall/

108. Interview with Kirill Semenov, October 2019.

109. Interview with author, June 2021.

110. Ravil Mustafin, 'Sudanskiy krizis svyazal Moskvu i arabskiye stolitsy' (Sudanese Crisis Links Russia and Arabian Capitals), 6 May 2019, https://www.ng.ru/kartblansh/2019-06-05/3_7591_kart.html

111. 'Sovet Federatsii zayavil o nedopustimosti nasil'stvennoy smeny vlasti v Sudane' (The Federation Council Announced the Inadmissibility of a Violent Change of Power in Sudan), RIA Novosti, 11 April 2019, https://ria.ru/20190411/1552573705.html

112. 'Russian Lawmakers Criticize Sudan Coup as "Unconstitutional"', The Moscow Times, 11 April 2019, https://www.themoscowtimes.com/2019/04/11/russian-lawmakers-criticize-sudan-coup-as-unconstitutional-a65190

113. Harding and Burke, 2019.

114. Elena Teslova, 'Russia Welcomes Sudan's Branding Ties "Strategic"', Anadolu Agency, 18 April 2019, https://www.aa.com.tr/en/africa/russia-welcomes-sudan-s-branding-ties-strategic-/1457104

115. Elnar Bainazarov, 'Maydan v Sudane: prezident strany arestovan, u vlasti voyennyye' (Maidan in Sudan: The Country's President Was Arrested, the Military is in Power), Izvestia, 11 April 2019, https://iz.ru/866846/elnar-bainazarov/maidanom-po-sudanu-prezident-strany-arestovan-u-vlasti-voennye

116. 'Glyadya na Sudan kak na Maydan' (Looking at Sudan as Maidan), Kommersant, 6 June 2019, https://www.kommersant.ru/doc/3992180

117. McGregor, 2019.

118. 'baed taeliq aleisyan, hadhih hi shurut almuearadat alsuwdaniat lilhiwar maratan 'ukhraa mae aleaskariiyn' (After the disobedience was suspended, these are the conditions of the Sudanese opposition for dialogue again with the military), Sputnik Arabic, 12 June 2019,

pp. [222–225]  NOTES

https://arabic.sputniknews.com/arab_world/201906121041636157-
/بعد-تعليق-العصيان-هذه-شروط-المعارضة-السودانية-الحوار-مجددا-العسكري

119. Sergei Seregichev, 'Business as Usual for Russia in Sudan', *The Moscow Times*, 17 April 2019, https://www.themoscowtimes.com/2019/04/17/business-as-usual-for-russia-in-sudan-a65272

120. 'Toll in Sudan Army Attack Jumps as China, Russia Block UN Action', Al Jazeera, 6 June 2019, https://www.aljazeera.com/news/2019/6/5/toll-in-sudan-army-attack-jumps-as-china-russia-block-un-action

121. 'Bogdanov zayavil, chto RF vystupayet protiv vmeshatel'stva izvne v situatsiyu v Sudane' (Bogdanov Says that the Russian Federation Opposes Outside Interference in the Situation in Sudan), TASS, 6 June 2019, https://tass.ru/politika/6515281

122. Elena Teslova, 'Russia Welcomes Deal Between Sudan's Army, Opposition', Anadolu Agency, 19 August 2019, https://www.aa.com.tr/en/europe/russia-welcomes-deal-between-sudan-s-army-opposition/1559808

123. 'Sudan mozhet konsolidirovat' tol'ko voyennyye, schitayet ekspert' (Only the Military Can Consolidate Sudan), RIA Novosti, 19 August 2019, https://ria.ru/20190819/1557631341.html

124. Interview with author, September 2021.

125. 'Did Russia Meddle in Madagascar's Elections?', BBC, 8 April 2019, https://www.bbc.co.uk/news/av/world-africa-47830161

126. Ibid.

127. Meduza, 8 April 2019.

128. Michael Schwirtz and Gaelle Borgia, 'How Russia Meddles Abroad for Profit: Cash, Trolls and a Cult Leader', *New York Times*, 11 November 2019, https://www.nytimes.com/2019/11/11/world/africa/russia-madagascar-election.html

129. Luke Harding, 'Pragmatism and Ideology Drive Kremlin's Interest in Africa', *The Guardian*, 11 June 2019, https://www.theguardian.com/world/2019/jun/11/pragmatism-and-ideology-drive-kremlins-interest-in-africa

130. Sergey Guryanov, 'Vyyavleno "vmeshatel'stvo" Rossii v vybory na Madagaskare' (Russian 'Interference' Revealed in Elections In Madagascar), Vzyglad, 8 April 2019, https://vz.ru/news/2019/4/8/972276.html

131. Interview with author, September 2021.

132. Luke Harding and Jason Burke, 'Leaked Documents Reveal Russian Effort to Exert Influence in Africa', *The Guardian*, 11 June 2019, https://www.theguardian.com/world/2019/jun/11/leaked-documents-reveal-russian-effort-to-exert-influence-in-africa

133. Schwirtz and Borgia, 2019.

134. Frida Ghitis, 'What is Russia Up to Across Africa', *World Politics Review*, 2 May 2019, https://www.worldpoliticsreview.com/articles/27809/what-is-russia-up-to-across-africa

135. Meduza, 8 April 2019.

136. Schwirtz and Borgia, 2019.

NOTES pp. [225–229]

137. Stephen Paduano, 'Putin Lost his African Great Game Before it Started', *Foreign Policy*, 31 October 2019, https://foreignpolicy.com/2019/10/31/putin-russia-africa-great-game-china-united-states/

138. Ibid.

139. 'Peskov zayavil, chto Rossiya ne vmeshivalas' v vybory prezidenta Madagaskara' (Peskov Said that Russia did not Intefere in the Presidential Elections in Madagascar), TASS, 11 November 2019, https://tass.ru/politika/7101059

140. 'Madagaskar atakovan "feykovymi novostyami"' (Madagascar Under Attack by 'Fake News'), Federal News Agency, 22 December 2018, https://riafan.ru/1134582-madagaskar-pod-udarom-feik-nyus

141. 'Kibervoyna i yuristy: kto iz grazhdan SSHA pytayetsya svergnut' prezidenta Madagaskara. Spetsial'noye rassledovaniye FAN' (Cyberwar and Lawyers: Which of the US Citizens is Trying to Overthrow the President of Madagascar. FNA Special Investigation), Federal News Agency, 8 January 2019, https://riafan.ru/1139029-kibervoiny-i-yuristy-kto-iz-grazhdan-ssha-pytaetsya-svergnut-prezidenta-madagaskara-specialnoe-rassledovanie-fan

142. 'SSHA vmeshalis' v vybory na Madagaskare' (US Intervened in the Elections In Madagascar), News.ru, 9 January 2018, https://news.ru/world/ssha-vmeshalis-v-vybory-v-madagaskare/

143. 'Mozambik gotov rabotat' s Rossiyey v energeticheskoy sfere' (Mozambique is Ready to Work with Russia in the Energy Sector), RIA Novosti, 3 July 2018, https://ria.ru/20180307/1515968685.html?in=t

144. 'Rosneft Signs Agreements on Offshore Gas Field Development in Mozambique', TASS, 22 August 2019, https://tass.com/economy/1074649

145. 'Posol RF: Rossiya mozhet uvelichit' eksport promyshlennoy produktsii v Mozambik' (Ambassador of the Russian Federation: Russia can Increase the Export of Industrial Products to Mozambique), 18 October 2019, https://tass.ru/ekonomika/7018100

146. Kachur, 2020.

147. 'Russia, Mozambique to Step Up Military-Technical Cooperation', TASS, 7 March 2018, https://tass.com/defense/993217

148. 'Minoborony Rossii i Mozambika dogovorilis' o razvitii sotrudnichestva v voyenno-morskoy sfere' (The Russian and Mozambican Defence Ministries Agreed to Develop Cooperation in the Naval Area), Russian Ministry of Defence, 4 April 2018, https://function.mil.ru/news_page/country/more.htm?id=12169888@egNews

149. Tim Lister and Sebastian Shukla, 'Russian Mercenaries Fight Shadowy Battle in Gas-Rich Mozambique', CNN, 29 November 2019, https://edition.cnn.com/2019/11/29/africa/russian-mercenaries-mozambique-intl/index.html

150. 'Inostrannyye CHVK pozhalovalis' na porazheniye v konkurentnoy bor'be s rossiyanami' (Foreign PMCs Complained of Defeat in Competition with Russians), *Vzglad*, 19 November 2019, https://vz.ru/news/2019/11/19/1009275.html

406

pp. [229–232]                    NOTES

151. TASS, 7 March 2018.
152. 'Mozambik zamanivayet Rossiyu v opasnyy i pribyl'nyy proyekt' (Mozambique Lures Russia into a Dangerous and Lucrative Project), *Vzyglad*, 21 August 2019, https://vz.ru/politics/2019/8/21/993589.html
153. '5 Russian Mercenaries Reportedly Killed in Mozambique Ambush', *The Moscow Times*, 29 October 2019, https://www.themoscowtimes.com/2019/10/29/5-russian-mercenaries-reportedly-killed-in-mozambique-ambush-a67963
154. Sergei Karamaev, 'Krizis v Mozambike i regional'nyye i global'nyye ugrozy' (Crisis in Mozambique and Regional and Global Threats), *Asia and Africa Today*, Issue 6, 2021, pp. 35–41, https://asaf-today.ru/s032150750015263-1-1/?sl=en
155. Interview with Co-Founder and Director of Burnham Global John Siko, December 2020.
156. Sergey Sukhankin, 'Russian Mercenaries Pour into Africa and Suffer More Losses (Part One)', Jamestown Foundation Eurasia Daily Monitor Volume 17, Issue 6, 21 January 2020, https://jamestown.org/program/russian-mercenaries-pour-into-africa-and-suffer-more-losses-part-one/
157. 'Èluósī wǎgénà jítuán zài fēizhōu de yèwù bùjǐn jǐn xiànyú lìbǐyǎ' (Russia's Wagner Group's Business Extends Beyond Libya, Dajunshi, 5 March 2021, http://www.dajunshi.com/lishi/202103/0514451.html
158. Interview with former French Ministry of Defence Official, November 2020.
159. 'No Russian Military Servicemen in Mozambique, Kremlin Says', TASS, 8 October 2019, https://tass.com/politics/1081988
160. 'SMI Mozambika rasprostranyayut feyki o gibeli rossiyan iz CHVK "Vagner"' (Mozambican Media Spread Fakes About the Death of Russians from PMC 'Wagner'), Federal News Agency, 1 November 2019, https://riafan.ru/1224241-smi-mozambika-rasprostranyayut-feiki-o-gibeli-rossiyan-iz-chvk-vagner
161. 'Glava FZNTS Shugaley podelilsya svoim mneniyem o khaose v Mozambike' (The Head of FZNTs Shugaley Shared his Opinion on the Chaos in Mozambique), Veka, 29 July 2021, https://wek.ru/glava-fznc-shugalej-podelilsya-mneniem-o-xaose-v-mozambike
162. Jasmin Opperman, 'An Expanded Russian Interest in Northern Mozambique Could be a Game-Changer', *Daily Maverick*, 14 October 2019, https://www.dailymaverick.co.za/article/2019-10-14-an-expanded-russian-interest-in-northern-mozambique-could-be-a-new-game-changer/
163. 'Mozambique Elections: Russians help Frelimo Backers to Break the Law- CIP Eleicoes, Club of Mozambique', 10 October 2019, https://clubofmozambique.com/news/mozambique-elections-russians-help-frelimo-backers-to-break-the-law-cip-eleicoes-144220/
164. 'Russian Disinformation Campaigns Target Africa: An Interview with Shelby Grossman', Africa Center for Strategic Studies, 18 February 2020, https://

407

NOTES pp. [232–237]

africacenter.org/spotlight/russian-disinformation-campaigns-target-africa-interview-shelby-grossman/

165. Kachur, pp. 47–48.

166. Emma Rumney, 'Russia's VTB Sues Mozambique Over Loan in $2 Billion Debt Scandal', Reuters, 6 January 2020, https://www.reuters.com/article/us-mozambique-credit-suisse-vtb-idUKKBN1Z527M

167. 'Mozambique Queried $535 Million Loan Guarantee, VTB Says in Court Filing', Reuters, 16 March 2020, https://www.reuters.com/article/mozambique-credit-suisse-vtb-idUSL8N2B96GK

168. 'Russia's VTB Demands US$817.5 Million from Mozambican State', Club of Mozambique, 4 May 2020, https://clubofmozambique.com/news/russias-vtb-demands-us817-5-million-from-mozambican-state-159138/

8. RUSSIA'S AFRICA POLICY IN THE AGE OF COVID-19

1. Mary Ilyushina, 'Why Does Russia, Population 146 million, Have Fewer Coronavirus cases than Luxembourg', CNN, 23 March 2020, https://edition.cnn.com/2020/03/21/europe/putin-coronavirus-russia-intl/index.html

2. Andrei Kortunov and Natalia Zeiser, 'Budushcheye Afriki v usloviyakh pandemii: dva stsenariya' (Africa's Future Amid a Pandemic: Two Scenarios), Russian International Affairs Council, 9 April 2020, https://russiancouncil.ru/activity/workingpapers/budushchee-afriki-na-fone-pandemii-dva-stsenariya/#short

3. Anna Juranets, 'Ambitsioznyye plany': pomozhet li Rossiya Afrike v bor'be s koronavirusom' (Ambitious Plans: Will Russia Help Africa in the Fight Against the Coronavirus), Gazeta.ru, 2 May 2020, https://www.gazeta.ru/politics/2020/05/01_a_13069387.shtml

4. Kortunov and Zeiser, 2020.

5. Ibid.

6. 'Koronavirus vpervyye obnaruzhen v Afrike' (Coronavirus First Detected in Africa), Interfax, 11 February 2020, https://www.interfax.ru/world/694865

7. 'Neskol'ko afrikanskikh stran obratilis' k Rossii za pomoshch'yu v bor'be s koronavirusom' (Several African Countries have Asked Russia for Help in the Fight Agaisnt Coronavirus), TASS, 21 April 2020, https://tass.ru/obschestvo/8292415

8. 'V MID postupilo 12 zaprosov o pomoshchi Rossii iz-za koronavirusa' (Foreign Ministry Receives 12 Requests for Russian Assistance due to Coronavirus), RIA Novosti, 28 April 2020, https://ria.ru/20200428/1570688790.html

9. 'COVID-19: A Test for Russia's African Ambitions', European Council for Foreign Relations, 29 April 2020, https://ecfr.eu/article/commentary_covid_19_a_test_for_russias_african_ambitions/

408

pp. [237–240]    NOTES

10. 'South Africa's Ramaphosa Meets Putin at G20', *Africa News*, 28 June 2019, https://www.africanews.com/2019/06/28/south-africa-s-ramaphosa-meets-putin-at-g20/

11. 'Ethiopia Looks Forward to Aid from Russia to Battle Pandemic, says Ambassador', TASS, 18 June 2020, https://tass.com/world/1169257

12. Addis Getachew, 'COVID-19: Ethiopia Premier Seeks Debt Relief from Africa', Anadolu Agency, 24 March 2020 https://www.aa.com.tr/en/africa/covid-19-ethiopia-premier-seeks-debt-relief-for-africa/1777564

13. 'Putin i prem'er Efiopii obsudili borbu s koronavirusom' (Putin and Ethiopian Prime Minister Discuss Fight Against Coronavirus), RIA Novosti, 7 April 2020, https://ria.ru/20200407/1569683726.html

14. 'Russia Joins UN's Appeal for Global Ceasefire, Lists Conflicts by Name', Euractiv, 25 March 2020, https://www.euractiv.com/section/global-europe/news/russia-joins-uns-appeal-for-global-ceasefire-lists-conflicts-by-name/

15. Simon Tisdall, 'US and Russia Blocking UN Plans for a Global Ceasefire Amid Crisis', *The Guardian*, 19 April 2020, https://www.theguardian.com/us-news/2020/apr/19/us-and-russia-blocking-un-plans-for-a-global-ceasefire-amid-crisis

16. 'African Ambassadors Complain to China over "Discrimination" in Guangzhou', Reuters, 11 April 2020, https://www.reuters.com/article/us-health-coronavirus-africa-idUSKCN21T0T7

17. Dmitry Kosyrev, 'Kto takoy rasist, ili Kak plokho obrashchalis' s afrikantsami v Guanchzhou' (Who is Racist or How Africans Were Mistreated in Guangzhou), RIA Novosti, 16 April 2020, https://ria.ru/20200416/1570094315.html

18. 'Potential COVID-19 Vaccine Hub in Africa: Russian Trade Envoy Says Morocco Mulling Sputnik V Registration', RT, 20 November 2020, https://www.rt.com/russia/507252-russian-vaccine-morocco-talks/

19. Hagar Hosny, 'How Egypt Became Hub for Russian COVID-19 Vaccine', Al-Monitor, 16 December 2020, https://www.al-monitor.com/originals/2020/12/egypt-russia-coronavirus-vaccine-sputnik-manufacture-africa.html

20. 'Rayiys Al-sunduq Al-Ruwsii Lilaistithmarat Al-Mbashrt: Yumkinuna Al-bad' fi 'iintaj Liqah 'Sbwtnyk 5' fi Misr Waljazayir' (Head of Russian Fund for Direct Investments: We can Start Production of Sputnik V vaccine in Egypt and Algeria), RT Arabic, 2 December 2020, https://arabic.rt.com/middle_east/1179343-في-مصر-والجزائر-v-الصندوق-الروسي-بإمكاننا-بدء-إنتاج-لقاح-سبوتنيك/

21. 'Algeria Becomes First African Nation to Approve Russia's Sputnik V Vaccine', RT, 10 January 2021, https://www.rt.com/russia/512091-sputnik-vaccine-algeria-coronavirus/

22. 'Russia and Russia Complete Ebola Vaccinations in Guinea', *Pharmaceutical Technology*, 14 December 2018, https://www.pharmaceutical-technology.com/news/rusal-ebola-vaccinations-in-guinea/

NOTES pp. [240–242]

23. Kester Klomegah, 'Russian Aluminum Delivers Sputnik V Vaccine to Guinea', *Modern Diplomacy*, 26 March 2021, https://moderndiplomacy.eu/2021/03/26/russian-aluminium-delivers-sputnik-v-vaccine-to-guinea/

24. 'Guinea's President Conde Receives Sputnik V Vaccine', TASS, 16 January 2021, https://tass.com/world/1245701

25. Alexander Winning and Joe Bavier, 'African Union Says Russia Offers 300 million Doses of Sputnik V vaccine', Reuters, 19 February 202,1 https://www.reuters.com/article/us-health-coronavirus-africa-idUSKBN2AJ0Y3

26. 'Fi Aitisal Gatifiin Rayiys Al-hukumat Biwazir Al-kharijiat Al-Ruwsi: Al-Aitifaq Ealaa Mazid Min Al-Taeawun Limujtamae Aintishar Fayruskuruna' (In Phone Call, the Prime Minister and Russian Foreign Minister Gathered: Agreement on Further Cooperation to Confront Spread of Coronavirus), Presidency of the Government, 9 March 2021, http://www.pm.gov.tn/pm/actualites/actualite.php?id=13007&lang=ar

27. "First Drop of Rain': Libya Receives Russia's Sputnik Vaccine', Al Jazeera English, 4 April 2021, https://www.aljazeera.com/news/2021/4/4/first-drop-of-rain-libya-receives-covid-vaccine-delivery

28. 'Algeria to Start Russia's Sputnik V vaccine production in September', Reuters, 7 April 2021, https://www.reuters.com/article/us-algeria-russia-vaccine-idUSKBN2BU3HG

29. 'Egypt to Produce Russia's Sputnik V, Rollout Expected in Q3 – Statement', Reuters, 22 April 2021, https://www.reuters.com/world/middle-east/egypt-produce-russias-sputnik-v-rollout-expected-q3-statement-2021-04-22/

30. Ray Ndlovu, 'Alrosa to Donate Sputnik Vaccines to Angola, Zimbabwe', Bloomberg, 10 February 2021, https://www.bloomberg.com/news/articles/2021-02-10/russian-diamond-giant-to-donate-vaccines-to-angola-zimbabwe

31. 'Sputnik Light Approved for Use in Angola', Pharmiweb, 13 May 2021, https://www.pharmiweb.com/press-release/2021-05-13/sputnik-light-vaccine-approved-for-use-in-angola

32. Adam Abu-bashal, 'Ghana to receive over 1M Doses of Sputnik V Vaccine', Anadolu Agency, 3 May 2021, https://www.aa.com.tr/en/africa/ghana-to-receive-over-1m-doses-of-sputnik-v-vaccine/2227628

33. 'Russia, Ethiopia to Ink Deal on Sputnik V Supplies, Says Ambassador', TASS, 30 April 2021, https://tass.com/economy/1285521

34. 'Russia's Coronavirus Jabs more Expensive for Africa than Western Jabs-FT', *The Moscow Times*, 26 February 2021 https://www.themoscowtimes.com/2021/02/26/russias-coronavirus-vaccine-more-expensive-for-africa-than-western-jabs-ft-a73080

35. Joe Bavier and David Lewis, 'Africa Proves Rocky Terrain for Russian and Chinese COVID-19 Vaccines', Reuters, 12 March 2021, https://www.reuters.com/business/healthcare-pharmaceuticals/africa-proves-rocky-terrain-russian-chinese-vaccines-2021-03-12/

pp. [242–245]  NOTES

36. Interview with Egyptian Analyst, May 2021.
37. Daria Litvinova, 'Putin Touts Russian Vaccines at BRICS Summit', Associated Press, 17 November 2020, https://apnews.com/article/summits-india-coronavirus-pandemic-vladimir-putin-china-63b174580063da09912890ffd167eca6
38. 'South Africa Should be Using all the COVID-19 Vaccines Available to it – Urgently', *South African Medical Journal*, Volume 111, Number 4, April 2021, ttp://www.scielo.org.za/scielo.php?script=sci_arttext&pid=S0256-95742021000400002
39. 'Tsentr Gamaleya ob'yavil ob effektivnosti "Sputnika V" protiv novykh shtammov COVID-19' (The Gamaleya Center Announced the Effectiveness of Sputnik V Against New Strains of COVID-19), *Vedomosti*, 27 February 2021, https://www.vedomosti.ru/society/news/2021/02/27/859528-v-tsentre-gamalei-zayavili-effektivnosti-sputnika-v-protiv-novih-shtammov-covid-19
40. 'Russia says Sputnik Shot Less Effective vs. S. Africa Variant but Better than Others', Reuters, 9 April 2021, https://www.reuters.com/business/healthcare-pharmaceuticals/russia-says-sputnik-shot-less-effective-against-south-africa-variant-ifax-2021-04-09/
41. Paul Vecchiatto, 'South Africa to Add Sputnik, Sinopharm Shots to Vaccine Arsenal', Bloomberg, 28 April 2021, https://www.bloomberg.com/news/articles/2021-04-28/south-africa-to-add-sputnik-sinopharm-shots-to-vaccine-arsenal
42. Interview with author, April 2021.
43. Interview with author, June 2021.
44. Ibid.
45. 'Rwanda: Opposition Grows to Russian-Backed Nuclear Power Plants', 29 November 2020, https://www.aa.com.tr/en/africa/rwanda-opposition-grows-to-russian-backed-nuclear-plants/2059467
46. Ray Ndlovu, 'Zimbabwe, Russia's Rosatom Sign Pact to Tap Nuclear Energy', Bloomberg, 14 April 2021, https://www.bloomberg.com/news/articles/2021-04-14/zimbabwe-signs-mou-with-russia-s-rosatom-to-tap-nuclear-energy
47. Stephen Kafeero, 'Uganda's Popular Boda-Bodas are Now Part of the Government's Surveillance System', 6 August 2021, https://qz.com/africa/2043622/ugandas-controversial-surveillance-contract-with-a-russian-firm/
48. 'Iran, Ghana Among Those Hardest Hit by Russia's Vaccine Delivery Delays-BBC', *The Moscow Times*, 4 August 2021, https://www.themoscowtimes.com/2021/08/04/iran-ghana-among-those-hit-hardest-by-russias-vaccine-delivery-delays-bbc-a74688
49. 'Emmanuel Macron Urges Europe to Send Vaccines to Africa', *Financial Times*, 18 February 2021, https://www.ft.com/content/15853717-af6c-4858-87d4-58b1826895a8

411

NOTES pp. [245–248]

50. Interview with author, April 2021.
51. Interview with author, May 2021.
52. Adam Kadomtsev, 'Vaktsina protiv geopolitiki? Politicheskiye ambitsii mogut zamedlit' bor'bu s global'noy pandemiyey' (Vaccine vs. Geopolitics? Political Ambition Could Slow Fight Against Global Pandemic), *International Affairs*, 30 November 2020, https://interaffairs.ru/news/show/28291
53. 'Lavrov otritsayet "vaktsinnuyu diplomatiyu" Rossii' (Lavrov Denies Russia's 'Vaccine Diplomacy'), Vedomosti, 23 March 2021, https://www.vedomosti.ru/politics/news/2021/03/23/862680-lavrov-oproverg-vedenie-vaktsinnoi-diplomatii
54. 'Kremlin Disagrees with Macron's Remark that Russia, China Use Vaccines as Leverage', TASS, 26 March 2021, https://tass.com/politics/1270715
55. 'Vaktsinnaya diplomatiya – novyy format mezhdunarodnykh otnosheniy' (Vaccine Diplomacy: A New Format of International Relations), Russian International Affairs Council, 5 April 2021, https://russiancouncil.ru/blogs/lea/vaktsinnaya-diplomatiya-novyy-format-mezhdunarodnykh-otnosheniy/
56. 'Factbox – US's New Actions Against Russia Reach from Africa to Crimea to Pakistan', Reuters, 15 April 2021, https://www.reuters.com/article/usa-russia-sanctions-idUSL1N2M81AP
57. C. Todd Lopez, 'Leaders Committed to Transparency with African Partners', Department of Defence, 1 July 2021, https://www.defense.gov/Explore/News/Article/Article/2679003/leaders-committed-to-transparency-with-african-partners/
58. 'Online Event: A New US Policy Towards Africa: A Conversation with Gregory Meeks and African Activists', 1 February 2021, https://www.csis.org/analysis/online-event-new-us-policy-toward-africa-conversation-chairman-gregory-meeks-and-african
59. Zainab Usman, 'How Biden Can Build US-Africa Relations Back Better', Carnegie Endowment for International Peace, 27 April 2021, https://carnegieendowment.org/2021/04/27/how-biden-can-build-u.s.-africa-relations-back-better-pub-84399
60. 'Kak izmenitsya politika SSHA v Afrike v sluchaye pobedy Baydena – prognoz' (How US Policy in Africa will Change if Biden Wins- Forecast), *Krasnaya Vesna*, 6 November 2020, https://rossaprimavera.ru/news/70a4d741
61. 'Afrikanskaya lovushka Trampa dlya Baydena' (Trump's African Trap for Biden), *International Affairs*, 14 February 2021, https://interaffairs.ru/news/show/29071
62. 'Macron Blames Russia and Turkey for Bolstering Anti-French Sentiments in Africa', France-24, 20 November 2020, https://www.france24.com/en/france/20201120-macron-blames-russia-and-turkey-for-bolstering-anti-french-sentiment-in-africa
63. Vasily Flippov, "Plokhiye novost' dlya Emmanuelya Makrona' ('Bad News' for Emmanuel Macron), *Asia and Africa Today*, Issue 4, 2020, pp. 4–12.

412

pp. [248–251]　　　　　　　　　　　NOTES

64. 'China and Russia Hold the Third Round of Director-Level Video Consultation on African Affairs', Ministry of Foreign Affairs of the People's Republic of China, 24 December 2020, https://www.fmprc.gov.cn/mfa_eng/wjbxw/t1843163.shtml

65. Olga Kuikova et al., 'Rossiysko-kitayskoye sotrudnichestvo v Afrike' (Russian-Chinese Cooperation in Africa), Russian International Affairs Council, 29 March 2021, https://russiancouncil.ru/activity/publications/rossiysko-kitayskoe-sotrudnichestvo-v-afrike/

66. Ibid, pp. 60–61.

67. 'Foreign Ministry Spokesperson Zhao Lijian's Regular Press Conference on 19 August 2020', Ministry of Foreign Affairs of the People's Republic of China, 19 August 2020, https://www.fmprc.gov.cn/mfa_eng/xwfw_665399/s2510_665401/t1807490.shtml

68. Paul Goble, 'China and Russia Cooperating and Competing in Africa', Jamestown Foundation, 29 June 2021, https://jamestown.org/program/china-and-russia-both-cooperating-and-competing-in-africa/

69. David Shinn, 'China in Africa, Testimony Before the US-China Economic and Security Review Commission', 8 May 2020 https://www.uscc.gov/sites/default/files/Shinn_Testimony.pdf

70. Interview with author, June 2021.

71. Ibid.

72. 'Cairo Counts on Russia in Resolving Grand Renaissance Dam Crisis – Foreign Minister', TASS, 11 April 2021, https://tass.com/world/1276585

73. 'Disputes Around Renaissance Dam Should be Resolved Via Dialogue – Russian Top Diplomat', TASS, 12 April 2021, https://tass.com/politics/1276821

74. Emad Eddin Hussein, "uwlayik aladhin khadhiluna fi majlis al'amn' (Those Who Let Us Down on the Issue of the Dam), *Al-Shorouk*, 10 July 2021, https://www.shorouknews.com/columns/view.aspx?cdate=10072021&id=2483a096-204a-4429-a5c5-fe670f49cafd

75. 'Why Did Putin Turn Against Sisi in the Renaissance Dam File', Middle East Monitor, 13 July 2021, https://www.middleeastmonitor.com/20210713-why-did-putin-turn-against-sisi-in-the-renaissance-dam-file/

76. Interview with Egyptian diplomat, June 2021.

77. 'Egypt, Ethiopia, Sudan Should Negotiate Mutually Beneficial Agreement over Management of Nile Waters, Top Official Tells Security Council', UNSC 8816th Meeting, 8 July 2021, https://www.un.org/press/en/2021/sc14576.doc.htm

78. Interview with author, July 2021.

79. Ibid.

80. 'Russia Floats Arctic Shipping Route as "Viable" Suez Canal Alternative', *The Moscow Times*, 25 March 2021, https://www.themoscowtimes.com/2021/03/25/russia-floats-arctic-shipping-route-as-viable-suez-canal-alternative-a73369

## NOTES pp. [251–254]

81. 'Northern Sea Route's Significance Growing in Light of Suez Incident – Rosatom', Interfax, 25 March 2021, https://interfax.com/newsroom/top-stories/71429/

82. 'Suez Canal Incident Highlights the Need for North-South ITC, Says Lavrov', TASS, 12 April 2021, https://tass.com/politics/1277033

83. Interview with author, June 2021.

84. 'Egypt Moves Ahead with Purchase of Russian Arms Despite US Warnings', Al-Monitor, 3 March 2021, https://www.al-monitor.com/originals/2021/03/egypt-us-tension-sanctions-russia-arms-deal.html

85. Baher al-Kady, 'Russia Resumes Flights to Egyptian Resorts After Six-Year Halt', Al-Monitor, 13 July 2021, https://www.al-monitor.com/originals/2021/07/russia-resumes-flights-egyptian-resorts-after-six-year-halt

86. 'Egypt Suspends Meetings with Russia's Rosatom Nuclear Firm Building El-Dabaa Power Plant', *New Arab*, 19 July 2021, https://english.alaraby.co.uk/news/egypt-suspends-meetings-russias-rosatom-nuclear-firm

87. 'Russia's Ambassador to Egypt Visits the El-Dabaa NPP Construction Site', Rosatom, 10 March 2021, https://rosatom.ru/en/press-centre/news/russia-s-ambassador-to-egypt-visits-the-el-dabaa-npp-construction-site/

88. Sergei Volkov, 'Novyy etap rossiysko-yegipetskogo sotrudnichestva' (New Stage of Russian-Egyptian Cooperation), *Asia and Africa Today*, Issue 1, 2021, pp. 11–14.

89. Konstantin Volkov, 'Spor mezhdu Yegiptom i Efiopiey iz-za vody Nila ugrozhayet vsey Yevrope' (The Dispute Between Egypt and Ethiopia Over the Water of the Nile Threatens All of Europe), *Rossiyskaya Gazeta*, 16 June 2020, https://rg.ru/2020/06/16/spor-egipta-i-efiopii-za-vodu-nila-ugrozhaet-vsej-evrope.html

90. Danila Moiseev, 'Voyna v Efiopii grozit pererasti v polnomasshtabnuyu' (War in Ethiopia Threatens to Become Full-Blown), *Nezavisimaya Gazeta*, 9 November 2020, https://www.ng.ru/world/2020-11-09/6_8009_ethiopia.html

91. 'Diplomat: UN Fails to Approve Call to End Tigray Violence', Associated Press, 6 March 2021, https://apnews.com/article/russia-violence-india-humanitarian-assistance-ethiopia-f93a9a6bc7c0845a37cf7e3e3757e1e7

92. 'Statement by Permanent Representative Vassily Nebenzia at UN Security Council Briefing on Peace and Security in Africa (The Situation in Tigray)', Permanent Mission of the Russian Federation to the United Nations, 2 July 2021, https://russiaun.ru/en/news/tigray_020721

93. Interview with Institute for Security Studies researcher Dawit Yohanes, June 2021.

94. Interview with author, May 2021.

95. Interview with Teshome Borago, June 2021.

96. 'Ethiopia, Russia Agree to Strengthen Cooperation in Security Service', FANA, 9 June 2021, https://www.fanabc.com/english/ethiopia-russia-agree-to-strengthen-cooperation-security-service/

## pp. [254–259]　NOTES

97. RIA Novosti, 27 July 2021, https://ria.ru/20210727/efiopiya-1743053419. html

### 9. NEW FRONTIERS OF RUSSIAN SECURITY POLICY IN AFRICA

1. Patrick Wintour, 'Libya Fighting Intensifies as Rival Forces Defy UN Call for Global Ceasefire', *The Guardian*, 27 March 2020, https://www.theguardian. com/world/2020/mar/27/libya-fighting-intensifies-rival-forces-defy-un-call-global-ceasefire

2. 'Moscow's "Shadow Army" Recruiting Syrian Youth to Fight in Libyan Conflict', Caravanserai, 21 April 2020, https://central.asia-news.com/en_GB/articles/cnmi_ca/features/2020/04/21/feature-01

3. 'Hundreds More Mercenaries Flee Western Libya: GNA Forces', Al Jazeera, 25 May 2020, https://www.aljazeera.com/news/2020/5/25/hundreds-more-russian-mercenaries-flee-western-libya-gna-forces

4. Jared Szuba, 'Wagner has Already Crashed Two Russian Jets in Libya, AFRICOM Says', Al-Monitor, 11 September 2020, https://www.al-monitor.com/originals/2020/09/russia-libya-fighter-crash.html

5. 'Russia Sends Fighter Jets to Libya to Support Mercenaries', France-24, 26 May 2020, https://www.france24.com/en/20200526-russia-sends-fighter-jets-to-libya-to-support-mercenaries

6. 'V Livii net rossiyskikh istrebiteley – glava komiteta Soveta Federatsii po oborone' (No Russian Fighter Jets in Libya- Head of Federation Council Defence Committee), Interfax, 27 May 2020, https://interfax.com/newsroom/top-stories/68850/

7. Edith Lederer, 'Experts: Libya Rivals UAE, Russia, Turkey Violate Arms Embargo', AP News, 9 September 2020, https://apnews.com/article/turkey-north-africa-qatar-libya-united-arab-emirates-20a2ad9c585f40ec29 1585dbf8e9ed22

8. 'sanae allah yakshif: musalahun "ajanib dakhaluu mina" sadrat waladayna 'adilat ealaa wujud "faghnar" fi alsharara' (Sanalla Reveals: Foreign Gunmen Entered the Port of Sidra, And We Have Evidence of the Presence of 'Wagner' in the Spark), *Al-Ahrar*, 5 July 2020, https://libyaalahrar.tv/2020/07/05/ صنع-الله-يكشف-مسلحون-أجانب-دخلوا-ميناء/

9. 'Libyan Mufti Calls for Resisting Russian "Invasion"', *Yeni Safak*, 1 July 2020, https://www.yenisafak.com/en/news/libyan-mufti-calls-for-resisting-russian-invasion-3533442

10. 'Landmine Planted by Wagner Mercenaries Wounds Child, Another Civilian in Libya's Tripoli', *Daily Sabah*, 21 July 2020, https://www.dailysabah.com/politics/landmine-planted-by-wagner-mercenaries-wounds-child-another-civilian-in-libyas-tripoli/news

11. Interview with author, April 2021.

12. 'Russian Mercenaries are Fighting in Libya, UN Diplomats Confirm', *The Moscow Times*, 7 May 2020, https://www.themoscowtimes.com/2020/05/

NOTES pp. [259–262]

07/russian-mercenaries-are-fighting-in-libya-un-diplomats-confirm-a70204

13. Edith Lederer, 'Russia, China Block Release of UN Report Criticizing Russia', Associated Press, 26 September 2020, https://apnews.com/article/libya-china-archive-united-nations-russia-383b41a5735567031226 5c05672153e5

14. Interview with Andrey Chuprygin, November 2020.

15. Konstantin Volkov, 'Lavrov: My ne odobryayem zayavleniye Khaftara o peredache vlasti v Livii' (Foreign Minister Lavrov: We do not Approve of Haftar's Statement on the Transfer of Power in Libya), *Rossiyskaya Gazeta*, 28 April 2020, https://rg.ru/2020/04/28/lavrov-my-ne-odobriaem-zaiavlenie-haftara-o-perehode-vlasti-v-livii.html

16. 'Spiker Palaty predstaviteley Livii zayavil, chto yego mirnyye initsiativy podgotovili "rossiyane"' (The Speaker of the House of Representatives of Libya Said that his Peace Initiatives were Prepared by the 'Russians'), *Kommersant*, 1 May 2020, https://www.kommersant.ru/doc/4335501

17. Mark Katz, 'What's the Meaning of Moscow's Murky Moves in Libya?', *Responsible Statecraft*, 30 May 2020, https://responsiblestatecraft.org/2020/05/30/whats-the-meaning-of-moscows-murky-moves-in-libya/

18. Hamdi Yildiz and Leila Thabti, 'Russia Asked Haftar to Declare Truce: Saleh', Anadolu Agency, 2 May 2020, https://www.aa.com.tr/en/middle-east/russia-asked-haftar-to-declare-truce-saleh/1826200

19. Associated Press, 9 September 2020.

20. Yasmina Allouche, 'Acrimony Follows UAE and Egypt's Scuppering of new UN Libya Envoy', *Middle East Eye*, 22 April 2020, https://www.middleeasteye.net/news/algerian-diplomat-denied-un-role-libya-after-egypt-uae-pressure

21. Interview with author, April 2020.

22. 'Turkish, Russian Officials Nearing Deal on Libya Ceasefire, Political Process – Minister', Reuters, 16 September 2020, https://www.reuters.com/article/uk-libya-security-turkey-russia-idUKKBN2673FR

23. Interview with Kirill Semenov, July 2020.

24. 'Bratskaya voyna: Liviya zhdet vtorzheniya yegipetskoy armii' (Fraternal War: Libya Awaits the Invasion of the Egyptian Army), Gazeta.ru, 14 July 2020, https://www.gazeta.ru/politics/2020/07/14_a_13152697.shtml

25. 'Yegipet nachinayet svoyu voyennuyu igru v Livii' (Egypt Starts its Own War Game in Libya), *Vzyglad*, 22 June 2020, https://vz.ru/world/2020/6/22/1046333.html

26. 'Macron Slams Turkey's "Criminal" Role in Libya, Putin's Ambivalence', Reuters, 29 June 2020, https://www.reuters.com/article/us-libya-oil-russia-macron-idUSKBN2402KB

27. 'Turkey: "France is Trying to Increase Russia's Presence in Libya"', *TRTWorld*, 30 June 2020, https://www.trtworld.com/turkey/turkey-france-trying-to-increase-russia-s-presence-in-libya-37746

NOTES

28. 'Ob'yasneniye nevozmozhnosti osvobodit' plennykh russkikh v Livii' (The Inabiltiy to Free the Captured Russians in Libya Explained), Lenta.ru, 21 September 2020, https://lenta.ru/news/2020/09/21/explained/

29. Torrey Clark and Samer al-Atrush, 'Russia Welcomes Libya Deal on Oil Exports, Revenue Distribution', Bloomberg, 19 September 2020, https://www.bloomberg.com/news/articles/2020-09-19/russia-welcomes-libya-deal-on-oil-exports-revenue-distribution

30. 'MID Rossii prokommentiroval otkaz Sarradzha pokinut' post glavy Natsional'noy natsional'noy politsii Livii' (Russian Foreign Ministry Commented on Sarraj's Refusal to Leave the Post as Head of Libya's GNA), RIA Novosti, 5 November 2020, https://ria.ru/20201105/sarradzh-1583126536.html

31. Marianna Belenkaya, 'Moskva i Tripoli razbegayutsya v blagodarnosti' (Moscow and Tripoli Scattered in Gratitude), Kommersant, 30 December 2020, https://www.kommersant.ru/doc/4638034

32. Marianna Belenkaya, 'Marsh, marsh Liviya' (March, March of Libya), Kommersant, 30 January 2021, https://www.kommersant.ru/doc/4670655

33. Kirill Semenov, 'Russia Seeks to Outplay the US in Libya', Al Monitor, 9 February 2021, https://www.al-monitor.com/originals/2021/02/russia-us-libya-strategy-lpdf-menfi-elections-hifter-moscow.html

34. Anton Mardasov and Kirill Semenov, 'Russia on the Eve of a Collapse in Libya', Riddle, 6 March 2021, https://www.ridl.io/en/russia-on-the-eve-of-a-collapse-in-libya/

35. 'Russia Calls for Deeper Military Ties with Libya', Arab News, 17 April 2021, https://www.arabnews.com/node/1844191/middle-east

36. 'Russia Stops UN Blacklisting of Notorious Libyan Militia', Al Jazeera, 21 November 2020, https://www.aljazeera.com/news/2020/11/21/russia-stops-un-blacklisting-of-libyas-al-kaniyat-militia

37. Belenkaya, 30 January 2021.

38. 'Russian Wagner Group to Send 300 Syrian Fighters to Libya', Daily Sabah, 12 April 2021, https://www.dailysabah.com/world/africa/russian-wagner-group-to-send-300-syrian-fighters-to-libya

39. 'Fathi Bashaga: ofitser, agent Zapada, drug Turtsii, ministr v Tripoli' (Fathi Bashagha: Officer, Agent of the West, Friend of Turkey, Minister in Tripoli), Federal News Agency, 24 April 2020, https://riafan.ru/1270937-fatkhi-bashaga-oficer-agent-zapada-drug-turcii-ministr-v-tripoli

40. Mardasov and Semenov, 8 March 2021.

41. 'President Putin's Envoy Bogdanov Met with Aref Nayed in Moscow Today', Al-Marsad, 13 August 2021, https://almarsad.co/en/2021/08/13/president-putins-envoy-bogdanov-met-with-aref-nayed-in-moscow-today/

42. 'Putin's "Chef" Pays Russian Operatives Released by Libya', The Moscow Times, 14 December 2020 https://www.themoscowtimes.com/2020/12/14/putins-chef-pays-russian-operatives-released-by-libya-a72352

NOTES pp. [265–269]

43. 'Pochemu Rossiya vozvrashchayet Liviyu Kaddafi' (Why Russia is Turning Libya to Gaddafi), RIA Novosti, 3 August 2021, https://ria.ru/20210803/liviya-1744056142.html

44. Nader Ibrahim, 'Wagner: Gaddafi's Son Faces Arrest Over Russian Mercenaries', BBC, 12 August 2021, https://www.bbc.co.uk/news/world-africa-58191433

45. Interviews with Moscow-based experts, December 2021.

46. Interview with author, April 2021.

47. 'Russia Accuses Operation IRINI of Being Biased', *Libyan Express*, 20 January 2021, https://www.libyanexpress.com/russia-accuses-operation-irni-of-being-biased/

48. Interview with author, May 2021.

49. Interview with Assistant Professor at Qatar University Ali Bakeer, May 2021.

50. Ibid.

51. 'Russia Sends 300 Military Instructors to Central African Republic', BBC, 22 December 2020, https://www.bbc.co.uk/news/world-africa-55412720

52. 'Russia, Rwanda Sent Troops' to Central African Republic', Al Jazeera, 21 December 2020, https://www.aljazeera.com/news/2020/12/21/russia-rwanda-send-troops-to-central-african-republic

53. John Lechner and Alexandra Lamarche, 'Outside Powers are Making the Conflict in Central African Republic Worse', *Foreign Policy*, 22 January 2021, https://foreignpolicy.com/2021/01/22/outside-powers-are-making-the-conflict-in-the-central-african-republic-worse/

54. 'Russia Pulling "Military Instructor" out of Central African Republic: Diplomats', France-24, 15 January 2021, https://www.france24.com/en/live-news/20210115-russia-pulling-military-instructor-out-of-central-african-republic-diplomats

55. 'CAR Troops, Russian Mercenaries Kill 44 Rebels Outside the Capital Bangui', RFI, 26 January 2021, https://www.rfi.fr/en/africa/20210126-car-troops-russian-mercenaries-kill-44-rebels-outside-the-capital-bangui-africa-humanitarian-crisis-elections

56. 'Rival Disinformation Campaigns Targeted African Users, Facebook Says', *The Guardian*, 15 December 2020, https://www.theguardian.com/technology/2020/dec/15/central-african-republic-facebook-disinformation-france-russia

57. 'The Central African Republic is a Hub for French and Russian Disinformation', *TRT World*, 16 December 2020, https://www.trtworld.com/magazine/the-central-african-republic-is-a-hub-for-french-and-russian-disinformation-42422

58. Interview with Western defence consultant in CAR, January 2021.

59. 'Frantsiya mozhet v blizhaysheye vremya uyti iz TSAR' (France May Leave CAR in the Near Future), Federal News Agency, 20 May 2021, https://riafan.ru/1449015-franciya-mozhet-v-blizhaishee-vremya-okonchatelno-pokinut-car

pp. [269–271]  NOTES

60. Interview with CAR official, June 2021.
61. 'France Halts Aid to Central African Republic over Anti-French Campaigns', *Daily Sabah*, 8 June 2021, https://www.dailysabah.com/world/africa/france-halts-aid-to-central-african-republic-over-anti-french-campaigns
62. 'France Slams Russia's "Seizure of Power" in C. African Republic', *Daily Sabah*, 18 June 2021, https://www.dailysabah.com/world/africa/france-slams-russias-seizure-of-power-in-c-african-republic
63. 'Luke Harding and Jason Burke, Russian Mercenaries Behind Human Rights Abuses in CAR, Say UN Experts', *The Guardian*, 30 March 2021, https://www.theguardian.com/world/2021/mar/30/russian-mercenaries-accused-of-human-rights-abuses-in-car-un-group-experts-wagner-group-violence-election
64. 'France, UK and US Accuse Russian Mercenaries of Human Rights Violations in CAR', France-24, 24 June 2021, https://www.france24.com/en/africa/20210624-france-uk-and-us-accuse-russian-mercenaries-of-human-rights-violations-in-car
65. 'Russia Insists CAfrica "Instructors" are Unarmed', France-24, 28 May 2021, https://www.france24.com/en/live-news/20210528-russia-insists-cafrica-instructors-are-unarmed
66. 'Private Russian Military Company May Sue News Agency for First Time Over "Fake" Report', Sputnik, 11 March 2021, https://sputniknews.com/world/202103111082316179-private-russian-military-company-may-sue-news-agency-for-first-time-over-fake-report/
67. Peter Kum, 'Russia to Deploy 600 More Soldiers in Central African Republic', Anadolu Agency, 30 June 2021, https://www.aa.com.tr/en/africa/russia-to-deploy-600-more-soldiers-in-central-african-republic/2290366
68. 'Peskov dal otsenku publikatsii otcheta SB OON o prichastnosti rossiyan k ubiystvam v CAR' (Peskov Assessed the Release of the UN Security Council Report on the Involvement of Russians in the Killings in CAR), *Izvestia*, 28 June 2021, https://iz.ru/1185130/2021-06-28/peskov-otcenil-doklad-sovbeza-oon-o-prichastnosti-rossiian-k-ubiistvam-v-tcar
69. 'Anti-Russia Political Hit Job: Moscow Rejects Claim of Troop Abuses in Central African Republic', Sputnik, 26 June 2021, https://sputniknews.com/africa/202106251083237262-anti-russia-political-hit-job-moscow-rejects-claim-of-troop-abuses-in-central-african-republic/
70. Interview with Central African Republic Member of Parliament Jean-Pierre Mara, April 2021.
71. Interview with author, June 2021.
72. 'Par sa politique étrangère, la RCA doit s'allier à des partenaires sérieux' (Through its Foreign Policy, the CAR Must Combine with Serious Partners), *Ndjoni Sango*, 29 June 2021, https://ndjonisango.com/2021/06/29/a-travers-sa-politique-etrangere-la-rca-doit-conjuguer-avec-des-partenaires-serieux/
73. Interviews with Bangui-based experts and officials, May 2021.

419

74. Ibid.

75. 'Russia Bolsters Presence in Central African Republic with 600 More Military Instructors', Voice of America, 2 July 2021, https://www.voanews.com/africa/russia-bolsters-presence-central-african-republic-600-more-military-instructors

76. 'La coopération militaire entre la RCA et la Russie pour "s'étendre davantage" – exclusive' (Military Cooperation Between CAR and Russia to 'Expand Further' – Exclusive), Sputnik France, 17 February 2021, https://fr.sputniknews.com/afrique/202102171045236111-la-cooperation-militaire-entre-la-rca-et-la-russie-va-selargir-davantage---exclusif/

77. Interview with CAR official, June 2021.

78. 'Reconstruction de la République centrafricaine: "La première aux entreprises russes"' (Reconstruction of the Central African Republic: 'The First to Russian Companies'), Sputnik France, 23 April 2021, https://fr.sputniknews.com/afrique/202104231045513710-reconstruction-de-la-centrafrique-la-primeur-aux-entreprises-russes/

79. 'Rossiya postavit vooruzheniye i voyennuyu tekhniku v Sudan i Laos' (Russia will Supply Weapons and Military Equipment to Sudan and Laos), TASS, 27 August 2020, https://tass.ru/armiya-i-opk/9309173

80. 'byvshiy glava vedomstva Minoborony RF schitayet, chto sobytiya v Sudane nesut riski dlya sozdaniya voyenno-morskoy bazy na Krasnom more' (Former Head of the Ministry of Defence of the Russian Federation Believes that the Events in Sudan Carry Risks for the Creation of a Naval Base on the Red Sea), Interfax, 25 October 2021, https://www.militarynews.ru/story.asp?rid=1&nid=559371&lang=RU

81. 'Zamestitel' predstavitelya Rossii v OON otsenil situatsiyu v Sudane' (Russian Deputy Representative to the UN Assessed the Situation in Sudan), RIA Novosti, 26 October 2021, https://ria.ru/20211026/sudan-1756403669.html

82. 'Lavrov prizval prekratit' lyuboye vneshneye vmeshatel'stvo v dela Sudana' (Lavrov Called for an End to Any External Interference in the Affairs of Sudan), TASS, 18 October 2021, https://tass.ru/politika/12691165

83. 'Russia Plans Naval Base in Sudan', Al Jazeera, 13 November 2020, https://www.aljazeera.com/news/2020/11/13/russia-plans-naval-base-in-sudan

84. 'Russia Plans Red Sea Naval Base in Sudan', RFE/RL, 12 November 2020, https://www.rferl.org/a/russia-plans-naval-base-on-sudan-strategic-red-sea/30943645.html

85. 'Russian Government Approves Agreement on Russian Navy Logistics Center in Sudan', TASS, 25 June 2021, https://tass.com/defense/1307377

86. Mohammed Alamin, 'Sudan's Civilians Sidelined in Army Overtures to Russia, Israel', Bloomberg, 11 December 2020.

87. 'Zachem Rossii voyennyy ob'yekt na Krasnom more' (Why Does Russia Need a Military Facility on the Red Sea), RBC, 19 November 2020, https://www.rbc.ru/politics/19/11/2020/5fb431d29a7947b75f06e721

pp. [275–277]  NOTES

88. Interview with Cameron Hudson, December 2020.
89. Ibid.
90. Ibid.
91. RBC, 19 November 2020.
92. 'Rossiyskaya voyenno-morskaya baza v Krasnom more' (Russian Naval Base in the Red Sea), *Expert*, 16 November 2020, https://expert.ru/expert/2020/47/baza-rossijskogo-vmf-v-krasnom-more/
93. Vladimir Mukhin, 'Platsdarm dlya rossiyskikh atomnykh podvodnykh lodok gotovitsya v Krasnom more' (A Foothold for Russian Nuclear Submarines is Being Prepared in the Red Sea), *Nezavisimaya Gazeta*, 12 November 2020, https://www.ng.ru/armies/2020-11-12/2_8013_submarine.html
94. 'Poyavleniye rossiyskoy voyennoy bazy v Sudane ob'yasnil ekspert' (The Emergence of a Russian Naval Base in Sudan Explained by the Expert), Mk.ru, 12 November 2020, https://www.mk.ru/politics/2020/11/12/poyavlenie-rossiyskoy-voennoy-bazy-v-sudane-obyasnil-ekspert.html
95. 'Èluósī zài fēizhōu 'bǎo diǎn' de fǎn zhì yìyì' (The Countermeasure Significance of Russia's 'Guarantee Points' in Africa), *People's Liberation Army Daily*, 26 November 2020, http://military.people.com.cn/n1/2020/1126/c1011-31945524.html
96. Interview with author, December 2020.
97. 'Russia Naval Base in Sudan Could Expand its Partnership with India in Indo-Pacific region', *The Economic Times*, 4 December 2020, https://economictimes.indiatimes.com/news/defence/russia-naval-base-in-sudan-could-expand-its-partnership-with-india-in-indo-pacific-region/articleshow/79571684.cms?from=mdr
98. 'U Rossii byla prikhot', no budet li' (Russia Had a Fad but Will There Be?), *Kommersant*, 3 June 2021, https://www.kommersant.ru/doc/4838828
99. 'Èluósī shuàixiān zài sūdān jiànlì hǎijūn jīdì quánqiú shǒu jiā jiāng kòngzhì zhòngdiǎn dìqū' (Russia is the First to Establish a Naval Base in Sudan, the first in the world, which will control key areas), *Sohu*, 16 November 2020, https://www.sohu.com/a/432141231_494439
100. 'Rossiya gotovit ryad krupnykh sdelok s Sudanom' (Russia is Preparing a Number of Major Deals with Sudan), *Rossiyskaya Gazeta*, 30 March 2021, https://rg.ru/2021/03/30/rossiia-gotovit-riad-krupnyh-sdelok-s-sudanom.html
101. 'Sudan's Silence About Russian Base Reflects Divergences in Khartoum', *The Arab Weekly*, 20 November 2020, https://thearabweekly.com/sudans-silence-about-russian-base-reflects-divergences-khartoum-0
102. Alamin, 11 December 2020.
103. 'aikhtilaf alara' hawl mawqie alqaeidat aleaskariat fi alsuwdan wamasdaru: aljaysh yaqtarib min musku tahasubana libaydin' (Opinions Differ over the Location of the Military Base in Sudan and a Source: The Military is Approaching Moscow in Anticipation of Biden), Al-Quds, 15 November 2020, https://www.alquds.co.uk/تباين-الرأي-حول-تحديد-موقع-القاعدة-الر/

NOTES pp. [278–281]

104. Jeremy Binnie, 'Russian Navy Ships Continue to Visit Sudan', Janes Intelligence, 5 May 2021, https://www.janes.com/defence-news/news-detail/russian-navy-ships-continue-to-visit-sudan

105. *Kommersant*, 3 June 2021.

106. 'Military Chief Says Sudan Reviewing Naval Base Deal with Russia', Al Jazeera, 2 June 2021, https://www.aljazeera.com/news/2021/6/2/military-chief-says-sudan-reviewing-naval-base-deal-with-russia

107. 'Sudan Lawmakers to Review Russian Navy Base Deal – FM', *The Moscow Times*, 12 July 2021, https://www.themoscowtimes.com/2021/07/12/sudan-lawmakers-to-review-russian-navy-base-deal-fm-a74497

108. Marianna Belenkaya, 'Voyenno-morskaya baza privedena v deystviye' (A Naval Base is Brought Under Cooperation), *Kommersant*, 13 July 2021.

109. Interview with author, June 2021.

110. Ibid.

111. 'Strategicheskiy Sudan' (Strategic Sudan), *Kommersant*, 12 November 2020, https://www.kommersant.ru/doc/4567734?from=doc_vrez

112. Interview with author, June 2021.

113. Gennady Petrov and Denis Moiseev, 'Moskva ne namerena otstupat' v Afrike pered Vashington' (Moscow Does not Intend to Retreat from Africa in Front of Washington), *Nezavisimaya Gazeta*, 2 June 2021, https://www.ng.ru/world/2021-06-02/1_8163_moscow.html

114. *Kommersant*, 3 June 2021.

115. Ibid.

116. *Kommersant*, 12 November 2020.

117. *Kommersant*, 3 June 2021.

118. Abdul Qadir Muhammad Ali, "amn albahr al'ahmaru: alsiyasat alkharijiat al'iiritriat fi biyat mutaghayira' (Red Sea Security: Eritrean Foreign Policy in a Changing Environment), Al Jazeera Center for Studies, 21 April 2021, https://studies.aljazeera.net/ar/article/4977

119. Andrew Korybko, 'Can Somaliland be Alternative for Russia's Troubled Sudanese Naval Base Plans?', Russian International Affairs Council, 9 June 2021, https://russiancouncil.ru/en/blogs/andrew-korybko/can-somaliland-be-alternative-for-russias-troubled-sudanese-naval-base/

120. Correspondence with author, September 2020.

121. Korybko, June 2021.

122. Interview with author, August 2021.

123. 'Vorota Indiyskogo okeana' (Indian Ocean Gate), *Nezavisimaya Gazeta*, 19 November 2020, https://nvo.ng.ru/nvo/2020-11-19/1_1118_ocean.html

124. 'Central Sahel: Spike in Violence Leads to Higher Deaths, More than 1 Million Fleeing Homes', International Committee of the Red Cross, 14 September 2020, https://www.icrc.org/en/document/central-sahel-spike-violence-leads-higher-deaths-more-1-million-fleeing-homes

pp. [281–284]  NOTES

125. 'Russia Calls for Negotiations to End Mali Crisis', CGTN, 22 August 2020, https://newsaf.cgtn.com/news/2020-08-22/Russia-calls-for-negotiations-to-end-Mali-crisis-T93O1dTph6/index.html

126. 'Posol Rossii vstretilsya s putchistami v Mali' (Russian Ambassador Meets with Putchists), *Izvestia*, 21 August 2020, https://iz.ru/1051160/2020-08-21/rossiiskii-posol-vstretilsia-s-putchistami-v-mali

127. 'Portyakova, Skorbi Mali: iz-za chego voyennye snyali prezidenta strany' (Mali Sorrows: Because the Military Removed the President of the Country), *Izvestia*, 19 August 2020, https://iz.ru/1050130/nataliia-portiakova/pechali-mali-iz-za-chego-voennye-smestili-prezidenta-strany

128. Raul Redondo, 'Russia and the coup d'etat in Mali,' *Atalayar*, 29 August 2020, https://atalayar.com/en/content/russia-and-coup-d%C3%A9tat-mali

129. 'Russia Trained the Mali Coup Leaders', *The Daily Beast*, 21 August 2020, https://www.thedailybeast.com/russia-trained-the-mali-coup-leaders

130. 'Senator prokommentiroval slukhi o prichastnosti Rossii k perevorotu v Mali' (Senator Commented on Rumors about Russia's Involvement in the Coup in Mali), RIA Novosti, 22 August 2020, https://ria.ru/20200822/prichastnost-1576125740.html

131. 'Was Russia Behind the Coup in Mali?', DW, 26 August 2020, https://www.dw.com/en/was-russia-behind-the-coup-in-mali/a-54705282

132. 'V Mali protesty osudili Frantsiyu i podnyali rossiyskiye flagi' (In Mali, Protests Condemned France and Raised Russian Flags), *Krasnya Vesna*, 27 March 2021, https://rossaprimavera.ru/news/78268c1c

133. Nathaniel Gleicher, 'Removing Coordinated Inauthentic Behaviour from France and Russia', Facebook, 15 December 2020, https://about.fb.com/news/2020/12/removing-coordinated-inauthentic-behavior-france-russia/

134. 'V posol'stve Rossii rasskazali o situatsii v Mali posle voyennogo perevorota' (The Russian Embassy Spoke About the Situation after the Military Coup), Lenta.ru, 25 May 2021, https://lenta.ru/news/2021/05/25/mali_rusemb/

135. 'Mali Strongman Goïta Reaches Out Amid International Pressure', Voice of America, 28 May 2021, https://www.voanews.com/africa/mali-strongman-goita-reaches-out-amid-international-pressure

136. 'Voyennyy perevorot 2.0 v Mali: chto proiskhodit v samom serdtse Sakhelya' (Mali Military Coup 2.0: What's Happening at the Heart of the Sahel), Federal News Agency, 31 May 2021, https://riafan.ru/1456325-voennyi-perevorot-v-mali-versiya-2-0-chto-proiskhodit-v-serdce-sakhelya

137. Vladimir Kulagin, '"Lyudi ustali ot bezyskhodnosti": pochemu zhiteli Mali zovut na pomoshch' Rossiyu' ('People are Tired of Hopelessness:' Why the Citizens of Mali are Calling for Help from Russia), Gazeta.ru, 29 May 2021, https://www.gazeta.ru/politics/2021/05/28_a_13612196.shtml

138. Danila Moiseev, 'Rossiya mozhet ukrepit' svoi pozitsii posle perevorota v Mali' (Russia can Strengthen its Position in Mali), *Nezavisimaya Gazeta*,

423

30 May 2021, https://www.ng.ru/world/2021-05-30/5_8160_mali. html

139. 'Exclusive: Deal Allowing Russian Mercenaries into Mali is Close – Sources', Reuters, 13 September 2021, https://www.reuters.com/world/africa/exclusive-deal-allowing-russian-mercenaries-into-mali-is-close-sources-2021-09-13/

140. Interview with author, October 2021.

141. Michelle Nichols, 'Lavrov Says Mali Asked Private Russian Military Company for Help', Reuters, 26 September 2021, https://www.reuters.com/world/africa/mali-asked-private-russian-military-firm-help-against-insurgents-ifx-2021-09-25/

142. 'Mali Receives Helicopters and Weapons from Russia', Al Jazeera, 1 October 2021, https://www.aljazeera.com/news/2021/10/1/mali-receives-helicopters-weapons-from-russia

143. 'Mali Accuses France of Abandonment, Approaches "Private Russian Companies"', France-24, 26 September 2021, https://www.france24.com/en/africa/20210926-mali-accuses-france-of-abandonment-approaches-private-russian-companies

144. 'Mali Denies Deployment of Russian Mercenaries from Wagner Group', France-24, 25 December 2021, https://www.france24.com/en/africa/20211225-mali-denies-deployment-of-russian-mercenaries-from-wagner-group

145. 'France Criticizes Deal Bringing Russian Mercenaries into Mali', Reuters, 15 September 2021, https://www.reuters.com/world/france-criticises-deal-bringing-russian-mercenaries-into-mali-2021-09-14/

146. Interview with author, September 2021.

147. 'VOA Exclusive: US AFRICOM Commander Says Russian Mercenaries in Mali', VOA, 20 January 2022, https://www.voanews.com/a/voa-exclusive-us-africom-commander-says-russian-mercenaries-in-mali/6406371. html

148. 'Macron Warns of "Predatory" Russian Mercenaries in Mali', France-24, 17 February 2022, https://www.france24.com/en/live-news/20220217-macron-warns-of-predatory-russian-mercenaries-in-mali

149. France-24, 25 December 2021.

150. 'Russian Troops Deploy to Timbuktu in Mali After French Withdrawal', Reuters, 6 January 2022, https://www.reuters.com/article/mali-security-russia-idAFL8N2TM47J

151. 'Russia: Gold Firm Revives Former Soviet Mines', RFE/RL, 9 May 1997, https://www.rferl.org/a/1084806.html

152. Raphael Parens, 'The Wagner Group's Playbook in Africa: Mali', Foreign Policy Research Institute, 18 March 2022, https://www.fpri.org/article/2022/03/the-wagner-groups-playbook-in-africa-mali/

153. *Vedomosti*, 18 February 2022.

pp. [287–289]   NOTES

154. 'Maliytsy Privetstvuyut Obrashcheniye Svoyego Prezidenta k Rossiyskim Voyennym Kompaniyam' (Malians Welcome their President's Appeal to Russian Military Companies), Foundation for National Values Protection, 1 January 2022, https://web.archive.org/web/20220101095249/https://fznc.ru/o-fonde/nashi-issledovaniya/malijczy-privetstvuyut-obrashhenie-svoego-prezidenta-k-rossijskim-voennym-kompaniyam/

155. 'Mali – Interview exclusive d'un spécialiste militaire Russe sur les activités des SMP et Wagner au Mali' (Mali- Exclusive Interview with a Russian Military Specialist on the Activities of PMCs and Wagner in Mali), *Maliactu*, 5 October 2021, https://maliactu.net/mali-interview-exclusive-dun-specialiste-militaire-russe-sur-les-activites-des-smp-et-wagner-au-mali/

156. 'Doubt Cast on Photos Alleged to Show Wagner Mercenaries Training Wagner Soldiers', France-24, 26 November 2021, https://observers.france24.com/en/africa/20211129-wagner-mercenaries-train-malian-soldiers-photos-doubts

157. 'Frantsiya vyvodit voyska iz Mali, gde oni borolis' s terrorizmom' (France withdraws troops from Mali where they fought terrorism), *Vedomosti*, 18 February 2022, https://www.vedomosti.ru/politics/articles/2022/02/17/909877-frantsiya-vivodit-voiska-mali

158. 'Saymondi: Frantsiya soznatel'no otkazalas' ot pomoshchi Mali v bor'be s terroristami' (Saimondy: France deliberately refused to help Mali in the fight against terrorists), Federal News Agency, 10 January 2022, https://riafan.ru/22671992-Saimondy_Frantsiya_namerenno_otkazalas_pomogat_Mali_v_bor_be_s_terroristami

159. *Vedomosti*, 18 February 2022.

160. 'Strannaya smert' prezidenta Chada. Kto vinovat: CHVK Vagnera ili Frantsiya?' (The Strange Death of the President of Chad. Who is to Blame: PMC Wagner or France?), *Krasnya Vesna*, 29 April 2021, https://rossaprimavera.ru/article/37e10d0e

161. James Tasamba, 'Russia refutes Arms Trafficking Claims Against Chad', Anadolu Agency, 7 April 2021, https://www.aa.com.tr/en/asia-pacific/russia-refutes-arm-trafficking-claims-against-chad/2200700

162. Samer al-Atrush, 'Chad Rebels Trained by Russia March on Heart of Africa', *The Times*, 23 April 2021, https://www.thetimes.co.uk/article/chad-rebels-trained-by-russia-march-on-heart-of-africa-n8gzkgk0q

163. 'Who are Chad's FACT Rebels and What are Their Goals', Al Jazeera, 21 April 2021, https://www.aljazeera.com/news/2021/4/21/who-are-chads-fact-rebels-and-what-are-their-goals

164. 'Chad FM Warns Against Russian Interference', France-24, 24 September 2021, https://www.france24.com/en/live-news/20210923-chad-fm-warns-against-russian-interference

165. *Krasnya Vesna*, 29 April 2021.

166. 'Vse v Chad' (All to Chad), Lenta.ru, 29 April 2021, https://lenta.ru/articles/2021/04/29/on_debys_death/

425

NOTES pp. [289–294]

167. 'Russia to Support G5 Sahel Group by Providing Weapons, Training Peacekeepers – Lavrov', TASS, 7 December 2021, https://tass.com/world/1371879

168. 'Chad, Central African Republic Call for Investigation of Border Incident', Reuters, 2 June 2021, https://www.reuters.com/world/chad-central-african-republic-call-international-investigation-into-border-2021-06-02/

169. 'Russian Aluminum Giant Says Could Recall Personnel from Guinea if Crisis Worsens', Reuters, 6 September 2021, https://www.reuters.com/world/russia-calls-release-guineas-conde-2021-09-06/

170. 'Deripaska priznal, chto perevorot v Gvineye mozhet potryasti rynok alyuminiya' (Deripaska Admitted that the Coup in Guinea Could Shake the Aluminium Market), Interfax, 6 September 2021, https://www.interfax.ru/business/788727

171. Danila Moiseev, 'Boksitovaya imperiya riskuyet grazhdanskoy voynoy vmesto zastoya' (Bauxite Empire Risks Civil War Instead of Stagnation), *Nezavisimaya Gazeta*, 6 September 2021, https://www.ng.ru/world/2021-09-06/1_8244_guinea.html

172. Ekaterina Postnikova, 'Ruda ne nakrasitsya: pochemu Rossiyu bespokoit perevorot v Gvineye' (Ore Will Not Make Up: Why Russia is Worried about the Coup in Guinea), *Izvestia*, 6 September 2021, https://iz.ru/1217885/ekaterina-postnikova/ne-sostavit-ruda-pochemu-rossiiu-bespokoit-perevorot-v-gvinee

173. 'Triumf zakona: novyye vlasti Gvinei privlekut k ugolovnoy otvetstvennosti eks-prezidenta Al'fa Konde' (Triumph of Law: New Authorities in Guinea will Prosecute Ex-President Alpha Conde), Federal News Agency, 14 September 2021, https://riafan.ru/1521227-torzhestvo-zakona-novye-vlasti-gvinei-predadut-sudu-eks-prezidenta-alfa-konde

174. *Postnikova*, 6 September 2021.

175. Tom Fowdy, 'The Coup in Tiny Guinea Matters at a Geopolitical Level. The US-China "Cold War" is a Race for Strategic Dominance of Commodities', RT, 7 September 2021, https://www.rt.com/op-ed/534165-guinea-military-coup-doumbouya/

176. 'Examining Neocolonial Interests in the Guinea Coup', Sputnik, 9 September 2021, https://sputniknews.com/20210909/examining-imperialist-ties-and-neocolonial-interests-in-the-guinea-coup-1088895756.html

177. Federal News Agency, 14 September 2021.

10.  THE UKRAINE WAR AND RUSSIA'S AFRICA STRATEGY

1.  Hilary Kumuyu, 'Museveni Son Backs Russia Assault on Ukraine', *Nairobi News*, 2 March 2022, https://nairobinews.nation.africa/museveni-son-backs-russia-assault-on-ukraine/

2.  'Uganda Leader Says China-Style Diplomacy "Better than" the West's', Nikkei, 17 March 2022, https://asia.nikkei.com/Editor-s-Picks/

pp. [294–297]  NOTES

Interview/Uganda-leader-says-China-style-diplomacy-better-than-the-West-s

3. 'S Africa's Ramaphosa: NATO to Blame for Russia's War in Ukraine', Al Jazeera, 18 March 2022, https://www.aljazeera.com/news/2022/3/18/update-1-s-africas-ramaphosa-blames-nato-for-russias-war-in-ukraine

4. Countries that condemned the war (Egypt, Libya, Tunisia, Mauritania, Sierra Leone, Liberia, Côte d'Ivoire, Ghana, Benin, Niger, Nigeria, Chad, Sao Tome and Principe, Gabon, Rwanda, Democratic Republic of Congo, Kenya, Somalia, Malawi, Zambia, Botswana, Lesotho, Comoros, Mauritius, and Seychelles). Countries that abstained (Algeria, Mali, Senegal, Sudan, South Sudan, Central African Republic, Equatorial Guinea, Congo, Uganda, Burundi, Tanzania, Angola, Mozambique, Zimbabwe, Namibia, South Africa, Madagascar). Countries that declined to vote (Morocco, Guinea, Guinea-Bissau, Burkina Faso, Togo, Cameroon, and Ethiopia).

5. Hannah Ryder and Etsehiwot Kebret, 'Why African Countries Had Different Views on the UNGA Ukraine Resolution, and Why This Matters', CSIS, 15 March 2022, https://www.csis.org/analysis/why-african-countries-had-different-views-unga-ukraine-resolution-and-why-matters

6. 'Kenyan UN Ambassador Compares Ukraine's Plight to Colonial Legacy in Africa', NPR, 22 February 2022, https://www.npr.org/2022/02/22/1082334172/kenya-security-council-russia

7. Patrick Gathara, 'The Kenyan UN Ambassador's Ukraine Speech Does Not Deserve Praise', Al Jazeera, 23 February 2022, https://www.aljazeera.com/opinions/2022/2/23/what-the-kenyan-un-ambassador-got-wrong-about-colonialism

8. Aanu Adeoye, 'UN Vote on Russia Invasion Shows a Changing Africa', Chatham House, 7 March 2022, https://www.chathamhouse.org/2022/03/un-vote-russia-invasion-shows-changing-africa

9. Tafi Mhaka, 'Africa Should Not Help Putin Whitewash his Crimes', Al Jazeera, 18 March 2022, https://www.aljazeera.com/opinions/2022/3/18/africa-should-not-help-putin-whitewash-his-crimes-in-ukraine

10. Patrick Ryan, 'African Leaders Tell Forum in Dubai Why they did not Condemn Russian Invasion of Ukraine', The National, 30 March 2022, https://www.thenationalnews.com/uae/government/2022/03/30/african-leaders-tell-forum-in-dubai-why-they-did-not-condemn-russian-invasion-of-ukraine/

11. 'AU Chairperson Says Africa a "Collateral Victim" of Ukraine War', Al Jazeera, 25 May 2022, https://www.aljazeera.com/economy/2022/5/25/au-chairperson-says-africa-a-collateral-victim-of-ukraine-war

12. Kester Kenn Klomeagh, 'Significance of Russian Officials and African Ambassadors Meetings on Russia-Ukraine Crisis', Pressenza, 27 March 2022, https://www.pressenza.com/2022/03/significance-of-russian-officials-and-african-ambassadors-meetings-on-russia-ukraine-crisis/

NOTES pp. [297–300]

13. 'Why Russia Wins Some Sympathy in Africa and the Middle East', *The Economist*, 12 March 2022, https://www.economist.com/middle-east-and-africa/2022/03/12/why-russia-wins-some-sympathy-in-africa-and-the-middle-east

   A 7 March 2022 *Economist* opinion poll showed approximately 60% support for Russia as an important economic partner in Kenya, South Africa and Uganda, and over 80% in Mali and Côte d'Ivoire. Nigeria was the sole outlier in countries polled, as only 30% viewed Russia as a key economic partner.

14. 'S Africa's Ramaphosa: Russia Sanctions Hurting "Bystander" States', Al Jazeera, 24 May 2022, https://www.aljazeera.com/economy/2022/5/24/update-2-s-africas-ramaphosa-russia-sanctions-hurt-bystander-countries

15. Ryan, 2022.

16. Mark Kapchanga, 'Africa's Neutrality over Ukraine Justified', *Global Times*, 28 March 2022, https://www.globaltimes.cn/page/202203/1257045.shtml

17. Tafi Mhaka, 'Can the African Union be a Neutral Arbiter of Peace in Ukraine?', Al Jazeera, 28 May 2022, https://www.aljazeera.com/opinions/2022/5/28/can-the-african-union-broker-peace-in-ukraine

18. Ibid.

19. 'Ekonomist ukazal na neobkhodimost' uvelicheniya prisutstviya Rossii v Afrike' (The Economist Pointed to the Need to Increase the Presence of Russia in Africa), *Izvestia*, 3 June 2022, https://iz.ru/1344463/2022-06-03/ekonomist-ukazal-na-neobkhodimost-narashchivaniia-prisutstviia-rossii-v-afrike

20. Andrey Maslov and Dmitry Suslov, 'Vozvrashcheniye v Afriku: kak sdelat' eto prioritetom dlya Rossii' (Return to Africa: How to Make it a Russian Priority), *Russia in Global Affairs*, 10 January 2022, https://globalaffairs.ru/articles/vozvrashhenie-v-afriku-prioritet/

21. Yuri Sigov, 'Afrikanskaya povestka Moskvy' (Moscow's African Agenda), *Nezavisimaya Gazeta*, 15 May 2022, https://www.ng.ru/dipkurer/2022-05-15/9_8435_africa.html

22. 'Strany Afriki i Blizhnego Vostoka pereydut na torgovlyu s RF v natsional'noy valyute' (The Countries of Africa and the Middle East will Switch to Trade with the Russian Federation in National Currency), *Izvestia*, 25 May 2022, https://iz.ru/1340014/2022-05-25/strany-afriki-i-blizhnego-vostoka-pereidut-na-torgovliu-s-rf-v-natcvaliute

23. 'Kak Rossiya vyvedet Afriku iz-pod vliyaniya Zapada' (How Russia will Take Africa out of the Influence of the West), *Vzglyad*, 4 June 2022, https://vz.ru/politics/2022/6/4/1161521.html

24. Declan Walsh and Valerie Hopkins, 'Russia Seeks Buyers for Plundered Ukrainian Grain, US Warns', *New York Times*, 5 June 2022, https://www.nytimes.com/2022/06/05/world/africa/ukraine-grain-russia-sales.html

428

pp. [301–304]                    NOTES

25.  Khalil al-Anani, 'Russia's War on Ukraine: Egypt's Limited Room for Maneuver', Arab Center, 6 April 2022, https://arabcenterdc.org/resource/ russias-war-on-ukraine-egypts-limited-room-for-maneuver/

26.  Ahmed Aliba, 'harb 'uwkrania walsirae aljiusiasiu bayn rusia wahilf shamal al'atlasii' (The Ukraine War and the Geopolitical Conflict between Russia and NATO), Al-Ahram Center for Political and Strategic Studies, 28 February 2022, https://acpss.ahram.org.eg/News/17417.aspx#

27.  Amr Kandil, 'Egypt Urges Quick Political Solution to Russia-Ukraine Crisis, Rejects Unilateral Economic Sanctions', Ahram Online, 2 March 2022, https://english.ahram.org.eg/NewsContent/1/1234/462137/Egypt/ Foreign-Affairs/Egypt-urges-quick-political-solution-to-RussiaUkra.aspx

28.  'Russia-Ukraine War: Egypt Seeks Support from Arab States, IMF to Curb Capital Flight', *Middle East Eye*, 9 April 2022, https://www.middleeasteye. net/news/russia-ukraine-war-egypt-arab-states-imf-foreign-capital-flight-curb

29.  Azza Guergues, 'Ukraine War Drives More Traffic to Egypt's Suez Canal, Increasing Revenues', Al Monitor, 14 May 2022, https://www.al-monitor. com/originals/2022/05/ukraine-war-drives-more-traffic-egypts-suez-canal-increasing-revenues

30.  'Russia-Ukraine War: Italy Signs New Gas Deal with Algeria in Bid to Cut Moscow Reliance', *Middle East Eye*, 11 April 2022, https://www. middleeasteye.net/news/russia-ukraine-war-italy-signs-new-gas-deal-algeria-bid-cut-moscow-reliance

31.  Andrew Farrand, 'Algeria's Fate is Tied to the Ukraine Crisis. Will a War Extinguish Hope for the Country's Popular Movement?', Atlantic Council, 17 February 2022, https://www.atlanticcouncil.org/blogs/menasource/ algerias-fate-is-tied-to-the-ukraine-crisis/

32.  Ijeoma Ndukwe, 'Ukraine Crisis: Can Africa Replace Russian Gas Supplies to Europe', BBC, 16 May 2022, https://www.bbc.co.uk/news/world-africa-61334470

33.  'Neftegazovyye interesy Rossii zastrakhuyet Blizhniy Vostok' (Oil and Gas Interests of Russia will be Insured by the Middle East), *Vzgylad*, 14 May 2022, https://vz.ru/world/2022/5/14/1158402.html

34.  Jasper Hamann, 'Morocco Feels Impact of Conflict Between Ukraine and Russia', *Morocco World News*, 26 February 2022, https://www. moroccoworldnews.com/2022/02/347316/morocco-feels-impact-of-conflict-between-russia-and-ukraine

35.  Souad Anouar, 'Survey: Despite Ukraine War, 37% of Moroccans Want to Keep Ties With Russia', *Morocco World News*, 31 May 2022, https://www. moroccoworldnews.com/2022/05/349407/survey-despite-ukraine-war-37-of-moroccans-want-to-keep-ties-with-russia

36.  Giorgio Cafiero and Emily Miliken, 'Russians Unlikely to Leave Libya Despite Ukraine War', Al Jazeera, 15 April 2022, https://www.aljazeera. com/news/2022/4/15/russians-unlikely-leave-libya-despite-ukraine-war

NOTES pp. [304–306]

37. 'Liviyskiy stsenariy' (Libyan Scenario), Federal News Agency, 27 December 2021, https://riafan.ru/1578250-kak-sryv-vyborov-obedinil-liviyu-protiv-vmeshatelstva-zapada
38. 'LNA Denies Kyiv's Allegation of Sending Mercenaries to Ukraine', *The Libya Update*, 21 March 2022, https://libyaupdate.com/lna-denies-kyivs-allegation-of-sending-mercenaries-to-ukraine/
39. Nerea Belmonte, The Wagner Group in Libya: An Added Problem for Gas Exports to Europe, Atalayar, 29 September 2022, https://atalayar.com/en/content/wagner-group-libya-added-problem-gas-exports-europe
40. UN Report: Libya Faces Serious Security Threat from Foreign Fighters, Russia's Wagner, Euronews, 28 May 2022, https://www.euronews.com/2022/05/28/un-report-libya-faces-serious-security-threat-from-foreign-fighters-russia-s-wagner
41. Russia Blocks Long Extension of UN Libya Mission, Daily Sabah, 29 July 2022, https://www.dailysabah.com/world/africa/russia-blocks-long-extension-of-un-libya-mission
42. Interview with Jalel Harchaoui, October 2022.
43. Federal News Agency, 27 December 2021.
44. 'Mustafa Fetouri, Libya Turns on Russia over Ukraine War but Does it Matter?', Al Monitor, 11 March 2022, https://www.al-monitor.com/originals/2022/03/libya-turns-russia-over-ukraine-war-does-it-matter
45. Samuel Ramani, 'How has the Ukraine War Affected Russia's Ties with Libya and Sudan', Middle East Institute, 25 April 2022, https://www.mei.edu/publications/how-has-ukraine-war-affected-russias-ties-libya-and-sudan
46. 'Sudan Remains Open to Naval Base Deal with Russia', Al-Monitor, 4 March 2022, https://www.al-monitor.com/originals/2022/03/sudan-remains-open-naval-base-deal-russia
47. 'Digital Press Briefing with the Commander of the US Africa Command, US Army General Stephen J. Townsend', US Department of State, 3 February 2022, https://www.state.gov/digital-press-briefing-with-the-commander-of-the-u-s-africa-command-u-s-army-general-stephen-j-townsend/
48. Hamza Hendawi, 'Moscow Hosts Sudan's Gen Dagalo Amid War in Ukraine', *The National*, 24 February 2022, https://www.thenationalnews.com/mena/2022/02/24/moscow-hosts-sudans-gen-dagalo-amid-war-in-ukraine/
49. 'Hemeti Visit Prompts Protests in Port Sudan', *Dabanga*, 16 March 2022, https://www.dabangasudan.org/en/all-news/article/hemeti-visit-prompts-protests-in-port-sudan
50. Mat Nashed, 'Sudan: Russian Influence and Ukraine War Stir Domestic Tensions', Al Jazeera, 18 March 2022, https://www.aljazeera.com/features/2022/3/18/sudan-russian-influence-and-ukraine-war-stir-domestic-tensions
51. Declan Walsh, 'From Russia with Love: A Putin Ally Mines Gold and Plays Favorites in Sudan', *New York Times*, 5 June 2022, https://www.nytimes.com/2022/06/05/world/africa/wagner-russia-sudan-gold-putin.html

pp. [307–309]    NOTES

52. Ibid.
53. 'Sudan's Foreign Ministry Denies Presence of Wagner Group', Reuters, 22 March 2022, https://www.reuters.com/world/africa/sudans-foreign-ministry-denies-presence-russian-wagner-group-2022-03-22/
54. Mattia Caniglia and Theodore Murphy, 'Khartoum's Autocratic Enabler: Russia in Sudan', European Council on Foreign Relations, 15 December 2021, https://ecfr.eu/article/khartoums-autocratic-enabler-russia-in-sudan/
55. Jason Burke and Zelnab Mohammed Salih, 'Russian Mercenaries Accused of Deadly Attacks on Mines on Sudan-CAR Border', The Guardian, 21 June 2022, https://www.theguardian.com/world/2022/jun/21/russian-mercenaries-accused-of-deadly-attacks-on-mines-on-sudan-car-border
56. Ibid.
57. Gelmo Dawit, 'Ethiopia Calls for Restraint in Ukraine Crisis', 3 March 2022, https://www.voanews.com/a/6468646.html
58. Dawit Endeshaw, 'Ethiopians Queue Up to Volunteer for Russia's Fight in Ukraine', Reuters, 21 April 2022, https://www.reuters.com/world/ethiopians-queue-up-volunteer-russias-fight-ukraine-2022-04-21/
59. 'Eritrea Seeks to Evade Sanctions Through Russia, China Alliances', Harrnet, 26 February 2022, https://www.harrnet.org/index.php/articles-corner/english-articles/item/7961-eritrea-seeks-to-evade-sanctions-through-russia-china-alliances
60. 'Kenya: Russia Says Sanctions Derailing Trade with Kenya, Refutes Claims Moscow to Blame for Rising Commodity Prices', All Africa, 28 March 2022, https://allafrica.com/stories/202203280588.html
61. David Thomas, 'Kenya will Lose $100m but I Support Russia Sanctions, says Odinga', African Business, 17 March 2022, https://african.business/2022/03/trade-investment/kenya-will-lose-100m-but-i-support-sanctions-says-odinga/
62. 'Tanzania Economy Feels the Heat from Ukraine War', The East African, 24 May 2022, https://www.theeastafrican.co.ke/tea/business/tanzania-economy-feels-the-heat-from-ukraine-war-3822258
63. 'War in Ukraine: To Seduce Africa, Putin Supporters Rewrite History', The Africa Report, 23 March 2022, https://www.theafricareport.com/186149/war-in-ukraine-to-seduce-africa-putin-supporters-rewrite-history/
64. 'Leap into Bitcoin Bemuses People of Central African Republic', Daily Sabah, 8 May 2022, https://www.dailysabah.com/business/finance/leap-into-bitcoin-bemuses-people-of-central-african-republic
65. 'Une attaque de mercenaires russes sur des sites miniers à Kouki fait des morts et des blesses' (An Attack by Russian Mercenaries on Mining Sites in Kouki Leaves People Dead and Injured), Corbeau News, 21 April 2022, https://corbeaunews-centrafrique.org/une-attaque-des-mercenaires-russes-sur-des-chantiers-miniers-a-kouki-fait-des-morts-et-des-blesses/
66. 'Zhurnalisty TSAR vysoko otsenili deyatel'nost' Kloda Ramo Biro na postu ministra oborony' (CAR Journalists Highly Appreciated the Activities

431

NOTES       pp. [309–312]

of Claude Rameau Biro as Minister of Defence), Federal News Agency, 3 February 2022, https://riafan.ru/22805407-zhurnalisti_tsar_visoko_otsenili_deyatel_nost_kloda_ramo_biro_na_postu_ministra_oboroni

67. Philip Obaji Jr, 'Survivors Say Russian Mercenaries Slaughtered 70 Civilians in Gold Mine Massacre', *Daily Beast*, 31 January 2022, https://www.thedailybeast.com/wagner-group-accused-of-killing-70-at-mine-in-aigbado-central-african-republic

68. 'Central African Republic: Abuses by Russia-Linked Forces', Human Rights Watch, 3 May 2022, https://www.hrw.org/news/2022/05/03/central-african-republic-abuses-russia-linked-forces

69. Ibid.

70. 'Cameroon Signs Agreement with Russia in Further Boost to Military Ties', RFI, 22 April 2022, https://www.rfi.fr/en/africa/20220422-cameroon-signs-agreement-with-russia-in-further-boost-to-military-ties-wagner-ukraine

71. Juan Pena, 'Cameroon-Russia Miltiary Deal Puts France on Alert', Atalayar, 13 May 2022, https://atalayar.com/en/content/cameroon-russia-military-deal-puts-france-alert

72. 'War in Ukraine: The Congolese in the Ranks of the Pro-Russian Militia in Luhansk', France-24, 9 June 2022, https://observers.france24.com/en/europe/20220613-war-in-ukraine-the-congolese-in-the-ranks-of-the-pro-russian-militia-in-luhansk

73. Colum Lynch, Amy Mackinnon and Robbie Gramer, 'Russia Flounders in Ukraine but Doubles Down in Mali', *Foreign Policy*, 14 April 2022, https://foreignpolicy.com/2022/04/14/russia-ukraine-mali-wagner-group-mercenaries/

74. 'Mali Receives Two Russian Helicopters', *Africa News*, 18 April 2022, https://www.africanews.com/2022/04/18/mali-receives-two-russian-military-helicopters/

75. 'Reported Massacre in Mali: UK Minister for Africa's Statement', Government of the United Kingdom, 5 April 2022, https://www.gov.uk/government/news/minister-for-africa-statement-reported-massacre-in-mali

76. 'German FM Urges End to Mali's Cooperation with Russian Forces', Al Jazeera, 13 April 2022, https://www.aljazeera.com/news/2022/4/13/german-fm-urges-end-to-malis-cooperation-with-russia

77. 'Frantsiya opravdyvayet zverstva boyevikov, chtoby diskreditirovat' maliyskiye vlasti' (France Justifies Militant Atrocities to Discredit Malian Authorities), Federal News Agency, 13 April 2022, https://riafan.ru/23016992-frantsiya_opravdivaet_zverstva_boevikov_dlya_diskreditatsii_vlastei_mali

78. Jason Burke and Emmanuel Akinwotu, 'Russian Mercenaries Linked to Civilian Casualties in Mali', *The Guardian*, 4 May 2022, https://www.theguardian.com/world/2022/may/04/russian-mercenaries-wagner-group-linked-to-civilian-massacres-in-mali

432

pp. [312–315]    NOTES

79. Peter Mwai, 'What Are France's Accusations Over a Mass Grave Found in Mali', BBC, 30 April 2022, https://www.bbc.co.uk/news/61257796

80. Annie Risemberg, 'France Blames Russian Mercenaries in Mali for False Claims About Mass Graves', Voice of America, 22 April 2022, https://www.voanews.com/a/france-blames-russian-mercenaries-in-mali-for-false-claims-about-mass-graves/6541258.html

81. Danila Moiseyev, 'CHVK Vagnera possorila Zapad s Mali' (PMC Wagner Quarreled Between the West and Mali), *Nezavisimaya Gazeta*, 12 April 2022, https://www.ng.ru/world/2022-04-12/1_8415_mali.html

82. Jason Burke, 'Facebook Struggles as Russia Steps up Presence in Unstable West Africa', *The Guardian*, 17 April 2022, https://www.theguardian.com/world/2022/apr/17/facebook-struggles-as-russia-steps-up-presence-in-unstable-west-africa

83. 'Russia-West Tensions Inflame UN Debate on Mali Peacekeepers', Voice of America, 19 June 2022, https://www.voanews.com/a/russia-west-tensions-inflame-un-debate-on-mali-peacekeepers/6624137.html

84. Christophe Chatelot and Cyril Bensimon, 'Paris Fails to Counter Russian Propaganda in the Sahel', *Le Monde*, 21 May 2022, https://www.lemonde.fr/en/international/article/2022/05/21/paris-fails-to-counter-russian-propaganda-in-the-sahel_5984236_4.html

85. 'Rossiyu prosyat spasti yeshche odnu stranu v Afrike' (Russia is Asked to Save Another Country in Africa), *Vzyglad*, 27 January 2022, https://vz.ru/world/2022/1/27/1140800.html

86. Henry Wilkins, 'Pro-Russia Sentiment Grows in Burkina Faso After Coup', VOA, 28 January 2022, https://www.voanews.com/a/pro-russia-sentiment-grows-in-burkina-faso-after-coup/6416363.html

87. *Vzyglad*, 27 January 2022.

88. Ibid.

89. Telegram, 1 October 2022, https://t.me/boris_rozhin/65754

90. Manukyan: perevorot v Burkina-Faso stal primerom izbavleniya Afriki ot vliyaniya neokolonizatorov (Manukyan: The Coup in Burkina Faso was an example of Africa's deliverance from the neocolonialists, RIAFAN, 2 October 2022). See https://riafan.ru/23674881-manukyan_perevorot_v_burkina_faso_stal_primerom_izbavleniya_afriki_ot_vliyaniya_neokolonialistov

91. Telegram, 1 October 2022. https://t.me/logikamarkova/3659

92. David Lawler, Inside the French Effort to Counter Russian Mercenaries in Africa, Axios, 14 October 2022, https://www.axios.com/2022/10/13/france-west-africa-wagner-group-disinformation

93. 'Russian War on Ukraine Hits Poorer Countries with Surging Wheat, Energy Prices: Niger President', Anadolu Agency, 12 March 2022, https://www.aa.com.tr/en/antalya-diplomacy-forum-2022/russian-war-on-ukraine-hits-poorer-countries-with-surging-wheat-energy-prices-niger-president/2532549

433

94. Williams Anuku, 'Russia Forfeited \$2 bn Ajaokuta Steel Renovation Contract over war with Ukraine- Adegbite', *Daily Post*, 31 March 2022, https://dailypost.ng/2022/03/31/russia-forfeited-2bn-ajaokuta-steel-renovation-contract-over-war-with-ukraine-adegbite/

95. Akin Irede, 'Nigeria: Russia-Ukraine War Threatens Completion of the \$8 Billion Ajaokuta Steel Plant', *Africa Report*, 2 March 2022, https://www.theafricareport.com/181142/nigeria-russia-ukraine-war-threatens-completion-of-the-8bn-ajaokuta-steel-plant/

96. Benjamin Fox, 'Nigeria Offers to Plug EU's Russian Gas Supply Gap', Euractiv, 28 March 2022, https://www.euractiv.com/section/energy-environment/news/nigeria-offers-to-plug-eus-russian-gas-supply-gap/

97. Souad Anouar, 'Russia Wants to Invest in Morocco-Nigeria Gas Pipeline', *Morocco World News*, 3 May 2022, https://www.moroccoworldnews.com/2022/05/348773/russia-wants-to-invest-in-morocco-nigeria-gas-pipeline

98. 'Government Must Provide Reasons to the Public Why Zambia Voted Against Russia at the UN', *Lusaka Times*, 5 March 2022, https://www.lusakatimes.com/2022/03/05/government-must-provide-reasons-to-the-public-why-zambia-voted-against-russia-at-the-un/

99. 'South Africa Skates on Diplomatic Thin Ice Over Russia-Ukraine War', France-24, 28 March 2022, https://www.france24.com/en/live-news/20220328-south-africa-skates-on-diplomatic-thin-ice-over-russia-ukraine-war

100. Ibid.

101. Alvin Botes, 'Ukraine – South Africa is not Neutral, we are non-aligned', *Daily Maverick*, 16 May 2022, https://www.dailymaverick.co.za/opinionista/2022-05-16-ukraine-south-africa-is-not-neutral-we-are-non-aligned/

102. James Hamill, 'South Africa has Clearly Chosen a Side on the war in Ukraine', *World Politics Review*, 16 March 2022, https://webcache.googleusercontent.com/search?q=cache:zFcT9hDakE0J:https://www.worldpoliticsreview.com/articles/30399/south-africa-has-chosen-a-side-on-ukraine-invasion-by-russia+&cd=22&hl=en&ct=clnk&gl=uk

103. France-24, 28 March 2022.

104. Ibid.

105. 'Activists Head to Russian Embassy in Pretoria, Demanding Immediate Release of Anti-War Activists', IOL, 20 May 2022, https://www.iol.co.za/news/politics/activists-head-to-russian-embassy-in-pretoria-demanding-immediate-release-of-anti-war-activists-01c8547b-abeb-4f22-8b2d-4a5c47ba2821

106. 'South Africa is Pursuing a Major Gas Deal- and Russia Wants In', *Daily Maverick*, 27 March 2022, https://www.dailymaverick.co.za/article/2022-03-27-south-africa-pursuing-major-gas-deal-and-russia-wants-in/

## NOTES

107. 'Mabuza Moves to Defend SA's Decision to Buy Gas from Russia', *Eyewitness News*, 1 April 2022, https://ewn.co.za/2022/04/01/mabuza-moves-to-defend-sa-s-decision-to-buy-gas-from-russia

108. Farai Shawn Matiashe, 'Historic Friends, Zimbabwe Remains Neutral to Russia, Despite Hard Hit to Fragile Economy', *The Africa Report*, 25 March 2022, https://www.theafricareport.com/186769/historic-friends-zimbabwe-remains-neutral-to-russia-despite-hard-hit-to-fragile-economy/

109. Zvamaida Murwira, 'Zimbabwe: Russia-Ukraine Conflict Wake Up Call – President', *The Herald*, 11 April 2022, https://allafrica.com/stories/202204110422.html

110. 'Mnagagwa Looks to Putin Example in Bid to Revive Floundering Zim \$', *New Zimbabwe*, 2 May 2022, https://www.newzimbabwe.com/mnangagwa-looks-to-putin-example-in-bid-to-revive-floundering-zim/

111. 'Kremlin Says Putin Updated Angola on its Goals in Ukraine', TASS, 28 April 2022, https://tass.com/politics/1444895?utm_source=google.com&utm_medium=organic&utm_campaign=google.com&utm_referrer=google.com

112. 'Angolan Diamond Mine Says Russia Sanctions Could Hurt Operations', Al Jazeera, 9 May 2022, https://www.aljazeera.com/economy/2022/5/9/angolas-endiama-says-sanctions-against-russia-could-hurt-its-diamond-operations

113. 'Italy Signs Deal with Angola in Bid to Boycott Russia', *Africa News*, 21 April 2022, https://www.africanews.com/2022/04/21/italy-signs-gas-deal-with-angola-in-a-bid-to-boycott-russia//

## EPILOGUE TO THE PAPERBACK EDITION: RUSSIA'S AFRICA POLICY IN 2023—SEISMIC SHOCKS, SMALL TRANSFORMATIONS

1. 'Putin Promises Grains, Debt Write-Off as Russia Seeks Africa Allies', Al Jazeera, 28 July 2023, https://www.aljazeera.com/news/2023/7/28/putin-promises-grains-debt-write-off-as-russia-seeks-africa-allies

2. 'Vstrecha s prezidentom Ugandy Yoveri Kagutoy Museveni' (Meeting with president of Uganda Yoweri Kaguta Museveni), President of Russia, 27 July 2023, http://kremlin.ru/events/president/news/page/17

3. 'Diplomat iz Gvinei priyekhal na sammit Rossiya-Afrika v futbolke s Putinym' (A diplomat from Guinea came to the Russia-Africa Summit wearing a Putin T-shirt), *Izvestia*, 27 July 2023, https://iz.ru/1550242/2023-07-27/diplomat-iz-gvinei-prishel-na-sammit-rossiia-afrika-v-futbolke-s-putinym

4. Korir Sing'Oei, Twitter, 17 July 2023, https://x.com/SingoeiAKorir/status/1680995973311393792?s=20

5. Kester Kenn Klomegah, 'Sergey Lavrov's Working Visit to Africa', *Modern Diplomacy*, 24 July 2022, https://moderndiplomacy.eu/2022/07/24/sergey-lavrovs-working-visit-to-africa/

NOTES pp. [322–325]

6. 'Macron Calls Russia "One of the Last Imperial Colonial Powers" on Africa Visit', France-24, 28 July 2022, https://www.france24.com/en/africa/20220728-marcon-calls-russia-one-of-last-imperial-colonial-powers-in-benin-visit

7. Susie Blann, 'Russia Says It Wants to End Ukraine's "Unacceptable Regime"', Associated Press, 25 July 2022, https://apnews.com/article/russia-ukraine-zelenskyy-kyiv-black-sea-arab-league-b5c583e8d057897cfdef6b40 7e113339

8. 'Uganda's Museveni Extols Russia-Africa Ties during Lavrov Visit', Al Jazeera, 26 July 2022, https://www.aljazeera.com/news/2022/7/26/ugandan-leader-extols-africa-russia-friendship-during-visit-by-lavrov

9. Robert Plummer, 'Ukraine War: Russia Denies Causing Global Food Crisis', BBC, 24 July 2022, https://www.bbc.co.uk/news/world-middle-east-62284377

10. 'Rossiya pobezhdayet Zapad v bor'be za Afriku' (Russia defeats the West in the fight for Africa), *Vzgylad*, 28 July 2022, https://vz.ru/politics/2022/7/28/1169676.html

11. Al Jazeera, 26 July 2022.

12. 'Lavrov, Back from Africa, Says West Has Failed to "Isolate" Russia', Reuters, 10 February 2023, https://www.reuters.com/world/europe/lavrov-back-africa-says-west-has-failed-isolate-russia-2023-02-10/

13. 'Russia's Lavrov Gets Controversial Welcome in South Africa', *The Moscow Times*, 23 January 2023, https://www.themoscowtimes.com/2023/01/23/russias-lavrov-gets-controversial-welcome-in-south-africa-a80015

14. Kate Bartlett, 'What Joint Drills with South African, Russian Navies Mean for China', VOA, 21 February 2023, https://www.voanews.com/a/what-joint-drills-with-south-african-russian-navies-mean-for-china-/6972341.html

15. Ibid.

16. Pearl Matibe, 'US Republican Lawmakers Launch Bill Denouncing South Africa's Naval Exercises with China and Russia', Defence Web, 28 February 2023, https://www.defenceweb.co.za/featured/us-republican-lawmakers-launch-bill-denouncing-south-africas-naval-exercises-with-china-and-russia/

17. Julian Borger, 'South Africa's President and ANC Sow Confusion over Leaving ICC', *The Guardian*, 25 April 2023, https://www.theguardian.com/world/2023/apr/25/south-africas-president-and-party-sow-confusion-over-leaving-icc

18. Carien Du Plessis, 'South Africa Asks ICC to Exempt It from Putin Arrest to Avoid War with Russia', Reuters, 18 July 2023, https://www.reuters.com/article/safrica-russia-icc/south-africa-asks-icc-to-exempt-it-from-putin-arrest-to-avoid-war-with-russia-idUSKBN2YY1E7/

19. Interview by author with Steve Gruzd, November 2023.

20. 'US Accuses South Africa of Providing Arms to Russia', *The Guardian*, 11

pp. [325–328]  NOTES

May 2023, https://www.theguardian.com/world/2023/may/11/us-accuses-south-africa-of-providing-arms-to-russia-reports

21. 'US Lawmaker Group wants S Africa Punished over Russia Ties', Al Jazeera, 13 June 2023, https://www.aljazeera.com/news/2023/6/13/us-lawmakers-want-s-africa-to-lose-trade-summit-over-russia-ties

22. 'Arms-to-Russia Inquiry: What Has the South African Investigation Revealed', Africa News, 12 September 2023, https://www.africanews.com/2023/09/06/arms-to-russia-inquiry-what-has-the-south-african-investigation-revealed//

23. 'Russia's Lavrov in Angola to Seek International Support', Africa News, 26 January 2023, https://www.africanews.com/2023/01/25/russias-lavrov-in-angola-to-seek-international-support//

24. 'Moscow Offers Mauritania "Help"', VOA, 8 February 2023, https://www.voaafrica.com/a/moscow-offers-mauretania-help-/6953912.html

25. 'Russia's Lavrov Pledges Security Training to Eswatini', *The Moscow Times*, 25 January 2023, https://www.themoscowtimes.com/2023/01/25/russias-lavrov-pledges-security-training-to-eswatini-a80032

26. 'The Plenary Session "Russia-Africa in a Multipolar World" Was Held in Moscow', The State Duma, 20 March 2023, http://duma.gov.ru/en/news/56646/

27. 'African Sentiment Is Favouring Ukraine', Ipsos, 21 June 2023, https://www.ipsos.com/en-za/african-sentiment-favouring-ukraine

28. Moira Fagan, Jacob Poushter and Sneha Gubbala, 'Overall Opinion of Russia', Pew Research Center, 10 July 2023, https://www.pewresearch.org/global/2023/07/10/overall-opinion-of-russia/

29. Gerald Imray, 'Putin, Zelensky Agree to Meet with "African Leaders Peace Mission," Says South Africa President', Associated Press, 17 May 2023, https://apnews.com/article/russia-ukraine-peace-africa-putin-zelenskyy-2e082ce281d405d94451cab9dad4212f

30. Samuel Ramani, 'Africa's Mission Chases the Chimera of Peace for Ukraine', CEPA, 31 May 2023, https://cepa.org/article/africas-mission-chases-the-chimera-of-peace-for-ukraine/

31. 'V MID RF ne podtverdili informatsiyu SMI otositel'no afrikanskogo mirovogo plana' (The Russian Foreign Ministry did not confirm media information regarding African peace plan), *Izvestia*, 19 May 2023, https://iz.ru/1515109/2023-05-19/v-mid-rf-ne-podtverdili-informatciiu-smi-otositelno-afrikanskogo-mirnogo-plana

32. Strelkovii, Telegram, 18 May 2023, https://t.me/strelkovii/4905

33. Interview with Gruzd, November 2023.

34. Evan Hill et al., 'Egypt Secretly Planned to Supply Rockets to Russia, Leaked U.S. Document Shows', *The Washington Post*, 10 April 2023, https://www.washingtonpost.com/national-security/2023/04/10/egypt-weapons-russia/

35. 'War in Ukraine: Behind Closed Doors with Zelenskyy and the African Union', Africa Report, 21 June 2022, https://www.theafricareport.

NOTES  pp. [328–331]

com/215651/war-in-ukraine-behind-closed-doors-with-zelenskyy-and-the-african-union/.

36. Aggrey Mutambo, 'Ukraine's Zelensky: Africa Gains Nothing from Russian Ties', *The East African*, 4 August 2022, https://www.theeastafrican.co.ke/tea/news/east-africa/ukraine-zelensky-africa-gains-nothing-from-russian-ties-3903336

37. Owei Lakemfa, 'Africans Have No Inheritance in the House of Zelensky', *Premium Times*, 8 July 2022, https://www.premiumtimesng.com/opinion/541558-africans-have-no-inheritance-in-the-house-of-zelensky-by-owei-lakemfa.html

38. Elian Peltier and Mady Camara, 'Ukraine's Top Diplomat Tries to Counter Russia's Narrative on Africa Tour', *New York Times*, 4 October 2022, https://www.nytimes.com/2022/10/04/world/africa/kuleba-africa-tour.html

39. 'Ukraine's Kuleba Promises to "Free Africa from Russia's Grip"', Al Jazeera, 17 August 2023, https://www.aljazeera.com/news/2023/8/17/ukraines-kuleba-promises-to-free-africa-from-russias-grip

40. Interview by author with Hassan Sheikh Mohamud, November 2023.

41. 'Russia Has Sent First Free Grain Shipments to Africa', *The Moscow Times*, 17 November 2023, https://www.themoscowtimes.com/2023/11/17/russia-has-sent-first-free-grain-shipments-to-africa-a83141

42. Joshua Surtees, 'Growing Foothold: How Russia Donates Fertiliser to Deepen African Alliances', *The Guardian*, 13 March 2023, https://www.theguardian.com/global-development/2023/mar/13/russia-fertiliser-donates-deepen-african-alliances-malawi

43. Anthony Kitimo, '34,000 Tonnes of Fertiliser Donated by Russia Firm Received at Mombasa Port', *Nation* (Kenya), 1 June 2023, https://nation.africa/kenya/business/34-000-tonnes-of-fertiliser-donated-by-russia-firm-received-at-mombasa-port-4253682

44. 'Egypt, Reliant on Imports, Buys More Russian Wheat', Al Jazeera, 5 September 2023, https://www.aljazeera.com/news/2023/9/5/egypt-reliant-on-imports-buys-more-russian-wheat

45. 'Article by Vladimir Putin "Russia and Africa: Joining Efforts for Peace, Progress and a Successful Future"', President of Russia, 24 June 2023, http://en.kremlin.ru/events/president/news/71719

46. 'Rossiya i Turtsiya dogovorilis' o postavke 1 mln tonn zerna' (Russia and Turkey agree to supply 1 million tons of grain), RBC, 6 September 2023, https://www.rbc.ru/politics/06/09/2023/64f8ad7d9a794749320488bb

47. Panina, Telegram, 5 September 2023, https://t.me/EvPanina/10959

48. Interview by author with Qatari diplomat, November 2023.

49. 'Lavrov Says Egypt Become "Global Player," Praises its Efforts on Gaza', *Egypt Today*, 16 November 2023, https://www.egypttoday.com/Article/1/128540/Lavrov-says-Egypt-become-%E2%80%9Cglobal-player%E2%80%9D-praises-its-efforts-on

50. Interview by author with Mohamed Hassan, November 2023.

438

## NOTES

51. 'Russia, Algeria Hold Naval Exercises in Mediterranean Sea', *Asharq al-Awsat*, 6 December 2023, https://english.aawsat.com/arab-world/4711446-russia-algeria-hold-naval-exercises-mediterranean-sea

52. Interview by author with Ahmed Dahshan, November 2023.

53. Miles Johnson, 'Wagner Leader Generated $250mn from Sanctioned Empire', *Financial Times*, 21 February 2023, https://www.ft.com/content/98e478b5-c0d4-48a3-bcf7-e334a4ea0aca

54. Michael Rubin, 'Wagner's Next Targets in Africa: Liberia, Sierra Leone, and Ivory Coast', *Washington Examiner*, 8 February 2023, https://www.washingtonexaminer.com/opinion/wagners-next-targets-in-africa-liberia-sierra-leone-and-ivory-coast

55. Digital Forensic Research Lab, 'Russian War Report: Wagner Group Fights French "Zombies" in Cartoon Propaganda', Atlantic Council, 20 January 2023, https://www.atlanticcouncil.org/blogs/new-atlanticist/russian-war-report-wagner-group-fights-french-zombies-in-cartoon-propaganda/

56. Prigozhin's Hat, Telegram, 7 April 2023, https://t.me/Prigozhin_hat/3019

57. 'Kremlin Continues to Undermine Wagner Group Financier's Operation', *Ukrainska Pravda*, 11 April 2023, https://www.pravda.com.ua/eng/news/2023/04/11/7397315/

58. 'Contract Terms between African Countries, Wagner PMCs Not Russia's Concern- Lavrov', TASS, 1 July 2023, https://tass.com/russia/1641361

59. Shugaley, Telegram, 31 July 2023, https://t.me/max_shugaley/785

60. Natasha Bertrand, 'Wagner Forces have not Withdrawn from Africa in "Meaningful Numbers", Defence Official Says', CNN, 24 September 2023, https://edition.cnn.com/2023/09/24/europe/wagner-forces-african-withdrawal-intl/index.html

61. 'How Russia is Restructuring Wagner Group's Africa Operations', *Wall Street Journal*, 2 November 2023, https://www.wsj.com/video/series/in-depth-features/how-russia-is-restructuring-wagner-groups-africa-operations/32272869-3B47-4037-9135-1FA4F2004B4E

62. Two Majors, Telegram, 20 November 2023, https://t.me/dva_majors/29354

63. Interview by author with Andrey Chuprygin November 2023.

64. Nicole Wolkov et al., 'Russian Offensive Campaign Assessment', Institute for the Study of War, 20 November 2023, https://www.understandingwar.org/sites/default/files/Nov%2020%20Russian%20Offensive%20Campaign%20Assessment%20PDF.pdf

65. Samy Magdy, 'US Seeks to Expel Russian Mercenaries from Sudan, Libya', Associated Press, 3 February 2023, https://apnews.com/article/russia-ukraine-putin-politics-libya-government-b4218ab0163e6c5e271a3902cd893759

66. Benoit Faucon et al., 'The Last Days of Wagner's Prigozhin', *Wall Street Journal*, 24 August 2023, https://www.wsj.com/world/russia/prigozhin-wagner-plane-crash-last-days-2c44dd5c

## NOTES
pp. [334–338]

67. Ibid.
68. VchK-OGPU, Telegram, 28 August 2023, https://t.me/vchkogpu/41302
69. Russian MoD, Telegram, 22 August 2023, https://t.me/mod_russia/29689
70. 'Putin's Move to Secure Libya Bases Is New Regional Worry for US', Bloomberg, 5 November 2023, https://www.bloomberg.com/news/articles/2023-11-05/putin-s-move-to-secure-libya-bases-is-new-regional-worry-for-us
71. Interview by author with Yuri Lyamin, November 2023.
72. Ibrahim Senusi, 'Tatneft Confirms Good Exploratory Results in the Ghadames Basin', *Libya Herald*, 31 July 2023, https://libyaherald.com/2023/07/tatneft-confirms-good-exploratory-results-in-the-ghadames-basin/
73. Interview by author with Jalel Harchaoui, November 2023.
74. Ibid.
75. Zeinab Mohammed Salih and Jason Burke, 'Wagner Mercenaries Sustain Losses in Fight for Central African Republic Gold', *The Guardian*, 2 February 2023, https://www.theguardian.com/world/2023/feb/02/wagner-mercenaries-sustain-losses-in-fight-for-central-african-republic-gold
76. Ibid.
77. Prigozhin's Hat, Telegram, 9 May 2023, https://t.me/Prigozhin_hat/3287
78. RSOTM, Telegram, 5 July 2023, https://t.me/rsotmdivision/8661
79. Elian Peltier, 'Xi Condemns Killings in African Nation Where Russian and Chinese Interests Compete', *New York Times,* 20 March 2023, https://www.nytimes.com/2023/03/20/world/europe/central-african-republic-russia-china.html
80. *Wall Street Journal*, 24 August 2023.
81. Elian Peltier, 'Battle for Influence Rages in Heart of Wagner's Operations in Africa', *New York Times*, 26 November 2023, https://www.nytimes.com/2023/11/26/world/africa/wagner-russia-central-african-republic.html
82. 'Foreign Minister Sergey Lavrov's News Conference Following his Visit to the United States within the Framework of Russia's Presidency of the UN Security Council', Ministry of Foreign Affairs of Russia, 25 April 2023, https://mid.ru/en/foreign_policy/news/1865546/
83. 'Statement by Deputy Permanent Representative Anna Evstigneeva at UNSC Briefing on the Situation in Sudan', Permanent Mission of the Russian Federation to the UN, 25 April 2023, https://russiaun.ru/en/news/250423_evst
84. Militarist, Telegram, 25 April 2023, https://t.me/infantmilitario/97212
85. Sergei Markova, Telegram, 23 April 2023, https://t.me/logikamarkova/6097
86. Interview by author with Sergei Seregichev, November 2023.
87. 'Sudan's Leader Agrees to Host Russian Naval Base on Red Sea', The Maritime Executive, 12 February 2023, https://maritime-executive.com/article/sudan-s-leader-agrees-to-host-russian-naval-base-on-red-sea
88. Nima Elbagir et al., 'Exclusive: Evidence Emerges of Russia's Wagner Arming

pp. [338–341]  NOTES

Militia Leader Battling Sudan's Army', CNN, 21 April 2023, https://edition.
cnn.com/2023/04/20/africa/wagner-sudan-russia-libya-intl/index.html

89. *Wall Street Journal*, 24 August 2023.

90. 'Wagner PMC Founder Offers Mediation Services for Settlement in Sudan', TASS, 20 April 2023, https://tass.com/politics/1607431?utm_source=newarab.com&utm_medium=referral&utm_campaign=newarab.com&utm_referrer=newarab.com

91. Interview with Seregichev, November 2023.

92. 'Sudan's al-Burhan, Ukraine's Zelensky Discuss Security Challenges', *Sudan Tribune*, 23 September 2023, https://sudantribune.com/article277588/

93. Joe Barnes, 'Ukrainian Special Services Launch Strikes on Wagner-Backed Militia in Sudan', *The Telegraph*, 20 September 2023, https://www.telegraph.co.uk/world-news/2023/09/20/ukrainian-special-services-drone-strikes-wagner-sudan/

94. Interview by author with Cameron Hudson, November 2023.

95. Wassim Nasr, 'How the Wagner Group is Aggravating the Jihadi Threat in the Sahel', *CTC Sentinel*, Volume 15, Number 11, November/December 2022, pp. 21–30, https://ctc.westpoint.edu/wp-content/uploads/2022/12/CTC-SENTINEL-112022.pdf

96. RSOTM, Telegram, 5 July 2023, https://t.me/rsotmdivision/8661

97. Anthony J. Blinken, 'Imposing Sanctions on Malian Officials in Connection to the Wagner Group', US Department of State, 24 July 2023, https://www.state.gov/imposing-sanctions-on-malian-officials-in-connection-with-the-wagner-group/

98. Elian Peltier, 'Wagner Group May Have Committed War Crimes in Mali, U.N. Experts Say', *New York Times*, 31 January 2023, https://www.nytimes.com/2023/01/31/world/africa/mali-wagner-civilian-killings.html

99. *CTC Sentinel*, Volume 15, Number 11, November/December 2022.

100. Ilya Lakstygal, 'Sergey Lavrov vpervyye posetil Mali' (Sergey Lavrov visited Mali for the first time), *Vedomosti*, 8 February 2023, https://www.vedomosti.ru/politics/articles/2023/02/08/962088-sergei-lavrov-vpervie-posetil-mali

101. Max Fras, Twitter, 28 February 2023, https://x.com/maxfras/status/1630496745359568896?s=20

102. Katarina Hoije and Antony Sguazzin, 'Russia Sends African Ally Mali Wheat, Strengthening Ties', Bloomberg, 25 July 2023, https://www.bloomberg.com/news/articles/2023-07-25/russia-sells-wheat-to-african-ally-mali-as-ties-strengthen

103. 'Russia Vetoes UN Resolution to Extend Sanctions, Monitoring in Mali', Al Jazeera, 31 August 2023, https://www.aljazeera.com/news/2023/8/31/russia-vetoes-un-resolution-to-extend-sanctions-monitoring-in-mali

104. 'Wagner Revolt in Russia Dims Outlook for Its Operations in Africa', Al Jazeera, 24 June 2023, https://www.aljazeera.com/news/2023/6/24/wagner-revolt-in-russia-clouds-outlook-for-its-operations-in-afri

NOTES

pp. [341–343]

105. Catrina Doxsee, Joseph S. Bermudez Jr. and Jennifer Jun, 'Base Expansion in Mali Indicates Growing Wagner Group Investment', CSIS, 15 August 2023, https://www.csis.org/analysis/base-expansion-mali-indicates-growing-wagner-group-investment

106. Nicholas Ward, 'Mali and Russia Troops Relocate Following Departure of UN Mission', VOA, 15 October 2023, https://www.voaafrica.com/a/mali-and-russia-troops-relocate-following-departure-of-un-mission/7311803.html

107. 'Retaking Kidal: A Potential Path to Victory for Mali's Junta', VOA, 17 November 2023, https://www.voaafrica.com/a/retaking-kidal-a-potential-path-to-victory-for-mali-s-junta/7358842.html

108. Tiemoko Diallo, 'Mali Signs Agreement with Russia to Build Gold Refinery', Reuters, 22 November 2023, https://www.reuters.com/markets/commodities/mali-signs-agreement-with-russia-build-gold-refinery-2023-11-22/

109. 'Burkina Faso Summons Ghana's Envoy over President's Claim on Wagner', Al Jazeera, 16 December 2022, https://www.aljazeera.com/news/2022/12/16/burkina-faso-summons-ghanaian-ambassador-over-wagner-allegations

110. Oleg Kusov, 'Novaya simfoniya Vagnera? Burkina-Faso nadeyetsya na zashchitu ot islamistov' (A new Wagner symphony? Burkina Faso hopes for protection from Islamists), News.ru, 5 October 2022, https://news.ru/africa/novaya-simfoniya-vagnera-v-burkina-faso-nadeyutsya-na-zashitu-ot-islamistov/

111. L.M. Sadovskaya, 'Ocherednoy voyennyy perevorot v Burkina-Faso' (Another military coup in Burkina Faso), IMEMO RAN, 12 December 2022, https://www.imemo.ru/news/events/text/ocherednoy-voenniy-perevorot-v-burkina-faso

112. 'Interim Burkina Faso President Hails Russia as "Strategic Ally"', Al Jazeera, 5 May 2023, https://www.aljazeera.com/news/2023/5/5/interim-burkina-faso-president-hails-russia-as-strategic-ally

113. Gloria Aradi, 'Russia to Build Nuclear Plant to Meet Burkina Faso's Energy Needs', BBC, 13 October 2023, https://www.bbc.co.uk/news/world-africa-67098444

114. Wayuwa Kimathi, '35-Year-Old President Who Called African Leaders "Beggars"', Kenya Times, 1 August 2023, https://thekenyatimes.com/latest-kenya-times-news/35-year-old-president-who-called-african-leaders-beggars/

115. 'Russia Urges Conflicting Parties in Niger to Refrain from Using Force-Diplomat', TASS, 27 July 2023, https://tass.com/coup-attempt-in-niger/1652789

116. Alexander Dugin, Telegram, 27 July 2023, https://t.me/Agdchan/11201

117. Tim Lister, 'Prigozhin Celebrates Niger Coup, Says His Wagner Group Can

442

pp. [343–345]    NOTES

Help', CNN, 29 July 2023, https://edition.cnn.com/2023/07/29/africa/prigozhin-niger-coup-wagner-intl/index.html

118. J.C. Okechukwu, Twitter, 5 August 2023, https://x.com/jcokechukwu/status/1687784019209912320?s=20

119. Sergey Savchuk, 'Na grani katastrofy: Frantsiya teryayet uran iz Nigera' (On the brink of disaster: France loses uranium from Niger), RIA Novosti, 1 August 2023, https://ria.ru/20230801/afrika-1887485153.html

120. Sam Mednick, 'Niger's Junta Asks for Help from Russian Group Wagner as It Faces Military Intervention Threat', Associated Press, 6 August 2023, https://apnews.com/article/wagner-russia-coup-niger-military-force-e0e1108b58a9e955af465a3efe6605c0

121. Mykhailo Podolyak, Twitter, 1 August 2023, https://x.com/Podolyak_M/status/1686320697465868288?s=20

122. Boureima Balima and Abdel-Kader Mazou, 'Niger Hit with More Sanctions as Junta Rebuffs Latest Diplomatic Mission', Reuters, 8 August 2023, https://www.reuters.com/world/africa/niger-coup-hopes-mediation-before-west-african-blocs-thursday-summit-2023-08-08/

123. Mark Anderson, Khadija Sharife and Nathalie Prevost, 'How a Notorious Arms Dealer Hijacked Niger's Budget and Bought Weapons from Russia', OCCRP, 6 August 2020, https://www.occrp.org/en/investigations/notorious-arms-dealer-hijacked-nigers-budget-and-bought-arms-from-russia

124. 'Pochemu perevorot v odnoy iz bedneyshikh stran mozhet byt' polezen Rossii' (Why a coup in one of the poorest countries could be useful for Russia), RBC, 27 July 2023, https://www.rbc.ru/politics/27/07/2023/64c22bc09a79476a8db3b134

125. 'Russia Calls on ECOWAS to Refrain from Invasion of Niger—Foreign Ministry', TASS, 13 September 2023, https://tass.com/politics/1674379

126. Petr Akopov, 'Interventsii ne budet: Rossiya pomogla Nigeru' (There will be no intervention: Russia helped Niger), RIA Novosti, 2 August 2023, https://ria.ru/20230802/niger-1887688390.html

127. 'Niger is Moscow's Next Target', MENAS Associates, 29 September 2022, https://menas.co.uk/blog/niger-is-moscows-next-target

128. Jason Burke, 'Russia Uses Social Media Channels to Exploit Niger Coup', *The Guardian*, 27 August 2023, https://www.theguardian.com/world/2023/aug/27/russia-uses-social-media-channels-to-exploit-niger-coup

129. 'Poll Reveals over 60% of Nigeriens Consider Russia Country's Most Reliable Partner', TASS, 8 August 2023, https://tass.com/world/1658097

130. Interview by author with Moscow-based defence expert, November 2023.

131. Ibid.

132. Ibid.

# INDEX

Note: Page numbers followed by '*n*' refer to notes.

Abacha regime, 45
Abacha, Sani, 41
Abdelaziz, Mohammed, 152–3
Abdel-Khalek, Osama, 301
Abdi, Rashid, 84, 324
Abkhazia, 202
Aboul-Gheit, Ahmed, 85
Abravitova, Liubov, 298
Abu Dhabi, 170, 212, 217, 261
Accra, 294–5
Achinov, Nikolay, 9
Adamishin, Anatoly, 39
Addax, 89
Addis Ababa, 9, 250–1, 253–4, 307
Aden clashes, 212
Aden, 8
Aden, Abdirisak, 84
Afanasyeva, Yulia, 247
Afghanistan, 18, 70, 207, 211, 296, 316
Africa
    Kozyrev visit to, 30–3
    Russia's relationship with, 244–50

Soviet influence in, 7, 11, 16
    *See also* Russia
African Action Plan (AAP), 57
African National Congress (ANC), 22
African Union (AU), 54, 223, 240, 253, 281, 289, 296
    Libya, Russia's intervention on, 206–12
African Union's Mechanism for Police Cooperation (AFRIPOL), 188–9
AFRICOM, 222, 257–9, 282, 286
Afrika Sevodnya (Today's Africa), 58
Afrikaners, 182–3
Afwerki, Isaias, 47
Agadir International Airport, 303
Ahmed, Abdullahi Yusuf, 83
Ahmed, Abiy, 235, 237, 251, 253, 307
Ain Zara, 304
Ajaokuta steel plant, 315
Ajaokuta, 187
Ajbadiya, 304

445

# INDEX

Al Ahrar (TV channel), 258
Al Jazeera (TV network), 214, 295
Al Jufra Airbase, 256
*Al-Ahram* (newspaper), 137
*Al-Ain*, 278
*Al-Arabiya* (news channel), 144, 220–1, 263
Al-Azhar University, 68
Alden, Chris, 3
Aleppo, 131
Alfano, Angelino, 158
Algeria, 269, 295, 297, 302–4, 315, 326
  Libya partnership with, 161
  Russia's vaccine diplomacy, 238–44
  Russian-Algerian business forums, 70
  Soviet Union signed an agreement with, 14
Algerian Hirak Protest Movement, 172
Algerians, 147
Algiers Summit (1973), 18
Ali, Wasil, 279
Aliba, Ahmed, 301
Al-Jazeera (TV network), 221, 278
Al-Jufra, 258
Al-Kadim, 258
Alkhanov, Alu, 71
Allison, Roy, 99
Al-Qaeda in the Islamic Maghreb (AQIM), 209–10, 265, 311
al-Qaeda, 50
Alrosa, 241
al-Shabab, 273
Alshateri, Albadr, 211–12
*al-Shorouk* (newspaper), 250
Aluminium Smelter Company of Nigeria (ALSCON), 60
Am Daga, 307

Amharic language, 9
  Amur class repair ship PM-138, 278
ANC government, 317
Anglo-Boer War II (1899–1902), 10
Angola, 17, 31
  Rogozin visit to, 114–15
  Russia signed an agreement with, 44
  trade between Russia and, 88
AngoSat1, 176
AngoSat2, 176
Ankara, 246
Anokhin, Vladimir, 217–18
Ansar al-Sharia, 152
Ansar al-Sunna, 229
Antananarivo, 224, 226–7
anti-apartheid movements, 316
Anti-Balaka, 205
anti-Western regimes, 55–6
António, Téte, 57–8
Antonov An-124 plane, 229
Antonov, Anatoly, 142
Arab League Summit, 322
Arab League, 86
Arab Misseriya tribes, 117
Arab Spring 2.0, 220
Arab Spring (2011), 75, 212–13, 221–2
Arab-Israeli conflict, 32
Argentina, 29–30
Arik, Mawien, 112
Aristide, Jean-Bertrand, 36
Arkhangelskaya, Alexandra, 123, 167
Arman, Abukar, 83–4
Armed Conflict Location and Event Data Project (ACLED), 311–12
Armed Islamic Group (GIA), 28

446

# INDEX

Armenia, 117
Army-2020 Forum, 273
Asmara, 17
al-Assad, Bashar, 101, 217
al-Assar, Muhammad Said, 142
Association for Free Research and International Cooperation (AFRIC), 231–2
Astana Peace Process, 145, 217
AstraZeneca, 241–2, 243
Aswan High Dam, 252
Atlantic Ocean, 111
Aziz, Tariq, 63

Bab el-Mandeb Strait, 275
Babakin, Alexander, 71
al-Badri, Abdelbassat, 158
Bah, Amadou, 200
Bakassi, 296
Baker, James, 30, 249
Balcha Hospital, 9
Balmasov, Sergei, 146, 303
Bamako, 282, 284
Bambari, 270
Bandung Conference (1955), 11
Bang, 270
Bangui, 267–9
Bani Walid, 257
Barabanov, Mikhail, 148
Barabanov, Oleg, 172–3
el-Baradei, Mohammed, 95
'Barbarian Imperialist Aggression', 74
al-Barghati, Mahdi, 157
Barrow, Adam, 111
Bashagha, Fathi, 263, 264–5, 305
al-Bashir, Omar, 51, 79–80, 218–19
    meetings with Russian officials, 119
Bastrykin, Alexander, 215

battalion tactical groups (BTGs), 304
Battle of Adwa (1895), 9
Bayoumi, Gamal, 171
Bazoum, Mohamed, 315
Béavogui, Mohamed, 296
Beijing, 117, 238, 246
Belarus, 294, 310
Belenkaya, Marianna, 263
Belmokhtar, Mokhtar, 146
Belt and Road Initiative (BRI), 6
Ben Ali, Zine Abedine, 92
Bendjedid, Chadli, 20, 28
Benghazi, 208, 211, 264, 304
Benghazi-to-Marsa-Matrouh rail-line, 266
Benghazi-to-Sirte railway project, 266
Benhamed, Lotfi, 241
Benin, 297, 323
Bensalah, Abdelkader, 173–4
Berengo training centre, 206
Beriziky, Omer, 224
Berlin Conference, 266
Bialer, Seweryn, 16
Biden, Joe, 246–7, 266, 277, 303
Bigot, Christophe, 310
Bitcoin, 309
Biti, Tendai, 179
Black Sea grain export agreement, 325
Black Sea ports, 297
Black Sea, 299
Blackwater, 206
Blinken, Anthony, 252, 286, 302
Blue Nile, 272–3
Boeing F-15 Advanced Fighter Jets, 326
'Boer Lives Matter' movement, 183
Boer War, 10

447

## INDEX

Bogdanov, Mikhail, 92–3, 151, 195, 207, 222–3, 262–3, 299
Bokassa (emperor), 287
Bokassa era, 268
Boko Haram, 128, 129, 310
Bolad, Kamal, 277
Bolotnaya Square, 100
Bolshevik Revolution (1917), 10
Bolton, John, 165–6, 206
Bondarev, Viktor, 257–8
Bongo, Omar, 65
Borgia, Gaelle, 224
Borisenko, Georgy, 252
Borisova, Jana, 86
Bortnikov, Alexander, 154–5
Bosnia, 74
Bossangoa massacre, 310
Botes, Alvin, 316–17
Botha, Pik, 31–2
Boukadoum, Sabri, 174
Bout, Viktor, 48, 326
Bouteflika, Abdelaziz, 69, 102
Bovin, Aleksandr, 27
Bovt, Georgy, 74
Boyarishchev, Vladimir, 224
Bozizé, François, 131, 267–8, 288
Brak, 258
Brasília, 184
Brazil, 29–30
Bregadze, Alexander, 201–2
Brezhnev era, 19
Brezhnev, Leonid, 187
BRI investments, 249
BRI. See Belt and Road Initiative (BRI)
BRICS (Brazil, Russia, India, China and South Africa), 52
BRICS summit (2009), 90–1
BRICS summit (2013), 137
BRICS summit (2014), 122
BRICS summit (2018), 163, 195

BRICS summit (2019), 184–5
Britain, 31, 223, 246, 269–70, 272
vaccines, 235–6
Broadcasting company (BBC), 224, 304
Brookings Institution report, 325
Brown, Brittany, 106
Bucha Massacre, 311
Bucharest Summit (2008), 78
Buhari, Muhammadu, 131, 186
Bulgaria, 16
el-Burhan, Abdel Fattah, 218, 222–3, 274, 276, 306
Burkina Faso, 18, 281, 313–14
Burundi, 112, 295
Bush administration, 68
Bush, George W., 59
Buthelezi, Mzayifani, 184
Byschkov, Petr, 247

Cabo Delgado, 227–30
Cairo Declaration, 260
Cairo, 250–2, 261, 266, 273, 301, 322
mass protests, 170
Putin's visit to, 68
California, 310
Camara, Sadio, 282, 285
Cameroon, 269, 296, 310, 323
Campbell, John, 59, 129
Canada, 286, 305
Cape Town, 31
CAR (Central African Republic), 1, 106, 131–3, 199, 232, 278
Africa and Russia, 244–50
Central and West Africa, 308–16
Chad and Guinea, Russia's influence in, 288–91
Russia's consolidation, 267–72, 305–8
Russia's intervention, 202–6

448

## INDEX

Carnegie Moscow Center, 204
Castro, Fidel, 18
Caucasus Strategic Research
Center, 217
Çavu͵soˇglu, Mevlüt, 261–2
Cedar Revolution (2005), 69
Centers for Disease Control
(CDC), 237
Central Asia, 9
Central Energy Fund, 317
Central Independent Election
Commission, 226
Chad, 247–8, 255, 259, 278, 281
Russia's influence, 288–91
Chad-CAR border, 289
Chamisa, Nelson, 179
Chechen War II, 53, 55, 66–7
Chemezov, Sergei, 72, 141
China National Nuclear
Corporation (CNNC), 197
China, 238, 301, 318, 321, 324,
329n9, 330n8
Africa and Russia, 244–50
Port Sudan facility, 276
PPE, 235
Russia aligned with, 111
signed deal for minerals, 200
vaccines, 235–8
China's National Offshore Oil
Corporation (CNOOC), 113
China-Africa Cooperation Forum,
54
Chinese naval bases, 276
Christians, 137
Chuprygin, Andrey, 209, 212, 217,
259, 261
Churkin, Vitaly, 32, 39, 79, 97–8
views on Russia's policies, 154–5
Cinar, Huriye Yildrim, 217
clandestine agreement, 304
Clinton, Bill, 51

Clinton, Hillary, 108
Clunan, Anne, 330n8
CNN (Media company), 226, 235
Coalition of Patriots for Change
(CPC), 270
Coega special economic zone, 317
Cohen, Herman, 191
Cold War, 7, 8, 85
Colonial Era (Pre-1960), 7
Committee for State Security
(KGB), 36
Communist Party of the Soviet
Union (CPSU), 19, 20
Comoros, 277
Conakry, 202
Condé, Alpha, 110, 200, 201–2,
240, 281, 289–90
Congo crisis (1960), 12
Congo War I, 48
Congo, 13, 241, 295, 321–2
Conkar, Ahmet Berat, 217
Constantine, 241
Conte, Lansana, 64–5
Coptic Christians, 68
Cornegay, Francis, 91
Cossa, Constantino, 231
Côte d'Ivoire, 103–4, 297
COVAX, 242
COVID-19 pandemic, 170, 233,
267, 299, 322
Africa and Russia, 244–50
Russia's vaccine diplomacy,
238–44
Russia-Africa relations, 236–8
vaccines, 192
CPSU. See Communist Party of the
Soviet Union (CPSU)
Credit Suisse, 232
Crimea, 121, 294, 301, 316–17
Crimean Peninsula, 105
Crocker, Chester, 19

449

# INDEX

CSIS report, 295
Cuban Missile Crisis, 294
Cup of Hope campaign, 205
Cyprus, 153
Cyrenaica, 209, 260
Czech Republic, 129, 285
Czechoslovakia, 16

Dahshan, Ahmed, 144
*Daily Maverick, The* (online
newspaper), 121, 317–18
*Daily Sabah* (newspaper), 216
*Dajunshi* (Chinese defence
website), 230
Damiba, Paul-Henri, 313
Dandykin, Vasily, 185
Daoud, Oumar Ibn, 288–9
Darfur, 64, 118, 272–3
Davydov, Oleg, 37
al-Dbeibah, Abdul Hamid, 240,
263–4
De Carvalho, Gustavo, 243
de Klerk, F.W., 31, 32
Déby, Idriss, 281
Déby, Mahamat, 281, 289
DeLisi, Scott, 113
Dembélé, Moussa, 287
Democratic Alliance Party, 125,
181, 317
Democratic Party, 316
Democratic Republic Congo, 310
Deng Xiaoping, 16
Dengov, Lev, 161–2, 214
Denisova, Tatyana, 290
Derg regime, 16, 254
Deripaska, Oleg, 5, 201, 290
Desalegn, Hailemariam, 188–9
Diallo, Cellou Dalein, 202
Dian-Dian mine, 200–1
Diaw, Malick, 282
al-Din, Omar Qamar, 275

Djemal, Orkhan, 203
Djibouti, 107, 254, 276, 297, 306
Dlamini-Zuma, Nkosazana, 62
Dmitriev, Kirill, 239
Dolgov, Boris, 69, 279
Donaldson, Robert, 34
Donbas, 118, 121, 304, 310
Dondra, Henri-Marie, 269
Donetsk People's Republics, 294,
303
Donetsk, 299
dos Santos, Isabel, 178
Dos Santos, José Eduardo, 30–1,
46–7
Dossier Center, 219, 225
Doumbouya, Mamady, 281
Draghi, Mario, 319
DRS. *See* Intelligence and Security
(DRS)
Dubai, 307
Dujarric, Stéphane, 259
Dumbuya, Mamadi, 290
Dunne, Michelle, 143
Dygalo, Igor, 81
Dzhabarov, Vladimir, 258

East Africa, 228, 250, 308
East Germany, 16, 17
eastern Africa, 276
Eastern Europe, 11, 71, 294
eastern Ghouta, 146
Eastern Indian Ocean region, 276
eastern Mediterranean, 275–6
Ebola, 201, 237, 239–40
ECFR report, 307
Economic Community of West
African States (ECOWAS), 57,
111, 287
Economic Freedom Fighters (EFF)
Party, 316
Economic Progress Party, 316

450

## INDEX

Egypt, 46, 68–9, 236–9, 297, 301–3, 326
  Russia's balancing strategy, 250–4
  Russia's partnership with, 8
  Russia's strategy recalibration, 256–67
  signed an agreement with Russia, 143
  Sputnik Light vaccine, 244
  Sputnik V, 239
  support for Haftar, 211
Egyptian military, 140
Egyptian Museum, 173
Egyptian Natural Gas Holding Company (EGAS), 142
Egyptian Revolution (2011), 95, 138
Egyptians, 92–3
El Dabaa Nuclear Power Plant, 143, 301–2, 323
El Salvador, 309
El-Sharara oil field, 258
Emam, Shaik, 318
Endiama, 177
Era of Soviet Adventurism (1975–85), 7
Erdoˇgan, Recep Tayyip, 215–16
Eritrea, 190–1, 273, 280, 294, 295, 307–8
Erkhov, Alexei, 216
Estonia, 269
Ethiopia, 47, 236, 247, 273, 295, 307, 322–4
  East Germany ties with, 17
  Italian invasion of, 10
  pro-Russian sentiments in, 92
  requested arms package from Russia, 61
  Russia's balancing strategy, 250–4

Ethiopia-Eritrea peace initiative, 57
Ethiopia-Eritrea War (1998–2000), 60
Ethiopian People's Revolutionary Democratic Front (EPRDF), 28
ethno-confessional conflicts, 61
EU-Africa Summit (2000), 54
Eurasian Economic Union (EAEU), 143
Europe, 25, 236, 330n8
European Union (EU), 217, 236–7, 240, 268, 285, 302–4, 322
  Russia and Southern Africa, 316–19
  Russia's military expansion, 206–12
  Sudanese revolution and democratic transition, 218–23
Everstov, Nikolai, 277
Evstigneeva, Anna, 313
ex-Seleka, 205
ExxonMobil, 81, 227
Eyrice, Elem, 249

Fabricius, Peter, 184, 185
Facebook accounts, 268, 287
Facebook, 210, 283
FACT rebels, 288–9
Fahmy, Nabil, 140
al-Fargh, 304
Farid, Mohamed, 251
Fayed, Abdelaziz, 239
Federal News Agency, 219, 226–7, 264–5, 284, 287
Federation Council, 6
Fedorenko, Nikolay, 13
Fedorov, Yuri, 59
Feltman, Jeremy, 247
Fezzan, 260
FIFA World Cup (2018), 145

451

## INDEX

Filatova, Irina, 290
Filipov, Vasily, 248
financial crisis (2008), 77
Fitin, Vladimir, 222
Fomin, Alexander, 278
Forces for Freedom and Change
    (FFC), 222, 277
Ford, Vicky, 311
Foreign Policy Concept (2000), 54
Fotyga, Anna, 166–7, 285–6
Fouad, Mahmoud, 239
Foundation for the Protection of
    National Values, 213–14, 287
Fradkov, Mikhail, 58
France, 204–5, 209, 211–12, 226,
    314, 321, 323–4
    Chad and Guinea, Russia's
        influence in, 288–91
    Operation Barkhane campaign,
        128
    Operation Sangaris campaign,
        132
    Russia's Involvement, 262–7
    Russian security involvement,
        281–8
    vaccines, 235–6
    views on Russia's vaccine
        diplomacy, 245–7
Free Officers Coup (1952), 11
Freedom and Justice Party (FJP),
    136
Frolovskiy, Dmitry, 215
Front for Change and Concord in
    Chad (FACT), 281

G20 countries, 237
G20 summit (2019), 183
G8 meeting (1999), 56
G8 summit (2002), 57
G8 summit (2008), 79
Gabon, 295

al-Gaddafi, Muammar, 20, 27, 74,
    96
Gaddafi, Saif al-Islam, 213, 265–6
Galenica, 239
Gamaleya National Center for
    Epidemiology and Microbiology,
    242–3
Gambia River, 111
Gambia, 111
GamEvac-Combi Ebola vaccine,
    239–40
Gardner, Anthony, 108
Gargash, Anwar, 212
Gas Exporting Countries Forum
    (GECF), 138
Gathara, Patrick, 295–6
Gavin, Michelle, 106, 116, 245
Gaydamak, Arcadi, 45
Gaza Strip, 137
Gazprom, 60, 75
Gazprombank, 317
Gbagbo, Laurent, 103–4
Geneva Convention, 101
Georgian War (2008), 6, 77
Gerasimov, Igor, 223
Gerasimov, Pavel, 217
Gerasimov, Valery, 219
GERD. *See* Grand Ethiopian
    Renaissance Dam (GERD)
Germany, 223, 259, 272, 285–6
Ghana, 11, 240, 241, 244
Ghanem, Dalia, 146
Ghardabiya, 258
Ghozlan, Mahmoud, 138
GIA. *See* Armed Islamic Group
    (GIA)
Gijima Technologies, 62
Gintsburg, Alexander, 243
GKChP. *See* State Committee
    on the State of Emergency
    (GKChP)

# INDEX

Global South, 3, 7, 27, 235, 240, 246, 293, 330n8
  Libyan revolution (2011), 95–101
  NATO airstrikes in, 98
  Russia and, 91
Goble, Paul, 249
Goïta, Assimi, 249, 313
  Russian security involvement, 281–8
Golts, Alexander, 27, 148
El-Gomati, Anas, 159–60, 209
Gorbachev, Mikhail, 8
Gorbachev-era policy, 20
Gordhan, Pravin, 122–3
Gordile village, 309
Gossi, 312
Gouend, Louis, 325–6
Government of National Accord (GNA), 135, 157, 210–16
  Russia's strategy recalibration, 256–67
Government of National Unity (GNU), 255
  Russia's involvement, 262–72
Grand Ethiopian Renaissance Dam (GERD), 189, 191–2, 236, 250–3, 273, 278, 302
Grand Inga Dam, 194
Greenfield, Linda-Thomas, 323
Grey, Robert, 18
Gromyko, Igor, 282
Grozny Conference (2016), 145
Guangzhou racism controversy, 238
Guangzhou, 238
Guardian, The (newspaper), 307
Guatemala, 244
Guevara, Che, 284
Guinea, 11, 14, 199, 232–3, 255
  Russia's hybrid intervention, 200–2

Russia's influence, 288–91
Russia's vaccine diplomacy, 238–44
  Sputnik V, 239–40
Gulf of Aden, 81, 82, 254
Gulf of Tadjoura, 9
Gulf War (1991), 43
Gumede, Robert, 62
Guterres, António, 237–8, 259
Gwanyanya, Persistence, 318

Habineza, Frank, 243–4
Hadfield, Gregory, 166
Hadi, Abd Rabbuh Mansur, 272
Haftar, Khalifa, 108, 153–4, 214, 288
  clandestine agreement, 304
  GNU and Russia's involvement, 262–72
  Libya, Russia's intervention on, 206–12
  Russia's strategy recalibration, 256–67
  stagnation in, Russia's intervention, 213–18
Haftar-Assad alliance, 217–18
Hagel, Chuck, 139
Hamdan, Mohammed, 221
Hamdok, Abdalla, 274, 276, 281
Hamid, Al-Hadi, 119
Handule, Mohammed, 83
Harare, 92
Harchaoui, Jalel, 212, 304
Hargeisa, 280
Harvard University, 245
Hemedti, 221, 306
HIV-AIDS, 243, 245
Hoffman, Jonathan, 257
Hokkaido, 79
Hong Kong, 238
'honorary consuls', 34

453

## INDEX

Horn of Africa, 9, 247, 250, 300, 305–8
Soviet influence in, 16–17
House of Representatives (HoR), 154
Houthi drone strikes, 273
Hoxha, Enver, 28
Hrytsak, Vasyl, 219
al-Hudhud, Ibrahim Salah, 145
Hudson, Cameron, 275
Human Rights Watch, 310, 311
Hussein, Abdel Rahim Mohammed, 63–4
Hussein, Emad Eddine, 250
Hussein, Hisham, 277
el-Hussein, Mohamed Osman, 274, 278
Hussein, Nur Hassan, 83
al-Huweij, Abdel Hadi, 264

ICC. *See* International Criminal Court (ICC)
Idlib, 215, 217
Idris (King), 156
Ignatenko, Alexander, 96–7, 138–9
Il-114, 277
Ilichev, Petr, 112
IMF. *See* International Monetary Fund (IMF)
India, 9, 246, 276–7, 296, 329n9
India-Brazil-South Africa (IBSA), 91
Indian Ocean Rim Association, 185
Indian Ocean, 120, 224, 273, 275–6, 280, 305–6
Indo-Pacific region, 8
Institute for International and Strategic Studies (IISS), 248
Institute of World Economy and International Relations (IMEMO), 38

Intelligence and Security (DRS), 36
Intergovernmental Development Authority (IGAD), 57
*International Affairs*, 55
International Anticrisis Center (IAC), 231
International Criminal Court (ICC), 79–81
International Crisis Group, 84
International Monetary Fund (IMF), 22, 237, 278
International Projects Centre (IPC), 31
'internationalist camp', 25
Iran, 79, 217, 325–6
Iranian Revolution (1979), 95
Iraq War (2003), 53, 119
Iraq, 238, 316
Ireland, 269
Islamic extremism, 61
Islamic Salvation Front (FIS), 28
Islamic State in the Greater Sahara (ISGS), 311
Islamic State of Iraq and the Levant (ISIS), 206–7, 210, 229–30, 238
Islamists, 138, 152
Israel, 226, 254
Israel-Gaza war (2008–09), 84
Israel-Hamas conflict, 84–5
Israel-Palestine conflict, 67
Issaev, Leonid, 66–7
Italo-Ethiopian War I (1895–96), 9
Italy, 212, 237, 324
Ivan IV, Tsar, 8
Ivanov, Alexander, 180, 270, 271, 287, 314
Ivanov, Igor, 67
Ivanov, Sergei, 98, 241
Ivashov, Leonid, 216, 274

454

# INDEX

Izmir, 249
*Izvestia* (newspaper), 27, 61, 271, 282

Jabal Amer gold mine, 275
Jabr, Abu-BakrYunis, 96
Jama'at Nasr al-Islam wal Muslimin (JNIM), 286
Jammeh,Yahya, 110, 111
Japan, 25, 246, 251
Joachim, Patriarch, 8
Johnson & Johnson, 241, 243
Joint Comprehensive Plan of Action (JCPOA), 325
Jokonya, Callisto, 179
Jonah, James, 165–6
Jonathan, Goodluck, 128
Jordan, 211
Jordan, Pallo, 62
Jufra, 257
Jumail, 256

al-Kabir, Siddiq, 157
Kaboré, Roch Marc Christian, 313
Kadomtsev, Andrey, 245–6
Kadyrov, Ramzan, 71, 145, 162, 215
Kagame, Paul, 195–6
Kainerugaba, Muhoozi, 294
Kalana gold project, 286
Kalibr anti-ship missiles, 208
al-Kani, Mohammed, 264
al-Kaniyat, 264
Kapchanga, Mark, 297–8
Karaganov, Sergei, 42
Karasin, Grigory, 38, 41
Kasrills, Ronnie, 62
Kasyanov, Mikhail, 61
Katz, Mark, 70, 143
Kaunda, Kenneth, 18
Kazagui, Maxime, 267–8

Kazakhstan, 117, 176
Keïta, Ibrahim Boubacar, 281–2
Keita, Modibo, 14
Kenya, 106, 192, 242, 289, 295, 303, 308, 323
Kenyatta, Uhuru, 192–3
Kerry, John, 157
Ketchley, Neil, 360n14
KGB. *See* Committee for State Security (KGB)
Khaddad, Mohammed, 151
Khalilzad, Zalmay, 79
Khannenje, Hassan, 299–300, 324
Kharief, Akram, 35–6, 174
Kharkiv University, 9
Khartoum Agreement, 190, 205
Khartoum massacre, 222–3
Khartoum, 204, 222, 273, 274, 275, 277–9, 281
Khelifa, Mohamed, 147
Kherson Region, 299
Khodorkovsky, Mikhail, 203, 219, 225
Khrushchev, Nikita, 11, 12, 15, 147
Kiir, Salva, 110, 111
Kimani, Martin, 295
Kirill, Patriarch, 137
Kiriyenko, Sergei, 86, 124
Klintsevich, Franz, 119–20
Klishas, Andrei, 221
Kolokolov, Boris, 40
*Kommersant* (newspaper), 59, 64, 136, 222, 263
Kondiano, Claude, 201
Konovalov, Ivan, 158
Korea, 153
Korendyasov, Evgeny, 282, 284
Kortunov, Andrei, 211
Kosachev, Konstantin, 99, 221
Kosovo War (1999), 6

455

# INDEX

Kostelyanets, Sergei, 280
Kouki, 309
Koyagbélé, Pascal Bida, 272
Koyara, Marie-Noëlle, 206, 271
Kozyrev, Andrei, 25, 27
    visit to Africa, 30–3
Kozyrev-era, 45
Kramar, Andrei, 224
Kramnik, Ilya, 280
*Krasnya Vesna* (newspaper), 289
Krasov, Andrei, 258
Kritinsyn, Oleg, 159, 208–9, 275
Krylova, Galina, 21
Kubinka, 117
Kuleba, Dmytro, 302, 324
Kurdish state, 147
Kuznetsov, Vasily, 69, 70, 210
    views on Arab Spring, 93
Kyrgyzstan, 26

L-29 fighter jets, 14
Lamamra, Ramtane, 173, 261
Laos, 273
'Late to the Party: Russia's Return to Africa', 4
Latin America, 29–30, 109
Lavrentiyev, Alexander, 145
Lavrov, Sergei, 50, 101, 207, 211, 217, 227–8, 321–3
    met with Desalegn, 188–9
    met with Mubarak, 84
    Russia's strategy recalibration, 256–67
    Russian security involvement, 281–8
    Ukraine war and Russia's vision, 298–300
    visit to Tunisia, 66
Le Drian, Jean-Yves, 285–6
*Le Fontenil* (newspaper), 194
*Le Monde* (newspaper), 205

Lefa gold mine, 201
Lenin Political-Military Academy, 175
Lenta.ru (online newspaper), 289
Lev Dengov, 208
Liberal Democratic Party of Russia (LDPR), 37
Liberia, 303
Libya National Army (LNA), 135, 157
    Russia's strategy recalibration, 256–67
Libya, 199, 232, 237, 255–6, 278, 297, 321, 348–9n86
    Africa and Russia, 244–50
    Chad and Guinea, Russia's influence in, 288–91
    GNU and Russia, 262–72
    Moscow's interventions in, 3
    Museveni on, 294
    North Africa, Russian influence in, 301–5
    partnership with Algeria, 161
    Russia relationship with, 72–5
    Russia's intervention, 206–12
    Russia's strategy recalibration, 256–67
    stagnation in, Russia's intervention, 213–18
    US bombing in, 74
Libyan civil war, 223, 236
Libyan government, 152
Libyan parliament, 153
Libyan Political Dialogue Forum (LPDF), 263
Libyans, 152, 160
Lisbon Agreement (1991), 31
Lisbon Peace Process (1991), 30–1
LNA forces, 304
LNA. *See* Libya National Army (LNA)

# INDEX

Lobaye Invest, 132
Logunov, Denis, 242–3
Lopatov, Vladimir, 43–4, 58
Lourenço, João, 319
Luanda Norte, 319
Luhansk People's Republics, 294, 310
Luhansk, 299
Lukyanov, Fyodor, 100, 104, 329–30n9
Lukyanov, Grigory, 287
Lumumba, Patrice, 12–13
Luo Jinyi, 168
Lusaka, 316
Lyamin, Yuri, 276
Lynn-White, Betty, 226–7

M Finans, 132
Maaraf, Ismail, 146
Mabote, Motsamai, 184
Mabuza, David, 318
Macedonia, 127
Machel, Samora, 308
Macron, Emmanuel, 245, 246, 248, 261–2, 269, 283, 286, 323
  attempt to de-escalate tensions with Russia, 166
  Putin consulted with, 167
  Timofeev on, 287–8
*Madagascar Tribune* (newspaper), 226
Madagascar, 85, 199, 232, 276–7
  Russia's political interference campaign, 224–7
Madrid Conference (1991), 32
Maduekwe, Ojo, 85
Maduro, Nicolás, 183
Maghreb, 8, 65, 240
Magna Carta PR company, 124
Mahamat, Moussa Faki, 296
Mahboub, Waiel, 279

Mahbuli, Faouzi, 108
al-Mahdi, Mariam al-Sadiq, 278
Mahjoub, Khaled, 304
Mahlobo, David, 122
Maïga, Choguel Kokalla, 285
*Mail and Guardian* (newspaper), 121
Mailhol (Pastor), 224–5
Mailhol, Andre, 224
Maiteeq, Ahmad, 157, 162, 262, 263
Makarevich, Oleg, 219
Makgoba, Thabo, 317
Makri, Abderrazak, 174
Makri, Noureddine, 302
Maksimychev, Dmitry, 308
Malanga, Christian, 194
Malashenko, Alexei, 95
Malema, Julius, 316
Mali, 11, 247–8, 255, 269, 304, 321
  France's withdrawals, 323
  Mali coup (2012), 126–7
  Russia's security, 308–16
  Russian security involvement, 281–8
Malian gold mines, 286
Malkevich, Alexander, 214
Mandela, Nelson, 31
  relations with Russia, 40
  Yeltsin met with, 51
Manga, 270
Mangoush, Najla, 305
Mansour, Adly, 139
Mantashe, Gwede, 183
Manturov, Denis, 115–16, 193, 263
Mao Zedong, 15
Maputo, 232
Marchenko, Vladimir, 178–9
Mardasov, Anton, 275

457

## INDEX

Margelov, Mikhail, 71, 80–1, 99
Markov, Sergei, 314
Marten, Kimberly, 3, 4
Marxism, 11
Marxist-Leninism, 13
Maskhov, V.F., 9
Maslov, Andrey, 179, 298, 300
Maslova, Elena, 155
Matoshin, Lev, 283
Mauritania, 69, 237
Mauritius, 276–7
Maximov, Yevgeny, 10
Mazov, Sergei, 13
Mbau region, 231
Mbeki, Thabo, 62
McKenzie, Kenneth, 326
Mechichi, Hichem, 240
Medelei, Murad, 102
*Meduza*, 214
Medvedev, Dmitry, 6, 77, 321
    embarked on four-country tour, 85–6
    views on UNSC resolution, 97
Medvedev-era, 111
Meeks, Gregory, 247
Mekele, 60
Mekonnen, Demeke, 254
memorandum of understanding (MOU), 72
MENA conflict zones, 238
MENA region, 95
Menelik I (Emperor), 9
al-Menfi, Mohammed, 263, 324
Meroe Gold, 307
Mersa Matruh, 252–3
Meskel, Yemane, 280
Messahel, Abdelkader, 172
Mexico, 30
Mfeketo, Nomaindia, 122
Mhaka, Tafi, 296
Mi-17 helicopter, 229

Mi-35M attack helicopters, 311
Middle East, 29, 215, 220, 236, 261, 283
MiG-15 fighter jets, 14
MiG-21 jets, 18
MiG-29 fighter jet, 72, 257–8
MiG-29SMT fighters, 72
Migranyan, Andranik, 42
Miliband, David, 79
Miller, Andrew, 143
Millett, Peter, 158
Minapharm, 241
Ministry of Defence (Russia), 6
Ministry of Foreign Affairs (MFA), 34–5
Ministry of Foreign Affairs (Russia), 6
MINUSCA. *See* Multidimensional Integrated Stabilization Mission in the CAR (MINUSCA)
M-Invest, 219–20
Mir Afriki (Africa World), 58
Mirzayan, Gevorg, 136
al-Mishri, Khalid, 217
Mishustin, Mikhail, 274
al-Mismari, Ahmed, 154, 162, 256
Misrata Brigades, 161
Misrata, 152, 209–10, 265
Miss Bangui beauty pageant, 205
Mitiga airport, 240
Mkhize, Zweli, 243
Mkuju River, 193
Mnangagwa, 180
Mnangagwa, Emmerson, 117, 308, 318
Modrzhinskaia, E.D., 12
Mohamed, Abdirisak, 280
Mohammed VI (King), 66, 150–1
Moldova, 26, 258
Mombasa, 192
Momoh, Joseph, 47–8

458

# INDEX

Mongolia, 273–4

Moran Security Group, 128

Morocco, 8, 237, 239, 242, 247, 303

Morozov, Oleg, 282

Morsi, Mohammed, 136–8

Moscow State Institute of International Relations (MGIMO), 38

*Moscow Times, The*, 93–4, 98

Moscow

Messahel visited to, 172

Sisi visit to, 168

Moscow-Tripoli relations, 213

Moussa, Amr, 33

Movement for Democratic Change (MDC), 78, 179

Movement for the Emancipation of the Niger Delta (MEND), 86

Mozambican National Resistance (Renamo), 21–2, 231–2

Mozambican National Resistance Movement (RENAMO), 21–2, 231–2

Mozambique Asset Management, 232

Mozambique Liberation Front (FRELIMO), 231

Mozambique, 199, 250

Russia's failure, 227–33

Mpahlwa, Mandisi, 91

Mpango, Philip, 297

Mphoko, Phelekezela, 117

MPLA. *See* People's Movement for the Liberation of Angola (MPLA)

MS-21 passenger aircraft, 263

MS-21s, 277

Mthembu, Jackson, 117

Mtumuke, Athanasius Salvador, 228

Mubarak, Hosni, 33, 45, 84

Mugabe era, 115

Mugabe, Robert, 18, 64

Look East strategy, 115

victory of, 78–9

Multidimensional Integrated Stabilization Mission in Mali (MINUSMA), 127

Multidimensional Integrated Stabilization Mission in the CAR (MINUSCA), 132, 133

Mumbengegwi, Simbarashe, 115

Munir, Mamdouh, 250–1

Murakhovsky, Viktor, 120

Musavuli, Kambale, 291

Museveni, Yoweri, 102, 110–11, 114, 294

Muslim Brotherhood, 67

N'Diaye, Mankeur, 271

Nabbanja, Robinah, 297

Nacala Airport, 229

al-Nadoori, Abdulrazek, 153–4

Nagy, Tibor, 109, 245

Naiya, Liu, 168

Namcor (Namibia), 88

Namibia, 88, 240

Nampula, 231

Narison, Stephen, 227

Naryshkin, Sergei, 150

Nasser, Gamal Abdel, 11

National Committee for the Salvation of the People (NCSP), 282

National Defense University (NDU), 5

National Front for the Liberation of Angola (FNLA), 17

National Intelligence and Security Services (NISS), 219

National Liberation Front (FLN), 15

459

# INDEX

National Oil Company (NOC), 75

National Transitional Council (NTC), 99

National Union for the Total Independence of Angola (UNITA), 17

NATO (North Atlantic Treaty Organization), 78, 251, 262, 301, 316, 318, 327
airstrikes in Libya, 98
Ramaphosa on, 294

NATO Parliamentary Assembly, 217

Naumkin, Vitaly, 210

Naval Force Mediterranean Operation Irini, 266

Nayed, Aref, 265

Ndah village, 309

Ndaw, Bah, 283

*Ndjoni Sango* (newspaper), 271

NDU. *See* National Defense University (NDU)

Nebenzia, Vasily, 190, 203–4, 251, 253

Nechai, Ruslan, 301

Nemtsov, Boris, 45

Nene, Nhlanhla, 126

neo-imperialism, 108

New Delhi, 276

New Partnership for Africa's Development (NEPAD) programme, 57

*New York Times* (newspaper), 5, 26, 224, 225, 306–7

*Nezavisimaya Gazeta* (newspaper), 64, 221, 279–80

Nguema, Sylvain, 271

Niaina, 224–5

Nicholas II, Tsar, 8

Nigaz, 87

Niger Delta, 86

Niger, 239, 242, 247, 271, 281, 289, 295–7, 314

Nigeria, 14, 41, 90

Nigerian Atomic Energy Commission, 187

Nigerian military, 129–30

Nigerian National Petroleum Corporation (NNPC), 87

Nile River, 254, 280–1

Nimeiry, Gafaar, 20

9/11 attacks, 67

Nioni, 312

Nishanov, Rafik, 28

Nizhny Novgorod, 6

Nkomo, Joshua, 18

Nkurunziza, Pierre, 110, 111

NNPC. *See* Nigerian National Petroleum Corporation (NNPC)

'No-Fly Zone', 348–9n86

Nokra Island, 17

Nordgold, 201

Norland, Richard, 266

Norov, A.S., 80

North Africa, 54, 220, 240–1, 287, 301–5
Arab Spring protests in, 92–5

North Caucasus, 33, 94, 137

North Korea, 294

Northeast Asia, 29

Norway, 71, 272

Novavax scheme, 241–2

*Novaya Gazeta* (newspaper), 203, 222

Nuclear Non-Proliferation Treaty (NPT), 40

al-Nur, Abdul Wahid, 222

Nyerere, Julius, 11, 15

Nyusi, Filipe, 228–9, 231–2

## INDEX

OAU. *See* Organization of African Unity (OAU)

Obama administration, 107

Obama, Barack, 77, 85, 245, 247

Obasanjo, Olusegun, 41, 59–60, 185

Oboronexport, 35

Obraztsova, Margarita, 34–5

Odesa port strike, 323

Odinga, Raila, 308

Officers Union for International Security (OUIS), 270

Ogaden War (1978), 17

Okitundu, Leonard, 194

Olivier, Darren, 184–5

Olivier, Gerrit, 39–40

Omer, Ibrahim, 118

Onishchenko, Gennady, 290

Ontikov, Andrei, 210

Operation Barkhane, 248, 285, 313–14

Operation Peace Storm, 256

Operation Serval, 127, 249

Operation Spring Shield Offensive, 217

Orabi, Mohammed, 251–2

Organisation for the Prohibition of Chemical Weapons (OPCW), 259

Organisation of Islamic Cooperation (OIC), 67, 150–1

Organization for Security and Cooperation in Europe (OSCE), 77

Organization of African Unity (OAU), 54, 56

Orthodox Christianity, 8

Ouagadougou, 313–14

Ouane, Moctar, 283

Ouattara, Alassane, 103–4

Ozerov, Oleg, 236, 254, 325

Ozerov, Viktor, 160

Pacheco, José, 227, 229

Palermo Conference, 208

Palestine, 296

Pan Am Flight (103), 33

Pandor, Naledi, 183

Panov, Vladimir, 251

Pantsir S-1 air defence system, 257

Paris Club, 44–5

Paris, 166, 287, 314

Parly, Florence, 205, 285

Patriot, 200

Patriotic Front, 316

Patrushev, Nikolay, 220, 263, 302

Paul, T.V., 330n8

Pazvakavambwa, Liberty (Zimbabwean commentator), 231

'Peace Through Eyes of Children', 205

Peking University (PKU), 248

*People's Liberation Army Daily, The* (newspaper), 276

People's Movement for the Liberation of Angola (MPLA), 14, 17

Perendzhiev, Alexander, 206

Persian Gulf, 33

personal protective equipment (PPE), 235

Peskov, Dmitry, 196, 206, 216–19, 226, 270, 284

Russia's failure, 227–33

Pfizer, 241

Piebalgs, Andris, 81

piracy, 61

Plekhanov Russian University of Economics, 206

PMCs. *See* private military contractors (PMCs)

461

## INDEX

Podtserob, Alexey, 37, 92
Pohamba, Hifikepunye, 87, 102
Polat, Ferhat, 266
Poluboyarenko, Vladimir, 182
Polyanskiy, Dmitry, 189–90, 223,
   270, 274, 304–5
Popov, Veniamin, 37, 98–9
Port Sudan agreement, 275–6
Port Sudan, 255, 306
   Russia's security presence,
   273–81
Portugal, 30
Possony, Stefan, 12
post-Arab Spring period, 135
post-Cold War era, 133
Post-Colonial Era (1960–75), 7
post-Soviet period, 4–5
Potekhin, Ivan, 11
Potepkin, Mikhail, 306–7
Power, Samantha, 323
Pozdnyakov, Roman, 224
Poznyakov, Vasily, 8
'pragmatist camp', 25
*Pravda* (newspaper), 29
*Premium Times* (online newspaper),
   324, 325
Pretoria, 22, 317, 325
Pribyshin, Taras, 247
Prigozhin, Yevgeny, 5, 200, 204–5,
   207, 208–9, 213–14, 224, 225
   fake Facebook accounts, 268
   Russia's consolidation, 305–7
   Russia's security, 308–16
   Russia's strategy recalibration,
   256–67
   Russian security involvement,
   281–8
   Sudanese revolution, 218–23
Prikhodko, Sergei, 88
Primakov era, 78
Primakov, Yevgeny, 25, 42–3, 66

Prince, Erik, 206–7
private military contractors
   (PMCs), 1
private security companies (PSCs),
   229
Psaki, Jen, 245, 246
PSC Black Hawk, 229
Pugo, Boris, 26
Pushkin, Alexander, 9
Pushkov, Alexey, 100–1
Putin, Vladimir, 224, 237, 253,
   261–2, 293–4
   Bongo met with, 65
   co-chaired first Russia-Africa
   Summit, 1
   consulted with Macron, 167
   emphasis on Russia-Africa
   relations, 55–6
   France's withdrawals, 323
   invited Museveni, 114
   Libya, Russia's intervention on,
   206–12
   meeting with Gaddafi, 74, 96
   met with Morsi, 137–8
   met with Shalkam, 72–3
   met with Zuma, 121
   Russia's security, 308–16
   stagnation in, Russia's
   intervention, 213–18
   trip to Abu Dhabi, 170
   views on Central African
   Republic, 202–6
   visit to Cairo, 68
Pyadushkin, Maxim, 61
Pyramids of Giza, 86

al-Qashat, Muhammad Saeed, 207
Qatar, 96, 212, 221, 227–8
Qiang Xiaoyun, 168

Rabaa Massacre, 139

462

# INDEX

*Rabochaya Tribuna* (newspaper),
31–2
Radchenko, Kirill, 203
Rajaonarimampianina, Hery,
224–5
Rajoelina, Andry, 85, 225
Ramaphosa, Cyril, 237, 294,
297–8, 316–17
Rapid Support Forces (RSF), 221
Raqqa, 160
RAS. *See* Russian Academy of
Sciences (RAS)
Rasheed, Olawale, 186
Rasolovoagy, Roseline, 227
Rastorguev, Alexander, 203
Ravalomanana, Marc, 226–7
Red Sea, 41, 275–6, 305–8
Russia consolidation, 273–81
Russia's expansion, 272–3
Regdalein, 256
RENAMO. *See* Mozambican
National Resistance Movement
(RENAMO)
Renova, 120
Renzi, Matteo, 155
Republic of Congo, 244, 319
Rhodesian Bush War, 17–18
RIA FAN, 227, 230–1
RIA Novosti (News agency
company), 205, 216, 265
RIAC report, 236
RIAC-PKU policy report, 248
Richards Bay Coal Facility, 318
Rio Tinto, 319
Rivière, Nicolas de, 270
Riyadh Agreement, 272–3
Roadmap for Peace plan, 67
Rogozin, Dmitry, 82–3, 114–15
Roll, Stephen, 360n14
Romanovsky, Kirill, 204
Rosatom agreement (2019), 126

Rosatom, 5, 251, 302, 323
*Rosbalt*, 270
Roscoe, James, 270
Rosneft, 227
Rosoboronexport, 5, 68, 148
Royal United Services Institute
(RUSI), 167, 212
Rozhin, Boris, 314
RSB Group, 208
RT Arabic (television news channel
broadcasting), 209–10, 216,
220–2, 226
RT article, 290–1
RT Global, 113
Rusakova, Vlada, 227
Rusal opaque contracts, 200–1
Rusal, 239–40, 290
*Russia in Global Affairs* (journal),
298
Russia
aligned with China, 111
annexed Crimean Peninsula, 105
Ethiopia requested arms
package from, 61
Mandela relations with, 40
military campaign in Syria, 131
military interventions in Crimea
and Donbas, 121
pipeline diplomacy against
Ukraine, 71
presence in Maghreb, 65
pro-Russian sentiments in
Ethiopia, 92
relations with Eritrea, 190–1
relationship with Libya, 72–5
relationship with Rwanda,
195–6
relationship with Zimbabwe,
115
response to Arab Spring protests
in North Africa, 92–5

463

## INDEX

resurgence in Africa, 2
scholarship programme (1996)
in Africa, 56
signed an agreement with
Angola, 44
South Africa and, 30
trade between Angola and, 88
*See also* Egypt
Russia-Africa Business Council, 58
Russian Academy of Sciences
(RAS), 6
Russian Air Force, 229
Russian Armed Forces, 82
Russian Central Bank, 43, 307
Russian Direct Investment Fund
(RDIF), 238–41
Russian Embassy, 278
*Russian Engagements: On Libyan
Politics and Libyan-Russian
Relations* (Nayed), 265
Russian Foreign Ministry, 237
Russian government, 43
Russian International Affairs
Council (RIAC), 139, 211, 237,
246, 280
Russian International Aid Agency,
91
Russian MFA, 203–4
Russian Ministry of Finance, 44
Russian Orthodox Church, 68
Russian State Duma, 6
Russian State University of the
Humanities, 221
Russian T-90 tanks, 96
Russian-Arab Cooperation Forum,
211
Russian-Libyan Trade House, 208
Russia-South Africa Business
Council, 120
Russia-Sudan bilateral relationship,
277

Rwanda, 42, 195–6, 243–4, 268,
271–2, 323
Rwandan MINUSCA bodyguards,
203

S-300 air defence missile systems,
208
S-400 anti-aircraft systems, 280
SA-6 missiles, 35
Sabha, 258
SADC. *See* South African
Development Community
(SADC)
Sahel, 233, 246, 255–6, 281,
288–9, 300
Sahin, Erkan, 249–50
Salafists, 139
Saleh, Aguila, 256, 259–60, 263,
265
Saleh, Osman, 308
Sall, Macky, 296, 297–8, 315–16
Saltanov, Alexander, 55, 84–5
Sanallah, Mustafa, 258
Sandinha, Carlos, 325
Sangwa, Jean-Claude, 310
Sankara, Thomas, 314
Sanya, Eduardo, 188
Sapronova, Maria, 127
Sarkozy, Nicolas, 213
al-Sarraj, Fayez, 214–15, 256, 260,
262–3
Satanovsky, Yevgeny, 94–5
Saudi Arabia, 137, 141–2, 218,
220–1, 273, 279, 302
*Saudi Gazette* (newspaper), 141–2
Savimbi, Jonas, 30
Scherbakov, Nikolai, 282
Scholz, Olaf, 297, 316
Scientific Electronic Database, 213
Security Service of Ukraine
(SSUA), 219

# INDEX

Seifan, Samer, 262, 265
Seifan, Samir, 213, 214, 262
Sékou Touré, Ahmed, 13
Selassie, Haile (Emperor), 16
Semenov, Kirill, 210, 220
Senkovsky, O.I., 80
Senoussi, Kag, 133, 206
al-Senussi, Abdullah, 99
Serbia, 273–4
Seregichev, Sergei, 221, 279
Serraj, 206, 207, 214, 215,
  216–17
Seychelles, 276–7
Shabayev, Yevgeny, 209, 230
Shagari, Shehu, 187
Shaimiev, Mintimer, 73
Shalkam, Abdel, 72–3
Shanghai Cooperation
  Organization (SCO), 168
Sharia law, 136
Sharpeville Massacre (1960), 14
Shenouda III (Pope), 68
Shevardnadze, Eduard, 21
Shinn, David, 249
Shirinsky, Mirgayas, 119
Shoigu, Sergei, 208, 217, 228, 263
Shoukry, Sameh, 156, 211, 250,
  252
Shubin, Vladimir, 55, 90, 180–1,
  243
Shugaley, Maxim, 213, 214, 224,
  231, 262–3, 265, 304
  pro-Touadéra propaganda, 269
Shumeleva, Tatiana, 173
Shvytkin, Yuri, 215
Sibut, 203
Sidiropoulos, Elizabeth, 3, 121–2
Siegle, Joseph, 5
Sierra Leone Civil War, 47
Sigov, Yuri, 298–9
Sinai Peninsula, 8

Sinopharm, 241
Sino-Soviet Split, 7, 15
Sinovac, 241
SIPRI, 228
Sirte Airbase, 256
Sirte, 160
el-Sisi, Abdel Fattah, 138–9,
  140–1, 301–2, 326, 360n14
  visit to Moscow, 168
Siyala, Mohamed, 211, 214, 263
Skhirat Agreement, 260
Slepnev, Andrey, 177
Slutsky, Leonid, 221–2
Smirnov, Alexander, 34
Smirnov, Yevgeny, 298
Soami, Rajesh, 276
SOCAR company, 317
Sochi Summit (2019), 163, 165–6,
  199, 205–6, 214–15, 228,
  232–3
  Russia's balancing strategy,
    250–4
  Russia's vaccine diplomacy,
    238–44
Sochi, 1, 214, 262, 298
Society for Worldwide
  Interbank Financial
  Telecommunication (SWIFT),
  297, 299, 308, 325–6
Socotra, 212
Solaiman, Hossein, 302
Somali government, 83
Somali National Army, 16
Somali piracy crisis, 82
Somalia, 6, 247, 273, 280, 297, 323
Sonara, 193
Sonatrach, 72
Sorokin, Pavel, 196
Sotnikov, Vladimir, 93
South Africa, 239, 242–3, 294,
  295, 297, 317–18, 323–4

## INDEX

exclusion from BRICS summit, 90–1

South Africa's Umbria Aviation, 229

South African Air Force (SAAF), 184

South African Communist Party, 317

South African Development Community (SADC), 57, 116

South African Institute of International Affairs (SAIIA), 121

*South African Medical Journal*, 242

South African variant, 243

South Kordofan, 272–3

South Korea, 251

South Ossetia, 78, 202

South Sudan, 80, 106, 112

South West Africa People's Organization (SWAPO), 87

Southern Africa, 21, 316–19

Southern African Development Community (SADC), 57, 116

Southern African Faith Communities Environment Institute (SAFCEI), 126

southern Europe, 208

Southern Transitional Council (STC), 272

Soviet Union-Benin Friendship Accord (1986), 20

Soviet Union, 10, 286, 314, 322
partnership with Somalia, 16
relationship with Uganda, 112
support to MPLA, 17
*See also* Algeria; Horn of Africa

Soviet-Afghan War, 314

Spetzvneshtechnika, 35

Sputnik Light vaccine, 244

Sputnik V vaccine, 235, 239, 241
Russia's balancing strategy, 250–4

Russia's vaccine diplomacy, 238–44

Sputnik, 204, 222, 226, 238

Sredin, Vasilii, 55

SSJ100 passenger aircraft, 263

St Petersburg Economic Forum, 211, 298

St Petersburg, 31, 224, 268, 299, 326

Stalin, Joseph, 28

Stalinism, 125

State Committee on the State of Emergency (GKChP), 26

State Duma Committee on Defence, 215

State Security Agency (SSA), 125

States Africa Command (AFRICOM), 108

Steenhuisen, John, 317

Stepanova, Ekaterina, 151–2

Stevens, J. Christopher, 152

Stockholm International Peace Research Institute (SIPRI), 63

Storchak, Sergei, 73

Stroitransgaz, 70

Stronski, Paul, 3, 4

Su-24 fighter jet, 257, 258

Su-30, 280

Su-35 jets, 252, 273, 280
Su-35 jet deal, 326

Su-75 Checkmate fighter jet, 326

Suakin port, 275–6

Sub-Saharan Africa, 59, 215, 230, 242, 308, 323

Suchkov, Maxim, 207

Sudan Liberation Movement (SLM-AW), 222

Sudan Revolutionary Front (SRF), 272–3

*Sudan Tribune* (news portal), 118, 279

# INDEX

Sudan, 199, 232, 237, 251, 272–3, 297, 321
  Africa and Russia, 244–50
  'positive neutrality' between South Sudan and, 112
  Red Sea and Horn of Africa, 305–8
  revolution, 218–23
  Russia's political interference campaign, 224–7
  Russia's security presence, 273–81
  Russia's strategy recalibration, 256–67
Sudanese Communist Party, 20
Sudanese National Assembly, 80
Sudanese revolution
  Russia's response, 218–23
Suez Canal Authority, 302
Suez Canal Industrial Zone, 144
Suez Canal Special Economic Zone, 143
Suez Canal, 8, 170, 251–2, 276
Suez Crisis (1956), 11
Sukhankin, Sergei, 3, 194
Sukhankin, Sergey, 3, 194
Sukhoi Superjet, 277
*Sun, The* (tabloid newspaper), 188, 208
*Sunday Independent* (newspaper), 121
al-Sunna, Asnar, 230
Supreme Council of the Armed Forces (SCAF), 136
Surikov, Mozambique Alexander, 228
Surur, Fathi, 86
Suslov, Dmitry, 298, 300
al-Suwayda, 256–7
Suweilam, Husam, 141
Svitzer, 81

Sylva, Timipre, 315
Syria, 118, 207, 215–16, 238, 261–2, 276, 283, 294, 311
  Russia's military campaign in, 131
  Sudanese revolution and democratic transition, 218–23

T-72 tanks, 35
Tabe, Crispin, 195
Tahnoon, Sheikh, 212
Tajikistan, 26
Takuba peacekeeping force, 286
al-Tamimi, Heiri, 264
Tangier, 8
Tanzania, 112, 193, 297
Tarhuna, 209, 260
Tartous, 276
Tarutin, Igor, 29
Tashkent, 254
Tatarov, Vladimir, 176
Tatarstan, 6
el-Tayeb, Ahmed, 145
Taylor, Charles, 48
Tegenu, Alemayehu, 254
Tehran, 326
*Telegraph, The* (newspaper), 209
Terekhin, Yevgeny, 254
Teshome, Grum, 189
al-Thani, Abdullah, 214
Third World, 25, 27
Tigray People's Liberation Front, 273
Tigray Province, 47
Tigray War, 253, 280, 308
Tigray, 21, 251, 253–4, 307, 324
Timbuktu, 285
Timofeev, Ivan, 287–8
Titorenko, Vladimir, 271, 288
Tkachenko, Vsevolod, 248

## INDEX

Tobruk, 154, 208
Tokmakov, Viktor, 205
Lengo Songo 98.9 FM radio, 205
Tolstoy, Leo, 10
Touadéra government, 309
Touadéra, 202–3, 204–6, 255, 309
   GNU and Russia, 262–72
Toungui, Paul, 104
*Tourist, The* (film), 271
Townsend, Stephen, 247, 257, 306
Transitional Military Council
   (TMC), 223, 281
Transvaal Republic, 10
Traore, Ibrahim, 314
Traore, Moussa, 14
Treaty of Friendship and
   Cooperation (1974), 16
Treaty of Rome, 80
Tripoli, 20, 73, 152, 209, 217, 240
   GNU and Russia's involvement,
     262–72
   Russia's strategy recalibration,
     256–67
*Trud* (newspaper), 63
Trump administration, 109, 112
Trump, Donald, 206–7, 222, 238,
   247, 253, 325
Tsegai, Petros, 280
Tselunov, Alexei, 312
Tselunov, Alexey, 290
Tsinamdzgvrishvili, Artyom, 239
Tu-154 jet, 286
Tu-154M airliners, 219
Tunisia, 66, 93237, 289, 303
   Russia's vaccine diplomacy,
     238–44
Tunisian revolution, 93
Turkey, 212–13, 215–18, 246,
   249–50, 261, 273, 275, 322–3
   Libya, Russia's involvement in,
     262–7

   Macron on, 248
   PPE, 235
   Turkey-Russia relations, 249–50,
     266
Tutu, Desmond, 317
Twitter, 231, 251
223rd Flight Unit, 229
224th Flight Unit, 229

UAE. *See* United Arab Emirates
   (UAE)
Udugov, Movladi, 51
Uganda, 112–13, 244, 247, 321–2
Ugbah, Steve, 185
Ukraine war, 287–8, 300–1, 326,
   409n4
   Africa's reaction, 294–8
   North Africa, Russia's influence
     in, 301–5
   Red Sea and Horn of Africa,
     305–8
   Russia and Southern Africa,
     316–19
   Russia's security, 308–16
   Russia's vision, 298–300
Ukraine, 26, 202, 258, 321–6
   Africa's reaction, 294–8
   North Africa, Russia's influence
     in, 301–5
   Red Sea and Horn of Africa,
     305–8
   Russia and Southern Africa,
     316–19
   Russia pipeline diplomacy
     against, 71
   Russia's security, 308–16
   Ukraine war and Russia's vision,
     298–300
Ukrainian Defence Ministry, 304
UN (United Nations), 209, 238,
   253, 259, 266–7, 323

# INDEX

peacekeeping operation in
Macedonia, 127
*See also* UN Security Council
(UNSC); Union of Soviet
Socialist Republics (USSR)
UN Conference (1985), 22
UN General Assembly (UNGA),
239, 301, 316
Africa's reaction, 294–8
UN Human Rights Council, 253,
295, 305
UN Multidimensional Integrated
Stabilization Mission in Mali
(MINUSMA), 312
UN Panel of Experts, 256,
258–9
UN report, 269–70
UN resolution, 202
UN Security Council (UNSC),
34, 209, 223, 237–8, 249, 263,
278, 289
Russia's balancing strategy,
250–4
UN World Food Programme
(WFP), 92
Union of Soviet Socialist Republics
(USSR), 298–9
UNITAF. *See* United Task Force
(UNITAF)
United Arab Emirates (UAE),
7, 118, 209, 211–12, 217,
220–21, 306
PPE, 235
Russia's strategy recalibration,
256–67
United Nations General Assembly
(UNGA), 106–7
United Nations Multidimensional
Integrated Stabilization Mission
in the Central African Republic
(MINUSCA), 270

United Nations Operation in Côte
d'Ivoire (UNOCI), 103
United States (US), 206, 209, 226,
237, 268, 274, 321, 323, 330n8
bombings in Libya, 74
Nagy on, 245
Russia's balancing strategy,
250–4
Russian security involvement,
281–8
US-Sudan relations, 279–80
vaccines, 235–6
United Task Force (UNITAF), 38
University of Pennsylvania, 245
UNSC Resolution (1054), 49
UNSC Resolution (1070), 50
UNSC Resolution (1957), 103
UNSC Resolution (1970), 97
UNSC Resolution (1973), 102–3
UNSC Resolution (2085), 127
UNSC Resolution (748), 36
UNSC Resolution (794), 38
UNSC Resolution (883), 37
UNSC. *See* UN Security Council
(UNSC)
Urnov, Andrey, 102
US government, 245
US Treasury Department, 247, 258
US. *See* United States (US)
US-China Cold War, 236
Uzbekistan, 26

Vasiliev, Alexei, 36
Vella, George, 159
Venezuela crisis, 221
Venezuela, 79, 184, 215, 222
Volin, Alexey, 114
Volodin, Duma Vyacheslav, 201
VTB bank, 232
Vybornov, Sergei, 89
Vystovsky, Vladimir, 82

469

## INDEX

*Vzyglad* (newspaper), 261, 299–300, 313, 322

Wadden, 258
Wagner Group, 200, 203–4, 230, 304–6, 307, 309, 311–14
   Africa and Russia, 244–50
   Chad and Guinea, Russia's influence in, 288–91
   Libya, Russia's intervention on, 206–12
   Russia and Sudan, 273–81
   Russia consolidation, 267–72
   Russia's security, 308–16
   Russia's strategy recalibration, 256–67
   Russian security involvement, 281–8
   stagnation in, Russia's intervention, 213–18
   Sudanese revolution, 218–23
Wahhabism, 145
Walubita, Keli, 50
Wang Jiahao, 168
War on Terror, 66
Washington, 247, 279, 306
Weatherington, Matthew, 226–7
Welch-Larson, Deborah, 330*n*8
West Africa, 14, 185, 201, 290
   Russia's security, 308–16
Western liberalism, 75
Western Sahara, 151, 174, 247, 303
Williams, Stephanie, 207, 259, 265–6, 304
Winer, Jonathan, 108
Wisner, Frank, 18
Wohlforth, William, 330*n*8
World Bank, 91, 237
World Health Organization (WHO), 237, 243

World War II, 10
World War III, 301
Wu Peng, 248

*Xinhua* (News agency company), 238
Xinjiang, 238
Xu Guoqing, 89

Yalta Economic Forum (2019), 195
Yanayev, Gennady, 26, 27
Yar'Adua, Umaru, 59–60, 86–7
Yasar University, 249
Yeltsin era, 55
Yeltsin, Boris, 28
   Ajaokuta Steel Project, 45
   met with Mandela, 51
Yemen, 211, 212, 273
Yemeni civil war, 272
Yibeltal, Kalkidan, 253–4
Yom Kippur War (1973), 14
Youssef, Khaled Omar, 278
Yugoslavia, 46, 316
Yushkov, Igor, 303

Zakharov, Valeri, 202–3, 205, 272
Zakharov, Valery, 202–3, 205, 272
Zakharova, Maria, 219, 222
Zambia, 18, 316
Zangaro Today Telegram channel, 290
ZANU-PF, 78–9
Zaporizhzhia, 299
Zarubezhvodstroi, 70
el-Zayat, Elhamy, 252
Zayed, Abdullah bin, 212
Zayed, Mohammed bin, 212
Zaytsev, Vadim, 179
Zeila, 188
Zelensky, Volodymyr, 297–8, 301, 303, 322, 324–5

# INDEX

Zenawi, Meles, 28, 60, 92
Zene, Chérif Mahamat, 289
Zheltov, Vladimir, 119
Zhirinovksy, Vladimir, 37, 50–1
Zhou En-Lai, 15
Zimbabwe African National Union (ZANU), 18
Zimbabwe African People's Union (ZAPU), 18, 115
Zimbabwe Consolidated Diamond Company (ZCDC), 180
Zimbabwe, 17–18, 79, 115, 241, 295, 318
Zinyama, Tawanda, 318
Zultun, 256
Zuma, Jacob, 103, 121–2, 175, 316
Zyuganov, Gennady, 50